# A GRAMMAR

OF

# OSCAN AND UMBRIAN

*WITH A COLLECTION OF INSCRIPTIONS*
*AND A GLOSSARY*

BY

## CARL DARLING BUCK, Ph.D.

PROFESSOR OF SANSKRIT AND INDO-EUROPEAN COMPARATIVE
PHILOLOGY IN THE UNIVERSITY OF CHICAGO

BOSTON, U.S.A.
GINN & COMPANY, PUBLISHERS
The Athenæum Press
1904

ENG

# PREFACE

The following work is an attempt to furnish in a single volume of moderate compass what is most essential for the study of the Oscan and Umbrian dialects. In spite of the meagreness of the material, as compared with languages like Greek and Latin, and in spite of the many questions of detail which are still unsolved, the main features of these two dialects are well understood. And such is their relation to Latin that some acquaintance with them is important, not to the Indo-Europeanist alone, but to the student of the Latin language, and, in a less degree, to the student of the history and antiquities of Italy. In order that a knowledge of the dialects should become more general, it is not enough that we have now such excellent works as Conway's Italic Dialects, with its full presentation of the existing material, and von Planta's exhaustive Grammatik der Oskisch-Umbrischen Dialekte. The fullness of v. Planta's treatment, the conscientious weighing of possibilities, and the liberal citation of authorities, all add to its value as a work of reference, but the resulting bulk of 1372 pages is likely to deter one who can devote only a moderate amount of time to the subject. That there is need of a briefer grammar has long been the author's conviction, which has only been strengthened by inquiries and suggestions from others in this country and abroad.[1]

In order to secure the desired brevity, it has been necessary to eliminate almost wholly any detailed discussion of disputed points, as well as special references for the views adopted or rejected. Any one for whom the ㅡㄷ ʰliography given below is not sufficient may ㅑㅕ ㅓㅁㄷ · ㅡ Only in a few cases, here and there, I have added references in footnotes, mostly to discussions more recent than v. Planta.  Generally I have simply stated the view which seemed to me on the whole the most probable, or else contented myself with a non liquet.  It is scarcely necessary to state that in matters of dispute I have had no predilection for my own previously expressed views, but have with equal freedom rejected them in favor of others or retained them against others, according to my present judgment.

That the treatment is historical and comparative, not merely descriptive, is a matter of course.  But the emphasis is on Italic, rather than on Indo-European, relations.  In the case of words which are peculiar to the dialects and not found in Latin, a fairly wide range of cognates is cited, as in sections 15, 16.  But ordinarily comparison within the Italic is deemed sufficient, and forms from other Indo-European languages are introduced only for special reasons.

The grammar is called a Grammar of Oscan and Umbrian, not of the Oscan-Umbrian dialects, for it does not pretend to treat systematically the minor dialects included under the name Oscan-Umbrian.  Most of the characteristics of these dialects (so far as they are clear) are mentioned incidentally, mainly in the Introduction.  But to discuss or even mention all the questions arising in the attempt to generalize from material consisting of only a few lines, would require an amount of space not justified by the results. Unless the material from these minor dialects is notably increased, our knowledge of the Oscan-Umbrian group will be almost coincident with what we know of its two principal dialects.  And in this approximate sense a grammar of Oscan and Umbrian is also a grammar of Oscan-Umbrian.

As the book has been practically ready for the press since the beginning of the year, and the Phonology in type since February, almost nothing in the literature of 1903 has been taken account of. But in what has appeared there is little which has entirely convinced me.  Special mention may be made of Brugmann's discussion of the negative prefix *an-* and *anter* 'inter' (I.F. 15, 70 ff.).  I have myself wished there were some way of equating these directly with the Latin, instead of assuming by-forms (as in **98** with *c*), which indeed seems out of the question in the case of **Anafríss** if = L. *Imbribus* (see **98**, *b*). But Brugmann's assumption that "initial *e* before nasal + consonant had a very open pronunciation in the Oscan-Umbrian period and had perhaps become identical in this position with Italic *a*" fails to convince me, in view of O. **embratur, Entraí**, and especially U. **iseçeles** 'insectis.' Nor do I see the necessity of separating O. **ant** from L. *ante* because of its meaning 'as far as' (see **299**, 2).

For assistance I am indebted to Professors J. C. Rolfe and Minton Warren, who kindly offered to read proof, and especially to my pupils, Mr. W. C. Gunnerson and Mr. R. B. Nelson, who have gone over the proof with great care, devoting no small amount of time to the verification of references, citations, etc., and contributing in every way to the accuracy of the text. The remarkable keenness and intelligence of the proof-reader in the office of the publishers has also saved the work from many blemishes.

C. D. B.

DECEMBER, 1903.

# TABLE OF CONTENTS

## FORMATION OF THE MOODS AND TENSES

The history of the study of the Italic dialects might be expected to date from the discovery of the Iguvinian Tables in 1444, but for several centuries all the attempts to decipher these were wholly worthless. The first sign of progress is found in Lanzi, Saggio di lingua Etrusca e di altre antiche d'Italia, Rome, 1789, in which the ritual character of the contents was recognized. In the first half of the nineteenth century fall, among others, the contributions of K. O. Müller, who in his great work on the Etruscans (Die Etrusker, 1828; 2d ed. by Deecke, 1877) definitely disposed of the error that Oscan and Umbrian were connected with Etruscan; of the Sanskritist Lassen, who gave a critical treatment of a section of the Iguvinian Tables in his Beiträge zur Deutung der eugubinischen Tafeln, Bonn, 1833; of Grotefend, celebrated for his decipherment of the Old Persian cuneiform, who treats selected passages in his Rudimenta linguae Umbricae, Hanover, 1835–1839; of Lepsius, the future Egyptologist, who in his dissertation, De tabulis Eugubinis, Berlin, 1833, cleared up the remaining difficulties of the alphabet and proposed a chronological arrangement of the tables which is still followed in the universally adopted numbering. Lepsius also brought out the first trustworthy edition of the Oscan inscriptions together with the Umbrian, the Inscriptiones Umbricae et Oscae, Leipzig, 1841.

A work of prime importance for the study of Oscan and the minor dialects was Mommsen's Unteritalische Dialekte, Leipzig, 1850. A similarly fundamental work for Umbrian was Aufrecht and Kirchhoff's Die umbrischen Sprachdenkmäler, 1849–1851, the first really critical attempt to interpret the Iguvinian Tables as a whole. Kirchhoff was also the first to recognize the true character of the longest Oscan inscription, the Tabula Bantina, in his elaborate commentary, Das Stadtrecht von Bantia, Berlin, 1853. In Huschke's Die oskischen und sabellischen Sprachdenkmäler, 1856, and Die iguvischen Tafeln, 1859, a wealth of knowledge on the side of antiquities

---

[1] A full bibliography is given by v. Planta, II, pp. xi ff. For the history of the interpretation of the Iguvinian Tables, see especially Bréal, Tab. Eug., pp. i ff.

is marred by a lack of critical judgment, especially in grammatical
points, so that while some of the many daring conjectures have
proved serviceable, his works in general mark a step backward.
Newman's Text of the Iguvine Inscriptions, London, 1864, is without
much value.   Grammatical questions were also discussed in numerous articles by Corssen, Ebel, Bugge, and others.   Bruppacher's
Oskische Lautlehre, 1869, and Enderis' Oskische Formenlehre, 1871,
were convenient little manuals for the time, though valueless to-day.

In the last quarter of the nineteenth century the most notable
advance in the interpretation of the dialect remains was made by
the works of Bréal and of Bücheler.   Besides their exhaustive commentaries on the Iguvinian Tables, cited below, each of these scholars
has discussed in one form or another most of the more important
Oscan inscriptions.   Important contributions were also made by
Bugge, Danielsson, Deecke, Jordan, Pauli, and others.   New editions
of the Oscan and Sabellian inscriptions with facsimiles were brought
out by the Russian scholar Zvetaieff in 1878 and 1884 (cited below).

The Italic dialects have always held an important place in the
interest of Indo-European philologists, and Brugmann especially
has done much to further their study, both as author and teacher.
It is not too much to say that the works of former pupils of his,
appearing from 1892 on, especially the treatises of Bronisch and the
present writer, von Planta's grammar, and Conway's edition of the
texts, all cited below, have put the whole subject on a new footing.
Contributions on special points, too numerous to specify here, have
been made in recent years by F. D. Allen, Bartholomae, Ceci,
Ehlich, Fay, Horton-Smith, Pascal, Skutsch, Solmsen, and others.

The following is a list of the works which are now the most
useful to the student.

*Indo-European Grammar*

BRUGMANN-DELBRÜCK, Grundriss der vergleichenden Grammatik
   der indogermanischen Sprachen.  5 vols.  Strassburg, 1886–1900.
   Vol. I in 2d ed., 1897.   Vols. I–II (Phonology and Morphology)
   by K. Brugmann (abbr. Brugmann, Grd.); vols. III–V (Syntax)
   by B. Delbrück (= Delbrück, Vergl. Syntax, I–III).

   The Oscan and Umbrian dialects are treated systematically and as fully
as the wide scope of the work permits.

BRUGMANN, Kurze vergleichende Grammatik der indogermanischen Sprachen. Parts I–II, Strassburg, 1902–1903.

In this shorter work, to be completed within the limits of a single volume, Oscan and Umbrian forms are mentioned only incidentally in connection with the treatment of Latin.

## Latin Grammar

LINDSAY, The Latin Language. Oxford, 1894.

SOMMER, Handbuch der lateinischen Laut- und Formenlehre. Heidelberg, 1902.

STOLZ, Historische Grammatik der lateinischen Sprache. Leipzig, 1894.

## Oscan-Umbrian Grammar

VON PLANTA, Grammatik der oskisch-umbrischen Dialekte. 2 vols. Strassburg, 1892–1897 (abbr. v. Planta).

A sound and exhaustive treatment, fundamental for all future work. Also contains the texts.

A brief sketch of Oscan-Umbrian grammar is included in Conway's Italic Dialects, and of Umbrian grammar in the commentaries of Bréal, Bücheler, and others, quoted below. Special chapters of the grammar are treated in:

BRONISCH, Die oskischen I- und E-Vocale. Leipzig, 1892.

BUCK, Der Vocalismus der oskischen Sprache. Leipzig, 1892 (abbr. Osk. Voc.).

BUCK, The Oscan-Umbrian Verb-System. Chicago, 1895 (abbr. Verb-System).

## Texts and Commentaries [1]

CONWAY, The Italic Dialects. 2 vols. Cambridge, 1897.

The most exhaustive collection of the material, containing the inscriptions with full epigraphical data, the glosses, lists of proper names, etc., together with a brief sketch of the grammar, and a glossary.

A concise but complete collection of the inscriptions is also included in v. Planta's Grammatik, cited above.

CONWAY, Dialectorum Italicarum Exempla Selecta. Cambridge, 1899.

Selections from the dialect inscriptions, with translation and brief notes.

AUFRECHT UND KIRCHHOFF, Die umbrischen Sprachdenkmäler. 2 vols. Berlin, 1849–1851.

See above, p. xiii. Still to be consulted with profit.

---

[1] References for particular Oscan inscriptions are given in the Collection of Inscriptions.

BRÉAL, Les Tables Eugubines.   Paris, 1875 (abbr. Tab. Eug.).
> This and the following are the two leading commentaries on the Iguvinian Tables.

BÜCHELER, Umbrica.   Bonn, 1883.
> On the whole the most convincing interpretation of the Umbrian remains, and followed in large measure in the present work.

MOMMSEN, Die Unteritalischen Dialekte.   Leipzig, 1850 (abbr. Unterit. Dial.).
> See above, p. xiii.   Still valuable for the epigraphical data and the geographical and historical notes.

ZVETAIEFF, Sylloge Inscriptionum Oscarum.   St. Petersburg and Leipzig, 1878.
ZVETAIEFF, Inscriptiones Italiae Mediae Dialecticae.   Leipzig, 1884.
> These two collections are now mainly valuable on account of the accompanying facsimiles.

Contributions on special points of grammar and interpretation are found in the various journals, proceedings of·learned societies, and series of studies, especially the following.

American Journal of Philology (abbr. Am. J. of Ph.).
Beiträge zur Kunde der indogermanischen Sprachen.   Ed. by A. Bezzenberger (abbr. B.B. = Bezzenbergers Beiträge).
Berichte über die Verhandlungen der königlichen sächsischen Gesellschaft der Wissenschaft zu Leipzig.   Philologisch-historische Classe (abbr. Ber. d. sächs. Gesell. d. Wiss.).
Classical Review.
Indogermanische Forschungen.   Zeitschrift für indogermanische Sprach- und Altertumskunde (abbr. I.F.), with the Anzeiger für indogermanische Sprach- und Altertumskunde (abbr. I.F. Anz.).
Mémoire de la Société de Linguistique de Paris (abbr. Mém. Soc. Ling.).
Pauli's Altitalische Studien.   5 vols.   Hanover, 1883–1887.
Rheinisches Museum für Philologie (abbr. Rh. M.).
Zeitschrift für vergleichende Sprachforschung auf dem Gebiete der indogermanischen Sprachen.   Founded by A. Kuhn (abbr. K.Z. = Kuhns Zeitschrift).

# EXPLANATIONS

**Black** type is used to transcribe words in the native alphabets, and *italics* for those in the Latin alphabet. The same distinction is commonly employed for separate letters or groups of letters. But sometimes, to save unnecessary repetition, italics are used referring to the spelling of both the native and Latin alphabets. Glosses cited are always indicated as such, except the frequently cited *famel*.

The meanings of words cited are usually given, though not always, especially where they can easily be inferred from the Latin cognates cited. Vice versa, Latin cognates are sometimes left to be inferred from the Latin translations. In the case of words of doubtful meaning these translations in the grammar are to be regarded as expedients, subject to amplification or correction in the glossary. In the texts uncertain letters are distinguished by a change of type, and where obvious mistakes are corrected the original reading is given in footnotes to the text. But in the grammar proper such matters are usually ignored except when bearing directly on the subject of discussion.

The signs $\underset{\sim}{i}$ and $\underset{\sim}{u}$ are used for consonantal *i* and *u*, English *y* and *w*; $\underset{\sim}{n}$, $\underset{\sim}{m}$, $\underset{\sim}{r}$, $\underset{\sim}{l}$, for the syllabic nasals and liquids assumed in Indo-European forms. The colon (:) is used to point out relationship, in the sense of "cognate with." Besides the abbreviations of works of reference mentioned above, the following are used.

Av. = Avestan.  
C.A. = Cippus Abellanus (no. 1).  
Eng. = English.  
Fal. = Faliscan.  
Germ. = German.  
Goth. = Gothic.  
Grk. = Greek.  
I.E. = Indo-European.  
Ital. = Italian.  
L. = Latin.  
Lith. = Lithuanian.  
Marruc. = Marrucinian.  
O. = Oscan.  

O.Bulg. = Old Bulgarian.  
O.Eng. = Old English.  
O.H.G. = Old High German.  
O.Ir. = Old Irish.  
O.Pruss. = Old Prussian.  
Pael. = Paelignian.  
Sab. = Sabine.  
Skt. = Sanskrit.  
T.A. = Tablet of Agnone (no. 45).  
T.B. = Tabula Bantina (no. 2.)  
U. = Umbrian.  
Vest. = Vestinian.

# OSCAN AND UMBRIAN GRAMMAR

## INTRODUCTION

### PEOPLES AND LANGUAGES OF ITALY

1. The Italian peninsula, in the earliest period of history, was occupied by various peoples speaking a variety of languages and dialects.

The **Ligurians** in the northwest have usually been regarded as relics of an aboriginal, pre-Indo-European, population, but are now thought by some to be Indo-European.[1] The linguistic remains, consisting largely of geographical names, are too meagre to be decisive.

The **Etruscans** (Latin *Etrūscī* or *Tuscī*, the latter from *\*Turscī;* cf. Umbrian **Turskum**, Greek Τυρσηνοί, Τυρρηνοί) occupied Etruria, and, previous to the Celtic invasions, much of the central part of northern Italy, in the valley of the Po. They were also masters of Campania from the eighth century B.C. down to the Samnite invasion in the last quarter of the fifth century B.C. The Etruscan inscriptions[2] number over six thousand, but only a few hundred contain anything more than proper names, and less than a dozen of these are of any considerable length. The interpretation is wholly uncertain and nothing positive can be affirmed as to the affinities of the language. But it is reasonably clear that it is not Indo-European. The riddle will probably remain unsolved until the discovery of a bilingual inscription of some length.

---

[1] Cf. Kretschmer, K.Z. 38, 108 ff.
[2] Now being collected in the Corpus Inscriptionum Etruscarum.

The **Veneti**, at the head of the Adriatic, and the **Messa-pians** and **Iapygians** in Calabria have commonly been grouped together as of Illyrian origin. There are several hundred short Venetian inscriptions,[1] and the Messapian is also represented by some hundred and sixty short inscriptions.[2] From these remains it appears that the two languages, though Indo-European, do not belong to the same group, and it is uncertain whether the Venetian, or the Messapian with the modern Albanian, should be classed as Illyrian.[3]

**Greek** colonies occupied nearly the entire southern portion of Italy, many of them dating from a period earlier than the beginnings of Roman history and retaining their Greek char-acter for several centuries after Christ.

**Celtic** tribes which poured in from the north, and in the early part of the fourth century B.C. sacked Rome, maintained themselves for some time in the central plains of northern Italy.

The rest of Italy was occupied by tribes speaking dialects akin to the Latin and with it constituting the **Italic** branch of the Indo-European family.

### Classification of the Italic Dialects

**2.** The Italic Dialects fall into two groups, the **Latin-Faliscan** and the **Oscan-Umbrian**.

The Latin-Faliscan comprises the **Latin**, of which there were local variations in the different towns of Latium, and the **Faliscan**, spoken in the Faliscan plain in the southeastern part of Etruria. The few short inscriptions[4] are sufficient to show that Faliscan differed but slightly from Latin.

The Oscan-Umbrian group is so named from its two most important members, the **Oscan** and the **Umbrian**, but includes

---

[1] Collected in Pauli, Die Veneter, Altitalische Forschungen III.

[2] Mostly in Fabrotti, Corpus Inscriptionum Italicarum.

[3] On the Illyrian question, cf. Pauli, l. c.; Kretschmer, Einleitung in die griechische Sprachgeschichte, 244 ff.; Hirt, Festschrift für Kiepert, 181 ff.; Pedersen, K.Z. 36, 299 ff.          [4] Collected in Deecke, Die Falisker.

also the dialects of most of the minor tribes of central Italy, which may be conveniently designated as **Sabellian**.[1] The best known of these is the **Paelignian**, which shows a very close resemblance to Oscan. Much the same are the dialects of the neighboring **Marrucinians** and **Vestinians**, of which there are some scanty remains. **Volscian**, known only from an inscription of four lines from Velitrae, is more strongly differentiated and in several particulars resembles Umbrian more than Oscan; but there is no sufficient reason for grouping it otherwise than among the Sabellian dialects. The **Marsians, Aequians**, and **Sabines** are connected historically with the other Sabellian tribes, and their dialects doubtless belong properly to the same group. But they were subjected to Latin influence from a very early period, and the meagre remains that we have give no satisfactory picture of their characteristics.

## Oscan — External Data

**3.** Oscan inscriptions have been found in Samnium (inclusive of the territory of the Frentani and Hirpini), Campania, northern Apulia, Lucania, and Bruttium, and in the Sicilian city of Messana from the period after its occupation by the Campanian Mamertines. These are precisely the regions which we know were occupied by Samnite tribes. In calling the language Oscan rather than Samnitic we are following the usage of the Latin authors, as when Livy (10, 20) relates how in one

---

[1] The etymological connection of *Sabellus* (from \*Saf-no-lo-), *Sabini* (from \*Saf-inoi), and *Samnium* (from \*Saf-nio-m; cf. Oscan Safinim), together with the tradition of the Sabine origin of the Samnites and the minor tribes like the Paeligni, is a witness to the tribal relations of these peoples. The Roman writers use *Sabellus* in the sense of Samnitic, and it is properly a generic term including Samnitic. Strictly speaking the Samnite tribes were Sabellian, and their language, the Oscan, a Sabellian dialect. But the Samnites and their language occupy such a preëminent position that they are best grouped by themselves, and we may, for convenience, reserve the name Sabellian for the closely related minor tribes and dialects.

The so-called Old Sabellian inscriptions, found in various parts of central Italy, are wholly unintelligible, and certainly are not in any of the Sabellian dialects. They possibly represent the language of some Illyrian tribes.

of the *Samnite* wars the Roman consul sent out spies who were acquainted with the *Oscan* language. Now the Oscans (Lat. *Oscī*, earlier *Opscī*, Grk. 'Οπικοί) were a Campanian tribe, and it has been held by some that Oscan was not the original language of the Samnites, but was adopted by them after their invasion of Campania. But this is altogether improbable. We must, rather, assume that the Oscans were simply a detached branch of the Samnites, speaking essentially the same language; and the principal reason why this language was called Oscan rather than Samnitic is that it was among the Oscans that the Greeks and Romans first came in contact with it. The Samnites entered the field of history as a politically distinct people from the Oscans; but their language, being the same, was called by the name already established. Moreover it was among the Oscans, by reason of their early contact with Greek and Etruscan civilization, that the language was first reduced to writing, so that while they did not give the Samnites a new language, they did give them its written form, and to a certain extent, probably, a sort of normalized standard of speech. This last supposition would help account for the fact that local variations of Oscan, outside of Campania, are far less marked than one would expect, considering the extent of the territory in which the language was spoken.

**4.** The Oscan inscriptions number over two hundred, but more than half of these contain only proper names or fragments of words. About three quarters of them come from Campania, where Pompeii, and in recent years Capua, have furnished the greatest number.

The period of time covered is nearly five centuries, the earliest remains being some coin-legends from the end of the fifth or first half of the fourth century B.C., while the latest are some of the graffiti of Pompeii, which there is reason to believe were scratched on the walls after the first earthquake in 63 A.D. But by far the greater part of the material falls between 300 B.C. and the Social War in 90–89 B.C. After the Social War Oscan ceased to be used in official documents, but continued to exist as a local patois for some time, — how long we cannot tell. If at Pompeii it was still spoken, to some extent at least, in the first century A.D., it very likely lingered on for several centuries in the remoter districts of Samnium.

Most of the inscriptions are written in the native Oscan alphabet, which is derived, through the medium of the Etruscan, from the Greek of the Chalcidian type. But a few from Lucania, including the longest Oscan inscription known, the Tabula Bantina, are in the Latin alphabet, and some from Sicily and various parts of southern Italy are in the Greek alphabet.

5. As regards contents, many well-known classes of inscriptions are represented. The Tabula Bantina, the longest inscription, itself only a fragment of the original, contains a series of municipal regulations. The next longest, the Cippus Abellanus, is an agreement between the cities of Nola and Abella touching certain temple property held in common. From Agnone in Samnium comes an inventory of statues and altars in a sacred grove. The Curse of Vibia, from Capua, together with a few shorter curses, belongs to the class of *devotiones* of which there are many examples among Greek and Latin inscriptions. There are several inscriptions on public works from Pompeii and elsewhere ; also dedications, including a peculiar series of *iovilae*-dedications, mostly from Capua, the nature of which is not fully understood. Certain inscriptions painted on house-fronts near some of the street-corners in Pompeii seem to be guides for the allied troops occupying the city in the Social War. There are numerous inscribed coins from various towns, some of them older than any of the inscriptions on stone; also several from the time of the Social War, bearing the legend Vítelíú 'Italia', and the names of the leaders of the allies. There are a few epitaphs, many bricks inscribed with names, and probably one of the well-known inscribed missiles; also some illegible electioneering notices, not to mention various other insignificant scrawls, on walls in Pompeii.

**6.** Besides the inscriptions, there are some secondary sources, such as the Oscan glosses, mostly in Varro and Festus, and the geographical and personal names from Oscan territory. But they contribute relatively little to our knowledge of the dialect.

**7.** Oscan was not a mere patois, nor was it so regarded by the earlier Roman writers. Ennius, in boasting of having three souls because he could speak Greek, Oscan, and Latin, gave to Oscan a position which he had no thought of giving to the local vernacular of his home, the Messapian. For a long time, while Latin was still confined to Latium and its immediate borders, Oscan was spoken over a vastly wider territory. It was the language of the people which gave the Romans the hardest fight for the hegemony of Italy. In the early centuries the Oscans of Campania, under the Etruscan rule, and close to the Greek colonies of Cumae, Naples, etc., stood on fully as high a plane of civilization as the Romans of the same period. Eminent scholars like Mommsen have expressed the conviction that there once existed an Oscan literature, and certainly the conditions for the rise of a native literature were as favorable as at Rome. But nothing has come down to us, not even a reference to anything more pretentious than the puppet-shows introduced in Rome from Campania under the name of *fabulae Atellanae* or *ludi Osci*. At Rome, of course, these were no longer given in Oscan, but in rustic Latin.

### UMBRIAN — EXTERNAL DATA

**8.** Aside from a few short inscriptions from various towns of Umbria, the Umbrian remains consist of the Iguvinian Tables, discovered at Gubbio, the ancient Iguvium, in the fifteenth century. These are seven small bronze tablets (originally nine, but two were lost soon after the discovery), most of them inscribed on both sides, and containing together between four and five thousand words. This makes a far more extensive document than any representing any other dialect except Latin.

**9.** Some of the tables are written in the native Umbrian alphabet, which like the Oscan is derived from the Greek through the Etruscan, others in the Latin alphabet. These two divisions of the material are conveniently distinguished as Old Umbrian and New Umbrian, but the differences are in part merely orthographic, and, at most, far less marked than those which are usually associated with the terms Old and New in such a connection. The New Umbrian tables may date from the early part of the first century B.C. How much earlier the Old Umbrian tables are it is impossible to say; different parts were inscribed at different times, and even the relative order is not fully determined. See the Commentary on the Iguvinian Tables.

**10.** The contents of the Tables consist of the acts of a certain corporation of priests known as the Atiedian Brothers, and in their general character resemble the Roman *Acta Arvalium*. They contain directions for various ceremonies, such as the Purification of the Sacred Mount and the Lustration of the People, as well as the more private functions of the brotherhood, with minute prescriptions as to the taking of auspices, manner of sacrificing the victims, etc.; also statements as to the duties of certain officials, perquisites of the priests, contributions to be made to the brotherhood by certain *gentes*, etc. Some of the older tables contain matter which is repeated in an expanded form in the later tables.

GENERAL CHARACTERISTICS OF THE OSCAN–UMBRIAN GROUP

#### Phonology

**11.** The most striking characteristics, as regards phonology, are:

Change of the labiovelars $q^u$ and $g^u$, which appear in Latin as *qu* and *v* (*gu* after *n*), to the labials *p* and *b*; e.g. O. *pis* 'quis', U. *pisi*, Volsc. *pis*, Marruc. *nipis*; — O. **bivus** 'vivi'; — U. *benust* 'venerit'; — U. **umen** (from *\*umben*) 'unguen'.

Extensive syncope of short vowels in non-initial syllables ; e.g. O. *actud* 'agito'; — U. fiktu 'figito'; — O. húrz 'hortus'; — U. Ikuvins 'Iguvinus'; — O. akkatus 'advocati'.

Assimilation of *nd* to *nn*; e.g. O. úpsannam 'operandam'; — U. *pihaner* 'piandi' (*n* for *nn*, 26).

Retention of *s* before nasals and liquids, where it is lost in Latin; e.g. O. fisnam 'fanum', U. fesnaf-e, Pael. *fesn.* ; — O. kersnu 'cena', U. *sesna* ; — Pael. *prismu* 'prima'.

Retention of *a* in medial syllables, where it is weakened in Latin to *e* or *i*; e.g. O. Anterstataí '*Interstitae'; — U. antakres 'integris'; — U. *procanurent* '*procinuerint'.

Representation of original *bh* and *dh* by *f*, not only initially as in Latin, but also medially, where Latin has *b* or *d*; e.g. O. tfei, U. tefe 'tibi'; — O. mefiaí 'in media'; — U. rufru 'rubros'.

Change of final *ā*, which in Latin is shortened, in the direction of *ō*; e.g. O. *molto*, U. mutu, muta 'multa'.

Change of *kt* to *ht*, and of *pt* to *ft* (Umbrian, further, to *ht*); e.g. O. Úhtavis 'Octavius'; — U. rehte 'recte'; — O. *scriftas* 'scriptae', U. *screhto*.

Assimilation of *ks* to *ss*, *s*; e.g. O. destrst 'dextra est', U. *destram-e*.

Change of *ns* to *f*, though under different conditions in Oscan and Umbrian; e.g. O. úíttiuf 'usus' from *oitiōn-s ; — U. Acc. Pl. *eaf* 'eas' (also Marruc. *iaf-c*) from *eans (but O. víass).

### Inflection

**12. DECLENSION.** The types of noun-declension are sufficiently like the Latin to fall naturally into the same grouping of Five Declensions. But the Fifth Declension is represented by only a few forms, and in the Third Declension the consonant-stems and *i*-stems are kept distinct in a greater number of case-forms than in Latin. The Cases are the same as in Latin, except that, in the Singular, the Locative exists as a distinct form with full syntactical functions. The important differences in case-formation are as follows (for examples, see the paradigms):

First Declension. The Gen. Sg. has the original ending -*ās*, which is preserved in Latin only in phrases like *pater familiās*; the Nom. Pl. has the original ending -*ās*, which is lost in Latin.

Second Declension. The Gen. Sg. has 'the ending -*eis*, from *i*-stems; the Dat. Sg. has the ending -*oi*, which occurs in Latin only in *Numasioi* of the Praenestine brooch; the Nom. Pl. has the original noun-ending -*ōs* for both nouns and pronouns, while the Latin has -*ī*, from -*oi*, the pronominal ending; the Gen. Pl. has only the original -*ōm* (L. -*um*), there being nothing to correspond to L. -*ōrum*, which is a specifically Latin development.

Third Declension. The Gen. Sg. always has -*eis*, the ending of *i*-stems, while Latin -*is* is the proper ending of consonant-stems; the Acc. Sg. of consonant-stems has -*om*, from *o*-stems; in the Nom. Pl. the consonant-stems and *i*-stems are kept distinct, the former having the original ending -*es* with syncope of the *e*, the latter -*ēs* as in Latin (O. **humuns** 'homines', but **trís** 'tres').

**13.** CONJUGATION. The conjugation-types are the same as in Latin, the material grouping itself under the Four Conjugations, leaving the relics of unthematic inflection as "Irregular Verbs." But the type represented by Latin *capiō* is, in origin, more closely connected with the Fourth Conjugation than with the Third, and in Oscan-Umbrian is better grouped with the Fourth.

The Moods are the same. As in Latin, the Subjunctive is a fusion of original Subjunctive and Optative forms, and the distribution of the forms is the same as in Latin, except in the Perfect Subjunctive (see below).

The Tenses are the same, except that, perhaps accidentally, there is no example of a Pluperfect.

The Voices are the same, but of the Passive there are only forms of the Third Singular and Third Plural.

Of the non-finite forms there are found a Present Active Participle, Perfect Passive Participle, Gerundive, Present Active

Infinitive, Perfect Passive Infinitive, and Supine.   The Ger-
und, Perfect Infinitive Active, Future Infinitives, Present Infinitive Passive, and Future Active Participle are lacking.   The
absence of examples of some of these forms is possibly a mere
accident, but it is probable that most of them are specifically
Latin formations.

The important differences in formation are as follows:

The Pres. Infin. Act. ends in -*om*; e.g. O. *ezum*, U. *erom* 'esse'.

The Future is an *s*-formation, in origin a short-vowel Subjunctive of an *s*-Aorist; e.g. O. *deiuast* 'iurabit', U. *ferest* 'feret'.

The Fut. Perf. is an *us*-formation, probably based on an
old Perf. Act. Partic. in -*us* combined with a short-vowel Subjunctive of the verb 'to be'; e.g. O. *dicust* 'dixerit', U. *benust*
'venerit'.

Among the different formations making up the Perfect
System, the *f*-Perfect is characteristic of Oscan-Umbrian; e.g.
O. **aikdafed** 'decrevit', U. *andirsafust* 'circumtulerit'. (Oscan-
Sabellian has also a *tt*-Perfect, and Umbrian an *l*-Perfect and
an *nki*-Perfect.)   The Latin *vī*- and *s*-Perfects are lacking.

The Perf. Subj. is a real Subjunctive form with the mood-
sign *ē*, not an Optative with mood-sign *ī* as in Latin; e.g. O. **tri-
barakattins** 'aedificaverint', U. *combifianśi* 'nuntiaverit'.

In the Third Singular and Third Plural there is a distinction between primary endings, which are -*t*, -*nt*, and secondary
endings, which are -*d* (lost in Umbrian), -*ns*; e.g. O. **faamat**
'habitat', but **fakiiad** 'faciat'; — O. **stahint** 'stant', U. *furfant*
'purgant', but O. *deicans* 'dicant', U. *dirsans* 'dent'.   Latin
shows -*d* in some of the earliest inscriptions, but nothing corresponding to -*ns*.

The unthematic form of the Third Plural, -*ent*, which in
Latin is always replaced by the thematic form -*ont*, -*unt*, is pre-
served, and even extended to thematic formations; e.g. O. **set**,
U. *sent* 'sunt', O. *censazet* 'censebunt'.

The Third Singular and Third Plural of the Passive have
an ending -*ter*, unknown in Latin, while the Latin -*tur* appears

only in Umbrian secondary tenses ; e.g. O. *vincter* 'convincitur', **karanter** 'vescuntur', U. **herter** 'oportet'; U. **emantur** 'accipiantur'.

The Third Singular Passive has also a peculiar set of forms in which the ending is neither *-ter* nor *-tur*, but simply *-r* ; e.g. U. *ferar* 'feratur', O. **sakrafir** (Perf. Subj.) 'sacrato'.

The Imperative Passive has an ending *-mō(d)*, O. *-mō-r*, which is of similar origin to the early Latin *-minō* ; e.g. O. *censamur* 'censetor', U. *persnihimu* 'precator'.

### Syntax

**14.** The Syntax shows a remarkably close resemblance to the Latin. There are no uses of the moods and tenses which cannot be paralleled in the Latin, the agreement being closest, in some respects, with early Latin prose. The Passive forms include both genuine Passives and Deponents, as in Latin, but the frequent impersonal use is characteristic of Oscan-Umbrian. In the use of the cases there are many interesting constructions, of which the following are the most noteworthy. The Locative, being preserved as a distinct case-form, is used where the Latin requires *in* with the Ablative, e.g. O. **eisei terei** 'in eo territorio'. The Partitive Genitive has a wider scope than in Latin, e.g. U. *iuenga peracrio tursituto* 'iuvencas ex opimis fuganto'. A Genitive of Time is seen in O. *zicolom* XXX *nesimum* 'in diebus XXX proximis'. The Genitive is used more freely than in Latin to denote the *matter involved* ; e.g. O. *eizazunc egmazum* 'in these matters', U. *pusi ocrer pihaner* 'as in the case of the purification of the mount'. The prepositions corresponding to Latin *inter* and *trāns* are used with both Accusative and Locative; those corresponding to *ob* and *post* are used with the Ablative.

### Vocabulary [1]

**15.** Of words which are characteristic of Oscan-Umbrian as compared with Latin, the following are the most important examples :

---

[1] Special attention is given here to the lexical peculiarities, since these are not, like the other characteristics, the subject of fuller treatment in the grammar proper.

1. *her-* 'velle'.   O. *herest* 'volet', **heriam** 'arbitrium, vim', **Herenta-**
   **teís** 'Veneris' (Pael. *Herentas*);   U. **heri** 'vult', *heriest* 'volet',
   etc., **herter** 'oportet', **heris** 'vel', *pis-her* 'quilibet'.   Cf. L. *horior*,
   *hortor*, Grk. χαίρω, Skt. *háryāmi* 'be gratified, delight in', Goth.
   *-gairns* 'eager', Eng. *yearn*.   This root completely displaces
   *uel-* (L. *volō*) in the meaning 'wish', the latter appearing only
   in a specialized meaning; e.g. U. **veltu** 'deligito', *ehueltu* 'iubeto'.

2. *toutā-* 'civitas, urbs, populus'.   O. *τωϝτο Μαμερτινο* 'civitas
   Mamertina', *toutad praesentid* 'populo praesente', *touticom*
   'publicum', etc.;   U. *totam Ïiouinam* 'civitatem Iguuinam',
   *tuderor totcor* 'fines urbici', etc.;   Marruc. *toutai Maroucai*
   'civitati Marrucinae';   Volsc. *toticu* 'publico'.   Cf. Lith. *tauta*
   'people', O.Pruss. *tauto* 'country', O.Ir. *tuath* 'people', Goth.
   *þiuda* 'people', O.Eng. *þéod* 'people, nation', etc. *Etruscan Influence*

3. *ais-* 'sacer, divinus'.   O. *aisusis* 'sacrificiis';   U. *esona* 'sacras', *Walde*
   *esono* 'sacrificium';   Marruc. *aisos* 'dis'(?);   Mars. *esos* 'dis'(?);
   Volsc. *esaristrom* 'sacrificium';   αἰσοί · θεοὶ ὑπὸ Τυρρηνῶν
   (Hesychius), *aesar* Etrusca lingua deus (Suetonius).   ~~Per-~~
   ~~haps~~ related to Germ. *Ehre* (Goth. *\*aiza*), and to Goth. *aistan*
   'revere', ~~L. aestimō,~~ from *aiz-d-*.   *S. Walde but not aestimo*

4. *komno-* 'comitium'.   O. *comono* 'comitia';   U. **super kumne**
   'super comitio', **kumnahkle** 'in conventu'.   From *kom* 'cum'
   + suffix *-no-* (cf. L. *prō-nus, trāns-trum*).

5. *hontro-* 'inferus'.   O. **hu[n]truis** 'inferis';   U. *hondra* 'infra',
   Superl. *hondomu* 'infimo'.   From *hom-*, related to L. *humus*,
   Grk. χαμαί, χθών, etc.   For meaning cf. L. *humilis*, Grk.
   χθαμαλός, Lith. *žėmas* 'low', *žemȳn* 'down', from *žėmė* 'earth'.

6. *medes-* 'ius'.   U. **meřs**, **mers** 'ius', *mersto* 'iustum', **mersuva**
   'iusta';   O. **meddíss** 'meddix', official title (cf. Festus "meddix
   apud Oscos nomen magistratus est"; Livy 26, 6, 13 "medix
   tuticus [O. **meddíss túvtíks**; see above, 2] qui summus magistratus apud Campanos est"; cpd. like L. *iūdex* from *\*iūs-dik-*),
   *medicim* 'magistracy', **meddíkiai** 'in the meddixship'; *medicatinom*
   'iudicationem', *medicatud* 'iudicato'; Pael., Volsc., *medix* (Nom.
   Pl.);   Mars. *medis*.   Cf. L. *modus, modes-tus*, Grk. μέδομαι, etc.

7. *ner-* 'vir, princeps', title of rank.   O. *nerum* (Gen. Pl.), **niir** (Nom. Sg.); U. *nerf* (Acc. Pl.), *nerus* (Dat. Pl.).   For related Sabine forms cf. Suetonius Tib. 1 "inter cognomina autem et Neronis adsumpsit, quo significatur lingua Sabina fortis ac strenuus"; Aul. Gellius 13, 23 "id autem, sive Nerio sive Nerienes est, Sabinum verbum est, eoque significatur virtus et fortitudo"; Lydus de Mens. 4, 42 "νερίκη γὰρ ἡ ἀνδρία ἐστὶ καὶ νέρωνας τοὺς ἀνδρείους οἱ Σαβῖνοι καλοῦσιν".   Cf. Grk. ἀνήρ, Skt. *nar-*'man', O.Ir. *nert* 'strength'.

8. *nessimo-* 'proximus'.   O. **nessimas** (Nom. Pl.), *nesimum* (Gen. Pl.), *nesimois* (Abl. Pl.); U. *nesimei* 'proxime' (adv.).   Cf. O.Ir. *nessam* 'nearest', etc.   Cf. also O. **nistrus** 'propinquos'.

9. *pert* 'trans'.   O. **pert viam** 'trans viam', *am-pert* 'not more than, dumtaxat'; U. **pert spiniam** 'trans columnam'(?).   An extension of *per*.   Umbrian also uses *traf* = L. *trāns*.

10. *postin* 'according to'.   O. **pústin slagím** 'according to the territory'; U. **pusti kastruvuf** 'per capita'(?) etc.   An extension of *\*posti* (early Latin *poste*).

11. *pŭr-* 'ignis'.   U. *pir* 'ignis', *pure-to* 'ab igne'; O. **purasiaí** 'in igniaria'.   Cf. Grk. πῦρ, πυρός, O.H.G. *fuir, fiur*, Eng. *fire*, etc.

12. *sēu̯o-* 'totus'.   O. *siuom* 'omnino'; U. *seuom* 'totum', **sev-akne** 'sollemne'.   Cf. L. *sō-lus*, Goth. *sē-ls*(?).

13. *tefro-* 'burnt-offering'.   O. **saahtúm tefúrúm** 'sacred burnt-offering'; U. **tefra** 'carnes cremandas', *tefru-to* 'ex rogo'.   Probably from *\*tepsro-*, related to L. *tepor*, Skt. *tápas*, etc.

14. *treb-* 'habitare'.   U. *trebeit* 'versatur', *tremnu* 'tabernaculo'; O. **trííbúm** 'domum', **tríbarakkiuf** 'aedificium', **tríbarakavúm** 'aedificare', etc.   Cf. O.Ir. *treb* 'dwelling-place', Lith. *trobà* 'building', Goth. *þaúrp* 'field', Germ. *Dorf*, etc.

15. *u̯ero-* 'porta'.   O. **veru** 'portam'; U. *uerof-e* 'in portam', etc.   Cf. Skt. *vr̥-* 'enclose', Goth. *warjan* 'ward off', Lith. *veriù* 'open, shut', *vartai* 'gate', L. *aperiō, operiō*.

For other examples, see, in the Glossary, O. **akeneí**, U. *acnu*; O. **aíkdafed**, U. **eitipes**; O. **eehiianasúm**, U. *ehiato*; O. *eizo-*, U. *ero-*; O. **púmperiaís**, U. **pumperias**.

**16.** Of the many words which are peculiar to Oscan (or Oscan-Sabellian) or to Umbrian, the following may be mentioned here.

A. OSCAN. 1. *aeteis* 'partis', **a]íttíúm** 'partium'. Cf. Grk. *aîσa* from *aἴτ-ἰα*.

2. **amnúd** 'circuitu', *amnud* 'causa' (prepos.). From *am-* ' amb-' + suffix *-no-*. (Cf. *kom-no-*, 15, 4.) Perhaps contained in L. *soll-emnis*.

3. *comparascuster* 'consulta erit', **kú]mparakineís** 'consilii'. From the same root as L. *poscō, precor,* but with the meaning which it has more commonly in other languages of 'ask, question' (Skt. *prcchámi* 'ask', *sam-prcchámi* 'consult', Germ. *forschen,* etc.).

4. *deiuā-* 'iurare' (*deiuatud* 'iurato', etc.). Denominative from *\*deiuo-* 'god'. Cf. Lettic *dîwati-s* 'swear', from *dîws* 'god'.

5. *egmo* 'res', *egmazum* 'rerum', etc. Etym. uncertain (L. *egeō*?).

6. *eituam,* **eítiuvam** 'pecuniam', *eituas* 'pecuniae', etc. Also Marruc. *eituam* 'pecuniam'. Etym. uncertain.

7. **feíhúss** 'muros', **feíhúís** 'muris'. Cf. Grk. τεῖχος, Skt. *dehí* 'heap, wall', etc. From the same root as L. *fingō, figūra,* etc.

8. **iním,** *inim* 'et'. Also Pael. *inim* and *inom* 'et'. Related to L. *enim,* U. *enom* 'tum'.

9. *ˈloufir* 'vel'. In form a 3d Sg. Pres. Pass. from the same root as L. *libet.* Cf. L. *vel* from *volō,* and U. **heris** 'vel' (15, 1).

10. **puklum** 'puerum, filium'. Also Pael. *puclois* 'pueris'. Cf. Skt. *putrá-* 'son', and, from the same root, L. *puer,* Grk. παίς.

11. *tanginom* 'sententiam', Abl. Sg. **tanginúd,** etc. Cf. Festus "tongere nosse est, nam Praenestini tongitionem dicunt notionem. Ennius 'Alii rhetorica tongent'". Cf. Goth. *pagkjan,* Eng. *think.*

For other examples, see, in the Glossary, **affukad, ampt, amvíannud, angetuzet, brateis,** *cadeis,* **karanter, deketasiúí, ehpeílatas, faamat, fertalís, heriiad, iúklei, iuvilu,** *lamatir,* **luisarifs, prupukid, serevkld, slagím, sullus, sverrunеí,** *trutum,* **usurs, ualaemom, vereiiaí.**

B. UMBRIAN. 12. *anglaf, ancla* 'oscines'. Cpd. of *klā-* (L. *clāmō*), as L. *oscinēs* from *canō.*

13. *anouihimu* 'induitor'.     From *\*an-ouiō* (Conj. IV);    cf.
L. *ind-uō* from *\*ind-ouō*, Lith. *aviù* 'wear (shoes)'.

14. *ape, appei* 'cum, ubi' (always temporal).    Probably from *ad*
+ *pe* (L. -*que*), and so in form like L. *adque, atque*.

15. *arsmor* 'ritus', *arsmatiam* 'ritualem', *arsmahamo* 'ordamini',
etc.    Etym. uncertain.

16. *combifiā-* 'nuntiare, mandare' (*combifiatu,* **kupifiaia,** etc.).
Probably from *fif-*, the same root as in L. *fīdō*, Grk. πείθω,
or possibly from *fuf-*, the same as in Grk. πυνθάνομαι.

17. *gomia* 'gravidas'.    Cf. L. *gemō*, and, for meaning especially,
Grk. γέμω.

18. *nertru* 'sinistro'.    Cf. Grk. νέρτερος 'lower, nether'.    According to Italic ideas *īmus* = *sinister*.

19. *purdouitu* 'porricito', *purditom* 'porrectum', etc.    From
*\*por-douiō*, with the root seen in L. *duim, duam*.

20. *tuder* 'finem', *tuderus* 'finibus', *tuderato* 'finitum', *eturstahmu*
'exterminato', etc.    Etym. uncertain.

21. *uend-* 'vertere' in *ahauendu* 'avertito', *preuendu* 'advertito'.
Cf. Germ. *wenden* (Eng. *wind*).

For other examples, too numerous to mention, see the
Glossary.    Many of them are technical terms, often of obscure
meaning.

**17.** Several words are used in a sense which is either
unknown or nearly obsolete in Latin.

1. O. **kasit** (L. *caret*) means 'decet' or 'oportet', e.g. **fakiiad kasit**
'faciat decet'.    Cf. Eng. "it wants to be done", that is "it
needs to be done".

2. O. *castrous*, U. *castruo* (L. *castrum*), mean either 'fundus,
landed property', or, more probably, 'head'.

3. O. *carneis*, U. **karu** (L. *carō*), have the general meaning 'part,
portion' (cf. also U. **kartu** 'distribuito'), e.g. *maimas carneis
senateis tanginud* 'maximae partis senatus sententia', U. **mestru karu fratru** 'maior pars fratrum'.    But Umbrian shows also
the specialized meaning 'piece of flesh', e.g. **aseçeta karne** 'non
secta carne'.

4. The forms corresponding to L. *operor* are used in the sense of 'make, construct', where Latin would employ *faciō*; e.g. O. ekass víass uupsens 'has vias fecerunt', trífbúm ekak úpsannam deded 'domum hanc faciendam dedit'; U. *capirse perso osatu* 'capidi fossam facito'; Pael. *Herec. fesn. upsaseter coisatens* 'Herculi fanum fieret curaverunt'.

5. O. ant (L. *ante*) means 'usque ad', e.g. ant púnttram 'usque ad pontem'.

6. U. *com* (L. *cum*), when postpositive, has developed a locative meaning, e.g. *ueris-co* 'at the gate', asa-ku 'at the altar'.

7. O. *op*, úp (L. *ob*), means 'apud', e.g. úp sakaraklúd 'apud templum', *op toutad* 'apud populum'.

8. *prō-* (L. *prō-*) sometimes has a temporal meaning 'before', for which in Latin *prae-*, or oftener *ante-*, is used; e.g. U. prupehast 'ante piabit', O. prupukid 'ex antepacto, by previous agreement'.

9. U. emantur (L. *emō*) 'accipiantur' shows the original meaning 'take' seen in Latin compounds and in the particle *em*. Cf. also Festus "emere, quod nunc est mercari, antiqui accipiebant pro sumere". The specialized meaning 'buy' is found in *emps* on one of the short inscriptions, where it is perhaps due to Latin influence.

10. U. prever (L. *prīvus*) means 'singulis', e.g. numer prever 'nummis singulis'. Cf. Festus "privos privasque antiqui dicebant pro singulis". So also O. *preiuatud* means 'reo, defendant' (as rarely in Latin, e.g. Livy 26, 3, 8, etc.), — the single man among the many making up the assembly.

11. U. *orto* (L. *ortus*) is sometimes used in the literal sense of 'rising, standing up', e.g. urtes puntis 'the pentads rising'. Cf. Velius Longus (Keil, Gram. Lat. VII, 74) "oriri apud antiquos surgere frequenter significat, ut apparet ex eo quod dicitur: oriens consul magistrum populi dicat, quod est surgens"; Livy 8, 23, 15 " consul oriens".

12. U. *tursitulo, tursiandu* (L. *terreō*), have the meaning 'drive off', which in Latin is only poetical; e.g. *ponne iuengar tursiandu* 'cum iuvencae fugentur'. But also *tursitu* 'terreto'.

13. U. *couertu* (L. *convertō*) always means 'return', with the intransitive meaning which is rare in Latin; e.g. *enom traha Sahatam couertu* 'tum trans Sanctam revertito'.

14. U. **vurtus** (L. *vertō*) has the meaning 'take a turn, change', which is rare in Latin (verterat fortuna, Liv. 5, 49, 5); e.g. **pune naraklum vurtus** 'cum nuntiatio mutaverit'.

15. U. *ostendu* (L. *ostendō*) has more nearly its etymological meaning than in Latin. It is used of 'stretching out', that is 'offering', fruits of the field or vessels; once of 'putting forward', that is 'choosing', an official.

16. O. *urust* (L. *ōrō*; see **21**) is used in the technical sense of 'plead, argue'; e.g. *com preiuatud actud,* ——, *in pon posmom con preiuatud urust* 'cum reo agito, ——, et cum postremum cum reo oraverit'. Cf. Festus "orare antiquos dixisse pro agere"; Cic. Brut. 12, 47 "oravisse capitis causam"; Livy 39, 40, 6 "si causa oranda esset", etc.

17. U. *comohota* (L. *commōtus*) means 'brought, offered', in *Di Grabouie, tio comohota tribrisine buo,* ——, *tiom subocau* 'Iuppiter Grabovi, te commoto ternione boum, —— te invoco'. Cf. Cato, De Agric. 144 "Iane pater, te hac strue commovenda (MSS. also ommovenda) bonas preces precor".

### Summary

**18.** The differences between Oscan-Umbrian and Latin are considerable. They are far greater, for example, than those between the Greek dialects, especially in the inflectional forms. But the resemblances with Latin, as compared with any other Indo-European language, are also notable, leaving no doubt that we have to do with two closely-related divisions of the same branch, sharing in many important characteristics which distinguish this among the various branches of the great family. This again is most marked in the inflectional system, so that we can maintain that the Latin inflectional system as a whole is also the Italic. The simplest proof of this lies in the fact that the general classifications which have been found most suitable for the treatment of Latin forms apply also to Oscan-Umbrian. For such classifications, as, for example, that of the verb-forms into the Four Conjugations with scattering Irregular Verbs, are not mere arbitrary devices, for which others equally good might be substituted, but actually reflect the distribution of the linguistic material in a given language.

A few specific examples of these resemblances are: merging of the Instrumental with the Ablative ; extension of the Ablative in *-d* from the *o*-stems to the other declensions ; partial fusion of *i*-stems and consonant-stems ; use of the Interrogative-Indefinite Pronoun as a Relative ; fusion of Aorist and Perfect; formation of the Imperfect Indicative ; formation of the Imperfect Subjunctive.

### SPECIAL CHARACTERISTICS OF OSCAN

**19.** Oscan is the Gothic of the Italic dialects. In the conservatism and transparency of its vowel-system it is rivaled only by Greek of all the Indo-European languages.

Diphthongs are preserved intact in all positions ; e.g. Dat.-Abl. Pl. *-ais* and *-ois*: L. *-īs* ; — Loc. Sg. *-ei*: L. *-ī* ; — Gen. Sg. of *u*-stems in *-ous*: L. *-ūs* ; — *deicum*: L. *dīcō* ; — **múiníkeí**: L. (*com-*)*mūnis*. So also Paelignian and Marrucinian.

The finer nuances of pronunciation are expressed by a highly-developed orthographical system. The qualitative difference between the long and short vowels (except the *a*-vowels), which is known to have existed in Latin, is more marked in Oscan than elsewhere. For example, the short *e* is denoted by the letter *e*, but long *e* has become so close in pronunciation as to be denoted by an *i*-character (in the Oscan alphabet by í, the sign of the relatively open *i*); e.g. *estud*: L. *estō*, but *ligud*, **lígatúís**: L. *lēx, lēgātus.* Note also *pod*, **púd**: L. *quod*, but *estud*, *estud*: L. *estō* ; also (in the Oscan alphabet) **píd**: L. *quid*, but Abl. Sg. -**íd**: L. *-īd*.

An original *s* between vowels, which becomes *r* in Umbrian as in Latin, remains a sibilant (also Paelignian); e.g. Gen. Pl. *-azum*: L. *-ārum*. Final *d* after long vowels is preserved, as in early Latin, while in Umbrian it is lost even after short vowels (**20**).

A specifically Oscan (also Paelignian) process is the development of an anaptyctic vowel between liquids or nasals and mutes; e.g. **aragetud** 'argento'; — **perek(aís)** 'perticis': U. *percam*. Among other secondary changes are the doubling of consonants before certain sounds, and the change of *u* after a dental; e.g. **kúmbenniéís** 'conventus', **alttram** 'alteram', **tiurrí** 'turrim'.

See also under **20**.

### Special Characteristics of Umbrian

**20.** Umbrian, as compared with Oscan, is characterized mainly by a number of secondary phonetic changes, of which the most important are:

Monophthongization of the original diphthongs in all positions; e.g. Dat.-Abl. Pl. **-es**, *-ir*, *-er*: O. *-ois*, L. *-īs*; — *ote*: O. *aut*, L. *aut*; — *pre*: O. **prai**, L. *prae*. So also Volscian.

Rhotacism, as in Latin, where Oscan preserves the sibilant; e.g. Gen. Pl. *-arum*: O. *-azum*.

Loss of final *d*; e.g. *-po* in *suepo* 'sive': O. *pod*, L. *quod*; — **façia** 'faciat': O. **fakiiad**. So also Volscian.

Loss of *l* before *t*; e.g. **muta**: O. *molta*, L. *multa*.

Assibilation of *k* before front vowels, as in late Latin and Romance; e.g. **façia**: O. **fakiiad**, L. *faciat*. So also Volscian.

Change of gutturals before *t* to *i*; e.g. **aitu**: O. *actud*, L. *agitō* (cf. French *fait* from L. *factum*).

Change of intervocalic *d* to a sound written *rs* (ř in Umbrian alphabet); e.g. *persi*, **peři**: L. *pede*.

Change of *ft* (in part from *pt*) to *ht*; e.g. *srehto* 'scriptum': O. *scriftas*, L. *scrīptus*.

Assimilation of secondary *ps*; e.g. *osatu* 'facito': O. **úpsannam**, L. *operor*.

Change of initial *l* to *u*; e.g. **vutu**: L. *lavitō*.

Among other Umbrian peculiarities are:

Development of original final *-ns* to *-f*, for which Oscan has *-ss*; e.g. U. *eaf* 'eas': O. **viass** 'vias'. So also Marrucinian.

Retention of intervocalic '*rs*; e.g. *tursitu* 'terreto'.

Ending of Abl. Sg. of consonant-stems in *-e*, as in Latin, while Oscan has *-ōd* after *o*-stems; e.g. **natine** 'natione': O. *tanginud* 'sententia'.

Ending of Dat.-Abl. Pl. of consonant-stems in *-us*, after *u*-stems, where Oscan has *-iss*, *-is*, after *i*-stems; e.g. *fratrus* 'fratribus' (as if L. \**fratrubus*): O. *ligis* 'legibus'.

Presence of pronominal forms with *sm*; e.g. **pusme** 'cui', *esmei* 'huic': Skt. *kásmāi, ásmāi*, etc.

Imperative *futu*, contrasted with O. *estud*, L. *estō* (also Volsc. *estu*).

Perfect in *l* and *nki̯*, contrasted with O. *tt*-Perfect (**13**).

Passive endings both *-ter* and *-tur*, Oscan having only *-ter* (**13**).

Use of *et* as the usual connective, as in Latin, for which Oscan has *inim* (**16**, 8).

Arrangement of the proper name, which is praenomen, father's name, gentile, while in Oscan it is the same as in Latin.

### Borrowed Words

**21.** The borrowed words consist mainly of Greek words in Oscan, introduced from the neighboring Greek colonies. These are mostly names or epithets of divinities, such as **Appelluneís** (Dor. Ἀπέλλων); — **Evklúí** (probably Εὔκολος, an epithet of Hermes in Magna Graecia); — **Herekleís** (Ἡρακλῆς, with syncope of the *a* and shortening of the vowel before *r* + consonant, whence, with anaptyctic vowel in different positions, come both the Oscan and Latin forms; the Oscan form, in contrast to the Latin, is an *o*-stem, Dat. Sg. **Hereklúí**; cf. also Vest. *Herclo*); — **Piístiaí** (Πίστιος; cf. Ζεὺς Πίστιος for *Iuppiter Fidius* in Dionys. Hal. 4, 58; the **íí** of the Oscan is perhaps due to contamination with some such form as **Piíhiúí**); — **Herukinaí**

('Ερυκίνη; **Herentateí Herukinaí** corresponds to the Sicilian 'Αφρο-
δίτη 'Ερυκίνη, the worship of whom as *Veñus Erycina* was also
introduced among the Romans in the second Punic war; cf.
Livy 22, 9, 10); — **Meeílíkiieís** (Μειλίχιος; **eeí** is merely the result
of an attempted correction of **ee** to **eí**); — **Arentika[í** (Hesych.
'Αράντισιν· 'Ερινύσι, Μακεδόνες).

But there are also a few common nouns of the same class
as those introduced into Latin at the same period, such as **thesavrúm** (θησαυρός; the Oscan form is neuter), **kúiníks** (χοῖνιξ),
**passtata** (παστάς), **tiurrí**, with L. *turris* (τύρρις); **limu** 'famem'
is also suspicious, since cognates of Grk. λῑμός are otherwise
unknown in Italic.

Latin influence shows itself in some official titles, as
O. **aídil** 'aedilis' (the *d* of L. *aedēs* comes from *dh*, which would
be *f* in Oscan); — O. **kenzstur** (cf. also **Kenssurineís**) beside the regular **keenzstur**, *censtur* 'censor' (see **244**, 1, *a*); — probably O. **kvaísstur**,
U. **kvestur** 'quaestor', though there is a possibility that the initial
was not *qᵘ*, but *ḱu*, and that this gives O.-U. *ku*, not *p* (**141**, *a*).

O. *urust* is best taken as a borrowed legal term (see **17**, 16),
since we should expect **uzust* (see **112**) as a cognate of L. *ōrō*
according to what is still the most probable derivation of the
latter, namely from *ōs*.

Some proper names show Latin or half-Oscanized Latin
forms, as **Niumeriis** 'Numerius', for which the genuine Oscan
form would be **Niumsiis** (cf. the praenomen **Ni]umsis**).

O. **Mener**, if, as is probable, an abbreviation of a form corresponding to
L. *Minervium*, shows that the Oscan, like the Etruscan, name of the divinity
was borrowed, together with the cult, from a dialect in which rhotacism took
place (**Menes-uā*). Though the cult of Minerva may have originated among
the Faliscans, as many suppose, it probably reached the Oscans through the
medium of the Romans, but at a time when the Latin form was still *Menerva*
(CIL. V 703, 799, VI 523, etc.)    Pael. *Minerua* is likewise borrowed.

U. **vinu** 'vinum' (and O. **Viínikiís** 'Vinicius', if related) must be borrowed
from *vīnum*, if the latter is from **ueino-*, earlier **uoino-* (οῖνος). For the change
of *uoi* to *uei* is probably Latin only (U. *uocu* : Grk. Φοῖκος ?), and even if it were
Italic, we should expect then U. **venu** (**65**).

A possible example of borrowing from one of the minor dialects is U. **felsva.**
See **149**, *b.*

# PHONOLOGY

## ALPHABET AND ORTHOGRAPHY

### OSCAN

**22.** The native Oscan alphabet consists of the following twenty-one characters:

| | | | | |
|---|---|---|---|---|
| A, a | ⅃, v | √, l | ⟨, s | |
| B, b | I, z(= ts) | M, m | T, t | |
| ⟩, g | ⊟, h | H, n | V, u | |
| Я, d | I, i | Π, p | 8, f | |
| Ǝ, e | Ж, k | ◘, r | ⊢(⊣ ⊦), í | V, ú |

The last two letters are simply differentiations of the ordinary characters for *i* and *u*, and are not found in the oldest inscriptions.[1] They are commonly transcribed by í and ú, but sometimes by ï and ů, the latter also by o. The í is used to indicate an open *i*-sound, representing etymologically a short *i* (44), an *ē* (41), a short *e* in hiatus (38, 1), and occurring regularly in *i*-diphthongs (61, 1) and in the combination ií representing *ī* (47). The ú denotes an *o*-sound, the character *o* being lacking in both Oscan and Umbrian.

Double consonants are indicated in the writing, except in some of the oldest inscriptions.

The length of vowels is often shown by a doubling of the vowel, as in **aasas**: L. *āra* ; — **Fluusaí**: L. *Flōra*.

**23.** The Latin alphabet of the Tabula Bantina is of the usual type. *z* does not denote the sound *ts* as in the native alphabet, but the voiced sibilant (English *z* in *zero*), which in

---

[1] The occurrence of ⊢ on a few Boeotian inscriptions (CIGS. I 1888, 1943, 2456), representing an open *ι* which comes from original *ει* or from *e* before vowels, but in the usual Boeotian orthography is not distinguished from *ι*, suggests that it may not be an Oscan invention after all, but possibly borrowed at a comparatively late period from some type of the Chalcidian alphabet in southern Italy.

the native alphabet is not differentiated from *s* ; e.g. Gen. Pl. *-azum* (-**asúm**).

Double consonants are only rarely indicated, and the doubling of vowels to denote length is unknown.

**24.** The Greek alphabet, used in a few inscriptions of Sicily and southern Italy, is of the Tarentine-Ionic type, such as appears in the Heracleian tables. This is the normal Ionic with the addition of ⊢ = h and ⊏ = v. Neither η nor ω is used to indicate quantity.

According to the system of orthography represented in no. 62 and some others, ηι and ωϝ are used to represent the diphthongs *ei* and *ou*, as in Gen. Sg. *-ηις* = -**eís**, τωϝτο = *touto*; while ει and ου represent monophthongs, the former the open *i*-sound, the í of the native alphabet, the latter the *u*-sound of original ō, e.g. μεδδειξ = **meddíss**, ουπσευς = **uupsens**.

But in some inscriptions ει and ου are used for diphthongs, and original ō then appears as *o*, e.g. Ϝερσορει 'Versori' (contrast the last two syllables with those of Απϝελλουνηι, no. 62), Λουκανοϝ 'Lucanorum' (cf. **Lúvkanateís** ; for the last syllable contrast Μαμερτινουϝ).

*a.* The spelling Διουϝει (cf. **Diúveí, Iúveí**) is probably due to the fact that the syllabic division was not clear. Cf. U. *auuei* beside usual *aueif* 'avis'.

*b.* A character S, occurring in Sεστιες and αϝαSακετ (nos. 65-66), is of disputed value, but is probably the equivalent of Oscan 8. Cf. also the coin-legend ⟩ЕΝϞЕΡ beside **Fensernu**.

*c.* In Νιυμσδιηις = **Niumsieís**, the σδ is probably connected in some way with the dialectic use of σδ for the usual ʒ, though in the latter case it represented the actual pronunciation.

### UMBRIAN

**25.** The native Umbrian alphabet consists of the following nineteen characters :

| | | | |
|---|---|---|---|
| Ⱥ, a | ⱦ, z(= ts) | Ɱ(Λ), m | Ⱦ(Ⴤ), t |
| Ⴊ, b | ⊘, h | Ⱨ, n | V, u |
| Ⴍ, ř | I, i | ꟼ, p | 8, f |
| ⴩, e | Ⴉ, k | ⊲, r | d, ç |
| Ⴑ, v | ↓, l | ⟩, s | |

There are no signs for *d* and *g*, the letters **t** and **k** answering for both surds and sonants.

The ꟼ represents a sound which comes from an original intervocalic *d* and appears in the Latin alphabet as *rs*. For convenience it may be pronounced simply as *rs*, but probably it was a sort of sibilant *r*, like the Bohemian *ř*, from which comes the usual transcription *ř*. It is also transcribed, with more regard for its origin than for its pronunciation, as ḍ or ṭ.

The ꟼ, transcribed ç, also sometimes ś, represents a sibilant derived from *k* before a front vowel.

Double consonants are not indicated. Vowel-length is sometimes shown by an added **h**, e.g. **kumnahkle** with suffix *-āklo-*.

> *a.* A by-form for **m**, ᴧ, occurring also in Etruscan, is regularly employed in Table V. The san, ᴍ, occurs twice for **s**, and the theta, ☉, is twice used for **t**. The appearance of **p** in place of **f** in **kutep, vitlup, turup** (I b 3, 4), for which there is no likely phonetic explanation, is perhaps to be accounted for by the existence of a by-form for **f** resembling the form of **p** (cf. Faliscan ↑).

**26.** The Latin alphabet is of the usual type, but with no *z*. The secondary sibilant, the ꟼ of the native alphabet, is denoted by Ś, which is transcribed *ś*. *q* is used before the vowel *u*, as often in Latin inscriptions (*pequnia*); e.g. *pequo, dequrier, peiqu*. Double consonants are rarely indicated. Vowel-length is shown by an added *h*, by vowel + *h* + vowel, rarely by doubling of the vowel; e.g. *spahmu, spahamu, eetu*.

> Note. For the probable origin of the use of an added *h* to denote vowel-length, which is characteristic of Umbrian of both alphabets, see **75**. The use of vowel + *h* + vowel is probably a combination of this with the double-vowel method.

### Relation of the Alphabets

> **27.** Both the Oscan and Umbrian native alphabets are derived from the Greek alphabet of the Chalcidian type, through the medium of the Etruscan. That they are not derived directly from the Greek is shown by the absence of the letter o, as well as by other evidence. At the same time, the presence of ꟻ points to an earlier type than that of the extant Etruscan inscriptions. Differences between Oscan and Umbrian may be attributed to both local and chronological variations of Etruscan, as well as to divergent development after borrowing. It is extremely probable that the Oscan development was influenced in some particulars by the neighboring Greek.

The fact that ⟩, g, is present in Oscan, but not in Umbrian, is sometimes explained by the supposition that the Oscan alphabet was borrowed earlier than the Umbrian. But at all periods Etruscan possessed both characters, ⟩ and 乂, used as by-forms for the surd. Umbrian took only 乂, possibly because this was preferred in the local type from which it was derived. Oscan took over both characters and differentiated them again. That in this process the original value of the signs in Greek was restored, instead of the opposite (see following), might be accidental, but is very likely due to the influence of Campanian Greek usage.

The apparent transposition of the signs for *d* and *r* is accounted for as follows. The Etruscans had no sound *d*, but used ⍌ as a by-form of ꟼ = *r*, in fact preferred it, as less likely to be confused with ꟷ = *p*; and with this value it was adopted by the Oscans and Umbrians. But the old signs for *r* were also taken over and employed for the sound *d*, — ꟼ by the Oscans, ꟼ by the Umbrians. This early Umbrian use of ꟼ as *d* is seen in some of the minor inscriptions. But with the change of intervocalic *d* the letter was retained for the new sound, that which we transcribe ř, and thenceforth the unchanged *d* was expressed by the letter t.

The origin of the sign 8, f, is disputed. Possibly it is a rounded form of ⊟, used first in combination with ⊏, and then alone, as vice versa in Latin first F⊟, then F. *Now found in Ludian Insc. — = Sabial*

The relation of the alphabets may be seen from the following[1]:

```
                    Chalcidian Greek
                          |
        +-----------------+--------------------+
      Latin                            Primitive Etruscan
                                              |
              +-----------+----------+----------------+
      Campano-Etruscan   Oscan    Etruscan        Umbrian
                                  (of Etruria)
```

### Notes on Orthography

**28. Résumé of methods of indicating vowel-length.** The length of a vowel may be indicated:

1) by doubling of the vowel sign, — in Oscan of the native alphabet, rarely in Umbrian of the Latin alphabet. See **22, 26**.
2) by vowel + *h*, — in Umbrian of both alphabets. See **25, 26**.
3) by vowel + *h* + vowel, — in Umbrian of the Latin alphabet. See **26**.

---

[1] From Conway's Italic Dialects, Part II, which also contains a comparative table of the alphabets with the variant forms of the letters.

But oftenest there is no designation of the length, and in such cases it is not customary to supply marks of quantity, as is done in the case of Latin, where metrical usage furnishes a criterion lacking in the dialects. For example, we write O. aasas, *eituas,* U. *totar,* though in this case there is no doubt of the vowel-length in the last syllable (Gen. Sg. ending -*ās*).

In Oscan the designation of length is, with a few exceptions, confined to root-syllables.

**29.** Use of ei, *ei,* in Umbrian. While in Oscan the digraph ei, *ei,* uniformly designates the diphthong *ei,* its uses in Umbrian, where the original *ei* had become a monophthong, are various. Sometimes it designates a secondary diphthong, the *i* of which comes from a guttural, e.g. teitu, *deitu* 'dicito' (**143**).

But it is frequently used in the Latin alphabet, and rarely in the native, much as in Latin inscriptions of the first century B.C., as one of the various spellings of a monophthong. It is notably frequent in the first thirty-odd lines of Table VI a. Oftenest it stands for original *ī,* e.g. *screihtor* (L. *scrīptus*); sometimes for the close *ē* resulting from *oi* in final syllables (**67,** 2), e.g. Dat.-Abl. Pl. *uereir,* or from original *ē,* e.g. *nesimei* 'proxime' (adverb in -*ē*), heriiei (Perf. Subj. with mood-sign *ē*). There are also a few reasonably certain instances of its use for a short *i,* namely Dat.-Abl. Pl. *aueis* (\*-*ifs*), Acc. Sg. *Fisei* (-*im*), 3d Sg. Pass. *hertei* beside *herti,* herter (-*tir* from -*ter*; see **39,** 2).

Puzzling is the use of *ei* in neip, *neip* 'nec' (with 'neiřhabas; see **84**), in eikvasese, eikvasatis, of uncertain meaning, and in *eiscurent* 'arcessierint'. For eitipes see **264,** 2.

*a.* For eikvasatis and eikvasese connection with L. *aequus* is plausible ; and for *eiscurent* the comparison with O.H.G. *eiscōn* (Germ. *heischen*), Lith. *jĕszkoti* 'seek', etc., pointing tȯ a Present \**ais-skō* (Skt. *icchámi* from \**is-skō* with reduced grade of root) is the most probable of all suggestions offered. Yet according to the usual orthography we should expect *e* for the open *ē* coming from *ai* (**63**). It is conceivable however that we have here isolated survivals of archaistic spelling, representing not the earliest period when *ei* was still pronounced as a diphthong, but a second period, in which the spelling *ei* was retained for the sound resulting from *ei* and extended to the same sound resulting from *ai* (both *ei* and *ai* resulted in an open *ē* ; see **63, 65**).  Cf. early Latin *deicō* and *inceidō*.

The ordinary use of *ei* for *ī*, close *ē*, etc., as described above, cannot be the result of any such orthographical development within the Umbrian, since it does not appear where the sound was originally *ei*.  It must rather be regarded as borrowed from contemporary Latin spelling.

*b.* For neip, *neip* we might also assume archaistic spelling (cf. O. *neip*), but its almost uniform appearance in this particular word (neip, *neip* 9 times, once *nep*) would remain to be accounted for.  A suggested derivation from \**nē* (from \**nē*, O. *ni*, or \**nei*, O. *nei*) + particle *-ī* + *p* would explain the spelling, as representing a genuine diphthong, but for various reasons seems improbable.

**30.**  While Oscan orthography, barring the inconsistency in the designation of vowel-length and a few other, mostly local, variations, is remarkably uniform, Umbrian orthography is as diverse as possible.  Various spellings of the same sound are used, sometimes wholly promiscuously, sometimes with a marked preference for one spelling in certain portions of the tables or in certain classes of forms.  Among the commonest variations are the following :

1. Variation between *e* and *i*.  In the great majority of instances this occurs where the sound lies between *e* and *i*, or, more correctly, between the extremes of an open *e* and a close *i* ; that is, it is either the open *i* from original short *i* (**45**), or the close *ē* from original *ē* (**43**) or from *oi* in final syllables (**67, 2**).  The spelling *e* is relatively more frequent in the native than in the Latin alphabet.  The use of *e* for closed *ī* from original *ī*, or, vice versa, of *i* for the open *e* from original short *e*, or for open *ē* from original *ai* or *ei*, is rare.  The variation between *e* and *i* corresponds then in general to the Oscan use of i.

2. Variation between *ei* and *e* or *i*.  See **29**.

3. Variation between *o* and *u* (only in the Latin alphabet, of course, since the native alphabet has no *o*), mostly in the case of original *ō* (**54**), sometimes for short *o*, especially before *r* (**51**).

4. Variation between *a* and *u* (in the native alphabet only ; in the Latin alphabet always *o*) for the rounded *a* (as in English *call*), coming from final *-ā* (**34**).

5. Variation in the designation of vowel-length, e.g. *ee*, *eh*, or *ehe* (in native alphabet only *eh*), or, oftenest, simply *e*, *e*, without indication of length.  See **25, 26, 28**.

6. Variation between p and b in the native alphabet, e.g. habina, hapinaf.  It is doubtless owing to the double value of t and k, which answer for both surds and sonants, that p is also used not infrequently for b.

7. Variation between single and double consonants.  Double consonants are not indicated in the native alphabet, and only occasionally in the Latin.

8. Presence or absence of *h*. The weak pronunciation of *h* in Umbrian is responsible for considerable inconsistency in spelling, just as is the case in Latin. See **149,** *a*. The use of *h* as a sign of hiatus is common to both Oscan and Umbrian, e.g. O. **stahínt** 'stant', U. **ahesnes** 'ahenis'.

9. Presence or absence of *n* before a consonant (**108,** 1).

10. Presence or absence of *r* before *s* (**115, 116**).

11. Presence or absence of most final consonants (**164,** 9).

**31.** An important difference between the orthography of the native alphabets and that of the Latin alphabet, in both Oscan and Umbrian, is the following. The glide sound which naturally intervenes between *i* or *u* and a following vowel is regularly expressed in the native alphabets, but nearly always omitted in the Latin alphabet, as in the spelling of Latin. So U. **triia,** but *trio* (L. *tria*); U. **tuves,** but *duir* (L. *duo*); O. **eítiuvam,** but *eituam*.

*a.* ii, *i.* In Umbrian, of words occurring in both spellings the examples are: **triia** (9), *trio* (2); **heriiei** (1), *heriei, herie* (4); **Atiieřiur** etc. (17), *Atiersur* etc. (5); **Klaverniie** (2), *Claverniur* (1); **Vehiies** (2), *Vehier* (4); in all, 46 occurrences with no exception to the distribution of the two spellings as stated. In Oscan too the spelling ii is employed consistently, as in the oblique cases of names in -iis, contrasted with i in the oblique cases of names in -is; e.g. **Dekkieis Rahiieis** Gen. Sg. of **Dekis Rahiis** (**174**).

Since ii is so evidently the normal spelling in the case of vowel *i*, there is the strongest presumption that, where the spelling in the native alphabets is simply i, this must represent something different, namely the consonantal *i*. And this is often corroborated by other evidence, such as doubling of consonants in Oscan, occasional omission of the i in Umbrian, etc. (**100,** 3).

Yet some exceptions must be admitted. In O. **Dekkviarím** and U. **tekvias** i cannot possibly represent a consonantal *i*; O. **Iúviass** is not to be separated from Iúviia; in O. **víú,** U. **via, vea,** consonantal *i* is of course impossible, and that the vowel is other than original *i* (cf. L. *via*) is improbable; consonantal *i* is also impossible in U. **arvia,** and improbable even after **v** preceded by a vowel, as in **aviekla** etc. It is perhaps for the very reason that there would be no ambiguity, that i is so often used in place of ii after **v**.

A different case is that of the Oscan *i* coming from original *e* before a vowel (**38,** 1). Here too in the earliest inscriptions the spelling is ii, but after the introduction of the character í this alone is used; e.g. **iiuk,** later **iúk** 'ea'.

*b.* uv, *u.* In Umbrian the contrasting examples are: **tuves** etc. (5), *duir* (2); **kastruvuf** (4), *castruo* (11); **prinuvatur** (5), *prinuatur* (8); **vatuva** (6), *uatuo* (6); in all 47 occurrences with no exception to the distribution of the two spellings as stated. But we find *saluuom, saluua,* once each beside 24 examples of *saluom* etc., and *tuua* 'tua' once beside 18 examples of *tua, tuer* (once also *touer*). The omission of v in **purtuetu** is doubtless accidental, and **aruvia** beside usual **arvia** is probably an engraver's error. In Oscan, v is used instead of uv in **sakrvist** beside **sakruvit**, in **eítiv.** for **eítiuv(ad)**, and probably in **minive** (no. 31 *b*). So possibly in U. **iveka** 'iuvencas', though here the omission of u seems much stranger, and many assume an actual phonetic change of *iuu-* to *iu-*.

## HISTORY OF THE SOUNDS [1]

### VOWELS

.a

. 32. 1. *a* in initial syllables remains unchanged, as in Latin. So O. *actud* : L. *agō* ; — U. *ager* : L. *ager* ; — O. *allo* : L. *alius* ; — O. **patir**, U. **patre**: L. *pater* ; — O. **fakiiad**, U. **façia** : L. *faciō* ; — O. *castrous*, U. *castruo* : L. *castrum* ; — O. **ant** : L. *ante*.

2. Final *a* is also unchanged, as in the Umbrian Vocatives *Tursa, Iouia*, etc. See **169, 5**.

3. Likewise in medial syllables, where in Latin *a* has been weakened to *i* or *e*, it is regularly preserved. So O. **Anterstataí**: L. *\*Interstita* (cf. *Praestitia*) ; — O. **tríbarakavúm** 'aedificare': L. *(co)-erceō* ; — U. **antakres** : L. *integer* ; — U. *procanurent* : L. *(oc)-cinuī* ; — U. **ařkani** 'cantum': L. *\*accinium* ; — U. **tuplak** 'furcam' (?) : L. *duplex* (cf. Grk. δίπλαξ). See **85**.

---

[1] The arrangement of the material and the choice of headings is dictated by considerations of convenience. Since we are dealing primarily with the relations of the sounds of the dialects to one another, rather than with their relations to the sounds of the other Indo-European languages, the material is arranged with reference to what belongs together from the Italic point of view. Thus, under the heading a is considered the history of Italic *a*, regardless of its various I.E. sources (*a, ǝ,* etc.); *en* from I.E. *ṇ* has the same history as original *en*, and need not be treated separately; similarly with *or, ol*, from *ṛ, ḷ, ou* from *eu*, etc. Only in the treatment of Vowel-Gradation is there any necessity of reverting to the I.E. vowel-system. But the headings do not always represent the Italic sounds. It is often simpler to take the I.E. sounds as the starting-point, as, for example, in the case of the sonant aspirates, *dh, bh*, etc., for which the precise stage of development reached in the Italic period is not in all cases certain. Or, again, it may be desirable to discuss in one place the history of a sound or group of sounds, which is partly of Indo-European, partly of Italic, and partly of still later origin, as, for example, in the case of *ns*. In general, the author has not hesitated to sacrifice consistency to convenience.

4. But a weakening in the direction of *u*, where a labial consonant precedes or follows, is seen in a few words. See **86.**

**ā**

**33.** *ā*, except when final, remains unchanged, as in Latin. So O. fratrúm, U. fratrum: L. *fråter* ; — O. Maatreís, U. *Matrer* : L. *måter* ; — O. aasas, U. asam: L. *åra* ; — Abl. Sg. of First Decl., O. *toutad*, U. *tota*: L. *-å* ; — suffix *-åno-*, O. Abellanús, U. *Treblanir*: L. *Rōmånus.*

**34.** Final *å*, which in Latin is shortened, preserves its quantity, but is changed in quality to a rounded sound like the *a* of English *call*. In Oscan it went so far in the direction of *ō* that it is never denoted by the letter *a*, but always by ú, o, o, or, rarely, by u, *u*. In Umbrian the sound is written both **a** and u in the native alphabet, but always *o* in the Latin. Examples are the forms of the Nom. Sg. of *å*-stems, which ended in *å*, as shown by Greek, Sanskrit, etc., and of the Nom.-Acc. Pl. Neuter, in which the *å*, belonging properly to *o*-stems, was extended in the Italic period to other stems.

OSCAN. víú 'via', fíísnú 'fanum' (Acc. fíísnam), iiu-k, íú-k, *io-c* 'ea', *molto* 'multa', *allo* 'alia', *touto* 'civitas'; — *comono* 'comitia', teremenniú 'termina', *petiru-pert, petiro-pert* 'quater' **(192, 2).**

UMBRIAN. muta, mutu 'multa', panta 'quanta', etantu 'tanta'; — veskla, vesklu 'vascula', vatuva, vatuvu, *uatuo* 'exta'(?), *proseseto* 'prosecta', atru, *adro* 'atra'. See also **235, 236, 2, 237, 300, 9.**

**35.** In Umbrian this rounding of the *å* takes place also before final *-ts* (from *-to-s* or *-ti-s* by vowel-syncope). So pihaz, *pihos* 'piatus', kunikaz, *conegos* 'conixus' (in form as if L. *\*cōnigåtus*), *Casilos* 'Casilas' (Dat. *Casilate*), -vakaz, *-uacos* 'vacatio, intermissio' from *\*u̯akåt(i)-s.*

*a.* A similar variation in spelling, which can hardly be separated from the phenomenon just described, is seen in Prestate, Prestote, and Tesenakes, *Tesenocir.* The former word, although L. *Praestitia* suggests *\*prae-ståtå-*, may be from a by-form *\*prae-ståtå-* (cf. L. *prae-ståtus* beside *prae-stitus*), and for the latter word a suffix *-āko-* is in itself more probable than *-ako-*, the existence of which is doubtful. But the explanation is difficult, since elsewhere there is no indication of a change of *ā* except under the conditions described above. It is possible that in the later Umbrian even the *ā* of medial syllables changed slightly in the direction of *ō*, but not enough to affect the usual spelling. Yet it is strange that the *o* is so consistently employed in these two words, and never found as a variant in the great majority of words containing *ā*. But to regard the *o* as standing for short *a* only increases the difficulty. Such a weakening of *a* where there is no contiguous labial consonant (86) is unsupported and unlikely.

A somewhat different, but equally difficult, case is *subotu* if this is the same word as subahtu 'deponito' with secondary *ā* (121, 75).

e

**36.** 1. *e* generally remains unchanged. So O. edum : L. *edō* ; — O. *ezum,* est, estud, U. *erom* : L. *esse,* etc.; — O. destrst 'dextra est', U. *destram-e* : L. *dexter* ; — O. mefiaí : L. *medius* ; — U. ferest, *fertu* : L. *ferō* ; — O. aragetud : L. *argentum.*

2. *e* also remains before *l* + consonant, or final *l*, where in Latin it becomes first *o*, then *u*. So U. *pelmner* : L. *pulmentum* ; — (also U. veltu 'deligito', eh-velklu 'sententiam', but in these *ụel-* is from *ụele-* : L. *volt, vult*); — O. *famel* : L. *famul* ; — U. sumel : L. *simul* (early inscr. *semol*).

3. *e* also remains generally in medial syllables, where in Latin before a single consonant it is weakened to *i*. So U. taçez, *tasetur* : L. *tacitus* ; — U. maletu : L. *molitus* ; — O. Genetaí : L. *genitus.*

4. But before a labial in medial syllables a weakening occurs, resulting, just as in Latin, sometimes in *u*, sometimes in *i*. See 86.

**37.** A change of *e* to *o* is seen in *\*pompe* 'quinque' (O. pumperias, U. pumpeřias '*\*quincuriae*', O. *pomtis* 'quinquiens') from *\*kᵘenkᵘe* (150), where it seems due to the position between two *kᵘ*'s.

*a.* The combination sụe which becomes *so* in Latin (*soror* from *\*sụesōr,* etc.) remains unchanged in O. sverrunei (96), but Umbrian shows the same change as Latin in *sonitu* : L. *sonō,* from *\*sụen-* (Skt. *svan-*).

*i for e*

**38.** OSCAN. 1. Before another vowel, *e* becomes an open *i* and is invariably denoted by an *i*-character (í in the native alphabet, earlier ii; see **31**, *a*). Compare Ital. *mio* from L. *meus*, *cria* from L. *creat*, etc. So **iiu-k, íú-k**, *io-c* 'ea', *ion-c* 'eum', *ius-c*, **iussu** 'iidem': L. *ea* etc. (cf. also Marruc. *iaf-c* 'eas'); — **fatíum** 'fari': L. *fateor*; — **putiiad, pútíad** 'possit', as if L. *\*poteat*; — **turumiiad** 'torqueatur', as if L. *\*tormeat*; — **Tíanud** 'Teano,' Loc. Sg. **Tiianei**; — **Tiiatium** 'Teatinorum'.

2. Before *r* the *e* had a closer pronunciation than usual, as is shown by *amiricatud* '\*immercato', with which may be compared rustic Latin *Mircurios, stircus*, etc.; further by **Tirentium** 'Terentiorum' and **Vírriis** 'Verrius'. But the change was so slight as to be commonly ignored in the spelling (cf. **pert, perek., pumperias**, etc.).

3. **Tintiriis**, if, as probable, from *\*Tinktrio-* and related to L. *tinguō, tīnctus* (Grk. τέγγω), is evidence of the same change as occurs in Latin before *n* + guttural.

4. In **nistrus** 'propinquos' beside **nessimas** 'proximae' etc., the i is probably only a misspelling.

5. For **íst** beside **est** 'est', see **217**, 2.

**39.** UMBRIAN. 1. Before another vowel *e* had a relatively close pronunciation, as shown by *farsio*, **fasiu** 'farrea', *tursiandu* 'terreantur', and by **iepi, iepru**, in case these are from the stem *eo-*. But the change did not go so far in the direction of *i* as in Oscan, and the spelling is regularly *e*, e.g. *eam, eaf, eo*, etc.

2. From *ostensendi* for *\*ostensender* (ending *-ter*, **238**, 1) and *herti* (4 times), *hertei* (once), beside **herter, herte**, we may assume that *e* before final *r* had a close pronunciation verging on *i*.

3. In *cringatro*, **krikatru** 'cinctum' beside **krenkatrum**, from *\*krengh-* (O.Eng. *hring*, O.Bulg. *krągŭ* 'circle'), we have a change of *e* in the direction of *i*, as in Latin before *n* + guttural (*tinguō, lingua*, etc.). See **38**, **3**.

4. In *isir* 'his' beside *esir*, — *iso*, *issoc* 'ita' beside *eso*, *esoc*, — *isec*, **isek** 'item', — **isunt** 'item', the *i* is perhaps due to a partial contamination of the stems *esso-* and *i-*. But see the following.

5. The single occurrence of *tasis* against 21 examples of *tases* etc., and of **vistiça** against 18 examples of **vestiça**, **vestiçia**, etc., show that in the following forms, which occur but once each, we may have, accidentally, the abnormal rather than the normal spelling: tiçit: L. *decet*; — iseçeles 'insectis', with i for *e(n)-*; — vaçetum-i se 'in vitiatum sit'(?) with i for postpositive *e(n)*. But it cannot be wholly accidental that in all these cases (cf. also *isir* etc., above) the vowel is followed by a sibilant. Apparently the *i*-quality of the sibilant has had some effect on the preceding *e* — but so slight that in most words it is never shown in the spelling.

6. In U. **vitlu** 'vitulum', *uitlu*, etc. the *i* is Italic (L. *vitulus*, also O. **Vīteliú** 'Italia'), though probably from original *e* ('yearling'; cf. L. *vetus*, Skt. *vatsd-* 'calf'). Where and how the change came about is unknown.

ē

**40.** *ē* had a closer pronunciation in Latin than the short *e*, as we know from its development in the Romance languages and from statements of the grammarians. It was the French *é* of *été* rather than the *è* of *mère*. It probably had this relatively close pronunciation in the Italic period, and in Oscan and Umbrian progressed still further in the direction of *ī*.

**41.** In Oscan it has gone so far that we may speak of a change to *ī*, since it is invariably denoted by an *ī*-character. This *ī* was a relatively open *ī*, indicated in the native alphabet by í or íí, being thus distinguished from original *ī*, which was close.[1] Examples: *ligud* 'lege', **ligatúís** 'legatis': L. *lēx*, *lēgātus*; — **fíísnú**, **fíísnam**, **físnam** 'fanum': L. *fēstus*, *fēriae* (99, 1); — **líkítud**, *licitud* 'liceto': L. *licētō*; — *hipid* 'habuerit', from *\*hēpēd*, belonging to the same Perfect-type as L. *cēpī*, *lēgī*, and with the Subjunctive-sign *ē*; — **fusíd** 'foret', **h]erríns** 'caperent' with the same mood-sign *ē* as the Latin Imperfect Subjunctive, but without the shortening seen in L. *-et, -ent* (78).

---

[1] This and similar statements as to the distinction in use between í and i refer to the normal Oscan orthography. It must be remembered that the í is lacking in the oldest inscriptions, and also that after its introduction it was so carelessly employed in some inscriptions, mostly those of Capua, that their evidence in this regard is to be ignored.

*a.* An *ě* which is the result of contraction in the Italic period has the same development as original *ě*. Thus **tris** : L. *trēs*, from *\*trejes* ; — **húrtin** 'in horto' from *\*hortej-en*. See **82, 1**.

*b.* But an *ě* resulting from some later process of vowel-lengthening retains the quality of the short *e*, and is not written *i*; e.g. **keenzstur**, *censtur*, **eestint**, etc. (**73, 77**).

**42.** In Umbrian the spelling *i* occurs frequently, especially in the Latin alphabet, but *e* is far more common.

The Imperatives of the Second Conjugation always have *i* in the Latin as against e in the native alphabet, but this distinction does not hold for other words. Thus *habitu*, **habetu** : L. *habētō* ; — *tursitu*, **tusetu** : L. *terrētō* ; — *filiu*, **feliuf** 'lactentes' from the *fē-* of L. *fē-mina* ; — *plener*, **plenasier** : L. *plēnus* ; — **rehte** : L. *rēctē*, earlier *\*rēctēd*. In a few cases the spelling *ei* occurs ; e.g. **herilei** 'voluerit' with the Subjunctive-sign *ē*; — *nesimei* 'proxime', adverb in *ē* like **rehte**; *sei-(podruhpei)* 'seorsum': L. *sēd-*.

Evidently *ē* in Umbrian had a very close pronunciation, but had not gone as far in the direction of *ī* as in Oscan.

i

**43.** *i* remains an open *i*. This open quality is shown by its designation **í** in the Oscan alphabet,[1] and for Umbrian by the frequent spelling *e* (**30, 1**). Final *i*, unless dropped, remains *i* in Oscan, but becomes *e* in Umbrian, as in Latin. Thus U. **ute**, *ote* 'aut': O. *auti* ; — U. **sakre**, *sacre*, etc. (Nom.-Acc. Sg. N. of *i*-stems).

**44.** OSCAN. Examples : **dadíkatted** 'dedicavit': L. *dēdicō* ; — **meddíss**, *meddis* 'meddix', Gen. Sg. **medíkeís**, Nom. Pl. **meddíss**, μεδδειξ (for ει see **24**; compare also εινειμ = **iním**), a compound of *dik-*, like L. *iūdex*, *iūdicis* (**15, 6**); — **líkítud**, *licitud* 'liceto': L. *liceō* ; — *uincter* 'convincitur': L. *vincō* ; — **tiurrí**: L. *turrim* ; — **pís**, *pis*, **píd**, *pitpit* : L. *quis*, *quid*, etc. ; — suffix *-iko*, e.g. **túv-tíks** 'publicus', *toutico* 'publica'.

*a.* When the consonantal *i* intervening between the vowel *i* and another vowel is expressed in the writing, as is nearly always the case in the native

---

[1] See footnote, p. 33.

alphabet (31), the vowel *i* is then written i, not í; e.g. fakiiad 'faciat', heriiad 'capiat', Heleviieís 'Helvii'.

*b.* An *i* arising from consonantal *i* by samprasāraṇa (91, 1) seems to have differed in quality from original *i*, judging from the spelling of púatiris 'posterius' with -is, not -ís, from -ios, in consequence of which the anaptyctic vowel is also i, not í. Cf. also the proper names like Vibis 'Vibius' etc. (172-174). For í in Maís etc., see 176, 3.

*c.* Isolated examples of *e* for *i* are : menvum 'minuere' on the carelessly written Curse of Vibia ; — esídum, esídu[m], for the usual ísídum 'ídem', on two inscriptions of Samnium, possibly due to a local contamination with the stem of essuf 'ipse'.

**45.** UMBRIAN. The spelling is either *i* or *e*, oftener the former. As is the case also with other sounds which are represented by both spellings, the *e* is more frequent in the native alphabet than in the Latin. See 30, 1. For the rare *ei*, see 29.

Examples: tiçel 'dedicatio', tikamne 'dedicatione': L. *dicātiō* etc.; — *dersicust* 'dixerit' from *\*de-dic-ust* : O. *dicust* (44, 95); — *uirseto* 'visum' from *\*uideto-* : L. *videō* ; — steplatu, *stiplatu*, *stiplo* : L. *stipulor* ; — sestu, seste : L. *sistō* ; — teřa, *dirsa*, *dersa* 'det' (from Redupl. Pres. *\*didō*) : O. *didest* 'dabit'; — piř-e, *pirs-i*, *pers-i*, etc.: L. *quid*, O. píd ; — suffix *-iko-*, e.g. Pupřike 'Publico' (?), fratreks, *fratrex* '\*fratricus'.

*a.* The Accusative Singular of *i*-stems nearly always appears as -e(m), -e(m), e.g. uvem, uve, *ocrem*, *ocre*, etc. (178, 4), indicating that before final *m* an *i* was more than ordinarily open. Contrast the -i(m), -i(m), -ei, of io-stems, in which the *i* comes from consonantal i by samprasāraṇa (91, 1). Cf. 44, b.

## ī

**46.** *ī* had a closer pronunciation in Latin than the short *i*, as is proved by the Romance development ; e.g. Ital. *chi*, *scritto* from L. *quī*, *scrīptus*, contrasted with *che*, *lece* from L. *quid*, *licet*. The same qualitative difference existed in Oscan-Umbrian, as is shown by the fact that original *ī* is indicated in Oscan by i, not í, and that in Umbrian the spelling *e*, so common for short *i*, is rare.

**47.** OSCAN. The spelling is i, not í, but where doubling is employed as a mark of length we find ií, not íí like aa, etc.

This spelling ií may possibly indicate a nuance of pronunciation something like *ie*, but more probably it is purely a matter of orthography, ii being avoided on account of its other uses.

Examples: **liímítú[m]** 'limitum': L. *līmes*; — **imad-en** 'ab imo': L. *īmus*; — *scriftas* 'scriptae': L. *scrīptus*; — Abl. Sg. **slaagíd** contrasted with Acc. Sg. **slagím**; — suffix -*īno*-, e.g. **deivinais** 'divinis', *Bantins* 'Bantinus', Μαμερτινο 'Mamertina'.

**48.** UMBRIAN. The spelling in the native alphabet is **i, ih**, rarely **e**; in the Latin it is *i, ihi, ei* (very frequent in the first thirty-odd lines of VI a), rarely *e*.

Examples: **persnimu, persnihmu**, *persnimu, persnihimu* 'precator', Imperative of the Fourth Conjugation; — *screhto, screihtor*: L. *scrīptus*; — *peica, peico, peiqu* (10 times in VI a 1–17): L. *pīca, pīcus*; — **pehatu**, *pihatu* 'piato', *pihaner, pehaner, peihaner* 'piandi': L. *piō* from \**pīō*, O. **Pííhiúí** 'Pio'; — suffix -*īno*-, e.g. **Ikuvins** 'Iguvinus', *Iouinam, Ioueine* (*ei* once only in over 100 occurrences).

o

**49.** *o* remains for the most part unchanged, and appears in the Latin alphabet as *o*, in the native Oscan alphabet as **ú**. But in the native Umbrian, and also in the earliest type of the Oscan, the V did duty for both *o* and *u*. All forms from these sources must therefore be ignored in distinguishing the sounds of *o* and *u*.

Examples: O. **úp**, *op*, U. *ostendu* 'ostendito' from *ops*-: L. *ob, obs*; — O. **púst**, *post*, U. *post*: L. *post*; — O. **púd**, *pod*, U. **puř-e**, *pors-e*: L. *quod*; — O. **úpsannam** 'faciendam', U. *osatu* 'facito': L. *operor*; — O. **húrz**: L. *hortus*; — U. *poplom*: L. *populus*.

The *o* is also preserved before *l* + consonant and before *n* + guttural, where in Latin, except in early inscriptions, it appears as *u*. Thus O. *molto* 'multa', **múltasíkad** 'multatica', U. *motar*: L. *multa*, early *molta*, *moltāticōd*; — O. **últiumam** 'ultimam': L. *ultimus* from \**oltimo*-; — O. *ionc* 'eum', with which compare L. *hunc*, early *honc*.

*u for o*

**50.** In Oscan, before final *m* the *o* became *u*, or at least was changed so far in the direction of *u* as to be commonly written *u*. Thus the Present Infinitive (ending *-om*, 241), with the possible exception of **tríbarakavúm** (ú not certain) on the Cippus Abellanus, shows *-um*, *-um*; e.g. *acum*, *deicum*, *ezum*, *censaum*, **deíkum**, **fatíum**. The enclitic particle *-om* (301, 5) always appears as *-um;* e.g. *pieis-um* 'cuiuspiam', **pídum** 'quidquam' (C.A.), **ísídum** 'ídem'. The Acc. Sing. of *o*-stems, however, though sometimes showing *-um*, as in *dolum*, *trutum*, **Núvellum**, etc., usually appears as *-om* (more frequent than *-um* on the Tabula Bantina) or *-úm* (always on the Cippus Abellanus). It is altogether probable that this spelling of the Acc. forms is a sort of pedantic orthography, due to the *o* of other case-forms (*-oi*, *úí-*, etc.), while the spelling of the other forms, which were not subject to such influence, represents more faithfully the actual pronunciation.

NOTE. In Umbrian not only does *o* remain unchanged before final *m*, but even *u* becomes *o* (57).

**51.** In Umbrian before *r* + consonant, or even before *r* alone, we find so many examples of the spelling *u*, although *o* also occurs, as to make it evident that the vowel was considerably modified in this position. Thus *curnaco*, *curnase* (5 times): L. *cornīx*; — prefix *pur-* in *purditom* 'porrectum' etc. (10 times, never *por-*): L. *por-*; — *tursitu* 'terreto' etc. (4 times) from *\*tor-seō* (97); — *courtust* 'reverterit' for *\*couurtust* beside *couortus*: early L. *vorsus*, *advortit*, etc. (97); — *furo* 'forum': L. *forum* (it is unnecessary, though possible, to assume that *furo* contains the reduced grade *dhur-*, like Grk. θύρᾱ, as compared with *dhu̯or-* in L. *forum*); — *tursiandu* 'fugentur' with *-du* for *-tur* from *-tor*; — *uru* 'illo' beside *orer* 'illius'(?).

*a.* Possible examples of *u* for *o* before *rs* from *d* (131) are *du-pursus*, *petur-pursus* (but see 94); also *atripursatu* 'tripodato', the explanation of which depends on the view taken of L. *tripudium* etc. beside early *tripodō* (late weakening of *o* to *u*, or contamination with a derivative of a root *pud-* related to *paviō?*).

*b.* An isolated instance of *u* elsewhere is *sunitu* beside *sonitu*: L. *sonō*.

## ō

**52.** The relation of *ō* to *o* is parallel to that of *ē* to *e*. We know that in Latin the *ō* had a closer pronunciation than the *o*, and the same is true of Oscan and Umbrian. But the development of *ō* in the direction of *ū* has gone further in Oscan than in Umbrian.

**53.** In Oscan, *ō* becomes *ū*, and is regularly denoted by u, uu, *u*, not by ú, o (except dúnúm 'donum', no. 53, which is doubtless due to an error). Examples: Fluusaí 'Florae': L. *flōs, Flōra*; — d]uunated 'donavit': L. *dōnō*; — *pru* 'pro': L. *prō*; — uupsens, upsens, ουπσενς 'fecerunt', Perf. with lengthened vowel to *\*opsā-* seen in úpsannam (49); — suffix *-tōr-* in Regaturei 'Rectori', kvaísstur 'quaestor', *censtur* 'censor', kenzsur, *censtur* 'censores'; — suffix *-ẓ̇ōn-* in tríbarakkiuf 'aedificatio', úíttiuf 'usus'; — Imperative ending *-tōd* in líkítud, *licitud*, estud, *actud, factud*.

The only exceptions to this orthography are case-forms in *ō* such as Abl. Sg. *-ōd*, Nom. Pl. *-ōs*, Gen. Pl. *-ōm*,[1] which on the Cippus Abellanus and other specimens of the standard Oscan orthography appear as -úd, -ús, -úm. But we also find -ud, -us, -um, and in the Latin alphabet always *-ud, -us, -um*. So that the spelling ú is probably another piece of pedantry in the standard spelling, due to the ú of other case-forms (see also 50). Examples: Abl. Sg. tanginúd, amnúd, sakaraklúd, Búvianúd, etc., but also tanginud, aragetud, tríbud, trístaamentud, *amnud, dolud, amiricatud*, etc.; Nom. Pl. Abellanús, Núvlanús, etc., but also *ius-c*; Gen. Pl. Abellanúm, Núvlanúm, fratrúm, etc., but also *nesimum* (once *zicolom*), *nerum, egmazum*, Μαμερτινουμ (ου as in ουπσενς; for Λουκανομ see 24).

*a.* The Pompeian inscriptions have Abl. Sg. in -ud, not -úd. Hence, in no. 3, Nom. Pl. íussu is more probable than íússu, though from the stone it is impossible to tell whether u or ú was intended.

**54.** In Umbrian both *u* and *o* are found, but not promiscuously. The spelling of individual words is uniform, likewise

---

[1] Here and in **54** it is assumed that *-ōm* had not been shortened to *-om*. See **78**, 4.

that of most formations. It is not clear whether we have to do with an actual difference in pronunciation, or with an artificial regulation of what was once a promiscuous use of both spellings for the same sound.

The spelling *u* is universal in the Imperative endings *-tōd*, *-mōd*, e.g. *fertu*, *deitu*, etc. (some 800 occurrences); likewise, with one or two exceptions (171, 6, *a*), in the Abl. Sg. ending *-ōd*, e.g. *poplu*, *pihaclu*, etc. (over 100 occurrences); in the suffix *-tōr-*, e.g. *arsferture*. The Nom. Pl. M. of *o*-stems, ending *-ōs*, has *-ur* (on the forms in *or* see 171, 13), e.g. *Atiersiur*, *tasetur*; note especially the contracted form *dur* 'duo' from \**duūr*, \**duōs*. The Acc. Pl. M. of *o*-stems, with secondary *ō* (74; but see also 74, note) usually shows *-u*, e.g. *toru*, *rofu*, but sometimes *-o*, e.g. *ueiro* (171, 11, *a*). Cf. also *du-pursus* 'bipedibus', *petur-pursus* 'quadrupedibus', probably containing *pōd-* (94); *bue* 'bove', Acc. Pl. *buf* (cf. Dor. βῶν, βῶς); the pronominal adverbs *pue* 'ubi' (202, 7), *podruhpei* 'utroque' (190, 2), *panupei* 'quandoque' (202, 12).

The spelling *o* is found in the Gen. Pl. ending *-ōm*,[1] with a single exception (*pracatarum*); in the suffix *-ōn-*, as *Acersoniem*, *homonus*, etc.; in the pronominal adverbs *ulo* 'illuc,' *ʒimo* 'retro,' *eso(c)* 'ita', etc. (190, 2); in the root-syllables of several words, as *nome* 'nomen' (nearly 100 occurrences): L. *nōmen*; *pone* 'posca': L. *pō-sca*, *pō-tus*, etc.

NOTE. Observing that the occurrences of *u* are in final syllables, or syllables which were final before the addition of enclitics (*podruh-pei* etc.), or before *r* (*arsferture* etc.), we may surmise that in these positions the *ō* actually had a closer pronunciation than elsewhere (for the position before *r* compare *u* for short *o*, 51). Further, the predominance of *o* even in final syllables before *m* might be attributed to the same influence of *m* which is seen in the change of original *u* to *o* (57). So much is reasonable, perhaps even probable. But to make further distinctions in final syllables — for example, to account for the *o* in *eso* etc. as compared with the *u* of the Ablatives on the ground that these adverbs are Instrumentals, and so ended in *-ō*, not *-ōd* — is to lay more stress on the spelling than Umbrian orthography will warrant, not to speak of the additional complication caused by *podruh-pei* etc. It is not unreasonable to

[1] See footnote, p. 38.

suppose that even in final syllables the sound was one which might be denoted by *o*, and that in the almost complete uniformity of spelling in the Ablatives there is something artificial, which would not necessarily affect the spelling of the adverbs, whether themselves of Ablative or Instrumental origin.

## u

**55.** Original *u* remains in general unchanged. Examples: O. supruis 'superis', U. super, *super-ne, subra* : L. *superus, super, suprā*; — O. purasiaí 'in igniaria', U. *pure-to* 'ab igne': Grk. πυρετός, πυρός, etc.; — O. puf, puz[1], U. *pufe, puse*: L. *ubi, uti*; — U. rufru, *Rufrer*: L. *ruber*.

### Oscan iu *for u*

**56.** In Oscan, after the dentals *t, d, n*, and once after *s*, is found the spelling iu. Thus Diumpaís 'Lumpis': L. *lumpa* from \**dumpā*; — tiurrí : L. *turrim*; — eítiuvam 'pecuniam': *eituam* in Latin alphabet; — últiumam 'ultimam' with secondary *u* (86, 1); — Niumsieís, Νιυμσδιηις 'Numerii'; — Siuttiís 'Suttius'. This spelling is not found in the Latin alphabet, and to judge from *eituam, eituas*, was not used. Just what modification of the sound this iu was intended to represent it is impossible to say. But the theory that it was *ịu* like our English pronunciation of *u* in *cube* etc. meets with the least objection.

### Umbrian o *for u*

**57.** In Umbrian, *o* appears regularly for *u* before *m*. Thus *somo*: L. *summus*; — Acc. Sg. of *u*-stems, e.g. *trifo* 'tribum'; — Supine in *-tum*, e.g. *aseriato* 'observatum'. Before *p* also, the spelling, though usually *u* (*superne, dupla*), is sometimes *o*, as in *sopa, sopam, sopo*, beside *supo*: L. *supīnus*. Here too the sound must have been open, but not so markedly as before *m*. Another example of *o* for *u*, the cause of which is not clear, is *sorser* 'suilli', *sorsom, sorsalem*, etc., probably from \**su-do-*, \**su-d-āli-* (cf. L. *pecu-d-, pecu-d-āli-*): L. *su-* in *su-bus* etc.

---

[1] Once *pous*, but the *ou* is probably a mere slip of the engraver, whose eye was caught by the *ou* of the following word on the copy, *touto*.

*a.* A change of initial *iu* to *i* is generally assumed on account of U. **iveka** 'iuvencas'. But possibly this is only a matter of spelling, as in O. **eitiv** for **eitiuv(ad)** etc. See **31**, *b.*

## ū

**58.** *ū* generally remains unchanged, as in Latin. Examples: O. **Fuutrei** 'Genetrici' from *bhū-* (cf. Grk. φῦμα, Skt. *bhū́ti-*, etc.); — O. **fruktatiuf** 'fructus': L. *frūx, frūctus*; — U. *mugatu* 'muttito': L. *mūgiō*. Note also the secondary *ū* in U. **struhçla**, *struŝla* 'struem, *struiculam*' from *\*struuikelā-*.

### ī for ū

**59.** It is probable that a change of *ū* to *ī* (through the intermediate stage of a *ū* pronounced like French *u*, German *ü*) is to be recognized for monosyllables in Umbrian and perhaps for final syllables in both Oscan and Umbrian. Examples: U. *pir* 'ignis': Grk. πῦρ; — U. **sim** 'suem' from *\*sū-m* (Grk. ῦ-ν), Acc. Pl. **sif** from *\*sū-f*; — U. *frif* 'fruges' from *\*frūg-f*: L. *frūx*; — Abl. Sg. of *u*-stems, e.g. U. **trefi** 'tribu', **ařputrati** 'arbitratu', **mani** 'manu', O. *castrid* 'capite'(?) (Gen. Sg. *castrous*).

NOTE. The author has elsewhere (Osk. Voc., p. 111 ff.) shown the possibility of explaining U. *pir* etc. without the assumption that they come from forms containing *ū*. But it must be admitted that the direct comparison with forms in *ū* (especially *pir*: πῦρ) is far simpler. The Ablatives might be explained as examples of heteroclism, but if the change is admitted at all, it may be assumed for these also. At best, however, the precise conditions under which the change took place cannot be formulated with certainty without more material.

## DIPHTHONGS

**60.** In the following sections are considered together not only the original diphthongs *ai, oi,* etc., but also those which, with shortening of the first element, come from I.E. *āi, ōi,* etc., as in the Dat. Sg. of *ā-* and *ō-*stems (Grk. -ᾱι, -ηι, -ωι). For there is no evidence of the preservation of a long diphthong as such even in Oscan, and the monophthongization in Umbrian presupposes an intermediate stage of short diphthongs.

But under certain conditions the long diphthongs, instead of shortening the first element, lost the second element, and in this case their further history became identical with that of the original long vowels. Thus the Dat. Sg. ending of *o*-stems, *-ōi* (Grk. *-ωι*), became on the one hand *-oi*, represented by the Oscan-Umbrian forms and by early Latin (Praenestine) *Numasioi*, on the other hand *-ō*, represented by the usual Latin form.

*a.* It is uncertain whether the Dat.-Abl. Pl. ending of *o*-stems, *-ois* (likewise Grk. *-οις*), represents the old Instrumental ending *-ōis* (Skt. *-āis*) or the Locative ending *-ois(i)* (Grk. *-οισι*) or both. After the analogy of *-ois* was formed the *-ais* of *ā*-stems.

**61.** Diphthongs are always preserved unchanged in Oscan, while in Umbrian they have become monophthongs, even such as are retained in Latin.

1. In the Oscan alphabet the *i*-diphthongs appear as **ai, ei, úi**, the **i**, as usual, denoting the open quality of the second element (cf. *ae, oe*, in Latin).

2. The *u*-diphthongs appear in the Oscan alphabet as **av** (rarely **au**), **ev, úv**, that is with the sign **⅃**, not **V**. But there is no reason to believe that this represents a pronunciation like that of modern Greek *av, ev*, in which the second element is a spirant (English *v* or *f*). The sign we transcribe **v** denoted simply the consonantal *u* (English *w*) and might with perfect propriety be used for the second element of a diphthong. Compare the occasional appearance in Greek inscriptions of *αϝ, οϝ*, for the usual *αυ, ου*; e.g. Ναϝπακτίων, σποϝδδάν.

*a.* In the Oscan inscriptions of the Greek alphabet we find likewise Αϝδεις, τωϝτο, but also ταυρομ, Αυσκλι, and beside the last the curious spelling Αυͱυσκλι, that is Αυͪυσκλι (cf. also **Ahvdiu** on a fragment).

3. But the history of *i*-diphthongs followed by consonantal *i* is exceptional, as it is also in Latin, and is not included in the following treatment of the several diphthongs. In Oscan the second element is written **i**, not **í** (compare **fakiiad, 44,** *a*), and in Umbrian the diphthong does not become a monophthong. Thus O. **Púmpaiians** 'Pompeianus', **Púmpaiianeís, Púmpaiiana**, etc.,

U. pernaiaf, pustnaiaf (pusnaes for *pusnaies, like pernaies), peřaia, *persaia, persaea* (for peřaem, peře, *persae*, see 173, 1), with suffix -*aiįo*- (253, 1); — O. Maiiúí 'Maio' (147, 3); — O. vereiiaí, vereias (once verehias?), U. Teteies(?), with -*eiįo*- (253, 2); — O. Kerríiaí, Kerríiúís, etc., with -*ēiįo*- (253, 3); — O. púiiu, púiieh : L. *quoius*, Grk. ποῖος, from *ʠ*uoi-įo*- (199, *b*). The pronunciation is most exactly represented by the spelling with two *i*'s, which is usual in Oscan and frequent in Latin inscriptions and early manuscripts (*Maiia* preferred by Cicero to *Maia, eiius, quoiius*, etc.). But a single *i*, representing a sound belonging equally to both sylla-ᵇᵇles, was also sufficient, and this spelling is regular in Umbrian, occasional in Oscan (Búvaianúd, Tantrnnaiúm, vereias ; *Maraies* beside Maraiieís, 176, 4), and usual in Latin.

*a.* With O. ai, ei, úi, not aí etc., compare L. *mai*(i)*us, quoi*(i)*us,* not *mae*(i)*us, *quoe*(i)*us,* and with the preservation of U. diphthongs in this position compare L. *ei*(i)*us* contrasted with *dīcō* from *deicō,* and *quoi*(i)*us, hoi*(i)*us,* contrasted with *ūnus* from *oinos* (the change to *cui*(i)*us, hui*(i)*us,* is much later than that in *ūnus* and of an entirely different character). L. *Pompeiānus* beside O. Púmpaiians shows that -*aiįo*- became -*eiįo* and so was merged with original -*eiįo.* That is, the diphthong *ai* became *ei,* as regularly in medial syllables (cf. *in-caidō, inceidō*), and this *ei* instead of passing on to *ī* (*incīdō*) retained its diphthongal value before the *į* (as in *ei*(i)*us*). At least it remained *ei* in *Pompeii, Pompeiānus.* But for many proper names which sometimes show -*eius,* as *Pobleiios, Publeius, Clodeius,* etc., and which seem to belong here, the normal Latin form has -*ius,* as *Publius, Clōdius,* etc. Cf. also *Marius* beside Faliscan *Mareio,* O. *Maraies.* One might assume that these names simply yielded to the analogy of the commoner type of proper names in -*ius.* But in view of L. *Boviānum* beside O. Búvaianúd,[1] it is worth while to consider the possibility that in medial sylla-bles, even before *į,* the *ei* became *ī,* which was then shortened to *i;* and that it was retained, as in *Pompeiānus,* only under certain (accentual?) conditions no longer understood.

### ai

**62. OSCAN.** Examples : kvaísstur, κϝαισ[τορ (borrowed? See 21): L. *quaestor* ; — aídil borrowed from L. *aedīlis* ; — a]íttiúm 'portionum', *aeteis* 'partis': Grk. αἶσα (*αιτ-ι̯α); — prai, *praesen-tid* 'praesente': L. *prae* ; — svaí, *suae* 'si'; — Dat.-Loc. Sg. of

---

[1] That this word, which occurs in an inscription found on the site of Bovianum, has nothing to do with the name of the town, as some assume, is incredible.

ā-stems (60), e.g. **Fluusaí** 'Florae', e]**ísaí víaí mefiaí** 'in ea via media', *Bansae* 'Bantiae'(Loc.); — Dat.-Abl. Pl. of ā-stems (60, *a*), e.g. **Diumpaís** 'Lumpis', **kerssnaís** 'cenis', *exais-c-en* 'in his'.

> *a.* The *ai* of the last example, as contrasted with usual *ae* in the Latin alphabet, is due to the following *s*. For *mais* see **91**, 1, for *maimas* **114**, *b*.

**63.** UMBRIAN. *ai* became an open *ē*. Its open quality is attested by the fact that the spelling *i*, so frequent in the case of original *ē*, or *oi* in final syllables, never occurs (cf. also **62**, 2, *a*). Examples: **kvestur**: O. **kvaísstur**; — **pre**, *pre*, **prehabia**, etc.: L. *prae*; — **sve**, *sve*: O. **svaí**, *suae*; — Dat.-Loc. Sg. of ā-stems, e.g. **ase** 'arae', **tute**, *tote* 'civitati', *Turse* 'Torrae'; Dat.-Abl. Pl. of ā-stems, e.g. **tekuries**, *dequrier* 'decuriis'; **semenies**, *sehmenier* 'sementivis.'

> *a.* For the possible appearance of ei as an archaistic spelling representing an intermediate stage in the development of ai, see **29**, *a*.

## ei

**64.** OSCAN. Examples: **deíkum**, *deicum* 'dicere', *deicans* 'dicant': L. *dīcō*, early *deicō*; — **Deívaí** 'Divae', **deivinais** 'divinis': L. *dīvus*, early *deivus*; — **feíhúss** 'muros': Grk. τεῖχος; — *preiuatud* 'reo': L. *prīvātus*; — **ehpeílatas** 'erectae, set up': L. *pīla*; — Gen. Sg. of *i*-stems, I.E. -*eis* (Skt. -*ēs*) transferred to consonant- and *o*-stems, e.g. **Maatreís** 'Matris', *carneis* 'partis', **eíseís**, *eizeis* 'eius', Κοττειης 'Cottii', Σταττιης 'Statii' (for ηι see **24**); — Loc. Sg. of *o*-stems like Grk. οἴκει, Lat. -*ī*, e.g. **múíníkeí tereí** 'in communi territorio', *comenei* 'in comitio'; Dat. Sg. of *i*- and consonant-stems, e.g. **Diúveí**, Διουϝει 'Iovi', **kvaístureí** 'quaestori', A]ππελλουνηι 'Apollini', etc.

> *a.* The form *ceus* 'civis': L. *cīvis*, early *ceivis*, if not merely a misspelling, indicates a special development of *ei* before *u*, such as is seen in L. *seu* beside *sīve*, early *seive*.
>
> *b.* In some Campanian inscriptions, mixed with Etruscan, we find *e* for *ei*, e.g. Gen. Sg. **Luvcies** 'Lucii'; cf. also Gen. Sg. **púíieh** 'quoius' (no. 39).

**65.** In Umbrian the *ei* appears regularly as **e**, *e*, the spelling *i* being of the utmost rarity. This indicates an open *ē*, like that from *ai* (63), as contrasted with the close *ē* from original *ē̆*, or *oi* in final syllables, for which the spelling *i* is so common.    Contrast the spelling of the Gen. Sg. ending, from -*eis* (64), which is regularly -*es*, -*er*, and only once -*ir*, with that of the Dat.-Abl. Pl. from -*ois*, which in the Latin alphabet is nearly always -*ir* (or -*eir*).    See also 82, 2, *a*.

Examples: prever 'singulis': L. *prīvus*, O. *preivatud*; — etu, *eetu*, from *ei-tōd*: L. *ītō*; — pronominal stem *ero-*, e.g. *erer* 'eius', *erar*, etc. (once, amid countless examples of *e*, *irer*): O. eíseís, *eizeis*, *eizois*, etc.; Gen. Sg. of *i*-stems etc. (see 64), e.g. *Matrer* 'Matris', katles 'catuli', *popler* 'populi'; — Dat. Sg. of *i*- and consonant-stems (64), e.g. Iuve 'Iovi', karne 'carni', *nomne* 'nomini'.

*a.* For the uses of the *spelling* ei, ei, in Umbrian see 29 with *a*.

### oi

**66.**    In Oscan, *oi* remains, both in initial syllables, where in Latin it becomes *ū*, and in final syllables, where in Latin it becomes *ī*.    Examples: múíníkú 'communis': L. *com-mūnis*, early *comoinem* (Goth. *ga-mains* etc.); — úíttiuf 'usus': L. *ūtor*, early *oetor*; — Dat. Sg. of *o*-stems (60), e.g. húrtúí 'horto', Abellanúí 'Abellano'; — Dat.-Abl. Pl. of *o*-stems (60, *a*), e.g. feíhúís 'muris', *eizois* 'eis', *nesimois* 'proximis'.    Cf. also Pael. *coisatens* (67, 1), *oisa* 'usa', Dat.-Abl. Pl. *puclois*, etc.

*a.* Since in all the examples in the Latin alphabet the *oi* is followed by a sibilant, in which case we also find *ai*, not *ae* (62, *a*), it is likely that the ordinary spelling was *oe*.

**67.**    UMBRIAN.    1.    In initial syllables *oi* becomes *ō*.    The most obvious examples are in the native alphabet, where ú might denote either *ū* or *ō*, namely: unu 'unum': L. *ūnus*, early *oinos*, *oenus*; — kuraia 'curet': L. *cūrō*, early *coiravere*, *coeravit*, Pael. *coisatens* 'curaverunt'; — muneklu 'sportulam': L. *mūnus*, related to *com-mūnis* etc. (66; cf. also Lith. *mainas* 'exchange'). But in the Latin alphabet there are several more or less certain examples, on the basis of which we assume that the sound was ō, namely: *pora* 'qua': O. *poizad* (thought by some to contain *ōi*, but see **199**, *d*) ; — Nom. Sg. *poei, poe, poi*, which probably contains *\*pō*, from *\*poi* (O. **pui**), with the enclitic *-ī* ; — *nosue* 'nisi', which is most naturally explained as containing *\*noi*, a by-form of *nei* (cf. O. *nei suae* 'nisi') ; — *uocu-cum*, **vuku-kum** 'ad aedem' (?), perhaps: Grk. ϝοῖκος, οἶκος (sometimes used of a temple or special shrine), L. *vīcus*.

2. In final syllables *oi* became a close *ē*, written **e**, *e*, **i**, *i*, *ei*. Examples: Dat. Sg. of *o*-stems (**60**), e.g. **Tefre, Tefri**, *Tẹfrei* 'Tefro', *pople* 'populo'; — Dat.-Abl. Pl. of *o*-stems (**60**, *a*), e.g. **pre veres Treplanes** 'ante portam Trebulanam', *uerir Treblanir, uereir Treblaneir*.

For the contrast with the open *ē* from *ai* or *ei*, see **63**, **65**; also **82**, 2, *a*.

### au

**68.** OSCAN. Examples: **avt**, *aut* 'at, aut', *auti* 'aut': L. *aut*; — **Avdiis**, Αϝδειες 'Audius'; — **Aukíl** 'Aucilus'; — ταυρομ 'taurum': L. *taurus*; — **thesavrúm**, from Grk. θησαυρός (**21**).

**69.** In Umbrian, *au* becomes *ō*. Examples: **ute**, *ote* 'aut': L. *aut* (see **68**); — **turuf**, *toru* 'tauros' (see **68**); — **uhtur**, official title: L. *auctor*; — *frosetom* 'fraudatum': L. *fraudō*.

### eu

**70.** Original *eu* became *ou* in the Italic period, so that its further history belongs with that of *ou*, given below. There are no examples of secondary *eu* resulting from contraction, as in L. *neu* etc. But it occurs in O. **Evklúí** borrowed from the Greek (**21**).

### ou

**71.** OSCAN. Examples: *touto*, τωϝτο 'civitas', **túvtíks** 'publicus', etc.: Goth. *þiuda* 'people' etc. (**15**, 2); — **Lúvkanateís** '\*Lucanatis', Λουκανομ 'Lucanorum', **Lúvkis** 'Lucius': L. *lūx* etc., Grk. λευκός; — Gen. Sg. of *u*-stems (L. -*ūs*, Goth. -*aus*, etc.), *castrous* 'capitis';—*loufir* 'vel' (96); — **lúvkeí** 'in luco': L. *lūcus* (early *loucom*); — **Lúvfreís** 'Liberi' (Pael. *loufir* 'liber'): L. *līber* (with dissimilation of *ou* to *oi, ei,* between *l* and labial; cf. *lubet, libet*), Grk. ἐλευθερός.

**72.** In Umbrian, *ou* becomes *ō*. Examples: **tuta,** *totam* 'civitatem': O. *touto* etc. (71); — *rofu* 'rufos' (96); — Gen. Sg. of *u*-stems (71), *trifor* 'tribus'.

*a.* If **Vuvçis** is 'Lucius' (O. **Lúvkis** etc.), as seems probable (104), it is an example of the archaistic spelling often found in proper names, in this case handed down from a period prior to the monophthongization of *ou*. The normal spelling is seen in **Vuçiia-per,** if 'pro Lucia'.

### Lengthening of Vowels

**73.** In Latin, vowels are regularly lengthened before *ns, nf, nct, nx,* and so also in Oscan-Umbrian, at least before *ns,* and, with accompanying loss of *n,* before *nct*. Thus O. **keenzstur** (**nz** = *nts* from *ns*; 110, 1) 'censor': L. *cēnsor*; — O. **saahtúm** 'sanctum', U. **sahta,** *sahatam*: L. *sānctus*; — U. *śihitu* 'cinctos', *ansihitu* : L. *cīnctus*.

*a.* For lengthening before *nf,* U. **aanfehtaf** 'infectas, non coctas'(?) is more doubtful evidence, since, with one **a** at the end of a line, the other at the beginning of the next, simple dittography is not unlikely.

**74.** In Latin, final *ns* loses its *n* with accompanying lengthening of the preceding vowel, as in the Acc. Pl. endings *-ōs, -īs,* etc. from *-ons, -ins,* etc. The Umbrian change of *-ns* to *f* (110, 2) seems to have been accompanied by lengthening of the preceding vowel, since the *o*-stem forms are usually written with *u* (for *ō*; 54), e.g. *toru, rofu,* and the *i*-stem forms sometimes with *ei* (for *ī*; 48), e.g. *aueif, treif*.

NOTE. If, as some suppose, the endings were originally *-ōns, -īns,* etc., and if, further, the shortening of vowels before *n* + consonant had not yet taken place, the long vowels in the forms cited might be regarded as original rather than secondary. This would have the advantage of enabling us to explain the *-f* from *-ef* in the Acc. Pl. of consonant-stems as due to regular syncope instead of to analogical influence. See **176,** 10. Nevertheless, in view of the uncertainty of the two premises, especially the second, the above statement has been preferred provisionally.

**75.** In Umbrian the $h$ resulting from $k$ before $t$ (148) or $f$ before $t$ (121) was weakly sounded or wholly lost, as is obvious from its frequent omission in the writing, and its time seems to have been added to that of the preceding vowel. For only on the supposition that the pronunciation was substantially that of a simple long vowel can we understand such a spelling as *sahatam* beside **sahta** (where, however, the vowel was already long before the reduction of $h$; see 78), or the extension of the spelling $h$ to cases where it had no etymological value but was only a mark of vowel-length. For example, by assuming that in **apehtre** 'ab extra' (cf. O. **ehtrad**) the *eh* was pronounced $\bar{e}$, we understand how the same characters could be used as a sign of length in **ampr-ehtu** 'ambito' beside *eetu*.

**76.** There are certain examples of lengthening, which, although not all on precisely the same plane, have this in common that the vowel is or had been followed by *rs*.

1. U. *meersta* 'iusta'. In Umbrian the *r* of *rs* was weakly sounded, as is shown by its frequent omission in the writing. And this is true not only of original *rs* (e.g. *fasio*, **fasiu** 'farrea' beside *farsio*; *sesna* 'cenam' beside **çersna-tur**), but also of the *rs* which in the Latin alphabet represents original *d* (e.g. *Acesoniam* beside *Acersoniem*: **Akeřunie**). In *meersta* the *rs* belongs to the latter class, for it is a derivative of *mers*, **meřs** (15, 6); moreover, in all examples of the word the *r* happens to be written. But the spelling with *ee*, though occurring only once, may fairly be taken as an indication that in general the reduction of *r* was accompanied by a lengthening, perhaps but slight, of the preceding vowel.

2. O. **peessl[úm** beside **pestlúm** 'templum' from *\*perstlo-*: U. .**persklum** 'sacrificium', *persclo*, *pescler*. In Oscan there is no such general reduction of *r* in *rs* as in Umbrian (cf. **kersnu** 'cena' always written with *r*), but apparently it was differently treated in the group *rstl*. That the lengthening is confined to **peessl[úm** and connected with the loss of *t* (139, 2), is unlikely.

3. U. *frateer* 'fratres' from *\*frāter(e)s* points to lengthening before final *rs*, the *s* then disappearing.

> NOTE. The early Latin use of *ter*, from *\*tĕrs*, as a long syllable is not parallel, since the form was not *tēr* with vowel-lengthening, but *terr*, like *hocc*, *miless*, etc. The same is true of *far*, from *fars*, which occurs as a long syllable in Ovid and is cited by Priscian (Keil II, 313) among words ending in *ăr*.

4. O. **teer[úm** 'territorium', related to L. *terra* from *\*tersa*. This form is commonly, and perhaps correctly, derived from *\*terso-*, it being assumed

from this that original *rs* between vowels in Oscan became *r* with lengthening
of the preceding vowel (**115**, 1). But as this is the only example for such a
development of *rs*, it is well to point out another possible explanation, which is
as follows : There once existed a simple neuter *s*-stem *\*ters-* with Nom.-Acc. Sg.
*\*ters* which became O.-U. *\*tĕr* according to 3. The oblique cases were affected
by the analogy of the Nom.-Acc., e.g. Gen. Sg. *\*terseis* being replaced by
*\*tĕreis* (tereís), just as U. Gen. Sg. *\*farser* was replaced by *farer* under the
influence of *far*. The word then went over completely to the commonest
neuter type, that of the *o*-stems, giving Nom.-Acc. *\*tĕrom*.

**77. 1.** The *ē* of O. **eestínt** 'exstant', **eehiianasúm** 'emittendarum', U. *eheturstahamu* 'exterminato', etc., like L. *ē-* beside
*ex-*, must be due to secondary lengthening, but the conditions
under which this took place cannot be the same as in Latin,
and are not yet clear.

NOTE. The *ē* in Latin is readily explained as due to the lengthening which
regularly accompanies the loss of *s* (in this case from *ks*) before *m, n, l*, etc.
But this cannot hold for Oscan-Umbrian, where *s* remains in these positions (**114**).
The Umbrian *ē* might be explained as coming from *ek-* before *t* according to
**75**, but there seems to have been no such reduction of *h* in Oscan, since in all
other forms it is uniformly written.

**2.** The *ā* of O. **aamanaffed** 'locavit', U. *ahauendu* 'avertito',
etc., like L. *ā* beside *ab, abs*, is likewise due to a secondary lengthening, the conditions of which for Oscan-Umbrian are not clear.

NOTE. It is possible here to assume a distinct prefix, original *ā-*,
but the difficulty in the derivation from *abs* is no greater than that
involved in the *ē* of O. **eestínt**, where original *ē*, even if there were
evidence for any such prefix, is out of the question (**41**).

**3.** The *ō* of U. *ooserclom*, if this is '*\*observaculum*,' offers the same difficulty. But meaning and etymology of the word are uncertain. The explanation as '*\*aviservaculum*' (*ō* from *au(i)-* ; **69**) is also possible.

### Shortening of Vowels

**78.** Vowel-shortening such as is seen in Latin before final
*r, l, t, m*, or when the vowel is itself final, is not observable in
Oscan or Umbrian. Positive evidence for the preservation of
the long vowel is furnished as follows :

**1.** For final *ā*, by the forms in -u, -ú, -o (**34**), since final
short *a* remains (**32**, 2).

2. Before *-r*, by O. patir[1] : L. *pater* (Grk. πατήρ), since the
ı points to *ē* (41); — O. keenzstur, *censtur* : L. *cēnsor* (Grk. -ωρ),
since the u, *u* points to *ō* (53); similarly by the Passive forms
O. *loufir* (Pres. Indic. of Second Conj.; **238**, 2), sakrafír (Perf.
Subj. with mood-sign *ē*; **234**).

3. Before *-t*, by O. kasit[1]: L. *caret* (**17**, 1), with ı for *ē* of
the Present Stem; cf. also (before *-d*) O. fusíd: L. *foret*, with ı
for *ē* of the Subjunctive.

4. Before *m*, by O. paam, L. *quam.*

> Note. As this form is a monosyllable, it would still be possible
> to assume shortening in polysyllables. But the analogy of the cases
> in 2 and 3 is against this, and moreover the forms of the Gen. Pl. are
> more easily understood as retaining *-ōm* than as having *-om*. The
> Oscan forms might indeed be taken as *-om* according to **50**, but in
> Umbrian even the single occurrence of *-um* in *pracatarum* is of weight
> in favor of *-ōm*, since *-om* never appears as *-um*.
>
> a. It is probable that the shortening of a long vowel before *n* + consonant,
> whether final or not, as in L. *amant* from *amā-nt*, Partic. *amant-* from *amā-nt-*,
> took place in the Italic period, but the evidence in Oscan-Umbrian is very
> meagre. See **215**, 2, on O. stahínt; **217**, 4, on O. amfret; also **74**, note. For the
> similar shortening before *r* + consonant, cf. O. Herekleís, L. *Herculēs*, from Grk.
> Ἡρακλῆς (**21**).
>
> The long vowel before the secondary ending *-ns* (e.g. Imperf. Subj.
> O. h]errins 'caperent'), which has replaced original *-nt*, may well be due to the
> analogy of the other forms (O. fusíd etc.). Or, if the explanation given in
> **128**, 1, is correct, the change of *nt* through *nd* to *n* may have antedated the
> shortening process.

## Anaptyxis in Oscan

**79.** Anaptyxis, or the development of a secondary vowel
between a liquid or nasal and another consonant either preceding
or following, is a wide-spread phenomenon in Oscan, though
unknown in Umbrian. It is necessary to divide the examples
into two classes according as the liquid or nasal precedes or
follows the other consonant. If it precedes, the quality of the
new vowel is that of the vowel preceding, while if it follows,
the new vowel has the quality of the following vowel. In

---

[1] We should expect patír, kasít, but the inscriptions containing these words
are careless in the use of í and ı.

other words, the newly developed vowel has the quality of the vowel of the syllable in which the liquid or nasal stands.

*a.* In the case of *mn* it is *n* which is parallel to the nasal in other groups, e.g. *comenei* from *\*komnei* (81). In fact there is no example of an anaptyctic vowel developed through *m*.

*b.* For the secondary vowel-development in connection with samprasā-raṇa see 91.

**80.** The liquid or nasal precedes. This type of anaptyxis is one of the marked characteristics of the Oscan (and Paelignian). The regularity with which it appears makes it well nigh certain that the newly developed vowel was not a mere glide, as in vulgar Latin *dulicia* for *dulcia*, etc., but formed a full syllable. An interesting parallel is seen in Russian, e.g. *golova* 'head' from *\*golva, bereg* 'bank' from *\*bergŭ.*

1. LIQUID. The vowel develops between a liquid and a guttural (including *h*) or a labial (including *u̯*); but not between a liquid and a dental. Examples: **aragetud** 'argento'; — **Herekleís** 'Herculis'; — Μαμερεκιες 'Mamercius'; — **tríbarakavúm** 'aedificare' from *\*trēb-ark-*: L. *arx*; — *amiricatud* '\*immercato' (38, 2); — **Mulukiis** 'Mulcius'; — **Verehasiúí** 'Versori' from *verh-*: L. *vergō*(?) ; — **kulupu** 'culpa'(?); — **Urufiis** 'Orfius'; — **Alafaternum** 'Alfaternorum'; — **turumiiad** 'torqueatur': L. *tormen*; — **teremníss** 'terminibus'; — **Salaviis** 'Salvius' (**salavs**, σαλαϝς 'salvus' owes its form to the oblique cases, for *\*saluos* would give *\*salus* in the O.-U. period; see 91, 1); — **Kalaviis** 'Calvius' (*Calavius* on Latin inscriptions is simply the Oscan form); — **Heleviieís** 'Helvii'; — **serevkid** 'auspicio' from *\*seru(i)kio-*; — **uruvú** 'flexa'(?): *urvum*(?). Cf. also Pael. *Herec., Alafis, Helevis, Salauatur.*

As examples of the lack of anaptyxis before dentals may be mentioned Μαμερτινο 'Mamertina', *molto* 'multa', **alttreí** 'alteri', *carneis* 'partis', **kerssnaís** 'cenis', Ϝερσορει 'Versori.'

2. NASAL. The vowel develops between *n* and *f*, and in some cases between *n* and a guttural. Examples:

**Anafríss** 'Imbribus'(?); — **aamanaffed** 'locavit', from *\*manf(e)-fed* (223); αϝαφακετ (for *f* see 24, *b*) 'dedicavit' from *\*anfaked*;

—Anagtiai 'Angitiae' from \**Ang(e)tiā-*; — Liganakdíkeí, name of
a goddess, from \**lēgān(i)ko-dik-* (or from \**lēgnāko-*, and so
belonging in 81?). Cf. also Pael. *Anaceta* 'Angitiae' beside
*Anceta, Anacta.*

NOTE. Usually there is no anaptyxis between *n* and a guttural, e.g.
tanginúd. The conditions under which it took place are not clear.

81. The liquid or nasal follows. This sort of anaptyxis,
the same that is seen in Latin *pōculum, piāculum*, etc., is of a
less determinate character than the preceding. It is subject to
local variation: at least in the inscriptions of Capua there is
no indication of it in the spelling. Elsewhere it occurs regularly after short syllables, but is not entirely confined to this
position, the more precise conditions not being clear.[1] Examples: pateref 'patri' (contrast maatreís 'matris'); — púteref-píd 'in
utroque', Nom. Pl. pútúrús-píd, etc., from \**potro-* (88, 4); — *petiro-
pert* 'quater' for \**petirio-pert* (100, 3, *c*), from \**petriā-pert* (192, 2);
— Sadiriis 'Satrius'; — pústiris 'posterius' from \**postrios* (88, 4),

[1] Thurneysen, who first assumed that anaptyxis occurred only after short
syllables (K.Z. 27, 181 ff.), has since modified his view to the extent of admitting
anaptyxis even after a long syllable in the case of *r* followed by consonantal *i* or *i*
in hiatus (I.F. Anz. 4, 38). This would cover pústiris, Aadiriís, etc. In this he
is followed by Brugmann, who however treats the development in these cases as a
distinct phenomenon (Grd. I², p. 825). But still further restrictions are necessary.
As regards *zicolom* 'diem', Acc. Pl. d]iikúlús, we agree with Thurneysen against
v. Planta that the suffix, though originally *-kelo-*, has passed through the stage *-klo-*,
and that the vowel of the penult is as truly anaptyctic as any other. But we can
see no plausibility in his view that the first syllable of this word, and also of Diíviiaí,
is to be taken as *dii-* from *dio-*. Such a change is without even the remotest analogy
in Oscan phonetics. And what of the preservation of (*d*)*io* not only in iúkleí and Iúviia,
with which Thurneysen equates *zicolom* and Diíviiaí, but also in Diúveí, Διουϝει,
Iúveís, etc.? Does he mean to assume a local change confined to Bantia, Samnium,
and the land of the Frentani? But Diúveí is also Samnitic. There is no real difficulty in assuming that anaptyxis in the case of *kl* took place without regard to the
quantity of the preceding syllable. Its absence in sakaraklúm may well be due to
the preceding anaptyxis (cf. Herekleís).
The author is convinced that the quantity of the preceding syllable is not the
only factor to be considered, but that others, such as relative rapidity of utterance,
local variations aside from that of Capua, inconsistency in the spelling of what was
perhaps not a full vowel, etc., are to be reckoned with. In Latin, where the material
is so much more plentiful, it is admitted that the factors are too complicated to allow
any precise formulation of the conditions of anaptyxis.

but Capuan **púatreí** 'in postero'; — **Aadiriís** 'Atrius' (whence by extension **Aadirans**); — **Vestirikiíúí** 'Vestricio'; — **sakaraklúm** 'sacellum' from *\*sakrā-klo-*, **sakarater** 'sacratur', σακορο 'sacrum', but Capuan **sakrím, sakrafír**, etc.; — **tefúrúm** 'burnt-offering' from *\*tefro-* : U. **tefra** 'carnes quae cremantur'; — **Pukalatúí** '\*Puclato', but Capuan **puklum** 'filium'; — *zicolom* 'diem', Abl. Sg. *ziculud*, Loc. Sg. *zicel[ei]*, Dat.-Abl. Pl. *zicolois*, Acc. Pl. **d]iíkúlús**, from *\*diē-klo-*[1]: L. *diēcula*; — **Patanaí** 'Pandae' from *\*Pat-nā-*; — **akeneí** 'in anno'(?), Gen. Pl. *acunum* (probable reading): U. *acnu* ; — *comono* 'comitia', Loc. Sg. *comenei*, from *\*komno-* (15, 4): U. **kumne**; — O. **Safinim** 'Samnium', from *\*Safniom*: L. *Samnium*. Cf. also Pael. *sacaracirix, pristafalacirix*, as if L. *\*sacrātrīx, \*praestibulātrīx*.

*a.* In **kú]mparakineís** 'consilii', *comparascuster* 'consulta erit', it is uncertain which *a* is anaptyctic; but if the second, and so falling under **80, 1**, it would be the only example before *s*. Against the assumption that the first *a* is anaptyctic, the preceding long syllable is not decisive. See footnote, p. 52.

### Contraction and Hiatus

**82.** Like vowels are contracted.

**1.** The loss of intervocalic *i̭* in the Italic period was attended by contraction of like vowels. Thus the ending of the Nom. Pl. of *i*-stems, originally *-ei̭es* (Skt. *-ayas*), became *-ēs*, and the *ē* had the same history as original *ē*. So O. **trís**: L. *trēs* ; — U. *pacrer* 'propitii', from stem *pakri-*. Another example of the same contraction is O. **húrtín** 'in horto' from *\*hortei̭-en* (Loc. Sg. with postpositive *en*; **171, 7**).

**2.** In Umbrian the close *ē* resulting from *oi* in final syllables (**67, 2**) was so near in quality to *i*, that in the Dat. Sg. and Dat.-Abl. Pl. of stems in *-i̭o-* and *-i̭o-* it contracted with the preceding *i* (and *i̭*). Contracted and uncontracted forms are found side by side, but the latter are due to the influence of the other case-forms. Thus Dat. Sg. **Iuve**, *Ioui*, beside **Iuvie**, *Iouie*, Dat.-Abl. Pl. *Atiersir* beside *Atiersier*, etc. Compare

---

[1] See footnote, p. 52.

Latin Nom. Pl. *fīlī* beside *fīliī*, Dat.-Abl. Pl. *auspicīs* beside *auspiciīs*, etc., the contracted forms being very frequent in inscriptions. Contraction of *u* with the sound resulting from *ō* is seen in U. *dur* 'duo' from *\*duōs* (**54**).

a. There are no such contracted forms in the case of the open *e* from original *e* (Voc. Sg. *arsie*), or the open *ē* from *ei* (Loc. Sg. *Fisie*, Gen. Sg. *Fisier*) or from *ai* (Dat.-Abl. Pl. of First Decl. *dequrier*).

**83.** Unlike vowels remain uncontracted, and sometimes *h* is used as a mark of the hiatus. Thus we find uncontracted:

*āo*, in Infinitives of the First Conjugation, O. *moltaum*, **tríbarakavúm** (**v** is simply the glide sound preceding the rounded vowel; cf. occasional Grk. ἀϝυτάρ for αὐτάρ, etc.).

*ăō*, in U. *stahu* 'sto' from *\*staiō*, U. *subocau*, *subocauu* 'invoco' from *-āiō* (*uu* = *uu* with glide as in **tríbarakavúm**; less probably doubling to indicate length, since this is very rare in final syllables).

*ae*, in U. **ahesnes** 'ahenis' from\* *a(i)esno* (Skt. *áyas*); — U. **staheren** 'stabunt' from *\*sta(i)esent*.

*āē*, in Present Subjunctive of First Conjugation, O. *deiuaid*, **sakahíter**, from *-āiē-*.

*eo*, *eā*, in O. *ioc*, *ionc*, **íak**, U. *eam*, etc.: L. *ea*, *eum*, etc., from *\*eio-*, *eiā-*. For O. *i*, see **38**, 1.

*oe*, in U. **Puemune**: Sabine *Poimunien*, L. *Pōmōna*, *pōmum* from *\*po-emo-* (cf. *cōmō* from *\*co-emō*).[1]

*ōī*, in U. *pue* 'ubi' from *\*pō* (L. *quō*) + *ī*; — U. *poei* 'qui' from *\*pō* (earlier *\*poi*) + *ī*.

*ai̯*, in O. **stahint** 'stant', U. *stahitu* 'stato'. But the retention of the hiatus here is probably due to analogy, partly of other forms of this verb, partly of the corresponding endings in forms of other verbs.

a. Between *i* and a following vowel there is no hiatus, but a glide *i̯* which is indicated in the spelling of the native alphabets (**31**). The consistent use of *h* in U. *pihatu* 'piato', **pehatu**, *pihaner*, etc. and O. **Píhiúí** 'Pio' (also Volsc. *pihom* 'pium') is remarkable, and without adequate explanation.

---

[1] Osthoff, I.F. 5, 317 ff.

**84.** Of the various phenomena which take place when vowels of two different words are brought together in the sentence, namely "crasis," "aphaeresis," "slurring," etc., we have but little evidence.

With L. *bonast* for *bona est* etc. are obviously parallel O. teremnatust 'terminata est' and destrst (for \*destrust) 'dextra est'. A more anomalous case is U. neiřhabas 'ne adhibeant', if for nei(-a)řhabas. With *animadvertō* from *animum advertō*, with slurring, is parallel U. eitipes 'decreverunt' from \**eitom* \**hipens* (264, 2).

*a.* For O. pússtíst (C. A. 33) the meaning 'positum est' is so much more suitable to the context than that of 'post est' that we cannot reject the possibility that the form comes from \*pústúm íst, in spite of the fact that the regularity with which final *m* is written in Oscan, except at Pompeii, would naturally point to its full pronunciation. That it is not the vowel of the enclitic that is absorbed, as in teremnatust, would be accounted for by the fact that the íst of the Cippus Abellanus is ĕst (217, 2).

### Vowel-Weakening in Medial Syllables

**85.** The wide-spread weakening of short vowels and diphthongs which occurs in Latin in medial syllables, such syllables being in the earlier system of accentuation unstressed, is unknown in Oscan-Umbrian. Examples of unchanged *a* and *e*, such as U. *pro-canurent* : L. *(oc)-cinuī*, or U. taçez : L. *tacitus*, have been cited in 32, 3, 36, 3.

**86.** But in the position before a labial, or in some cases after a labial, a weakening takes place, which results sometimes in *u*, sometimes in *i*. In the corresponding Latin. phenomenon the determining factor in the development to *u* or *i* respectively was the character of the vowels of the surrounding syllables (cf. *occupō*, *nuncupō*, but *anticipō*, *occipiō*, etc., from *cap*-), but so many secondary changes have taken place, owing to the mutual influence of forms belonging to the same system or formation, that the original distribution is only partially reflected in the actual forms. Much the same is true for Oscan-Umbrian.

1. The superlatives, formed from the suffix -*(t)emo*- (I.E. -*(t)m̥mo*-), show the influence of the preceding vowel. Thus

with L. *optumus, maxumus, proxumus, ultumus* (eventually *optimus* etc., under the influence of the commoner type) may be compared O. últiumam 'ultimam' (iu from *u*; see 56) and U. *hondomu* 'infimo' (*o* from *u* before *m;* see 57); while with the Latin forms in *-imus* may be compared O. nessimas 'proximae', *nesimois,* U. *nesimei,* and O. messimass 'medioximas'(?). But note U. nuvime 'nonum' from *\*nouemo-* (Skt. *navamá-*).

2. In O. *pertumum* 'perimere' from *\*pert-emom.* the following vowel seems to have been a factor, though in *pertemust, peremust,* as well as in *pertemest,* the *e* is retained, apparently under the influence of the simplex ("recomposition").

3. In O. sifei 'sibi' (cf. Pael. *sefei,* U. *tefe*), as in L. *sibi,* the weakening is due to the enclitic use of the pronoun, to which points also O. tfei. In L. *simul,* early *semol, semul,* from *\*semel* the weakening in the first syllable is likewise due to enclitic use, and to this probably corresponds U. sumel 'simul', although it is possible to see in the latter an original *som-* (Grk. ὁμαλός).

NOTE. The single occurrence of O. tfei is not sufficient warrant for assuming actual syncope of the *e,* but on the other hand, taken in connection with sifei, it cannot be regarded as a mere graver's error without any foundation in the actual pronunciation. It is doubtless a careless spelling, but one that is due to the reduced pronunciation of the vowel.

4. U. prehubia 'praehibeat' beside prehabia may owe its *u* to the existence of such forms as *\*prehubust* (cf. *habus*), just as the *u* of early Latin *dērupiō* is probably due to a *\*dērupuī.*

Although there are no examples of *i* for original *a,* it is altogether probable that, as in Latin, the *a* had the same double development as the *e,* as seen in the superlatives cited above ; in this case we must regard prehabia as an example of recomposition for *\*prehibia.*

5. O. *praefucus* 'praefectus' beside *facus* 'factus', where the labial precedes, is different from any case known in Latin, but here too the vowel of the following syllable is obviously a factor. A still different, though uncertain, example is O. prupukid 'ex ante pacto', which is most naturally derived from

*prō-pakio-*, although it is possible that this is a case of vowel-gradation (u = *ō* in interchange with *a*, *ā*).

6. A change of *o* to *u* is seen in O. *amprufid* 'improbe'.

7. In Latin we find a similar interchange of *u* and *i*, where the original vowel is either *u* or *i*. A parallel to L. *dissipō* beside the more original *dissupō*, or *lacrima* beside *lacruma*, would be U. *combifiatu* 'nuntiato', if this were related to Grk. πυθ- (πυνθάνομαι etc.); but this is uncertain, since connection with Grk. πιθ- (πείθω etc.) is also possible. Vice versa, with L. *pontufex* beside *pontifex* we may compare U. *atropusatu* beside *gtripursatu* 'tripodato', if the former spelling is not simply a mistake.  *a̅r fśu bra̅tȷ*

8. A change of *ou* to *u*, such as is seen in L. *dēnuō* from *dē novō*, has been assumed for Oscan-Umbrian, but on insufficient evidence.

### Syncope in Medial Syllables [1]

**87.** Syncope of short vowels in medial syllables, as in L. *caldus* beside *calidus*, *rettulī* from *retetulī*, etc., is far more extensive in Oscan and Umbrian than in Latin, yet there are numerous examples of the retention of short vowels. We must confine ourselves to a statement of the facts.

NOTE. Even in Latin the factors involved are so complex and have been so obscured by subsequent leveling that it is impossible to formulate the precise conditions, though much progress has been made in this direction. For Oscan-Umbrian, with the limited amount of material before us, it is almost useless to speculate upon the original conditions of the syncope.

**88.** Syncope of *e*. 1. In the Imperatives of the Third Conjugation the original *e*, which in Latin is changed to *i* (*agitō*), is always lost, except after *n*. Thus O. *actud*, U. aitu (ai from *ak*, 143): L. *agitō*; — U. kuvertu: L. *convertitō*; similarly U. ostendu, fiktu, *ninctu*, etc.; — but U. kanetu: L. *canitō*.

2. In the Participles in *-eto-* the *e* is retained, e.g. U. *tasetur* 'taciti', maletu 'molitum', etc. (244, 4).

3. Further examples are: O. prúffed 'posuit' from *pro-fefed*, aamanaffed 'locavit' from *man-fefed*: L. *prō-didit*, etc.; — O. upsed 'fecit', úpsannam 'faciendam', U. osatu 'facito', from *opesā-*: L. *operor*; O. *cebnust* 'venerit': U. *benust*; — O. Dekmanniúís

'*Decumaniis': L. *decumānus, decimus* from *\*dekemo-*; — O. **fruk-tatiuf** 'fructus' from *\*frūgu̯etātiōn-*, as if L. *\*fruitātiō*; —U. **mersto** 'iustum' from *\*medes-to*: L. *modes-tus.*

4. Syncope is usual in the suffixes *-kelo-, -elo-, -tero-, -ero-, -men-*. In some few cases the short form may be an inherited variety of the suffix, such as *-tro-* beside *-tero-, -lo-* beside *-elo-,* etc. But for the majority of the examples this is improbable, and for some distinctly impossible, e.g. in U. **tiçlu** on account of the ç (**144**), in U. **katlu** because original *tl* becomes *kl* (**129**, 2), etc. Examples: U. **tiçlu** 'dedicationem' from *\*dikelo-* (in Nom. Sg. **tiçel** the *o* of the final syllable is lost and the *e* remains); — U. **veskla** 'vascula' from *\*ves-kelo-*; — *\*diē-klo-* (whence O. **zicolom** 'diem' etc., **81**) from *\*diē-kelo-*; — U. **katlu** 'catulum' from *\*katelo-* (Nom. Sg. **katel** like **tiçel**); — U. **vitlu** 'vitulum' from *\*u̯itelo-* (cf. O. **Víteliú** 'Italia', **250**); — O. **pústreí**, U. **postra**, *\*postrios* (whence O. **pústiris**, **81**, **91**, 1): L. *posterus, posterius*; — *\*potro-* (U. **podruhpei** 'utroque', O. **púterei-píd** by **81**): Grk. πότερος; — O. **alttram**: L. *altero-*; — O. **teremniss**: L. *terminibus* (but O. **teremenniú**: L. *\*terminia*); — U. **nomner**: L. *nōminis.*[1]

**89.** 1. Loss of *i* is seen in O. **minstreis** 'minoris': L. *minister*; — O. **Pupdiis** 'Popidius' beside **Púpidiis**; — U. **totcor, todceir**: O. **túvtíks, toutico** (**15**, 2). The loss is common to Latin also in *dexter*, O. **destrst**, U. **destram**, etc.: Grk. δεξίτερος, and in the prefix of L. *amb-igō, am-plector*, O. **am-víannud**, U. **an-ferener**, etc.: Grk. ἀμφί.

2. Loss of *a* is seen in O. **eestint** 'exstant' from *\*eks-stahint* (cf. **stahínt** 'stant'); — O. **embratur**: L. *imperātor*, from *\*em-parātor* (*parō*); — O. **prúftú** 'posita' from *\*pro-fato-* (**244**, 1).

3. Loss of *o* is seen in O. **akkatus** 'advocati' from *\*ad-u̯okāto-* through *\*adokāto-* (cf. **102**, 3; otherwise we should expect *\*adukatus* by **91**, 1); — perhaps in O. **meddíss** (**263**, 1, with footnote) and O. **Vezkeí** (**256**, 8).

---

[1] In O. **teremníss**, U. **nomner, tikamne**, etc., it is possible to assume the retention of the reduced grade -*mn*- instead of syncope. But the probability is that these have the same grade as the Latin forms. That the latter owe their -*min*- to anaptyxis (Sommer, Lat. Laut- und Formenlehre, 154) we are not convinced.

### Syncope in Final Syllables

**90.** In final syllables also, syncope is far more wide-spread than in Latin.

1. A short *o*, *e*, or *i* is dropped before final *s*.   Examples: Nom. Sg. of *o*-stems, e.g. O. húrz 'hortus' from *\*hortos*, Bantins 'Bantinus', Púmpaiians 'Pompeianus', túvtíks 'publicus', Mutíl 'Mutilus', U. Ikuvins 'Iguvinus', fratreks '\*fratricus', pihaz, *pihos* 'piatus' from *\*piãtos*, U. tiçel 'dedicatio' from *\*dikelos* ; — Nom.-Acc. Sg. N. of *s*-stems, e.g. O. *min*[*s* 'minus' from *\*minos*, U. mers 'ius' from *\*medos* ; — Dat.-Abl. Pl. (ending -*fos* : L. -*bus*), e.g. O. luisarifs 'lusoriis', teremníss 'terminibus', *ligis* 'legibus', U. avis 'avibus', *fratrus* 'fratribus'; — Nom. Sg. of *i*-stems, e.g. O. *ceus* 'civis', aídíl 'aedilis', U. *fons* 'favens' (suffix -*ni*-; cf. Nom. Pl. *foner*); — Nom. Pl. of consonant-stems (ending -*es* : Grk. -ες), e.g. O. humuns 'homines', meddíss 'meddices', *censtur* 'censores', U. *frater* 'fratres'.   (See also 2.)

*a.* Before final *m* vowels are retained, e.g. Acc. Sg. O. húrtúm, *touticom*, slagím, U. *poplom*, etc.

*b.* That *u* was not dropped even before final *s* is in itself probable. Cf. its universal retention in Latin, and likewise in Gothic (*dags* from *\*dagas*, *ansts* from *\*anstis*, but *sunus*). So O. *sipus* 'sciens', which in its relation to L. *sapiō* evidently contains the form of the root which characterizes Perfects like L. *cēpī* to *capiō*, etc. (**225**), may be a stereotyped Perfect Active Participle with Nom. Sg. in -*us*, like Skt. *vidus*, Avest. *viduš*. But it is also possible that it comes from *\*sēp-u̯os*, like O. *facus* from *\*fak-u̯os* (**91**, 1); cf. Volsc. *sepu* 'sciente' from *\*sēp(u̯)ōd*.

2. Syncope of *e* before final *s* and also before a final dental is seen in the 2d Sg. and 3d Sg. Fut. and Fut. Perf. as in U. heries 'voles', *heriest* 'volet', from *\*herieses*, *\*herieset*. See **221**, **230**.

But *e* remains in the 3d Sg. Perf. Indic. (O. kúmbened 'convenit', etc.; **223** ff.); also in the 3d Sg. Pres. Indic. of the Third Conjugation, though the only examples are from the minor dialects (Marruc. *feret* 'fert', Vest. *didet* 'dat'). U. seste also, though variously taken, is probably 'sistis', with *e* retained, perhaps under the influence of a *\*sistet*. In U. *pis-her* 'quilibet', probably from *-herit* (216), the syncope is due to the enclitic use of the verb.

NOTE. Assuming that under conditions no longer apparent both syncopated and unsyncopated forms existed in the Present and Perfect, the survival of the latter may be due to the fact that many of the syncopated forms would have lost their distinctive character, e.g. *kúmben(e)d would have become *kúmben. The Fut. and Fut. Perf. forms retained or seemed to retain the characteristic endings -s, -t.

### Samprasāraṇa

91. In those cases of syncope in which the consonant preceding the syncopated vowel itself assumes the function of a vowel, so that there is no reduction in the number of syllables, the phenomenon is known as samprasāraṇa. Such cases are best kept apart from the preceding, not only on account of the additional process involved, but because, when samprasāraṇa is possible, syncope may take place in positions where it does not otherwise occur. Thus, in general, syncope does not occur before final *m* (O. húrtúm, etc. 90, 1, *a*), but this need not prevent our assuming that -*iom* becomes -*im*.

1. *ụo* to *u*; *ịo* to *i*. Examples: O. *facus* 'factus' from *fak-ụos* (suffix -*ụo*-; 258, 1); — O. *fortis* 'potius': L. *fortius*; — O. *pústiris* from *postrios* (81): L. *posterius*; — so probably *mais* 'plus' from *maiios* (*magịos*; see 147, 3): L. *maius*, like Mais 'Maius' beside Dat. Sg. Maiiúí; — Nom. and Acc. Sg. M. and Nom.-Acc. Sg. N. of *ịo*-stems, e.g. O. Pakis 'Pacius', Acc. Pakim, *medicim* 'magisterium', U. Fisim 'Fisium', etc. (see 172 ff.).

2. *ro* and *ri* to *ṛ* (syllabic *r*), later *er*. Examples: U. *ager*: L. *ager*, from *agros*; — U. *pacer* 'propitius' from *pakris* (cf. L. *ácer* from *ákris*); — U. -*per* 'pro', as in *tota-per* 'pro populo', etc., from -*pro*; — O. Aderl. 'Atella' from *Átro-lá* (cf. L. *agellus* from *agro-los*); — O. Abella- (Abellanús) probably from *Apro-lá*- (L. *aper*). Observe also O. trstus 'testes' from *tristo-*[1]: L. *testis* from *tristi-* (but O. trístaamentud: L. *testámentum*); — O. Tantrnnaium from *Tantrinnaio-*(?). See also 239 on O. -*ter*.

---

[1] That is, 'third party'. See Skutsch, B.B. 23,100, Solmsen, K.Z. 37,18.

*a.* The parallel change of *no* (cf. L. *Sabellus* from *\*Safno-lo-*) is seen in U. *Padellar* from *\*Padenlā*, *\*Padn̥lā*, *\*Patno-lā* (cf. O. **Patanaí**). For the corresponding development of *lo* there are no certain examples, since U. **tiçel**, **katel**, perhaps also O. *famel*, contain the suffix *-elo-* (**88**, 4). O. **Fíml**, **Mítl** probably stand for *\*Fímel*, *\*Mítel* (*\*Mítel* : L. *Mitulus* = O. *famel* : L. *famulus*).

*b.* U. *ocar*, **ukar** 'mons', although its oblique cases are from the stem *okri-*, is not from *\*okris*, but from a by-form with suffix *-ari-*, or *āri-*.

> NOTE. The chronology of this process is a difficult problem. The agreement between Latin and Oscan-Umbrian would lead us to infer that it took place in the Italic period. But O. **Aderl.** and **Abella-**, with the change of surd to sonant which is observed elsewhere before *r* (**157**), would indicate that in the Oscan-Umbrian period the development had not passed beyond the stage *r̥*, and now comes the Latin form s]*akros* = *sacer* on the newly discovered forum-inscription, which, unless an analogical restoration, proves that the whole process took place independently in Latin.
>
> The reduction of *ri* in accented syllables (L. *ter* from *\*tris*, etc.[1]) was doubtless later than the change in unaccented syllables, and this is borne out by the existence in Oscan of **trístaamentud**. But here too the development seems to have begun in Oscan, judging from **trstus**.

### Loss of Final Short Vowels

**92.** As in Latin, final short vowels are sometimes dropped, sometimes retained. It may be assumed that in the Italic period sentence-doublets arose, of which the dialects inherited now the form with the vowel, now the one without it.

The primary personal endings *-ti*, *-nti* (Grk. *-τι*, *-ντι*) are without the final vowel in Oscan-Umbrian, as in Latin, e.g. O.-U. **est** 'est', O. **stahínt** 'stant', etc. Further examples are: U. *et* : L. *et*, from *\*eti* (Grk. *ἔτι*) ; — O. *nep*, *neip*, U. *neip* : L. *nec* beside *neque* ; — O. **avt**, *aut* 'at, aut', but also O. *auti* 'aut', U. *ote* : L. *aut* ; — O. **ant** : L. *ante* ; — O. **puf**, but U. *pufe* : L. *ubi* ; — O. *pan*, but U. *pane* : L. *quamde* ; — O. **pún**, but U. *ponne* : L. *\*quomde*.

---

[1] The contrast between *ter*, *testis*, and *tribus*, not to speak of *triplex*, etc., shows that in Latin the change was conditioned by the nature of the following sound. It took place before *s* (cf. change of final *-ros*, *-ris*), and possibly before *n*, though *cernō* is not decisive.

### Vowel-Gradation

**93.** In many cases the difference in the vowel of related words is not due to any of the regular vowel-changes of a particular dialect, such as have been described in the preceding sections, but is inherited from a system of Vowel-Gradation, or Ablaut, already existing in the parent speech. It is unnecessary here to enter into any discussion of the subject as a whole, but will be sufficient to mention such of these inherited variations as show themselves in the relation of Oscan-Umbrian forms to one another or to the cognate Latin forms.

**94.** *e, o,* etc. The interchange of *e* and *o* (L. *tegō* : *toga*) is seen in L. *gemō* : U. *gomia* 'gravidas'; — U. **meřs** 'ius', O. **meddíss**, etc. (15, 6): L. *modus*,[1] *modestus*; — U. **nuřpener** '-pondiis': L. *pondus, du-pondius.* Less certain examples are U. **sukatu** 'declarato'(?), probably a denominative from *\*soko-* : L. *insece* ; — U. **pruzuře** 'praestante'(?), possibly for *\*prō-sode* : L. *sedeō.*

The *ē*-grade is seen in U. **prusikurent** 'pronuntiaverint': L. *insece* (cf. L. *sēdī* : *sedeō*) ; — O. **trííbúm** 'domum' etc. (15, 14): U. *trebeit* 'versatur', *tremnu* 'tabernaculo' (L. *trabs*, if related, has a reduced grade).

The *ō*-grade is probably seen in U. *du-pursus* 'bipedibus', *petur-pursus* (cf. Dor. πώς, Goth. *fōtus*): L. *ped-, pēd-*, although the *o*-grade is possible.

**95.** *ei, i,* etc. The interchange of *ei* and *i* (L. *deicō, dīcō* : *dictus*) is seen in O. *deicans* 'dicant': O. *dicust*, U. *dersicust* 'dixerit', U. **tiçel** 'dedicatio', etc. ; — O. **feíhúss** 'muros' (Grk. τεῖχος) : L. *fingō, figūra*, etc.

An example of the *oi*-grade is U. *nosue* 'nisi', if from *\*noisuai* (67, 1) : O. *nei*, L. *nei, nī.*

Nouns formed with the suffix *-ien-* show an interchange between the strengthened grade *-iŏn-* and the long reduced grade *-īn-* (181, *a*).

*a.* O. **Diíviiaí** 'Diae' beside **Deívaí** etc. would point to a reduced grade *dīu-.* But this, although not inconceivable in view of such forms as Skt. *dívyati*

---

[1] But some regard the *o* in *modus* as due to assimilation.

'plays', *sívyati* 'sews', is regarded with suspicion, since the cognates such as Skt. *divyá-* point rather to *diu̯-*. Possibly the Oscan form is due to an error.[1]

**96.** *ou, u,* etc.   Since *eu* becomes *ou* in Italic (**70**), *ou* may represent either this or the original *ou*-grade.   Examples : O. *loufir* 'vel': L. *lubet, libet* ; — U. *iouies* 'iuvenibus': L. *iuvenis* ; — U. *rofu* 'rufos': U. *rufru* 'rubros', L. *ruber* ; — U. *purdouitu* 'porricito': U. *purditom* from *\*du̯īto-* (cf. L. *duam*).

The interchange of *u̯e* and *u* is seen in O. **sverrunef** 'spokesman'(?) from *\*su̯ereśōn* :  L. *susurrus* from *\*su-sur-eso-*, the root *su̯er-, sur-*, being the same as in Skt. *svárati* 'sounds' and Eng. *swear* and *answer*.

**97.** *er (el), or (ol),* etc.   Since I.E. *r̥* becomes *or* in Italic, *or* may represent either this reduced grade or the original *or*-grade.   Examples : U. *couertu* 'revertito': Fut. Perf. *couortus* etc. (early L. *vorsus, advortet,* etc.); — L. *terreō* : U. *tursitu* 'terreto'; — U. *persclo* 'sacrificium', *persnimu* 'precator': U. **pepurkurent** 'poposcerint', L. *poscō* from *\*porkskō* (Skt. *pr̥cchámi*) ; — L. *circulus* (*i* from *e*): U. **kurçlasiu** '*\*circulario, extremo*'(?).

The *ē*-grade is seen in the Nom. Sg. of nouns of relationship, as in O. **patir** 'pater' (**78**, 2), beside Dat. Sg. O. **paterei** from *\*patrei* (**81**), U. **patre**, with reduced grade as in L. *patrī*, Grk. πατρί ; — O. **niir** 'vir', beside Gen. Pl. *nerum* with the *e*-grade (cf. Skt. *nā́*, Vedic Gen. Pl. *narā́m*).

The *ō*-grade is seen in the *-tōr-* of agent-nouns, which belonged originally to the Nom. Sg., but was extended to all cases, as in Latin.   See **53, 54, 180, 1**.   The reduced grade *-tr-* is seen in some derivatives, as U. **kvestr-etie** beside **kvestur**, etc. (cf. L. *victr-īx*).   See **246, 1,** *a*.

The long reduced grade *r̥̄* becomes *ar* or *rā* in Italic.   Probable examples are : O. **kú]mparakineís** 'consilii', *comparascuster* 'consulta erit', with *park* or *prāk* (**81,** *a*) : L. *poscō* (see above); — U. **mantrahklu** from *\*man-trāg-klo-* : L. *mantēle* from *\*man-tergsli-* (*tergeō*).

──────────

[1] See Solmsen, Stud z. lat. Sprachgeschichte, 112.  Neither the explanation of v. Planta, I, 173, nor that of Thurneysen, I.F. Anz. 4, 38 (see footnote, p. 52) is at all probable.

U. *comatir*, **kumates** 'commolitis', with loss of *l* as in **mutu** 'multa', is an example of *al* for *l̥* (cf. Skt. *mūrṇá-*), while the *ol*-grade[1] (cf. Goth. *malan*, Lith. *malù*) is seen in Pres. Imperat. *comoltu*, **kumultu** (**kumaltu** is probably due to confusion with the preceding). For **maletu** see following.

The antevocalic form of the reduced grade, that is *r̥r*, becomes *ar* in Italic, as in L. *carō*, U. **karu**, from the root *ker-* (Grk. κείρω etc.); — O. **karanter** 'vescuntur', *caria* 'panis' (gloss) (cf. Grk. κορέννυμι, Lith. *szeriù* 'feed'). Of similar origin is *al* in U. **maletu** 'molitum' and in O. *ualaemom* 'optimum': L. *volō*.

    *a.* The relation of O. **aflukad** 'deferat'(?) to Fut. Perf. **aflakus** is wholly uncertain, as is the etymology, though connection with L. *flectō* seems probable. They might contain the root in the forms *flok* and *flāk* from *fl̥k* (cf. L. *falx*), but such an interchange between Present and Perfect stems is without parallel in Italic. A more natural interchange would be that of *flak* and *flāk*, but the assumption of weakening of *a* to *u* in **aflukad** is somewhat bold, in spite of the uncertainty as to the precise conditions of this phenomenon (**86**).

**98.** *en, on, an.* Italic *en* may represent either original *en* or the reduced grade *n̥*; and *an* may represent either the long reduced grade *n̥̄*, or, according to a view which we regard as probable, the antevocalic reduced grade *n̥n* (L. *canis*, etc.; cf. *carō* with *ar* for *r̥r*, **97**). The negative prefix, which represents the reduced grade of the *ne* seen in O. *ne*, L. *ne-fas*, etc., appears in Latin as *in-*, from *en-*, *n̥*, but in Oscan-Umbrian always as *an-*; e.g. O. *ancensto* 'incensa', U. *anhostatu* 'non hastatos'. That this *an-* represents *n̥̄*, for which there is no other evidence,[2] is less likely than that it is a generalization of the antevocalic form (Grk. ἀν-, Skt. *an-*) as compared with the generalization in Latin of the anteconsonantal form (Grk. ἀ-, Skt. *a-*).

    *a.* In O. *tanginom* 'sententiam' beside L. *tongeō*, *tongitiō*, the *an* might represent *n̥̄* (cf. *n̥* and *on* in Goth. *þugkjan* beside *þagkjan*), but the assumption of a grade *n̥̄* in this root meets with difficulty. Perhaps it is a case of secondary gradation, with interchange of *a* and *o* (**99**, 3).

---

    [1] L. *molō* is commonly derived from *melō (O.Ir. *melim*), but U. *ol* cannot have this origin (**36**, 2).

    [2] On Grk. νηκέρδης see now Brugmann, Sitzungsberichte d. königl. sächs. Gesellschaft d. Wiss. 1901, p. 102.

*b.* O. **Anafriss**, if related to L. *imber* (*ṃ-bhri-*; cf. Skt. *abhrá-* 'cloud', Grk. *ἀφρός*) would seem to point to a by-form **ṃ̄-bhri-*, but this is regarded with rightful suspicion. The connection of the two words is entirely uncertain.

*c.* The relation of O.-U. *anter* to L. *inter* is almost certainly a different one. It is probable that **en-ter*, containing *en* 'in' (L. *in*, Grk. *ἐν*), was replaced by a similar formation from *an-* (L. *an-* in *an-hēlō*, Grk. *ἀνά*), which in Umbrian is used interchangeably with *en-* (*andendu, endendu*). Cf. O.Bulg. *ǫtrĭ* 'within' (as against *jętro* 'liver': Grk. *ἔντερον*), which is of similar origin.

**99.** Other variations are:

1. *ē, a* (I.E. *ə*).   U. *fetu* 'facito': O. **fakiiad**, U. **façia** (cf. L. *fēcī : faciō*) ; — O. **fíísnam**, U. **fesnaf-e**, from **fēs-nā-* (cf. L. *fēstus, fēriae*): L. *fānum* from **fas-no-*.  Cf. also the *ē*-Perfects to Presents with *a*, O. *hipid* 'habuerit', *sipus* 'sciens' (**90,** 1, *b*).

2. *ā, a* (I.E. *ə*).   O. **Staatiis**: **stahínt** (short *a* shown by **eestínt**), **statíf, statús**, probably also with short *a* (cf. L. *stāre, prae-stātus*, etc.: *statiō, praestitus*, etc.) ; — L. *fārī* : O. **fatíum**, L. *fateor* (denominative from a Partic. **fato-*, replaced in Latin by *fāto-*) ; — O. **faamat** 'habitat, tendit': L. *famulus, familia*, O. *famel, famelo*.

3. *a, o, ā*.   L. *acies, acuō*, etc. (Grk. *ἄκρος*): L. *ocris*, U. *ocar* (Grk. *ὄκρις*): L. *ācer* (so probably O. **akrid**, but possibly **āk-*) ; — O. **kahad**: L. *incohō* ; — L. *hasta* : U. *hostatu*, etc.

4. *e, a*.   Of this variation, which is seen in the relation of L. *pateō, pandō*, O. **patensíns**, to Grk. *πετάννυμι*, the following are uncertain examples: L. *tepor* : U. **tapistenu** 'caldariolam'(?); — U. **erietu** (or *ē*?): L. *ariēs*.

5. *i, ī*.   L. *vir* (Goth. *waír*, O.Ir. *fer*): U. **ueiro, uiro** (Skt. *vīrá-*, Lith. *výras*).

NOTE. The three occurrences of the spelling *ueiro* make it less likely that this is to be added to the rare cases of *ei* for short *i* (**29**). Cf. also Volsc. *couehriu* 'curia' from **co-uīrio-* (L. *cūria* from **co-uiriā-*).

6. *u, ū*.   U. *pure-to*, O. **purasiaí** : U. *pir* 'ignis' (**59**).

7. The relation of U. **veskla** 'vascula' to U. *uaso*, L. *vās*, is not clear.  A variation of *e* or *ē* with *ā* is not well established.

8. *o, ō*.   O. **úpsannam**, etc. (**49**): O. **uupsens**, etc. (**53**).  But see **225,** *a*.

### Consonantal i (i̯)

**100.** 1. Initial i̯ remains unchanged, as in Latin. Thus U. *iouies* 'iuvenibus': L. *iuvenis* (Skt. *yúvan-*).

For i̯ from di̯, see **134**.

2. Intervocalic i̯ was lost in the Italic period, and of the resulting vowel-combinations some are contracted, while others remain in hiatus. See **82, 83**. But between *i* and a following vowel there naturally intervenes a glide, or transition sound, i̯, which is shown in the spelling of the native alphabets, but not in the Latin; e.g. U. **triiu-per**, but *trio-per*: L. *tria.* See **31**, *a.*

The i̯ following an *i*-diphthong is also retained. See **61, 3**.

*a.* For U. *portaia*, **kuraia**, etc., see **232**; for U. **fuia, fuiest**, **215**, 3; for O. **staiet, 215**, 2.

3. Postconsonantal i̯, which in Latin becomes a vowel (e.g. *medius* for original dissyllabic \**medh-i̯o-*), retains its consonantal function. In the Latin alphabet it is impossible to know whether an *i* stands for consonantal or vocalic *i*, but in the native alphabets, where the latter regularly appears as ii, a single i is evidence of consonantal value, though there are some few cases in which it is used carelessly in place of ii. See **31**, *a.* .

But more direct evidence of the consonantal function is furnished in those cases in which a preceding consonant has been affected, as follows:

*a.* Gemination of consonants before i̯ is frequent in Oscan, e.g. **kúmbennieís** 'conventus', **Mamerttiais** 'Martiis', **tríbarakkiuf** 'aedificatio', etc. See **162**, 1.

*b.* In Umbrian, i̯ palatalizes a preceding *n* and *k*, and the *i* is then sometimes omitted in the writing. So **spina** beside **spinia**, *Rubine* beside **Rupinie**; **façu** beside **façiu**, etc. (**144**).

*c.* In the local dialect of Bantia, i̯ unites with a preceding *l, r, t, d, k,* to form *l(l̨), r(r̨),* **s, z, x**. Thus *allo* from \**ali̯ā*: L. *alia;* — *famelo* from \**fameli̯ā*: L. *familia;* — so perhaps *mallom, mallud, malud* from a stem \**maljo-* beside L. *malo-*; — *herest* 'volet' from \**heriest* : U. *heriest* ; — *petiro-pert* 'quater' from \**petirio-pert*, this from \**petriā-pert* (81, 192, 2); — *Bansae* from \**Bantjae*; — *zicolom* 'diem' from \**diēkolom* : L. *diēcula* ; — *meddixud* 'magistratu' from \**meddikjōd* (250, 2).

NOTE. In some cases the *j* itself is the result of a local change of vocalic *i*. So \**petriā-pert* must have had *i*, not *j*, and probably \**diēkolom* (184, *a*).

### Consonantal u (ṷ) [1]

**101.** Initial and intervocalic *ṷ* remain, as in Latin. Examples:

O. víú, U. **via, vea,** *uia* : L. *via* ; — O. Ϝερσορει '\*Versori', U. **ku-vertu,** *co-uertu* 'convertito': L. *vertō*.

O. **Iuveí,** U. **Iuve**: L. *Iovī* ; — O. **bivus**: L. *vīvus;* — O. **deivinais**: L. *dīvīnus* ; — U. **uvem,** *oui* : L. *ovis* ; — U. **avif,** *auif* : L. *avis.*

The glide *ṷ*, which was regularly sounded between *u* and a following vowel, shows itself in the spelling in the native alphabets, but not in the Latin; e.g. U. **tuves,** but *duir* : L. *duo.* See 31, *b.*

**102.** 1. Postconsonantal *ṷ* generally remains unchanged. Thus O. **svaí,** *suae* 'si' (L. *sī* is from a form without *ṷ*); — O. **dekkviarím** 'decurialem'; — U. *arvia* 'frumenta': L. *arvum.*

2. After labials *ṷ* is lost, as in Latin. Thus O. **fufans** 'erant': L. *-bant* from *-bhṷā-*; — O. *amprufid* 'improbe', **prúfatted** 'probavit': L. *probus* from \**pro-bhṷo-* ; — U. *subocau* 'invoco' from \**sub-uocāiō* ;[2] — O. **Piíhiúí** 'Pio', U. *pihatu* 'piato': L. *pius* from \**puṷṷo-* (cf. L. *pūrus*).

3. *dṷ*, in Latin *b* (and *v*), becomes *d*. Thus U. *di-fuè* 'bifidum': L. *bis* etc., from \**dṷi-*; — U. *dia* 'det' from \**dṷ-iiō* (cf. L. *duam*) ; — U. *pur-ditom* 'porrectum' from \**dṷ-īto-* beside

---

[1] In the citation of Oscan and Umbrian forms it is customary to use the v only for forms written in the native alphabets, in which there was a distinct character for it, and not for forms written in the Latin alphabet. But for Latin words we continue to use the *v*, in spite of the resulting inconsistency.

[2] L. *subveniō* etc., under the influence of the simplex (but *aperiō* from \**apṷeriō*, the simplex being lost). See **164,** *a.*

*pur-douitu* (**96**); — O. **akkatus** 'advocati' from *\*ad(o)kāto-* (**89**, 3), this from *\*ad-uokāto-*.[1]

4. An apparent loss of *u* after *r* is seen in U. *seritu* 'servato', *anseriato* 'observatum', and *caterahamo* '\*catervamini', as compared with L. *servō*, *caterva*. But the precise explanation is not clear. In *seritu* etc. it may be due to the position between *r* and *i̯*, i.e. *\*seri̯ō* from *\*serui̯ō*.

5. For *su̯e*, see **37**, *a*.

r

**103.** 1. *r* usually remains unchanged, as in Latin. Examples: O. **Regaturei** 'Rectori', U. **rehte** 'recte': L. *regō* ; — O. **teremniss** 'terminibus', U. *termnom-e* : L. *termen* ; — U. **fertu**, *ferar*, etc.: L. *ferō*.

2. It is also retained in some combinations in which it is lost in Latin, as *rsk*, *rsn*. But in Umbrian, in these combinations, and in general before *s*, the *r* was faintly sounded and often omitted in the writing. See under *rs*, **115, 116**.

a. In O. **Falenias**, beside **Faler.** on a companion inscription, the omission of *r* is due to carelessness in spelling, though the sound of *r* is naturally somewhat less distinct before consonants than elsewhere.

3. The combination *rl* appears unassimilated in O. **Aderl.** 'Atella' of an old coin, but has become *ll*, as in Latin, in **Abella-** (**Abellanús**), probably from *\*Aberlā-*, *\*Apro-lā-* (**91**, 2).

4. Final *r* is frequently omitted in Umbrian, mostly in the forms of the Passive. So **herte**, *herti*, *hertei*, beside **herter** ; — **emantu** beside **emantur**; — *pihafi*, *pihafei* : O. **sakrafir** ; — **tuta-pe** beside usual **tuta-per** 'pro populo'.

l

**104.** Initial *l* is seen in O. *ligud* 'lege'; — **likitud**, *licitud* 'liceto'; — *loufir* 'vel': L. *libet* ; — **Lúvfreis** 'Liberi'; — **lúvkei** 'in luco', etc.

In Umbrian there is no example of an initial *l* on the Iguvinian Tables, and a change of initial *l* to *u̯*, though disputed, is

---

[1] L. *advocō*, etc., under the influence of the simplex. See **164**, *a*.

probably to be recógnized in **vutu** 'lavato': L. *lavō*;—**vapeř-**, *uapers-* 'sella': L. *lapis* (cf. *subsellis marmoreis* of the Acta Arvalium); — **Vuvçis** 'Lucius' (**72**, *a*).   Other examples are very doubtful.

NOTE. A change of *l* to *u* before consonants is seen in many languages, e.g. French *autre* from L. *alter* ; Dutch *koud* : Eng. *cold*.  In such cases, and likewise in Umbrian, the change must have been through the medium of a strongly guttural *l*.

**105.** 1. Medial *l* is generally preserved in both Oscan and Umbrian.   Examples: O. **Fluusaí** 'Florae'; — O. *allo* 'alia'; — O. **Alafaternum**, U. **alfu** 'alba': L. *albus* ; — U. *plener* 'plenis'; — U. *saluom* 'salvum'.

*a.* O. **Fiuusasiaís** 'Floralibus' beside **Fiuusaí**, if not simply due to the care-lessness of the engraver, would point to the beginning of a change similar to what has taken place in Italian *flore, piano*, etc.   But all other evidence is against this.

2. In the combination *lt* the *l* is lost in Umbrian.   So **muta**, *motar*, etc.: O. *moltam*, L. *multa* ; — **kumates**, *comatir* 'commoli-tis'.   But in the Imperatives **kumultu**, *comoltu* 'commolito', **veltu** 'deligito', etc., in which the *l* and *t* were formerly separated by a vowel, the *l* is always written.

*a.* The Oscan *atrud* beside *altrei* on the Tabula Bantina is an indication that in the dialect of Bantia the *l* was not fully sounded, though in the numerous occurrences of *molta* it is never omitted.

3. U. *Uoisiener* 'Volsieni', on an inscription of Assisi, shows a local pala-talization of *l* before *s*, or else is due to Etruscan influence.

**106.** In a number of Umbrian words an original *l* is repre-sented by ř, *rs*, which commonly stands for an intervocalic *d* (**131**). This points to a change of *l* to *d*, with which we may compare the opposite change of *d* to *l* in L. *lingua, lacrima*, etc.   The most certain examples are **kařetu**, *carsitu* 'calato', **uřetu** 'adoleto', **fameřias** 'familiae'.

*a.* Whether *arsir* (VI a 6, 7) is 'alius' or Dat.-Abl. Pl. 'caerimoniis' belonging to Voc. Sg. *arsie* 'sancte', is uncertain.  That **Pupřike, Pupřiçe**, epi-thet of **Puemune**, is 'Publico' is extremely probable, in view of L. *Publica Fides, Publica Fortuna*, etc.   The old explanation of **tribřiçu** 'ternio' as = L. *\*tripliciō* cannot be considered impossible, but Brugmann's derivation from *\*tri-p(e)d-ikiōn-* 'band of three' (L. *pedica*) offers a plausible substitute for this.

No satisfactory statement can be made as to the conditions under which the change took place.

### n and m

**107.** 1. Initial and intervocalic *n* and *m* remain unchanged, as in Latin. Examples: O. **ni, nep, neip,** U. **neip**: L. *nē, nec,* etc.; — U. *nome*: L. *nōmen*; — O. **dunum,** U. **dunu**: L. *dōnum*; — O. **Maatreís,** U. **Matrer**: L. *māter*; — O. *moltam,* U. *motar*: L. *multa*; — O. *pertemest,* U. **emantur**: L. *emō.*

2. Similarly postconsonantal *n* and *m*; e.g. O. *egmo* 'res'; — O. **Patanaí** 'Pandae' from \**Pat-nā-* (**81**); — O. *comono* 'comitia', U. **kumne,** from \**komno-* (**15, 4, 81**).

*a.* A change of *mn* to *m* is perhaps to be recognized in the Passive Imperative ending, O. -*mur,* U. -*mu,* though this is by no means certain. See **237.** This would involve the supposition that in all the numerous examples of *mn* the combination is of secondary origin, as indeed it probably is in many cases, e.g. U. *nomner* 'nominis' etc. (**88, 4**).[1]

3. Assimilation of *nl* to *ll,* as in Latin, is seen in O. **Vesulliaís** from \**Vesōn-liā-*: U. **Vesune**; — U. *Padellar* from \**Paden-lā* (**91, 2,** *a*); also in U. **apelust** etc. with *l* from *nl,* earlier *ndl* (**135**).

### *Omission of nasals before consonants*

**108.** 1. In Umbrian, nasals were not fully sounded before mutes and spirants, as is evident from their frequent omission in the writing. The circumstance that in the Latin alphabet this omission is to be noted only before *s* (once before *f*) is perhaps due to the influence of Latin orthography, the omission of *n* on Latin inscriptions being far more common before *s* than elsewhere. Examples: **ustetu** beside **ustentu,** *ostendu* 'ostendito'; — **iveka** beside *iuenga* 'iuvencas'; — **kupifiatu** beside **kumpifiatu,** *combifiatu* 'nuntiato'; — **azeriatu,** *aseriatu* beside **anzeriatu,** *anseriato* 'observatum'; — *dirsas* beside *dirsans* 'dent'; — **sis** beside *sins* 'sint'; — **Saçe** beside *Sansie* ; — **aferum,** *afero,* beside *anferener* 'circumferendi'.

2. In Oscan, *n* is regularly omitted in the case of final *ent.* Thus **set** 'sunt', **fiiet** 'fiunt', **staíet** 'stant', *censazet* 'censebunt', etc.:

---

[1] Admitting the change, we should hold to the derivation of O. *comono* etc. and **amnúd** 'circuitu' from \**kom-no-,* \**am-no-* (v. Planta prefers \**kom-beno-,* \**am-beno-*), and assume that the words came into existence at a later period.

U. *sent, benurent,* etc.   Note that in this case the *n* is always written in Umbrian, while, vice versa, in the case of final *-ns,* where it is frequently omitted in Umbrian (above), it is always written in Oscan (*deicans,* uupsens, etc.).

The same omission is frequent, though not universal, in the case of medial *ent,* e.g. aragetud 'argento', Aret[ikai] beside Arentikai, deketasiúí (degetasis etc.) '*decentario'.

a. Isolated examples of omission elsewhere are *mistreis* beside *minstreis* 'minoris' and Λαπονις 'Lamponius'(?).

In ekak 'hanc' and íak 'eam' beside *ionc* 'eum', eisunk 'eorum', etc., the omission is probably due to the influence of Accusatives with final *m* omitted. All the certain occurrences of ekak are on Pompeian inscriptions, which have vía 'viam' etc. (109, 2).

3. A special case in which *n* is lost in both Oscan and Umbrian is in the combination *nkt.* See 73.

### *Final n and m*

**109.** 1. In Umbrian, final *n* and *m* were so faintly sounded that they are far oftener omitted than written.   Thus Acc. Sg. puplu, *poplo,* beside puplum, *poplom;* — *nome*: L. *nōmen;* — *-e* beside *-en* 'in'.   For final *n* we also find *m* written.   This is not merely the result of confusion caused by the reduction of both nasals, since we never find *n* for *m,* but is due to the influence of a preceding *m,* as in numem beside *nome,* and in Akeŕuniam-em etc. beside esunum-en, esunum-e, etc.   From its use with the Acc. Sg. the *-em* came to be used elsewhere too, as in Loc. Sg. *Acersoniem* etc.

2. In Oscan, final *n* is never omitted.   Final *m* is nearly always written except on inscriptions of Pompeii, where it is oftener omitted than written, e.g. vía 'viam', tiurrí 'turrim'.   But it is possible that even where *m* was regularly written it was reduced in pronunciation.   See 84, *a.*

### *ns*

**110.** The history of the combination *ns* is somewhat complicated.   It is necessary to separate the cases of original *ns* from those in which it is of later origin, and again to distinguish these latter according to the period at which the *ns* arose.

1. Original medial *ns* becomes *nts*, as appears from the spelling **nz** in the native alphabets, though this is not constant. In the Latin alphabet *ns* is written. Cf. *z* : *s* for final *-ts* in U. taçez : *tases* 'tacitus', etc. (**137**, 2). Thus O. keenzstur (for zs see **162**, 2), *censtur* 'censor' from *\*kens-tōr* ; — U. anzeriatu, *anseriato* 'observatum' from *\*an-seriā-*; — U. menzne 'mense' (from stem *\*mens-en-* ; cf. Sab. *mesene*), antermenzaru 'intermenstrium' ; — U. uze, *onse* 'in humero' from *\*om(e)so-*.

2. Original final *ns* becomes *-ss* in Oscan, but *-f* in Umbrian. Thus Acc. Pl. O. viass, *eituas*, feíhúss, U. vitlaf, vitluf, etc.

*a.* Umbrian final *f* was so weakly sounded as to be frequently omitted in the writing, e.g. *uitla, uitlu*. In the oldest tables the omission is comparatively infrequent, while in those written in the Latin alphabet the *f* is omitted nearly ten times as often as it is written, except in monosyllables, where it is written nearly four times as often as omitted.

3. Secondary medial *ns* from *nss*, originating in *nt-t* or *nd-t* (**138**), becomes *f* in Umbrian, there being no examples in Oscan. Thus spefa 'sparsam' from *\*spensso-, \*spend-to-*[1] (cf. Grk. σπένδω): L. *spōnsus* from *\*sponsso-, \*spond-to-*[1]; — similarly mefa 'mensam' from *\*menssā-*: L. *mēnsa, mēnsus* ; — subra spafu 'superiectum' from *\*spansso-*.

*a.* *\*mensso-* is not from *\*mend-to-* (cf. L. *mētior*, Skt. *mā-*, etc.), but is formed after the analogy of Participles of related meaning such as *\*pensso-* (L. *pēnsus*), *\*tensso-* (L. *tēnsus*), from roots in *-nd*. *\*spansso-* may be of similar origin, but it is possible that beside the *\*spā-* of U. *spahatu, spahamu* (cf. Grk. σπάω) there was another root-form *\*spand-* and that L. *pandó* represents a contamination of this with the root seen in L. *pateō*. In this case U. spafu could be compared directly with L. *pānsus*.

4. Secondary final *ns* from *-nss*, earlier *-nts*, becomes *f* in Umbrian, there being no examples in Oscan. See **243**. Thus zeřef, *serse* 'sedens': L. *sedēns* from *\*sedent-s* ; — restef, *reste* 'instaurans'; — *traf*, tra 'trans'. For omission of *f*, see above, 2, *a*.

5. Secondary final *ns* in the Nom. Sg. of *n*-stems (**181**) appears as *f*. Thus O. úíttluf, tríbarakkiuf, statíf, and probably

---

[1] See p. 86, footnote.

O. essuf, *esuf* 'ipse', U. esuf (197, 5). On the strength of esuf we assume that Umbrian had the same formation and that in tribřiçu and karu the f is omitted, as often (above, 2, *a*).

6. Secondary final *ns* resulting from syncope of vowels (90) remains unchanged. Thus O. *Bantins* 'Bantinus', U. Ikuvins 'Iguvinus', O. humuns 'homines' from *hōmōnes*, etc. See 90, 1.

7. Final *ns* appears also in the secondary ending of the Third Plural, as in O. *deicans*, U. *dirsans*, etc. On its origin see 128, 1.

In tabular form the representation is as follows:

|  |  | O. | U. |
|---|---|---|---|
| I. | 1. Orig. *-ns-* | *-nts-* | *-nts-* |
|  | 2. Orig. *-ns* | *-ss* | *-f* |
| II. | 3. *-ns-* from *-nss-* (*-ntt-*) | — | *-f-* |
|  | 4. *-ns* from *-nss* (*-nts*) | — | *-f* |
|  | 5. *-ns* in Nom. Sg. of *n*-stems | *-f* | *-f* |
| III. | 6. *-ns* by Syncope | *-ns* | *-ns* |

NOTE. Although there are no Oscan examples for 3 and 4, the probability is that Oscan agreed with Umbrian and that 3, 4, and 5 belong together. This change of secondary *ns* must have antedated the appearance of what might be called the tertiary *ns* of 6, which doubtless belongs to the close of the Oscan-Umbrian period. Again, the change of original *ns* must have antedated the appearance of the secondary *ns*, else they would have had the same development. Here arises a complication in the case of original final *ns*. · The divergence between Oscan and Umbrian shows that the development could not have been completed in the Oscan-Umbrian period. The only solution is to assume that final *ns*, either in Italic or in the earliest Oscan-Umbrian period, was so changed as to remain distinct from both secondary and tertiary *ns* throughout the Oscan-Umbrian period, and also in Oscan, though in Umbrian finally yielding the same result as secondary *ns*.

**s**

111. Initial *s* and *s* in connection with a surd mute remain, as in Latin. Examples: O. súm, set, U. *sent*, *sins* : L. *sum*, *sunt*, etc.; — O. sakrim, U. sakre : L. *sacer* ; — O. staít, U. *stahu* : L. *stō* ; — O. est, U. est, *est* ; L. *est* ; — O. púst, U. *post* : L. *post*.

### *Intervocalic s. Rhotacism*

**112.** Rhotacism of intervocalic *s* occurs in Umbrian as in Latin, but not in Oscan. In the latter the *s* has become *z*, written *z* in the Latin alphabet, but *s* in the native alphabet, in which *z* had the value of *ts*. This change of *s* to its corresponding sonant *z* is a necessary stage in the development of rhotacism, and was probably reached in the Italic period, Oscan then remaining on this stage. Examples: Gen. Pl. of *ā*-stems, O. -asúm, -*azum*, U. -aru, -*arum* : L. -*ārum* (Skt. -*āsām*, Hom. -*άων* from *-*ά̆σων*; — O. *ezum*, U. eru, *erom* 'esse': L. *erō*, etc.; — O. eíseís, *eizeis*, U. erer 'eius' from *eiso-*; — O. kasit 'decet': L. *caret* ; — forms of Imperf. Subj., Fut. Indic., and Fut. Perf. Indic., in which *s* is a part of the tense-sign (see under Inflection), e.g. O. fusíd 'esset': L. *foret* ; — O. *censazet* 'censebunt', U. furent 'erunt'; — O. tríbarakattuset 'aedificaverint', U. *benurent* 'venerint'. Cf. also Pael. *coisatens* 'curaverunt' (U. kuraia 'curet'), *upsaseter* 'operaretur, fieret'.

*a.* In most cases where *s* is found between vowels in Umbrian, this *s* is obviously not original but comes from a group of consonants, such as *ss*, *tt*, *ts*, *ks*, *ps*. But there are some forms the explanation of which is not so apparent. Nothing satisfactory can be said of asa-, *asa*-: O. aasaí, L. *āra*. For *esono*- 'sacer', related to O. aisusis 'sacrificiis' etc. (15, 3), it is possible to assume an extension of an *s*-stem, i.e. *ais(e)s-ōno-*, while erus 'magmentum'(?) and ereçlu 'sacrarium', if cognate, show the regular change of simple *s*. In plenasier, urnasier, etc., as compared with Latin words in -*ārius*, the *s* is probably due to the fact that the following *i* was consonantal, that is they contain the suffix -*asjo-*, while the by-form -*asio-* is perhaps to be recognized in ezariaf 'escas'(?), from *ed(e)s-āsio-*(?).

### *Final s*

**113.** Final *s* remains in Oscan, and in Umbrian on the older Tables I–IV, but on Tables V–VII it appears as *r*. Thus Nom. Pl. of *o*-stems (O. -ús, -*us*), U. prinuvatus, *prinuatur*, Atiieřiur (V), etc. ; — Dat.-Abl. Pl. of *o*-stems (O. -úís, -*ois*), U. veres, uerir, tripler (V), etc. ; — 2d Sg. U. *sir* 'sis'. These *r*-forms doubtless represent sentence-doublets, arising before words beginning with a vowel, but finally coming into general use without regard to the following word.

a. Before enclitics an *s* is treated in the same way as in the interior of a word. So U. funtler-e, *fondlir-e* 'in fontulis', but esunes-ku 'apud sacra', ueris-co 'apud portam'. But pis-i kept its *s* under the influence of pis (svepis 'si quis'), and retained it even after the latter had become *pir* (*pisi*, but *sopir*). Similarly *pis-est*.

b. The final *s* of Tables I–IV is sometimes omitted, e.g. Ikuvinu beside Ikuvinus, prinuvatu beside prinuvatus, snate beside snates, antakre beside antakres, etc. The later *r* is also occasionally omitted, as in *sei, si*, beside *sir* 'sis', *heri* 'vel' beside heris, but scarcely ever in noun-forms.

c. In Oscan there are two examples of *h* for final *s*, where the next word begins with *s*, namely upsatuh sent 'operati sunt', púiieh súm 'cuius sum'. The occasional omission of *s* in the Nom. Sg. of proper names in -is, -iis, etc., e.g. Steni, Paapi, Paapii, Paapií, is merely graphic, perhaps due to the influence of Latin orthography (*Claudi = Claudius*, etc.).

### *sn, sm, sl, zd*

**114.** The combinations *sn, sm, sl, zd*, which in Latin lose the sibilant (if medial, with lengthening of the preceding vowel), remain unchanged.

sn.   U. snata 'umecta': L. *nāre* ; — O. fíisnú 'fanum', U. fesnaf-e (also Pael. *fesn.*): L. *fānum* from \**fas-no-* (99, 1); — U. ahesnes 'ahenis': L. *ahēnus* from \**a(i)es-no-* (aes, Skt. *áyas*, etc.); — O. kersnu 'cena', U. *śesna* : L. *cēna* ; — O. *casnar* 'senex' (Festus, Varro; also Pael.): L. *cānus, cascus.*

sm.   U. pusme 'cui', *esmei* 'huic' (Skt. *ásmāi* etc.); so also O. *posmom* 'postremum' with *sm* from *stm* (139, 2). Cf. also Pael. *prismu* 'prima'.

sl.   O. slaagid 'fine' (derivation uncertain); — O. Slabiis 'Labius'; — U. *dis-leralinsust* 'inritum fecerit' (cf. L. *dīligō* from \**dis-ligō*, etc.); — so also O. peessl[úm with *sl* from *stl* (139, 2).

zd.   U. sistu 'sidito', *ander-sistu*, is best explained as from \**sizd(e)tōd*: L. *sīdō* from \**si-zdō* (cf. *nīdus* from \**nizdos*, Eng. *nest*).

*a.* U. *ninctu* 'ninguito', the root of which appears in other languages with initial *s* (Eng. *snow*, Lith. *snēgas*, etc.), may represent a by-form without *s*, like Grk. τέγος beside στέγος, etc.

*b.* O. *maimas* 'maximae' is probably from *maisemo-* (147, 3, *a*, 189, 3), through the stages *maizemo-* (112), *maizmo-*, with loss of *z*, in contrast to the preservation of *s*.

*c.* U. *sumtu* 'sumito', which cannot be explained in the same way as L. *sūmō* from *susmō, *sups-(e)mō*, is probably from *summō, *sup-(e)mō* (125, 1).

*d.* That O. *imad-en* 'ab imo' comes from *ins-mo-*, often assumed as the derivation of L. *īmus*, is unlikely.

### *Intervocalic rs*

**115.** 1. Original intervocalic *rs*, which becomes *rr* in Latin, remains unassimilated in Umbrian, while in Oscan it appears as *r* with lengthening of the preceding vowel. In Umbrian *rs* the *r* was weakly sounded and often omitted in the spelling. Examples: U. *tursitu*, *tusetu* 'terreto': L. *terreō* from *terseō*; — U. *farsio, fasio,* fasiu 'farrea': L. *farreus* from *fars-eo-* (see 117), O. *terúm,* teer[úm 'territorium': L. *terra* from *tersā*.

*a.* U. Gen. Sg. *farer* instead of *farser* (L. *farris*) is due to the influence of the Nom.-Acc. *far* (117).

2. Intervocalic *rs* arising from syncope, in Latin not distinguished from the preceding, appears in Umbrian as *rf*, in Oscan as *rr*. Examples: U. **Cerfe,** *Serfe*: L. *Cerus* (i.e. *Cerrus*), from *Ker(e)so-*; — O. **Kerrí** 'Cereri' from *Ker(e)s-ē-*; — U. *parfa* 'parram' from *paresa-*; — O. h]erríns 'caperent' from *her(i)sênt* (216); — O. sverruneí from *sueres-ōn-*: L. *susurrus* (96).

NOTE. For the development of original *rs* in Oscan, as given above, the following stages must be assumed: *rs — rz — rr — r* with compensative lengthening. The later *rs* of 2 passed through the first two stages, but stopped at *rr* (the still later *rs* of 3 remained unchanged, though in Umbrian the *rs* of 2 and 3 have the same history). But it should be pointed out that the assumption of a double development in Oscan, according as the *rs* was original or arose through syncope, rests wholly on the form teer[úm, and that for this a different explanation is at least possible, though somewhat complicated (see 76, 4). Barring this word, we should assume that Oscan, like Latin, had *rr* for the *rs* of 1 as well as for that of 2, and at least one of the examples under 2, namely sverruneí, would be more naturally put under 1. Further material, such as a form corresponding to U. *tursitu*, is necessary to settle the matter conclusively. (O. teras 'terrae'(?), from the Curse of Vibia, might stand for *terrās as well as for *tĕrās.)

3. Intervocalic *rs* from *rss*, earlier *rts* or *rtt* (**137**, 1, **138**), remains in Oscan as in Latin, but appears as *rf* in Umbrian. Thus O. Fερσορει '*Versori', U. *trahuorfi* 'transverse': L. *versus*.

### *rs before consonants*

**116.** *rs* before consonants, which in Latin loses *r*, or in some combinations *s*, is retained, though in Umbrian the *r*, as in the case of intervocalic *rs*, was weakly sounded and often omitted in the spelling.

1. *rsk.* U. **persklu**, *persclu, pesclu* 'precatione': L. *poscō* from *\*porscō* ; — here also O. *comparascuster* 'consulta erit' if from *parsc-*, not *prasc-* (see **81**, *a*); — U. **Turskum**, *Tuscom* 'Tuscum' (cf. Grk. Τυρσηνοί, Τυρρηνοί).

2. *rsn.* O. **kersnu** 'cena', **kerssnais, kerssnasias**, etc., U. **ŝesna**, **çersnatur** : L. *cēna* from *\*kesnā, \*kersnā* (earlier *\*kers-snā-, \*kert-snā*, from root *qert-* 'cut', Skt. *kṛt-*, etc.; for meaning, cf. Grk. δαίς beside δαίομαι) ; — U. **persnihmu, pesnimu**, *persnihimu, pesnimu* 'precator', denominative from *\*persk-ni-* (**146**).

NOTE. For original *rsn*, which gives L. *rn* (*cernuus*), there is no example.

3. *rst.* U. **perstu, pestu** 'ponito' (?) from *\*persktōd* (**146**). But O. **pestlúm, peessl[úm**, indicates that in Oscan the *r* was lost in the combination *rst*, or at least in *rstl* (**76**, 2).

### *Final rs*

**117.** Final *rs* becomes -*r*, as in Latin. Thus O. **far**, U. *far* : L. *far* from *\*fars* (cf. Gen. Sg. *farris* from *\*farsis*, Goth. *barizeins* 'of barley') ; — likewise in the case of *rs* arising from syncope, U. *ager* : L. *ager* from *\*agers, \*agros* (**91**, 2) ; — Nom. Pl. O. *censtur* 'censores' from *\*censtōr(e)s*, U. **frater**, *frateer* 'fratres' from *\*frāter(e)s* (**90**, 1). The spelling *frateer* points to compensative lengthening. See **76**, 3.

*a.* In O. **usurs**, Acc. Pl., -*rs* is from -*r(e)ss*.

*b.* Before an enclitic beginning with a vowel U. *rs* is preserved, like medial *rs*. Cf. **113**, *a*. Thus U. *pars-est* 'par erit'.

*sr*

**118.** A change of *sr* to *fr*, whence in Latin initial *fr*,
medial *br* (*fūnebris* from *\*fūnes-ris*), belongs doubtless to the
Italic period, and in Oscan-Umbrian we should expect *fr* in all
positions (as, from *bh*, O.-U. *f* = L. *f*, *b*). A probable example
is O. tefúrúm 'burnt-offering', U. *tefru-to* 'ex rogo', tefra 'carnes
cremandas', from *\*tesro-*, *\*teps-ro* : L. *tepor*, Skt. *tápas*, etc.

*ls*

**119.** 1. Of original intervocalic *ls*, which becomes *ll* in
Latin, and which we should expect to find unchanged in
Umbrian (like *rs*), there is no certain example. For the *ls* is
probably secondary in U. *pelsatu* etc. (see 262, 1, *a*).

2. Final *ls* (from *-l(i)s*, *-l(o)s*) becomes *-l*. Thus O. aidil
'aedilis', O. *famel* 'famulus', U. katel 'catulus', O. Mutíl 'Mutilus',
Paakul 'Paculus', etc. O. Upfals and Upils have *-ls* from *-lls* (cf.
Gen. Sg. Upfalleis).

**p**

**120.** *p* remains, as in Latin. Examples: O. pateref, U. patre
'patri'; — O. prai, U. pre 'prae'; — O. supruis 'superis', U. super
'super'; — U. *dupla* 'duplas'. For *br* from *pr*, see 157, 1.

*pt*

**121.** *pt* becomes *ft*, just as *kt* becomes *ht* (142), and this
remains in Oscan. In Umbrian this *ft*, together with the *ft* in
which *f* comes from *dh* (136, *a*), becomes *ht*, and this has the
same further history as the *ht* from *kt* — that is, the *h* was almost
or wholly lost in pronunciation (75, 142). Examples: O. *scriftas*
'scriptae', U. *screhto*, *screihtor*: L. *scriptus* ; — O. ufteis 'voluntatis', uhftis, from *\*opti-*: L. *optiō* ; — so probably, with the same
change of secondary *pt*, U. hahtu, hatu, *hatu* 'capito' (also subahtu
'deponito', *subator* 'omissi') from *\*haftōd*, *\*haptōd*, *\*hapitōd* (cf.
O. *hipid* ; see 218).

NOTE. The peculiar spelling of O. uhftis perhaps indicates the beginning
of a development like that in Umbrian.

*ps*

**122.** 1. Before consonants *ps* becomes *s*, as in Latin. Thus U. *ostendu* 'ostendito': L. *ostendō* from *\*ops-tendō*.

2. Original intervocalic *ps* is assimilated to *ss*. Thus O. *osii[ns* 'adsint': L. *ob-sint*; — so perhaps O. **essuf**, *esuf*, U. **esuf** 'ipse', as if L. *\*ipsō* (197, 5).

3. Secondary intervocalic *ps* remains unchanged in Oscan, but is assimilated in Umbrian. Thus O. **upsed** 'fecit', **úpsannam**, etc., but U. *osatu, oseto*, from *\*opesā-*: L. *operor*.

**b**

**123.** *b* remains, as in Latin. So O. **trííbúm** 'domum', **tríbarak-kiuf** 'aedificatio', U. *trebeit* 'versatur' (15, 14); — U. **kebu**: L. *cibus*.

**bh**[1]

**124.** *bh*, which appears in Latin initially as *f*, medially as *b*, is always *f*. Examples : O. **fust**, U. **fust** 'erit', O. **fusíd** 'esset', U. *futu* 'esto', etc.: L. *fuī, forem*, Grk. ἔφῡ, Skt. *bhū-*; — U. *fertu, ferest, ferar*, etc.: L. *ferō*, Grk. φέρω, Skt. *bhar-*; — O. **fratrúm**, U. **fratrum** 'fratrum': L. *frāter*, Skt. *bhrā́tar-*; — U. **alfu** 'alba', O. **Alafaternum**: L. *albus*, Grk. ἀλφός; — O. *loufir* 'vel': L. *libet*, Skt. *lubh-*; — O. **tfei**, U. **tefe**: L. *tibi*, Skt. *túbhyam*; — Dat.-Abl. Pl. ending *-fs* seen in O. **luisarifs** 'lusoriis' (?): L. *-bus* (cf. also Skt. *-bhyas*).

*a.* This final *-fs*, except in the example cited, which is from one of the earliest Oscan inscriptions, is assimilated to *-ss, -s*; e.g. O. **teremniss** 'terminibus', *ligis* 'legibus', U. **avis** 'avibus'.

*b.* For Umbrian *mb* from *mf*, see 161.

**Labials and Nasals**

**125.** 1. As in Latin, *p* or *b* followed by a nasal becomes *m*. So U. *somo* 'summum' from *\*sup-mo-*; — U. *pelmner* 'pulmenti': L. *pulmentum* from *\*pulpmentum* (*pulpa*); — U. *tremnu* 'tabernaculo' from *\*treb-no-* (cf. L. *somnus* from *\*sop-no-*, *\*suep-no-*).

*a.* But *fn* remains. Thus O. **Safinim** from *\*Safniom* (81): L. *Samnium*.

---

[1] For the development of sonant aspirates in general, see 160-161.

2. *mb* becomes *mm* (cf. *nn* from *nd* ; **185**). Thus U. **umen** 'unguen' from *\*omben*, with *b* from *g*$^{u}$ (**151**). Cf. L. *commurat* = *comburat* (Orelli-Henzen 6404), *commuratur* = *comburatur* (CIL. VI 19267).

a. U. **menes** 'venies' might have arisen in a compound *\*kommenes* from *\*kom-benes* (O. **kúmbened** with recomposition), but as all other forms show *b* (*benust, benurent*) the m may be merely a graver's error.

t

**126.** In general, *t* remains unchanged, as in Latin. Thus O. **trís**, U. **trif** : L. *três* ; — O. **estud** 'esto', U. **etu** 'ito'; — O. *scriftas* 'scriptae', U. *screihtor* 'scripti', etc.

a. At Bantia *t*ĭ becomes *s*, as in *Bansae* 'Bantiae'. See **100, 3, c.**

b. For change of *nt* to *nd* and *tr* to *dr* in Umbrian, see **156, 157, 2.**

*Final t*

**127.** 1. Original final *t*, as in the secondary ending of the Third Singular, became *d* in the Italic period (early L. *feced*, *sied*, etc.); and this *d*, like original *d*, remains in Oscan but is regularly dropped in Umbrian. Thus O. **deded**, U. **dede** 'dedit' ; — O. **fakiiad**, U. **façia** 'faciat', etc. See also **133.**

a. In O. *tadait* 'censeat' the *t* is due to an error, as in *pocapit* beside p]*ocapid*, **púkkapíd** (**201, 4**).

2. But final *t* from earlier -*ti* (**92**), as in the corresponding primary ending, remains *t* in both Oscan and Umbrian, though in Umbrian it was not fully sounded, and, in a few instances, is omitted in the writing. Thus O. **faamat** 'tendit', U. **tiçit** 'decet', U. *trebeit* 'versatur', U. **habe**, *habe* 'habet', **heri** 'vult'.

3. The *t* of final -*st* and -*rt* is also frequently omitted in Umbrian. Thus *fus, heries*, etc. for usual *fust, heriest*; — *trioper* 'ter' (cf. also L. *sem-per*): O. *petiro-pert* 'quater'; — U. *pis-her* 'quilibet' from *\*-hert*, this probably from *\*-herit* (**216**).

*Final nt*

**128.** 1. The history of original final *nt* is a matter of dispute. The secondary ending of the Third Plural in

Oscan-Umbrian is *-ns*, e.g. O. *deicans* ' dicant', U. *dirsans, dirsas* 'dent' (for omission of *n* see **108**, 1), O. **fufens** 'fuerunt', U. **eitipes** 'decreverunt', etc. (also Pael. *coisatens* 'curaverunt'). It has been held that this comes by regular phonetic change from the original ending *-nt*, and that the same change is seen in Latin in the numeral adverbs like *quōtiēns* etc. coming from *-ient, -int* (Skt. *kíyat*, etc.). But the Latin forms admit of another explanation, and for Oscan-Umbrian the fact that the *-ns* is retained and does not appear as O. *-ss*, or even as *-f*, indicates that it is of comparatively late origin and could not have come from *-nt* in the Italic period. See **110** with note.

A more probable view is the following. As original *-t* changed to *-d* (**127**, 1), so original *-nt* to *-nd*, and this became *-n*. In Latin this was mostly replaced by the primary ending, *-nt*, as was *-d* in the Third Singular by *-t*; but a trace of it remains in the old forms like *danunt, explēnunt*, etc., in which *-unt* is added after the analogy of *legunt* etc. In the Oscan-Umbrian period the forms in *-n* were remodeled in another way, namely by the addition of *s*, under the influence of the plural endings of nouns, or perhaps more specifically of the Nom. Pl. of *n*-stems like O. **humuns** 'homines' etc.[1]

2. Final *nt* from earlier *-nti* (**92**), as in the corresponding primary ending, remains unchanged. Thus O. **stahínt** 'stant', O. **set** (for omission of *n* see **108**, 2), U. **sent** 'sunt', U. **furent** 'erunt', etc.

*a.* In Umbrian there are three examples of omission of final *nt*, namely *surur-o* 'item' (VI b 48) beside the usual *surur-ont*, **eru-hu** 'eodem' (II b 22) beside usual *-hunt*, and *fefure* 'fuerint' (II a 4) for \*fefurent (cf. **benurent**). The latter form is more commonly taken as 3d Sg. Perf. Indic. 'turbavit' from a root *fur-*, but against this view is the obvious parallelism of the passage with VI a 26. In **staheren** 'stabunt' the omission of *t* is due merely to the fact that the following word begins with *t*.

---

[1] The above explanation combines a suggestion of Ehrlich, I.F. XI, 299 ff., who thinks that the whole ending *-ns* was adopted from nouns, with Johansson's assumption of a secondary ending *-nd, -n*, preserved in L. *danunt* etc.

*tl*

**129.** 1. Initial *tl*, which becomes *l* in Latin, as in *lātus* from *\*tlātos*, is seen in U. *Tlatie*, perhaps connected in form with L. *Latium*.

2. Medial *tl* becomes *kl* except after *s*, as in Latin; and the change may well belong to the Italic period. Thus, with the suffix which was once -*tlo-* (**248**, 3), O. **sakaraklúm** 'templum', U. *pihaclu* 'piaculo', etc.: L. *piāculum*, *pōculum*, etc.; — but O. **pestlúm** 'templum' (for **peessl[úm** see **139**, 2). U. *persclo* 'precationem' is probably *persc-lo* with suffix -*lo-*, not -*tlo-*.

Note. Cf. the Paelignian change of *tr* to *kr* in *sacaracirix*, *pristafalacirix*, as if L. *\*sacrātrix*, *\*praestibulātrix*.

**d**

**130.** *d* remains in Oscan in all positions, and initially in Umbrian. Examples: O. **deíkum**, *deicum* 'dicere', U. **teitu**, *deitu* 'dicito'; — O. **destrst** 'dextra est', U. *destram-e* 'in dextram'; — U. **tuves**, *duir* 'duobus'. —— O. **edum** 'edere'; — O. **deded**, δεδετ 'dedit'; — O. **píd** 'quid', *pod* 'quod', etc.

*Umbrian ř, rs, from d*

**131.** In Umbrian an intervocalic *d* regularly appears as ř, *rs*. For the pronunciation and origin of the character transcribed ř see **25**, **27**. Examples: **teřa**, *dirsa* 'det': O. *didest* 'dabit' from a Reduplicated Present as if L. *\*didō*, *\*didere* ; — **a-teřafust**, *an-dirsafust* 'circumdederit'; — **peři**, *persi* 'pede', *peturpursus* 'quadrupedibus'; — **zeřef**, *serse* 'sedens'.

a. In a few words intervocalic *d* remains. Except for a single form of doubtful meaning and origin (*tesedi*, *tenzitim*), these contain an *r*, so that the failure to change to ř, *rs*, seems due to the dissimilatory influence of this *r*. Thus *Coredier*, *Kureties* 'Coredii'; — *utur* 'aquam': Grk. ὕδωρ; — *tuder* 'finem', *tuderato* 'finitum', etc. This last is from an original *s*-stem *\*tudes-*, and where the *s* is preserved the change of the *d* takes place, as shown by *etuřstamu*, *eturstahmu* 'exterminato', from *\*tur(e)stā-*, denominative from *\*tudes-to-* (cf. L. *modes-tus*).

*b.* The occasional omission of r from *rs*, as in *Acesoniam* beside *Acersoniem* (**Akeřunie**), is parallel to the omission in the case of original *rs*. See 76, 1.

*c.* A few of the minor inscriptions antedate the change of intervocalic *d*, and show the sign ꟼ with its original value of *d* (27), as in **dunum dede** 'donum dedit'.

**132.** The occasional presence of ř, *rs*, before and after consonants is due to syncope of an intervening vowel or to transfer from the intervocalic position. So **ařpes** beside **ařepes** 'adipibus'; — **tribřiçu** 'ternio' from *tri-p(e)d-ikiōn-* (? see 106, *a*); — **ař-fertur**, *ars-fertur*, **ař-peltu**, **ařveitu**, etc., with the prefix **ař-**, *ars-* 'ad-', which gained this form before words beginning with a vowel; — **meřs**, *mers* 'ius' from *med(o)s*, with ř from other forms (not extant) in which the vowel was not lost; — **teřtu**, *dirstu* 'dato', **teřte** 'datur', with ř from forms like **teřa** (131).

> NOTE. In the last two examples we cannot explain the ř as having arisen in the unsyncopated forms *medos* and *didetōd*, since the syncope here took place in all probability in the Oscan-Umbrian period. The normal development of *did(e)tōd*, namely *dittōd*, is probably to be recognized in **titu**, *ditu*, which interchange with **teřtu** etc., although these can also be regarded as standing for *dītōd* and connected with *dia* 'faciat'.
>
> *a.* We find r, *r*, in place of ř, *rs*, in **mersus**, Dat.-Abl. Pl. of **meřs**, and **mersuva**, derivative of the same (*medes-ṷo-*); — **tertu** beside **teřtu**; — **armamu** beside *arsmahamo* 'ordinamini'; — *tribrisine* beside **tribřiçu**; — **ar-veitu**, *ar-ueitu* (once even a-veitu) beside **ař-veitu**, *ars-ueitu*; — *arfertur* beside *ars-fertur*.
>
> The difference between **mersus**, **mersuva**, and **meřs** is probably only one of spelling. In the Latin alphabet we have regularly *rs* for *rss*, as in **mers** = **meřs** (and even *mersi* 'ius sit' for *merss-si*). The sound of ř was not far from *rs*, and we may assume that when followed by *s* it was still nearer *rs*, so that the combination might be written either řs (**meřs**, **etuřstamu**, in I b) or **rss**, whence **rs** (**mersus**, **mersuva**, in III). Perhaps **tertu**, **armamu**, are mere mistakes in spelling (ꟼ for ꟼ; cf. **řanu** corrected by graver to **ranu**). The r for *rs* in *tribrisine* may be due to the following *s*.
>
> But the resemblance of **ar-veitu**, *ar-fertur*, etc. to early Latin *ar-vorsum*, *ar-fuerunt*, etc. suggests that *ar-* is the form which the prefix regularly assumed before *v*, *f*, and does not come from **ař-**, *ars-*, which in **ař-veitu** etc. is analogical (see above), as is the *ad-* of L. *ad-fuī*.
>
> *b.* According to the most probable explanation of *dersua*, **desua** 'prosperam' (*ded(e)s-ṷo-* 'giving, granting', from *dedos* 'gift'), **tesvam** would stand for *tersvam*, this to be explained precisely like **mersuva** (*a*).

### *Final d*

**133.** Final *d*, including the *d* from earlier *t* (127, 1), remains in Oscan, but is dropped in Umbrian, in both cases without regard to the quantity of the preceding vowel. Examples: O. *pod* 'quod', *píd* 'quid', but U. **svepu** 'sive' (= O. *suae pod*); — O. **deded** 'dedit', but U. **dede**; — Abl. Sg. O. *toutad, dolud,* **slaagid,** but U. *tota, poplu, mani*; — Imperat. O. **estud,** *actud*, but U. **futu, aitu**; — 3d Sg. Subj. O. **fakiiad,** *hipid*, but U. **façia,** *combifianśi*.

> *a.* In Oscan there are two examples of *h* for *d*, both on the Curse of Vibia, indicating a weakening of the final *d* in the Capuan dialect. These are: **svai puh** 'sive' = *suae pod* of the Tabula Bantina; — **suluh** 'omnino', an Ablative used adverbially.
>
> *b.* By combination with an enclitic beginning with a vowel, an original final *d* becomes intervocalic and so is preserved in Umbrian as **ř, rs**. Thus **pří-i,** *pirs-i*: O. **píd,** L. *quid*; — **puř-e,** *pors-i*: O. *pod*, L. *quod*; — **eř-ęk**: O. *id-ic*.
>
> Similarly U. **-ař** 'ad' in the only examples (two) where the next word begins with a vowel, and twice also even when it begins with a consonant. In all other examples the form is *-a*.

### *Initial dị*

**134.** The history of initial *dị* is the same as in Latin. It is preserved in a few Oscan inscriptions of early date, as in early Latin *Diovis*, but elsewhere the *d* is lost. So O. **Diúveí,** Διουϝει, **diuvilam,** but **Iúveís, Iuveí, iúvilam,** U. **Iuve,** *Ioui*.

> *a.* It is doubtful if the *\*dịěkolom* to which Bantian *zicolom* 'diem' points contains original *dị*. It may be from *diě-*, like L. *diēs*, with dialectic change of *i* to *ị*. See note to **100, 3, c.**

### *nd, dn*

**135.** *nd* becomes *nn*, usually written *n* in Umbrian (**25, 26**). So the Gerundives O. **úpsannam** 'operandam,' **sakrannas, eehiianaśúm,** U. *pihaner, anferener,* etc.; — O. *pan, pam* 'quam': L. *quamde*; — U. *ponne, pone,* O. **pún,** *pon* 'cum', from *\*pomde* as if L. *\*quomde* like *quamde*; — U. *ostendu,* **ustentu** from *\*ostennetōd*: L. *ostendito* (see also **156**); similarly **ampentu** 'impendito', *endendu* 'intendito', etc.

Consonants [137

In the case of *ndl* the change to *nnl*, *nl*, with the further change of *nl* to *ll* (107, 3), led to such forms as U. apelust 'impenderit', entelust 'intenderit', which are based upon -pend-lo-, -tend-lo- (226).

a. U. une is probably from *udne, Abl. Sg. of utur, i.e. *udōr : Grk. ὕδωρ. The relation of O. Perkens to Gen. Perkedne[ís is not clear.

*enbeimeden /Form Minius Perkednicio... Echt oskisch ist auch der Sentilename Per̄dh¹nius, ableilet von dem gerade in*

**136.** *dh*, which appears in Latin initially as *f*, but medially as *d* or *b* according to the surrounding sounds, is *f* in both positions. Examples: O. fakiiad, *factud*, U. façia, fakust, etc.: L. faciō, Grk. τίθημι, Skt. dhā- (root dhē-); — O. fiisnú 'fanum', U. fesnaf-e: L. fānum, fēstus, etc. (probably from the same root as the preceding); — O. feíhúss 'muros': L. fingō, Grk. τεῖχος, Skt. dih- (root dheigh-); — U. furu: L. forum, Grk. θύρα, Eng. door. —— O. mefiaí 'in media': L. medius, Skt. mádhya-; — O. Aiífineís: L. Aedinius, aedes, Grk. αἶθος, Skt. édha-; — U. combifiatu 'nuntiato': L. fīdō, Grk. πείθω, or: Grk. πυνθάνομαι (86, a; in either case the *f* represents *dh*). —— U. rufru 'rubros': L. ruber, Grk. ἐρυθρός, Skt. rudhirá-; — O. Lúvfreís 'Liberi': L. līber, Grk. ἐλευθερός; — O. staflatas 'statutae', U. staflarem '*stabularem': L. stabulum, stabilis, with suffix -flo-, Grk. -θλο-, orig. -dhlo-; — U. uerfale 'templum': L. verbālis, verbum, Goth. waurds, Eng. word.

a. Here belong also U. Acc. Pl. uef 'portiones' from *ueif-f, and U. vetu 'dividito' from *ueif(e)tod : L. dī-vidō, Skt. vindháte, etc. In vetu the *f* has passed through the same development as that of *ft* from *pt* (121).

### Dental + s

**137.** 1. A dental is assimilated to a following *s*, as in Latin, and the change to *ss* doubtless belongs to the Italic period. Thus U. revestu 'revisito': L. vīsō from *ueid-sō ; — U. Fiso 'deo Fidio', O. Fiísíaís '*Fisiis': L. fīsus from *fid-s-o- (cf. fīdus-tus).

---

¹ For the development of sonant aspirates in general, see 160-161.

2. But secondary *ts*, due to the syncope of an intervening vowel or to a late combination, remains under the designation *z* in the native alphabets, appearing as *s* in the Latin alphabet. Thus O. húrz 'hortus' from *\*hortos* (90, 1); — U. taçez, *tases* 'tacitus' from *\*taketos* ; — O. az 'ad' from *\*ad-s* (cf. L. *ab-s* etc.); — O. puz, *pous* 'ut', U. puze, *puse*, from *\*put-s* (202, 6). O. *aserum* 'adserere' is ambiguous, since it is not found in the native alphabet, but probably belongs here rather than under 1; here also U. *ostensendi* 'ostendentur' from *\*ostend(e)senter.*

NOTE. It is uncertain whether the *s* of the Latin alphabet also denoted *ts*, or whether the sound had actually become *s*. It has been suggested that U. zeřef 'sedens' with *z* for *s* is an indication that even before the native alphabet was abandoned, a change had taken place so that the sound of *z* was practically *s*. But there are no examples of *s* in place of *z* in the native alphabet, and U. zeřef has also been explained as arising in a compound like *\*anzeřef (cf. anzeriatu, 110, 1). Still, if the analysis of U. pruzuře as *\*prō-sode (94) were more certain, it would add weight to the first suggestion.

### Dental + Dental

**138.** The combination of the final dental of a root with the *t* of a suffix shows the same treatment as in Latin, and had doubtless become *ss*, or *st* before *r*, in the Italic period. Examples: O. Fερσορει '\*Versori' (U. *trahuorfi* 'transverse' with *rf* from *rss* ; see 115, 3): L. *versus*, earlier *\*verssus*, from *\*vert-to-*[1]; — U. *sesust* 'sederit', probably based on a participial stem *\*sesso-*: L. *sessus* (*\*sed-to-*[1]); — O. usurs probably: L. *ōsor* (*\*ōd-tōr*[1]); — U. *frosetom* 'fraudatum': early L. *fraussus* (*\*fraud-to-*[1]). O. luisaříls probably as if L. *\*lūsāribus* from *lūsus* (*\*loid-to-*[1]); — O. castrous, U. *castruo* : L. *castrum* (*\*cat-tro-*[1]; cf. *cassis* from *\*cat-ti-*).

*a.* In the case of *dh + t*, the normal phonetic development is different, the combination becoming *ddh* in Indo-European, and resulting in *st* in Italic, e.g. L. *custōs* : Grk. κύσθος, Goth. *huzd* 'hoard', from *\*kudh-to-*[1] (for root cf. κεύθω, Eng. *hide*). So L. *hasta*, U. *hostatu* 'hastatos', from *\*ghadh-tā*[1] (cf. Goth. *gazds* 'sting'); — probably U. ufestne 'operculatis'(?) from *\*op-fest(i)no-*, an extension of *\*festo-* from *\*bhendh-to-*[1] (root *bhendh-*, Eng. *bind*, seen also in L. *offendix* 'knot').

---

[1] So written for convenience in showing the root. These combinations were partially transformed even in the parent speech.

But in most cases this development has been interrupted by an analogical restoration in prehistoric times of the *t* of the suffix, so that *ddh* was replaced by *dt* (*tt*), which then became *ss* in Italic, as usual.  Thus L. *iussus*, not *\*iustus*, though from a root ending in *dh*.  There is, then, no difficulty in the assumption (189, 1) that O. **messimass** 'medioximas'(?) comes from *\*medh-tm̥mo-* (Skt. *mádh-ya-*), and O.-U. *nessimo-* 'proximus' (cf. O.Ir. *nessam* 'next') from *\*nedh-tm̥mo-* (Skt. *nah-* 'tie', Partic. *naddhá-*), though the latter may also come from *ned-*, a by-form of *nedh-*, seen in Skt. *nédiṣṭha-* 'next', Av. *nazdiśta-*.  O. **nistrus** 'propinquos' is also, probably, from *\*nedh-tero-* (*\*neddhero-*), either through *\*nestero-* with the same development as in L. *custōs*, or through *\*nettro-* with restored suffix and syncope, and subsequent development as in L. *castrum* (in the latter assumption there is a chronological difficulty, though not an insurmountable one).

### Other Combinations of Dentals

**139.  1.**  A dental is assimilated to a following *k*, *p*, or *f*, as in Latin.  Thus O. **púkkapíd**, *pocapit* 'quandoque', a compound of *pod*, probably *\*pod-kād-pid* ; — O. **perek.**, U. *percam*, from *\*pertkā* :  L. *pertica* ; — O. **akkatus** 'advocati' (89, 3, 102, 3); — U. *appei*, *ape* 'ubi' probably from *\*ad-pe* (202, 8) ; — U. Acc. Pl. *capif* 'capides' from *\*kapid-f* (**kapiř** is a mistake due to ř in other case-forms); — O. **aflukad** from *\*ad-flok-* (? see 97, *a*).

*a.*  A remarkable assimilation of *d* to a preceding *k* or *s* must be assumed for O. **ekkum** 'item' and O. **íussu** 'iidem', if these contain the enclitic *dom*.  But see 201, 5.

**2.**  A loss of *t* in the combinations *stm*, *stn*, and *stl*, subject to special local or chronological conditions, is seen in O. *posmom* 'postremum' beside **pustm[as** ; — U. **pusnaes** beside **pustnaiaf** 'posticas' ; — O. **peessl[úm** (for *ss*, see 162, 2) beside **pestlúm** 'templum'.  So in Latin, with subsequent loss of *s*, *pōmērium* from *\*post-moiriom*, *pōne* from *\*post-ne* (U. *postne*), *lis* from *slis*, *stlis*.  Cf. also U. **pusveres** beside *post uerir* 'post portam'.

### The Gutturals

**140.**  It is necessary to distinguish between the two series of gutturals known as the palatals and the labiovelars.  The palatals appear as simple *k*-sounds in the western languages (Greek,

Latin, Celtic, Germanic), conveniently known as the *centum*-languages, while in the eastern group (Indo-Iranian, Balto-Slavic, Armenian, Albanian), known as the *satem*-languages (Avestan *satəm* = L. *céntum*), they develop into sibilants (like L. *c*, *g*, before *e*, *i*, in the Romance languages). The labiovelars, which were pronounced well back on the soft palate and with an accompanying rounding of the lips, appear as simple *k*-sounds in the satem-languages, while in the centum-languages the rounding of the lips has resulted in a distinct *u̯*-sound closely following the guttural, giving what may be called *ku̯*-sounds. This *u̯*-element may remain distinct, as in Latin *qu*, or may unite with the guttural to form a labial, as in the Oscan-Umbrian *p*. It is one of the chief characteristics of Oscan-Umbrian as compared with Latin that the labiovelars appear regularly as labials.

There is still a third series of gutturals, called the pure velars, which remain simple *k*-sounds in both groups, showing neither the *u̯*-element in the centum-languages nor the development to sibilants in the satem-languages. But since within either group this series is identical with one of the other two, it will be necessary here, where we are for the most part only comparing Oscan-Umbrian with Latin, to distinguish only two series, the one which shows the *u̯*-element and the one which does not.

We shall treat, then, the *k*-sounds, which include the Indo-European palatals (*k̑* etc.) and the pure velars (*q* etc.), and the *ku̯*-sounds, which represent the labiovelars (*qu̯* etc.).

**k**

**141.** *k* appears as **k**, *c*, as in Latin. Examples: O. *censaum*, **keenzstur**: L. *cēnseō*, *cēnsor*, etc.; — U. **kanetu**, *procanurent*: L. *canō*; — O. **deikum**, *deicum*, *dicust*, U. *dersicust* (from *\*dedicust*): L. *dīcō*; — O. **Dekmanniúis** '*\*Decumaniis*', U. **tekuries**, *dequrier* 'decuriis': L. *deoem*.

*a*. It is uncertain whether *ku̯* (i.e. I.E. *k̑* + *u̯*) remained unchanged or became *p* like *ku̯* (I.E. *qu̯*). Cf. L. *equus* from *ek̑u̯o*- and *sequor* from *sequ̯*-. For the former would speak U. **ekvine**, if connected with L. *equinus*, — for the latter, the gentiles *Epidius* etc., found in Latin inscriptions from Oscan-Umbrian territory, if they belong with L. *Equitius* etc. and are genuine O.-U. forms.

*b.* In Umbrian a final *k* is often omitted in the writing, e.g. ere, *ere*, beside erek, *erec*: O. *izic*. See 201, 1.

## *kt*

**142.** But before *t* a *k* became a spirant and then simply *h*, so that the combination *kt* appears as *ht* in both Oscan and Umbrian. In Umbrian, however, the *h* was weakly sounded or wholly lost, as is evident from its frequent omission in the writing, and the preceding vowel was lengthened. See 75. Examples: O. ehtrad, U. ap-ehtre, from *\*ek-tro-*: L. *extrā*, etc.; — O. Úhtavis: L. *Octāvius*; — U. rehte: L. *rēctē*; — O. saahtúm, U. sahta, satam, *sahatam*: L. *sānctus*; — U. uhtur: L. *auctor*; U. speture: L. *(in-)spector*.

*a.* It is possible that the same change from *k* to *h* should be recognized before *p*, examples of which would be O. ehpeilatas 'erectae', and ehpreivid, of uncertain meaning, on a fragmentary inscription. But the *eh* may be due to extension from compounds of words beginning with *t*.

**143.** Secondary *kt*, resulting from the syncope of an intervening vowel, has an entirely different history. It remains unchanged in Oscan, while in Umbrian it appears as *it*, the *k* having passed through the same development as in French *fait* from L. *factum*. Examples: O. *factud*: L. *facito*; — O. *actud*: L. *agito*; — O. *uincter*: L. *vincitur*; — U. aitu, *aitu*: O. *actud*; — U. teitu, *deitu* 'dicito' from *\*deik(e)tōd* (the original diphthong is represented by the *e* only; see 65); — U. feitu, *feitu*, fetu, *feetu* 'facito' from *\*fēk(e)tod* (219). Here belongs also U. -veitu (arveitu, *arsueitu* 'advehito', kuveitu 'convehito') from *\*yektōd*, this from original *\*yeghetōd* (160).

## *Umbrian palatalization of k*

**144.** In Umbrian a *k* before the vowels *e* and *i*, and before consonantal *i*, becomes a sibilant, written ç, ś, or often simply *s*. This recalls the development of Latin *c* before palatal vowels in the Romance languages, as in French *cent* etc. The precise pronunciation of the Umbrian sound, the difference between it and the ordinary *s*, is of course uncertain. It may have been *š* (i.e. Eng. *sh*) or *ś* (palatal *s*). As regards the use of *s* for *ś*, it is comparatively rare initially, but between vowels vastly more common than *ś*. Examples : *śesna* 'cenam', *çersnatur* 'cenati' : L. *cēna*, O. kersnu ; — *śihitu, sihitu* : L. *cīnctus* ; — *pase* (15 times, always *s*): L. *pāce* ; — taçez, *tases* (14 times, always *s*): L. *tacitus* ; — *desenduf*: L. *decem* ; — tiçit : L. *decet* ; — ançif : L. *ancus, uncus* ; — skalçe-ta, *scalse-to* : L. *calice* ; — *curnase* 'cornice' (Acc. Sg. *curnaco*). Observe also *pesetom* 'peccatum' from *\*pecceto-*: L. *peccō* from *\*petcō*. Further, with consonantal *i*, which is frequently omitted in the writing, façia, façiu, façu : L. *faciō* ; — *Sanśie, Sansie,* Saçe: L. *\*Sancius* (*Sancus*); tribřiçu 'ternio' beside Abl. Sg. *tribrisine* (*-ik-ịōn-, -ik-īn*, 181); — *purdinśiust* 'porrexerit', *purdinsust,* purtinçus, etc. (*nkị-*Perfect, 239).

We find also çị, *śl,* in a number of words, but in these the palatalization of the *k* is due to a following *e* which has been lost by syncope after having affected the *k*. Thus tiçlu 'dedicationem' from *\*dik-elo-* ; — *preuiślatu* (also *preuilatu* by engraver's error) '*\*praevinculato*', denominative from *\*ụink-elo-* : L. *vinculum* ; — struhçla, *strušla* '*\*struiculam*' from *\*struụikelā-*. But when *k* is preceded by *s* it is not affected, e.g. veskles, *uesclir* 'vasculis' from *\*ụes-kelo-*. The instrumental suffix *-klo-* remains unchanged, since this does not come from *-kelo-* like the diminutive suffix. So pihaklu, *pihaclu* 'piaculum', etc.

*a.* In several words we find *k* unchanged before *e* or *i*. In some this is due to the analogical influence of other cases in which the *k* is followed by another vowel, as Gen. Sg. *Naharcer* after *Naharcom.* So probably also forms of the Dat. Sg. and Dat.-Abl. Pl. like *fratreci, todceir,* etc. though in these *e, i,* comes from earlier *oi.* Cf. also Pupřike beside Pupřiçe etc. A few forms occurring in the oldest tables may be regarded as survivals from a period antedating the process of palatalization, e.g. kebu: L. *cibus.* The origin of Akeřunie, *Acersoniem,* and its relation to O. Akudunniad are obscure. For *cehefi* 'accensum sit'(?), ku-kehes, there is no satisfactory etymology (connection with Grk. καίω from *\*καϝ-ịω impossible).

*b.* For original *kị,* which regularly appears as çị, *śị,* or ç, *ś, s* (façiu, façu, etc., above), we find simply *i* in usaịe beside usaçe, and in peiu, *peiu,* from *pik-io-* (for *e* for *i* see **45**): L. *piceus*. The reason for this is not apparent, and some prefer to assume an error in *usaie* and to reject the comparison of *peiu* with L. *piceus*. But *peiu* denotes some color, contrasted with *rufru* 'rubros', and the meaning 'piceos' is so strikingly suitable that in spite of the difficulty in the form, we prefer to accept the connection. Cf. also *feia* 'faciat' (**219**).

## *ks*

**145.** 1. Before consonants *ks* becomes *s*. Thus O. **destrst** 'dextra est', U. *destram-e* 'in dextram'; — U. **sestentasiaru** 'sextantariarum'; — **\*persk-, \*porsk-**, etc. (**97**) from *\*perk-sk-* (cf. L. *poscō*, *\*porscō* from *\*pork-sk-*, beside *precor*), in U. *persclo* 'precationem', *persnihimu* 'precator' (see **146**), etc., beside **pepurkurent** 'poposcerint', and in O. *comparascuster* 'consulta erit' beside **kú]mparakineís.**

NOTE. The reduction to *s* in the examples given belongs to different periods. In *\*persk-* it is probably Indo-European, in **sestentasiaru** Italic, in **destrst** Oscan-Umbrian.

2. Final *ks*, both original and secondary, becomes *ss, s*. Thus O. **meddíss**, *meddis* 'meddix' (Gen. Sg. **medíkeís**); also Nom. Pl. **meddíss** from *\*meddik(e)s* (**90**, 1); — U. *uas* 'vitium' from *\*uak(o)s* (cf. L. *vacō*). But sometimes the *k* is restored under the influence of the oblique cases, e.g. O. Nom. Pl. μεδδειξ = **meddíss**, O. **túvtíks** 'publicus', U. **fratreks**, *fratrexs* '\*fratricus'.

3. Intervocalic *ks* is seen in O. **eksuk** 'hoc', *exac* 'hac', etc., to which corresponds U. **esu**, *esu, essu* 'hoc', *esa* 'hac', etc. It is uncertain whether this *ks* is original or secondary. If the latter, compare O. **úpsannam**: U. *osatu* (**122**, 3).

### *Loss of k between consonants*

**146.** Loss of *k* (in part from *kʷ* by **153**) between consonants is seen in O. *molta*, U. **muta**: L. *multa, mulcta* (*mulcō*); — O. *fortis* 'potius': L. *fortis, forctis* ; — U. **Urnasier** '\*Urnariis': L. *urna* from *\*urcnā* (*urceus*); — O. **turumiiad** 'torqueatur', denominative from *\*torkmo-, \*torkʷ-mo-*: L. *tormentum* (*torqueō*); — U. *persnihimu* 'precator', denominative from *\*persk-ni-* (*\*persk-* from *\*perk-sk-*, **145**); — U. **perstu** 'ponito'(?) from *\*persk(e)tōd* (cf. *peperscust*); — O. Púntiis, U. puntès 'pentads', from *\*ponk-t-*, *\*ponkᵘ-t-* (153), beside O. Πομπτιες and *pomtis* 'quinquiens' from *\*pomptis*, with *p* after *\*pompe* 'quinque' (cf. L. *Quīntus, Quīnctus*); — similarly, where the combination is due to syncope, U. anstintu 'distinguito' from *\*-stinktōd, \*-stinkᵘtōd* (153), but *ninctu* 'ninguito' with the guttural restored from unsyncopated forms prior to the labialization in the latter (or were *n* and *nc* two spellings for the same sound, namely the guttural nasal?).

*a.* In the examples of *nt* from *nkt* the *k* of the latter is from *kᵘ* (153). In the case of original *nkt* (i.e. with I.E. *k̑*) the nasal was lost and the *kt* became *ht*, as elsewhere. See 73, 142.

*b.* U. kunikaz, *conegos* 'conixus' shows the same reduction of *nkn* to *n* as L. *cōnīveō* (root *kneigᵘh-*, Goth. *hneiwan*).

## g

147. 1. Original *g* is for the most part unchanged. Examples: O. Genetaí 'Genitae'; — O. aragetud 'argento'; — O. *ligud* 'lege'; — O. tanginúd 'sententia': L. *tongitiō*; — U. *ager* 'ager'.

2. Initial *gn* remains in Oscan, but appears as *n* in Umbrian. Thus O. Gnaivs 'Gnaeus'; — U. natine : L. *nātiō* from *\*gnātiō (gēns)*; — naratu, naraklum : L. *nārrō, gnārus*.

3. An Italic change is that of intervocalic *gi̯* to *i̯i̯*, the first *i̯* then forming a diphthong with the preceding vowel. For to L. *maior* from *\*magi̯ōs (magis, magnus)*, *maius, Maius*, etc. belong O. Maiiúí 'Maio' (see 100, 2), with Nom. Sg. Mais, and *mais*[1] 'magis, plus', from *\*maii̯os* (91, 1). Cf. also U. aiu 'agitationes, disturbances'(?), probably from *agi̯o*.

*a.* In *\*maistero-* (whence U. mestru 'maior') and *\*maisemo-* (whence O. maimas 'maximae', 114, *b*), the *\*mais-* may also be from *\*mai̯i̯es* (cf. L. *maiestās*), but more probably has replaced *magis* (cf. L. *magister*) under the influence of forms like O. *mais*.[1] O. *Maesius* 'mensis Maius' (Festus) seems also, in contrast to L. *Maius*, O. Maiiúí, to be formed directly from *mais*.

4. Assimilation of *g* to a following *f* is seen in U. Acc. Pl. *frif* 'fruges' from *\*frūg-f* (59).

---

[1] According to another view, once held by the author also, these words are not cognate with L. *magis, maior*, etc. but with Goth. *mais* (Eng. *more* etc.).

## Umbrian palatalization of g

**148.** Corresponding to the palatalization of *k* before *e* and *i* is the Umbrian change of *g* to a sound which is represented by *i*. Thus *muieto* 'muttitum' beside *mugatu* 'muttito' (cf. pruseçetu, *proseseto* 'prosecta' beside prusekatu 'prosecato'); — eveietu 'voveto' from *\*ē-ụēgētōd*, *\*ē-ụeigētōd* (L. *victima*, Germ. *weihen*).[1]

*a.* An apparent example of palatalization of *g* by a preceding *i* is seen in Iiuvina, *Iiouinur, Iouinur*, etc. beside Ikuvina 'Iguvinus'. But the mediæval and modern forms of the name preserve the *g*, and it has been suggested that the spelling cited is due to a "pious fraud" of the priests who wished to connect the name of the city with that of the divinity. Cf. Iuve, *Iouie, Iiouie*, etc.

### gh

**149.** *gh* appears as *h*, as in Latin. Examples: O. húrz, húrtúm: L. *hortus*, Grk. χόρτος ; — O. humuns 'homines', U. *homonus* 'hominibus': L. *homō* ; — O. hu[n]truis 'inferis', U. *hondra* 'infra', *hondomu* 'infimo': L. *humus* etc. (15, 5); — O. *herest* 'volet', U. *heriest* 'volet', etc.: L. *horior* etc. (15, 1); — O. heriiad 'capiat', h]errins 'caperent': L. *hērēs*, Grk. χείρ, Skt. *hárāmi* 'hold'; — O. feihúss 'muros': Grk. τεῖχος (L. *fingō* with *g* for *gh* after *n*); — O. kahad 'capiat': L. *incohō* ; — O. Verehasiúí 'Versori'(?), perhaps : L. *vergō* (*g* for *gh* after a consonant); — O. eehiianasúm 'emittendarum', U. *ehiato* 'emissos' (used of the victims 'let out' for the sacrificial hunt): L. *hiō* (occasionally transitive 'emit'), Lith. *žióju* 'gape'. For U. -veitu 'vehito', see **148**.

*a.* Umbrian *h* was so weakly sounded that, as in Latin, the letter is sometimes omitted, or, vice versa, employed where it has no etymological value. Thus eretu beside usual *heritu* 'optato' (: *heriest* 'volet' etc., above); — *an-ostatu* beside *an-hostatu, hostatu* 'hastatos': L. *hasta ;* — enclitic *-ont* after consonants beside *-hont* after vowels (*er-ont, eri-hont* 'idem' etc., 195); eitipes from *\*eitom hipens* (84, 264, 2); — *hebetaf-e* beside *ebetraf-e* 'in exitus' from *\*ē-baitrā* (L. *baetō*); — *habina* 'agnas': L. *agnus* (? or: Skt. *chágā* 'goat', in which case the *h* is etymological); — Hule, *holtu* 'aboleto'(?), perhaps from a root *ol-* (Grk. ὄλλυμι etc.).

In O. Herukinai 'Erycinae' the *h* is due to the influence of Herentatei, of which it is an epithet.

---

[1] Osthoff, I.F. 6, 39 ff.

*b.* The substitution of *f* for *h*, in *folus* for *holus* and other forms cited by Latin writers, and in Faliscan *foied* 'hodie', seems to have been characteristic of rustic Latin and some of the neighboring minor dialects. It is possible that U. **felsva** is a borrowed technical term originating in regions where this change was made. For, certainly, the comparison with L. *holus* is more attractive than any other explanation offered.

For U. *era-font* beside *era-hunt* 'eadem', see **201, 6.**

## k͜ʯ

**150.** *k͜ʯ*, L. *qu*, appears as *p*. Examples: O. **púd**, *pod*, U. **puř-e**: L. *quod*; — O. **píd**, U. **pïř-e**: L. *quid*; — U. **panta**: L. *quanta*; — O. *petiro-pert* 'quater', U. *petur-pursus* 'quadru-pedibus': L. *quattuor*; — *\*pompe* (O. **púmperiaís**, U. **pumpeřias**): L. *quīnque*.

*a.* Both O.-U. *\*pompe* and L. *quīnque* are from an Italic *\*k͜ʯenk͜ʯe*, though this comes by consonant-assimilation from an earlier *\*penk͜ʯe* (cf. Grk. πέντε, Skt. *páñca*).

## g͜ʯ

**151.** *g͜ʯ*, Latin *v* or (after *n*) *gu*, appears as *b*. Examples: O. **kúmbened** 'convenit,' U. **benust** 'venerit': L. *veniō* (Eng. *come*); — O. **bivus** 'vivi': L. *vīvus* (Eng. *quick*); — U. **berus** 'veribus': L. *verū*; — U. **bum** 'bovem' (Eng. *cow*; L. *bōs* is borrowed from some O.-U. dialect); — U. **umen** 'unguen' from *\*omben* (**125, 2**): L. *unguen*; — U. *habina*: L. *agnus* (? see **149, a**).

## g͜ʯh[1]

**152.** *g͜ʯh*, Latin *f* (initially), *v* (between vowels), or *gu* (after *n*), appears as *f*. Thus U. **vufru** 'votivum', **vufetes** 'votivis': L. *\*u̯ou̯eto-* (whence *vōtus*, like *mōtus* from *\*mou̯eto-*), *voveō* (cf. Skt. *vāghát-* 'sacrificer', Grk. εὔχομαι, root *u̯eg͜ʯh-* and *eug͜ʯh-*). Unquestionable examples of initial *f* from *g͜ʯh* are wanting.

*a.* U. *uouse* is commonly translated 'voto' and regarded as corresponding in form to a L. *\*vovicio-*. But there is no adequate explanation of the *uou-* in its relation to the *vuf-* of the other forms.

---

[1] For the development of sonant aspirates in general, see **160-161.**

**Loss of ꭒ in kꭒ etc.**

**153.** The ꭒ of *kꭒ* etc. is lost before another consonant, as in Latin *coctus* beside *coquō*, *quīntus* beside *quīnque*, etc. Thus O. **Púntiis**, U. **puntes** 'pentads', from \**ponk-t-* (**146**), \**ponkꭒ-t-*, beside \**pompe* with the usual development of *kꭒ* (**150**), while in O. Πομπτιες and *pomtis* the labial is analogical. See also **146**. The same loss occurs in combinations resulting from syncope, showing that the latter process antedates the change of *kꭒ* etc. to *p* etc. Thus U. **fiktu** 'figito' from \**fīkꭒtōd*, \**fīgꭒetōd*[1]: L. *fīgō*, earlier *fīvō* ; — O. **fruktatiuf** 'fructus' from \**frūkꭒt-*, *frūgꭒetātiōn-*[1]: L. \**fruitātiō*, *fruitiō* ; — U. **anstintu** 'distinguito' from \*-*stinktōd* (**146**), \*-*stinkꭒtōd*, \*-*stingꭒetōd*[1] ; — U. *ninctu* 'ninguito' from \**ninkꭒtōd*, \**ningꭒetōd* (originally *gꭒh*; see **161**).

*a.* U. **umtu** 'unguito' instead of \***untu** or \***unktu** is an analogical form like O. *pomtis*, *m* in this case coming from forms like \***ummō**, \***umbō** (cf. **umen** from \***omben** : L. *unguen*; **151**).

*b.* U. **subocau** 'invoco' agrees with L. *vocō*, the *k* probably originating in Nom. Sg. \**ꭒōks* (L. *vōx*) from \**ꭒōkꭒs* (Grk. ἔπος, ὄψ). In U. **kunikaz**, **conegos** 'genu nixus' (as if L. \**cōnigātus* for \**cōnivātus*): L. *cōnīveō*, Goth. *hneiwan* 'kneel' (root *kneigꭒh-*), the simple guttural might be attributed to the influence of forms such as L. *nīxus*, *nīctō*, but in that case it is not clear why we have not \**conecos*.

**154.** Loss of the ꭒ before a following *u*, as seen in L. *quīncuplex* beside *quīnque*, etc., is perhaps to be recognized for Oscan-Umbrian also, and so attributed to the Italic period. But the material is meagre and indecisive. Examples would be U. **prusikurent** 'pronuntiaverint': L. *inseque* (but it is fully as likely that the *k* in this, as in the probably related U. **sukatu** and in L. *insece* beside *inseque*, is due to the influence of forms like L. *insectiō*, in which the ꭒ was lost before the following consonant) ; — U. \**arkelo-*, whence **arçlataf** 'arculatas' (**144**), instead of \**arpelo-*, perhaps due to the analogy of \**arku-* as L. *arcitenēns* for *arquitenēns* is due to *arcu-*.

---

[1] We are justified in assuming that the Oscan-Umbrian forms go with the Latin, even though the *gꭒ* in these forms is not Indo-European. See Brugmann, Grd. I², p. 603.

The *p* in O. **puf**, U. **pufe** 'ubi' and O. **puz**, U. **puze** 'ut' must then be attributed to the influence of forms like O. **púd, píd**, etc.

<small>*a.* L. *ubi, ut,* etc. are variously explained, but there are no serious objections to the view that they represent the regular Latin development of initial *k*$^u$*u.*</small>

### Change of Surd Mutes to Sonants

**155.** The change of *nkl* to *ngl*, seen in L. *angulus* from *\*anklo-* (*ancus*), doubtless belongs to the Italic period. Thus O. *ungulus* 'anulus' (Festus): L. *uncus* ; — U. *anglom-e* 'ad angulum' ; — U. *anglaf* 'oscines' (*g* 6 times, but twice *c*) from *\*an-klā-* (L. *clāmō* ; cf. *oscen* from *canō*).

**156.** In Umbrian, *nk, nt,* except when final, become *ng, nd.* Thus *iuengar*: L. *iuvenca* ; — *ander*: O. **anter**, L. *inter* ; — Passives *tursiandu, ostensendi,* with endings *-tor* (L. *-tur*), *-ter* (U. **her-ter**, O. *uincter*); — *ostendu* 'ostendito' from *\*os-tentu*, this from *\*os-tennetōd* (**135**), similarly *andendu, endendu* 'intendito' from *\*an-tentu, \*en-tentu* ; — *hondra* 'infra': O. **hu[n]truis** 'inferis' ; — *hondomu* 'infimo': L. *-tumo-.*

<small>NOTE. This change is later than the palatalization of *k*, as is shown by **ançif** and *preuiślatu* (**144**).</small>

**157.** 1. A change of medial *pr* to *br* is regular in Umbrian. Thus *subra*, **subra** 'supra', **kabru** 'caprum', *cabriner* 'caprini', *abrof* 'apros', **abrunu** 'aprum'. In **supru, kaprum** etc., **apruf**, the **p** probably stands for **b**, as not infrequently elsewhere (**30, 6**). In Oscan also we find **embratur** 'imperator' and **Abella-** (**Abellanús**) probably from *\*Apro-lā-* (**91, 2**), but usually *pr* remains (**supruis** etc.).

2. A similar change of *tr* to *dr* is seen in a few words, though usually *tr* remains (U. *fratrom*, O. **fratrúm**, etc.). Thus U. **podruh-pei** 'utroque': O. **pútúrús-píd** from *\*po-tro-* (**81**) ; — O. **Sadiriis** 'Satrius' (**81**) ; — U. *adro* 'atra', O. **Aderl.** 'Atella' from *Ātro-lā* (see **91, 2**, and note; but it is possible that *dr* in this case is original, becoming *tr* in Latin, as in *taeter* from *\*taed-ro-*).

<small>NOTE. The reasons for the variation in the representation of *tr* and (in Oscan) of *pr* are obscure.</small>

**158.** Other, more isolated examples are U. *Padellar* from *Patno-lā-* (91, 2, a), with which may be compared L. *scabellum* from *scap-no-lo-* (*scāpus*), *dignus* from *dec-no-*, etc. ; — O. **degetasis, degetasiús,** beside **deketasiúí,** from *dekentāsio-*, the explanation of the g being doubtful (cf. L. *vīgintī?*) ; — U. *todcom-e* 'in urbicum', *todceir*, beside *totcor* (cf. O. *touticom*), the *d* being probably a graphic vagary due to the following *tuder*.

## Change of Sonant Mutes to Surds

**159.** The change of sonant to surd before a following surd mute is an Indo-European process, but repeats itself in the case of combinations arising through syncope in the Oscan-Umbrian period. Thus O. *actud* 'agito' from *ag(e)tōd*, U. **fiktu** 'figito' from *figu(e)tōd* (153), etc.

a. O. **akenei,** U. *acnu, peracni-*, etc., if the frequently assumed connection with L. *agō* is correct, indicate that *ak-* in place of *ag-* was generalized from such forms as L. *āctus, āctiō* (cf. U. **ahtim**), reinforced in the Oscan-Umbrian period by forms like O. *actud*. With this view would agree O. *acum* on the Tabula Bantina, though no great weight can be attached to this on account of the frequent misspellings (e.g. *licud* for *ligud*).

The words in question have also been connected with L. *annus* from *atno-* (Goth. *aþn*), and on the side of meaning this is most attractive, especially for the fairly certain *acunum VI nesimum* of the Tabula Bantina and the **akun.** **CXII** of no. 13. Moreover the resemblance of the compounds U. *per-acni-* and *seu-acni-* (cf. U. *seuom* 'totum', O. *siuom* 'omnino') to L. *per-ennis* and *soll-ennis* (the by-form *sollemnis* contains a different word, perhaps one related to O. *amnúd* 'circuitu') is too striking to be ignored, though *peracni-* is not 'perennis' in meaning, but is used, like *seuacni-*, in the same sense as L. *sollennis*. Now an Oscan-Umbrian change of medial *tn* to *kn* is not sufficiently paralleled by the change of *tl* to *kl*, which is Italic (129, 2); and it is, moreover, opposed by O. **Patanaí** 'Pandae' from *Pat-nā-* (or earlier *Patenā*?). But there may be an indirect connection; that is, the O.-U. *akno-* may represent a contamination of *atno-* with some other form, perhaps an *agno-* or *akno-* coming from *ag-* and meaning 'ceremony' (occurring at fixed periods).

## Changes of the original Sonant Aspirates

**160.** In the Italic period the Indo-European sonant aspirates became first surd aspirates, as likewise in Greek, and then the corresponding spirants. That is, *bh, dh, gh, guh*, became first *ph, th, kh, kᵘh,* then *f, þ* (= Eng. *th* in *thin*), χ (= Germ. *ch*), χᵘ. The further changes of *þ* to *f*, of χ to *h*, and of χᵘ to *f*, even where common to Oscan-Umbrian and Latin, probably took place independently in each branch. The *d* of L. *medius* (O. mefiaí) must come directly from *þ* (cf. also λίτρα̃ borrowed from *lĩprā̃*, whence L. *lĩbra*); and since in this position Italic *f* is impossible, it is improbable in the others. Intervocalic χ appears as *h* in all dialects, but U. -veitu 'vehito' makes it unlikely that it had reached this stage at the time of the Oscan-Umbrian syncope, for this implies *u̯ektōd* (see 148), which can come from *u̯eχetōd*, but hardly from *u̯eh(e)tōd.*

**161.** In Latin we find regularly a sonant mute after a nasal; that is, not only *mb* and *nd* (in which the sonant would not necessarily be due to the nasal), but also *ng* and *ngu*, e.g. *lingō* (λείχω), *ninguit* (νείφει). The same holds true for Umbrian. Thus:

*mb* from *mf*: *ambr-(ambr-etuto* 'ambiunto') beside O. amfr-(amfret 'ambiunt'), from *amfer,* which is formed from *amf(i)-* (L. *amb-,* Grk. ἀμφί) after the analogy of *anter, super,* etc. (i.e. *amfer-eō* after *anter-eō,* L. *inter-eō*; cf. L. *comb-ūrō* after *amb-ūrō*);— here probably also *amb-oltu* 'ambulato' (Grk. ἀλδομαι?); — *com-bifiatu* 'nuntiato' from *com-fif-*: L. *fīdō,* Grk. πείθω, root *bheidh-* (or Grk. πυνθάνομαι, root *bheudh-*; see 86, 7). For the operation of the process even in composition, see 164, *a.*

*ng* from *nχ*: *cringatro* 'cinctum': O.Eng. *hring* 'ring', O.Bulg. *krągŭ* 'circle', root *krengh-.*

> For *nd* from *nþ* and for *ngᵘ* from *nχᵘ* there are no certain examples. It would be attractive to derive -*uendu* (*ahauendu* 'avertito', *preuendu* 'advertito') from *u̯enþetōd* (Germ. *winden, wenden,* root *u̯endh-*) through the medium of *u̯endetōd* (like *ostendu* from *ostendetōd,* 156), and *ninctu* from *ninχᵘetōd* (Grk. νείφει etc.) through *ningᵘetōd* (like fiktu from *fĩgᵘetōd,* 153). But the vowel-syncope belongs in all probability to the Oscan-Umbrian period, whereas the change to sonant seems to be Umbrian only, not Oscan (see *a* with footnote). It is better, then, to assume the development *u̯enþ(e)tōd, *u̯entōd, uendu,* and *ninχᵘ(e)tod, *ninkᵘtōd* (cf. *u̯eχetōd, *u̯ektōd,* 160), *ninctu.*

*a.* O. ampt 'circum' is obviously connected with *amf(i)-,* L. *amb-,* etc., being formed by the addition of the same -*t(i)* seen in *pos-t, per-t,* etc. But we cannot well derive it from *amf-t* with a change of *ft* to *pt*, since Oscan shows, rather, the opposite change of *pt* to *ft* (121). Nor can we start from *amb-t*, since *amb-* from *amf-* is confined to Latin and Umbrian (O. amfr-; see above)[1]. The explanation is as follows : In the Italic period *amf-* became *am-* before certain consonants, e.g. before *f* (cf. U. *an-ferener*). This *am-* was extended to other forms, and became a regular by-form of *amf-* as in L. *am-iciō* etc. Oscan-Umbrian examples are O. am-viannud 'vico' (cf. Grk. ἄμφοδον); — O. amnúd 'circuitu' (16, 2); — probably O. ampu[l]ulum 'ministrum'(?), diminutive from *am-polo-* (*p* from *kʷ*): L. *an-culus*, Grk. ἀμφί-πολος ; — U. *an-ferener* 'circumferendi' ; — U. *an-dirsafust* 'circumtulerit'; — U. aplenia 'impleta, full on both sides' ; — possibly U. am-peṛia (see Glossary).

From this by-form am- was formed *am-t*, which became ampt with the same secondary *p* which is seen in L. *ēm-p-tūs*, *sūm-p-tus*, etc. (cf. also *amptermini* in Festus).

### Doubling of Consonants in Oscan

**162. 1.** Doubling of consonants is to be observed in Oscan frequently before consonantal *i*, and occasionally before *r* and *v*. Examples : Mamerttiais 'Martiis'; — úíttiuf 'usus' from *oitiōn-; — a]íttiúm 'portionum', Gen. Pl. beside Gen. Sg. *aeteis* (í instead of i is due to the influence of other case-forms, as -ím, -íss, etc.); — meddikkiai 'in *meddicia' from *meddik-iā-; — tríbarakkiuf 'aedificatio' from *trēbark-iōn-; — Dekkieis 'Decii' (Nom. Dekis); — kúmbenníeís 'conventus' from *kom-ben-io-; — teremenniú 'termina' as if L. *terminia ; — Dekmanniúís '*Decumaniis';—Vítelliú 'Italia', etc..—— alttram 'alteram', alttreí 'alteri' ; — púnttram 'pontem'. —— Dekkviarím 'Decurialem'.

**2.** Doubling of *s* before *t* is seen in kvaísstur 'quaestor' (once kvaízstur; influence of keenzstur ?); — keenzstur 'censor' (nz = *nts*, 110, 1) ; — pússtíst 'positum est' (? see 84, *a*), passtata 'porticum' (31). Probably kerssnaís 'cenis' and kerssnasias are also examples of similar doubling, in spite of the fact that they once had etymological *ss* (116, 2); also peessl[úm (139, 2).

**3.** Appellúneís 'Apollinis', Αππελλουνηι, remind us of L. *Appuleius* beside *Apuleius*, etc., and the spelling is perhaps due to

---

[1] The possibility of separating the *f* of O. amfret from that of *amf(i)-*, as advocated by some, and assuming an Italic change of sonant aspirate to sonant after a nasal, has been considered, but given up as improbable. Cf. also O. Verehasiúí : L. *vergō* (? 149).

the influence of compounds like L. *appellō* etc. **Helleviis** for usual **Heleviis** is simply a mistake.

NOTE. Even for words falling under 1 and 2, the doubling is by no means universal, the spelling sometimes varying for the same word. It is probably an attempt to indicate that the consonant was sounded both at the end of one syllable and at the beginning of the next. Cf. L. *quattuor*, and the occasional inscriptional spellings such as *frattre*, *aggro*, *mattrona*, *asstante*, *iussta*, *Vessta*, etc. In Greek, σστ for στ is especially common, and doubling before ι and ρ is found in dialectic inscriptions.

### Simplification of Double Consonants

**163.** In Oscan, which in general, apart from the oldest inscriptions and the Tabula Bantina, faithfully represents double consonants in the writing, there are some examples of single in place of double consonants. But even in these cases it is not clear how far we have to do with anything more than irregularity in spelling. Examples: **dadíkatted** 'dedicavit' from \**dad-dik-* (cf. *dat* 'de') ; — **eehiianasúm** 'emittendarum' beside **úpsannam** etc.; **amvíanud** 'vico' beside **amvíannud**; — **medíkeís**, **medíkeí**, beside **meddíss** 'meddix'; **medikkiai** beside **meddikiai**; — further, on the Tabula Bantina, *medicim*, *medicatinom*, *medicatud*, beside *meddis*, *meddixud*.

### Changes in Sentence-Combination. Sandhi.

**164.** The history of initial and final sounds has been included in the general treatment. For crasis etc., see **84**. Following is a résumé of the changes of finals.

1. Final short vowels are sometimes lost (**92**).
2. Final *ā* is changed in the direction of *ō* (**34**).
3. Final *rs*, *ls*, become *r*, *l* (**117, 119, 2**).
4. Final *fs*, *ks*, become *ss*, *s* (**124, a ; 145, 2**).
5. Final *ns* in certain cases becomes *f* (**110, 2, 4, 5**).
6. Final *t* becomes *d* (**127, 1**).
7. Final *d*, including preceding, is lost in Umbrian (**133**).
8. Final *s* becomes *r* in later Umbrian (**113**).

9. Final consonants were weakly sounded in Umbrian, and, with more or less frequency, omitted in the spelling. This is true of all except *r* from *rs*, *l* from *ls*, and *s* from *fs*, *ks*. Thus *m*, *n* (109, 1), *r* (103, 4; 113, *b*), *f* (110, 2, *a*), *t* (127, 2), *k* (141, *b*), *s* (113, *b*). Omission of final *nt* is rare (128, 2, *a*).

*a.* CHANGES IN COMPOUNDS. Noteworthy is the extent to which phonetic changes affecting the initial of the second member of a compound take place in Oscan-Umbrian without interference from the analogical influence of the simplex, if such still existed. Cf. U. *subocau* from *\*sub-ṵok-* (102, 2), O. **akkatus** from *\*ad-ṵok-* (102, 3), U. *endendu* from *\*en-tend-* (156), U. *combifiatu* from *\*com-fif-* (161), U. **anzeriatu** from *\*an-ser-* (110, 1). A possible, but uncertain, example of such a change even reacting on the simplex is U. **menes** (125, 2, *a*).

But the influence of the simplex is sometimes seen, e.g. U. *an-ferener* (not *mb* by 161), U. *an-dirsafust* (not *nn* by 135), O. **kúm-bened** (not *mm* by 125, 2).

## Accent

**165.** 1. WORD-ACCENT. The Latin accentual system, based on the quantity of the penult, is comparatively late, having been preceded by a system, dating from the Italic period, according to which the accent stood always on the first syllable. Whether this initial accent was preserved in Oscan-Umbrian or replaced by some such system as arose in Latin, cannot be determined.

*a.* There are certain phonetic changes, such as the simplification of double consonants (163), which with added material may prove to be connected with an accentual system like the Latin, but at present the evidence is far from conclusive.

2. SENTENCE-ACCENT. There is substantial agreement with the Latin. For pronominal enclitics, see 201; for enclisis of personal pronouns, see 86, 3; for that of the indefinite pronouns cf. O. *suaepis* (usually so written), U. **svepis**, etc.; — for that of the verb ‘to be’, cf. O. **teremnatust, destrst** (84), **pússtíst** (84, *a*), and also O. **prúftúset, staflatasset, ehpeílatasset**, U. *peretomest, ortoest, parsest* (117, *b*), *mersest, mersi* (132, *a*), etc. (the writing as two words is also found, but less frequently). With L. *quīlibet* compare U. *pisher* (90, 2). The enclitic use of prepositions is far more common than in Latin (299 ff.).

SUMMARY OF THE OSCAN AND UMBRIAN SOUNDS[1]

**166.**      OSCAN

### a

a, written a, *a*,

    = orig. *a*, e.g. ant 'ante'. **32.**

    = anaptyctic *a*, e.g. aragetud 'argento'. **80, 81.**

### ā

ā, written a, aa, *a*,

    = orig. *ā*, e.g. aasas 'arae' (Gen. Sg.). **33.**

    = orig. *a* with secondary lengthening, e.g. saahtím 'sanc-
        tum'. **73.**

### ę

ę, written e, *e*,

    = orig. *e*, e.g. estud, *estud* 'esto'. **36.**

    = anaptyctic *e*, e.g. Herekleís 'Herculis'. **80, 81.**

    in *er* = *ro* or *ri*, e.g. Aderl. 'Atella'. **91, 2.**

### ę̄

ę̄, written e, ee, *e*,

    = orig. *e* with secondary lengthening, e.g. keenzstur, *censtur*
        'censor'. **41,** *b*, **73, 76, 77, 1.**

### i̧

i̧, written í, *i*,

    = orig. *i*, e.g. pis, *pis* 'quis'. **44.**

    = orig. *e* in hiatus, e.g. íúk, *ioc* 'ea'. **38, 1.**

    = anaptyctic *i*, e.g. *amiricatud* '*immercato'. **80, 81.**

    = orig. *e* in medial syllables before labials, e.g. *nesimois*
        'proximis'. **86.**

---

[1] A survey of the Oscan and Umbrian sounds, with their *normal* spellings, and their various *regular* sources. No account is taken here of the spelling of Old Oscan, or of that in the Greek alphabet, for which see **24**; and no attempt is made to cover all the details of the preceding sections. Attention is called by means of asterisks to some of the most important differences between Oscan and Latin. Open and close vowels are distinguished by a hook or a dot placed beneath the letter, e.g. ę = open *e*, ẹ = close *e*.

## į̄

į̄, written í, íí, *i*,
   = orig. *ē*, e.g. **ligatúís** 'legatis', *ligud* 'lege', **fíísnú** 'templum'. 41.
   = *ē* from contraction, e.g. **trís** 'tres'. 41, *a*, 82.

## į

į, written í, *i*,
   = orig. *į* by samprasāraṇa, e.g. **púatirís** 'posterius'. 44, *b*, 91, 1.
   = orig. *i* before *i̯*, e.g. **fakiiad** 'faciat'. 44, *a*.
   NOTE. Or is the difference from í only graphic ?

## ị̄

ị̄, written í, íí, *i*,
   = orig. *ī*, e.g. Abl. Sg. **slaagid, líímítú[m** 'limitum', *scriftas* 'scriptae'. 47.
   ? = orig. *ū* in final syllables, e.g. *castrid*. 59.

## ǫ

ǫ, written ú, *o*,
   = orig. *o*, e.g. **púd,** *pod* 'quod'. 49.
   = orig. *e*, in *\*pompe* 'quinque'. 37.
   = anaptyctic *o*, e.g. **tefúrúm** 'burnt-offering'. 80, 81.

## ǭ

ǭ, written ú, *o*,
   = orig. final *ā*, e.g. **víú** 'via', *allo* 'alia'. 34.

## u

u, written u, *u*,
   = orig. *u*, e.g. **puf** 'ubi'. 55.
   = anaptyctic *u*, e.g. **Mulukiis** 'Mulcius'. 80, 81.
   = orig. *o* before final *m*, e.g. *ezum* 'esse'. 50.
   = orig. *a, e,* or *o* in medial syllables before (or after) labials,
        e.g. *praefucus* 'praefectus', *pertumum* 'perimere'. 86.
   = orig. *u̯* by samprasāraṇa, e.g. *facus* 'factus'. 91, 1.

ịu (*precise sound uncertain*)

ịu, written iu, *u*,
   = *u* after dentals, e.g. eítiuvam, *eituam* 'pecuniam'. 56.

ū

ū, written u, uu, (ú), *u*,
   = orig. *ū*, e.g. Fuutreí 'Genetrici'. 58.
   = orig. *ō*, e.g. estud, *estud* 'esto', Fluusaí 'Florae'. 53.

ai

ai, written aí, *ae* (*ai*),
   = orig. *ai* (or *āi*), e.g. svaí, *suae* 'si'. 62 (60), (61, 3).

ei

ei, written eí, *ei*,
   = orig. *ei* (or *ēi*), e.g. deíkum, *deicum* 'dicere'. 64 (60), (61, 3).

oi

oi, written úí, *oi*,
   = orig. *oi* (or *ōi*), e.g. lígatúís 'legatis', *nesimois* 'proximis'.
   66 (60), (61, 3).

au

au, written av, au, *au*,
   = orig. *au*, e.g. avt, *auti* 'aut'. 68, 61, 2.

eu

eu occurs only in the borrowed Evklúí. 70.

ou

ou, written úv, *ou*,
   = orig. *ou* or *eu*, e.g. túvtíks 'publicus', *touto* 'civitas'. 71,
   61, 2.

### i̯ (*consonantal i*)

i̯, written i, *i*,

  = orig. i̯, e.g. **kúmbennieís** 'conventus'. 100.

  = initial *di̯*, e.g. Iúveí 'Iovi'. 134.

### u̯ (*consonantal u*)

u̯, written v, *u*,

  = orig. u̯, e.g. **svai**, *suae* 'si'. 101, 102.

Note. But when i̯ and u̯ are merely glides following a vowel *i* or *u* they are written in the native alphabet, but not in the Latin. 31.

### r

r = orig. *r*, e.g. **Regatureí** 'Rectori'. 103.

  = intervocalic *rs*, e.g. **terúm** 'territorium'. 115, 1.

  = final *rs*, e.g. *censtur* 'censores'. 117.

rr = intervocalic *rs*, e.g. h]erríns 'caperent'. 115, 2.

  = *ri̯* at Bantia, e.g. *herest* 'volet'. 100, 3, *c*.

### l

l = orig. *l*, e.g. *ligud* 'lege'. 104, 105.

  = final *ls*, e.g. **aídil** 'aedilis'. 119, 2.

ll = orig. *rl*, e.g. **Abellanam** 'Abellanam'. 103, 3.

  = orig. *l* by secondary doubling, e.g. **Vítelliú** 'Italia'. 162, 1.

  = orig. *nl*, e.g. **Vesulliaís** 'Vesulliais'. 107, 3.

### n

n = orig. *n*, e.g. *ni* 'ne'. 107.

nn = orig. *nd*, e.g. **úpsannam** 'operandam'. 135.

  = orig. *n* by secondary doubling, e.g. **kúmbennieís** 'conventus'. 162, 1.

For omission of *n* before consonants, see 108, 2, 3.

### m

m = orig. *m*, e.g. **Maatreís** 'Matris'. 107.

For rare omission of final *m*, see 109, 2.

### s

s  = orig. *s*, e.g. *estud* 'esto'. **111, 114.**

  = *ks* before consonants, e.g. **destrst** 'dextra'st'. **145, 1.**

  = *ti̭* at Bantia, e.g. *Bansae* 'Bantiae'. **100, 3,** *c.*

**s(s)**= final *ks*, e.g. **meddíss,** *meddis* 'meddix'. **145, 2.**

    = final *fs* from -*bh*(*o*)*s*, e.g. **teremníss** 'terminibus', *ligis* 'legibus'. **124,** *a.*

    = final *ns*, e.g. Acc. Pl. **víass,** *eituas.* **110, 2.**

    = *ps*, e.g. *osii*[*ns* 'adsint'. **122, 2.**

    = dental + *s*, e.g. **Fíísíais** '\*Fisiis'. **137, 1.**

    = dental + dental, e.g. Fερσορει '\*Versori'. **138.**

    = *s* by secondary doubling, e.g. **kvaísstur** 'quaestor'. **162, 2.**

**ks,** written **ks,** *x,*

    = intervocalic *ks*, e.g. **eksuk** 'hoc', *exac* 'hac'. **145, 3.**

    = *ki̭* at Bantia, e.g. *meddixud* 'magisterio'. **100, 3,** *c.*

**ts,** written **z,** *s,*

    = secondary *ts*, e.g. **puz,** *pous* 'ut'. **137, 2.**

    **nts** = orig. *ns*, e.g. **keenzstur,** *censtur* 'censor'. **110, 1.**

**ns**  = secondary *ṅs*, e.g. *Bantins* 'Bantinus'. **110, 6, 128, 1.**

### z (*as in Eng. zero*)

z, written **s,** *z,*

  = intervocalic *s*, e.g. Gen. Pl. **-asúm,** -*azum.* **112.**

  = *di̭* at Bantia, e.g. *zicolom* 'diem'. **100, 3,** *c.*

### p

p  = orig. *p*, e.g. *post* 'post'. **120.**

  = orig. *ku̯*, e.g. *pod* 'quod'. **150.**

### b

b  = orig. *b*, e.g. **trííbúm** 'domum'. **123.**

  = orig. *gu̯*, e.g. **kúmbened** 'convenit'. **151.**

  **br** = orig. *pr*, e.g. **embratur** 'imperator'. **157, 1.**

### t

t  = orig. *t*, e.g. **trís** 'tres'. **126.**

## d

d  = orig. *d*, e.g. *deicum* 'dicere'. **130, 133.**

  = final *t*, e.g. **deded** 'dedit'. **127, 1.**

  dr = orig. *tr*, e.g. **Sadiriis** 'Satrius'. **157, 2.**

## k

**k**, written **k**, *c*,

  = orig. *k*, e.g. **deikum**, *deicum* 'dicere'. **141.**

  = orig. *ku̯* (*gu̯*), e.g. **fruktatiuf** 'fructus'. **153, 154.**

  kl = orig. *tl*, e.g. **sakaraklúm** 'sacellum'. **129, 2.**

## g

g  = orig. *g*, e.g. **aragetud** 'argento'. **147, 1.**

  ngl = orig. *nkl*, e.g. *ungulus* 'anulus'. **155.**

## f

**f**  = orig. *bh* (L. *f*, *b*), e.g. **fratrúm** 'fratrum', **sifei** 'sibi'. **124.**

  = orig. *dh* (L. *f*, *b*, *d*), e.g. **fakiiad** 'faciat', **Lúvfreis** 'Liberi',

      **mefiai** 'mediae'. **136.**

  = orig. *gu̯h* (L. *f*, *v*, *gu*). **152.**

  = final *ns* of secondary origin, e.g. **úittiuf** 'usus'. **110, 5.**

  fr = orig. *sr*, e.g. **tefúrúm** 'burnt-offering'. **118.**

  ft = orig. *pt*, e.g. *scriftas* 'scriptae'. **121.**

## h

h  = orig. *gh* (L. *h*), e.g. **humuns** 'homines'. **149.**

  = *k* before *t*, e.g. **ehtrad** 'extra'. **142.**

**167.**                 **UMBRIAN**

## a

**a**, written **a**, *a*,

  = orig. *a*, e.g. **patre** 'patri'. **32.**

## ā

**ā**, written **a**, **ah**, *a*, *ah*, *aha*,

  = orig. *ā*, e.g. **fratrum** 'fratrum'. **33.**

  = orig. *a* with secondary lengthening, e.g. **sahta**, *sahatam*

      'sanctam'. **73.**

### å̊

å̊ (long rounded *ā*), written **a, u,** *o,*
  = orig. final *ā*, e.g. **vatuva, vatuvu,** *uatuo.* **34.**

### e

e, written **e,** *e* (rarely **i,** *i*),
  = orig. *e,* e.g. **fertu** 'ferto'. **36.**
  = final *i,* e.g. *ote* 'aut'. **43.**

### ę̄

ę̄, written **e, eh,** *e, ee, eh, ehe* (very rarely **i,** *i*),
  = orig. *ai* (or *āi*), e.g. **pre,** *pre* 'prae'. **63 (60).**
  = orig. *ei* (or *ēi*), e.g. **etu,** *eetu* 'ito'. **65 (60).**
  = orig. *e* with secondary lengthening, e.g. **e-, eh-,** *e-, ehe-*
    'ex'. **75-77.**

### ē̦

ē̦, written **e,** *e,* **i,** *i,* **ei** (rare), *ei,*
  = orig. *ē,* e.g. **habetu,** *habitu* 'habeto'. **42.**
  = orig. *oi* (or *ōi*) in final syllables, e.g. Dat.-Abl. Pl. **-es,** *-ir,*
    *-eir.* **67, 2 (60).**

### į̄

į̄, written **i,** *i,* and, in the case of orig. *i,* frequently **e,** *e,*
  = orig. *i,* e.g. **pire, pere,** *pirsi,* etc. 'quid'. **45.**
  = orig. *e* in medial syllables before labials, e.g. *nesimei*
    'proxime'. **86.**

### į̦̄

į̦̄, written **i, ih,** *i, ihi,* **ei** (rarely **e,** *e*),
  = orig. *ī,* e.g. **persnimu,** *persnihimu,* etc. 'precator'. **48.**
  ? = orig. *ū* in monosyllables etc., e.g. *pir* 'ignis'. **59.**

NOTE. For the five preceding sounds both the letters *e* and *i* are employed,
but with different relative frequency, as indicated.

## ǫ

ǫ, written **u**, *o*,

    = orig. *o*, e.g. *post* 'post'. **49.**

    = orig. *u* before *m*, e.g. *somo* 'summum'. **57.**

    = secondary *u* before *m*, from *e*, e.g. *hondomu* 'infimo'. **86.**

## ǭ

ǭ, written **u**, *o*,

    = orig. *au*, e.g. **ute**, *ote* 'aut'. **69.**

    = orig. *ou* (*eu*), e.g. **tuta**, *totam* : O. *touto*. **72.**

    = orig. *oi*, e.g. *pora* 'qua' : O. *poizad*. **67, 1.**

## ọ

ọ, written **u**, *o*, *u*,

    = orig. *ō*, e.g. *nome* 'nomen', Abl. Sg. -*u*. **54.**

## u

u, written **u**, *u*,

    = orig. *u*, e.g. **pufe** 'ubi'. **55.**

    = orig. *a* or *e* in medial syllables before labials, e.g. **prehubia**
          'praehibeat'. **86.**

    = orig. *o* before *r*, e.g. *curnaco* 'cornicem'. **51.**

## ū

ū, written **u**, **uh**, *u*,

    = orig. *ū*, e.g. *mugatu* 'muttito'. **58.**

## ai

ai, written **ai**, *ai*,

    = orig. *ak* before *t*, e.g. **aitu**, *aitu* 'agito'. **143.**

    = orig. *ai* before *i̯*, e.g. **pernaiaf** 'anticas'. **61, 3.**

## ei

ei, written **ei**, *ei*,

    = orig. *ek*, or *ēk* with *ē* from *ei* or *ai*, e.g. **teitu**, *deitu*
          'dicito'. **143.**

    = orig. *ei* before *i̯*, e.g. **Teteies**(?). **61, 3.**

    For the *spelling ei*, see **29** with *a*.

## i̯

i̯, written ı, *i*,
     = orig. i̯, e.g. *iouies* 'iuvenibus'. **100.**
     = initial di̯, e.g. **Iuve**, *Ioui*. **134.**

## u̯

u̯, written **v**, *u*,
     = orig. u̯, e.g. **via**, *uia* 'via'. **101, 102.**
     = initial *l*, e.g. **vutu** 'lavato'. **104.**

But when i̯ and u̯ are merely glides following a vowel *i* or *u*, they are written in the native alphabet, but not in the Latin. **31.**

## r

**r**  = orig. *r*, e.g. **rehte** 'recte'. **103.**
     = intervocalic (and sometimes final) *s*, e.g. Gen. Pl. *-arum*. **112, 113.**
     = final *rs*, e.g. *ager* 'ager'. **117.**
       For omission of *r*, see **115, 116.**

## l

**l**  = orig. *l*, e.g. *plener* 'plenis'. **105, 1.**
       For omission of *l*, see **105, 2.**
     ll = orig. *nl*, e.g. *Padellar* 'Patellae'. **107, 3.**

## n

**n**  = orig. *n*, e.g. *nome* 'nomen'. **107.**
       For omission of *n*, see **108, 1, 109, 1.**
     = initial *gn*, e.g. **natine** 'natione'. **147, 2.**
     nn, written n, *n*, rarely *nn*,
       = orig. *nd*, *dn*, e.g. *pihaner* 'piandi'. **135.**

## m

**m**  – orig. *m*, e.g. **Matrer** 'Matris'. **107.**
       For omission of final *m*, see **109, 1.**

## s

**s** = orig. *ṣ*, e.g. *est* 'est'. **111, 113** ff.

   = *ks* before consonants, e.g. *destram-e* 'in dextram'. **145, 1.**

   = *ps* before consonants, e.g. *ostendu* 'ostendito'. **122, 1.**

   = final *ks*, e.g. *uas* 'vitium'. **145, 2.**

   = final *fs* from *-bh(o)s*, e.g. **avis** 'avibus'. **124,** *a.*

**s(s)** = intervocalic *ks*, e.g. *essu*, **esu** 'hoc'. **145, 3.**

     = intervocalic *ps*, e.g. *osatu* 'facito'. **122, 2, 3.**

     = dental + *s*, e.g. *Fiso* 'deo Fidio'. **137, 1.**

     = dental + dental, e.g. *sesust* 'sederit'. **138.**

**ts,** written **z, s,**

       = secondary *ts*, e.g. **taçez,** *tases* 'tacitus'. **137, 2.**

     **nts** = orig. *ns*, e.g. **antermenzaru** 'intermenstrium'. **110, 1.**

**ns** = secondary *ns*, e.g. **Ikuvins** 'Iguvinus'. **110, 6, 128, 1.**

## ç, ś (*precise sound uncertain*)

The sibilant written **ç, ś, s,**

   = orig. *k* before *e, i,* etc., e.g. **taçez,** *tases* 'tacitus'. **144.**

## ř, rs (*precise sound uncertain*)

The sound written **ř, rs** (sometimes **r,** *r,* *s*),

   = intervocalic *d*, e.g. **peři,** *persi* 'pede'. **131, 132.**

   = (rarely) intervocalic *l*, e.g. **kařetu,** *carsitu* 'calato'. **106.**

## p

**p** = orig. *p*, e.g. *pre* 'prae'. **120.**

   = orig. *ku̯*, e.g. **piř-e** 'quidquid'. **150.**

## b

**b,** written **b** (sometimes **p**), *b,*

   = orig. *b*, e.g. **kebu** 'cibo'. **123.**

   = orig. *gu̯*, e.g. *benust* 'venerit'. **151.**

   **mb** = orig. *mbh*, e.g. *ambr-* 'amb-'. **161.**

   **br** = orig. *pr*, e.g. *subra* 'supra'. **157, 1.**

## t

**t** = orig. *t*, e.g. **etu** 'ito'. **126.**

     For omission of final *t*, see **127, 2.**

## d

**d**, written t, *d*,

= orig. *d*, e.g. **tuves**, *duir* 'duobus'. **130**.

= orig. *d̯ꭐ*, e.g. *di-fue* 'bifidum'. **102, 3.**

**dr** = orig. *tr*, e.g. *podruhpei* 'utroque'. **157, 2.**

**nd** = orig. *nt*, e.g. *ander* 'inter'. **156.**

= orig. *ndh*, e.g. *ahauendu* 'avertito'. **161.**

## k

**k**, written **k**, *c* (rarely *q*),

= orig. *k*, e.g. **kanetu** 'canito', *procanurent* '*procinuerint'. **141.**

= orig. *kꭐ* (*gꭐ, gꭐh*), e.g. **fiktu** 'figito'. **153, 154.**

**kl** = orig. *tl*, e.g. *pihaclu* 'piaclo'. **129, 2.**

## g

**g**, written **k**, *g*,

= orig. *g*, e.g. *ager* 'ager'. **147, 1.**

**ng** = orig. *nk*, e.g. *iuengar* 'iuvencae'. **156.**

= orig. *ngh, ngꭐh*, e.g. *cringatro* 'cinctum'. **161.**

## f

**f** = orig. *bh* (L. *f, b*), e.g. **fratrum** 'fratrum', **alfu** 'alba'. **124.**

= orig. *dh* (L. *f, b, d*), e.g. **façiu** 'facere', **rufru** 'rubros'. **136.**

= orig. *gꭐh* (L. *f, v, gu*), e.g. **vufetes** 'votis'. **152.**

= *ns*, e.g. **vitluf** 'vitulos'. **110, 2, 3, 4, 5.**

For omission of final *f*, see **110, 2, a.**

**fr** = orig. *sr*, e.g. *tefru-to* 'ex rogo'. **118.**

**rf** = *rs* (from *r(e)s, rss*), e.g. *trahuorfi* 'transverse'. **115, 2, 3.**

## h

**h** = orig. *gh* (L. *h*), e.g. *homonus* 'hominibus'. **149.**

(**h**)t = orig. *kt*, e.g. **rehte** 'recte'. **142.**

= *ft* from *pt*, e.g. **screhto** 'scriptum'. **121.**

= *ft* from *dht*, e.g. **vetu** 'dividito'. **136, a.**

As the *h* in *ht* was almost or wholly lost in pronunciation (**75, 121**, etc.), it does not properly belong under the *sound h*, but is placed here for convenience.

For the use of the letter *h* as a sign of hiatus, see **83.**

For the omission of initial *h*, see **149, a.**

# INFLECTION

## NOUNS [1]

On the general system of declension, see 12.

### FIRST DECLENSION

**168.** Examples of Declension.

|  | OSCAN | UMBRIAN |
|---|---|---|
|  | *Singular* |  |
| NOM. | víú, *touto*, τωϝτο | muta, mutu |
| GEN. | vereias, *eituas* | tutas, *totar* |
| DAT. | deívaí | tute, *tote* |
| ACC. | víam, *toutam* | tuta, *totam* |
| VOC. |  | *Tursa* |
| ABL. | eítiuvad, *toutad* | tuta, *tota* |
| LOC. | viaí, *Bansae* | tafle, *tote* |
|  | *Plural* |  |
| NOM. | aasas, *scriftas* | urtas, *iuengar* |
| GEN. | eehiianasúm, *egmazum* | urnasiaru, *pracatarum* |
| D.-A. | kerssnaís | tekuries, *dequrier* |
| ACC. | víass, *eituas* | vitlaf, *uitla* |

### Remarks on the Case-Forms

**169.** 1. NOM. SG. The original ending *-ā* is not shortened as in Latin, but is changed in quality. See **34**.

2. GEN. SG. The original ending *-ās*, preserved in Latin only in the phrases *pater familiās* etc., remains unchanged, except for the rhotacism in the later Umbrian. See **113**.

---

[1] As the declension of adjectives is like that of nouns (see **187**), some adjective forms are included in the paradigms.

In the Plural, the case which is called simply the Dative-Ablative is of course in reality the Dative-Ablative-Locative.

3. DAT. SG. The original ending -*āi* was shortened to -*ai*, which remained in Oscan, but became -*ē* in Umbrian. See **60, 62, 63.**

4. ACC. SG. The original ending -*ām* retains the long vowel. See **78**, 1. For the omission of final *m*, see **109.**

5. VOC. SG. This is found only in the Umbrian proper names *Tursa, Iouia, Prestota, Serfia.* These forms certainly represent the old Voc. in -*a*, not the Nom. in -*ā*, since in all the occurrences, nearly fifty in number, the spelling is uniformly *a*, never *o*.

6. ABL. SG. The ending is -*ād*, which arose in the Italic period after the analogy of -*ōd*. In Oscan the *d* is retained, as in early Latin *sententiād* etc., but is lost in Umbrian. See **133.**

7. LOC. SG. The ending is identical with that of the Dative. But in Umbrian, in this and other declensions, the postpositive *en* 'in' is frequently employed, either separately as in **tafle e**, or with contraction, yielding a form in -*en*, as **arven**, or oftener in -*em*, as *Acersoniem* (see **109**, 1). And since a final nasal is oftener omitted than written, many, perhaps all, of the noun-forms in -*e* are to be regarded as compounded with -*en*, rather than as simple Locatives.

   *a.* Noteworthy are the phrases *ocrem Fisiem* beside *ocre Fisie*, and *toteme Iouinem, toteme Iouine*, beside *tote Iouine*. The extension of *m* to the adjective forms, as if it were a part of the real case-ending (cf. O. **húrtín Kerriín, 171,** 7), was probably favored by the parallelism between Locatives with and without *m* and Accusatives with and without *m*, where the *m* of course appears in the adjective also. That is, the Loc. *ocre(m) Fisie* became *ocre(m) Fisie(m)* after Acc. *ocre(m) Fisi(m)*. In *toteme* with *e(n)* added again to the already compounded *totem* the influence of Acc. forms like *totam-e* (cf. *destram-e* etc.) is also probable.

8. NOM. PL. The ending is the original -*ās*, which is seen in Sanskrit and Gothic, but which in Latin and Greek has been supplanted by -*ai* modeled after the -*oi* of the Second Declension. The only change is the rhotacism in the later Umbrian (**113**).

9. GEN. PL.   The ending is *-āsōm*, seen in Homeric *-άων* and belonging originally to the Pronouns (Skt. *tấsām*).   The Umbrian shows rhotacism like the Lat. *-ārum*, while in Oscan only the intermediate stage *z* has been reached.   See 112.   The *o* of the last syllable was probably still long (78, 4, note).

10. DAT.-ABL. PL.   The ending is *-ais* like the Greek *-αις*, both modeled after the *-ois* of the Second Declension.   The *ai* remains in Oscan, but changes to *ē* in Umbrian, as in Latin to *ī*.   See 62, 63.   Rhotacism occurs in later Umbrian,[1] and also in Old Umbrian before the postpositive *en*, e.g. fesner-e 'in fano'.   See 113 with *a*.

11. ACC. PL.   All forms of Italic (as well as of Greek) go back to an ending *-ans*, which, modeled after the *-ons* of the Second Declension, has replaced an older *-ās*.   The *ns*, which in Latin loses the *n* with lengthening of the preceding vowel, becomes O. *-ss*, *-s*, U. *-f*, the latter being very frequently omitted.   See 110, 2.

12. MASCULINE ă-STEMS.   There are several examples of the Nom. Sg. of Masculine proper names belonging to this declension.   Some are borrowed from the Greek, but are without the final *s*; e.g. Santia, Arkiia — Ξανθίας, Ἀρχίας.   But there are also some which seem to represent a genuine Italic formation in *-as*; e.g. Tanas, Markas, Maras, Μαραϛ.   For the oblique cases there is little material.   An Acc. form is seen in Velliam.   The Gen. Sg. Maraheis, if not simply a mistake for *Marahieis from Nom. Marahis (176, 4), stands for *Marā-eis, with the same adoption of the *o*-stem ending that is seen in Grk. *-āo*, and also in L. *-āī*, except that in the latter it is not restricted to Masculines.

---

[1] The term later Umbrian is used instead of the specific New Umbrian, so as to include V a–V b 7, which is Old Umbrian, but later than I–IV, and in the rhotacism of final *s* goes with the New Umbrian (see 113), e.g. plenasier urnasier (V a 2). Similarly in 2 and 8, above, though there happen to be no examples of the Gen. Sg. or Nom. Pl. of this declension in V a–V b 7. The -r forms of 171, 2, 8, 10, are all from this passage.

## SECOND DECLENSION

**170.** Examples of Declension.

|        | OSCAN | UMBRIAN |
|--------|-------|---------|
|        | *Singular* | |
| Nom.   | húrz, *Bantins* | Ikuvins, *ager* |
| Gen.   | sakarakleís | katles, *popler* |
| Dat.   | húrtúí | kumnakle, *pople* |
| Acc.   | húrtúm, *dolom* | puplu(m), *poplo(m)* |
| Voc.   |  | Serfe, *Tefre* |
| Abl.   | sakaraklúd, *dolud* | puplu, *poplu* |
| Loc.   | tereí, *comenei* | kumne, *onse* |

|        | *Plural* | |
|--------|----------|---------|
| Nom.   | Núvlanús | Ikuvinus, *Iouinur* |
| Gen.   | Núvlanúm, *zicolom* | pihaklu, *pihaclo* |
| D.-A.  | Núvlanúís, *zicolois* | veskles, *uesclir* |
| Acc.   | feíhúss | vitluf, *uitlu* |

|        | *Nom.-Acc. Neuter* | |
|--------|--------------------|---------|
| Sg.    | sakaraklúm, *touticom* | persklum, *persclo* |
| Pl.    | prúftú, *comono* | iuku, iuka, *uatuo* |

### Remarks on the Case-Forms

**171.** 1. Nom. Sg. The *o* of the original *-os* (so in the earliest Latin inscriptions) is everywhere dropped (90, 91). For forms like O. húrz, U. taçez, *tases*, see 137, 2; — U. *ager* from *\*agros*, 91, 2, 117; — O. *famel*, U. katel (Acc. katlu), tiçel (Acc. tiçlu), from *-elos*, 36, 2, 88, 4, 119, 2; — similarly O. Aukíl, Mutíl, from *-ilos*, Paakul from *-ulos* (cf. gentiles Muttillieis, Pakulliis, with doubling of *l*), 119, 2; — O. Mitl, Fiml, probably for *\*Mitel*, *\*Fimel* (like *famel*), 91, 2, *a*; — O. Upfals, Upils, from *-llos* (cf. Gen. Sg. Upfalleis), 119, 2; — O. *facus*, *praefucus*, from *-ṷos*, 91, 1. For *ịo*-stems, see 173, 1.

2. Gen. Sg. The ending is *-eis*, borrowed from the Third Declension, where it represents the original ending of *i*-stems, as vice versa the Acc. Sg. of consonant-stems follows that of

the *o*-stems.   In Umbrian the *-eis* appears as -es, -er, *-er* (65, 113), rarely -e, *-e* (113, *b*).   For O. Πακϝης etc., see 24.

3. DAT. SG.   The original ending *-ōi* has been shortened to *-oi*, which remains unchanged in Oscan and becomes a monoph-thong in Umbrian.   The only corresponding form in Latin is *Numasioi*, the usual ending *-ō* coming from *-ōi* by a different process.   See 60, 66, 67, 2.   The Umbrian forms usually show e, *e*, but occasionally i, *i* or *ei*, e.g. **Tefri**, *fratreci*, *Tefrei*.

a. U. **Trebo**, **Fiso**, for earlier **Trebe**, **Fise**, show a transfer to the Fourth Declension.   In O. **Pakiu** and **Verehasiú** the omission of i is simply a mistake.

4. ACC. SG.   The original ending was *-om*, as in the earliest Latin inscriptions.   In Oscan it is usually written **-úm**, *-om*, occasionally -um, *-um* (50).   In Umbrian the vowel is always *o* in the Latin alphabet.   For omission of the final *m*, see 109.

5. VOC. SG.   The original ending *-e* is preserved as in Latin.   The only examples are from the Umbrian.   With *Tefre* compare *puere* in Plautus.

6. ABL. SG.   The *d* of the original *-ōd* is retained in Oscan, as in early Latin *preivātōd* etc., but dropped in Umbrian.   See 133.   The vowel is written **ú** or u in the Oscan native alphabet, but always *u* in the Latin, and in Umbrian also nearly always *u*.   See 53, 54.

a. On the Iguvinian Tables, among over 100 occurrences, there is only one certain instance of an Ablative in *-o* (*somo*, VI a 10), apart from adverbs like *eso* (see 54, note, 190, 2, note).   But as there seems to be something artificial in this uniformity of spelling (see l. c.), there is no objection on this score to taking *maronato* (no. 83) as Abl. Sg. of an *o*-stem (cf. Loc. Sg. *maronatei*, no. 84), though some assume that it is Loc. Sg. of a *u*-stem.   See 302.

7. LOC. SG.   The original *-ei* from which comes the Lat. *-ī* is retained in Oscan, becoming an *-ē* in Umbrian.   See 64, 65.   A fusion of this Locative with the postpositive *-en* is to be seen in O. **húrtín Kerríín**, where the apparent ending *-ín* (from *-ēn*, *-ei-en*; 41, *a*, 82, 1) is extended to the adjective.   Otherwise Oscan has the simple Locative.   In Umbrian the combination with *-en* is frequent, perhaps even universal.   See 169, 7.

8. Nom. Pl. In Latin, as in Greek, the pronominal ending *-oi* has completely displaced the old noun-ending *-ōs*, but in Oscan-Umbrian the leveling has been in the opposite direction, and both nouns and pronouns show *-ōs*. This appears in Oscan as *-ús, -us* (*ius-c* 'ii'), in Umbrian as *-us, -u, -ur, -ur*. See 53, 54, 113.

9. Gen. Pl. The ending is *-ōm*, which in Latin becomes *-om, -um* (*deum* etc.), so far as it is not replaced by the secondary *-ōrum*. It appears in Oscan as *-úm, -um*, once *-om, -ουμ*, or *-oμ*, in Umbrian as *-u, -o(m)*. See 53, 54, 78, 4, 109, 1.

10. Dat.-Abl. Pl. The ending is *-ois* (Grk. *-οις, -οισι*; see 60, *a*), which becomes L. *-īs*. It appears in Oscan as *-úís, -ois*, in Umbrian as *-es* (*-er-e*), *-e, -er* (once *-is*), *-ir* (*-is-co*), *-er, -eir*, the usual forms being *-es* and *-ir* (over 100 examples of *-ir* including *-isco*, 7 of *-eir*, 6 of *-er*). See 66, 67, 2, 113 with *a, b*.

11. Acc. Pl. The ending is *-ons* (or *-ōns*; see 74, note), whence L. *-ōs* by loss of *n* and vowel-lengthening. For the change of *-ns* to O. *-ss*, U. *-f*, and the frequent omission of the latter, see 110, 2. For the long vowel in Umbrian, usually written *u*, rarely *o*, see 74, 54.

*a*. Several Umbrian forms with *o* which were once taken as Masc. are more probably Neuter (see below, 13), and the existence of any Masc. forms with *o* is denied by some. But there is nothing incredible in the appearance of U. *o* for *ō* (see 54), and any other explanation than as Acc. Pl. Masc. is too forced in the case of *uiro, ueiro* 'viros', and *pesondro* 'figmenta'(?) in VI b 37 (Masc., as shown by *pesondro sorsalem* VI b 39; Pl., as shown by *sufuf* in the parallel passage I a 33). Probable examples also are *ehiato* 'emissos' VII b 2, agreeing with *pifi* 'quos' (other explanations less likely), and *abrof*, **apruf** 'apros' (regarded by some as for *abronf*; cf. abrunu, abrons, 181, *b*).

12. Nom.-Acc. Sg. Neuter. This has exactly the same history as the Acc. Sg. Masc.

13. Nom.-Acc. Pl. Neuter. The ending is *-ā*, and in the Italic period this was extended to the Neuters of the Third and Fourth Declensions. This *-ā*, which thus became the ending of all Neuters, has the same history as that of the Nom. Sg. of the First Declension, being shortened in Latin, and appearing in Oscan as *-ú, -o*, in Umbrian as *-a, -u, -o*. See 34.

But in Umbrian there are also some Nom. Pl. forms in -*or* and some Acc. Pl. forms in -u(f), -*o*(*f*), which seem to be Neuters (of various declensions) with *r* and *f* added after the analogy of the corresponding cases of Masc. *o*-stems. This extension probably started with the Acc., where it was favored by the existence of Masc. forms with and without *f*, and spread to the Nom. Examples are: Nom. *uasor* (stem *u̯ās*-, Abl. Pl. **vasus**); — *tuderor* (stem *tuder*-, Acc. Sg. *tuder*, Abl. Pl. *tuderus*), with the adjectives in agreement *totcor* and *screihtor*: — so probably *arsmor* with *dersecor subator* in agreement; — Acc. **krematruf** beside **krematru**, **krematra**: — **kastruvuf** beside **kastruvu**, *castruo* (*u*-stem, O. Gen. Sg. *castrous*); — *uerof-e*, **veruf-e** (O. **veru** Acc. Pl. Neut., rather than Acc. Sg. Masc.; cf. **veruis**).[1]

14. GENDER. An example of a Fem. *o*-stem is O. **Eídúís** 'Idibus' (**Eídúís Mamerttiaís**), the Latin cognate being a Fem. *u*-stem. O. **trííbúm** is also Fem. (**trííbúm ekak**), but as only the Acc. Sg. and Abl. Sg. (**tríbud**) occur, it may be taken as a consonant-stem.

### i̯o-STEMS

172. Examples of Declension.

|      | OSCAN *Singular* | | UMBRIAN |
|------|-------------------|---|---------|
| NOM. | Pakis, degetasis | | *Atiersir* |
| GEN. | Dekkieis, kúmbenniefs | | **Marties**, *Fisier* |
| DAT. | deketasiúí | | **Iuvie**, *Fisi* |
| ACC. | Pakim | | *Fisi*(*m*) |
| VOC. | | | *arsie* |
| ABL. | *meddixud* | | *Fisiu* |
| LOC. | | | *Fisie* |

---

[1] I have adopted Thurneysen's view (K.Z. 32, 554 ff.; cf. also I.F. Anz. 9, 185), but am more thoroughly convinced of its truth for the Acc. forms cited than for the Nom. forms, for which the older explanation is by no means impossible (-*or* graphic variant of -*ur*; for *vasor*, *tuderor*, metaplasm as in L. *vās*, *vāsa*, *vāsōrum*, and in *terminus*, *terminōs*, *termina*, which occur side by side in the Sententia Minuciorum). I do not follow Thurneysen in assuming that all Acc. forms in -*o*(*f*) must be Neuter. See above, 11, *a*.

|  | OSCAN | UMBRIAN |
|---|---|---|
|  | *Plural* |  |
| Nom. | degetasiús | Atiieřiur, *Atiersiur* |
| Gen. | Tirentium | Atiieřiu, *Atiersio* |
| D.-A. | Dekmanniúís | Atiieřies, *Atiersier, Atiersir* |
| Acc. |  | feliuf, *filiu* |

### *Nom.-Acc. Neuter*

| Sg. | *medicim*, memnim, Safinim    ařkani, *tertim* |
|---|---|
| Pl. | arvia, arviu |

### Remarks on the Case-Forms

**173.** 1. Nom. and Acc. Sg. M. and Nom.-Acc. Sg. N. The forms come from -*įos*, -*įom* by samprasāraṇa (**91**, 1). For the quality of the resulting *i* (O. i, not í, U. -*i(m)*, not *e(m)*), see **44**, **45**, *a*. U. *Fisei*, which occurs once, is one of the few examples of *ei* for short *i* (**29**). Like O. Mais from *\*Maijos* (Dat. Sg. Maiúí) are U. peřaem (Acc. Sg. M.), peřae, *persae* (Nom.-Acc. Sg. N.), from *\*pedaijom* (Acc. Pl. F. peřaia, *persaea*), but with -*e(m)* for -*i(m)* after the preceding vowel; here perhaps U. *difue* 'bifidum' (Acc. Sg. N.) from *\*duį-fuįom* (or *i*-stem?).

2. Dat. Sg. In Umbrian, uncontracted and contracted forms are found side by side (**82**, 2), about evenly divided in Old Umbrian, but with a great preponderance of contracted forms in New Umbrian. Thus *Fisie* (1), *Fisi* (12), *Fisei* (1). Once *Sansii* beside *Sansie, Sansi*.

3. Dat.-Abl. Pl. Contracted forms (**82**, 2) are found only in New Umbrian, as *Atiersir, Clauerni*. Variations of the final are the same as in other *o*-stems (171, 10, 113 with *a*, *b*), e.g. Atiieřies, Atiieřier (V), Atiieřie, Klaverniie, etc. But *Clauerni* is the only case of omitted -*r* in a noun-form (see 113, *b*).

4. The other case-forms are like those of the ordinary *o*-stems, with the usual Umbrian variations in spelling, for which see **171**. For the absence of contracted forms of the Gen., Voc., and Loc. Sg., see **82**, 2, *a*. For O. *meddixud* from *\*meddikįōd*, see 100, 3, *c*.

5. But there are some examples of transfer to the *i*-stem forms. Thus in the Abl. Sg., beside the forms given in the paradigms, we find O. **serevkid, prupukid, medikid** (probable reading), probably from *\*seruikio-, \*prō-pak-io-, \*meddik-io-*, rather than from original *i*-stems. A similar transfer is probable in U. **arvis, arves,** Dat.-Abl. Pl. to **arvia** '*\*arvia, frumenta', since a contracted form, even if such were otherwise known in Old Umbrian (see 3), would not have -**es**. As an *i*-stem form the -**es** would not be without parallel (**aves, punes**), though its relative frequency (**arves** 11, **arvis** 2) is surprising.

### Oscan Gentiles in -iis etc.

**174.** Many of the examples of *io*-stems are to be found among the proper names, for which Oscan furnishes copious material. Of forms like O. **Pakis, Dekis,** etc., some are gentiles and some praenomina. But there is also in Oscan, with some few examples in Umbrian, a distinct class of names in -**iis** (-**iís,** -**ies,** -**ιες**), Gen. -**iieís** (-**iíeís**). With the exception of a few forms on carelessly written inscriptions, these are all gentiles. The combination of praenomen in -**is** with gentile in -**iis** is frequent. Thus:

| | |
|---|---|
| Pakis Kluvatiis | Vibis Smintiis |
| Pakim Kluvatiium | Vibis Urufiis |
| Dekis Rahiis | Stenis Kalaviis |
| Dekkieis Rahiieis | Dekis Seppiis |
| Sepis Helevi(is) | Σπεδις Μαμερεκιες |
| Sepíeís [1] Heleviieís | Τρεβις Σεστιες |

Note also praen. **Sepis**: gent. **Seppiis**; — praen. Τρεβις: gent. **Trebiis.**

Further examples from the oblique cases of -**iis** are Gen. Sg. **Aadiieís, Saidiieís, Vírriieís** (also U. **Kluviier, Kastruçiie,** the only Umbrian examples of the type): — Gen. Pl. **Kluvatiium, Magiium, Viriium.** The only Acc. Sg. form is **Kluvatiium.**

---

[1] The first í is simply a mistake. The word occurs on one of the *iovilae* inscriptions, which are notoriously inexact in the use of í.

Examples of forms in -iis are **Aadiriis** (also **Aadíriis**, probably a mistake), **Atiniis, Kiípiís, S]puriis, Viínikiís**; Gen. Sg. **Spuriíeís, Kastríkiíeís**; — Dat. Sg. **Iúvkiíúí, Vestiríkiíúí.**

In the Greek alphabet we find -ιες, as Πομπτιες = **Púntiis**, Μαμερεκιες, etc.; also Αϝδειες = **Avdiis**. The few examples in the Latin alphabet have -*ies*, as *Afaries*, and ·such forms are common also in Paelignian, as *Ponties*, *Loucies*, etc. The spelling -**ies** in the native alphabet is very rare.

**175.** As is well known, the Latin gentiles are in origin patronymic adjectives formed with the ?o- suffix from individual names (that is, in terms of the fully developed system the praenomina), just as in certain Greek dialects patronymics in -ιος are regularly used in place of the usual Genitives of the father's name. So *Mārcius* from *Mārcus*, *Tullius* from *Tullus*, etc. To such forms correspond the Oscan gentiles in -**is**. But there are also in Latin praenomina in -*ius*, as *Lūcius*, *Servius*, etc., and in Oscan the praenomina in -**is** are very numerous. From such praenomina, it is clear, are formed the Oscan gentiles in -**iis** etc. That is, the gentile **Trebiis** stands in the same relation to the praenomen Τρεβις, as gent. **Heírennis** to praen. **Heírens**, or as Latin gent. *Mārcius* to praen. *Mārcus*. The only uncertainty is as to the precise form of the suffix and the actual pronunciation.

There are three possibilities for the suffix, namely 1) -*iio*-, 2) -*iio*-, 3) both -*iio*- and -*iio*-, the latter in the case of forms in -iis. The probability is in favor of the first. Not only is -*iio*- the suffix most natural to assume, whether as the inherited by-form of -*io*- thus turned to special account, or as actually formed from -*io*- in the Italic[1] or Oscan-Umbrian period, but it is also the one which best harmonizes with the usual spelling of the oblique cases. That is, in **Dekkieís Rahiieís** we have the same relation between i = *i* and ii = *ii* that is elsewhere observed (**31**).

---

[1] Any such differentiation between -*io*- and -*iio*-stems would necessarily be lost in Latin in most cases, since postconsonantal *i* becomes vocalic (e.g. *medius* from \**medhio*-). A possible trace is the difference between praen. *Gāius* (from \**Gāuios* before the change of *i* to *i*) and gent. *Gāvius*, but even this is uncertain, as *Gāvius* might be regarded simply as the older form retained in use in the gentile.

The Nominative in -iis from -*ijos* is best explained by the assumption of samprasāraṇa in the last syllable. That is, as \**Pak-jos* became **Pakis** (173, 1), so \**Kluvati-jos* became **Kluvatiis**. Against this it may be urged that we should then expect also Acc. \***Kluvatiim**,like **Pakim**, but it is possible that **Kluvatiium**, if this single occurrence is representative of the usual form, involves a restoration under the influence of **húrtúm** etc.

But in the Nom. forms, owing probably to dissimilation, the second vowel differed somewhat in quality from the first, and this is brought out in the spelling -ies, -ies. The same thing is indicated by the spelling -iis, and wherever this was in vogue the ií in place of ii was extended to the oblique cases. The forms in -iis, -iieis, then, which are preferred in the Cippus Abellanus and many of the Pompeian inscriptions, but are not found elsewhere, represent simply a graphic variation of the usual type and not an independent formation.

**176.** 1. Although the interchange of -iis with -is reflects in general an earlier interchange of -*ijos* with *jos*, yet in many instances the Nom. in -iis may be formed, at a comparatively late date, directly from the Nom. in -is, after the analogy of the usual relation between the two. Thus **Mahii[s** is formed from **Mais**, **Mais**, or rather from \***Mahis** with the spelling implied by the abbreviation **Mh.** For **Mais** comes through \**Maijos* (Dat. Sg. **Maiiúí**), from \**Mag-jos* (147, 3), and an inherited by-form \**Mag-ijos* would yield O. \***Magiis**, which is actually represented by Gen. Pl. **Magiium**. So probably **Ieiis** from praen. \***Ieis** (like **Mais**) from \**Ieijos*, \**Iegjos*, the original by-form \**Ieg-ijos* surviving in L. *Iegius*.

2. Similar examples are **Rahiis** 'Raius' (Gen. **Rahiieis**) from praen. \***Rahis**, \**Raijos*, and **Staiis** 'Staius' from praen. \***Stais**, \**Staijos*, except that in these *ij* does not come from *gj*.

3. The spelling í instead of i (44, *b*) in \***Stais**, **Staiis**, \***Ieis**, **Ieiis**, as in **Mais** beside **Mais**, and in **Vesulliais**, is due to the influence of the many words containing the diphthongs aí, eí.

4. The relation of gent. *Maraies*, Gen. Sg. **Maraiieis** to praen. **Marahis**, Gen. Sg. **Marahieis** is probably the same as that of **Mahii[s** to **Mais**, \***Mahis** (**Mh.**), except in the matter of spelling, the examples being from different localities and showing an extension of the *h*, which belongs to the Nom. Sg. as a mark of hiatus, to the oblique cases of the praenomen rather than to those of the gentile. The forms then go back to \**Maraijos*, related to Fal. *Mareio* and L. *Marius*. For the praen. **Maras**, Μαραϛ (with Gen. **Maraheis** ?), from the simpler stem *Marā-*, see 169, 12.

5. In **Dekis Hereiis**, Gen. **Dekkieis Heriieis** (no. 40), either **Hereiis** is a mistake for \***Heriis**, or **Heriieis** for \***Hereiieis** (with suffix -*eijo*-, 253, 2). The former is more probable. **Virriiis** (no. 20) beside **Virriis**, **Virriieis**, etc., is simply a careless spelling, rather than a different form with suffix -*eijo*- (253, 3). For U. **Teteies** (II a 44), probably 'Tetteius', see 61, 3, 253, 2.

## THIRD DECLENSION

**177.** The Latin Third Declension represents a partial fusion of consonant-stems and *i*-stems. In Oscan-Umbrian too there is a fusion in certain cases, but the distinction between the two classes is more faithfully preserved than in Latin. In the Acc. and Abl. Sg. there is no encroachment of the consonantal forms upon the *i*-stems, as in L. *-em*, *-e*, beside *-im*, *-i*; and in the Nom. Pl. the forms are as distinct as in the Gen. Pl. In the Dat.-Abl. Pl. the fusion exists in Oscan as in Latin, while in Umbrian consonant stems follow the *u*-stems. The relation of the two types may be seen from the following:

|  | *A.* CONSONANT-STEMS | *B.* I-STEMS |
|---|---|---|
| | *Singular* | |
| NOM. | O. meddíss | O. aídil, U. *fons* |
| GEN. | O. medíkeís (U. -es, -er) | O. *aeteis* (U. -es, -er) |
| DAT. | O. medíkeí (U. -e, -e) | O. Fuutreí (U. -e, -e) |
| ACC. | O. *tanginom* (U. -u, -o) | O. slagím (U. -e(m), e(m)) |
| ABL. | O. *ligud* (but U. kapiře) | O. slaagid (U. -i, -i) |
| LOC. | U. ferine, *ferine*(?) | U. *ocre* |
| | *scalsi-e*(?) | |
| | *Plural* | |
| NOM. | O. meddíss, humuns | O. trís, aídilis (U. -es, -er) |
| GEN. | O. fratrúm (U. -u(m), -o(m)) | O. a]íttíúm, U. *peracnio* |
| D.-A. | O. *ligis* (but U. *fratrus*) | O. luisarifs, Anafríss (U. -is, -is) |
| ACC. | O. malaks, usurs, U. *nerf* | U. trif, *trif*, *auif* |
| | *Nom.-Acc. Neuter* | |
| SG. | U. tuplak, *pir*, *nome* | U. *uerfale*, *sehemeniar* |
| PL. | (see 178, 12) | U. triia, triiu-per, *trio-per* |

### Remarks on the Case-Forms

**178.** 1. NOM. SG. Owing to the syncope of *i* in the *-is* of *i*-stems, the ending becomes identical with that of most consonant-stems. For the loss of *s* in aídil, see 119, 2. For peculiarities in the different classes of consonant-stems, see 179–182.

2. GEN. SG.  The *-eis*, representing the normal formation for *i*-stems as seen in various languages, has been extended to consonant-stems.  In Latin, vice versa, the *-is* from *-es*, which belongs properly to the consonant-stems, has been extended to *i*-stems.  For U. -es, -er, see **65**.

3. DAT. SG.  The *-ei* belongs properly to the *i*-stems, of which it is an old Loc.  The Latin *-ī*, early *-ei*, may be the same, or may stand for *-ai*, the old Dat. of consonant-stems, or may represent both.  For U. -e, -e, see **65**.

4. ACC. SG.  The *-im* of *i*-stems, only partially preserved in Latin, remains undisturbed.  In Umbrian the spelling *-im* occurs in a few instances, but nearly always we find -e(m), -e(m), indicating the open quality of the *i* before final *m* (**45**, *a*).  Thus **spantim, ahtim-em**, but **uve(m), perakne(m), Tařinate**, *ocre(m)*, *stafla-re(m)*, *Tarsinatem*, etc.  This *-em* has of course no connection with the Latin *-em*, which is not from *-im* but represents the ending of consonant-stems.

In consonant-stems the original *-em* (from -m̥) has wholly disappeared in favor of *-om*, which is borrowed from the *-o*-stems.

5. ABL. SG.  The ending of *i*-stems is *-īd*, identical with L. *-ī*, early *-īd*.  In Umbrian the spelling is usually -i, -i (-ei), rarely *-e* (cf. **48**); e.g. **puni** (22 times), *poni* (12), *pone* (1), **ukri-pe(r)** (9), *ocri-per* (16), *ocre-per* (3).

In consonant-stems there is a difference between Oscan and Umbrian.  In Oscan we find the ending of *o*-stems, as in the Acc.; e.g. **tanginúd, tanginud**, *tanginud*.  But in Umbrian it is *-e* as in Latin, e.g. **kapiře, karne**, *curnase, frite* (from *\*frēt-* : L. *frētu-* ; Abl. more likely than Loc., see **294**), etc.  This is probably a Loc. in origin, with *-e* for original *-i*.

*a.* O. *praesentid* shows the form of an *i*-stem, just as in Latin the Present Participles show *-ia*, *-ium*, regularly, and often -ī beside -e in the Abl.  U. **peři**, *persi, persei-co* (aes *persti-co*), is also an example of the encroachment of the *i*-stem ending, as in early Latin *airīd* etc.

6. LOC. SG.  The proper endings are *-ei* (from *-ēi* or *-eii*) for *i*-stems, and *-i* for consonant-stems.  Owing to the absence

of Oscan examples and the ambiguity of the Umbrian -*e*, which
may come from -*ei* (65) or -*i* (43), the history of the case is not
altogether certain, but there is no objection to supposing that
*ocre* contains the ending -*ei* (for *ocrem* see 169, 7), and that in
*ferine* the -*e* comes from -*i*. This last is favored by *scalsie*,
apparently for *scalsi-e(n)* (cf. *scalse-to* 'ex patera') with the original *i* retained before the enclitic.

NOTE. U. *ferine* is obviously a consonant-stem as if L. *\*feriōne* (see 181),
but the phrase in which it occurs is so obscure that it is uncertain whether it is a Loc.
'in feretro' (L. *ferō*) or Abl. 'cultro' (L. *feriō*), though the former is more probable.

7. NOM. PL. The ending of consonant-stems is -*es* (Grk. -ες,
Skt. -*as*, etc.), which in Latin is completely displaced by the -*ēs*
of *i*-stems. With syncope of the *e* it appears in O. **humuns** etc.
See 90, 1. For *i*-stems the ending is -*eies* (Skt. -*ayas*), whence -*ēs*
which appears in Latin and in O. **trís** and in U. **puntes**, *pacrer, foner*.
See 82, 1, 41, *a*. But O. **aídilís** (also **fertalis**, if Nom. Pl.), with **i**
instead of **í**, points to a different formation, probably -*īs*, following
the analogy of -*ās*, -*ōs*, in the First and Second Declensions.

8. GEN. PL. The endings are -*ōm* and -(*i*)*ŏm*. For
O. a]**íttíúm**, see 162, 1.

9. DAT.-ABL. PL. The ending of *i*-stems is -*ifos*, from -*ibhos*,
whence comes the Latin -*ibus*. This becomes by syncope -*ifs*,
which is found in a single Oscan form of very early date, **luisarifs**.
All other examples show assimilation of the *fs* (124, *a*). Thus
O. **Anafríss**, **sakriss**, U. **avis**, **puntis**, *sacris*, etc., also **aves**, **punes**, with
**e** for **i** (45), and once **sevakne** with omission of the **s** such as
occurs elsewhere only in the case of original final *s* (113, *b*). The
single occurrence of *ei* in *aueis* is not sufficient ground for supposing that the simplification of *fs* was accompanied by vowel-
lengthening. See 29.

Consonant-stems show the *i*-stem form in Oscan as in Latin,
but in Umbrian follow the *u*-stems. Thus O. *ligis*, but U. *fratrus, homonus*, **karnus**, etc.

10. ACC. PL. The ending of *i*-stems is -*ins* (or -*īns*; see
74, note), whence L. -*īs* by loss of *n* and vowel-lengthening.

This would give O. -*iss*, like -*ass*, -*úss*, of the First and Second Declensions, but examples are wanting. Umbrian examples are trif, tref, tre, *trif*, *treif*, avif, *auif*, *aueif*, *auuei*, etc. For the change of final *ns* to *f* and the frequent omission of the latter, see 110, 2. For the long vowel indicated by the spelling *ei*, see 74.

For consonant-stems the ending is -*ens* (from -*n̥s*), whence L. -*ēs* by the same process as -*īs* from -*ins*. This would give O. -*ess*, U. -*ef*, for which, however, we find O. -*s*, U. -*f*. The Oscan form might be the result of syncope, but this could not be assumed for Umbrian, if the vowel in -*ef* was long (74). The change may be due to the analogy of the Nom. Pl. in -*s* (from -*es*), since in the other declensions the -*f* stands in the same relation to the stem as the -*s* of the Nom. Pl. But see 74, note.

The probable Oscan examples are usurs 'osores'(?) and malaks 'malevolos'(?). In Umbrian we have *nerf* (ner-, 180, 2), manf (man-, otherwise *manu*-), capif, kapi (also kapiř by mistake) from \**kapid-f* (189, 1), *uapef-e* from \**u̯aped-f*, *uef* from \**u̯eif-f* (186, *a*), *frif* from \**frūg-f* (147, 4). For U. *abrons*, see 181, *b*.

11. Nom.-Acc. Sg. Neuter. The -*i* of *i*-stems may remain as U. -*e* (43), or be dropped (92), just as in Latin we have *sedīle*, but *animal* etc. Thus U. *sacre*, *uerfale*, etc., but *sehemeniar*. Examples of consonant-stems are U. tuplak (192, 1), *pir* (180, *d*), nome (181), etc.

12. Nom.-Acc. Pl. Neuter. The ending -*ā*, belonging properly to *o*-stems, has been generalized, giving -(*i*)*i̯ā* for *i*-stems and -*ā* for consonant-stems, which then undergo the usual change of final *ā*. See 34, 171, 13. Examples from *i*-stems are U. triia, triiu-per, *trio-per* (192, 2), sakreu, perakneu (e for i, 45). From consonant-stems the only Umbrian examples are of the secondary type in -*or*, as *tuderor* from *tuder*- etc. See 171, 13. O. teremniú beside teremnïss 'terminibus' is either an example of the encroachment of the *i*-stem ending, or else comes from a stem *termeni̯o*-, an extension of *termen*-. An original *i*-stem *termeni*- is less probable. For O. *petora* 'quattuor' (Festus), which may possibly contain the old ending of consonant-stems, -*a*, I.E. -*ə*, see 191, 4.

## Types of Consonant-Stems

**179.** **Mute-Stems**

|  | OSCAN | UMBRIAN |
|---|---|---|
| | | *Singular* |
| Nom. | meddíss, *meddis* | zeřef, *serse* |
| Gen. | medíkeís | —— |
| Dat. | medíkeí | kapiře, *capirse* |
| Acc. | —— | *capirso*, erietu, *curnaco* |
| Abl. | *ligud* | kapiře, *curnase* |
| Nom.-Acc. Neut. | | tuplak, huntak |

*Plural*

|  | OSCAN | UMBRIAN |
|---|---|---|
| Nom. | meddíss, μεδδειξ | —— |
| Gen. | líímítú[m | —— |
| D.-A. | *ligis* | kapiřus, *uapersus* |
| Acc. | malaks | *capif, uapef-e, uef, frif* |

*a.* For the consonant-changes in Nom. Sg. meddíss and Nom. Pl. meddíss, see 145, 2; for U. zeřef, 110, 4; for U. Acc. Pl. *capif* etc., 178, 10.

### Liquid Stems

**180.** 1. Agent-nouns in -*tōr*-, like Latin *victor, victōris.*

|  | OSCAN | UMBRIAN |
|---|---|---|
| | | *Singular* |
| Nom. | *censtur*, keenzstur, kvaís- stur, embratur | ařfertur, *arsfertur*, kvestur, uhtur |
| Gen. | —— | —— |
| Dat. | kvaístureí, Regatureí | ařferture, speture |
| Acc. | —— | *arsferturo*, uhturu |
| Abl. | —— | —— |

*Plural*

|  | OSCAN | UMBRIAN |
|---|---|---|
| Nom. | kenzsur, *censtur*, kvaízstur | —— |
| Acc. | usurs | —— |

## 2. Nouns of Relationship, like Latin *pater, patris*

| | OSCAN | | UMBRIAN |
|---|---|---|---|
| | | *Singular* | |
| NOM. | patir, niir | | —— |
| GEN. | Maatreís | | *Matrer* |
| DAT. | Pateref | | Iuvepatre |
| ACC. | —— | | —— |
| VOC. | —— | | Iupater |
| ABL. | —— | | —— |

| | | *Plural* | |
|---|---|---|---|
| NOM. | —— | | frater, *frateer, frater* |
| GEN. | fratrúm, *nerum* | | fratru(m), *fratrom* |
| D.-A. | —— | | fratrus, *fratrus, nerus* |
| ACC. | —— | | *nerf* |

*a.* The Nominative Singular preserves the original long vowel (Grk. -ηρ, -ωρ, Skt. -ā, etc.), which is shortened in Latin. See **78**, 2. In the other cases we have, as in Latin, -tōr- in agent-nouns, but -tr- in nouns of relationship, except in the Vocative Singular. See **97**.

O. **Fuutreí, Futreí** 'Genetrici', Gen. **Futre[ís**, apparently follows the declension of nouns of relationship, but the existing case-forms may belong equally well to an *i*-stem, and the word is perhaps a relic of the old Feminine formation of agent-nouns (Skt. -tr-ī), which in Latin nearly always appears in an extended form (*gene-tr-ī-x* etc.).[1]

*b.* For the Nom. Pl. in -*r* from -*r*(*e*)*s*, see **117**; for U. *frateer*, see **76**, 3; for O. -*rs* in the Acc. Pl., see **117**, *a.*

*c.* O. **niir**, *nerum*, U. *nerf, nerus*, etc., correspond to Grk. ἀνήρ, Skt. *nar-*, Nom. Sg. *nā́* 'man', Gen. Pl. *narā́m* (Vedic).

*d.* Neuter *r*-stems are: U. **utur** 'aquam' (Grk. ὕδωρ), with Abl. Sg. **une** (*udne*; see **135**, *a*) from an *n*-stem (cf. L. *femur, feminis*); — U. Nom.-Acc. **pir**, *pir* 'ignis' from *pūr (Grk. πῦρ; see **59**), with Abl. Sg. **pure**, *pure-to*, from a stem *pur-*. From *pure-to* arose, after the analogy of the Masculines, Acc. Sg. *purom-e* beside the regular *pir.*

---

[1] The history of the word would be simplified, could we accept the suggestion of De Saussure and Thurneysen (I.F. Anz. 9, 184) that it is not, as commonly supposed, a derivative of *fŭ-* with causative meaning 'cause to be, create', but the equivalent of Grk. θυγάτηρ, Skt. *duhitā́*, etc. But, without attempting to discuss here the complicated phonetics of this group of words, it is safe to say that we should expect in Oscan either *Fuktreí or *Fuhtreí. That the latter should appear three times without h would do for Umbrian, but not for Oscan (**142**).

### 181. Nasal Stems

| MASCULINES AND FEMININES | NEUTERS |
|---|---|

**Singular**

| | | |
|---|---|---|
| NOM. | O. fruktatiuf, úíttiuf, tríbarak-kiuf, U. tribřiçu, karu | U. numem, *nome*, umen |
| GEN. | O. *tangineis*, kú]mparakineís, *carneis* | U. *nomner, pelmner* |
| DAT. | O. leginei, sverrunei, U. karne | U. *nomne* |
| ACC. | O. leginum, *tanginom, medicatinom*, U. abrunu | U. numem, *nome* |
| ABL. | O. tanginúd, tanginud, *tanginud*, U. natine, *tribrisine*, karne | U. *nomne*, umne, tikamne |
| LOC. | U. ferine, *ferine* (?) | |

**Plural**

| | | |
|---|---|---|
| NOM. | O. humuns | [O. teremenniú] |
| GEN. | O. —— | —— |
| D.-A. | U. *homonus*, karnus | O. teremníss |
| ACC. | U. manf | —— |

a. Most of the Masc. and Fem. forms belong to the type of L. *legiŏ, -iŏnis*, but in the oblique cases show the suffix in the reduced grade -*ĭn*- (95 ; the vowel-length is shown by the Oscan spelling i, not í ; see 47). In O. **statíf** 'statua' (in form L. *statiŏ*) the reduced grade appears also in the Nom., but the í is strange (hardly -*ĭn*- beside -*ĭn*-).

b. The type of L. *sermŏ, -ŏnis* is represented by O. sverrunei, humuns (cf. early Latin *hemŏnem*), U. *homonus*, abrunu (as if L. *aprŏnem*). U. *abrons*, VIIa 43, used as Acc. Pl., is probably the Nom. form written by mistake for *abronf*.

c. U. karu, Gen. Sg. O. *carneis*, etc., agree with L. *carŏ, carnis* in showing the reduced grade of the suffix in the oblique cases.

d. The Oscan Nom. Sg. in -f represents -*ns*, with n introduced from the oblique cases, and s added after the analogy of other Nominatives. The Umbrian forms probably represent the same type with the final f omitted, rather than the formation in -*ŏ* like the Latin. See 110, 5.

### S-Stems

**182.** Examples of *s*-stems are : U. meřs, *mers* 'ius', Dat.-Abl. Pl. mersus (132, *a*) ; — O. Dat.-Abl. Pl. aisusis 'sacrificiis' ;—

U. Dat.-Abl. Pl. **vasus** 'vasibus' (cf. L. *vās*), Nom. Pl. *uasor* (171, 13);
— O. **far**, U. *far* 'far' (from *\*fars* ; see 117), Gen. Sg. *farer* (instead
of *\*farser*, under the influence of the Nom.); — U. Acc. Sg. *tuder*
'finem' (see 181, *a*), Dat.-Abl. Pl. *tuderus*, Nom. Pl. *tuderor* (171,
13), Acc. Pl. *tudero* ; — U. *ose* 'opere'(?).   U. *pars* in *pars-est* 'par
est' seems to be like *\*fars, far*, with *rs* preserved before the
enclitic (117, *b*), but the relation to L. *pār, paris* is not wholly
clear.

### Irregular Nouns

**183.** The nouns corresponding to L. *Iuppiter, bōs*, and *sūs*
show the following forms :

1. Gen. Sg. O. **Iúveís** ; Dat. Sg. O. **Diúveí**, Διουϝει, **Iuveí**,
U. **Iuve**, *Iuue* ; Acc. Sg. U. *Dei* ; Voc. Sg. U. **Iupater**, *Di, Dei*.

2. Acc. Sg. U. **bum** ; Abl. Sg. U. *bue* ; Gen. Pl. U. *buo* ;
Acc. Pl. U. **buf**, *buf*.

3. Acc. Sg. U. **sim**, **si** ; Acc. Pl. U. **sif**, *sif, si*.

*a.* The relation between O. **Iúveís** and **Diúveí** is the same as between
L. *Iovis* and early *Diovis* (see **134**). For O. Διουϝει see **24**, *a*.   U. *Iuue* for
*\*Ioue* is due to the influence of the Old Umbrian spelling.   U. **Iupater**, like
L. *Iūpiter* (*Iuppiter*), is from *\*Dįeu-pater* (Grk. Ζεῦ πάτερ).   U. *Di, Dei*, are prob-
ably from the stem seen in L. *diēs, Diēs-piter*, with contraction (**82**, 2).

*b.* U. **bum**, *buf*, are from *bō-* (cf. Grk. Dor. βῶν, βῶs), and this form of the
stem has spread to the other cases, replacing *bou-* of L. *bove* etc.

*c.* For U. **sim**, **sif**, etc., see **59**.

## FOURTH DECLENSION

**184.** Examples of Declension.

|      | OSCAN | UMBRIAN |
|------|-------|---------|
|      | *Singular* | |
| Nom. | —— | —— |
| Gen. | *castrous* | *trifor* |
| Dat. | —— | *trifo*, **Ahtu** |
| Acc. | [*manim*] | **trifu**, *trifo* |
| Abl. | [*castrid*] | [**mani**, *mani*, **trefi**, **ařputrati**] |
| Loc. | —— | **manuv-e** |

|  OSCAN | UMBRIAN |
|--------|---------|
| | *Plural* |
| N.-A. NEUT. | berva, *castruo*, kastruvuf |
| GEN. | *pequo(?)* |
| D.-A. | berus |

### Remarks on the Case-Forms

**185.** 1. GEN. SG. Oscan shows the original ending -*ous* (Skt. -*ōs*, Goth. -*aus*, etc.), whence U. -*or* (72, 113), and L. -*ūs*.

2. DAT. SG. U. *trifo* (also *Fiso*, *Trebo*, with transfer from the *o*-stems; see 171, 3, *a*) may be combined with the Latin Dative in -*ū* on the basis of a form in -*ou*. This is probably an old Locative, seen in U. manuv-e with the diphthong preserved before the enclitic, the -*ou* coming from -*eu* (70), this from -*ēu* (60; cf. Skt. -*āu*).

3. ACC. SG. For U. -*o* from -*um*, see 57. O. *mánim* cannot be reasonably explained from \**manum* and must be an *i*-stem form, due perhaps to the Ablatives in -*id*.

4. ABL. SG. See 59 with note.

5. LOC. SG. For U. manuv-e, see above, 2.

6. NOM.-ACC. PL. NEUTER. The ending is -*uā* with -*ā* from *o*-stems (171, 13), showing the usual change of final -*ā* (34). For U. kastruvuf beside *castruo*, see 171, 13.

7. DAT.-ABL. PL. The ending -*us* is from -*ufs*, -*ufos*, -*ubhos* (L. -*ubus*), and this has been extended to consonant-stems (178, 9).

8. GENDER. As in Latin, *u*-stems are regularly Fem. (cf. U. trefiper Iiuvina) or Neuter. But U. *mani*, in contrast to L. *manus*, is Masc. (*mani nertru*).

### FIFTH DECLENSION

**186.** The Fifth Declension is represented by only a few scattering forms, namely:

DAT. SG. O. Kerrí 'Cereri'; — U. rí 'rei'; — U. *auie* 'augurio' (stem *auiē*- more probable than *auiā*- or *auio*-, on account of aviekate, *auiecla*).

ABL. SG.   U. **ri** 're'.
ACC. PL.   U. *iouie.*
DAT.-ABL. PL.   U. *iouies.*

*a.* The ending of the Dat. Sg. is *-ē*, from *-ēi*, like L. *-ō* from *-ōi* in the Second Declension (**60**). Cf. L. *faciē* etc. quoted by grammarians.

*b.* O. **Kerrí** represents a transfer from an original *s*-stem. Nom. Sg. \**Kerēs* (L. *Cerēs*) became \**Kerrēs* under the influence of Gen. Sg. \**Kerreis* from \**Ker(e)seis* etc., and this was drawn into the analogy of forms of the Fifth Declension, just as was in part L. *plēbēs.*

## ADJECTIVES

### DECLENSION

**187.** As in Latin, adjectives are declined according to the First and Second Declensions or according to the Third.

1. A large proportion of the existing forms follow the First and Second Declensions. Examples:

O. **túvtíks** 'publicus', Nom. Sg. F. *toutico,* Acc. Sg. N. *touticom ;* — U. *todcom* (Acc. Sg. M.), Nom. Pl. N. *totcor* (**171**, 13), Dat.-Abl. Pl. *todceir.*

O. **múiníkú** 'communis' (Nom. Sg. F.), Acc. Sg. F. **muinikam**, Abl. Sg. F. **múiníkad**, Loc. Sg. N. **múiníkei**.

U. **Ikuvins** 'Iguvinus', Gen. Sg. F. **Iiuvinas**, Dat. Sg. F. **Ikuvine**, Acc. Sg. F. *Iiouinam,* Abl. Sg. F. **Ikuvina**, Loc. Sg. F. *Iiouine, Iouinem* (**169**, 7, *a*), Nom. Pl. M. **Ikuvinus**.

*a.* Just as the pronominal adjectives in Latin show pronominal forms in the Gen. Sg. and Dat. Sg., so in Oscan we find Dat. Sg. *altrei* 'alteri', not \**altroi.* See **195**, *c.*

But in the Gen. Sg. there is no special pronominal ending, and Masc. and Fem. forms are kept distinct (**195**, *b*). Hence it is useless to assume pronominal declension for O. *minstreis* to account for its use with *aeteis* (*minstreis aeteis* 'minoris partis'), a word which is elsewhere Fem. (cf. a]**ittiúm alttram** 'portionum alteram'). We must rather assume local variation in the gender of the noun.

2. Adjectives of the Third Declension are mostly *i*-stems. Thus O.-U. *sakri-* beside *sakro-* (cf. early L. *sacrēs porcī* etc.; the Oscan and some of the Umbrian examples are used substantively, while the forms of *sakro-* are all adjectives), e.g. O. **sakrím**

(Acc. Sg. M.F.), U. sakre, *sacre* (Acc. Sg. N.), O. sakrid (Abl. Sg.), U. sakreu (Acc. Pl. N.), O. sakriss, U. *sacris* (Abl. Pl.). Cf. also the forms of U. *pacri-, peracni-, seuacni-, peracri-,* etc. Consonant stems are seen in U. tuplak (192, 1) and O. malaks 'malevolos' (?).

a. Observe that U. *pacer* (Nom. Sg.) is both Masc. and Fem., like many early Latin forms in *-er*.

## COMPARISON

### The Comparative

**188.** 1. Corresponding to the Latin Comparative in *-ior* (suffix *-ịes*) are found only a few adverbial forms in *-is* from *-ịos* (L. *-ius*); e.g. O. pústiris : L. *posterius*; — O. *fortis* : L. *fortius*; — O. *mais* 'magis': L. *maius*. See 91, 1.

2. The suffixes *-ero-* and *-tero-*, regular Comparative suffixes in Greek and Sanskrit, are used, as in Latin, in adjectives of time and place, but without the force of Comparatives in the grammatical sense; and, as O. pústiris shows, a regular Comparative could be formed from such adjectives, as in Latin. Examples, including some adverbial forms, are: O. supruis 'superis', U. *subra* 'supra'; — O. pústreí 'in postero', U. *postra* 'posteras, posteriores'; — O. ehtrad 'extra', U. ap-ehtre 'ab extra'; — O. *contrud* 'contra'; — O. Entraí '*Interae'; — U. *pretra* 'priores' from *prai-tero-* (for the form cf. L. *praeter*); — O. *pruter (pan)* 'prius(quam)' from *prō-ter* formed from *prō* like Grk. πρότερος from πρό (cf. also Skt. *prātár*); — O. destrst 'dextra est', U. *destram-e* etc.; — O. hu[n]truis 'inferis', U. *hondra* 'infra', from *hom-tero-* or *homi-tero-* (cf. L. *humus, humilis*); — U. *nertru* 'sinistro': Grk. ἐνέρτερος, νέρτερος (cf. ἔνεροι); — O. nistrus 'propinquos' from *nedh-tero-*[1] (138, *a*; cf. *nessimo-*, 189).

[1] Others derive O. nistrus from *nedh-is-tero-* (cf. 188, 3) and O.-U. *nessimo-* from *nedh-is-ṃmo-* (cf. 189, 3); also O. messimass from *medh-is-ṃmo-*. But it is better not to separate these from the other adjectives of similar use. It is true of course that *-tero-* and *-tṃmo-* are not suffixes of primary derivation; but by the assumed *ned(h)-tero-*, *ned(h)-tṃmo-*, we do not imply derivatives from the verbal root but from an adverbial form, similar to Grk. ὕσ-τερος, Skt. *út-tara-, ut-tamá-,* from *ud-tero-, *ud-tṃmo-*. With the assumed *medh-tṃmo-* compare Goth. *miduma*, Av. *maδəma-*, from *medh-ṃmo-*.

a. The suffix -*tero*- is also frequent, as in Latin and elsewhere, in pronominal adjectives. Thus O.-U. \**potro*- (O. pútúrús-píd etc.): L. *uterque*, Grk. πότερος, etc. (200, 2); — O. alttram 'alteram', alttrei, *altrei*, etc. : L. *alter*; — U. *etru* 'altero', etre, etram-a, etc. from \**e-tero*-: O.Bulg. *jeterŭ* 'some one' (contained also in L. *cētero*- from \**cej-etero*-).

3. A suffix -*is-tero*-, a combination of -*is*-, the reduced form of the suffix -*ies*-, and the -*tero*- just mentioned, is seen in O. minstreis 'minoris' from \**min-is-tero*-, and U. mestru 'maior' from \**maistero*- (with regular monophthongization of the diphthong) for \**mag-is-tero*- (see 147, 3, *a*). Cf. L. *minister, magister*, used substantively.

### The Superlative

189. 1. Nearly all the forms occurring are from adjectives of time and place, corresponding to L. *sum-mus, prox-imus, ul-timus*, etc. with the suffixes -*mo*-, -*emo*- (I.E. -*ṃmo*-), and -*temo*- (I.E. -*tṃmo*-). Thus U. somo 'summum' (57, 125, 1); — O. imad-en 'ab imo' (derivation uncertain; see 114, *d*); — O. pustm[as 'postremae', posmom (139, 2); — O. últiumam 'ultimam'; — U. hondomu 'infimo' (cf. U. *hondra*, 188, 2; for *d*, see 156); — O.-U. *nessimo*- 'proximus' (O. nessimas etc., 15, 3), cognate with O.Ir. *nessam* 'next', from \**nedh-tṃmo*-[1] (138, *a*); — O. messimass 'medioximas'(?) from \**medh-tṃmo*-.[1]  For the vowel-changes in the suffix, see 86, 1.

a. The same suffix -*mo*- appears in ordinals, as U. promom 'primum' etc. (191, 1, 9, 10); — also in U. çimu, *simo* 'retro' from a stem \**ki-mo*-: L. *ci-trā* (cf. also U. çive 'citra', from a stem \**ki-yo*-). Under the influence of the adjectives in -*mo*- was formed \**sēmo*- (U. semu, sehemu 'medio'; see 305) from an adverb \**sēmi* (Skt. *sāmí*, adv., L. *sēmi*-, Grk. ἡμι-, in cpds.).

2. O. ualaemom 'optimum' (also Valaimas) differs from the preceding in meaning and formation.  It seems to contain -*mo*- added to a case-form (Dat.-Loc. Sg.), as perhaps also L. *postrēmus*.  But neither this nor any other explanation is certain.

3. O. maimas 'maximae' from \**maisemo*- (114, *b*) for \**mag-is-ṃmo*- (147, 3, *a*) is parallel to O. minstreis, L. *minister* (188, 3).

---

[1] See footnote, p. 134.

## ADVERBS

**190.** The most common adverbial endings represent stereotyped case-forms. Formations of more obscure origin are seen
in many of the Pronominal Adverbs and Conjunctions (see under
Pronouns, **195** ff. passim, **202**), and in Prepositions (**299** ff.), which
are, in origin, Adverbs of Place.

1. Ablatives in *-ēd* (L. *-ē*, early *-ēd*). Thus O. *amprufid*
'improbe'; — U. prufe 'probe', rehte 'recte', nuvime 'nonum', *nesimei* 'proxime', preve 'singillatim', *trahuorfi* 'transverse', çive 'citra'
(**189**, 1, *a*), etc.

2. Ablatives in *-ōd* (L. *-ō*, early *-ōd* in *porōd*). Thus
O. *contrud* 'contra' (cf. L. *contrō-versus*), *amiricatud* '*immercato'
(see **294**, *a*), suluh 'omnino' (**133**, *a*); — U. *heritu* 'consulto' (**294**, *a*,
**307**), *eso(c)* 'ita', *tertio* (*postertio*) 'tertium', *ulo* 'illuc', çimu, *èimo*
'retro' (**189**, 1, *a*), supru sese 'sursum', testru sese 'dextrorsum'
(cf. *dextrō-vorsum* etc.; for use of sese see **307**), *podruh-pei*
'utroque', etc.

NOTE. Since the Instrumental was merged with the Ablative in prehistoric
times, it is quite possible that this formation is of Instrumental origin. But
that the old Instrumental *form*, without the *d*, is to be recognized in the Umbrian
adverbs, is unlikely, in view of the *d* in Oscan and Latin. We assume, e.g., that
U. *supru* comes from *suprōd*, like O. *contrud*, L. *porōd*. See also **54**, note.

3. Ablatives in *-ād* (L. *-ā*, early *-ād*). Thus O. ehtrad
'extra', s]úllad 'ubique'; — U. *subra* 'supra', *hondra* 'infra'.

*a.* Here belongs also O. *dat* 'de', da(d)-, U. *da-* (**300**, 3), while L. *dē* is from
an *o*-stem (cf. O. *contrud*: L. *contrā*), either Ablative (above, 1) or Instrumental.[1]
The final *t* in O. *dat* arose before words beginning with a surd and was generalized (cf. the opposite process in L. *ob*), a contributory factor being the influence
of ant, ampt, pert, post. A simple error, as in *pocapit* (**127**, 1, *a*), is unlikely,
as the form occurs four times.

4. Ablatives in *-īd* (L. *-ī*, mostly replaced by *-iter*). A
probable example is O. akrid 'acriter'(?).

---

[1] In favor of taking L. *dē* as an Instrumental form may be urged its appearance
as *dē*, not * dēd*, in the S. C. de Bacchanalibus, in which the retention of final *d*, although
archaistic, is absolutely consistent in the body of the inscription.

5. Neuter Accusatives in -*om* (L. -*um*, e.g. *multum*), especially frequent in adverbs of time.   Thus O. *siuom* 'omnino',
*posmom* 'postremum', U. *promom* 'primum'; — similarly U. *duti*
'iterum', *tertim* 'tertium', from *\*dutiom*, *\*tertiom* (172, 173, 1).
Here belong also the pronominal adverbs such as U. *enom*
'tum' and O. *pon* 'cum', U. *ponne*, from *\*pom-de*.   Cf. L. *tum*,
*quom*, *cum*.

6. Neuter Accusatives are also the adverbs of the Comparatives like O. *pústiris* 'posterius' etc. (188, 1), and the conjunctions
O. *pod*, U. *puř-e*, *pirs-e*, etc. (202, 1, 2), U. *eřek*, *erse* 'tum'.   The
Acc. Sg. F. in -*am* is seen only in pronominal forms, like O. *pan*
'quam', U. *pane*, from *\*pam-de*.   Cf. L. *tam*, *quam*.

   a. A probable example of the Acc. Pl. N. is U. *postro*, *pustru* 'retro'
(VIIa 43, 44, Ib 34, 36), since this is hardly to be separated from *postro*, *pustru*,
*pustra*, appearing elsewhere (VIb 5, VIIa 8, IIa 32, IIb 19) as an adjective used
predicatively in the sense of 'retro'.   See 306.

## NUMERALS

### CARDINALS AND ORDINALS

**191.** 1. Cardinal, U. *unu* 'unum'.   Ordinal, U. *prumum*, *promom* 'primum' (adv.) from *\*pro-mo-* (cf. Grk. πρό-μος 'foremost').
The stem *\*prīsmo-*, whence L. *prīmus*, is seen in Pael. *prismu*
'prima'.

2. The cardinal is declined like the Plural of an *o*-stem, the
old Dual inflection being given up even in the Nom., where it
is retained in Latin.   The following forms occur in Umbrian:
Nom. M.F. *dur*, Dat.-Abl. **tuves**, tuver-e, *duir*, Acc. M.F. **tuf** (cf.
also *desen-duf* 'duodecim'), Acc. N. **tuva**.   For the contraction
in *dur*, **tuf**, see 54, 82, 2.

For the ordinal the pronominal **etram-a**, *etru*, etc. (188, 2, *a*)
is used in Umbrian, like *alter* in Latin.   The adverb *\*du-tiom*,
U. *duti* 'iterum' is formed after *\*ter-tiom*, U. *tertim* (3).

   a. The stem *du-* is also seen in U. *du-pla*, tu-**plak** (192, 1), and U. *du-pursus*
'bipedibus'; and *\*dui-* (L. *bi-*, Skt. *dvi-*; see 102, 3) in U. *di-fue* 'bifidum': Grk.
δι-φυής.

3. The cardinal has the regular declension of an *i*-stem, as in Latin. Thus in Oscan Nom. M.F. **tris** (41, *a*, 82, 1), in Umbrian Dat.-Abl. **tris**, Acc. M.F. *trif* etc. (178, 10), Acc. N. **triia** (also *trio-per*, 192, 2).

The ordinal appears in U. **tertiam-a**, *tertiu*, etc., and in the adverb *tertim* from *\*tertiom*.

4. O. *petora* (Festus) is a Nom.-Acc. Pl. N. from a stem *\*qu̯etu̯or-*. Cf. L. *quattuor*, with *a* of doubtful explanation, and Dor. *τέτορα*. If exactly quoted, it retains the old ending of consonant-stems, *-a* (I.E. *-ə*), escaping the usual substitution of *-ā* (171, 13) from the fact that it was no longer felt as an inflected form (cf. L. *quattuor*). But it is also possible that it stands for *\*petoro* with the usual *-ā*, being quoted with Latinized ending. For O. *petiro-pert*, see 192, 2.

The ordinal is probably to be recognized in O. *trutum*, though the translation 'quartum' is disputed. As such it can readily be explained as from *\*ktru-to-* with a reduced form of I.E. *\*qu̯etru-* (cf. L. *quadru-*, Av. *čaθru-*), just as Skt. *turī́ya-* 'fourth' is from *\*kturīya-* (cf. Av. *ā-χtūirya-* beside *tūirya-*).

a. U. *petur-pursus* 'quadrupedibus' shows another form of the stem, namely *\*qu̯etur-* (Skt. *catur-* in cpds.; cf. also *\*qu̯etru-* above).

5. The cardinal *\*pompe* and the ordinal *\*ponto-* are to be assumed from O. **púmperiaís** 'quincuriis', U. **pumperias**, O. **Púntiis**, Πομπτιες 'Quintius', O. *pomtis* 'quinquiens', and U. **puntes** 'pentads.' See 37, 146, 150, 153.

6. The ordinal *\*sesto-* (L. *sextus*; cf. O.-U. *destro-*: L. *dextro-*) is to be assumed from U. **sestentasiaru** 'sextantariarum'.

8. The ordinal stem is seen in O. **úhtavis** 'Octavius'.

9. An ordinal *\*nou̯emo-*, like Skt. *navamá-* but in contrast to L. *nōno-* from *\*nou̯eno-*, is seen in U. **nuvime** 'nonum'.

10. The cardinal is seen in U. *desen-duf* 'duodecim' (144).

An ordinal corresponding to L. *decimus* is implied by O. **Dekmanniúís** '\*Decumaniis'; also a *\*dekento-* (Grk. δέκατος) by O. **deketasiúí** '\*decentarius' according to one interpretation.

*a.* U. **tekvias** 'decuriales' and O. **Dekkviarim** 'Decurialem' are formed with the suffix -*io*- from a stem **deku-** (cf. L. *decussis* and late *decu-plex*), which, like *centu-* in L. *centu-plex* etc., is due to the analogy of **q̆etru* (4). Cf. also U. *dequrier*, **tekuries** 'decuriis'.     *Lith peukeria*

12. U. *desenduf* 'duodecim'.   See 10.  *kelveria*

## DISTRIBUTIVES AND NUMERAL ADVERBS

**192.** 1. Distributives are U. **prever** 'singulis' (17, 10), **tupler** 'binis', *dupla* 'binas', **tripler** 'trinis'. The last two agree with L. *duplus, triplus*, in form but not in meaning. The only multiplicative is U. **tuplak**, Acc. Sg. N. used substantively ('furcam'?): L. *du-plex*, Grk. δί-πλαξ.

2. Numeral Adverbs are U. **triiu-per**, *trio-per* 'ter', O. *petiro-pert, petiru-pert* 'quater'; O. *pomtis* 'quinquiens', U. **nuvis** 'noviens'. With -*pert*, -*per* (127, 3) compare L. *sem-per* etc. It is added to the Neuter Plural in U. **triiu-per** from **triā-pert*, and after the analogy of this form arose **petriā-pert*, whence O. *petiro-pert* (81, 100, 3, *c*). O. *pomtis* and U. **nuvis** cannot be connected with the Latin formation in -*iens* and are probably formed after the analogy of **duis* (L. *bis*) and **tris* (L. *ter*). For the *m* of O. *pomtis*, see 146.

## PRONOUNS

## PERSONAL PRONOUNS

**193.** The few occurring forms of the Personal Pronouns are: FIRST PERSON. U. *mehe* 'mihi'.

SECOND PERSON. O. **tiium**, **tiú** 'tu'; — O. **tfei**, U. **tefe**, *tefe* 'tibi'; — U. **tiu**, *tiom, tio, teio*, 'te'.

REFLEXIVE. O. **sifei** 'sibi'; — U. *seso* 'sibi'; — O. *siom* 'se'.

*a.* The Dative forms *mehe, tefe*, **sifei**, correspond to L. *mihi* etc. and represent **meghei, *tebhei, *sebhei*. The enclitic use of the forms explains the weakening of the vowel in the first syllable in Latin and in O. **tfei, sifei**. See 86, 3.

*b.* U. *seso* is perhaps *se-so, se* being from **s(u̯)oi* (Grk. *oi*) and *so* a particle of unknown connection.

*c.* The Acc. forms U. *tiom*, O. *siom*, perhaps contain *tē* and *sē* with the addition of the particle *-om* seen in O. *píd-um* etc. (**201**, 5). O. **tiium** would then be the same form, used as a Nom., just as, vice versa, in some Doric dialects *τύ* is used as an Acc. Another possibility is that the Nom.-Acc. Sg. Neuter of the Possessive *me(i̯)o-* (L. *meus*) came to be used substantively for both 'ego' and 'me' and that after *meom* arose Nom.-Acc. *teom*, *seom*. For *i* from *e*, see **38**, 1, **39**, 1.

### POSSESSIVE PRONOUNS

**194.** The following forms are found:

SECOND PERSON.    O. **tuvai** 'tuae'; — U. *touer, tuer* 'tui'; — *tuua, tua* 'tua'; — U. *uestra* 'vestra'.

THIRD PERSON.    O. **suveís** 'sui'; — **suvam** 'suam'; — **súvad** 'sua'; — U. *sueso* 'suo' (Loc.).

*a.* The contrast in spelling between U. *touer* and *tuer* and between O. **súvad** and **suveís** (suvam and tuvai, no. 19, are ambiguous) seems to point to the existence of both the stems which are found in other languages, namely *teu̯o-*, *seu̯o-* (early Latin *tovos*, *sovos*), and *t(u)u̯o-*, *s(u)u̯o-* (Skt. *tvá-*, *svá-*). Cf. Grk. *τεός, ἑός*, beside *σός, ὅς*.[1]

*b.* U. *sueso* is probably a Locative *suei + so* (cf. *seso*, **193**, *b*).

## DEMONSTRATIVE PRONOUNS

**195.** The pronoun corresponding in use to the Latin *is* agrees with the latter in the Nominative and Accusative forms (stems *i-* and *e(i̯)o-*, *e(i̯)ā-*; for the *i* in O. **íúk**, *ioc*, etc., see **38**, 1), but the other cases show a stem *eiso-*, O. *eizo-*, U. *ero-*. This perhaps has its origin in a Gen. Pl. *eisōm* (O. **eisun-k**), properly *ei-sōm*, with the regular pronominal ending *-sōm* (Skt. *-sām*; also Italic in *-ā-sōm*), but felt as *eis-ōm* on account of the usual noun-ending. The enclitic *-k* is attached to many of the forms, as in L. *hic*. See **201**, 1.

For the sake of a more complete representation of the cases, the forms corresponding in use to L. *idem* are included in the paradigm, but inclosed in brackets. On the enclitics used, see **201**, 5, 6.

---

[1] The author is unable to accept the view of v. Planta and of Solmsen, Studien z. lat. Sprachgeschichte, 151 ff., that *ou̯* becomes *uu̯* in unaccented syllables. See Verb-System, 175.

| | OSCAN | | | UMBRIAN | | |
|---|---|---|---|---|---|---|
| | M. | N. | F. | M. | N. | F. |
| | | | *Singular* | | | |
| NOM. | *izic* [isídum, (esídum, 44, c)] | ídík | iiuk, íúk, *ioc* | ere(k), *ere(c)* [er-ont, eri-hont] | eřek, *erse* | —— |
| GEN. | eíseís, *eizeís* | —— | | *erer, irer,* erer-ek | | *erar* [erar-unt] |
| DAT. | —— | | —— | | | |
| ACC. | *ionc* | idik, *idic* | íak (108, 2, a) | —— | eřek, *erse* | *eam* |
| ABL. | eísúd, *eizuc* | | eísak, *eizac* | eru-ku, *eru-com* [eru-hu] | | erak [era-hunt, era-font] |
| LOC. | eíseí, *eizeic* | | e]ísaí | —— | | —— |
| | | | *Plural* | | | |
| NOM. | *iusc* [iussu, iusu][1] | —— | —— | [eur-ont] | —— | —— |
| GEN. | eisunk | | *eizazunc* | eru, *ero(m)* | | —— |
| DAT. | *eizois* | | *eiza(i)sc*[2] | [erer-unt[3], erir-ont] | | —— |
| ACC. | —— | *ioc* | —— | —— | *eu, eo* | eaf, *eaf* |

a. U. *erec* and *erse* are certainly equivalent to O. *izic* and *idic*, but, although *e* for *i* is common enough in Umbrian (45), the consistency of the spelling *e* is probably due to the influence of the other case-forms, *erer* etc.

b. The Gen. Sg. U. *erar*, together with O. *ulas* 'illius' (197, 3), shows that, in contrast to Latin, the Feminine was kept distinct from the Masculine.

c. The Dat. Sg. M. and N. of pronominal *o*-stems had the Locative ending *-ei*, as is shown by the pronominal adjective O. *altrei* 'alteri', thus agreeing with the Latin (*illī* etc.). Cf. also U. *esmei* 'huic' (197, 1). The Feminine form was doubtless kept distinct, as in the Genitive. Cf. Loc. Sg. O. e]ísaí.

d. U. *iepi* and *iepru* have been thought to contain case-forms of *erec*, but this is very uncertain.

e. U. eřek, *erse*, Acc. Sg. N., is sometimes used as an adverb 'tum', e.g. VIa 6, where it is correlative with *pirsi* 'cum'.

f. The stem *i-* is seen also in the following adverbs: U. *ife* 'ibi' with the same ending as *pufe* (202, 5), to which belongs perhaps *ef* VIa 4, with loss of

---

[1] See 53, a.     [2] Aes *eizasc*.     [3] Aes *erererunt*.

the final vowel (cf. also *ifont* 'ibidem', **201**, 6); — O. *ip* 'ibi' (Pael. *ip*) probably from *\*i-pe* with the same enclitic as *neip*, L. *neque*; — U. *itek* 'item' from *\*i-te-k* or *\*i-t'-ik* (cf. L. *ita*, *item*, Skt. *iti*, etc., which however differ in the final vowel).

**196.** The pronoun corresponding in use to the Latin *hic* is in Oscan formed in part from a stem *eko-*, in part from *ekso-*, in Umbrian wholly from the latter in the form *es(s)o-* (**145**, 3). In most of the Oscan forms the enclitic *-k* (**201**, 1) is used.

*Singular*

| | M. | N. | F. |
|---|---|---|---|
| NOM. | —— | —— | O. ek., U. *eso* |
| GEN. | | —— | —— |
| DAT. | O. *exeic* of *ex* 363 | | |
| ACC. | —— | O. ekík | O. ekak (108, 2, *a*) |
| ABL. | O. eksuk, | | O. *exac*, U. *esa* |
| | U. *essu, esu*, esu-ku | | |
| LOC. | O. *exeic* | | —— |

*Plural*

| | M. | N. | F. |
|---|---|---|---|
| NOM. | —— | —— | O. ekas, ekask |
| GEN. | U. *esom-e*, esum-ek(?) | | —— |
| D.-A. | U. *esis-co*, | | O. *exaisc-en* |
| | *esir, isir* | | |
| ACC. | —— | —— | O. ekass |

*a.* The Oscan Acc. Sg. N. ekík (Pael. *ecic*) is from *\*ekid-k* formed after the analogy of íd-ík. Cf. also U. *este* (**197**, 4).

*b.* The stem *eko-* or *ekso-* is seen also in O. ekss, *ex* 'ita', but the precise formation is uncertain (*\*ek(e)s* or *\*eks(e)s* with the same *-s* as in puz, or *\*eks(e)?*). For O. ekkum 'item', see **201**, 5.

*c.* The Umbrian stem *es(s)o-* is also seen in *eso, esoc, iso, issoc* 'ita' (adv. in -*ô*; see **190**, 2), *isec, isek* 'item' (cf. *itek*, **195**, *f*), and *isunt* 'item' (**201**, 6). For the *i* in these forms and in Dat.-Abl. *isir*, see **39**, 4.

**197.** There are some scattering forms from other stems.

1. U. *esmei* 'huic', esmik 'ei'; Loc. Sg. *esme*. These, together with U. pusme 'cui', are the sole relics in Italic of a type of pronominal case-forms found in various languages, most clearly in

Sanskrit, e.g. Dat. Sg. *ásmāi, tásmāi, kásmāi,* Loc. Sg. *ásmin,* etc. The stem of *esmei* is *e,* the same as in Skt. *á-smāi,* the two forms being identical except that in *esmei* the Locative ending is used for the Dative, as usual (**195**, *c*).

2. U. **uru,** *uru* 'illo'; Abl. Sg. F. **ura-ku**; Dat.-Abl. Pl. **ures**; here also probably, as Gen. Sg. M., *orer* VIa 26, etc., though there are various interpretations of the phrase. For *u* in *uru* see **51**. The stem may be \**oro-,* \**oso-,* or even \**oiso-,* cognate forms being unknown.

3. U. **ulu,** *ulo* 'illo, illuc', adv.; here also probably, as Gen. Sg. F., O. **ulas** (no. 19). Stem *ōlo-* as in L. *ōlim,* to which early L. *olle* is also related.

4. U. **estu** 'istum'; Acc. Sg. N. **este,** *este*; Acc. Pl. N. *esto,* **estu.** Stem *esto-,* whence L. *iste* with *i* under the influence of *is.* The neuter *este* is from \**estid* formed after the analogy of *id, pid.*

5. O. **essuf,** *esuf* 'ipse', U. **esuf.** The meaning 'ipse' is reasonably certain (cf. T. B. 19, 21), so that it is difficult not to assume connection with L. *ipse,* though inconsistent with the usual derivation of the latter from \**is-pse.* The stem would then be \**epso-* (for *ss* see **122**, 2), and the -uf perhaps represent a transfer to the inflection of *n*-stems (O. **úíttiuf** etc., **181**) as if we had in Latin \**ipsō* formed after agent-nouns in *-ō, -ōnis.* But the whole matter is problematical.

6. U. **surur** 'item' (whence *sururont, suront,* **201**, 6) is of uncertain origin, but perhaps represents a reduplicated formation \**sŏ-sŏ-s* or \**sŏ-sŏ-r, sŏ* being from the stem *so-* seen in L. *sīc,* earlier *sei-ce.*

## INTERROGATIVE, RELATIVE, AND INDEFINITE PRONOUNS

**198.** The use of the I.E. Interrogative-Indefinite Pronoun, stems \**qu̯o-* (\**qu̯ā-*), \**qu̯i-,* and, in adverbs, \**qu̯u-,* for the Relative is characteristic of Italic. The Latin distinction between *quī, quod,* and *quis, quid,* is also common to the dialects. The *o*-stem forms are used for the ordinary Relative (with definite ante-cedent), the *i*-stem forms for the Interrogative (only one example),

Indefinite, and Indefinite Relative. For the distinction between the Definite and Indefinite Relative, cf. O. **thesavrúm púd eseí tereí íst . . . iním píd e[iseí] thesavreí púkkapíd ee[stít** 'thesaurum qui in eo territorio est . . . et quidquid in eo thesauro quandoque exstat'. In Latin, too, *quis* was originally used for the Indefinite Relative (Neue, Formenlehre II⁸, p. 430), and Cato's *quesquomque* is evidence for *\*quisquomque* (U. **pisi-pumpe**). Cf. also *quisquis*, and *quisque* in its Relative use.

How far there was any corresponding differentiation in the other case-forms cannot be determined from the limited number of occurrences.

**199.** Examples of Declension. Some of the compound forms (**200,** 1) and conjunctions (**202**) are included.

| | STEM *po-, pā-* (L. *quo-, quā-*) | | | STEM *pi-* (L. *qui-*) | |
|---|---|---|---|---|---|
| | *Singular* | | | | |
| | **M.** | **N.** | **F.** | **M. F.** | **N.** |
| NOM. | O. **pui,** U. *poi, poe, poei* | O. **púd** | O. **paí, pai,** *pae, paei* | O. **pís, pis,** *pis,* U. **pis-i,** *pis-i, pis-est, pis-her,* **sve-pis,** *so-pir* | O. **píd,** U. **piř-e** |
| GEN. | O. **púiieh** | —— | —— | O. *pieis-um* | —— |
| DAT. | U. **pusme** | —— | —— | O. *piei* | |
| ACC. | —— | O. *pod,* (U. *sue-po,* **puř-e,** *pors-e,* etc., conj.) | O. **paam,** **pam** | O. *phim*[1] | O. **píd, pid,** **píd-um,** **pid-um,** (U. **piř-e,** *pirs-e,* etc., conj.) |
| ABL. | —— | —— | O. *poizad,* U. *pora* | —— | —— |

[1] Misspelling for *pim*, probably due to the influence of Latin orthography with its not infrequent confusion of *p* and *ph*, *t* and *th*, etc. Cf. also O. **Aphinis, Perkhen.** (beside **Perkens**).

*Plural*

| | M. | N. | F. | M. F. | N. |
|---|---|---|---|---|---|
| Nom. | O. pús,<br>U. pur-e,<br>pur-i | O. paí | O. pas, *pas* | —— | —— |
| Acc. | —— | O. pai | U. *paf-e* | U. *pif-i* | —— |

*a.* O. pui is from *q̯̈oi, whence L. *quī*, while U. *poi* is to be explained as the same form (*pŏ from *poi) with the addition of the particle -*ī*, seen in *pur-i*, *paf-e*, etc. O. *paei* beside *paí* is probably only a careless spelling for *pae*, since the particle -*ī* is not found in the other Oscan forms.

*b.* O. púiieh, for *púiieis (see **64**, *b*, **113**, *c*), is in origin the Gen. Sg. of the Possessive Adjective, like L. *nostrī*, *vestrī*, etc.[1] The adjective is seen in O. púiiu 'cuia': L. *quoius*, Grk. ποῖος, all from a stem *q̯̈oi-i̯o- (**253**, note).

*c.* U. puame is a form like *esmei* and so almost identical with Skt. *kāsmāi*. See **197**, 1.

*d.* O. poizad, U. pora, are from a stem *poiso-, standing in the same relation to po- as *eiso- to *i-, *e(i)o-, and probably of similar origin. See **195**. Nothing is gained by assuming a compound *pŏ-eiso-.

*e.* O. pieis, piei, instead of which we should expect *peis, *pei, are due to the influence of *pis*, which as a monosyllable retained the *i* in contrast to other *i*-stem Nominatives. That is, we have *slag-s, Gen. *slag-eis, but *pi-s* and so Gen. *pi-eis*. The analogy of *i̯o*-stems (Nom. -is, Gen. -ieis) may also have been a factor.

*f.* A form *porsi, porse, porsei*, which occurs in place of certain case-forms, e.g. Nom. Sg. M. (VI a 6, 9, etc.), Nom. Pl. N. (VI a 15, 19), Acc. Pl. N. (VI b 40), although usually explained in various other ways, is best taken as the conjunction (cf. puř-e II a 26), used loosely as a sort of indeclinable Relative.

**200. 1.** Indefinite and Indefinite Relative Pronouns compounded of *pis* are:

U. *pis-i* (piř-e etc.). Indefinite and Indefinite Relative. But *pif-i* VII b 2 has a definite antecedent.

O. *pis-um* (píd-um, pid-um, *pieis-um*). Indefinite.

O. pis-pis (*pit-pit* Festus). Indefinite Relative. Cf. L. *quis-quis*.

U. *pis-her*. Indefinite. Formed like L. *quī-libet*, *her* being 3d Sg. Pres. Indic. from *her-* 'velle' (**216**).

---

[1] The suggestion of Sommer, Lat. Laut- und Formenlehre, 472, that púiieh is Nom. Sg. M. of the adjective, would be attractive if it could be shown that the order of the inscription (no. 39) might be púiieh súm | perkium, in which case we could translate 'cuius sum? Perkiorum' (cf. no. 55). Yet on the analogy of **Maís** beside **Maiiúí** (**173**, 1) one would expect Nom. Sg. M. *puis.

2. The pronoun corresponding to L. *uterque* is seen in O. Nom. Pl. **pútúrús-píd**, Loc. Sg. **púterei-píd**, etc., U. Gen. Sg. **putres-pe**, adv. *podruh-pei*; also in U. *sei-podruhpei* 'seorsum utroque', with which compare L. *sēd-utraque* (Plautus, Stich. 106). All these forms come through *\*potro-* (**81, 88,** 4) from *\*qu̯otero-* (Grk. πότερος, Skt. *katará-*), that is, *\*qu̯o-* with the suffix *-tero-* (**188,** 2). L. *uterque* owes its *u* to the influence of adverbial forms containing the stem *\*qu̯u-* (see 3).

*a.* O. **alttreí pútereípíd akeneí,** if **akeneí** is 'year' (**159,** *a*), must mean 'in every other year', where the Romans said 'in anno altero quoque' (Col. R.R. 5, 8).

3. Besides the stems *\*qu̯o-* and *\*qu̯i-*, a stem *\*qu̯u-*, frequent in the adverbial forms of various languages (e.g. Skt. *kú-tas* 'whence?', *kú-tra* 'where?', etc., Cretan ὅπυι etc.), is to be recognized in O. **puf** 'ubi', U. *pufe*; — O. **puz** 'ut', U. **puze, puse,** etc. See **154** with *a*, **202,** 5, 6.

## PRONOMINAL ENCLITICS

201. The enclitic particles used with pronominal forms are as follows:

1. *-k*, like L. *-ce*, *-c*, in *hic*, *hunc*, etc. In contrast to Latin, this is very common in forms of the pronoun corresponding to L. *is* (see **195**); it occurs also in most of the Oscan forms of **eko-, ekso-** (see **196**); further in U. **esmik** (**197,** 1), and various adverbs, as **esoc, isec, itek, inum-k,** etc. In general it is more frequent in Oscan than in Umbrian. It has become an integral part of some of the forms, just as in L. *hic, hunc,* e.g. O. **iúk, ioc** (but U. **eu, eo**), while in others its use is optional, e.g. O. **eísúd** and **eizuc.** In Umbrian, however, the absence of *-k*, *-c*, is not always proof that the formation without the enclitic is intended. It is altogether unlikely that **ere, ere,** is to be separated from **erek, erec** (O. **izic**), or **erse** from **erek** (O. **idic**), or **eso** from **esoc.** Probably the final *k*, like other final consonants in Umbrian, was weakly sounded and so, frequently, omitted in the writing.

2. *-ik*, a combination of the preceding. This is seen in the forms just mentioned, O. **iz-ic, id-ík, id-ic,** U. **er-ec,** etc., also in **esum-ek, esom-e,** and in the adverbs **enum-ek** etc. The particle to which the *k* is added probably stands for *id* (like *pid*). For the change of *\*id-k* to *-ik*, cf. Abl. Sg. **eísak, eizac.**

3. *-ī*, as in Grk. οὗτοσ-ί. This is found in Umbrian in nearly all forms of the Relative-Indefinite Pronoun (**199**), including the adverbs **puz-e, pus-ei, pu-e,** etc.

201] *Pronominal Enclitics* **147**

4. *-pid*, used like the Latin generalizing *-que* in *quisque* etc. This is seen in the forms corresponding to L. *uterque* (**200**, 2), and in the adverbs O. púkkapíd, *poca-pit* 'quandoque', U. *panu-pei* 'quandoque', U. pum-pe in pisi pumpe 'quicumque'. It corresponds in form to L. *quid* and stands in the same relation to L. *-que* as Skt. *-cid* to *-ca*, both of these being used as generalizing particles though in different combinations. The three occurrences of U. *-pei* (*panupei*, *podruhpei*, *seipodruhpei*) make it probable that in Umbrian, in the adverbs at least, the particle *-í* (above, 3) was added to *-pi* from *-pid*.

5. *-om* (or *-dom* ?). This is found in Oscan, 1) as a particle of Identity, in ísídum 'idem' etc. (**195**), where Umbrian has *-hont* (6), and in the adverb ekkum 'item'; — 2) as an Indefinite particle, in píd-um 'quidquam' etc. (**200**, 1), where Umbrian has *-í* (3), and in the conjunction pun-um 'quandoque'. It is probably the same element in O. *per-um* 'sine', and perhaps in O. tiium, U. *tiom*, etc. (**193**, c). For O. *-um* from *-om*, see **50**.

There is a difference of opinion as to whether the particle is properly *-om* or *-dom*, as it is also a matter of dispute whether in L. *idem* etc. the *-dem* is original or due to a wrong division of *id-em*, Abl. *eōd-em*, etc. On general grounds there is no objection either to *-dem*, *-dom*, from the same stem *do-* that is seen in various enclitics, e.g. *-de* in L. *quamde*, U. *pane*, or to *-em*, *-om*, to be compared with Skt. *-am* in *id-ám*. The question is which suits better the actual forms. In the Indefinite forms there is no evidence for *-dom*, in fact it is very unlikely that píd-um comes from *píd-dom*. In ísídum we may divide ís-íd-um (as we have assumed *is-id-k* for *izic*) as well as ís-í-dum. The chief support for *-dom* is found in ekkum and íussu, but the changes involved (*kd* to *kk* and *sd* to *ss*) are otherwise unknown (**139**, a), and it is quite possible that ekkum is for *ekk'-om* with *ekk'* for *ekke* (L. *ecce*), and that of the two spellings íussu and íusu the latter is the more correct, the former being a slip due to the existence of an Acc. Pl. form *íúss-u or else to an uncertainty as to the syllabic division (íus-u with etymological, íu-su with phonetic syllabification). At any rate the derivation from *ek-dom* and *eōs-dom* is not so obvious as to constitute proof of the particle *-dom* in Oscan.

6. *-(h)ont*. This is found in Umbrian only, namely in eront, erihont 'idem' etc. (**195**), and in the adverbs ifont 'ibidem', isunt 'item', sururont 'item' (whence also suront by haplology). It probably contains *hom*, from the same stem as L. *hic*, with the *-t* of pos-t, per-t, etc. We find *-hont* after vowels, but *-ont* after consonants (**149**, a). For sururo and eruhu, occurring once each, see **128**, 2, a. The Abl. Sg. F. erafont which occurs twice beside erahunt owes its *-font* to a wrong division of other forms, e.g. *if-ont* (ife 'ibi') taken as *í-font*.

7. Here may be mentioned the pronominal prefix *e* in O. *e-tanto* 'tanta': L. *tantus*. Cf. L. *e-quidem*.

8. For enclitics found only in adverbs, see the following.

## RELATIVE ADVERBS AND CONJUNCTIONS

**202.** Many of the pronominal adverbs have been cited among the forms of the various pronominal stems (195–200), but it is desirable to treat separately the forms of the Relative (and Indefinite) Adverbs, most of which serve as Conjunctions; and for the sake of convenience the Conjunctions not formed from the stems of Relative Pronouns are included.

1. O. *pod* in *suae pod* 'sive', **svai puh** (133, *a*), with which is identical U. *suepo*, **svepu**; also in O. *pod — min[s* 'quo minus'. This is Acc. Sg. N. like L. *quod*, not Abl. Sg. as in L. *quō minus*. The same form with the enclitic -ĭ is seen in U. **puř-e** 'quod, cum, quomodo' (II a 26, III 5, V a 7), with which is identical *pors-i* etc. used in place of certain case-forms (199, *f*). Cf. also O. **adpúd**, U. *arnipo* (below, 9, 10).

2. U. **piř-e**, *pirs-i*, etc. 'quod, si, cum', e.g. *sersi pirsi sesust* 'sede cum sederit' (VI a 5), *persei pir orto est* 'si ignis ortus est, in case fire has broken out' (VI a 26 etc.; similarly **peře** II a 3), *persei mersei* 'si ius sit, in so far as is right' (VI a 28 etc.), with which compare L. *quod opus siet* (Cato). In form this is the Acc. Sg. N. of *pis-i*. It is not always to be distinguished with certainty from **piř-e** 'quidquid' (V a 5).

3. O. *pon*, **pún**, U. *ponne*, *pone*, **pune** 'cum'; also O. **pun-úm** 'quandoque'. From *\*pom-de*: L. *\*quom-de* (cf. *quam-de*). See **92, 135**. Another combination of *pom* (L. *quom, cum*) is to be recognized in U. **(pisi)pumpe**: L. *(quī)quomque*, *(quī)cumque*. See also **201, 4**.

4. O. *pan* 'quam', *pruter pan* 'priusquam' (cf. Grk. πρό-τερον ἤ), U. *pane* in *postertio pane* 'postquam tertium'. From *\*pam-de*: L. *quam-de*. See **92, 135**. The simple *\*pam* (L. *quam*) appears in U. *pre-pa* 'priusquam'. (In O. *pruter pam* beside *pruter pan* the *pam* probably stands for *pan*, the next word beginning with *m*.)

5. O. **puf**, U. *pufe* 'ubi'. From stem *\*qʷu-* (200, 3) and an adverbial ending *-dhe* (cf. Skt. *kú-ha* 'where?', O.Bulg. *kŭ-de* 'where'), or *-dhi* (Grk. -δι). U. *ife* 'ibi' has the same ending, the *b* in L. *ibi* being due to the analogy of *ubi* (*b* = *dh* after *u*).

In L. *ubi*, *ibi*, the final *i* is not the original short vowel, but is shortened from -*ī*, this from -*ei* (cf. early L. *ubei*), which arose under the influence of the adverbs in -*ei* representing Locatives of *o*-stems. U. *pufe* might also represent such a form, but it is far more likely that it preserves the original -*dhe*, only without syncope as in Oscan (cf. O. *pon*: U. *ponne*).

6. O. **puz**, *pous* (mistake for *pus*; see footnote, p. 40), U. **puz-e**, *pus-e*, *pus-ei*, etc. 'ut' (in Umbrian also 'quasi'). This stands for *\*pu-t-s* (137, 2), in Umbrian with added -*ī*, containing the stem *\*qu̯u-* (200, 3) and an adverbial ending -*the* (cf. Av. *ku-θa* 'how') or -*ti* (as in *au-ti* etc.), with loss of the final vowel and addition of -*s* (as in L. *ab-s*, O. *az*, i.e. *ad-s*, etc.).

L. *ut* is the same form without the added *s*, the latter appearing in *usquam* etc. L. *utei*, *utī*, is like *ubei* etc.

7. U. *pue*, **pue** 'ubi, where'. From *\*pō* (L. *quō*) with enclitic -*ī*.

8. U. *ape*, *appei*, **ape**, **api**, **ap** 'ubi, cum' (always temporal). From *\*ad-pe*, in form like L. *atque*, but with a different force of the particle (cf. Grk. dial. ἔσ-τε, ἔν-τε 'until'). In U. **ap** the final vowel is lost as in L. *ac*, while the other forms probably contain the enclitic -*ī*, like *pusei*, **puz-e**, etc.

9. O. **adpúd** 'quoad'. Formed like L. *quo-ad* (rarely *ad-quō*), except that **púd** is probably the same as *pod* (above, 1), and so cognate with L. *quod* rather than with *quō*.

10. U. *arnipo* 'donec, until'. From *ar* 'ad' (132, *a*) and -*ne* (as in *per-ne* etc., or negative?) + *\*pom* or *\*pod*. Cf. L. *dōnicum*, *dōnec*.

11. U. *nersa* 'donec, until', used after a negative clause. From *\*ne-dām*; cf. L. -*dam* in *quon-dam* etc., and *dum*.

12. U. *panupei* 'quandoque'. From *\*pan-dō-pid*: L. *quan-dō-que*. For -*pei* see 201, 4.

13. O. **púkkapíd**, *pocapit*, *p]ocapid* 'quandoque'. From *\*pod-kād(?)-pid*, the second element being perhaps Abl. Sg. F. of the stem seen in L. -*ce*, like O. *dat* 'de' from *do*- (190, 3, *a*).

14. O. **svaí**, *suae*, U. **sve**, *sue* 'si', *no-sue* 'nisi'. From *\*su̯ai*, Loc. Sg. F. of *su̯o*-, while L. *sī* is from *\*sei*, Loc. Sg. N. of *so*-. Cf. Grk. *ai* and *ei* from stem *so*- or *o*-.

a. The relation of U. *sopir*, VI b 54, to **svepis** 'siquis' of the parallel passage I b 18, is puzzling. That it cannot be regarded as a later form of the same word is obvious from *sue* beside **sve**. The first syllable may be *sŏ* from *\*soi*, and it is conceivable that this *\*soi* is from an earlier *\*syei*, though such a change is only imperfectly paralleled by that seen in *sonitu* (37, a). Another view is that *sopir* is not 'siquis', but an Indefinite Relative 'quisquis', and contains a generalizing particle *\*sod* or *\*syod*, related to the *so* in Eng. *whoso, whosoever*. But the chief support for this, the derivation of Grk. ὅτις from *\*σϝοδ-τις*, is not beyond question.[1]

15. U. **et** 'et': L. *et*, Grk. ἔτι, etc.

16. O. **ínim**, *inim*, εινειμ (44), abbr. *in.* 'et'; U. **enem**, *eine*, **ene**, **inen-ek** (for *\*inem-ek*), and *ennom*, *eno(m)*, **enum-ek**, **inum-ek**, etc. 'tum, deinde'. These forms, together with Pael. *inom* 'et', are obviously connected with L. *enim* (*einom* of the Duenos inscription is best left out of account) in some way,—exactly how is not so clear.

The ending -*im* of L. *enim* is seen in the Oscan forms and in U. *enem* etc., while U. *enom* etc. with Pael. *inom* show -*om*. The difficulty is with the initial vowel. The Oscan forms point to *i* or *ē*, not *e*. Pael. *inom* also points to *i* or (possibly) *ē*. The various Umbrian spellings are most easily combined on the basis of *ē*, but *i* is also possible. On the whole, in view of L. *enim*, the probability is perhaps in favor of *\*ēnim* and *\*ēnom*, but the matter is quite uncertain. The *nn* in *ennom* is very likely due to the influence of the correlative *ponne*.

17. O. *auti, aut*, **avt** 'aut, at', U. *ote*, **ute** 'aut': L. *aut, autem*. From *\*au* (Grk. αὖ, αὖ-τε), with the same -*ti* as in *\*eti* (*et*), *\*toti* (L. *tot*), etc. The Oscan forms with and without apocope (92) were differentiated in meaning at Bantia, where *auti* is 'aut', *aut* 'at'. Elsewhere we find only **avt**, usually 'at', once 'aut'.

18. O. *loufir* 'vel'. In form this is a 3d Sg. Pass. of the root seen in L. *libet* (96, 238, 2), in the impersonal use (239). For the development of meaning, cf. L. *vel*, Imperat. of *volō*, and the following.

19. U. **heris** . . . **heris**, *heri* . . . *heri, herie* . . . *herie*, etc. 'vel . . . vel'. These are from *\*heriō* 'volo', partly 2d Sg. Pres. Indic. (**heris**, *heri*), partly 3d Sg. Perf. Subj. (*herie, heriei*).

---

[1] See Delbrück, Vergl. Syntax, III, pp. 339 ff.

20. The negatives.  Oscan has (1) *ne* (L. *ne-fas*, *ni-si* from *ne-sei*, etc.), (2) *ni* (L. *nē*), (3) *nei* (L. *nī*); and for each of these a corresponding form with the enclitic *-p*, corresponding to *-c*, *-que*, in L. *nec*, *neque*, namely 1) *nep*, nep, 2) nip, 3) *neip*, neip. As regards use, *ne* occurs in *ne pon* 'nisi cum' and as a prohibitive with a pronoun in *ne phim pruhipid* 'ne quem prohibuerit', while *ni* is always prohibitive, and *nei* occurs in conditional clauses, *suaepis nei, nei suae*.  But all three compounded forms have the prohibitive force, 'neve', though neip is also used like *nei*, e.g. svai neip.

Umbrian has nei in neiřhabas 'ne adhibeant' (84), otherwise *neip*, neip (once *nep*), both prohibitive and simple negative. Whether this corresponds to O. *neip* or nip or both is not clear, the spelling *ei* being remarkable in any case.  See 29, *b*. U. *no-sue* 'nisi' probably contains *\*noi*, a by-form of *nei*.

## VERBS

On the general system of conjugation, see 13.

### THE PERSONAL ENDINGS

**203.** The personal endings of the Indicative and Subjunctive Active are:

| PRIMARY | SECONDARY | | PRIMARY | SECONDARY |
|---------|-----------|---|---------|-----------|
| *Singular* | | | *Plural* | |
| 1. *-ō* | *-m* | 1. —— | —— |
| 2. *-s* | *-s* | 2. —— | —— |
| 3. *-t* | *-d* (lost in U.) | 3. *-nt* | *-ns* |

For the endings of the Imperative, see 235-237; for those of the Passive, see 238-239.

Primary and secondary endings, which, in contrast to Latin, are clearly distinguished in the Third Singular and Third Plural, are used as follows: primary in the Present, Future, and Future Perfect Indicative, — secondary in the Imperfect and Perfect Indicative and in all tenses of the Subjunctive.

### Remarks on the Endings

**204.** 1. The original endings of the Third Singular and Third Plural were primary *-ti*, *-nti*, secondary *-t*, *-nt*. By the loss of the final *i* (92) the former became *-t*, *-nt*, but in the meantime the original *-t*, *-nt*, had undergone a change, as follows:

The *-t* became *-d*, which is preserved in Oscan, and existed in early Latin (*feced* etc.) until the primary ending was generalized. In Umbrian this, like every final *d*, was lost; but since even final *t* is sometimes omitted in the writing, the distinction is less clear in Umbrian than in Oscan. See 127, 1, 2, 133.

The *-nt* probably became first *-nd*, then *-n* (cf. L. *dan-unt* etc.), and to this an *s* was added under the influence of the plural ending of nouns. See 128, 1.

2. In *-nt* the *n* is regularly written in Umbrian (the only exception is furfaθ (25, *a*) beside *furfant*), while in Oscan it is omitted in the case of *-ent* (the only exception being one occurrence of **sent** beside **set**), but written in **stahint** and **eestint**, the only forms occurring which do not end in *-ent*. In *-ns* the *n* is always written in Oscan but frequently omitted in Umbrian. See 108, 1, 2. For U. **fefure** and **staheren**, see 128, 2, *a*.

3. The plural forms in *-ent*, *-ens*, represent the full endings, original *-enti*, *-ent*, which belong properly to unthematic formations like U. **sent**, O. **set** (cf. Dor. ἐντὶ for *ἐντὶ, Skt. *sánti*, Goth. *sind*, I.E. **senti*). But they have been extended at the expense of thematic forms, just as in Latin, vice versa, *-ont* (*-unt*) has completely driven out *-ent*. Thus we have *-ent* in the Future and Future Perfect, which are thematic formations; and *-ens* in the Perfect, which, while containing types of various origin, is always thematic in the Third Singular.

*a.* It is probable that the same encroachment of *-ent* upon *-ont* is to be recognized in O. **fliet** as compared with L. *fīunt*, and likewise in O. **staiet**. But some believe that the original ending of verbs of this class was *-jenti* or *-ịṇti*. For the double formation in the Fourth Conjugation, represented by O. **fliet**, **staiet**, and O. **stahint**, **eestint**, see also 215, 2.

4. In the Second Singular in Umbrian the -*s* is sometimes omitted or changed to -*r*. Thus **seste** 'sistis', **heri**, *heri* 'vel' beside **heris** (see **202**, 19), *sir*, *sei*, *si* 'sis'. See **113** with *b*.

. 5. The secondary ending of the First Singular occurs only in O. **manafum** 'mandavi', and in O. **súm** 'sum' (**217**, 1).

6. The primary ending of the First Singular, -*ō*, seen in U. **sistu** 'sisto', is not contracted with the preceding *ā* of the First Conjugation as in Latin. Thus U. *subocauu*, *subocau* 'invoco' from -*ā̧ō*. Cf. also U. *stahu* 'sto' from \**sta̧ō*. See **83**.

7. The Latin shortening of vowels before final *t* is unknown. See **78**, 3. So O. **faamat** is to be understood as *fāmāt*, O. **kasit** 'decet' as *kasīt* (with *ī* from *ē*), etc. For the vowel-quantity before -*nt*, -*ns*, see **78**, *a*.

8. The short *e* of the Second and Third Singular Present Indicative of the Third Conjugation, and of the Third Singular Perfect Indicative, does not suffer syncope. See **90, 2.**

## EXAMPLES OF CONJUGATION

The following paradigms include all the verb-forms occurring in Oscan or Umbrian (barring some variations in spelling), except where an " etc." is added, that is in the 2d and 3d Sg. Imperat. Act., the 3d Sg. Fut. Perf., and the Perf. Pass. Partic. (including the periphrastic Perf. Indic. Pass.). A few Paelignian (P.), Marrucinian (M.), and Vestinian (V.) forms are included.

In the Perfect System there are given under the First and Fourth Conjugations only those types which are characteristic of these conjugations, namely, in the following order, the *f*-, *tt*-, and *nkf*-Perfects (and, in the Fourth, U. **purtiius** etc.). The other types, which are found with verbs of all conjugations, but mostly with those of the Third, are given under the Third only, namely, in the following order, the reduplicated Perfect, the simple Perfect without vowel-change, the Perfect with lengthened vowel, and the *l*-Perfect.

Under the Fourth Conjugation are included the forms corresponding to the Latin type *capiō*. See **216**.

**205.**        FIRST CONJUGATION

| | ACTIVE | | PASSIVE | |
|---|---|---|---|---|
| | INDICATIVE | SUBJUNCTIVE | INDICATIVE | SUBJUNCTIVE |

PRESENT

| | INDICATIVE (Active) | SUBJUNCTIVE (Active) | INDICATIVE (Passive) | SUBJUNCTIVE (Passive) |
|---|---|---|---|---|
| 1. Sg. | U. *subocauu* | U. *aseriaia* | | |
| 2. Sg. | | U. **kupifiaia** (or 3. Sg.?) | | |
| 3. Sg. | O. **faamat** | O. *deiuaid,* *tadait,* U. *portaia,* **kuraia** | O. **sakarater** | O. **sakahíter,** **sakraífir**(?) |
| 3. Pl. | U. *furfant,* **furfaθ** | U. *etaians,* *etaias* | O. **karanter** | |

IMPERFECT

| | | | | |
|---|---|---|---|---|
| 3. Sg. | | | | P. *upsaseter* |

FUTURE

| | | | | |
|---|---|---|---|---|
| 3. Sg. | O. *deiuast,* U. **prupehast** | | | |
| 3. Pl. | O. *censazet* | | | |

PERFECT

| | | | | |
|---|---|---|---|---|
| 3. Sg. | O. **aíkdafed** | | O. **sakrafír,** U. *pihafi,* *pihafei* | |
| | O. **prúfatted,** **dadíkatted,** d]**uunated** | | O. *lamatir* | |
| | | U. *combifianŝi* | | |
| | | | O. **teremnatu-st,** U. **stakaz** est etc. | U. **kuratu si** |
| 3. Pl. | O. **prúfattens,** **teremnattens,** P. *ooisatens* | O. **tríbarakattíns** | | |
| | | | O. **staflatas-set** etc. | |

ACTIVE · PASSIVE

FUTURE PERFECT

3. SG. U. *andirsafust*
    U. *combifianšiust*

                  U. *pihos fust*

3. PL. O. **tríbarakattuset**

                  U. **cersnatur furent**

IMPERATIVE

PRES. 2. SG.   U. *stiplo, aserio*

FUT. 2. 3. SG. O. *deiuatud,*   O. *censamur,*
        U. *pihatu,*    U. *eturstahmu, spahamu*
        *portatu,* etc.

  2. (3.) PL. U. *etato*     U. *arsmahamo, caterahamo*

INFINITIVE

PRES. O. *censaum, moltaum,*  PERF. U. *erom ehiato,* **kuratu eru**
    **tríbarakavém**

PARTICIPLES

            PERF.     O. **staflatas** etc.,
                   U. **anzeriates,**
                   *pihos,* etc.

        GERUNDIVE O. **sakrannas,**
                   **úpsannam,**
                   **eehiianásum,**
                   U. *pihaner,*
                   **pelsans**

SUPINE

U. *anseriato*

**206.** SECOND CONJUGATION

| ACTIVE | | PASSIVE | |
|---|---|---|---|
| INDICATIVE | SUBJUNCTIVE | INDICATIVE | SUBJUNCTIVE |

PRESENT

3. SG. O. kasit,     O. pútiad,     O. *loufir*

    U. tiçit,        turumiiad,

    *habe,* habe,   U. habia

    *trebeit*(?)

3. PL.          O. pútians                  U. *tursiandu*

FUTURE

3. SG. U. *habiest*

IMPERATIVE

FUT. 2. 3. SG. O. *licitud,* líkítud,

            U. *habitu,* habetu,

                *tursitu,* tusetu,

                *carsitu,* kařetu, kařitu,

                *sersitu, tenitu,*

                uřetu, upetu, eveietu

    2. 3. PL. U. *habituto,* habetutu,

                *tursituto,* tusetutu,

                upetuta

INFINITIVE

PRES. O. fatíum

PARTICIPLES

PRES. U. *serse,* zeřef, kutef      PERF. U. *tases,* taçez, *uirseto,* etc.

**207.**                   THIRD  CONJUGATION

|  | ACTIVE | | PASSIVE | |
|---|---|---|---|---|
|  | INDICATIVE | SUBJUNCTIVE | INDICATIVE | SUBJUNCTIVE |

PRESENT

1. SG. U. sestu
2. SG. U. seste
3. SG. M. *feret,*        O. kahad, aflukad,  O. *uincter*   U. *ferar*
    V. *didet*        da[da]d, P. *dida,*
              U. *dirsa,* teřa    U. teřte    O. krustatar(?),
                                       kaispatar(?)
3. PL.              O. *deicans,*      M. *ferenter* U. emantur,
               U. *dirsans, dirsas,*          terkantur
               neiřhabas

IMPERFECT

3. PL.              O. patensíns

FUTURE

2. SG. U. menes, anpenes
3. SG. O. *didest, pertemest,*
    U. ferest
3. PL.                        U. *ostensendi*

PERFECT

1. SG. O. manafum
3. SG. O. deded,       O. *fefacid,* dadid
    U. dede,
    O. prúffed, aamanaffed
    O. kúmbened,
    *αναϕακετ*
    O. upsed        O. *hipid*
                      U. *srehto est* etc.
3. PL. U. eitipes,
    O. uupsens,
    *ουπσενς*
                      O. *scriftas set,*
                      prúftú-set,
                      U. *screihtor sent* etc.

ACTIVE               PASSIVE

INDICATIVE

FUTURE PERFECT

2. SG. O. fifikus

     O. aflakus,

     U. benus, kuvurtus

     U. entelus, apelus

3. SG. O. *fefacust*, U. *dersicust* etc.

     O. *dicust, cebnust*, etc.,      O. *comparascuster*,

     U. fakust, benust, habus, etc.      U. *benuso, couortuso*

     U. *entelust*, apelust

3. PL. U. *dersicurent*, pepurkurent

     O. *angetuzet*,

     U. *facurent, benurent,*
        *haburent, procanurent,*
        *eiscurent*

     U. prusikurent


IMPERATIVE

FUT. 2. 3. SG. O. *actud*,

          U. fertu, ustentu,
            aitu, *deitu*, kanetu, etc.

    2. 3. PL. U. fertuta, ustentuta,
            aituta, *hatuto*


INFINITIVE

PRES. O. defkum, *deicum, acum*, edum,
       menvum, *aserum, pertumum*,

     U. aferum, *afero*


PARTICIPLES

PRES. U. restef, *reste*        PERF. O. *scriftas*, prúftú, *censtom*,
                          U. *sorehto, sihitu, orto*, etc.

                   GERUNDIVE U. *anferener*

**208.**  FOURTH CONJUGATION

| ACTIVE | | PASSIVE | |
|---|---|---|---|
| INDICATIVE | SUBJUNCTIVE | INDICATIVE | SUBJUNCTIVE |

**PRESENT**

1. SG. U. *stahu*

2. SG. U. heris, heri, *heri*

3. SG. O. sakruvit, O. fakiiad, U. herter, herte,
   U. heri,   heriiad,  *herti, hertei*
   O. stait,   U. façia,
   U. *pis-her*  feia, fuia

3. PL. O. fiiet, staiet
   O. stahint, eestint

**IMPERFECT**

3. PL.     O. h]errins

**FUTURE**

2. SG. U. heries, purtuvies

3. SG. O. sakrvist
   O. *hafiest, herest,*
   U. *heriest, heries,*
   fuiest, kukehes(?)

3. PL. U. staheren

**PERFECT**

3. SG.     U. heriiei, *heriei, herie*

             U. herifi, *cehefi*(?)

**FUTURE PERFECT**

2. SG. U. purtiius
   U. purtinçus

3. SG. U. *purdinšiust, disleralinsust*

          U. *persnis fust,* purtitu fust

|  | ACTIVE | PASSIVE |
|---|---|---|

### IMPERATIVE

FUT. 2. 3. SG. O. *factud*,

    U. *stahitu, seritu,*     U. *persnimu,* **persnimu,**

       *purdouitu,* **amparitu**    *anouihimu,* **amparihmu**

    2. 3. PL. U. *stahituto*     U. *persnimumo*

### INFINITIVE

PRES. U. **façiu, façu**

### PARTICIPLES

              PERF. U. *persnis, purditom,*

                 *heritu,* etc.

## 209.     IRREGULAR VERBS

|  | THE VERB 'TO BE' | | THE VERB 'TO GO' | |
|---|---|---|---|---|
|  | INDICATIVE | SUBJUNCTIVE | INDICATIVE | SUBJUNCTIVE |
| **PRESENT** | | | | |
| 1. SG. | O. **súm** | | | |
| 2. SG. | | U. *sir, si, sei* | | |
| 3. SG. | O. **est, íst** | U. *si, si, sei* | | |
|  | U. *est,* **est** | | | |
| 3. PL. | O. **set, sent,** *set* | U. **sins, sis** | O. **amfret** | |
|  | U. *sent* | O. *osii[ns* | | |
| **IMPERFECT** | | | | |
| 3. SG. | | O. **fusid** | | |
| 3. PL. | O. **fufans** | | | |
| **FUTURE** | | | | |
| 3. SG. | O. *fust,* **fust** | - | U. *eest, est* | |
|  | U. *fust, fus,* **fust** | | | |
| 3. PL. | U. **furent** | | | |
| **PERFECT** | | | | |
| 3. SG. | | O. *fuid* | (Passive) U. *ier* | |
| 3. PL. | O. **fufens** | | | |
| **FUTURE PERFECT** | | | | |
| 2. SG. | | | U. **amprefuus** | |
| 3. SG. | O. *fust* | | U. *iust* | |
| 3. PL. | U. **fefure** | | U. *ambrefurent* | |

IMPERATIVE

Fut. 2. 3. Sg. O. *estud*, estud        U. *eetu, etu,* etu
        U. *futu,* futu
    2. 3. Pl. U. *fututo*        U. *etuto,* etutu, etuta
        O. *eítuns*(?)

PARTICIPLES

Pres. O. *praesentid*        Perf. U. *daetom, peretom*

INFINITIVE

Pres. O. *ezum,* U. *erom,* eru

## FORMATION OF THE MOODS AND TENSES

### THE PRESENT STEM

#### Conjugation I — Present Stem in ā

**210. 1.** As in Latin, this conjugation is made up mainly of Denominatives.   Thus O. *moltaum* 'multare' from *molto* 'multa', U. kuraia 'curet', etc.   See **262,** 1.

2. The Frequentatives, also of denominative origin, are represented; e.g. U. *etaians* 'itent': L. *itō.*   See **262,** 1.

3. Primary Verbs like L. *secō, domō,* etc., are: U. prusekatu 'prosecato', U. *mugatu* 'muttito', O. dadíkatted 'dedicavit', O. *censaum* 'censere' contrasted with L. *censeō* of the Second Conjugation; here probably O. sakahíter 'sanciatur' from *sakā-* (cf. *sak-* in L. *sacer* etc.).

*a.* The inflection of the Present is in the main that which belongs properly to the primary verbs, in which the endings were added directly to the *ā.*   The denominatives, which are formed from *ā*-stems with the *i̯o*-suffix, furnish the First Singular (**204,** 6).   In the other forms they would probably by regular contraction show partly *ā,* partly *ō,* before the endings; but under the influence of the primary verbs the *ā* is generalized.   However, whatever contraction took place here occurred in the Italic period, and the O.-U. forms throw no new light on the question.   Note that *\*sta-i̯ō,* U. *stahu* 'sto' follows the Fourth Conjugation (**215**).

*b.* The interchange of conjugation between O. dadíkatted 'dedicavit' and *deicum* 'dicere' is the same as between L. *dicō, dē-dicō,* etc., and *dīcō ;* and with L. *occupō* beside *capiō,* compare U. anzeriatu 'observatum' beside *seritu* 'servato'. Cf. also U. *andirsafust* 'circumtulerit' beside *dirsans* 'det' (O. *didest* etc., **213,** 4).

**211.** As in Latin, the *ā* is not confined to the Present System, but normally runs through the whole conjugation. So U. kuratu, pihaz, *pihafi*, çersnatur, O. *deiuatuns*, teremnatu, teremnattens, prúfatted, etc. But there are also some forms of the Perf. and Perf. Pass. Part. without the *ā*, as is the case with several of the Latin primary verbs, such as *domō, domuī, domitum, secō, secuī, sectum*, etc. Thus U. aseçeta 'non secta', pruseçetu, *proseseto* 'prosecta', beside Imperat. prusekatu (in prusektu which occurs in the same line with prusekatu and in the same meaning, the a is omitted by mistake); — O. *ancensto* 'incensa' beside Infin. *censaum*; — U. *muieto* 'muttitum' beside Imperat. *mugatu*; — *portust* 'portaverit' beside Imperat. *portatu*; — O. upsed 'fecit', 3d Pl. uupsens, Partic. U. *oseto* (but O. upsatuh), beside Gerundive O. úpsannam, Imperat. U. *osatu*. So doubtless O. *urust* 'oraverit', U. *frosetom* 'fraudatum' (**262**,1), *uasetom, uasetom* 'vitiatum' (L. *vacō*; *ə, s*, by **144**), *pesetom* 'peccatum' (**144**), though Present forms are lacking.

### Conjugation II — Present Stem in ē

**212.** Verbs of this conjugation comprise the same classes as in Latin, namely:

1. Denominatives like L. *albeō* from *albus*. So O. turumiiad 'torqueatur' from *tormo-* (cf. L. *tormentum*), O. fatíum 'fari', O. pútíad 'possit'. See **262**, 2.

2. Causatives like L. *moneō*. So U. tursitu 'terreto' with the regular *o*-grade (**51, 97**) as in L. *moneō* beside *meminī* etc.

3. Primary Verbs like L. *liceō, sedeō*, etc. So O. líkítud, *licitud* 'liceto', kasit 'decet'; U. *habe* 'habet', tiçit 'decet', sersitu 'sedeto', *tenitu* 'teneto', uŕetu 'adoleto'.

a. The relation of the inflection of the Present to that which belonged originally to the primary verbs in *ē* on the one hand and the denominatives and causatives in -*eio*- on the other is similar to what is seen in the First Conjugation (see **210**, *a*). For the *i* in O. pútíad, U. habia, etc., and in O. *licitud*, U. tursitu, etc., see **38**, 1, **39**, 1, and **41, 42**.

b. Owing to the ambiguity of the spelling (*i* = *ē* or *ī*, *e* = *ē* or, rarely, *ī*) there are several Umbrian forms, without precise cognates in Latin, of which it is impossible to say with certainty whether they belong to the Second or Fourth

Conjugation. To the Second belong probably *tremitu* (L. *tremō*), *sonitu* (L. *sonō*), *nepitu* (cf. L. *Neptūnus*), which are used transitively ("overwhelm with terror, noise, and water") and may be modeled after the causative type (*tursitu*); perhaps also *sauitu* in the same passage, but of uncertain meaning and derivation ('sauciato'?). That *sonitu* is of the Third (early L. *sonit* etc.) is less likely, for, though the short vowel is not lost after *n* (88, 1), we should expect *sonetu*. In *trebeit* 'versatur' the *ei* points to ī (46), but may also stand for ē (42), and the meaning rather favors the Second Conjugation. To the Second belong also, without much doubt, **eveietu** 'voveto' (148); *carsitu*, **kařetu, kařitu** 'calato' contrasted with L. *calō* of the First ; **upetu** 'optato, deligito', with Perf. Pass. Partic. *opeter* 'lecti, choice', of which L. *optō* represents the iterative formation (*optō* from *opeto-*,[1] the same stem as in U. *opeter*, whence also L. *optimus*).

## Conjugation III — Present Stem in ᵉ/₀

**213. 1.** Most verbs of this conjugation, as in Latin, show the simple root with the thematic vowel. Thus O. *acum* 'agere', O. *actud*, U. **aitu**, from *agetōd* (143); O. **edum** 'edere'; U. **emantur** 'accipiantur'; O. *pertumum* 'perimere'; O. **deíkum** 'dicere', *deicans*, U. *deitu* (143), etc.

*a.* Here also, in contrast to their Latin cognates, O. **kahad** 'incohet', U. *amboltu* 'ambulato', and U. **vutu** 'lavato' (but also L. *lavit* beside *lavat*).

**2.** Presents in *-nō* like L. *cernō* are represented by O. **patensíns** 'aperirent' from *patnō* or *patenō* (as if L. *patinō*).

**3.** Presents with inserted nasals like L. *rumpō, vincō*, are represented by O. *uincter* 'vincitur', U. *ninctu* 'ninguito'.

**4.** Reduplicated Presents like L. *sistō, gignō*, are represented by U. **sestu** 'sisto'; and by *didō*, seen in O. *didest* 'dabit', U. **teřa,** *dirsa* 'det', *dirsans* (131), **teřtu,** *dirstu*, **titu,** *ditu* 'dato' (132 with note), **teřte** 'datur' (also Vest. *didet* 'dat', Pael. *dida* 'det').

*a.* Here also, with loss of reduplication in composition, O. **da[da]d** 'dedat' from *dad-didō* (cf. L. *reddō* from *re-didō*); and U. **restef,** *reste* 'instaurans, renewing' from *re-sistō*. On account of the meaning this view of U. **restef** is far more probable than connection with U. *stahu* 'sto' etc. (215, 1). For the same reason U. **restatu** 'instaurato, offer' is also best taken as a reduplicated formation (cf. Volsc. *sistiatiens*, Pael. *sestatiens*(?) 'statuerunt'), with transfer to the First Conjugation (see 210, *b*), or, less probably, with retention of original *sistā-* (Grk. ἴστημι).

---

[1] Also recognized by Hempl, with great probability, in the Duenos inscription. See Trans. Am. Phil. Ass. 33, 157.

5. There are no examples of Presents like L. *crēscō*, in which the termination is confined to the Present System. But there are some forms parallel to L. *poscō* in which the original Present-suffix has become a part of the verb-stem. Thus U. **perstu** 'ponito'(?) from *\*persketōd* (**146**), to which belongs the Fut. Perf. *peperscust*; — O. *comparascuster* 'consulta erit' (**145**); — U. *eiscurent* 'arcessierint' (**29**, *a*).

6. For Presents like L. *capiō*, see **216**.

### Conjugation IV — Present Stem in i

**214.** The verbs of this conjugation comprise:

1. Denominatives like L. *fīniō*. So U. *persnihimu* 'precator' from *\*persni-*. See **262**, 3.

2. Primary Verbs like L. *veniō*. So O. **heriiad** 'capiat', **fakiiad** 'faciat', U. **façia** etc.; — U. **heris** 'vel' (2d Sg. Pres. Indic. used as adverb; see **202**, 19), with Fut. *heriest*, Perf. Pass. Partic. *hereitu*, Perf. Subj. **herifi**. As appears from this last example, the *ī* is not confined to the Present System as in most of the Latin primary verbs.

3. Denominatives from *u*-stems, which in Latin follow the Third Conjugation. So at least O. **sakruvit** 'sacrat', Fut. **sakrvist**, from *\*sakru-i̯ō* (cf. L. *statuo* from *\*statu-i̯ō*).

**215.** 1. The inflection of the Present is that which belongs properly to the primary verbs, and to a type of these, to be recognized in other languages also, in which the suffix [1] -(*i*)i̯o- interchanges with -*ī*-. The length of the *i* is shown by the absence of syncope and in part by direct evidence of the spelling. Thus U. *an-ouihimu* 'induitor' (cf. Lith. *aviù* 'wear (shoes)'; L. *induō, exuō*, from *\*ind-ou̯ō, \*ex-ou̯ō*, of Conj. III); — U. *pur-douitu* 'porricito' (**96**); — U. **am-paritu** 'conlocato', **amparihmu** (L. *pariō, -periō*); — also, outside the Present System, U. *hereitu*, **herifi** (**214**, 2). Likewise in U. *stahitu* 'stato', beside *stahu* 'sto' from *\*stai̯ō*, the *i* is almost certainly long, and it is

---

[1] That the *i* and the *i* or *i̯* of -(*i*)i̯o- may belong ultimately to the root need not concern us here.

probably long also in O. **staít** 'stat' in spite of the í, which may be
due to the influence of the regular spelling of the diphthong **aí.**

2. The Third Plural shows two formations. O. **fiíet** 'fiunt'
and **staíet** 'stant' (**aí** perhaps due to **staít**, above, 1; from *\*staíent*
would come regularly *\*staent*) are like L. *veniunt* except for the
usual substitution of unthematic *-ent* for *-ont* (**204**, 3, *a*); while
O. **stahínt, eestínt** (**89**, 2) are as if we had in Latin *\*venint* like
*amant*, *monent*, and a trace of such a formation is probably to
be seen in L. *prōdīnunt* etc. (**128**, 1). This double formation is
paralleled by that seen in the Future, where we find U. *heriest*
(like **ferest**) and O. **sakrvíst** (like *deiuast*), and also by the Latin
Imperfects in *-iēbam* and *-ībam*.

NOTE. It is uncertain which of the two formations is the earlier. The
-int may represent original *-īnti* with vowel-shortening before *nt*, or *-inti* (see
**216**, note), or may be due to the analogy of *-ant, -ent (-ānt, -ēnt)*, of the First
and Second Conjugations. The corresponding Slavic verbs end in *-ętŭ*, which
points to *-inti* or *-īnti*, but here again it is uncertain whether this is original or
due to an extension of *i* from the other forms.

3. In U. **fuia** 'fiat' (Fut. **fuiest**) from *\*fu-įō* (: L. *fīō* from
*\*fuįįō*) the retention of intervocal *į* is of course due to the
analogy of forms like U. **façia** etc.

### Forms of the type of L. capio

**216.** In Latin many primary verbs in *-iō*, like *capiō* etc.,
have short *i* instead of *ī*, and after the thematic vowel *e* of
the Third Conjugation had become *i*, such verbs had so many
forms in common with those of the Third Conjugation that they
are commonly and conveniently grouped únder it. In Oscan-
Umbrian the great majority of the primary verbs have *ī*. See **215**.

Nevertheless there are some few forms which point to a
short *i* which has been lost by syncope, this bringing about
identity with the forms of the Third Conjugation. Thus
O. *factud* 'facito' from *\*fakitōd*, beside O. **fakiiad** 'faciat'; —
O. h]**erríns** 'caperent' beside O. **heriiad** 'capiat'; — U. **herter** 'oportet', U. *pis-her* 'quilibet', probably from *heri-*, beside U. **heris,**

*hereitu*, **herifi** (**215**, 1) with *herī*-; — U. **hahtu**, *hatu*, probably from
*\*hapitōd* (**218**). Whether O. **staít, stahínt**, belong here is doubtful
(see **215**, 1, 2).

NOTE. The short *i* in Latin has been recently explained as having arisen
in *capis*, *fugis*, etc. by iambic shortening (all the verbs of this type have the
first syllable short), from which it spread to the other forms. That the iambic
shortening has been a contributory factor is altogether probable. But there
was already a nucleus of forms with inherited short *i*, for which there is evidence in other languages. Otherwise, since iambic shortening is a purely Latin
phenomenon, we should have to separate O. *factud* from **fakiiad** and L. *faciō*
and assume for it a different Present Stem.

### Irregular Verbs

**217.** Irregular verbs, that is such as do not conform to
any of the four regular types and are mainly characterized
by the presence of the unthematic forms, are confined to the
two verbs 'to be' and 'to go' given in the paradigm (**209**). For
U. *fertu* is, in view of the Subj. *ferar* and Marruc. *feret* 'fert',
*ferenter* 'feruntur', better taken as thematic, from *\*feretōd*;
and U. **veltu** 'deligito', *ehueltu*, are from *\*ueletōd* (**105**, 2). The
Perfect System of U. *fertu* is supplied, not by a form corresponding to L. *tulī*, but by a form belonging to *\*didō* 'do', at
least in *andirsafust* (**210**, *b*), which belongs in use with U. *anferener* 'circumferendi'.

1. O. **súm** points to *\*som*, whence also L. *sum*. This is
apparently a thematic form with secondary ending, which as an
Injunctive has come to be used in place of the original form
of the Present Indicative.

2. O. **est**, U. **est**, agree with L. *est* (Grk. ἔστι etc.). But
O. **íst**, which is the invariable spelling of the Cippus Abellanus
(7 occurrences) and so cannot possibly be a mere graphic variation of **est**, must be a different form. It can represent *\*ēst*
(í = *ē*, **41**) with *ēs*- standing in the same relation to the usual
*es*- as the *ēd*- in L. *ēst* to the usual *ed*- of *edō* etc.

3. As regards the distribution of the roots *es*- (Grk. εσ-,
Skt. *as*-, etc.) and *fū*- (Grk. φŭ-, Skt. *bhū*-, etc., **124**), observe

O. **fusíd** agreeing with L. *foret* rather than with *esset*, O.-U. *fust* contrasted with L. *erit*, and U. *futu* contrasted with O. *estud*, L. *estó*.

4. O. **amfret** 'ambiunt', for which one would expect *\*amfríiet* or *\*amfrínt*, is probably a form of the Second Conjugation, into the analogy of which the Present had been drawn by the First Singular *\*amfreó*, just as in Latin, vice versa, *ambiō* follows the Fourth Conjugation, starting from *ambīs*, *ambit*, etc. In both cases the isolation from the simplex is due to the fact that the prefixes were unusual, making the composition less obvious.

U. *ambretuto* 'ambiunto' etc. may also belong to the Second Conjugation, but here there is no difficulty in assuming the original unthematic inflection, the *e* corresponding to *ī* in L. *itó* and both representing original *ei*.

### Remarks on the Forms Connected with L. habeō

218. U. *habe* 'habet', Pres. Subj. **habia**, Imperat. *habitu*, **habetu**, belong with L. *habeō* to the Second Conjugation. But the Future U. *habiest* shows a formation which belongs properly to the Fourth Conjugation. This might have arisen by analogy, owing to the resemblance between forms like **habia** (with *i* for *e*, 39, 1) and those of the Fourth Conjugation. However, the intimate relation between *i̯o-* and *ē-*formations is well known, and *habiest* may belong to a lost present *\*habi̯ō*.

U. **neiȓhabas** 'ne adhibeant' may be compared with early Latin *advenat*, *tagam*, etc., in which the usual Present Stem does not appear.

The *hēp-* of O. *hipid* 'habuerit', *pruhipid* 'prohibuerit', Fut. Perf. *hipust*, *pruhipust* (cf. also U. **eitipes**, 264, 2) is best explained as a contamination of the roots seen in L. *habeō* and *capiō*, *cēpī*.

A Present *\*hapi̯ō* is also to be assumed with great probability for U. **hahtu**, *hatu* 'capito', from *\*hapitōd* (216) through *\*haptōd*, *\*haftōd* (121); to which belong further U. **subahtu** 'deponito', *subotu* (? see 35, *a*), and *subator* 'omissi' (for the lack of the initial *h*, cf. *an-ostatu* beside *an-hostatu* etc., 149, *a*).

O. *hafiest* 'habebit' is very likely a mistake for *\*hapiest*, formed from *\*hapiō*, like U. *heriest* from *\*heriō*. In this case all the Oscan forms would belong to *\*hapiō*.

Note. L. *habeō* has often been connected with Gothic *haban*, Eng. *have*, etc., on the basis of a root *khabh-*. But the Umbrian forms point unmistakably to a root ending in *b*, not *bh*, and the Germanic words are probably from the same root as Goth. *hafjan*, L. *capiō*. O. *hafiest* with *f* stands absolutely alone, and is irreconcilable with U. *habe* etc., except on the assumption of a by-form of the root. Without further evidence for *f* it seems more likely that it is a mistake for *\*hapiest* (cf. *fepacid* for *fefacid*; even as it stands *hafiest* contains one obvious correction, the reading being *hafiert*).

### Remarks on the Forms Connected with L. faciō

**219.** The Pres. Subj. O. **fakiiad**, U. **façia**, Infin. **façiu, façu**, Imperat. O. *factud*, agree entirely with the Latin inflection. But the Umbrian Imperat. *fetu, feitu*, cannot correspond to O. *factud*, for we should have *\*faitu* like aitu to O. *actud* (**143**). It must rather come from *\*fēk(e)tōd* or *fēk(i)tōd* with the form of the root seen in L. *fēcī*.

The participles U. **aanfehtaf** and **feta**, if belonging here, are also from *fēk-*.

U. **feia** 'faciat', beside **façia**, is also, probably, from *fēk-*. We should expect *\*feçia*, but see **144**, *b*, on U. *peiu*.

Note. It is noteworthy that in the Imperative form the spelling with *e* is far more common than that with *ei* (fetu 48 times, *fetu* 52 times, *feetu* once: feitu 20 times, *feitu* 5 times), while in all other examples the diphthong resulting from the change of *k* to *i* remains unchanged, not only in aitu, but also in -veitu and *deitu* (**143**). The reason for the difference lies in the quality of the first vowel. The *e* was an open *e* in both -veitu (orig. *e*) and *deitu* (open *ē* from *ei*; see **65**), and did not contract with the following *i*, while in *feitu* the *ē* was a close *ē* (orig. *ē*; see **42**) and did suffer contraction. In the same way *ie* was contracted only when the *e* was close (**82**, 2, with *a*). Thus the spelling *fetu*, fetu, represents the contracted form, while feitu, which is nearly as common as fetu in Old Umbrian, is a retention of the old spelling prior to the contraction.

In all the examples where we have assumed *fēk-*, some prefer *fē-*. This is somewhat easier for feia, but less satisfactory for fetu, *feitu*. Moreover it is probable that in the meaning 'do, make' the Italic root is always *fēk-, fak-*, though this, of course, is an extension of an earlier *fē-, fa-* (Grk. *θη-*, Skt. *dhā-*, etc.), which is preserved in L. *condō* etc. and in O. **prúffed, prúftú** (see **223** with footnote).

## The Imperfect Indicative

**220.** The only extant form is O. **fufans** 'erant', showing the same formation as in Latin. A form serving as the past tense of the verb 'to be', namely *\*bhu̯ā-*, whence O. *fā-*, L. *-bā* (**124**), was added to case-forms in *-ā*, *-ē*, giving a periphrastic formation, and this was then extended to root-forms, as in L. *dabam*, *ībam*, with which O. **fufans** is most closely connected.

## The Future Indicative

**221.** This is in origin a short-vowel Subjunctive of an *s*-Aorist, identical with the Homeric short-vowel forms of the Aorist Subjunctives. In the Second and Third Singular the *e* suffers syncope (**90, 2**), and in the Third Plural the *-ont* is supplanted by *-ent*, as regularly (**204, 3**). Thus O. *deiuast* 'iurabit', *censazet* 'censebunt', U. **prupehast** 'piabit', from *-āset*, *-āsent*; — U. **ferest** 'feret' from *\*fereset*; — U. *ostensendi* 'ostendentur' from *\*ostendesenter* (**137, 2, 156**); — O. **fust**, U. *fust* (*fus*, **127, 3**) 'erit', **furent** 'erunt', from *\*fuset*, *\*fusent*; — U. *eest*, *est* 'ibit' from *\*eiset*, etc.

Although the *s*-aorist is properly formed from the Verb-Stem, the Future has come to follow the Present Stem even where it differs from the former. So O. *didest* 'dabit' with the Present reduplication, U. *heriest* (*heries*, **127, 3**) 'volet', O. *herest* (**100, 3, c**), U. **purtuvies** 'porricies', **fuiest** 'fiet', with the *-i̯o-* of the Present Stem. In the Fourth Conjugation there are two formations, as regards the stem, related to one another as the Latin Imperfects *leniēbam* and *lenībam*; e.g. U. *heriest* etc., — but O. **sakrvist** 'sacrabit' (Pres. **sakruvit**). The latter is analogous to *deiuast*.

## The Perfect Indicative

**222.** This tense, as in Latin, includes various formations. While the *vī-* and *s*-Perfects of the Latin are lacking, their place is taken by others specifically Oscan-Umbrian. The *f-*, *tt-*, and *nkị-*Perfects (227-229), though having no formal connection with the Latin *vī-*Perfect, resemble it in scope, in that they are mainly confined to the First and Fourth Conjugations.

NOTE. An *s-*Perfect, that is, an *s-*Aorist in origin, is assumed by some for U. *sesust* 'sederit', *andersesust*. But this is probably based on the participial stem *sesso-* with *ss* from two dentals (138). A *vī-*Perfect is also assumed by some, but with even less justification.

The endings are the same as in other secondary tenses. In illustrating the different types, forms of the Perfect Subjunctive and Future Perfect are included.

**223.** Reduplicated Perfect. Examples: O. **deded** 'dedit', U. **dede** (131, *c*), with Fut. Perf. U. **teřust**, *dirsust*, from *\*dedust* (by 131); — O. *fefacid* 'fecerit'; — U. *peperscust* 'posuerit'(?); — U. **pepurkurent** 'poposcerint'; — U. **fefure** 'fuerint' (128, 2, *a*); — U. *dersicust* 'dixerit' from *\*dedikust* (by 131); — O. **prúffed** 'posuit' from *\*pro-fefed*: L. *prō-didit*,[1] *con-didit*, etc. (for the *ff* cf. L. *rettulī*, *reppulī*, for *\*re-tetulī* etc.); — O. **aa-manaffed** 'mandavit, locavit' from *\*man-fefed* (80, 2), as if L. *\*mandidit* like *condidit* etc. (see 264, 2); **manafum** 'mandavi'; — O. **fifikus** 'decreveris'(?).

*a.* In all examples but the last the vowel of the reduplication is *e*. This is the original vowel of the Perfect reduplication, but in Latin, after the analogy of *tetendī* to *tendō*, etc., it was replaced by an *i*, *u*, or *o*, of the root-syllable wherever the latter was the same in both Perfect and Present; e.g. *momordī* for earlier *memordī*, *cucurrī*, etc., but *pepulī*. O. **fifikus**, if connected with L. *fīgō*, U. **fiktu**, is an example of a similar, though independent, development in Oscan-Umbrian. None of the other Perfect forms is necessarily at variance with such an assumption, for in U. *dersicust* and *fefure* there is no identity in the root-syllable of Present and Perfect, and for U. **pepurkurent** the Present is unknown.

**224.** Simple Perfect without reduplication. Examples: O. **kúmbened** 'convenit', O. *cebnust* (*ce-* prefix as in L. *cedo*), U. *benust* 'venerit'; — O. *dicust* 'dixerit'; — O. *avaφακετ* 'dedicavit' (80, 2), U. **fakust** 'fecerit'; — U. *habus* 'habuerit'; — O. **dadid**

---

[1] The meaning of O. **prúffed** and **prúftú** (244, 1) agrees more nearly with that of Grk. προτίθημι than with that of L. *prōdō*. In the Latin compounds in *-dō* are merged forms of the roots *dhē-* 'put' and *dō-* 'give', and the existence of the former is less obvious in *prōdō* than in *condō*, which is therefore a more certain cognate of the Oscan forms.

'dediderit'; — U. *couortus, courtust* 'converterit'; — O. *pertemust* 'peremerit', *peremust* 'perceperit'; — U. *procanurent* '*proci-nuerint'; — U. *eiscurent* 'arcessierint'; — U. *portust* 'portaverit'; — O. *urust* 'oraverit'; — O. *comparascuster* 'consulta erit'; — O. **aflakus** 'detuleris'(?).

*a.* As in Latin, it is impossible to distinguish always between forms which are in origin simple thematic Aorists, like Grk. **ἔλιπον** etc., and those which belong historically to the Reduplicated Perfect, but have lost the reduplication in composition or, by analogy, in the simplex, as L. *scidī* beside earlier *scicidī* etc. Loss of reduplication is most evident in cases like O. *dicust* beside U. *dersicust* or U. *fakust* beside O. *fefacid.* O. *dadid* and U. *procanurent* are doubtless examples of loss of reduplication in composition. O. *urust* and U. *portust* from verbs of the First Conjugation (see **211**) are, of course, not original formations.

*b.* U. *iust* 'ierit' is parallel to L. *it*, and U. *purtiius* 'porrexeris' is an extension of the same type, like L. *audiī* after *iī*. With *purtiius* belongs also U. **heriiei** 'voluerit' (**234**, note).

**225.** Perfect with lengthened vowel in the root-syllable. Examples: O. *hipid* 'habuerit', *hipust*, etc. (**218**), U. **prusikurent** 'pronuntiaverint' (cf. also O. *sipus* 'sciens', **90**, 1, *b*), with *ē*, like L. *cēpī, vēnī,* etc.; further O. **upsed** 'fecit', **uupsens, upsens,** *ουπσενς,* with *ō* (**53**) in contrast to *o* of the Present (**úpsannam** etc.).

*a.* By lengthened vowel is meant here simply a long vowel in contrast to a short vowel of the Present. It represents an inherited variation; e.g. *ĕ* : *a* in O. *hipid, sipus,* as in L. *cēpī* to *capiō* (see also **218**), or *ĕ* : *e* in U. **prusikurent**, as in L. *vēnī* to *veniō.* O. **upsed** belongs to a denominative of the First Conjugation, from which one would expect Perf. *\*úpsatted* or *\*úpsafed,* but is formed after the analogy of Perfects of primary verbs, and the *ō* in contrast to the *o* of the Present must be due to Perfects like L. *ēmī, ōdī,* etc.

*b.* Observe that the forms corresponding to L. *ĕmī, vēnī,* and *fēcī* do not follow this type. Thus O. *pertemust* (**224**); O. *kúmbened,* U. *benust* (**234**); O. *fefacid* (**223**), U. *fakust* (**224**), like *fhefhaked* of the Praenestine brooch (cf. L. *pepigī* beside *pēgī*).

**226.** The *l*-Perfect. This is found in Umbrian only, the examples being Fut. Perf. **entelust** 'imposuerit', 2d Sg. **entelus,** and **apelust** 'impenderit', 2d Sg. **apelus.** These are based on participial forms *\*en-tend-lo-, \*am-pend-lo-* (*-lo-* is a regular participial suffix in the Slavic languages; cf. also L. *pendulus, crēdulus,* etc.), with the change of *ndl* through *nnl, nl,* to *ll* (**135**).

The type doubtless arose in the Future Perfect, which is of participial origin, and as the only examples are in this tense it is impossible to say whether it ever extended to the Perfect, giving such forms as *enteled etc. If not, its mention here among the Perfect types is only justified by convenience.

**227.** The *f*-Perfect. Examples: O. aíkdafed 'decrevit'(?);— O. sakrafír 'sacrato'; — U. *andirsafust* 'circumtulerit'; — U. *pihaft* 'piatum sit'; — U. herifi 'oportuerit'; — probably U. *cehefi* 'accensum sit'; — O. fufens 'fuerunt'; — U. amprefuus 'ambieris', *ambrefurent* 'ambierint'.

This *f*-Perfect is a periphrastic formation like the Imperfect, the second element in this case being *bhu̯om*, *bhu̯es*, *bhu̯et*, etc., that is, a past tense formed from the root 'to be' with the thematic vowel. The Latin Futures like *qmābō* contain the same form, but in its Subjunctive function.

**228.** The *tt*-Perfect. This is found in Oscan (with Paelignian, Marrucinian, and Volscian) but not in Umbrian. Oscan examples, all of the First Conjugation, are: prúfatted 'probavit', Pl. prúfattens; — dadíkatted 'dedicavit'; — teremnattens 'terminaverunt'; — tríbarakattíns 'aedificaverint'; — lamatir, *lamatir* 'caedatur'(?); — d]uunated 'donavit'. Cf. Pael. coisatens 'curaverunt', Marruc. *amatens*, Volsc. *sistiatiens* 'statuerunt'. This formation is probably based on the *to*-Participle through the medium of the Future Perfect (cf. the Umbrian *l*-Perfect), but so long as the double *t* is left unexplained its history must remain obscure.

> NOTE. It is possible that a contamination of the *to*-Participle and the *u̯es*-Participle resulted in a form with *tu̯* (e.g. -*tu̯ōs*) which then became *tt*. But it is difficult to support the change of *tu̯* to *tt*.

a. O. *angetuzet* 'proposuerint', the etymology of which is wholly uncertain, has sometimes been taken as a *t*-Perfect. But without further evidence of a *t*-Perfect in the Third Conjugation, it seems more probable that the *t* belongs to the root (*get*- or *gent*- with prefix *an*-). By any theory the fragmentary *angitu*.., if related, is puzzling on account of the *i*.

**229.** The *nki*-Perfect. This is found in Umbrian only, the examples being Fut. Perf. purdinśiust 'porrexerit', *purdinśust*, *purdinśus*, 2d Sg. purtinçus; — *combifianśiust* 'nuntiaverit', *combifianṣiust, combifianṣust*, Perf. Subj. *combifianṣi*; — *dislera-linṣust* 'inritum fecerit'.   These forms point clearly to a forma-tion containing *nkị* (see 144), but its precise origin is uncertain.

Taking *purdinṣiust* as the earlier formation, one may assume that it is based on an adjectival stem *purdinkio-*, again through the medium of the Future Perfect (**226**).   Such a form would contain an *-inko-* based on the O.-U. suffix *-in-* (O. leginum etc.) like L. *-iunco-* based on the corresponding *-iōn-* (cf. L. *rati-uncula* to *ratiō*).   But neither this nor any of the other explanations is entirely convincing.

### The Future Perfect

**230.**  For examples, see **205-209** (especially **207**) and **223-229**. For the omission of final *t* in U. 3d Sg. *habus* and *couortus*, cf. **127, 3.**

The origin of this formation is disputed, but the most prob-able explanation is that it is periphrastic, a combination of a short-vowel Subjunctive of the verb 'to be' with an old Nom. Sg. of a Perf. Act. Partic. in *-us*, a possible relic of which is O. *sipus* 'sciens' (**90,** 1, *b*).   The forms would then be 2d Sg. *-us-ses*, 3d Sg. *-us-set*, whence by syncope *-us(s)*, *-ust*.   After the analogy of the Future, e.g. after *-azent* to *-ast*, would arise beside *-ust* the 3d Pl. in *-uzent* (O. *-uzet*, -uset, U. *-urent*).

> NOTE.  Another possibility is that the type is formed from the Perfect Stem after the analogy of the Future *fust* 'erit'.   Connection with the Latin *vĭ-* and *uĭ-*Perfect, which is strongly urged by some, seems to the author the least likely view.  *Now more p..·+·'·· .*

*a.*  U. *uesticos* 'libaverit' (VI b 25) beside Imperat. *uesticatu* is taken by some as coming from *uestikaust*, but we should expect rather *uesticafust*, or *uesticust* like *portust*.   It probably stands for *uesticos fust*,[1] and is a *to*-Participle, like U. *pihos* 'piatus', but used here in the Active sense like U. çersnatur, L. *cēnātus*.

### THE SUBJUNCTIVE

**231.**  The Italic Subjunctive represents a fusion of the old Subjunctive and Optative, which are kept distinct in Greek and in Vedic Sanskrit.

---

[1] Such an ellipsis, though perhaps without parallel in Latin, is natural enough where the Future Perfect has been used in a clause immediately preceding, and where the conjunction *arnipo* 'donec' prevents any ambiguity.   But it is also possible that the omission is a mere error.

The Optative mood-sign was $i\bar{e}$, $\bar{\imath}$, for unthematic verbs, as seen in L. *sim*, *sīs*, etc. (early L. *siem*, *siēs*, etc.), *velim*, *edim*, etc., and also in the Perfect Subjunctive in *-im* etc. In thematic verbs the mood-sign, including the thematic vowel, was *oi*, as in Grk. φέροι etc., but of this formation there is no trace in Italic.

The Subjunctive mood-sign for unthematic verbs was identical with the thematic vowel of the thematic Indicatives. This type, which may be called the short-vowel Subjunctive, is seen in Latin in *erō* and in the Future Perfect, and in Oscan-Umbrian in the Future and probably in the Future Perfect (230), but has not survived in any forms which are Subjunctives from the Italic point of view. For thematic verbs there were two mood-signs, $\bar{a}$ and $\bar{e}$. The $\bar{a}$ is seen in Latin in the Present Subjunctive of Conjugations II, III, and IV. The $\bar{e}$ is seen in the Present Subjunctive of Conjugation I (probably, see below) and in the Imperfect and Pluperfect Subjunctive, also in the Future of Conjugations III and IV except in the First Singular. In general, then, the Italic Subjunctive forms represent either unthematic Optatives with $i\bar{e}$, $\bar{\imath}$, or thematic Subjunctives with $\bar{a}$ or $\bar{e}$. In Oscan-Umbrian their distribution is the same as in Latin except in the Perfect Subjunctive (234).

### The Present Subjunctive

232. For examples, see 205-209. In the First Conjugation the Oscan forms *deiuaid* 'iuret', *tadait* 'censeat', **sakahíter** 'sacrificetur', contain *-āē-*, from which comes L. *-ē-* by contraction. This *-āē-* from *-āie-* is probably the $\bar{e}$-Subjunctive of *-āio-*, though it might also be wholly or in part the $i\bar{e}$-Optative of an unthematic stem in *-ā*. The Umbrian forms *portaia* 'portet' etc. represent a departure from the original type and are due to the influence of such forms as U. **façia**, **feia**, **fuia**, etc., of the Fourth Conjugation. The forms of Conjugations II–IV agree entirely with the Latin. Of the unthematic forms, U. *si*, *sins*, etc., show the same generalization of the $\bar{\imath}$ as is seen in L. **sīs** etc. (early *siēs* etc.); while O. *osii[ns* with *ii* for *ie* shows the

opposite extension of *iē*, or, more exactly, represents the original
*\*si-ent* (ending *-ent*) with *e* changed to *ē* under the influence of
forms containing *-iē-*.

## The Imperfect Subjunctive

**233.** The only examples are O. **fusíd** 'foret', h]**erríns** 'caperent', **patensíns** 'aperirent' (with Pael. *upsaseter* 'operaretur, fieret').
The **í** is identical with the *ē* in L. *essēs*, *amārēs*, *agerēs*, etc., and
the formation represents an *ē*-Subjunctive of an *s*-Aorist. The
*s*-Aorist, as an unthematic formation, would take the short-vowel
Subjunctive, and this is preserved in the O.-U. Future (**221**).
But, used as Subjunctives, the forms followed the analogy of
the long-vowel type, which had become characteristic of Italic
Subjunctives.

## The Perfect Subjunctive

**234.** For examples, see **205-209** and **223-229**. The **í** of
O. **sakrafír** and **tríbarakattíns** points to *ē* rather than *ī*, so that
the formation is an *ē*-Subjunctive.

NOTE. Some maintain that the two Oscan forms with **í** are not sufficient
evidence to justify us in assuming a divergence from the Latin formation, which
is an *ī*-Optative; that the **í** of **sakrafír** may be a mistake such as is found in the
class of inscriptions to which it belongs, and that the **í** of **tríbarakattíns** may stand
for *i*, shortened from *ī* before *nt*. As regards the latter point, the Imperf. Subj.
forms like h]**erríns** etc. beside **fusíd** show that before the ending *-ns* a long vowel
was either retained or restored by analogy (**78**, *a*), and so we are reasonably
justified in assuming from **tríbarakattíns** a 3d Sg. *\*tríbarakattíd. As for U. heriiei,
which is best taken as a Perf. Subj. 'voluerit' (and *heriei*, *herie* 'vel', which is the
same form), the spelling ei is otherwise unknown for either *ĕ* or *ī*, but may stand
for *ē*, like the *ei* in *nesimei* (**42**). It must be admitted that the material bearing
on the question is scanty, but so far as it goes it points decidedly, we think, to
an *ē*-Subjunctive.

## THE IMPERATIVE

**235.** Two probable examples of the Present Imperative
are: U. *aserio* 'observa' and *stiplo* 'stipulare', both of the First
Conjugation, with *o* for final *ā* (**34**). Here also Pael. *eite* 'ite'.

**236.** All other forms are such as correspond to the Latin
Future Imperative.

1. The ending of the Second and Third Singular is O. *-tud*, U. *-tu*, corresponding to L. *-tō*, early *-tōd*, Grk. *-τω*, etc. (**53, 54**). For examples, see **205-209**. All the Oscan forms are of the Third Person. In the Third Conjugation the thematic vowel suffers syncope except after *n* (**88, 1**). For U. **aitu**, *deitu*, **-veitu**, see **143**; for U. *feitu, fetu*, **219**.

2. There is no unquestioned example of a Plural in Oscan, but **eítuns** (nos. 14–18) has often, and perhaps correctly, been taken as 'eunto'. As such it is easily explained as formed from the Singular after the analogy of the Third Plural of other tenses, where *-ns* corresponds to Sg. *-d*, e.g. Subj. *-ans* beside *-ad*, **-íns** beside **-íd**, etc. It is no objection to this that the Latin and Umbrian formations are different, for both are secondary.

In Umbrian a Second and Third Plural has been formed by the addition of *-tā* (written **-ta, -tu, -to**; see **34**), of uncertain origin. So *fututo* 'estote', **aituta** 'agunto', **habetutu**, *habituto* 'habento', **tusetutu**, *tursituto* 'terrento', etc.

   *a.* The form **etatu**, *etato* 'itatote' comes from *\*etatutu, \*etatuto*, by haplology, as L. *sēmēstris* from *\*sēmi-mēstris* etc.

**237.** There is also a Passive Imperative, ending in Oscan in *-mur*, in Umbrian in *-mu*, Pl. *-mumo*. Thus O. **censamur** 'censetor'; — U. **persnihmu**, *persnihimu* 'precator', Pl. **persnihimumo**; **anouihimu** 'induito', *eheturstahamu* 'exterminato', etc. (the Umbrian forms are all Deponents). The history of the ending is like that of early Latin *-minō*, in *fruiminō* etc., which is related to the *-minī* of the Second Plural (originally an Infinitive form), but modeled after the Active ending *-tō(d)*. Similarly O.-U. *\*-mōd* was formed after *-tōd*, and in Oscan the *d* was replaced by the *r* of the Passive. The Umbrian pluralizing *-mā* is modeled after the *-tā*.

   NOTE. This *\*-mōd* may come from *\*-mnōd* and so be almost identical with L. *-minō*. But, in the absence of other evidence for a change of *mn* to *m* in Oscan-Umbrian, the possibility must be granted that, while formed in the same way as L. *-minō*, it started from a by-form with *m*, perhaps one of the cases in which an I.E. interchange of *mn* and *m* has to be recognized.

*a.* U. **armamu**, *arsmahamo* 'ordamini' comes from \**arsmamumo* by haplology, as *etato* 'itatote'. And this has effected a reduction in the following
word, **kateramu**, *caterahamo* 'catervamini'.

THE PASSIVE

**238.** The Imperative forms have just been mentioned.   In
the Indicative and Subjunctive only the Third Singular and
Third Plural are represented, but two different types of formation are to be distinguished.   For omission of the final *r* in
Umbrian, see **103, 4.**

1.  Forms in -*ter* and -*tur*, answering to the Latin formation
with -*tur*.   In Oscan only -*ter* is found, while in Umbrian -*ter*
is used in primary tenses, -*tur* in secondary.   Examples:

Indicatives.   O.  *uincter* 'convincitur', **sakarater** 'sacratur',
**karanter** 'vescuntur', *comparascuster* 'consulta erit'; — U. **herter**
'oportet', **terte** 'datur'(?), *ostensendi* 'ostendentur' (**39, 2, 156**).
Cf. also Marruc. *ferenter* 'feruntur'.

Subjunctives.   O. **sakahíter** 'sanciatur'; — U. **emantur, emantu**
'accipiantur', **terkantur** 'suffragentur', *tursiandu* 'terreantur' (**156**).
Cf. also Pael. *upsaseter* 'operaretur, fieret'.

2.   Forms in which *r* alone appears as the ending of the
Third Singular.   This type is unknown in Latin.   The most certain examples are:  Pres. Subj. U. *ferar*; — Perf. Subj. O. **sakrafír**, with which belong O. **lamatir**, *lamatir*, U. *pihafei*, **herifi**, *cehefi*,
and probably U. *ier* (cf. Fut. Perf. *iust*); — Pres. Indic. O. *loufir*
(from \**loufēr* beside Act. \**loufēt*: L. *libet*; for meaning 'vel',
see **202, 18**).   For the meaning of forms of this type, see **239.**

The Future Perfects U. *benuso, couortuso*, probably belong
here, standing for \**benusor* and \**couortusor*, though their precise
origin is doubtful.

*a.* The view that U. *hertei, herti*, stands for \**hertēr*, and represents a Present Subjunctive of a still different type from those cited under 1 and 2, is to be
given up.   Though *ei* usually stands for a long vowel, there are a few instances
of its use for short *i* (**29**) which, taken in connection with U. *ostensendi* with *i*
for *e* before final *r* (**39, 2**), show that it is unnecessary to separate *hertei* from
**herter** and other forms in -*ter*.   Nor is the Subjunctive demanded by the syntax.

*b.* O. sakraitir 'sacretur', for which one would expect \*sakraiter like saka-hiter, possibly owes its i to contamination with forms like sakrafir. Or shall we adopt the other possible reading sakrattir in spite of the fact that this would give us a *tt*-Perfect and an *f*-Perfect from the same verb?

*c.* For O. kaispatar 'caedatur'(?) and krustatar 'cruentetur'(?), apparently related to L. *caespes* and *crūstus*, there is no satisfactory explanation. If they are taken as Subjunctives of the *tt*-Perfect from denominatives of the First Conjugation, the *-ar* instead of *-ir* cannot be accounted for. It is more probable that they are Present Subjunctives of the Third Conjugation, from \*kaispō, \*krūstō, the *-tar* in place of *-ter* being due, possibly, to contamination with the type of U. *ferar*. Another suggestion is that they are from Presents in *-atō* or *-ātō*, in which case they belong to the same type as U. *ferar*.

**239.** A Passive and Deponent formation characterized by *r* is the common possession of the Italic and Celtic languages. This *r* is unquestionably to be connected with a series of Third Plural secondary endings containing *r*, which are preserved in Sanskrit (*-ur, -ran, -ranta*, etc.). But the precise starting-point and the various steps in the development are necessarily obscure. The following view seems most probable.[1]

We start from an Active ending *-r*, parallel to the usual *-nt*, and a Middle ending *-ro* parallel to the usual *-nto*.

The forms in *-r*, though originally Plural and Active, came to be used only when the subject was indefinite, and in this way lost their specifically Plural force. Cf. Eng. 'they say' or 'one says', but Germ. 'man sagt', Fr. 'on dit', etc. From such a meaning it is but a step to an Impersonal Passive (cf. Eng. 'it is said'), and from that again to a fully developed Passive with definite subject; and this development would be assisted by the existence of other forms containing *r* which were based on a Middle ending and so had partly Passive force from the outset. In the O.-U. forms in *-r* the impersonal meaning prevails, there being only one form with subject expressed, namely O. *esuf lamatir* 'let him be beaten'(?). In O. Iúviass . . . sakriss sakrafir, avt últiumam kerssnaís 'the Ioviae are to be consecrated with sacrifices, but the last one with banquets', sakrafir has the Accusative construction which goes with the meaning 'let one consecrate', 'let there be consecration of'. O. *loufir*, U. *ier*, *herifi*, *benuso*, and *couortuso* are impersonal, while in the case of U. *ferar*, *pihafei*, and *cehefi* it is impossible to say whether the word or clause to which they refer is to be taken as Nominative or Accusative.

[1] I follow Thurneysen, K.Z. 37, 92 ff., in his explanation of forms in *-ter*, but for forms like U. *ferar* I still hold to what is substantially the view of Zimmer, K.Z. 30, 276 ff., and this without regard to the question of how far an Active impersonal use is actually to be recognized in the corresponding Celtic forms.

The forms in *-ter* sprang from a Third Plural in *-ntro* representing a contamination of the Middle endings *-nto* and *-ro* (cf. Skt. *-ranta*, a combination of the same elements in the reverse order). After this the Third Singular ending *-to* became *-tro*; and *-tro, -ntro*, became *-ter, -nter*, in the same way as U. *ager*, L. *ager*, from *\*agros* (91, 2).

The forms in *-tur*, undoubtedly from *-tor*, are the most difficult, but perhaps originated in a combination of *-nto* with the simple *-r*, giving *-ntor*, whence the Singular *-tor*.

All the formations mentioned, though originating in secondary endings, came to be used in primary tenses as well. The distinction of primary *-ter* and secondary *-tur* is unoriginal and confined to Umbrian. In Latin, *-tur* prevailed in all tenses; in Oscan, *-ter*.

### The Periphrastic Passive

**240.** In the Perfect System of the Passive, periphrastic forms are more common than the *r*-forms. Thus: Perf. Indic. O. **teremnatust** 'terminata est', **prúftúset** 'posita sunt', *scriftas set* 'scriptae sunt', U. *screhto est* 'scriptum est', *screihtor sent*, etc.; Perf. Subj. U. **kuratu si** 'curatum sit'; Fut. Perf. U. **pihaz fust** 'piatus erit', *muieto fust* 'muttitum erit', **çersnatur furent** 'cenati erunt', etc.; Perf. Infin. U. **kuratu eru** 'curatum esse', *ehiato erom* 'emissum esse'.

### The Present Infinitive

**241.** For examples, see **205-209**. The ending was *-om*, doubtless an Accusative form in origin, with change to *-um* in Oscan (**50**). In the First Conjugation *-aum* remained uncontracted, and in **tríbarakavúm** the **v** is simply a glide sound. See **33**.

For the Perfect Infinitive Passive, see **240**.

### The Supine

**242.** The one certain example of the Supine is U. **anzeriatu**, *aseriato* 'observatum', showing the same formation and use as the Latin Supine. On *o* for *-u(m)*, see **57**.

*a.* U. *aso* VI b 50 is often regarded as a Supine, but is more probably a Perf. Pass. Partic. ("Let the same person carry it lighted on the right shoulder").

## The Present Active Participle

**243.** The formation is the same as in Latin. Examples are:
O. *praesentid* 'praesente' (**178**, 5, *a*), U. zeřef, *serse* 'sedens', U. restef,
*reste* 'instaurans' (**213**, 4, *a*), U. kutef 'murmurans' (**262**, 2). For
the -*f*, see **110**, 4.

*a.* The existence of an O. staief 'stans' is altogether doubtful, owing to
the uncertainty of the reading and division of words (no. 29).

## The Perfect Passive Participle

**244.** The formation is the same as in Latin.

1. -*to*-. O. *scriftas* 'scriptas', U. *screihtor*;—U. *šihitu* 'cinctos'; — O. statús 'stati'; — O. prúftú 'posita' from *pro-fa-to- (*fa*-
reduced grade of *fē*-, as in *fak*- beside *fēk*-); L. *prō-di-tus*,
*con-di-tus*, Grk. πρό-θε-τος (see **223** with footnote); — U. *daetom*
'delictum' (as if L. *dē-itum*); — O. *ancensto* 'incensa', *censtom-en*
'in censum', to *censaum* (**211**). For forms in -*so*- from roots ending in a dental, see **138**; and for U. *spefa* etc., see **110**, 8.

*a.* O. *ancensto*, *censtom-en*, represent the normal formation, as compared
with L. *cēnsus* which is one of the examples of the analogical extension of -*so*-.
Similarly O. *censtur* : L. *cēnsor* (O. kenzsur, occurring once, is due to Latin
influence).

*b.* A probable example of the analogical -*so*- is *pelso-, assumed from
U. *pelsatu* etc. See **262**, 1, *a*. So also U. *sepse*, which may well mean 'sane'
(*sepse sarsite* 'sane sarteque'), is perhaps an adverb formed from *saipso- :
L. *saeptus*. Cf. L. *lāpsus*.

*c.* U. *aso* 'arsum' (**242**, *a*) is commonly connected with L. *assus*, which
seems to contain *asso- in place of *asto-. But it might also be connected with
L. *ārsus*, if the *r* of *ārdeō*, *āreō*, were original and not from *s*, as is often assumed.
That is, its *s* might stand in the same relation to the *rf* of U. *trahuorfi* (**115**, 3)
as that of L. *rūsum* to the restored *rs* of *rūrsum*, *versus*, etc. This of course is
impossible if L. *āreō* is connected with *āra*, O.-U. *asa-*, but the history of this
whole class of words is obscure.

2. -*āto*-. O. teremnatust 'terminata est', staflatas 'statutae',
ehpeílatas 'erectae'; — U. pihaz, *pihos* 'piatus' (**35**, **137**, 2), çersnatur
'cenati', anzeriatas 'observatis', etc.

*a.* O. doiuatuns 'iurati', if the *n* is not merely a mistake, must owe its
form to the influence of agent-nouns in -*ōn*- like L. *praedō*, O. averrunei (**247**, 2).

3. *-īto-*.  U. *purditom* 'porrectum', *heritu* 'optato', *stahmito* 'statutum', *persnis* 'precatus' from *\*persnīt(o)s*, etc.  Like *persnis* in formation and use is U. *uestis, uesteis* 'libans', beside *uesticatu* etc. from an extended stem *\*uestikā-*.  Here belongs also U. *sarsite* 'sarte' (see above, 1, *b*), as if L. *\*sarcītus* instead of *sartus*.

4. *-eto-* (see **36, 3, 88, 2**).  U. **taçez**, *tases* 'tacitus' (**137, 2**), *uirseto* 'visum', *opeter* 'lecti' (**212,** *b*), **maletu** 'molitum' (beside *comatir* 'commolitis' with *-to-*); — further, in the First Conjugation, U. **pruseçetu**, *oseto*, etc. (**211**).

a. U. *comohota* 'commota' probably belongs here, coming from *\*moueto-* by syncope and change of *ou* to *ō* (**72**).  L. *mōtus* also comes from *\*moueto-*, but independently.  For it is not to be separated from *vōtus* from *\*uoueto-*, earlier *\*uoghꭎeto-*, U. **vufetes** (**152**), in which, obviously, the process is specifically Latin.

### The Gerundive

**245.** The forms correspond to the Latin, with the change of *nd* to *nn* (**135**).  The origin of the formation is still unsettled.  Examples : O. **úpsannam** 'faciendam', **sakrannas** 'sacrandae', **eehiianasúm** 'emittendarum'; — U. *pihaner* 'piandi', *anferener* 'circumferendi', **pelsans** 'sepeliendus'(?).

Note.  The Oscan-Umbrian forms bear upon the much-disputed question of the origin of the Gerundive to this extent, that they are unfavorable to any theory which assumes that the original form contained *ndh.*  For there are too serious difficulties, we think, in the way of assuming that the representation of an original sonant aspirate after a nasal by a simple sonant is not only Latin and Umbrian (**161**) but also Oscan, and so may belong to the Oscan-Umbrian or even the Italic period.  See **161**, *a* with footnote, and **264, 2** (O. **aa-manaffed** from Pres. *\*manfō*), not to mention O. **Anafríss.**  Otherwise Fay, Trans. Am. Phil. Assoc. 29, pp. 15 ff.

# WORD-FORMATION[1]

## DERIVATION OF NOUNS AND ADJECTIVES

### NOUNS

**246.** 1. *-tōr-* in agent-nouns (L. *victor*). O. *censtur* 'censor', U. aïfertur '*adfertor, flamen', O. embratur 'imperator', O. Regaturei 'Rectori' (with *-ā-tōr-* after derivatives of *ā*-verbs). See **180, 1**.

*a.* Derivatives of agent-nouns are regularly formed from the reduced grade of the suffix (**97**), like L. *victr-īx*; e.g. U. kvestretie, uhtretie (**251, 1**), beside kvestur, uhtur, O. Fuutrei (**180**, *a*). Here belong the Oscan proper names Sadiriis 'Satrius' (**81, 157, 2**; cf. L. *sator*), Vestirikiiúí 'Vestricio' (**81**; cf. L. *Vestōrius* with *-tōr-*), Tintiriis '*Tintrius'' (cf. L. *Tintōrius* with *-tōr-*; *Tintirius* is simply the Oscan form, like *Pontius, Popidius, Calavius*). But the later formation with *-tōr-* (cf. L. *amātōrius, auctōritās*) is also represented, e.g. U. speturie '*spectoriae' beside Speture '*Spectori', O. Kenssurineís beside kenzsur 'censores'.

2. *-ter-* (*-tēr-, -tr-*) in nouns of relationship (L. *pater*). O. patir 'pater', U. frater 'fratres'. See **180, 2**.

**247.** 1. *-iōn-* (*-īn-*), *-tiōn-* (*-tīn-*), in abstracts denoting action, or, with a transfer to the concrete sense, the result of the action (L. *legiō, āctiō*). O. tríbarakkiuf 'aedificium', *tanginud* 'sententia', fruktatiuf 'fructus', *medicatinom* 'iudicationem', U. natine 'natione'. See **181**, with *a*.

*a.* *-ti-*, of which *-tiōn-* is an extension, is seen in some words where the Latin has the extended form. Thus U. ahtim-em 'ad caerimonium'(?): L. *āctiō*; — O. uhftis 'voluntates': L. *optiō*; — U. -vakāz, -uacos, from *uakāt(i)s : L. *vacā-tiō*. Cf. also U. puntes 'pentads' from *pomp-ti- (**146, 153**); — U. spanti 'latus' from *span-ti (root *span-*, Eng. *span*, Germ. *spannen*, related to *spā-* in U. spahatu (**110, 3**, *a*).

---

[1] That is, the formation of the word as a whole, irrespective of inflectional variations. Some matters which belong strictly under this head, such as the formation of adverbs, of the comparative and superlative, etc., have been treated, for greater convenience, in connection with Inflection. There remain, then, Derivation of Nouns and Adjectives by means of suffixes, Secondary Verbal Derivation, and Composition. No attempt is made to present the material in full, but examples are given of all the more important formations.

2. *-ōn-* in agent-nouns (L. *praedō*). O. **sverrunei** 'spokesman' (? see note to C. A. 2; cf. L. *susurrō*); — U. *marōn-*, name of an official (see note to no. 84). For other nouns in *-ōn-*, see **181**, *b*.

*a.* *-ōnā-*, probably an extension of *-ōn-*, and frequent in names of divinities (L. *Bellōna*), is seen in U. **Vesune**. In the parallel names of male divinities, U. **Ahmune, Puemune,** *Uofione*, all Dat. Sg., it is not clear whether the suffix is *-ōno-* or simply *-ōn-*.

3. *-men-* (*-mn-*) in nouns denoting action or result of the action (L. *fragmen*). U. *nome* 'nomen'; — O. **teremniss** 'terminibus' (but U. *termnom-e* etc., like L. *terminus* beside *termen*); — U. **tikamne** 'dedicatione' (from *dikā-*; cf. L. *certāmen* etc.). The extended form *-mento-* is seen in O. **tristaamentud** 'testamento'. But U. *pelmner*: L. *pulmentum*.

**248.** *-lo-, -elo-, -flo-, -klo-, -tro-,* in nouns denoting means or instrument, or sometimes place or result.

1. *-lo-,-elo-*(L. *vinculum*). U. *\*uiðlo-* (*preuiðlatu* '*\*praevinculato*') from *\*uinkelo-* ;— U. **tiçel** 'dedicatio', Acc. Sg. **tiçlu**, from *\*dikelo-*. See **88, 4, 144**.

2. *-flo-* (L. *pābulum*; orig. *-dhlo-*, Grk. *-θλο-*). A *\*staflo-* (L. *stabulum*) is implied by O. **staflatas** 'statutae', U. **staflarem** '*\*stabularem*', Pael. *pristafalacirix* '*\*praestibulatrix*'. Cf. the adjective suffix *-fli-* (**261**, 1).

3. *-klo-, -klā-* (L. *piāculum*; orig. *-tlo-*, Grk. *-τλο-*; see **129**, 2). O. **sakaraklúm** 'templum', U. *pihaclu* 'piaculo', U. **naraklum** 'narratio'; — U. **kumnahkle** 'in conventu', from *\*komno-* (U. **kumne**, O. *comono*), either directly, after the analogy of other forms in *-āklo-*, or through a denominative verb-stem *\*komnā-* ; — U. **ehvelklu** 'sententiam' from *\*ueleklo-* (*ehueltu*, **veltu**; cf. L. *vehiculum*);—U. **muneklu** 'sportulam' from *\*moinī-klo-* (cf. L. *perīculum*), containing a denominative verb-stem *\*moinī-* (cf. L. *mūnia, commūnis,* O. **múiní-kú**); — (Masc.) O. **puklum** 'puerum', Pael. *puclois* (Skt. *putrá-*); — U. **fikla** 'offam' from *\*fig-klā* (L. *fingō*). For O. **pestlúm** 'templum' with *-tlo-* preserved, and U. *persclo*, belonging probably under 1, see **129**, 2.

*a.* Is U. *aviekla, auiecla* 'augurali' simply an adjective form of a noun *\*auiē-klo-*, formed from a denominative verb-stem *\*auiē-* (cf. U. *auie* 'augurio')?

We should expect an additional adjectival suffix, as in L. *perĭculōsus, piāculāris,* etc. But on the other hand, a diminutive form *\*ayiĕkelo-,* whether with -*kelo-,* or from an *\*ayiĕko-* (cf. U. aviekate), would give U. \*avieçla. Cf. U. arçlataf and struhçla, 249, 1, 2, and 144.

　　4. -*tro-, -trā-* (L. *arātrum*). U. krematru '\*crematra' (L. *cremō*); — *cringatro* 'cinctum' (39, 3); — kletram 'lecticam' (L. *clī-nō, clī-tellae,* etc.).

　　*a.* A transfer to the *u*-Declension is seen in O. *castrous,* U. *castruo,* etc.: L. *castrum.*

　　**249.** -*lo-, -elo-, -kelo-,* in diminutives.

　　1. -*lo-, -elo-* (L. *porculus*). U. Funtler-e, *Fondlir-e* 'in \*Fontulis' from *\*fontelo-* (L. *fōns*); — U. arçlataf 'arculatas', derived from *\*arkelo-* (L. *arcus, arculus*; see 154); — O. iúklei probably 'formula of consecration, consecration' from *\*iokelo-* (L. *iocus,* U. iuka 'preces').[1]

　　2. -*kelo-* (L. *ōsculum*). O. ziculud 'die', Acc. Pl. d]iikúlús (cf. L. *diēcula*); — U. veskla 'vascula', struhçla '\*struiculam'. See 88, 4, 144.

　　**250.** -*io- (-i-), -iā-.* For the inflection of the Neuters in -*io-,* see 172, 173, 1, 5.

　　1. In primary derivatives (L. *studium, furia*). O. kúmbenniefs 'conventus'; — O. memnim 'monumentum' from *\*me-men-io-;* — U. arkani 'cantum'; — O. heriam 'arbitrium, vim'.

　　2. In secondary derivatives (L. *magisterium, familia*). O. *medicim* 'magistracy', Abl. Sg. *meddixud* (100, 3, *c*), and meddikkiai 'in the meddixship', both derived from *meddik-* 'magistrate, meddix', the suffix having here the same force as L. -*ātus* in *iūdicātus, magistrātus* (L. *iūdicium, vindicia,* are primary derivatives from *iūdicō, vindicō*); — O. *famelo* 'familia' from *\*famelia* (100, 3, *c*), derived from *\*famelo-* (O. famel, L. *famulus*); — O. Víteliú 'Italia' (also Vítelliú, 162, 1) from * Uiteliā,[2] probably derived from *\*uitelo-* (U. vitlu, L. *vitulus*); — here also probably O. prupukid 'by previous agreement' (173, 5).

---

[1] The derivation from a *\*diuo-kelo-* 'day', though attractive on the side of meaning, is on the whole less likely.

[2] From some such form was borrowed the Grk. 'Iταλία, which became the source of L. *Italia.*

**251.** 1. *-itiā-* (L. *dūritia*). U. **kvestretie** 'in quaestura', **uhtretie** 'in *auctura', beside **kvestur**, **uhtur** (see **246,** 1, *a*).

*a.* That these are Locatives of the First Declension and not Ablatives of the Fifth with the suffix *-itiĕ-* (L. *dūritiĕs*), is shown by the form of the adjective agreeing with **kvestretie**.

2. *-no-*, *-nā-* (L. *dōnum*, *urnā*). O. **dunum**, U. **dunu** 'donum'; —U. *tremnu* 'tabernaculo' from **treb-no-* (**125**, 1); — O. **fíísnú** 'fanum', U. **fesnaf-e**, from **fēs-nā-* (**99**, 1). O. *comono* 'comitium', U. **kumne**, and O. **amnúd** 'circuitu', *amnud* 'causa', are formed from the prepositional adverbs *kom* and *am*, like L. *trānstrum* from *trāns*. For *-no-* in adjectives, see **255**.

*a.* *-snā-* is to be assumed for O. **kersnu** 'cena', U. *šesna*, etc. See **116**, 2. *-ni-* is seen in U. *poni* 'posca' (*pō-ni-*).

3. *-mo-*, *-mā-* (L. *armus*, *spūma*). O. **tormo-*, whence **turumiiad** 'torqueatur', from **torkʸ-mo-* (**146**); — O. *egmo* 'res' (L. *egeō*?); — U. *arsmor* 'ritus,' whence also *arsmatiam* 'ritualem', *arsmahamo* 'ordamini', without any certain cognates, but probably coming from **ad-mo-*, with a root *ad-* used of 'orderly arrangement'. For *-mo-* in adjectives, see **189**.

4. *-uriā-*, *-eriā-*, in derivatives of numerals. U. **tekuries**, *dequrier* 'decuriis' (**191**, 10); — O. **púmperiaís** '*quincuriis' (in U. **pumperías** the ř is probably an error).

5. *-tāt(i)-* (L. *bonitās*). O. **Herentateís** 'Veneris' (Pael. *Herentas*; cf. also 'Ερμέντης · 'Αφροδίτης ἐπώνυμον. — Hesychius) from **herenti-tāt(i)-* by haplology, like L. *voluntās* from **ʋolonti-tāt(i)-*.

6. *-tu-* (L. *cantus*). U. **Ahtu** '*Actui'; — U. **arputrati** 'arbitratu' with *-ātu-*, like L. *cōnsulātus* etc., but with this force more commonly *-i̯o-* (**250**, 2) or *-āto-* (**259**, 2).

### ADJECTIVES[1]

**252.** 1. *-i̯o-*, *-ii̯o-* (L. *patrius*). This is especially common in praenomina and gentiles, for which see **174-176**; also in derivatives of names of divinities, as O. **Mamerttiaís** 'Martiis', O. **Iúvíla**

---

[1] Including many substantives of obviously adjectival origin.

'Ioviam', U. **Iuvie**, U. **Çerfie** beside **Çerfe**, O. **Fiisiais**, U. *Fisier*, etc., beside U. *Fiso*.

a. Many of these are used as epithets of other divinities, as in U. **Prestate Çerfie**, **Tefre Iuvie**, etc. (cf. L. *Hercules Iovius*, *Venus Iovius*, etc.). They sometimes stand alone as independent names, e.g. U. **Iuvie** (II a 6, 8), **Saçi** (II b 10).

2. *-eo-* (L. *aureus*) from *-eio-*. U. **fasiu**, *farsio* 'farrea' (*i* from *e*, 39, 1).

**253.** \**-aiio-, -eiio-, -ēiio-*. See 61, 3.

1. *-aiio-*. O. **kersnaiias** '\*cenariae'; — U. **pernaiaf** 'anticas', **pustnaiaf** 'posticas', from *perne* 'ante', *postne* 'pone'; — **pefaia**, *persaia* 'humi stratas'(?) from **pefum**, *perso* 'fossam'; — in names of persons, O. **Tantrnnaiúm**, **Vesulliaís** (176, 3), *Maraies*, Gen. Sg. **Maraiieís** (176, 4); — extended by the suffix *-āno-*, O. **Púmpaiians** 'Pompeianus', O. **Búvaianúd** 'in Boviano'.

a. Like *Veii* etc., *Pompeii* was named from a gens, in this case the \***Púmpaiius** (derived from \**pompe* 'quinque'; cf. *Quintii*).

2. *-eiio-*. O. **vereiiaí** 'iuventuti', Gen. Sg. **vereias**, **verehias** (? reading uncertain) from \**uero-* 'defense' (see note to no. 4); — U. **Teteies** 'Tetteius'(?). It is doubtful whether U. *deueia* 'divinam' belongs here, though if it contains the simple *-io-* suffix (252, 1), like O. **Diíviiai**, the spelling *ei* in both occurrences is remarkable.

3. *-ēiio-* (L. *plebēius*). O. **Kerríiaí** 'Cereali', **Kerríiúís**, etc.

Note. The suffixes *-aiio-, -ciio-*, and *-ēiio-* probably originated in the addition of the suffix *-io-* to the Loc. Sg. of *ā-, o-*, and *ē-*stems. With *-aiio-* is to be compared Grk. *-αιος* (δίκαιος); and Grk. *-ειος* (οἰκεῖος), though coming from various sources, corresponds in part to *-eiio-*. Similarly O. **púiiu** 'cuia', L. *quoius, cuius*, are, like Grk. ποῖος, from \**quoi-io-*.

**254.** *-āsio-* (L. *ōrdinārius*). O. **purasiaí** 'in igniaria', **degetasis** '\*decentarius'; — frequent in substantive use, denoting certain ceremonies, as O. **Fiuusasiaís** 'Floralibus', **kerssnasias** '\*cenariae', **sakrasias** '\*sacrariae', U. **plenasier urnasier** '\*plenariis \*urnariis', etc.; — with an added *-iko-*, O. **múltasíkad** 'multaticia'. For the retention of *s* in Umbrian, and for U. **ezariaf** 'escas'(?), see 112, *a*.

Note. It is not unlikely that this suffix originated in the addition of the suffix *-io-* to the Gen. Sg. of *ā-*stems.

**255.** 1. *-no-* in primary derivatives. U. *plener* 'plenis'; — O. **sullus** 'omnes', **sullum**, etc. (L. *soll-emnis* etc.; cf. also Pael. *solois* 'omnibus'), probably from *\*solno-*[1]. For *-no-*, *-nā-* in nouns, see **251, 2.**

2. *-ni-* in primary derivatives. U. *fons* 'favens', Nom. Pl. *foner*, etc. (cf. L. *Fōnēs* beside *Faunus*).

3. *-no-* in secondary derivatives. U. **ahesnes** 'ahenis'.

4. *-āno-* (L. *Rōmānus*). O. **Abellanús** 'Abellani', U. *Treblanir* 'Trebulanis', etc.; — with added *-io-*, O. **Dekmanniúís**, name of a festival.

*a.* O. **amvianud** 'detour' would seem to be a derivative in *-āno-*, used substantively, were it not for the spelling **amviannud**, which occurs twice, and is probably the more correct (n for nn can be paralleled, but not nn for n; see **162, 163**). The form looks like a Gerundive used substantively, as if L. *\*amviandum*, and meaning a 'circuitous route'. But there is apparently nothing like this in Latin.

5. *-īno-* (L. *dīvīnus*). O. **deivinais** 'divinis', *Bantins* 'Bantinus', Μαμερτινο 'Mamertina'; U. *cabriner* 'caprini', **Ikuvins** 'Iguvinus', etc.

6. *-ōno-*. U. *esono-* 'sacer' is possibly from *\*ais(e)s-ōno-* (**112, a**), though there is little support in Italic for such an adjective-suffix. The noun-suffix *-ōno-*, *-ōnā-*, originated in an extension of *-ōn-* (**247, 2, a**).

**256.** 1. *-ko-* in names of peoples (L. *Opscī, Oscī, Faliscī,* etc.). U. **Turskum**, *Tuscom* 'Tuscum'; — U. **Iapuzkum**, *Iapusco* '\*Iapudicum' from *\*Iapud(i)sko-* (cf. *Iapydes*, Ἰάπυδες, name of an Illyrian- people); — U. **Naharkum**, *Naharcom* '\*Narcum' (cf. L. *Nār, Nahartēs, Nārtēs*).[2]

2. *-iko-* (L. *bellicus*). O. **túvtiks** 'publicus', *toutico*, U. *totcor*, etc.; — O. **múiníkú** 'communis', **muinikam**, etc.; — U. **fratreks**, *fratrexs* '\*fratricus, magister fratrum'.

3. *-ikio-* (L. *patricius*). O. **serevkid** 'auspicio' probably from *\*seruikio-* (**173, 5**); — O. **Kastríkiíeís** 'Castricii'; — with syncope O. **Iúvkiíúí** '\*Iovicio'.

---

[1] Some derive from *\*solio-*, but the change of *lu* to *ll* is one which we do not accept.

[2] The uniform spelling with *h* in both alphabets shows that the *h* is not merely a sign of vowel-length, and that L. *Nār* is from *\*Nahar*, like *cōrs* from *cohors*.

4. *-īkio-* (L. *novīcius*, but otherwise rare except in the type *-tīcius*). O. **Vestirikiíúí** 'Vestricio', **Viínikiís** ' Vinicius' (*-īkio-* rather than *-ikio-* is assumed here on account of the spelling with i, not í).

5. *-ukio-* (or *-ūkio-?*). U. **Kastruçiie** (cf. O. *castrous*, U. *castruo*, from *kastru-*) in contrast to O. **Kastríkiíeís**.

6. *-āk-* (L. *audāx*). O. **malaks** 'malevolos'(?); — U. **huntak** 'puteum'(?), probably Acc. Sg. N. of *\*hondāk-* meaning 'underground' (cf. *hondra* 'infra') and used substantively of a 'well'; — U. *curnaco* 'cornicem', *curnase*: L. *cornīx* with *-ik-*.

7. *-āko-* (L. *merācus*; cf. also Celtic names like *Teutobodiācī* etc.). U. **Tesenakes**, *Tesenocir* (see **35**, *a*).

8. *-k-*. O. **Vezkeí** is most easily derived from *\*U̯etes-k-* or *\*U̯etos-k-* with *-k-* beside *-ko-* in L. *vetuscus*, yet the connection with the latter word must be regarded as wholly uncertain.

**257.** 1. *-ro-* in primary derivatives. O.-U. *sakro-* 'sacer' (O. σακορο, U. *sacra*, etc.); — U. **rufra** 'rubra'; — U. **vufru** 'votivum' (*u̯of-*; cf. **vufetes** 'votis').

2. *-ri-* in primary derivatives. O.-U. *sakri-* beside *sakro-* (see **187**, 2); — U. **pacer** 'propitius', Nom. Pl. **pacrer** (*păk-*; cf. L. *păx* etc.); — O. **akrid** (**99**, 3); — O. **ocrer** (**99**, 3; for *ocar* see **91**, *b*).

3. For *-ero-*, *-tero-*, see **188**, 2.

4. *-āli-*, *-āri-*, in secondary derivatives (L. *rēgālis*, *populāris*). O. **fertalis** '(ceremonies) celebrated with sacrificial cakes' (L. *fertum*); — O. **luisarifs** (see **138**, and note to no. 21); — O. **Dekkviarím** 'Decurialem'; — U. **furu sehmeniar** 'forum seminarium' (cf. *forum piscārium* etc.). Cf. also U. *disleralinsust*, **262**, 3.

5. *-īlo-* (cf. L. *-īli-* in *hostīlis* etc.). O. **iuvilu** '\*iovila', **diuvilam**, **iúvilam**, etc., is probably an adjective form used substantively, from *\*di̯ou̯īlo-*, a derivative of *Di̯ou̯-* (O. **Diúveí** etc.). Cf. L. *Iūlus*, *Iūlius*, from *\*Iou̯ilo-*, *Iou̯ilio-*; and *Iuīliús* (inscr.), which is perhaps *Iuīlius*.

**258.** 1. *-u̯o-* in primary derivatives. O. **salavs** 'salvus' (**80**, 1), U. **suluom** 'salvum', etc.; — O. **siuom** 'omnino', U. **seuom** 'totum', etc., from *\*sē-u̯o-* (**15**, 12); — U. **çive** 'citra' (**189**, 1, *a*, **190**, 1); —

with participial force, O. *facus* 'factus', *praefucus* 'praefectus', from
*\*fak-ŭo-* (cf. L. *mortuus* etc.).

2. *-ŭo-* in secondary derivatives. U. **mersuva** 'iusta' from
*\*medes-ŭo* (**132**, *a*); — U. **tesvam**, *dersua* 'prosperam' probably
from *\*dedes-ŭo-* (**132**, *b*); — U. **felsva** 'holera'(?) from *\*feles-ŭo-*
(L. *holus*? see **149**, *b*).

3. *-ŭio-*, an extension of *-ŭo-*, in proper names. O. **Salaviis,
Kalaviis, Helleviis, Heleviieís**, for which see also **80**, 1; — O. **Akviiai,**
U. *Piquier*.

4. *-oŭio-* in proper names. O. **Kaluvis**, Gen. Sg. **Kalúvieís** ; —
U. *Fisouie, Grabouie.* · U. *Ikuvinus, Iiouinur*, etc. also implies an
*\*Igoŭio-* : L. *Iguvium*. Cf. Mars. *Cantouios*, and *Vitrovius, Sal-
lovius*, etc., which occur in Latin inscriptions but are dialectic,
the regular Latin forms being *Vitruvius, Salluvius*, etc.

Note. *-oŭio-* is an extension of *-oŭo-*, earlier *-eŭo-*, as *-ŭio-* is of *-ŭo-*.
For *-eŭo-* beside *-ŭo-*, cf. Ion. κενεός from *\*κενεϝός and κεινός from *\*κενϝός. In
Latin the two forms of the suffix become identical.[1]

**259.** 1. *-to-*, the suffix of the Perf. Pass. Partic. (**244**), is
also used, as in Latin (*barbātus*), to form adjectives directly
from noun-stems. U. *hostatu* 'hastatos', *mersto* 'iustum' (**88**, 3),
**petenata** 'pectinatam, comb-shaped', etc. ; — U. *ponisiater*, **puniçate**,
name of an official, perhaps named from a purple costume
(*\*poiniki-āto-* : L. *pūnicus*). Cf. also proper names from participles or adjectives in *-to-*, as O. **Minaz, Pukalatúí** (*\*puklāto-*
from *puklo-* 'puer', O. **puklum** etc.), **Kluvatiis, Betitis**, etc.

2. *-āto-* is used in substantives denoting office or official
body, like L. *-ātu-*. O. *senateis* 'senatus' (cf. also L. *senātī*); —
U. *fratrecate* (Loc. Sg.) 'office of fratrex'; — U. *maronatei* (Loc.
Sg.) 'office of maro' (see note to no. 84), *maronato* (Abl. Sg.;
see **302**). *[handwritten annotation]*

3. *-āti-* in derivatives of names of towns (L. *Arpīnās*).
O. **Saipinaz** 'Saepinas, of Saepinum', **Lúvkanateís** '\*Lucanatis'; —

---

[1] For the material see especially Solmsen, Studien zur lat. Lautgeschichte,
pp. 135 ff., who, however, goes too far in assuming that all such forms as are cited
above in 1, 2, and 3 contain *-eŭo-*, not *-ŭo-*. See author's Verb-System, p. 175.

U. **Taŕinate**, *Tarsinatem* 'Tadinatem, of Tadinum'; — used substantively as names of *gentes*, U. **Atiieŕiate, Kaselate,** *Casilate,*
**Talenate,** etc. (II b 1-7).

   **260.** 1. *-do-*. U. **kaleŕuf**, *calersu* 'with a white forehead'
(cf. L. *cal(l)idus*, Isidorus, Orig. 12, 1, 52), like L. *pallidus* etc.;
— probably U. *sorser* 'suilli', *sorsalem* 'suillam' (see 57).

   2. *-idio-, -edio-*, in proper names (L. *Calidius*).  O. **Húsidiis,**
**Púpidiis,** *Caisidis,* Pael. *Apidis* ; — also with syncope O. **Pupdiis,**
Pael. *Popdis* ; — with added *-īno-*, O. **Tafidins** ; — U. *Coredier,* **Kure-**
**ties** (Pael. *Uibedis*); — U. *Atiersiur*, **Atiieŕiur** (but L. *Attidium*),
Pael. *Ouiedis*.   The reason for O. ì (not í) and, in general, the
relation of the different forms are obscure.

   **261.** *-fli-* (L. *amābilis* ; orig. *-dhli-*, the adjective *i*-stem form
of *-dhlo-*, **248**, 2).   U. **façefele** (aes **façefete**) '*facibile, *sacrificabile',
**purtifele** '*porricibilem'.  Since anaptyxis is unknown in Um-
brian the first e in *-fele* is surprising.  Possibly it is due to the
Nom. Sg., in which *-fel* from *-flis* would be regular (cf. *pacer*
from *\*pakris* **91**, 2).

## SECONDARY VERBAL DERIVATION

### DENOMINATIVES

   **262.** 1. As in Latin, the great mass of denominatives,
whether or not derived from *ā*-stems, follow the First Conjugation.   Examples: U. **kuŕaia** 'curet', **kuratu** (Pael. *coisatens*) from
*\*koisā* (L. *cūra*); — O. *moltaum* 'multare' from *\*molktā* (O. *molto,*
L. *multa*); — O. **ehpeílatas** 'erectae, set up' from *\*peilā*: L. *pīla* ;
— O. *deiuaid* 'iuret', *deiuast, deiuatud*, etc. from *\*deiu̯o-* (L. *deus* ;
see 16, 4) ; — U. **stakaz** 'statutus' from *\*stāko-* (cf. L. *stāgnum*); —
U. *pihatu* 'piato', *pihos*, etc. from adj. *\*pīo-* (L. *pius*); — O. **prú-**
**fatted** 'probavit' from adj. *\*profo-* (L. *probus*); — O. **teremnattens**
'terminaverunt' from *\*termen-* (O. **.teremníss,** L. *termen*); —
U. **vepuratu** 'restinguito'(?) from adj. *u̯e-pur-* 'fireless' (U. **vepurus,**
**263**, 2); — O. **úpsannam** 'operandam, faciendam', U. *osatu*, etc. from
*\*opes-* (L. *opus*); — U. *tuderato* 'finitum' from *\*tudes-* (U. *tuder*);

— U. **eturstamu**, *eturstahmu* 'exterminato' from *\*tudes-to-* (cf. L. *modes-tus*).

There are also exâmples of the formation from the *to-*Participle, corresponding to the Latin iteratives. Thus U. *etaians* 'itent', *etato*, etc. from *\*ei-to-*, not from *\*i-to-* like L. *itō*; — U. **statitatu** 'statuito' from *statīto-* (U. **statita**, see below, 3); — U. *frosetom* 'fraudatum' from *\*frausso-* (L. *frausus*) as if L. *\*frausō*; — U. *preplotatu* of uncertain meaning, but perhaps '*\*praeplauditato*, strike down' from *\*plaudeto-*.

*a. U. pelsatu, pelsans, etc. is probably derived from a Partic. \*pelso-, like L. pulsō from pulsus, though its etymological connection is uncertain. The meaning 'bury' (in the trench ; cf. VI b 40) seems the most probable among various suggestions, and the connection with L. sepeliō may be maintained if we take the latter as se-peliō (for se- beside sē- cf. solvō from \*se-luō, socors from \*se-cors). In this case \*pelso- will be \*pel-so- for \*pel-to- with the same analogical -so- as in L. pulsus etc. (see also 244, 1, a, b).*

2. Denominatives of the Second Conjugation are : O. **turumiiad** 'torqueatur' from *\*tormo-* (cf. L. *tormentum*); — O. **fatíum** 'fari' like L. *fateor* from Partic. *\*fato-* (φατός), which was replaced in Latin by *fāto-*; — U. **kutef** 'speaking low' (**kutef pesnimu** equivalent to the more common **taçez pesnimu** 'tacitus precator') probably as if L. *\*cauteō* (*\*cautēns*) from *cautus*; — O. **pútíad, putiiad** 'possit', as if L. *\*poteō* (cf. *potēns, potuī*), from *poti-* (L. *potis*).

3. Denominatives of the Fourth Conjugation are: U. *persnihimu* 'precator', *persnis*, etc. from *\*persni-, \*persk-ni-* (146) (cf. Skt. *praç-ná-* from the same root, whence denom. *praçnayāmi*)[1]; — U. **statita** 'statuta' from *\*sta-ti-* (Grk. στάσις); — U. *stahmito* 'statutum', *stahmeitei*, from the stem of U. *stahmei* 'statui' (*\*stā-mo-* or *\*stā-mi-*); — O. **sakruvit** 'sacrat', **sakrvist**, from *\*sakru-* (214, 3); — U. *disleralinsust* 'inritum fecerit' from an adjective *\*dis-leisāli-* 'off the track' (L. *līra*, Germ. *Geleise*) and so 'wrong, void'.

---

[1] The assumption of a primary verb with a *ni*-suffix, a type of which there are no other relics in Italic, is altogether less probable.

## COMPOSITION

### Nouns and Adjectives

**263.** 1. The first element is a noun or adjective stem (L. *armi-ger*). O. **meddíss**, *meddis* 'meddix', Gen. Sg. **medíkeís**, etc., from \**medos* (U. **meřs** 'ius') and *dik-*,[1] precisely like L. *iūdex* from *iūs* and *dik-*; — **líganak-díkeí**, name of a goddess, the first part being a derivative related to L. *lēx* (**80**, 2; cf. Θεσμοφόρος an epithet of Demeter); — U. **man-trahklu**, *man-draclo* 'mantele'(**97**); — U. **tu-plak** (**192**, 1); — U. *du-pursus* 'bipedibus', *petur-pursus* 'quadrupedibus' (**94**, **191**, 2, *a*, 4, *a*); — U. *di-fue* 'bifidum' (**191**, 2, *a*); — U. **nuř-pener** '——pondiis', name of a small coin, the first part being obscure, while the second is from \**pendo-* (cf. L. *du-pondius*; **94**); — U. *seu-acni-* (**159**, *a*). O. **tríbarakkíuf** 'aedificatio' and the verb **tríbarakavúm** are probably derivatives of a \**trēbark-* or \**trēbarkio-*, compounded of \**trēbo-* or \**trēb-* (O. **tríbúm** 'domum'; see **171**, 14) and \**ark-* (L. *arx*, *arceō*), and so meaning first 'the closing in, i.e. the construction of, a building', then simply 'building', like L. *aedificatiō*.

*a.* U. *seuacni-*, *peracni-*, exemplify the same shifting to the *i*-stem form that is seen in L. *inermis*, *biiugis*, etc.

2. The first element is an adverbial prefix. Most of these prefixes are the same which are used in the composition of verbs (**264**, 1), and occur separately as prepositions, e.g. O. **kúm-benníeís** 'conventus'. For examples, see **299-302**. But the following occur only in noun and adjective (including participial) compounds.

The negative *an-* (L. *in-*; see **98**), corresponding to L. *in-*, in O. *an-censto* 'non censa', *am-prufid* 'improbe', *amiricatud* '\*immercato'; U. *an-hostatu* 'non hastatos', *an-takres* 'integris', *aanfehtaf* 'infectas' (**73**, *a*), *ansihitu* 'non cinctos', *auirseto* 'non visum', *asnata* 'non umecta', *aseçeta* 'non secta' (*n* omitted in last two examples by **108**, 1; for *auirseto* from *an-u-* cf. U. *co-uertu* etc. (**300**, 2).

U. *sei-* (L. *sēd-*, *sĕ-*) in *sei-podruhpei* 'seorsum utroque' (**200**, 2).

---

[1] O. **meddiss** may be from \**medes-dik-* through \**medsdik-*, *s* being lost between two mutes, or from \**medo-dik-* with the not infrequent substitution of the *o*-stem for the *s*-stem form.

U. **ven-** in **ven-persuntra, vem-pesuntres, ve-pesutra** 'ficticia' (?) beside *per-sontro-* 'figmentum' (?) is evidently connected with L. *vĕ-*,· but with a nasal, perhaps representing an added particle *ne*, and without distinctly negative force.[1] Another probable example of this prefix is U. **vepurus**, which is best explained as 'fireless' (cf. U. *pir, pure-to*, etc.), **esunes-ku vepurus** meaning 'at the sacrifices without fire' (cf. Grk. ἱερὰ ἄπυρα).

**3.** Juxtaposition (L. *senātusconsultum*).   U. **Iupater**, like L. *Iūpiter* from Voc. Sg. *\*Di̯eu-pater* (Ζεῦ πάτερ); — U. *desen-duf* 'duodecim'.

*a.* The juxtaposition of prepositions and adverbs of time and place, as in L. *ab-hinc, inter-ibi*, etc., is exemplified by U. **ap-ehtre** 'ab extra, extrinsecus'. For other examples of compound adverbs see **202**, passim.

VERBS

**264.** 1. The only extensive type of verbal composition is that in which the first element is an adverbial prefix. Most of these prefixes are such as occur separately as prepositions, and examples will be given in connection with the latter (**299-302**). Those not occurring separately are :

(L. *ă, ab*).  O. **aa-manaffed** 'mandavit, locavit', U. *aha-uendu* 'avertito', *aha-tripursatu, a-tripursatu*, **ah-trepuřatu, a-trepuřatu** 'tripodato'. See 77, 2. The preposition with a case-form does not happen to occur. But cf. U. **ap-ehtre** 'ab extra, extrinsecus' (**263**, 3, *a*).

(L. *amb-, am-*).  For *am-* and *\*amfer-*, for which, however, there is a related preposition, O. **ampt** (**300**, 1), see 161 with *a*.

(L. *an-* in *an-hēlō*).  U. **an-tentu**, *an-dendu*, with the same meaning as **en-tentu**, *en-dendu* 'intendito', **am-pentu, a-pentu** 'impendito', *an-ouihimu* 'induitor', **an-zeriatu**, *an-seriato* 'observatum', *a-seriatu*, etc., **an-stintu, a-stintu** 'distinguito', *an-stiplatu* 'stipulator', **am-paritu** 'conlocato', **am-parihmu** 'surgito' (in the last four examples connection with L. *am-, amb-*, is possible, but less likely); — O. αραfαϰετ 'dedicavit' (**80**, 2), probably *an-getuzet* 'proposuerint' (**228**, *a*). Cf. also U. **ancla, anglaf** 'oscines' (**155**).

(L. *dis-*).  U. *disleralinsust*. See **262**, 3.

(L. *por-*).  U. **pur-douitu, pur-tuvitu** 'porricito', *pur-dinšiust, pur-ditom*, etc.  See 51.

(L. *re-*).  U. **re-vestu** 'revisito', **re-statu** 'instaurato', **re-stef**, etc.

O. **ce-bnust** 'venerit' contains the particle seen in L. *ce-do, ce-tte*.

---

[1] So occasionally in Latin. See I.F. 10, 248 ff.

2. Juxtaposition.   A probable parallel to L. *animadvertō*
is U. **eitipes** 'decreverunt' from \**eitom* \**hipens* (see **84**), used like
L. 'ratum habuerunt'.   For \**hipens*, i.e. \**hēpens*, cf. O. *hipid*
etc. (**218**).

The first part is perhaps from \**aiketo-* with the same root as Skt. ĭç-
'have power', Eng. *own*, etc. (cf. also O. **aikdafed**, **264**, 3), the phonetic development being \**aikto-,* '*ēkto-*, \**eito-* (**143**).

O. **manafum** 'mandavi', **aa-manaffed** 'mandavit, locavit', from
\**manfefom*, \**manfefed* (**80**, 2, **223**), belong to a Pres. \**manfō*, earlier
\**mandhō*, whence also L. *man-dō*, which was originally inflected
like *abdō*, *condō*, etc., but passed over to the First Conjugation
(thus avoiding confusion with *mandō* 'chew').

This \**man-dhō* is formed after \**con-dhō* (L. *condō*) etc. from *man-*, seen
in U. **manf** 'manus' (Acc. Pl.), L. *man-ceps*, etc.   (If it is viewed thus as an
analogical formation, it is not necessary to assume a case-form in *man-*.)

A parallel formation is probably U. *hondu* 'pessumdato'(?), belonging to
a Pres. \**hondō*, this from \**hon-fō*, \**hom-dhō*, *hom-* being the same element that
is seen in U. *hondra* 'infra' etc. (L. *humus*).   The phonetic development is the
same as in U. *-uendu* (**161**).

3. O. **tribarakavúm** 'aedificare' is probably, like L. *aedificō*, a derivative
of a noun already compounded.   See **263**, 1.   Of O. **aikdafed** the most probable
explanation is that it means 'decrevit, authorized' and is derived from \**aiko-do-*,
the first part belonging to the root *aik-* seen in Skt. ĭç- 'have power' etc. (cf. also
U. **eitipes**, **264**, 2).

# SYNTAX [1]

## USES OF THE CASES

## THE GENITIVE

**265.** The Possessive Genitive in the various phases of possession and connection is common. Thus O. **sakaraklúm Hereklefs** 'templum Herculis'; predicative O. **Herentateís súm** 'Veneris sum';—O. **L. Pettíeis meddíkíaí** 'in the meddixship of L. Pettius';—O. *senateis tanginud* 'senatus sententia';—U. *farer agre Tlatie* 'farris agri Latii';—U. *popluper totar Iiouinar* 'pro populo civitatis Iguvinae'; predicative U. *pisest totar Tarsinater* 'quisquis est civitatis Tadinati'.[2]

The Objective Genitive. U. **katle tiçel** 'catuli dedicatio';—*arsier frite* 'sancti fiducia, with confidence in (thee) the holy one'.

**266.** The Partitive Genitive. U. **mestru karu fratru** 'maior pars fratrum';—O. *minstreis aeteis eituas* 'minoris partis pecuniae';—O. *idic tangineis* 'id sententiae', like L. *id temporis* etc.

The following are bolder than anything in Latin, but may be paralleled elsewhere. U. *iuenga peracrio tursituto* 'iuvencas ex opimis fuganto' (VII a 51);—U. **struhçlas fiklas sufafias kumaltu** 'prepare some sacrificial cake, etc.' (II a 41).

The use of the Partitive Genitive as subject, which is found in Avestan, Lithuanian, and rarely in Greek, is probably to be recognized in U. **eru emantur herte** '(whether) any of them are to be accepted' (V a 8).

---

[1] The treatment of the Syntax is brief, not through any intention to slight this side of the grammar, but because the syntactical material is relatively meagre. That is, owing to the nature of the remains only a limited number of constructions are met with. Moreover, in view of the general similarity to Latin syntax, it is needless to heap up examples of the common constructions, and some matters, such as the uses of the parts of speech, etc., may be passed over entirely.

[2] These last two examples belong to the class in which it is impossible to draw the line between the Possessive and the Partitive Genitive.

**267. Genitive with Adjectives.** O. **diuvilam Tirentium Magiium sulum muinikam** 'iovilam Terentiorum Magiorum omnium communem'.

**268. Genitive of Time.** This Genitive, which is found in Greek and elsewhere (νυκτός 'by night', τριῶν μηνῶν 'within three months', etc.), and which is a natural development of the Possessive Genitive (the time to which an action belongs), is to be recognized in O. *eisucen ziculud zicolom XXX nesimum comonom ni hipid* 'shall not hold the comitia within the next thirty days from that day' (T. B. 17). Cf. L. *in diebus V proxsumeis* in the Latin inscription of the Tabula Bantina.

NOTE. The *zicolom* is often taken as an Acc. Sg., as if 'from that day until the thirtieth day following', but there are serious objections to this, namely 1) the use of the Accusative without a preposition, 2) the use of the numeral signs for the ordinal, 3) the use of *nesimum* 'proximum' in such a phrase, as if L. *ad diem tricensimum proximum*.

**269. Genitive of the Penalty.** O. *ampert minstreis aeteis eituas moltas moltaum licitud* 'dumtaxat minoris partis pecuniae multae multare liceto' (T. B. 12, 13), and *moltaum licitud, ampert mistreis aeteis eituas licitud* 'multare liceto, dumtaxat minoris partis pecuniae liceto' (T. B. 18). That is, 'one may fine with (a fine of) not more than half the property'.

In the former passage *aeteis* may be the Genitive of the Penalty with *moltas* in apposition, or it may be taken as an explanatory Genitive with *moltas*, this last being the Genitive of the Penalty.[1] The preceding *ampert*, literally *nōn trāns*, is not a preposition (in this case, we should expect the Acc.), but an adverb used without effect on the case-construction, just as, frequently, L. *plūs, minus, amplius*. Similarly in the corresponding Latin phrase [*dum minoris*] *partus familias taxsat* (T. B. Latin side), *partus* is Genitive of the Penalty, and not governed by *taxsat*.

    *a.* A noteworthy construction, perhaps containing a sort of detached Genitive of the Penalty, is seen in U. *fratreci motar sins a. CCC* 'magistro multae sint asses CCC' (VII b 4), which is paralleled by L. *Iovei bovid piaclum datod et a. CCC moltai suntod* (CIL. XI, 4766), where *moltai* must be Gen. Sg. and not Nom. Pl., as is shown by the

---

[1] Some take *moltas* as a Cognate Accusative (Plural) and assume that it is to be understood in the shorter passage. But the Plural is unlikely. See also *a*.

following *eius piacli moltaique dicator*[*ei*] *exactio est*[*od*]. The construction might arise through a contamination of such expressions as *magistro a. CCC multa sint (sunto)* and *magistrum a. CCC multae multato*. Cf. the detached Abl. in U. **muneklu habia numer prever (292)**, and L. *Iupiter, tibi bove aurato voveo futurum* (Acta Arvalium).

**270.** Genitive of the Matter Involved, in legal phraseology. O. *suaepis . . . altrei castrous auti eituas zicolom dicust* 'siquis alteri capitis aut pecuniae diem dixerit', that is, on a charge involving the death penalty or a fine (T. B. 13, 14; on *castrous* see note to passage), contrasted with *dat castrid loufir en eituas* 'de capite vel in pecunias' (T. B. 8, 9). Cf. L. *quoad vel capitis vel pecuniae iudicasset privato* (Livy 26, 3, 8), beside *de capite*, etc. A bolder example is O. *aserum eizazunc egmazum pas exaiscen ligis scriftas set* 'to make a seizure involving these matters which are written in these laws' (T. B. 24). Cf. L. *eiq(ue) omnium rerum siremps lex esto* (T. B., Latin side). Note also the free use of the Genitive in the Law Code of Goṛtyna to denote the matter or person involved, e.g. τῶ ἐλευθέρω 'in the case of a freeman', τῶ χρόνω 'in the matter of time', ἢ ϝεκάστω ἐγράτται 'as is written in each case'.

NOTE. To take such Genitives as depending on a noun either expressed (e.g. *zicolom* in the first Oscan example) or understood, is forced. It is possible, of course, that they originated in connection with a noun and afterwards came to modify the sentence as a whole, thus going through the reverse of the process seen in the case of the Adnominal Dative. But even this assumption is unnecessary, and it is more probable that we have to do simply with certain phases of a broad use of the Genitive denoting the sphere to which an action belongs.

**271.** Free use of the Genitive of a noun with gerundive in agreement. With L. (*arma*) *quae cepit legum ac lîbertatis subvortundae* (Sallust) compare U. *uerfale pufe arsfertur trebeit ocrer peihaner* 'the *templum* where the flamen remains for the purification of the mount' (VI a 8). A more striking example is U. *sururo stiplatu pusi ocrer pihaner* 'let him make the same request as for the purification of the mount' (VI b 48).

NOTE. This Genitive, which obviously modifies the sentence as a whole, and not a noun expressed or understood, belongs historically with the preceding. See note to **270**.

## DATIVE

**272.** Dative of the Indirect Object with transitive verbs.
O. **Anagtiai Diíviiai dunum deded** 'Angitiae Diae donum dedit'; —
U. *buf trif fetu Marte Grabouei* 'boves tris facito Marti Grabovio'.

**273.** Dative with certain verbs used intransitively. U. **ri
esune kuraia** 'rem divinam curet' (cf. *cūrō* with Dative in early
Latin); — *arsferture ehueltu* 'flaminem iubeto' (cf. *iubeō* with
Dative in Tacitus); — **persnihmu Puemune** 'supplicato Pomono'.

**274.** Dative with prepositional compounds. U. *prosesetir
strusla ficla arsueitu* 'prosectis struem offam addito (advehito)',
U. **pir ase antentu** 'ignem arae imponito'.

**275.** The Dative of Reference or Concern. U. *aserio . . .
anglaf esona mehe, tote Iioueine* . . . 'observa . . . oscines divinas
mihi, civitati Iguvinae' (VI a 4, 5); — O. *piei ex comono pertemest*
'(the magistrate) in whose case the assembly shall be prevented
in this way' (T. B. 7); — O. *suaepis altrei . . . zicolom dicust*
'siquis alteri . . . diem dixerit' (T. B. 13, 14); — U. **pune karne
speturie . . . naraklum vurtus** 'cum carni *spectoriae . . . nuntiatio
mutaverit' (II a 1); — U. *ahauendu . . . atero pople* 'avertito . . .
malum populo' (VII a 27; cf. L. *solstitium pecori defendite* etc.); —
*preuendu . . . atero tote* 'advertito malum civitati' (VII a 11); —
O. **Maiiúí Vestirikiíúí . . . iním Maiiú[í] Iúvkiíúí . . . ekss kúmbened**
'Maio Vestricio . . . et Maio Iovicio . . . ita convenit' (C. A. 1 ff.;
observe the use of two Datives where Latin has one Dative and
*cum* with the Ablative); — O. **ekas iúvilas Iuveí Flagiuí stahínt** 'hae
*iovilae Iovi Flagio stant' (no. 25); — O. **aasas ekask eestínt
húrtúí** 'these altars are for (belong to) the sacred grove' (T. A.).

NOTE. Several of these Datives might of course be differently classified,
e.g. that with O. **kúmbened** and U. *preuendu* under **274**, that with *ahauendu*
under a special class of "verbs of taking away." The last two examples cited
are very close to the Dative of the Possessor (**276**), but this is only a special
variety of the Dative of Reference and in our usual terminology is restricted to
the use with the verb 'to be'.

**276.** Dative of the Possessor. U. **etantu mutu arferture si**
'tanta multa flamini sit' etc.

**277.** Dative with Adjectives of Relation. U. *futu fons pacer . . . pople* 'esto favens propitia . . . populo'; — O. **nessimas staiet veruis** 'proximae stant portae' (but **veruis** may also be taken as an Ablative of the Point of View, **288**).

**278.** Dative with Nouns. The Dative with nouns of verbal meaning (L. *obtemperatio legibus* etc.) is seen in U. **tikamne Iuvie** 'with a dedication to Iovius' (II a 8). The Dative of Reference with nouns is found only in brief clauses which are in the nature of headings, as O. **Evklúí statíf** 'Euclo statua' (T. A.).

## ACCUSATIVE

**279.** The Accusative of the Direct Object with transitive verbs and the Accusative with Prepositions (**299, 301**) are of course extremely common. The Cognate Accusative is seen in U. *teio subocau suboco* 'te invoco invocationes' (VI a 22 etc.; cf. *te bonas preces precor*, Cato, De Agric. 134). Note also U. *perca arsmatiam anouihimu* 'virgam ritualem induitor' (cf. L. *galeam induitor*); — O. *censamur eituam* 'censetor pecuniam' (cf. *voluisti magnum agri modum censeri, . . . cum te audisset servos suos esse censum*, Cic. pro Flacco, 32).

## LOCATIVE

**280.** In contrast to its restricted use in Latin, the Locative is widely used in Oscan-Umbrian. It has preserved a distinct form in the Singular, at least in the First and Second Declensions, to which nearly all the examples belong, while in the Plural it is merged with the Dative-Ablative-Instrumental. In Oscan it is ordinarily used without a preposition, but in Umbrian it is very frequently, perhaps always (see **169, 7**), combined with the postpositive *-en*. For the Locative with other prepositions, see **301, 302**.

**281.** Locative of Place. 1. OSCAN. *Bansae* 'at Bantia', **Tiianei** 'at Teanum', **eíseí terei** 'in this territory', *comenei* 'in the assembly', **viaí mefiaí** 'in the middle of the road', **aasaí purasiaí**

'on the fire-altar', lúvkeí 'in the grove', thesavreí 'in the treasury';
— with -*en*, húrtín 'in the grove' (171, 7), *exaisc-en ligis* 'in these
laws'.

2. UMBRIAN. Akeřunie, *Acersoniem* 'at Acedonia', *tote Iouine*,
*toteme Iouinem* (169, 7, *a*) 'in the city of Iguvium', *ocre Fisie*,
*ocrem Fisiem* (169, 7, *a*) 'on the Fisian mount', *destre onse*, testre
e uze 'on the right shoulder', arven 'in the field', tertie svieeve
'in the third pot', tafle e 'on the table', *ferine* 'on the stand'(?),
manuv-e 'in the hand', *Fondlir-e* 'at the Springs', fesner-e 'at the
fane'.

**282.** Locative of Time. 1. OSCAN. *eizeic zicel*[*ei*] 'on that
day', alttreí pútereípíd akeneí 'in every other year' (? see 200, 2, *a*),
púistreí iúkleí 'at the following ceremony'(?), medikkiaí 'in the meddixship', Fiuusasiaís 'at the Floralia' (similarly eídúís Mamerttiaís,
Fíísiaís púmperiais, used, in the iovilae-inscriptions, of certain
festivals). ·

2. UMBRIAN. sume ustite 'at the last period'(?), kvestretie,
uhtretie (251, 1, *a*), *fratrecate*, *maronatei* 'in the quaestorship' etc.,
plenasier urnasier, *sehmenier dequrier* 'at the festivals of —'.

**283.** A Locative of Circumstance is seen in O. *eizeic uincter*
'is convicted of this'. Cf. L. *in hoc scelere convictus* beside the
usual Genitive construction.


## ABLATIVE(-INSTRUMENTAL)

**284.** The fusion of the original Ablative and Instrumental
was accomplished in the Italic period, so that in Oscan-Umbrian,
as in Latin, they are no longer distinguished in form. For the
Ablative with prepositions, see also **300**, **302**.


### ABLATIVE USES

**285.** Ablative of the Place or Time Whence. O. Akudunniad 'from Acedonia', Tíanud Sidikinud 'from Teanum Sidicinum'
(both examples from coin-legends); — O. imad-en 'from the bottom up', *eisuc-en ziculud* 'from this day on' (the -*en* here is not

essential to the Ablative force). In Umbrian this Ablative is regularly accompanied by the preposition *e, ehe* 'ex' or the postpositive *-ta, -tu, -to* (300, 9), as *ehe esu poplu* 'from this people', **akru-tu** 'from the field', *anglu-to hondomu . . . anglom-e somo* 'from the lowest to the highest corner', *pure-to* 'from the fire'.

**286.** Ablative of the Source. O. **eítiuvad múltasíkad, aragetud multas[íkud]** 'from the money raised by fines'. Cf. L. (*ex*) *aere conlato, aere moltaticod.*

NOTE. These examples might also be classed under the Ablative of Means.

**287.** Ablative of Accordance. O. *senateis tanginud* (once with *dat*) 'in accordance with the judgment of the senate', U. **arputrati fratru Atiieřiu** 'in accordance with the judgment of the Atiedian brothers', O. **prupukid sverrunei** 'spokesman(?) by previous agreement', U. **fratru mersus** 'in accordance with the customs of the brothers' (III 6; cf. L. (*ex*) *moribus*).

NOTE. This Ablative is probably, in part, of Instrumental origin, and is not always to be distinguished clearly from the Ablative (Instrumental) of Attendant Circumstances, and of Means.

**288.** Ablative of the Point of View. U. *nesimei asa* 'next to the altar' (L. *proxime ab*), **testru sese asa** 'at the right of the altar' (see 307); — so probably U. *todceir tuderus seipodruhpei* 'on both sides, separately, of the city limits' (VI a 11).

**289.** Ablative after Comparatives. O. *mais zicolois X nesimois* 'more than the ten following days'. Although *mais* might be used without effect on the following case, as sometimes L. *plūs*, an Ablative of Time seems less probable here.

### INSTRUMENTAL USES

**290.** Ablative of Means. O. **sakriss sakrafír, avt últiumam kerssnaís** 'consecrate with victims, but the last with banquets'; — O. **trístaamentud deded** 'gave by will' (Ablative of Source also possible; cf. L. (*ex*) *testamento*); — U. *mani nertru tenitu* 'hold with the left hand'; — U. **kletra fertuta** 'carry on (by means of) a litter'; — U. *esu bue pihafei* 'expiate with this ox'; — U. **vinu**

**persnihmu** 'make supplication with wine', similarly, with verb understood, *tio esu bue* 'thee with this ox (I supplicate)'.

*a.* U. *herie uinu herie poni fetu* 'vel vino vel posca facito' (VI b 19, 20) is to be compared with L. *ture et vino fecerunt* (Acta Arvalium), etc. But the Accusative construction is the usual one, as in Latin also, and the use of the Ablative here is perhaps due to its denoting a subsidiary offering, thus approaching the uses mentioned in **293**.

*b.* With L. *quid hoc homine facias* compare U. *fetu uru pirse mers est* 'do with him what is right' (VI b 55).

**291.** Ablative of the Route. U. *uia auiecla etuto* 'go by the augural way'; — O. **eksuk amvíannud eítuns** 'let them go(?) by this detour' (see note to nos. 14–18). O. r[íhtúd] **amnúd** 'right around in a circle' (C. A. 16, 17) is to be compared with L. *sursum (deorsum) rivo recto (iugo recto)* 'right up (down) the stream (ridge)' (CIL. I 199).

**292.** Ablative of Measure and Price. O. **vía teremnattens perek(ais) III** 'laid out the roads three rods wide'. Note especially U. **muneklu habia numer prever pusti kastruvuf** 'spertulam habeat nummis singulis in capita, shall receive a perquisite of one sesterce for each person' (V a 17, 18; cf. also V a 13).

**293.** Ablative of Accompaniment. This is regularly accompanied by the preposition *com*. U. *com prinuatir stahitu* 'stand with the assistants', *eru-com prinuatur dur etuto* 'let the two assistants go with him', O. *com preiuatud actud, con preiuatud urust* 'deal (plead) with the defendant', *com atrud acum* 'have a lawsuit with another'. But it also appears without the preposition where the feeling of accompaniment has become subordinate to that of means or manner. Thus U. **apretu tures et pure** 'go about (i.e. perform the lustration) with the bulls and the fire' (I b 20). Note the Ablative with and without *com* in U. *eno com prinuatir peracris sacris ambretuto* 'let him together with the assistants go about with unblemished victims' (VI b 56; but also *etuto com peracris sacris*, VI b 52). The Ablative of Accompaniment without *com*, in close attachment to a noun, also appears in U. **arvia puni purtuvitu** 'offer fruits of the field with sour wine'

(II a 24) and U. **persutru vaputis mefa vistiça feta fertu** 'bring the *persontrum* with incense etc.' (II b 13), in which the feeling is much the same as in some of the examples given under the Ablative of Attendant Circumstances (**294**). See also **290**, *a*.

> *a.* In Umbrian, the Ablative with postpositive -*co(m)*, -**ku(m)**, has developed a distinctly locative sense, 'at', e.g. **asa-ku** 'at the altar', *termnu-co* 'at the boundary', **testru-ku peři**, *nertru-co persi* 'at the right (left) foot', **vuku-kum**, *uocu-com* 'at the temple', *ueris-co* 'at the gate', etc. In the sense of 'with' the postpositive occurs only with pronominal forms, as *eru-com* (in example above). Cf. L. *mēcum, quibuscum*, etc.

**294.** Ablative of Attendant Circumstances, Manner, etc. U. **eruhu tiçlu sestu Iuvepatre** 'present to Jupiter with the same dedication' (II b 22), **fetu tikamne Iuvie** 'offer with a dedication to Iovius' (II a 8), *arsier frite tio subocau* 'with confidence in (thee) the holy one I invoke thee' (VI a 24 etc.; *frite* could also be a Locative in form, but probably belongs here rather than in **283**), *futu fos pacer pase tua* 'be favorable and propitious with thy peace' (VI a 30 etc.), O. *dolud mallud* 'with guile'; — here also O. **medíkeís serevkid** 'under the inspection of the meddix', *pr. meddixud* 'under the magistracy of the praetor' (cf. Loc. **medikkiaí, 282**).

> *a.* Of the same origin are the adverbial O. *amiricatud* '*immercato, without remuneration' (cf. L. *immeritō, inauspicātō*, etc.), and U. *herita* 'consulto, intentionally' (see **307**).

**295.** Ablative of Time. U. **menzne kurçlasiu** 'in the last(?) month' (II a 17), *pesclu semu* 'in the middle of the prayer' (VI b 15, 36).

**296.** Ablative Absolute. O. *toutad praesentid* 'in the presence of the people', U. **aves anzeriates** 'when the birds have been observed' (I a 1 etc.).

### LOCATIVE USES

**297.** The sphere of meaning of the Ablative(-Instrumental) overlaps that of the Locative at certain points, and in several of the examples already given the Ablative expresses what might also be expressed by the Locative.   Thus Means and Place are often identical, and we find U. **mani kuveitu** 'bring with the hand', *mani tenitu* 'hold with the hand' (**290**), beside **manuv-e habetu** 'hold in the hand'; — U. **kletra fertuta** 'carry by means of a litter' (**290**), beside **tafle e fertu** 'carry on a table'.   The road by which one goes is also the road on which one is, and the Ablative of the Route may be used even where there is no word of motion. Cf. L. *iam consul via Labicana ad fanum Quietis erat* (Livy 4, 41, 8).   The Ablative of Time, originally an Instrumental denoting duration of time, comes to be used with much the same force as the Locative of Time.   See **295**.   The Ablative of Accompaniment with postpositive -*co* has developed a Locative force.   See **293**, *a*.   Cf. also the Ablative with *op* in Oscan in a strictly local meaning (**300**, **5**).

These and other points of contact in function, together with the identity of form in the Plural which exists in all branches of Italic, have led in Latin to the almost complete absorption of the Locative by the Ablative.   And even in Oscan-Umbrian, where in general the Locative preserves its identity,[1] there are examples of the Ablative which can only be viewed as encroachments on the Locative, namely:

**298.**   Ablative of the Place Where.   U. *tremnu serse* 'sitting in the tent' (VI a 2, 16), *sersi*[2] *pirsi sesust* 'when he has seated himself on the seat' (VI a 5); — so also probably *anderuomu sersitu* (VI b 41), though *anderuomu* is of unknown meaning, and is taken by some as *ander uomu* 'inter ——'; — O. **Búvaianúd** 'at Bovianum' (no. 46; see p. 43, footnote).

---

[1] In consonant-stems in Umbrian the Abl. Sg. and Loc. Sg. are not to be distinguished, both ending in -*e*, which, like the L. -*e*, is probably the old Loc. ending -*i*. In Oscan there are no examples of the Locative in the Third Declension.

[2] Abl. Sg. of an *i*-stem.  The Loc. Sg., whether of an *i*-stem or consonant-stem, would end in -*e*.

## PREPOSITIONS [1]

### (AND THE CORRESPONDING PREFIXES [2])

### With the Accusative only

**299.** **1.** (L. *ad*). O. **az** (*ad-s*, like L. *ab-s*; **137**, 2), U. -**ař**, -**a** (**133**, *b*). O. **az húrtúm** 'at the grove'; — U. **asam-a** '(return) to the altar', **asam-ař** '(offer etc.) at the altar', **spinam-ař** '(go) to the column', **spiniam-a** '(pray) at the column'.

CPDS. O. **adfust** 'aderit', *aserum* 'adserere' (**137**, 2), **akkatus** 'advocati' (**89**, 3, **102**, 3, **139**, 1), **aflukad**, **aflakus** (? **97**, *a*, **139**, 1), **adpúd** 'quoad' (**202**, 9); — U. **ařpeltu** 'adpellito', **ařveitu**, **arveitu**, **arsueitu**, etc. 'advehito', **aïfertur**, *arsfertur*, *arfertur*, etc. '*adfertor*, flamen', **neiřhabas** 'ne adhibeant' (**84**), **ařkani** '*accinium*, cantum', **ařputrati** 'arbitratu', *ape*, *appei*, etc. 'ubi' (**202**, 8), *arnipo* 'donec' (**202**, 10). For U. **ař-**, **ar-**, *ars-*, **ar-**, see **132** with *a*.

> NOTE. U. -**ař**, -**a**, occurs only in Tables III, IV, and II a. Elsewhere 'to' is expressed by -*e(n)* (**301**, 2) and 'at' by -**ku(m)**, -*co(m)* (**293**, *a*).

**2.** (L. *ante*). O. **ant** 'usque ad' (from *\*anti*; see **92**). The only example is **ant púnttram** (no. 3) 'up to the bridge' (i.e. 'up to in front of the bridge', and so 'close up to the bridge').

> NOTE. The meaning 'before' is expressed by O. **prai**, U. **pre** (**300**, 7).

**3.** (L. *extrā*). O. **ehtrad** (**142**, **190**, 3). Thus **ehtrad feíhúss** 'outside the walls'.

**4.** U. *hondra*, **hutra** 'infra' (**15**, 5, **188**, 2). Thus *hondra esto tudero* 'below these limits', *hondra furo*, **hutra furu** 'below the forum'.

*a.* O. **huntrus teras** (no. 19, 11) apparently means 'infra terram' and contains a related preposition, of obscure formation, followed by the Genitive. But the sentence is incomplete, and it is not wholly certain that **huntrus** cannot be simply Acc. Pl. 'inferos'.

**5.** (L. *per*). O. **pert**, U. **pert** 'trans' (from *\*per-ti*; cf. *post* from *\*pos-ti*). O. **pert viam** 'across the road', U. **pert spinia** 'beyond the column'. Cf. also O. *am-pert* 'not beyond, not more than',

---

[1] "Prepositions" is used here as a syntactical term and includes the postpositives.

[2] Given here for convenience. For prefixes which have no corresponding forms used as prepositions, see **263**, 2, **264**, 1.

which however is used adverbially, not as a preposition (see **269**). The same form, joined postpositively to the Acc. Pl., appears in the numeral adverbs O. *petiro-pert* 'quater', U. **triiuper**, *trio-per* 'ter' (**192**, 2; for the loss of *-t*, see **127**, 3).

CPDS.   O. *pert-umum* (*pert-emest*, *pert-emust*) 'perimere, prevent'. The simple *per-* appears in O. *per-emust* 'perceperit', also in U. **per-tentu** 'stretch out' ('protendito' may be used in translating, since L. *pertendo* is used only in a transferred sense, but this *per-* has nothing to do with *-per* 'pro'; for U. *perne* etc. see **300**, 3, *a*), *per-etom* 'peritum', *per-acni-* 'sollemnis' (**159**, *a*); with intensive force, in U. *per-acri-* 'opimus, in perfect condition' (in form like L. *per-ācer*, but with the meaning which the root shows in Grk. ἀκμή etc.).

> NOTE.   The meaning 'beyond, across', seen in O.-U. *pert*, is an easy development of 'through', and traces of a similar use are found elsewhere.   Cf. Lith. *peř tìlta* 'go over the bridge', *peř trìs mylès* 'over (more than) three miles', etc.   Here, probably, L. *perfīdus*.

6. O. *perum* 'sine' (*\*per-om*; see **201**, 5).   Thus *perum dolom mallom* 'without guile'.

> NOTE.   The meaning is simply a further specialization of that seen in *pert*.   Cf. Eng. 'beyond doubt' = 'without doubt'.

7. O. **pústin**, U. **pustin**, **pusti**, *posti* 'according to' (an extension of *post*, probably *\*posti-en*).   O. **pústin slagím senateís suveís tanginúd** 'by vote of the respective senates according to the territory' (see note to C. A. 34); — U. *posti acnu* '(four pounds of spelt) for each year' (or 'ceremony'; see **159**, *a*), **pusti kastruvu** '(one, two, or three sesterces) per head, for each person' (or 'estate'; but see note to T. B. 8, 13), **pustin ançif** 'by turns', **pustin ereçlu** '(to Pomonus and Vesuna) on their respective altars'.

> NOTE.   From a *\*posti-ne* (cf. U. *post-ne*) one would expect O. *\*púistin* with *i*, while from *\*posti-en* the i of **púistin** is regular (see **44**, *b*).   For the meaning, cf. Eng. *after* = *according to*, in 'after their value', 'after our sins', etc., L. *secundum*, Germ. *nach*, etc., and also the distributive force of L. *in* in 'in singulos annos' etc.

8. (L. *suprā*).   U. *subra* (**157**, 1, **190**, 3).   Thus *subra esto tudero* 'above these limits'.   Elsewhere the form is used adverbially (*subra screihtor* 'written above' etc.).

### With the Ablative only

**300.** **1.** (L. *amb-*, Grk. ἀμφί). O. **ampt** (see **161**, *a*). Thus **eksuk amvíannud eítuns ampt tríbud tuv. ampt Mener** 'by this detour let them go(?) around the Public Building (and) around the temple of Minerva' (no. 18). Except for this one example we find, as in Latin, only the prefix.

CPDS. The prefix appears usually as *am-*, rarely as *amb-* (Umbrian), and also in an extended form *\*amfer-* (after *anter-*), O. **amfr-**, U. **ambr-**. See **161** with *a*.

**2.** (L. *cum*). O. *com*, U. *com*, *-co(m)*, *-ku(m)*. See **293** with *a*.

CPDS. O. **kúmbened** 'convenit', **kúmbęnnieís** 'conventus', *comparascuster* 'consulta erit', **kú]mparakineís** 'consilii'; — U. *combifiatu* 'nuntiato', *couertu* 'revertito' (17, 13), **kuveitu** 'convehito, congerito' (for *co-* before ų cf. early Latin *coventiōnīd*, Volsc. *couehriu* 'curia'), *comoltu* 'commolito', *comohota* 'commota' (17, 17), *conegos* 'genu nixus', **kukehes** 'incendat'(?). Cf. also O. *comono* 'comitia', U. **kumne** 'comitio' from *\*kom-no-* (15, 4, 251, 2).

**3.** (L. *dē*). O. *dat* (190, 3, *a*). Thus *dat eizaíc egmad* 'concerning this matter', *dat eiza(i)sc* 'concerning these matters', *dat sena[teis] tanginud* 'in accordance with the judgment of the senate' (also *senateis tanginud*, 286; cf. L. *dē sententiā* beside *sententiā*), *dat castrid* 'in a matter involving the death penalty' (also *castrous*, 270).

CPDS. O. **dadíkatted** 'dedicavit', **da[da]d** 'dedit', **dadid** 'dediderit', all with *dad-* for *dad-d-* (163); — U. *da-etom* '\*de-itum, delictum' (*da* from *\*dād* by 133, and extended to cpds.).

**4.** (L. *ex*, *ē*). U. *e*, *ehe*. There are only two examples, **e-asa** 'from the altar' and *ehe esu poplu* 'from this people', the meaning being commonly expressed by the postpositive *-tā* (below, 9).

CPDS. O. **ehpeílatas** 'erectae', **ehpreívíd** (142, *a*); **eestínt** 'exstant', **ee[stit]** 'exstat', **eehiianasúm** 'emittendarum' (77, 1); — U. *ehueltu* 'iubeto', **ehvelklu** 'sententiam', **eveietu** 'voveto', *eheturstahamu*, *eturstahmu* 'exterminato', *efurfatu* 'expurgato'(?), *ehiato* 'emissos', *ebetraf-e* 'in exitus'. Cf. also O. **ehtrad** 'extra' and U. **ap-ehtre** 'ab extra' (142).

NOTE. The conditions under which the *ē* of O. **eestínt** etc. arose are not clear. See **77**, 1, with note.

5. (L. *ob*).    O. **úp**, *op* (from \**opi*- by **92**; cf. Grk. ἐπί, Skt. *ápi*).    Thus **úp eísúd sakaraklúd** 'at this temple', [**úp**] **slaagid** 'at the boundary', *op toutad, op eizois* 'in the presence of the people, of these persons', 'apud populum', 'apud eos'.

CPDS.   O. *osii*[*ns* 'adsint' (**122**, 2); U. *ostendu* 'ostendito' (**122**, 1), probably **ufestne** (**138**, *a*), perhaps *ooserclom* (**77**, 3).

6. (L. *post*).    O. **púst**, *post*, U. *post*, **pus** (from \**pos-ti*; cf. Lith. *pàs* etc.).    O. **púst feíhúís** 'behind the walls', *post eizuc, post exac* 'after this'; — U. *post uerir*, **pusveres** (**139**, 2) 'behind the gate'. Cf. L. *posteā, posthāc*.    In origin this is probably an Ablative of the Point of View.

*a.* In U. *postertio pane* 'postquam tertium' *tertio* is not an Ablative after *post*, but an independent adverb of time, *post* being here an adverb, forming together with *pane* a conjunction.    ·

Cf. the derivatives U. *postne* 'pone' (cf. *perne* 'ante'), whence **pustnaiaf** 'posticas'; O. *posmom* 'postremum', **púst**iris 'posterius', etc.   See **139**, 2, **188**, 2, **189**, 1.

7. (L. *prae*).    O. **prai**, U. **pre**, *pre* (**63**).    O. **prai Mamerttiais** 'before the Martian festival', U. *pre uerir* 'before the gate.'    As only plural forms occur, the Locative is also possible, but it is far more probable that the case is the same as that used with *pru, post*, etc.

CPDS.   O. *praesentid* 'praesente,' *praefucus* 'praefectus'; — U. **prehabia** 'praehibeat', **prepesnimu** 'praefator', **preuendu** 'advertito' (used in contrast to *ahauendu* 'avertito'), etc.   Cf. also *prepa* 'priusquam' (**202**, 4) and *pretra* 'priores' (**188**, 2).

8. (L. *prō*).    O. **pru** (**53**), U. **-per**, **-pe**(r) (from *-pro*, **91**, 2; for -pe, see **103**, 4).    O. **pru meddixud** 'by virtue of magistracy' (L. *prō imperiō* etc.), *pru medicatud* 'in place of judgment', that is 'as if judgment had been rendered' (cf. L. *prō ioudicatōd*, CIL. IX 782); — U. *tota-per*, **tuta-per**, **tuta-pe** 'for the city', *poplu-per* 'for the people', *ocri-per* 'for the mount', **fratrus-per** 'for the brothers', etc.

CPDS.   O. *pruhipid* 'prohibuerit', **prupukid** 'by previous agreement' (**86**, 5, **173**, 5); — U. **prusekatu** 'prosecato', *procanurent* '\*procinuerint', **prupehast** 'ante piabit', etc.   Note the distinct temporal force of the prefix in O. **prupukid**, U. **prupehast**.   Cf. also O. *pruter pan* 'priusquam' (**188**, 2, **202**, 4).

*a.* In U. *perne* 'ante', **pernaiaf** 'anticas', O. **Pernaí** 'Prorsae', the *per-* is not from *pro-*, like U. *-per*, but is original.   Cf. Lith. *pérnai* 'in the previous year', Grk. πέρυσι, etc.

9.  U. **-ta, -tu,** *-to* (for *-tā* ; see **34**), of uncertain origin.   Thus **skalçe-ta** 'from the bowl', **akru-tu** 'from the field', *pure-to* 'from the fire', etc.   See **285**.

**With the Accusative and Locative**

301.  1. (L. *inter*).   O. **anter** (U. **anter-,** *ander-,* **98,** *c,* **156** ; no certain example of prepositional use).   Thus O. **anter slagím [A]bellanam iním Núvlanam** 'between the territory of Abella and that of Nola' (C. A.; cf. also nos. 14–17); — but **anter teremníss** 'within the boundaries' (that **teremníss** is an Ablative is much less likely).   If we may judge from the single example, the Locative was used where the meaning is 'within'.   In all examples of the Accusative the meaning is 'between (two points)'.

CPDS.  O. **Anterstataí** ' *Interstitae' ;— U. *andersistu* 'intersidito', **antermenzaru** 'intermenstruarum', *anderuacose,* **antervakaze** ' *intervacatio' (? see note to VI b 47, I b 8), *anderuomu* (? see **298**).

2. (L. *in*).   O. *en,* -*en,* U. *-en* (*-e,* *-em,* **109,** 1 ; once *-i,* **39,** 5).

With Accusative.   O. *en eituas* 'for a fine', *censtom-en* 'to the census'; — U. *anglom-e* 'to the corner', **fesnaf-e** 'to the temple', etc.   Frequently *-en* is used where Latin would prefer *ad* 'to', and in a few cases even like *ad* 'at'.   Thus (VI a 10) *anglu-to somo uapef-e auiehclu todcom-e tuder* 'from the highest corner at the augural seats to the city limits' (*uapef-e auiehclu* resumes briefly the previous *porsei nesimei uapersus auiehcleir est*).

With Locative.   O. *exaisc-en ligis* 'in these laws'; —U. **manuv-e** 'in the hand', etc.   See **280-282**.   For O. **húrtín Kerríín** with *-en* added to both noun and adjective, see **171,** 7.

In O. **imad-en** 'from the bottom up', *eisuc-en ziculud* 'from this day on', *-en* is used adverbially.

CPDS.  O. **embratur** 'imperator', U. **enetu** 'inito', *endendu* 'intendito', **iseçeles** 'insectis' (**39,** 5).   Cf. also the derivative O. **Entraí** ' *Interae'.

3. (L. *super*). U. **super** with Locative, *super-ne* (cf. adverbs *per-ne*, *post-ne*, L. *pōne*, *super-ne*, etc.) with Accusative. Thus *superne adro* '(place the white vessels) over (on top of) the black'; — but **super kumne** '(let loose the heifer) above the place of assembly', **super ereçle** '(make libation) over the shrine'.

4. (L. *trāns*). U. *traf*, *trahaf*, *traha*, **tra** (110, 4). Thus *traf Sahatam etu* 'go across the Sacred Way' (similarly with *couertu* 'return', *combifiatu* 'announce'); — but *trahaf Sahate feetu* 'sacrifice on the other side of the Sacred Way' (similarly **tra ekvine 'fetu**).

CPD. U. *trahuorfi* 'transverse'.

## With the Locative and Ablative

**302.** (L. *sub*). O. συπ μεδικιαι 'in the meddixship'; — but U. *su maronato* (*su* by **125**, 1) 'in the maroship' (see note to no. 84). Some assume that *maronato* is Loc. Sg., from a *u*-stem, but more probably it is Abl. Sg. of the *o*-stem seen in the Loc. Sg. *maronatei*. A difference in construction is more likely than a difference in stem. For both Locative and Ablative are parall-eled by the corresponding constructions without the preposition (O. **medikkiai**, U. *maronatei*, etc., **282**; — O. *meddixud*, **294**). For the Abl. Sg. in -*o* see **171**, 6, *a*.

CPDS. U. *subocauu* 'invoco' (**102**, 2), **subahtu** 'deponito, set down', *subator* 'set aside, omitted' (**218**; for force of *sub* cf. L. *subdūcō* 'remove'), **sumtu** 'sumito' (**114**, *c*), **sutentu** 'subtendito' (su- by **121**), probably **sufafiaf** 'partis exsertas' (? cf. *faf-* in *ex-fafillātō*, Plautus Mil. Gl. 1180, and *ef-fafllātum* 'exertum', Festus ed. Thewrewk, p. 59), and **sufefaklu** of uncertain meaning.

*a.* In Umbrian, forms of the adjective *sopo-* are used predicatively in the sense of 'sub'. See **306**.

## With Other Cases

**303.** (L. *contrā*). O. *contrud* (**190**, 2). In O. *contrud exeic* 'contrary to this' *exeic* is commonly taken as a Locative, but is much more easily understood as a Dative, properly a Dative of Relation with *contrud* used adverbially. Cf. L. *siti contra pug-nandum* (Cels. 4, 5 (2)), *huic contra itum* (Tac. A. 11, 10).

**304.** The Genitive is found only with the so-called improper prepositions, as in O. *egm*[*as touti*]*cas amnud* 'rei publicae causa' (cf. **amnúd** 'circuitu'), U. *ocrer pehaner paca* 'montis piandi causa' (*paca* Abl. Sg. of \**pākā-*; cf. L. *pāctum* etc.).   Another possible example is O. **liímítú**[m] *pernúm* 'in front of the boundaries' (C. A. 29), but the reading here is wholly uncertain.   For O. *ampert mistreis aeteis*, where *aeteis* has been taken as a Genitive after *ampert,* see **269.**

## ADJECTIVES

**305.** Use of adjectives to denote a part.   With L. *summus mons* etc., cf. U. *pesclu semu* 'in the half of the prayer' (*semu*: L. *sēmi-*; see **189,** 1, *a*), that is, 'in the middle of the prayer, during the prayer'; — O. e]**ísaí viaí mefiaí** 'in the middle of this road'.

**306.** Predicative use of adjectives with the force of adverbs.[1] With L. *sciēns* 'wittingly', *libēns* 'willingly', etc., compare O. *deiuatud sipus* 'swear wittingly', U. *tases persnimu* 'pray silently', **kutef pesnimu** 'pray quietly', etc.   Similarly U. *postro* in *sopo postro peperscust* 'put the under parts behind' is an adjective agreeing with *sopo* (cf. **pustra, pustru,** II a 32, II b 19), but in effect an adverb.   U. *sopo-* is frequently used in the same way, like L. *supīnus,* Grk. ὕπτιος.   Thus **persuntru supu ereçle** (IV 17), where **supu,** though an adjective agreeing with **persuntru,** has the force of 'sub', in contrast to the 'super' of **persuntru . . . super ereçle** (IV 19); — *uestisia sopa purom-e* (VI b 17; cf. also VII a 38), where *sopa,* though agreeing with *uestisia,* goes in sense with the following, *sopa purom-e* meaning 'beneath, into the fire' and so 'beneath the fire, sub ignem'.

## ADVERBS

**307.** Predicate use of adverbs in the sense of adjectives[2] (L. *bene est,* etc.).   U. *porsei nesimei asa deueia est* 'which is next to the altar of the gods' (but O. **nessimas staíet veruís** 'stand

---

[1] That is, where an adverbial construction seems more natural to us.

[2] That is, where an adjectival construction seems more natural to us.

next to the gate'); — U. **esuf testru sese asa asam-a purtuvitu** 'himself standing at the right of the altar he shall place the offering
on the altar' (IV 15 ; cf. also III 23, IV 3), in which **sese** is probably an adverb, as if L. *\*sessē*, meaning 'situated' (cf. L. *dextrō-
vorsum* etc.); — U. **eřek prufe si** 'let this be approved', literally
'let this be (regarded as) properly (done)'[1]; — U. **fetu puze neip
eretu** (II a 4) and, in briefer form, *pusei neip heritu* (VI a 27
etc.) '(take it) as not intentionally (done)'.

## THE VERB

### VOICE

**308.** The Passive. Besides the Passive force, as seen for
example in O. *uincter* 'vincitur', *comparascuster* 'consulta erit',
U. **emantur** 'accipiantur', *ostensendi* 'ostendentur', the Deponent
use is frequent. So O. **karanter** 'vescuntur', U. **terkantur** 'suffragentur', U. *eturstahmu* 'exterminato', U. *persnihimu* 'precator',
*persnis fust* 'precatus erit', etc. Sometimes, however, the Active
form is used in contrast to the Deponent of the Latin, e.g.
U. *stiplo, stiplatu*: L. *stipulor*; — U. *osatu*, O. **upsed**, etc. : L. *operor*
(but O. **upsatuh sent** no. 44 is Deponent 'operati sunt', in contrast
to U. *oseto* 'operata, facta') ; — O. **fatíum** : L. *fateor*. Compare
the use of Active forms in early and late Latin parallel to
Deponents of the classical period.

*a.* With the Deponent use of L. *cēnātus* beside *cēnō*, *iūrātus* beside *iūrō*,
etc., compare O. *deiuatuns* 'iurati', U. **çersnatur furent** 'cenaverint', and also
U. *uesticos* (*fust*) 'libaverit' (**230,** *a*).

*b.* A Passive form with distinctly middle force is seen in U. **amparihmu**
'raise oneself, rise' beside the Active **amparitu** 'raise, set up (the litter)'. A
similar relation is sometimes assumed between U. *subra spahatu* 'spread out
over, throw on' (VI b 41) with object expressed (the vessels that have just been
used), and *subra spahmu* (VI b 17, VII a 39), *subra spafu* (V a 20), with no
objects expressed. But the meaning of the latter is probably not 'throw oneself over, walk over', but 'perform the ceremony of throwing on (the vessels)'.

---

[1] Cf. O. *izic amprufid facus estud* '(if any one has been made tribune of the
people contrary to this) let him be (regarded as) made so improperly'.

*c.* U. *uestis, uesteis* 'libans' is parallel to U. *persnis* 'precatus' both in formation and use. It comes from *\*u̯estito-s*, with verb-stem *\*u̯esti-*, of which *\*u̯estikā-* (U. *uesticatu* 'libato') is an extension. The etymology of this group of words, to which belong also U. **vestiçia** 'libamentum' and probably *Uestisier*, name of a god, is unknown.

**309.** The frequent impersonal use of the Passive (L. *itur, itum est,* etc.) is noteworthy, e.g. O. **sakarater** 'a sacrifice is made', U. *purdito fust* 'the offering shall take place', *muieto fust* 'a noise shall be made', **herter** 'it is desired, desirable' and so used like L. *oportet.* Nearly all of the forms in which *r* alone appears as the personal ending are used impersonally. See **239.**

**310.** Transitive use of verbs usually intransitive, and vice versa. U. *ninctu,* in form L. *ninguitō,* means 'overwhelm with snow'; similarly U. *sonitu* 'overwhelm with sound', *tremitu* 'make tremble', though these are not of the same conjugation as L. *sonō, tremō.* Cf. also U. *nepitu* 'overwhelm with water' from a root seen in L. *Neptūnus.* U. *habe* (VI b 54 = I b 18) is used intransitively, 'holds himself, remains'.

## TENSE

**311.** The use of the tenses shows no variation from what is found in Latin. The use of the Present Indicative to denote what is customary is frequent, as is natural in the language of ritual. It occurs with future meaning in some temporal and conditional clauses cited below. There is only one occurrence of the Imperfect Indicative, namely **fufans** 'erant', C. A. 10, where it simply denotes past situation, as so frequently in Latin. The Perfect Indicative occurs chiefly in dedications and inscriptions on public works, where it has the simple narrative force (Historical or Aoristic Perfect). The Future and Future Perfect are very frequent in temporal clauses, the difference between the two being the same as in Latin.

All the occurrences of the Imperfect Subjunctive are in clauses depending on an Historical Perfect, namely O. **ekss kúmbened . . . puz ídík sakara[klúm] . . . fusíd, . . . pún patensíns, . . .**

**patensíns**, . . . [h]**erríns** 'ita convēnit, ut id templum . . . esset, . . .
cum aperirent, . . . aperirent, . . . caperent' (C. A. 10–54); also
Pael. *upsaseter coisatens* 'fieret curaverunt'.   The Perfect Subjunctive is regularly used in prohibitions and occasionally in positive commands and expressions of wish.   See **312, 313**.   It occurs
also a few times in temporal and conditional clauses (**319, 320**).

## MOOD
### Commands and Prohibitions

**312.**  The Subjunctive of Command is frequent in Umbrian
in the passage V a 1–V b 7, where the Atiedian Brothers decreed
'*let* the flamen, whoever he shall be, *have the care* (**kuraia**) of the
ceremony, *let him furnish* (**prehabia**) whatever is necessary.   *Let
him receive* (**habia**) certain fees.   When the brothers shall have
feasted, *let* the magister or quaestor *take a vote* (**ehvelklu feia**) as
to whether the matter has been properly looked after.   And if
the majority pronounce it satisfactory *let it be appróved* (**eřek
prufe si**).   If not, *let* the magister or quaestor *take a vote* (**ehvelklu
feia**) as to the amount of the penalty, and whatever penalty they
demand, *let* the flamen's penalty *be* so great (**etantu mutu ařfer-
ture si**)'.   But even within the limits of this passage the Imperative occurs twice, and elsewhere the Imperative is almost
exclusively employed, occurring in hundreds of examples.   The
other examples of the Subjunctive are **ene tra Sahta kupifiaia** 'then
announce across the Sacred Way' (I b 35, in the midst of a series
of Imperatives; the corresponding clause in VII a 43 has the
Imperative *combifiatu*), and **terkantur** 'let them approve' (III 9,
also in the midst of Imperatives).

NOTE.  It is hardly accidental that the series of Subjunctives in V a is
immediately preceded by **eitipes** 'decreverunt.'  Although the clauses are not
actually dependent, they are so closely attached in feeling that the choice of
the Subjunctive rather than the Imperative may well be due to the exclusive
use of the former in dependent clauses.  Similarly *fos sei, pacer sei* 'be favorable
and propitious', belonging under **314**, always occurs immediately after the
phrase *teio subocau* 'I invoke thee', whereas elsewhere the Imperative *futu fos
pacer* is used.  Cf. VI a 22 ff.

In Oscan also, the Imperative is nearly always employed in positive commands. Examples of the Subjunctive are **saahtúm tefúrúm sakahíter** 'let a burnt-offering be made' (T. A.);— *lamatir* 'let him be beaten' (T. B.);—**sakrafír** 'let there be a consecration'. (nos. 29, 30). For the use of the Perfect in the last two examples, cf. L. *sit denique inscriptum in fronte unius cuiusque quid de re publica sentiat* (Cic. Cat. 1, 13, 32), and see **313**.

With the preponderance of the Imperative in both Oscan and Umbrian is to be compared the usage of early Latin inscriptions, in many of which (e.g. the Lex Bantina, Lex agraria) the Imperative is used exclusively, while in others (e.g. the Sententia Minuciorum) a Subjunctive of Command may now and then appear.

**313.** In prohibitions, Umbrian uses the Imperative regularly, the Present Subjunctive occurring once in **neiřhabas** 'let them not furnish' (IV 33). In Oscan, however, the Imperative is never used, but always the Perfect Subjunctive. Thus **nep Abellanús nep Núvlanús pídum tríbarakattíns** 'let neither the Abellani nor the Nolani build anything' (C. A. 46 ff.);—*izic eizeic zicel[ei]* *comono ni hipid* 'let him not hold an assembly on this day' (T. B. 7, 8);—*ne phim pruhipid* 'let him not prevent any one' (T. B. 25); — *nep fefacid* 'let him not cause' (T. B. 10), in contrast to the Imperative *factud* of a positive command in the same sentence; — *nep censtur fuid, nei suae pr. fust* 'let no one be censor, unless he has been praetor' (T. B. 28).

NOTE. This use of the Perfect Subjunctive is to be compared with the Greek use of μή with the Aorist Subjunctive, and, together with its occasional use in positive commands (**312**) and expressions of wish (**314**), is to be connected with the energetic force natural to the aoristic function. No temporal distinction is involved.

### The Subjunctive of Wish

**314.** The Subjunctive of Wish, though of different origin, is not always easily distinguished from the Subjunctive of Command. But certainly U. *fos sei, pacer sei* 'be favorable, propitious', alternating with *futu fos pacer* (see **312**, note), belongs

here, likewise the Oscan Subjunctives in the Curse of Vibia
and ·the shorter curse, no. 20, namely **turumiiad, krustatar, kaispatar, lamatir** 'may he be tortured, etc.', and, with the negative,
**nep pútiad, nep heriiad** 'may he not be able, etc.'[1] Here also
U. *pihafei* 'may it be expiated' (VI a 29 etc.). For the use of
the Perfect, as in the case of U. *pihafei*, O. **lamatir** (possibly **krustatar, kaispatar**; but see **238**, *c*), which is also frequent in early
Latin, see **313**, note.

### The Subjunctive in Substantive Clauses[2]

**315.** The Subjunctive is usually introduced by O. **puz**,
U. *pusi* 'ut' (**202**, 6), but in certain phrases, as in Latin, it may
also stand without any conjunction. Examples are: U. *stiplo
aseriaia* 'demand that I observe' (VI a 2); — U. *etaians deitu* 'let
him tell them to go' (VI b 64); — U. *combifiatu erus dersa* 'let
him give notice to add the *erus*' (VII a 44); but with an intervening clause as well as a different verb, *carsitu . . . puse erus
dersa* 'let him call out . . . to add the *erus*' (VII a 43); — with
U. *tiçit* 'decet', **herter** 'oportet', O. **kasit** 'decet' (in form L. *caret*),
as U. *façia tiçit* 'one ought to sacrifice' (II a 17), O. **fakiiad kasit**
'one ought to sacrifice' (no. 31), U. *dirsans herti* 'they ought to
give', etc.; — O. **ekss kúmbened . . . puz ídík sakara[klúm] . . . fusíd**
etc. 'it was agreed that this temple should be' etc. (C. A. 10 ff.;
see also **311**); — U. *eo iso ostendu, pusi pir pureto cehefi dia* (VI a
20), best taken as 'let him set them out in such a manner (*iso*)
that (*pusi*) he cause (*dia*) one fire to be lighted from the other',
*cehefi* depending directly on *dia*; — so probably U. **pepurkurent
herifi** (V b 6) 'shall have urged to be necessary' (as if L. *poposcerint oportuerit*); — O. *factud pous touto deiuatuns tanginom deicans* 'let him cause the people to declare their opinion under
oath' (T. B. 9).

---

[1] In Greek curses the Optative is used in both the positive and the negative form.
[2] For convenience the Subjunctives in Substantive Clauses are grouped together here, without regard to their specific origin (Volitive etc.).

A noteworthy construction is seen in O. *nep fefacid pod pis dat eizac egmad min[s] deiuaid dolud malud* 'let him prevent any one from swearing falsely in this matter' (T. B. 10 f.), in which *nep fefacid* is felt as the equivalent of a verb of preventing and followed by *pod mins*, which is identical with L. *quōminus* in meaning and nearly so in form (202, 1)[1].

### Clauses of Indirect Question

**316.** In U. *ehvelklu feia* . . . , *panta muta arferture si* 'take a vote as to what the flamen's penalty shall be' (V b 1 f.), the *si* is simply a dependent Subjunctive of Deliberation or Propriety. But an unquestionable example of a Subjunctive in an indirect question of fact, where the direct question would have the Indicative, is U. *ehvelklu feia* . . . , *sve rehte kuratu si* 'take a vote as to whether it has been arranged properly' (V a 23 ff.).

Noteworthy, because of the lack of any interrogative word, is U. *revestu . . . emantur herte* 'see whether they are to be accepted' (V a 8, 10). Since even in Latin the original Indicative may still stand in indirect questions of fact, there is no necessity of taking *herte* as a Subjunctive. See 238, 2, *a*.

### Relative Clauses [2]

**317.** In nearly all the relative clauses occurring, whether the relative is definite or indefinite, and whatever the mood of the principal verb, the Indicative is used. Thus U. *pisest* . . . , *eetu* 'whoever is . . . , let him go' (VI b 53 f.); — O. *sakaraklúm Herekleís [úp] slaagíd púd íst*, . . . *puz ídík sakara[klúm]* . . . *fusíd* 'that the temple of Hercules which is at the boundary . . . should be' (C. A. 11 f.); — U. *pisi pumpe fust* . . . , *ere ri esune kuraia* 'whoever shall be . . . , let him look after the ceremony' (V a 3 ff.); — O. *censamur esuf . . . poizad ligud iusc censtur censaum angetuzet*

---

[1] I cannot understand the objection of v. Planta (II, p. 482) to this view, nor his assertion that the construction does not correspond to L. *prohibeat quominus* but to *prohibeat quominus non* or *prohibeat ut non*.

[2] Except those of time, for which see 318.

'let him be rated according to the law by which the censors shall have proposed to take the census' (T. B. 19 f.), etc. (examples of the Future and Future Perfect are very numerous).

Hence in U. prehabia piře uraku ri esuna si herte, et pure esune sis 'let him furnish whatever is necessary for the ceremony, and whatever persons are necessary' (V a 5 f.) there is no necessity of taking herte as a Subjunctive (see **238**, 2, *a*), and in the second clause sis probably depends on a herte to be supplied from the preceding, though of course a Subjunctive would also be possible (cf. *cui iussus siet, auscultet,* Cato, De Agric. 5, 3, etc.).

A reasonably certain example of a Subjunctive in a descriptive relative clause is seen in O. *siom . . . idic tangineis deicum pod ualaemom touticom tadait ezum* '(having sworn) that they will render such judgment as they think to be for the best public good' (T. B. 9 f.)[1].

Here may be mentioned, though *persei* is in this case a conjunction (**202**, 2), U. *persei mersei* 'so far as is right' (VI a 28, 38, 48) beside *perse mers est* (VI b 31, 55), the main verb each time being a Subjunctive. Cf. L. *quod opus siet,* used by Cato even where the main verb is Indicative (e.g. De Agric. 16). The choice of the two expressions, 'so far as is right' or 'so far as may be right', has nothing to do with the mood of the principal verb.

### Temporal Clauses

**318.** All the temporal clauses which occur refer to future time, and in the great majority of cases, as in Latin, the Future or Future Perfect Indicative is used. The usual conjunctions are O. *pon,* U. *ponne* (**202**, 3) and U. *ape* (**202**, 8). The latter is far more common than *ponne* in the later Umbrian, and with the Future Perfect entirely displaces it (cf. *ape ambrefurent* VI b 56: puni amprefuus I b 20, etc.). U. puře (**202**, 1) and piře, *pirsi* (**202**, 2), also have temporal force sometimes, as in puře nuvime

---

[1] Better taken so than as an Indirect Question (Verb-System, p. 144), since *pod,* not *pid,* is used.

ferest 'when he shall bring them the ninth time' (II a 26), *sersi pirsi sesust* 'when he shall have taken his seat' (VI a 5).

But the Present Indicative with future meaning is also found. Thus U. *ponne oui furfant, uitlu toru trif fetu* 'when they purify(?) the sheep, sacrifice three bull-calves' (VI b 43; *furfant* Pres. Indic. of Conj. I, as shown by *efurfatu*); — U. *pune seste, urfeta manuve habetu* 'when you dedicate (the calf), hold the *orbita* in the hand' (II b 22 f.);—U. *ponne iuengar tursiandu hertei* 'when it is necessary to drive forth the heifers' (VII b 2; for *hertei* see 238, 2, *a*). Cf. also O. *adpúd fiiet* 'so long as they occur' (no. 31 a; for *adpúd* see 202, 9).

Compare the Latin use of the Present Indicative with future force after *antequam* and *priusquam*, and, especially in early Latin, in relative and conditional clauses (see also 319).

The Present Subjunctive is also found. Thus O. **pun far kahad, nip putiiad edum** 'when he takes food, may he not be able to eat' (no. 19, 8); — U. *pone esonome ferar pufe pir entelust, ere fertu, poe* . . . 'when that in which the fire has been placed is brought to the ceremony, let him bring it, who . . . ' (VI b 50).

This of course is the Anticipatory Subjunctive, which is frequent enough in such clauses in early Latin, and which in Oscan-Umbrian, as in Latin, was not completely displaced by the Future Indicative (itself a Subjunctive in origin).

The Imperfect Subjunctive occurs in G. A. 50, where the verbs of the surrounding clauses are also in the same tense, depending on **ekss kúmbened.** See above, 311.

**319.** With the Conjunctions meaning 'before', 'after', 'until', namely O. *pruter pan* (202, 4), U. *prepa* (202, 4), *post pane* (202, 4), *nersa* (202, 11), *arnipo* (202, 10), the Future Perfect is the commonest construction, but there is one occurrence each of the Future Indicative and the Perfect Subjunctive, the latter, as in Latin, with the same force as the Future Perfect. Thus:

Future. — O. *com preiuatud actud, pruter pam medicatinom didest* 'let him treat with the defendant before he gives judgment' (T. B. 15 f.).

Future Perfect. — U. *nep andersistu, nersa courtust porsi angla anseriato iust* 'one shall not interrupt(?) until the one who has gone to observe the birds has returned' (VI a 6) ; — U. *postertio pane poplo andirsafust, . . . persnihimumo* 'after he has performed the lustration of the people the third time, . . . let them pray' (VII a 46 f.) ; — *eam mani nertru tenitu, arnipo uestisia uesticos* 'let him hold it in the left hand until he has poured out the libation' (VI b 24 f.) ; — *anderuomu sersitu, arnipo comatir pesnis fust* 'let him sit in the . . . until he has prayed with the broken cakes' (VI b 41).

Perfect Subjunctive. — *neip amboltu, prepa desua combifiansi* 'one shall not go around before he has announced a propitious bird' (VI b 52).

### Conditional Clauses

**320.** In conditional clauses, introduced by O. **svai,** *suae,* U. **sve,** *sue* (**202,** 14), the commonest construction is the Future or Future Perfect Indicative, the main verb being usually an Imperative or Subjunctive of Command. The Tabula Bantina alone furnishes some sixteen examples. The Future Perfect in both condition and conclusion occurs once in Umbrian (VI a 7). U. **piře,** *pirsi* (**202,** 2), also, sometimes has conditional force 'in case that, if', e.g. *persei . . . pir orto est* 'if a fire has occurred' (VI a 26 etc.), **peře . . . aiu urtu fefure** 'if disturbances(?) shall have occurred' (II a 3 ; see **128,** 2, *a*).

The Present Indicative with future force, which is frequent in early Latin legal inscriptions and is found occasionally in Latin poetry (e.g. Verg. Aen. 3, 606), is seen in O. *suaepis censtomen nei cebnust, in eizeic uincter, esuf lamatir* 'if any one shall not have come to the census and is convicted of it, let him be beaten' (T. B. 20 f.). Cf. also U. **svepis habe** 'if any one remains' (I b 18), **svepis heri** 'if any one wishes' (IV 26).

The Present Subjunctive is found in U. **svepu . . . vakaze,** *suepo . . . uacose* (I b 8, VI b 47), according to the explanation as \**uacos-se* 'vacatio sit'. See note to passage.

The Perfect Subjunctive in future or future perfect sense, also found in Latin, is seen in O. **svai neip dadid, lamatir** 'if he does not give it up, let him be beaten' (no. 19, 4) ; — so probably U. *ier* (**238,** 2) in *noŝue ier ehe eŝu poplu*, . . . , *portatu* . . . 'if one does not go from this people, carry him . . . ' (VI b 54 f.).

Noteworthy, because of the lack of any conjunction, is U. **heriiei façiu aŕfertur,** . . . **façia tiçit** 'if the flamen wishes to make the sacrifice, it is proper' (II a 16 f.).

## INFINITIVES AND PARTICIPLES

**321.** The Present Infinitive is used as in Latin. The construction with subject Accusative is already developed, e.g. O. *deiuatuns . . . siom deicum* 'having sworn that they will say' (T. B. 9) etc. The Supine is used exactly as in Latin, e.g. U. *aseriato etu* 'go to observe.' For the *-to-* Participle without passive force, see **308,** *a.* The Gerundive is used as in Latin, e.g. **iúvilas sakrannas** 'the iovilae to be consecrated', **úpsannam deded** 'had made', etc. For the Genitive construction iņ U. *ocrer pihaner*, see **271.**

### AGREEMENT

**322.** Agreement óf adjectives belonging to nouns of different gender. Agreement with the Masculine is seen in U. *peiqu peica merstu* 'pico pica iusto' (VI a 1 ; but elsewhere with adjective repeated, *peico mersto peica mersta*, etc.). Agreement with the nearest noun is seen in the recurring passage (VI a 32 f. etc.) *saluo seritu ocrer Fisier, totar Ĩiouinar nome, nerf, arsmo, ueiro, pequo castruo, fri salua seritu* 'salvum servato arcis Fisiae, civitatis Iguvinae nomen, principes, ritus, viros, pecuum capita, fruges salvas servato', where *saluo* agrees with the first object *nome*, and *salua* with the last, *fri*.

**323.** Agreement by sense. As in Latin, the Plural may be used with a collective noun or a noun joined to another by *com.* Thus O. *pous touto deiuatuns tanginom deicans* 'ut populus

iurati sententiam dicant' (T. B. 9) ; — U. **sve mestru karu fratru
Atiieřiu, pure ulu benurent, prusikurent** 'si maior pars fratrum Atiediorum, qui illuc venerint, pronuntiaverint' (V a 24 ff.); —U. *com
prinuatir . . . ambretuto, . . . com prinuatir eso persnimumo* 'cum
legatis ambiunto, cum legatis sic precantor', 'let him (the flamen) with the assistants go about, pray' (VI b 56 f.).    Cf. also
U. *hondra furo sehemeniar hatuto totar pisi heriest* 'infra forum
seminarium capiunto civitatis quisquis volet' (VII a 52).

**324.** Attraction.   The attraction of a noun to the case of
the relative pronoun is seen in U. *uasor* (Nom. Pl.) *uerisco Treblanir, porsi ocrer pehaner paca ostensendi, eo iso ostendu* 'vasa
ad portam Trebulanam, quae arcis piandae causa ostendentur,
ea sic ostendito' (VI a 19 f.); — also in O. **eítiuvam paam . . . deded,
eísak eítiuvad** 'pecuniam quam dedit, ea pecunia' (no. 4), though
here the noun is repeated in its proper case.   In Latin such
attraction is mainly poetical in the best period (*urbem quam
statuo vestra est*, Verg. Aen. 1, 573), but not uncommon in early
prose.   Cf. *Vįturies quei . . . damnati sunt, . . . eos omneis* etc.
(CIL. I 199, 43 f.), *viatores praecones quei ex hac lege lectei sub-
lectei erunt, eis viatoribus praeconibus* etc. (CIL. I 202, col. II, 31 f.).

## OMISSION OF WORDS

**325.** Asyndeton.   The omission of the connective in a
series of coördinate words or clauses is, as in Latin and elsewhere, extremely common.   Noticeable is the frequency of
phrases consisting of pairs of words without connective, like
L. *volens propitius* etc.   Thus U. *fons pacer* 'favorable and propitious', **pernaiaf pustnaiaf** 'before and behind', **antakres kumates**
'whole and broken', **arepes arves** 'offerings of fat and the fruits
of the field', **atru alfu** 'black and white' (I b 29), *dupursus petur-
pursus* 'bipeds and quadrupeds', *perne postne* 'before and after',
*fato fito* 'success and good fortune' (as if L. *factum fitum*, the
first referring to 'efficiency, successful accomplishment', the
second to 'that which happens, turns out well, good fortune'),

*sepse sarsite* 'together and completely' (cf. L. *sane sarteque*; for
the forms see **244**, 1, *b*, **244**, 3)[1], **veskla snata asnata** 'vessels wet and
dry' (i.e. vessels for liquids and those not for liquids; cf. Eng.
'dry-measure' and 'liquid measure'). Note also O. *pr. censtur*
'praetor or censor' (T. B. 27).

**326.** Omission of the Subject. In the Iguvinian Tables,
as in early Latin prose, the subject is frequently left unexpressed, when it is well understood who is the proper person
to perform the action in question. Thus **ape apelust, muneklu
habia** etc. (V a 17 ff.) 'when one (i.e. the proper person, in this
case the flamen) shall have performed certain rites, he shall
receive certain fees'. Even when there is a change of subject,
it may be left unexpressed. Thus in VI b 48 ff. there is a series
of verbs with no subject expressed, though some of the actions
are performed by the augur and others by the flamen, as is seen
from the more detailed statements in VI a 1 ff.

**327.** Omission of the Verb. The verb *subocauu* 'invoco'
is omitted in U. *tio esu bue peracrei pihaclu* 'te hoc bove opimo
piaculo' (VI a 25 etc.), **tiu puni tiu vinu** 'te posca te vino' (II a 25),
with which compare L. *te hoc porco piaculo* (Cato, De Agric.
141, 4). Corresponding to *eno deitu arsmahamo* etc. 'tunc dicito:
"ordinamini"' etc. (VI b 56 etc.) the older version has simply
**enumek armamu** etc. 'tunc "ordinamini"' etc. (I b 19 etc.).

The omission of the verb or of the object in dedications is
of course common, likewise of the verb when it is readily
supplied from a preceding clause.

## ORDER OF WORDS

**328.** There is no fundamental difference from the Latin
order, the resemblance being closest with the style of early
prose such as that of Cato or the inscriptions. The following
points are perhaps worthy of mention.

---

[1] U. *sepse sarsite* is also taken as 'separately and together', *sepse* being explained
as from *se-pse*. But this is on the whole less likely.

1. As in Latin, the adjective regularly follows its noun, but may precede it if emphatic. Thus U. *ocri-per Fisiu, tota-per Iiouina* 'pro monte Fisio, pro civitate Iguvina', etc., but *destru-co persi, nertru-co persi* 'ad dextrum (sinistrum) pedem', *destram-e scapla* 'in dextram scapulam', etc. In the numerous sacrifices of three victims the numeral always follows its noun in VI a 22, 58, VI b 1, 3 etc., but always precedes it in the earlier version (I a 3, 7, 11, 14 etc.). Demonstrative pronouns precede, possessives follow their nouns, as in Latin.

2. As in Latin, words or even whole clauses belonging to a subordinate clause are sometimes introduced before the relative pronoun or conjunction. Thus O. **prai Mamerttiais pas set** 'which are before the Martian' (no. 27), beside the normal order in the companion inscription (no. 28) ; — O. **sakaraklúm Hereklefs [úp] slaagid púd íst** 'the temple of Hercules which is at the boundary' (C. A. 11 ff.). In this last passage all the words quoted, together with the succeeding four lines, belong to the clause introduced by **puz** (l. 17), which depends upon **ekss kúmbened** (l. 10). But in this case, owing to the length of the intervening relative clauses, the subjects are repeated after **puz**. Cf. L. *sei ques esent quei sibei deicerent necesus ese Bacanal habere, eeis utei ad pr. urbanum Romam venirent* (SC. de Bacch. 3 ff.).

3. With a series of objects the verb is sometimes placed before the first and repeated after the last. Thus U. **fertu** . . . **fertu** (II a 17 ff.), *pihatu* . . . *pihatu* (VI a 29 f.), *seritu* . . . *seritu* (VI a 32 f.; quoted in **322**).

# COLLECTION OF INSCRIPTIONS

The following collection contains all the more important inscriptions. Those omitted contain, for the most part, only proper names or mutilated words.

Uncertain letters are indicated by a change in type, italic in black-face text, roman in italic text.[1] Obvious mistakes are corrected in the text, the original reading being given in a footnote. Where there can be any reasonable doubt as to a correction, it is given in the footnote, the original reading being left in the text. Mistakes in the division of words (which is indicated by dots, usually one, sometimes two) are corrected without remark. Restorations are inclosed in brackets. The division of the lines is indicated by |, except where the printed lines follow those of the original.[2]

For the sake of convenience, capitals and marks of abbreviation and punctuation are supplied in the text, as well as in the translation.[3] The translation of the more uncertain words is given in italics, or sometimes omitted entirely; yet from the fact that a given translation is not italicized it does not follow that this translation is undisputed, but only that the author regards it as reasonably certain. A few fictitious Latin words are used for convenience, and marked with an asterisk. But transcriptions and translations of proper names, even when unknown in Latin, are not so marked, except in the Glossary. The brief comments to some of the inscriptions are merely supplementary to the Glossary.

For each inscription the corresponding numbers of the collections of Conway and v. Planta are given. Some slight variations from the reading of one or both of these are based upon autopsy. See the author's Critical Notes to Oscan Inscriptions, I.F. 12, 13 ff.

## OSCAN INSCRIPTIONS

The Cippus Abellanus and the Tabula Bantina are given first, as furnishing connected reading of some length and illustrating the spelling in each of the two alphabets. They are also commented upon more fully than the other inscriptions. After these numbers the arrangement is geographical.

---

[1] Many letters which are somewhat mutilated, but of which enough remains to make it perfectly clear what was intended, are printed without change of type. In the texts of Conway and v. Planta mutilated letters are marked more freely. I am not sure now that I have been entirely consistent in this matter, but think I have not failed to mark letters which are mutilated enough to be really doubtful.

[2] In the case of a one-line inscription covering more than one line of printed text, | is added at the end. So nos. 6, 41 b, etc.

[3] But in some cases where the interpretation is extremely doubtful, notably in no. 19, marks of punctuation are omitted from the text and given only in the translation.

225

## 1. Cippus Abellanus

A limestone tablet about 6 feet 5 inches high, 1 foot 8 inches broad, and 11 inches thick. Inscribed on both sides. Found in 1745 at Avella in use as a door-step, and believed to have been brought from Castel d'Avella, the probable site of the ancient Abella. Now in the Seminary at Nola. Conway no. 95, v. Planta no. 127.

### A

Maiiúí Vestirikiíúí Mai. Sír.
prupukid sverruneí kvaístureí Abellanúí iním Maiiú[í
Iúvkiíúí Mai. Pukalatúí
5 medíkeí deketasiúí Núvl[a-
núí] iním lígatúís Abell[anúís
iním lígatúís Núvlanúís,
pús senateís tanginúd
suveís pútúrúspíd lígat[ús
10 fufans, ekss kúmbened.
Sakaraklúm Herekleís [úp
slaagid púd íst iním teer[úm
púd úp eisúd sakaraklúd [íst
púd anter teremníss eh[trúís
15 íst, paí teremenniú mú[iníkad
tanginúd prúftúset r[íhtúd
amnúd, puz ídík sakara[klúm
iním ídík terúm múiní[kúm
múiníkeí tereí fusíd [iním
20 eiseís sakarakleís í[ním
tereís fruktatiuf, fr[ukta-
tiuf] múiníkú pútúrú[mpíd
fus]íd. Avt Núvlanú . . .
. . . . *H*erekleís fíí[sn . . .
25 . . . . *p*íspíd Núvla*n* . . . .
. . . . . . *gt* . . . . . . . . . .

Maio Vestricio Mai. f. Sír.,
ex antepacto *arbitro*, quaestori
Abellano, et Maio
Iovicio Mai. f. Puclato
meddici *decentario Nolano
et legatis Abellanis
et legatis Nolanis,
qui senatus sententia
sui utrique legati
erant, ita convenit.
Templum Herculis ad
finem quod est, et territorium
quod ad id templum est,
quod inter termina *exteriora*
est, quae termina communi
sententia posita sunt recto
circuitu, ut id templum
et id territorium commune
in communi territorio esset, et
eius templi et
territorii fructus, fructus
communis utrorumque
esset. At Nolani
. . . . Herculis fanum
. . . . . . . . . . .

**B**

Ekkum [*svaí píd herieset*
trííbarak[*avúm tereí púd*
líímítú[m] *pernúm* [*púís*
30 Hereklefs fíísnú mefi[ú
íst, ehtrad feíhúss *pú*[s
Hereklefs fíísnam amfr-
et, pert víam pússtíst
paí íp íst, pústin slagím
35 senateís suveís tangi-
núd tríbarakav*ú*m lí-
kítud.  Iním íúk tríba-
rakkiuf pam Núvlanús
tríbarakattuset¹ iním
40 úíttiuf Núvlanúm estud.
Ekkum svaí píd Abellanús
tríbarakattuset¹ íúk trí-
barakkiuf iním úíttiuf
Abellan*ú*m estud.  Avt
45 púst feíhúís pús físnam amfret, eíseí tereí nep Abellanús nep Núvlanús pídum
tríbarakattíns.¹  Avt thesavrúm púd eseí tereí íst,
50 pún patensíns, múíníkad t*a*[n-
ginúd patensíns, iním píd e[íseí
thesavreí púkkapíd ee[stit
a]íttíúm alttram alttr[ús
h]erríns.  Avt anter slagím
55 A]bellanam iním Núvlanam
s]úllad víú uruvú íst . edú .
e]ísaí viaí mefiaí teremen-
n]iú staíet.

Item [*si quid volent*
aedificare [*in territorio quod*
limit*um tenus* [*quibus*
Herculis fanum medium
est, extra muros qui
Herculis fanum ambiunt,
trans viam *positum* est
quae ibi est, pro finibus
senatus sui sententia,
aedificare liceto.
Et id aedificium
quod Nolani
aedificaverint et
usus Nolanorum esto.
Item si quid Abellani
aedificaverint, id
aedificium et usus
Abellanorum esto.  At
post muros qui fanum ambiunt, in eo territorio neque Abellani neque Nolani quidquam
aedificaverint.  At thesaurum qui in eo territorio est,
cum aperirent, communi sententia aperirent, et quidquid in eo
thesauro quandoque exstat,
portionum alteram alteri
caperent.  At inter finis
Abellanos et Nolanos
*ubique* via *flexa* est ——,
in ea via media termina
stant.

---

¹ tríbarakat tuset, tríbarakat tíns.

## COMMENTARY

Cf. Mommsen, Unterital. Dial., 121 ff. ; Bücheler, Commentationes philo-
logicae in honorem Th. Mommseni, 227 ff. ; Bartholomae, I.F. 6, 307 ff. ;
v. Planta II, 622 ff. ; Conway, Exempla Selecta, 10 ff.

The inscription contains an agreement between the cities
of Nola and Abella in regard to a temple of Hercules, which
was situated on the boundaries and owned in common. Such
joint ownership of temples was not uncommon in antiquity.
One may recall the temple of Artemis Limnatis on Mt. Tayge-
tus which caused endless trouble between the Laconians and
Messenians (Pausanias 4, 4, 2), the temple and grove of Juno
Sospita at Lanuvium common to the Romans and Latins (Livy
8, 14), and especially the temple which Servius Tullius built on
the Aventine for the use of Romans and Latins (Livy 1, 45;
Dion. Hal. 4, 26). For this temple on the Aventine we are told
that Servius Tullius made regulations and had them inscribed
on a bronze stele which was placed in the temple, where it
remained "until my time, with letters such as the Greeks once
used" (Dion. Hal. l. c.). The Cippus Abellanus is probably
one of two copies, the other having been set up at Nola.[1]

The precise date is unknown. The prominence of the
senate points to a period after 216 B.C., when the powers of
the senate of Nola were notably increased, while it can hardly
be later than the Social War, in which Nola was virtually ruined.
One may take 150 B.C. as an approximate date.

The general arrangement of the temple property here is
one that is well known elsewhere. The land immediately

---

[1] This was Mommsen's view and is distinctly favored by the provenance of
the tablet; Bücheler, as is evident from his explanation of slaagid, l. 12, as 'e regione',
supposes there was only one tablet, which was set up near the site of the temple; and
Conway urges that "the cost of erecting such a block and cutting such a long inscription would surely have been too considerable to allow of two copies where one would
do." But dual copies of even longer inscriptions are well attested. Cf., for example,
Dittenberger, Syll. Inscr. Graec.², no. 20, an inscription of over sixty lines on a marble
stele found at Eleusis, another copy of which was ordered set up on the Acropolis at
Athens; further, Collitz, Sammlung d. griech. Dialekt-Inschriften, no. 345 (over 90
lines, two copies authorized), Collitz, no. 3624 (325 lines, three copies authorized), etc.

surrounding the temple formed the sacred precinct proper and was inclosed by walls. Outside of this was the land which was a part of the temple property but not withheld from secular uses. This was marked off by a series of boundary-stones. Such land was often used for pasturage and thus made a source of considerable income. In the case of our inscription, building was to be permitted on this land, if properly sanctioned.

### Summary of Contents, and Notes

ll. 1–10. Agreed as follows between the quaestor of Abella and the meddix of Nola and the delegates of Abella and Nola, appointed by their respective senates:

l. 2. The word **sverrunei** does not refer to a special kind of quaestorship or to some other regular office held in addition to the quaestorship, but rather to a special appointment made 'by previous agreement' (**prupukid**) with reference to the business in hand. According to the very probable connection with Eng. *swear* and *an-swer* (see **96**), it may well have some such meaning as 'spokesman.'

l. 5. Besides the **meddíss túvtíks** which appears in inscriptions of Pompeii, Herculaneum, Capua, and Bovianum, and seems to designate the head of a league of cities, the title meddix (see **15**, 6) was also applied to municipal officers. Cf. **medíkeís Púmpaiianeís**, no. 3. At Nola (cf. also no. 42, from which it appears that there were two such officials, and no. 43) the title was defined by a word which corresponds in form to a L. *decentārius*. This may be explained either as related to L. *decēns* (cf. L. *dicentārius* from *dīcēns*) and meaning 'regularly appointed, ordinarius', or as related to L. *decem* (see **191**, 10) and referring to some organization of the city's territory or population of which we have no precise knowledge.

ll. 11–23. That the temple of Hercules, and the adjacent land within the outer boundaries which have been set around, be held in common, and the income from them be joint income of both cities.

l. 12. **slaagid** (perhaps related to O.Ir. *slicht* 'track', *slige* 'street') means properly 'boundary, border' as here, but the word was also used, like L. *fīnis* in the Plural, of 'territory, district', and this is the meaning of **slagím** in ll. 34, 54.

ll. 27–48. If any one wishes to erect a building on the land in front of the temple limits, outside the wall running about the fane and across the road, it may be done with the sanction of the senate under whose jurisdiction the land falls.  If the Nolans build, the building and its income shall belong to them; to the inhabitants of Abella, if they build.  But behind the wall surrounding the fane, no one shall erect a building.

l. 29.  The reading of the second word is very uncertain.  The best sense would be given by a word meaning 'inside of', the líímítú- being understood as equivalent to the teremenniú inclosing the whole temple property.  So if we accept pernúm it may mean 'in front of' looked at from the inside, as in the case of pert viam, l. 33.

l. 33.  To understand pert viam we must assume that a road skirted the walls.  Possibly the road connecting Nola and Abella ran up to the walls and then divided, passing around on each side.

ll. 34–35.  'By the vote of the respective senates according to the territory'.  As the temple was situated on the boundary, the adjacent land would include sections from the original territory of both cities, each city retaining jurisdiction over its own section in the matter of granting permission to build.

ll. 48-54.  When they open the treasury which is in this territory, they are to open it by common consent, and whatever is in the treasury they are to share.

ll. 54-58.  The boundary-stones are on the road between the territory of Abella and that of Nola.

This last sentence defines the locality of the boundary-stones, but the precise meaning is obscured by the uncertainty of the reading in l. 56.  At the beginning the old reading p]úllad taken as 'qua' gives a reasonable sense, but there is no support for such a word, as there is for s]úllad.  At the end the only really certain letters are edú, and, while the old reading tedur is out of the question, v. Planta's pedú X is only a possibility.  The old explanation of uruvú as 'flexa', related to L. *urvum*, the curved part of a plow (which is then not to be connected with Skt. *vṛj-* 'turn'), is in itself simpler than the connection with Grk. εὐρύς, Skt. *urú-* 'wide', though it must be confessed that either 'qua . . . flexa' or 'ubique . . . lata' seems a better combination than 'ubique . . . flexa'.  But the whole line is puzzling.  It is not even clear whether the road referred to is one connecting the two cities, or one which itself forms the boundary-line between their respective territories.

### 2. Tabula Bantina

Fragment of a bronze tablet, about 15 by 10 inches, containing also, on the other side, a Latin inscription (CIL. I 197).  The Oscan inscription was originally in two columns, a few letters of the right-hand column still showing.  The fragment represents the middle portion of the left-hand column, and probably

contains about one sixth of the whole inscription.  Found in 1793 at Bantia,
near the boundaries of Apulia and Lucania.  Now in the Museum at Naples.
Written in the Latin alphabet.  There are six paragraphs, divided by spaces.
Conway no. 28, v. Pl. no. 17.

## 1

1 . . . *onom ust izic ru* . . . |

2 . . . *suae* . . *nus q moltam*
  *angitu* . . . *nur*[1] . . . |

3 . . . . . . . . . . . . *deiuast*
  *maimas carneis senateis*
  *tanginud*[1] *am*[1] . . . . . . |

4 *XL osii*[*ns p*]*on ioc egmo*
  *comparascuster. Suae pis pert-*
  *emust, pruter*[1] *pan* . . . . . |

5 *deiuatud sipus comenei*
  *perum dolom mallom, siom ioc*
  *comono mais egm*[*as touti-*] |

6 *cas amnud pan pieisum*
  *brateis auti cadeis amnud,*
  *inim idic siom dat sena*[*teis*] |

7 *tanginud maimas carneis*
  *pertumum. Piei ex comono*
  *pertemest, izic eizeic zicel*[*ei*] |

8 *comono ni hipid.*

. . . . . . . . . . . *is* . . . . . . . .
. . . . *si* . . . quaestor multam
*proposuerit* . . . . . . . . . . . .
. . . . . . . . . . . . . . . iurabit
maximae partis senatus
sententia [*dummodo non minus*]
XL adsint, cum ea res
consulta erit.  Si quis peremerit, prius quam [peremerit],
iurato sciens in comitio
sine dolo malo, se ea
comitia magis rei publicae
causa quam cuiuspiam
gratiae aut inimicitiae causa,
idque se de senatus
sententia maximae partis
perimere.  Cui sic comitia
perimet (quisquam), is eo die
comitia ne habuerit.

## 2

  *Pis pocapit post*
*post exac comono hafiest*[2]
*meddis dat castrid loufir* |

9 *en eituas, factud pous*[3] *touto*
  *deiuatuns tanginom deicans,*
  *siom*[4] *dat eizasc*[5] *idic tangineis*|

  Quis quandoque
post hac comitia habebit
magistratus de *capite* vel
in pecunias, facito ut populus
iurati sententiam dicant,
se de iis id sententiae

---

[1] *nur, ud am, rut*, from a small fragment now lost.
[2] Aes *hafiert.* [Correct form probably *hapiest.*  *Later inscription with h.*]
[3] Probably for *pus*, *ou* being due to following word.  See footnote, p. 40.
[4] Aes *stom.*        [5] Probably for *eizaisc*.

10 *deicum, pod ualaemom* — dicere, quod optimum
    *touticom tadait ezum,* — publicum censeat esse,
    *nep fefacid*[1] *pod pis* — neve fecerit quo quis
    *dat eizac egmad min[s]* | — de ea re minus
11 *deiuaid dolud*[2] *malud. Suae-* — iuret dolo malo.   Si-
    *pis contrud exeic*[3] *fefacust* — quis contra hoc fecerit
    *auti comono hipust, molto etan-*| — aut comitia habuerit, multa tanta
12 *to estud: n.ⅭⅮ Ⅽ Ⅾ. In. suaepis* — esto: n. MM.   Et siquis
    *ionc fortis meddis moltaum* — eum potius magistratus multare
    *herest, ampert minstreis aeteis*| — volet, dumtaxat minoris partis
13 *eituas moltas moltaum licitud.* — pecuniae multae multare liceto.

### 3

    *Suaepis pru meddixud* —     Siquis pro magistratu
    *altrei castrous auti eituas* | — alteri *capitis* aut pecuniae
14 *zicolom dicust, izic comono* — diem dixerit, is comitia
    *ni hipid ne pon op* — ne habuerit nisi cum apud
    *toutad petirupert urust* — populum quater oraverit
    *sipus perum dolom* | — sciens sine dolo
15 *mallom in. trutum zico.* — malo et *quartum* diem
    *touto peremust. Petiropert,* — populus perceperit.   Quater,
    *neip mais pomtis,*[4] — neque plus quinquiens,
    *com preiuatud actud* | — cum reo agito
16 *pruter pam medicatinom di-* — prius quam iudicationem
    *dest, in. pon posmom con prei-* — dabit, et cum postremum cum
    *uatud urust, eisucen ziculud* | — reo oraverit, ab eo die
17 *zicolom XXX nesimum como-* — in diebus XXX proximis comi-
    *nom ni hipid. Suae pis con-* — tia ne habuerit.   Si quis con-
    *trud exeic fefacust, ionc suaepis*| — tra hoc fecerit, eum siquis
18 *herest meddis moltaum,* — volet magistratus multare,
    *licitud, ampert mistreis* — liceto, dumtaxat minoris
    *aeteis eituas licitud.* — partis pecuniae liceto.

---

[1] Aes *fepacid.*      [2] Aes *docud.*      [3] Aes *exeig.*
    [4] Following the spacing on the bronze, some punctuate after *pomtis*. Still others make the division after *petirupert*. The division adopted is the only one which admits a satisfactory interpretation.

**4**

| | |
|---|---|
| *Pon censtur* \| | Cum censores |
| 19 *Bansae[1] toutam[2] censazet, pis* | Bantiae populum censebunt, qui |
| *ceus Bantins fust, censamur* | civis Bantinus erit, censetor |
| *esuf in. eituam poizad ligud* \| | ipse et pecuniam qua lege |
| 20 *iusc[3] censtur censaum angetu-* | ii censores censere proposu- |
| *zet.[4]   Aut suaepis censtomen* | erint.   At siquis in censum |
| *nei cebnust dolud mallud* \| | non venerit dolo malo, |
| 21 *in. eizeic uincter, esuf* | et eius convincitur, ipse |
| *comenei lamatir pr.* | in comitio *caedatur* praetoris |
| *meddixud toutad prae-* | magistratu, populo prae- |
| *sentid perum dolum* \| | sente sine dolo |
| 22 *mallom, in. amiricatud allo* | malo, et \*immercato cetera |
| *famelo in. ei. siuom paei* | familia et pecunia omnino quae |
| *eizeis fust, pae ancensto fust,* \| | eius erit, quae incensa erit, |
| 23 *toutico estud.* | publica esto. |

**5**

| | |
|---|---|
| *Pr., suae praefucus* | Praetor, sive praefectus |
| *pod post exac Bansae fust,* | post hac Bantiae erit, |
| *suae pis op eizois com* \| | si quis apud eos cum |
| 24 *atrud ligud acum herest,* | altero lege agere volet, |
| *auti pru medicatud manim* | aut pro iudicato manum |
| *aserum eizazunc egmazum* \| | adserere de eis rebus |
| 25 *pas exaiscen ligis scriftas* | quae hisce in legibus scriptae |
| *set, ne phim[5] pruhipid* | sunt, ne quem prohibuerit |
| *mais zicolois X nesimois.* | plus diebus X proximis. |
| *Suae pis contrud* \| | Si quis contra |
| 26 *exeic pruhipust, molto* | hoc prohibuerit, multa |
| *etanto estud: n. ⅭⅠↃ.   In.* | tanta esto: n. **M.**   Et |
| *suaepis ionc meddis mol-* | siquis eum magistratus mul- |
| *taum herest, licitud,* \| | tare volet, liceto, |

---

[1] Aes *Sansae.*     [2] Aes *tautam.*

[3] The first two letters are mutilated, but there is no doubt of the reading.

[4] Aes *anget uzet.*     [5] For *pim.*  See footnote, p. 144.

27 *[ampert] minstreis aeteis*   ·   [dumtaxat] minoris partis
     *eituas moltas moltaum*          pecuniae multae multare
     *licitud.*                    liceto.

### 6

       *Pr. censtur Bansae* |         Praetor censor Bantiae
28 *[ne pis fu]id, nei suae q.*      [ne quis] fuerit, nisi quaestor
     *fust, nep censtur fuid,*         fuerit, neve censor fuerit
     *nei suae pr. fust. In. suae-*      nisi praetor fuerit.    Et si-
     *pis pr. in. suae-* |            quis praetor et si-
29 . . . . . . . . . . . . *q* . . . . .      [quis censor] . . . . . . *q* . . . . .
     . . .]*um nerum fust, izic post*      . . . . . ] virum fuerit, is post
     *eizuc tr. pl. ni fuid. Suaepis* |    ea tr. pl. ne fuerit.    Siquis
30 *[contrud exeic tr. pl. facus*      [contra hoc tr. pl. factus]
     *f]ust, izic amprufid facus*      erit, is improbe factus
     *estud. Idic medicim eizuc* |    esto.    Id magisterium eo
31 . . . . . . . . . . . . . . . . . . .      . . . . . . . . . . . . . . . . . . . . . .
     *[pocapid Bansae]* . . . . .      [quandoque Bantiae] . . . . . . .
     . . . . . . *medicim* acunum      . . . . . . magisterium *annorum*
     *VI nesimum* |               VI proximorum
32 . . . . . *um pod* |           . . . . . . quod-
33 . . . . . . *medicim.*[1]          . . . . magisterium.

### COMMENTARY

     Cf. Kirchhoff, Das Stadtrecht von Bantia ; Lange, Die oskische Inschrift
der Tabula Bantina ; Jordan, B.B. 6, 195 ff. (for the Avellino fragment) ; Bréal,
Mém. Soc. Ling. 4, 381 ff. ; Bücheler in Bruns, Fontes iuris Romani⁶, 48 ff. ;
Moratti, Archivio giuridico, 1894, 74 ff. ; v. Planta II, 599 ff. ; Conway, Exempla
Selecta, 2 ff.

     The inscription contains a series of municipal regulations
for the town of Bantia. Its date and relation to the Latin
inscription on the other side of the tablet are matters of dispute. But the probability is that the Latin inscription, the
date of which falls somewhere between 132 and 117 B.C., is

---

     [1] From l. 29 on so much is lost that, even with the help of an inexact copy of a
fragment containing a portion of what is now missing (called the Avellino fragment),
no certain restoration of the whole text can be made.

quite independent of the Oscan and somewhat earlier. The Oscan inscription belongs then to the last quarter of the second century B.C.

## Translation and Notes

### I

ll. 1–4. Only the conclusion beginning with *deiuast* is clear. "... he shall take oath with the assent of the majority of the senate provided that not less than forty are present when the matter is under advisement."

ll. 4–8. "If any one by right of intercession shall prevent the assembly, before preventing it he shall swear wittingly in the assembly without guile that he prevents this assembly rather for the sake of the public welfare than out of favor or malice toward any one, and that too in accordance with the judgment of the majority of the senate. The presiding magistrate whose assembly is prevented in this way shall not hold the assembly on this day."

The verb *pertemō* (*pertenqust* etc.) is used in the technical sense of 'prevent by intercession'. The *intercession* at Rome, while possible to any magistrate of a rank equal to or higher than that of the one in charge, was a prerogative employed especially by the tribunes of the people. These officials existed at Bantia, as is seen from l. 30. The intercession could be exercised, among other occasions, against calling together the assembly, no matter for what purpose summoned. But sometimes a particular law contained the special provision that no intercession should be allowed. In our inscription the right of intercession is conditioned upon an oath to the effect that the privilege is exercised in the public interest, and with the approval of the senate. Compare the voluntary oath taken by Tiberius Gracchus, when interceding against the imprisonment of Scipio Asiaticus, that it was not due to any friendship for Scipio Africanus (Aul. Gell. 6, 19); and also the fact that even at Rome, in the case of a comitia summoned for the election of magistrates, the intercession was dependent on the sanction of the senate (Cic. ad Att. 4, 16, 6). On the general subject of the intercession see Class. Dict. s.v.

l. 5. The phrase *sipus perum dolom mallom* is simply the reverse of the common Latin formula *sciens dolo malo*, which occurs with prohibitions, as 'let him not swear (or act) wittingly with guile'.

l. 6. The phrase *pieisum brateis auti cadeis amnud* is clearly the equivalent of *cuiuspiam gratiae aut inimicitiae causa* of Latin legal phraseology, and the Greek οὔτε χάριτος ἕνεκ' οὔτε ἔχθρας.[1]

---

[1] For *brateis* (also Pael. *bratom, brata*, Vest. *brat.*) no satisfactory etymology has been suggested, while *cadeis* may well be related to Goth. *hatis*, Eng. *hate*.

**2**

"Whatever magistrate shall hereafter hold an assembly in a suit involving the death penalty or a fine, let him make the people pronounce judgment after having sworn that they will render such judgment as they believe to be for the best public good, and let him prevent any one from swearing in this matter with guile. If any one shall act or hold an assembly contrary to this, let the fine be 2000 sesterces. And if any magistrate prefers to fix the fine, he may do so, provided it is for less than half the property of the guilty person."

This and the following section refer to the assembly in its judiciary function as a court of appeal.

With *dat castrid loufir en eituas* (ll. 8, 9) and *castrous auti eituas* (l. 13) compare the Roman *iudicia capitis* [1] and *iudicia pecuniae*. Cf. Livy 26, 3, 8 *quoad vel capitis vel pecuniae iudicasset privato* (note also in this passage *privato* = *reo*, as in ll. 15, 16).

With ll. 9, 10, compare *iuranto . . . neque se aliter consilium habiturum . . . neque sententiam dicturum, quam ut ex h(ac) l(ege) exque re communi municipum eius municipi censeat fore* (CIL. II 1963).

l. 10. For the construction with *nep fefacid*, see **315**, end.

For ll. 12, 13, see **269**.

---

[1] Nearly all commentators have taken *dat castrid* and *castrous* as 'de fundo', 'fundi'. But the objection raised long ago by Lange, Tab. Bant., 21 ff., has never been answered, namely that according to all Roman analogies we have to do with criminal procedure, in which a suit involving real estate would have no place. He translates 'capitis', but with an untenable explanation of the form. Recently Bréal, Mém. Soc. Ling. 11, 5, without recollection of Lange's view, quotes the opinion of a legal colleague that 'capitis', not 'fundi', gives the contrast to be expected, and suggests that *castrid, castrous*, were inscribed by mistake in place of a word corresponding to L. *caput*. But this last assumption is not necessary. For, retaining the formal connection with L. *castrum*, the meaning 'head', though apparently remote, is more easily explained than 'real estate'. The word is generally connected with L. *cassis*, and so would contain the root *(s)kat-, s(k)ad-* 'cover, protect', the cognate nearest in form being Skt. *chattra-m* 'parasol'. From the meaning 'protection', whence in L. 'fortress', may come 'cover' or 'summit', which frequently interchange with 'head'. Cf. Skt. *kakud* 'mountain-peak' and 'head'; — Germ. *Giebel*: Grk. κεφαλή; — Germ. *kopf* probably: Eng. *cop*, Dutch *kopje*; — and especially Germ. *Dach* 'covering, roof' (*decken*, στέγω, etc.), used dialectically in sense of 'head'.

The Umbrian *castruo*, *kastruvuf*, which cannot be separated from the Oscan forms, occur in two often repeated phrases. In V a 13 ff. the perquisite for the performance of certain ceremonies is fixed at so much *pusti kastruvuf*, commonly taken

### 3

" If any magistrate shall have appointed the day for another in a suit involving the death penalty or a fine, he must not hold the assembly until he has brought the accusation four times in the presence of the people without guile, and the people have been advised of the fourth day. Four times, and not more than five, must he argue the case with the defendant before he pronounces the indictment, and when he has argued for the last time with the defendant he must not hold the assembly within thirty days from that day. And if any one shall have done contrary to this, if any magistrate wishes to fix the fine, he may, but only for less than half the property of the guilty person be it permitted."

The Roman procedure, as described in Cic. pro domo, 17, 45, Livy 26, 3, etc., is followed closely except that, according to the usual understanding of the case (otherwise Lange, Tab. Bant., 65 ff.), the interval of the trinundinum at Rome occurred after the third preliminary hearing, the *quarta accusatio* being immediately followed by the decision of the comitia ; whereas at Bantia the interval of thirty days (this was also a recognized interval at Rome for certain classes of trials) was between the last hearing, which was the fourth or sometimes even the fifth, and the convocation of the comitia.

The *op toutad*, l. 14, refers to the informal assembly, the *contio*. The *trutum zico.*, l. 15 (cf. the *die prodicta*, Cic. l. c.), probably means the *fourth* day, that is the day for the fourth and (usually) final hearing, though *trutum* is also taken as 'definitum, fixed'.[1]

### 4

" When the censors shall take the census of the people of Bantia, whoever is a citizen of Bantia shall be rated, himself and his property, according to the law under which these

---

as 'in fundos', 'for each estate'. But the meaning 'in capita', 'for each person' (cf. Livy 2, 33, 11, etc.) is more appropriate (cf. *in hominem a. II*, CIL. VI 820). In the other passage, where the word occurs among a series of objects which the god is asked to preserve (VI a 30 etc.), the meaning 'capita' is less attractive, and were it a question of this passage alone we should prefer 'fundos'. But it is possible to take *pecuo castruo* together as 'pecuum capita', or else to assume that the word was also used for small animals, sheep, goats, etc., in contrast to *pecuo*, large animals, kine.

[1] With this meaning there is no nearer connection for *trutum* than Lith. *tvirtas* 'firm', while as 'quartum' its explanation is simple (**191**, 4). Moreover the analogy of the Roman *quarta accusatio* affords a strong presumption in favor of 'quartum', even though the procedure is not precisely the same.

censors shall have proposed to take the census.    And if any one·
fraudulently fails to come to the census, and is convicted of it,
let him be scourged(?) in the assembly, under the magistracy of
the praetor, in the presence of the people, and let the rest of his
household, and all his property which is not rated, become public
property without remuneration to him."                              ·

At Rome there was a *formula census* or *lex censui censenda dicta*.   According to the lex Iulia municipalis (CIL. I 206) the censors are instructed to find
out name, age, financial condition, etc., *ex formula census, quae Romae ab eo,
qui tum censum populi acturus erit, proposita erit* (cf. *poizad ligud* etc. here).
At Rome, too, each citizen had to appear in person (cf. *suaepis censtom-en nei
cebnust* here).

The penalty at Rome for non-appearance at the census without sufficient
excuse (cf. *dolud mallud* here) was death or slavery of the person and sale or
confiscation of his property.   Cf. Valer. Max. 6, 3, 4 *et bona eius et ipsum vendidit*
and Livy 1, 44, 1 *censu perfecto, quem maturaverat metu legis de incensis latae
cum vinculorum minis mortisque, . . .*   The meaning of *lamatir*, l. 21, which
occurs also in the Curse of Vibia (no. 19), is disputed, but 'caedatur' is more
probable than 'veneat'.[1]

## 5

"The praetor, or if there shall be a prefect at Bantia after
this, in case any one wishes to go to law with another before
them, or to make a forcible seizure, as if judgment had been
rendered, on these matters which are written of in these laws,
shall not prevent one for more than the ten succeeding days.
If any one contrary to this shall prevent, the fine shall be 1000
sesterces.   And if any magistrate wishes to fix the fine he may
do so, but only for a fine involving less than half the property
shall it be permitted."

The construction is awkward.   The subject of *pruhipid* (l. 25) is *Pr.* at
the beginning, the clause *suae . . . fust* being thrown in parenthetically.   Yet
*eizois* refers to the prefect as well as to the praetor.   With *pru medicatud manim
aserum* compare *pro ioudicatod n.* [L.] *manum iniect*[*i*]*o estod* (CIL. IX 782).

---

[1] The translation 'veneat' (Bücheler) for the passage in the Vibia Curse was
thought to receive some support from the presence of τετρημένος in the Cnidian
Curses, but it is now recognized that this is not from πιτράσκω, but from πίμπρημι,
and means 'consumed with fever' (cf. Rh. M. 49, 39).   Accepting the translation
'caedatur', *lamatir* may be connected with O.Bulg. *lomiti* 'break', Eng. *lame* and
(colloquial) *lam*.   Cf. Danielsson, Pauli's Altit. Stud. 3, 183.

## 6

"No one shall be praetor or censor of Bantia unless he has been quaestor, nor shall any one be censor unless he has been praetor. And if any one shall be praetor, and ......, he shall not become a tribune of the people after this. And if any one shall be made tribune contrary to this, he shall be made so wrongfully."

This section treats of the order of magistrates, which here is *quaestor — praetor — censor*, while at Rome it is usually *quaestor — censor — praetor*, though sometimes the praetorship precedes the censorship as here; cf. Livy 41, 9, 11. Except for the first sentence, the text is so fragmentary that the precise meaning is entirely uncertain.

### INSCRIPTIONS OF POMPEII [1]

#### 3-13. Inscriptions on Public Works, and Dedications

Most of these belong to the second century B.C. None is later than the Social War, after which Oscan ceased to be used in official inscriptions; and, on the other hand, with the exception of no. 9, from a temple believed to belong to the third century, there is probably none earlier than 200 B.C. Within these limits there are no evidences of date beyond the forms of the letters, which show, for example, that no. 3 is one of the earliest of this period, no. 4 one of the latest. All of these inscriptions are now in the Naples Museum.

3. Road-makers' tablet, found near the Porta Stabiana. Conway no. 39, v. Pl. no. 28.

| | |
|---|---|
| *M.* Siuttiis **M. N.** Púntiis **M.** | M. Suttius M. f. N. Pontius M. f. |
| a]ídilis eka*k* víam terem[na- | aediles hanc viam termina- |
| t]tens ant *pú*nttram Staf[ii- | verunt usque ad pontem Stabi- |
| anam. Víu te[r]emnatust per. | anum. Via terminata est perticis |
| 5 X. Í*u*ssu vía Púmpaiiana ter- | X. Iidem viam Pompeianam ter- |
| emnattens perek. III ant kaí- | minaverunt perticis III usque ad |
| la Iúveís Meefílkiieís. Ekass ví- | aedem Iovis Milichii. Has vi- |
| ass íní vía Iúviia íní Dekkvia- | as et viam Ioviam et Decuria- |
| rím medíkeís Púmpaiianeís | lem meddicis Pompeiani |
| 10 serevkid imaden uupsens, í*u*- | auspicio ab imo fecerunt, ii- |
| su² aídilis prúfattens. | dem aediles probaverunt. |

---

[1] For topographical matters cf. especially Nissen, Pompejanische Studien, and Mau's Pompeii translated by Kelsey (references are to the second edition, 1902).

² íu[s]su impossible; here and in l. 5 uncertain whether u or ú, but see **53**, *a*.

Cf. Nissen, Pomp. Stud., 531 ff., and Mau, Pompeii, 184.

The aediles laid out two roads, and these as well as two others they also constructed or repaired under the direction of the meddix of the city. One road, leading out from the Stabian gate where the inscription was set up, they laid out at a certain width as far as the Stabian bridge. The street leading from the same point into the city, and called, from its importance, the Via Pompeiana (now known as the Strada Stabiana), they laid out at a certain width as far as the temple or precinct of Jupiter Milichius. The Via Iovia was doubtless named from a temple of Jupiter, and the Via Decurialis from some public building. The phrase *viam terminare* is not used in Latin, but the reference is clearly to the laying out of the road, that is, marking off its exact width, delimiting it (on the sides). **Viass . . . imad-en uupsens** 'made from the bottom up' corresponds to the Latin *vias substruxerunt*.

**4.** A tablet found on the site of what is believed to have been a palaestra. Conway no. 42, v. Pl. no. 29.

| | |
|---|---|
| **V. Aadirans V. eítiuvam paam** | V. Adiranus V. f. pecuniam quam |
| **vereiiaí Púmpaiianaí trístaa-** | *iuventuti* Pompeianae testa- |
| **mentud deded, eísak eítiuvad** | mento dedit, ea pecunia |
| **V. Viínikiís Mr. kvaísstur Púmp-** | V. Vinicius Mr. f. quaestor Pom- |
| 5 **aiians tríibúm ekak kúmben-** | peianus domum hanc conven- |
| **nieís tanginud úpsannam** | tus sententia faciendam |
| **deded, ísídum prúfatted.** | dedit, idem probavit. |

Cf. Nissen, Pomp. Stud., 168 ff.

The quaestor had this building constructed from the money which V. Adiranus left by will to the Pompeian *vereiia*. This was probably an association of young men devoted to athletic and military training like the Greek ephebes. The word is best explained as a derivative with suffix *-eijo-* (**253**, 2) from a *\*uero-* 'defense', containing the same root as O. veru 'portam', Goth. *warjan* 'ward off', etc. (**15**, 15), so that the original meaning would be 'defensive body' (cf. Germ. *Landwehr*); but the military side of the association may have become entirely subordinate at the time of this inscription.[1]

**5.** Inscribed under a sun-dial found at the Stabian baths. Conway no. 43, v. Pl. no. 30.

| | |
|---|---|
| **Mr. Atiniís Mr. kvaísstur** | Mr. Atinius Mr. f. quaestor |
| **eítiuvad \| múltasíkad** | pecunia multaticia |
| **kúmbennieís tangi[n.] \| aamanaffed.** | conventus sententia locavit. |

With **eítiuvad múltasíkad** and **aragetud múltas[íkud]** (no. 43) compare L. *quaistores aire moltaticod dederont* (CIL. I 181).

---

[1] The spelling **verehias**, no. 30, if indeed this is the correct reading, I regard as a somewhat freakish variant of that seen in **vereiiaí** and not as sufficient ground for preferring connection with O. **Verehasiúí**.

**6.** Stamped in dots on the margin of the pavement in the temple of Apollo. Conway no. 52, v. Pl. no. 31.

Ú. Kamp[aniis . kvaí]sstur  
kúmbenn[ieís tanginud]  
Appelluneís eítiu[vad . . . . .  
úps]annu aaman[aff]ed. |

O. Campanius — f. quaestor  
conventus [sententia]  
Apollinis pecunia . . . . .  
faciendum locavit. -

Doubtless a word for pavement is to be supplied before úps]annu. With Appelluneís eítiu[vad compare L. *portic(um)* . . . *de stipe Dian(ae) emendum [fa]ciendum coeraver[e* (CIL. X 3781).

**7.** On a stone block with'cornice. Conway no. 44, v. Pl. no. 34.

V. Púpidiis V. med. túv.  
passtata ekak úpsan.  
deded, ísídu prúfattd.

V. Popidius V. f. meddix tuticus  
porticum hanc faciendam  
dedit, idem probavit.

Compare *V. Popidius Ep. f. q. porticus faciendas coeravit*, found in the forum of Pompeii (CIL. X 794).

**8.** On a marble slab formerly attached to a piece of sculpture representing a'female head. Conway no. 45, v. Pl. no. 35.

V. Púpidiis V.  
med. túv.  
aamanaffed,  
ísídu  
prúfatted.

V. Popidius V. f.  
meddix tuticus  
locavit,  
idem  
probavit.

**9.** On a block from the epistyle of a small building thought to be a well-house (Mau, 139 ; otherwise Nissen, 338). Conway no. 47, v. Pl. no. 36.

Ni. Trebiis Tr. med. túv.  
aamanaffed.

N. Trebius Tr. f. meddix tuticus  
locavit.

**10.** On a small pedestal. Conway no. 48, v. Pl. no. 36 a.

Mz. Avdiis Klí.  
Dekis Seppiis Úpf.  
kvaízstur upsens.

Mz. Audius Cle.·f.  
Decius Seppius Off. f  
quaestores fecerunt.

**11.** On a stone slab. Conway no. 50, v. Pl. no. 32.

. S]*p*uriís Ma.  
k]vaísstur  
kú]mparakineís  
ta]ngin. aamanaffed.

. Spurius Ma. f.  
quaestor  
consilii  
sententia locavit.

12. On a stone basis.   Conway no. 53, v. Pl. no. 40.

**V. Sadiriis V. aídil.**                        V. Satrius V. f. aedilis.

13. On a plaster slab.   Conway no. 59, v. Pl. no. 62.

**Ahvdiu Ņi. akun. CXII**                   ... Audio N. f. an. CXII

Formerly read **ahvdiuni** etc., no interpretation being attempted. But the
mark of separation is clear.[1] Apparently we have to do with an epitaph, the
praenomen being lost.[2] For the spelling of **Ahvdiu** see **61**, 2, *a*, and **171**, 3, *a*.

### 14–18.   The Eítuns Inscriptions

These are painted in red on the outside walls of houses standing near
street-corners. For their interpretation cf. Nissen, Pomp. Stud., 497 ff. ; Conway, I.F. 3, 85 ff. ; Degering, Mitt. d. deutsch. archäol. Inst., röm. Abt., 13,
124 ff. ; Mau, ibid. 14, 105 ff. ; Mau, Pompeii, 240 ff. The usual and more
probable view is that they are military notices, dating from the Social War,
when Pompeii was besieged by Sulla (89 B.C.). It is suggested that many of
the important streets were barricaded and that these inscriptions served as
guides to the soldiers, pointing out the shortest available route to their respective stations along the city walls. Nos. 14–16 are near streets leading to the
north wall, no. 17 is on a street leading to the western wall, while no. 18, unknown
until 1897, is near what at the time of the earthquake was a blind alley, but
which at an earlier period probably led through to the region of the "Triangular Forum" near the south wall. The **veru Sarínu** of nos. 14, 15, is not the
Sarnian gate, but what is now known as the Herculanean gate. The buildings
mentioned in no. 18 were probably in the Triangular Forum, the temple of
Minerva being perhaps the well-known Doric temple at that place.

The phrase **puf faamat** means 'where (the officer named) is stationed' (for
**faamat** : L. *famulus*, see **99**, 2 ; the officer's home is his command). The **amviannud** (see **255**, *a*) is not simply 'way', but 'way around, detour' (to avoid the
barricaded streets ; see above). For **eítuns** the common interpretation as Nom.
Sg. 'iter' is the most difficult to justify grammatically. If the form is a noun
at all it is Nom. Pl. of an *-ōn-* stem, meaning perhaps 'goers', that is 'patrols'.
But the author is now inclined to favor the old interpretation 'eunto', there
being no real difficulty in explaining the form as an Imperative (**236**, 2).

14. Conway no. 60, v. Pl. no. 47.

| | |
|---|---|
| **Eksuk amvíanud eítuns** | Hoc circuito *eunto* |
| **anter tiurrí XII íní ver.** | inter turrim XII et portam |
| **Sarínu, puf faamat** | Sarinam, ubi habitat |
| **Mr. Aadíriis V.** | Mr. Atrius V. f. |

---

[1] Dennison, Am. Jour. of Arch. 1898, 399 b, Buck, I.F. 12, 21.

[2] Neither the published reports nor my own recollection of the inscription serves
to confirm or refute the supposition that it is incomplete.

**15.** Conway no. 61, v. Pl. no. 48.

| | |
|---|---|
| Eksuk amvíannud eít. | Hoc circuitu *eunto* |
| anter tiurrí XII íní | inter turrim XII et |
| veru Sarínu, puf | portam Sarinam, ubi |
| faamat Mr. Aadiríís V. | habitat Mr. Atrius V. f. |

**16.** Conway no. 62, v. Pl. no. 50.

| | |
|---|---|
| *Ek*[s]uk am*v*ianu*d* eítu[ns | Hoc circuitu *eunto* |
| anter tiurr]í X íní XI, puf | inter turrim X et XI, ubi |
| faama]*t* T. Físanis Ú. | habitat T. Fisanius O. f. |

**17.** Conway no. 63, v. Pl. no. 49.

| | |
|---|---|
| Eksuk amv[í]anud | Hoc circuitu |
| eítuns an[ter tr]íísbu | *eunto* inter domum |
| Ma. Kastríkiíeis íní | Ma. Castricii et |
| Mr. Spuriíeís L., | Mr. Spurii L. f., |
| puf faamat | ubi habitat |
| V. Sehsímbr*iís* L. | V. Sexembrius *L.* f. |

**18.** Notizie degli scavi 1897, p. 465, Mitt. d. deutsch. archäol. Inst., röm. Abt., 13, 124 ff., I.F. 12, 13 ff.

| | |
|---|---|
| Eksuk amvíannud | Hoc circuitu |
| eítuns ampt tríbud | *eunto* circum Villam |
| túv. ampt Mener. | Publicam, circum Minervium. |

18*a*  *see page* 352.

## INSCRIPTIONS OF CAPUA

### 19. The Curse of Vibia

On a lead plate about 8¼ by 8 in., found in 1876 near a tomb. Now in the Naples Museum. Conway no. 130, v. Pl. no. 128.

| | |
|---|---|
| 1 Keri Arent[íkai man]afum pai | Cereri Ultrici mandavi, quae |
| pu*í* [p]*uí* heriam suvam | quive vim suam, |
| legin[um suvam a*í*]*akad* | cohortem suam *adferat* |
| . . . . . , | |
| 2 usurs inim malaks nistrus | *osores* et *malevolos* propinquos |
| Pakiu Kluvatiu*í*[1] Valamais[2] | Pacio Clovatio Valaemae |
| p[uklui] an*íkad*um damia*d* | filio. *occidionem, damnum* |

---

[1] Final letter almost certainly i, not d as usually read, so Dat. with nistrus (cf. 277). For Pakiu see 171, 3, *a*.    [2] Read Valaimas.

3 leginum aflukad idik tfei | cohortem adferat, id tibi
manafum Vibiiai prebai- | mandavi. Vibiae ——
-ampu[l]ulum da[da]d Keri | ministrum reddat. Cereri Ultrici
Ar[entikai Pakim Kluvatiium]| | (mandavi) [Pacium Clovatium]

4 Valaimas puklum inim ulas | Valaemae filium, et illius
leginei svai neip dadid | cohorti. Si nec reddiderit,
lamatir akrid eiseis dunte | caedatur acriter eius ——

5 inim kalspatar i[nim] | et glebis tundatur et
krustatar svai neip avt | cruentetur. Si nec, aut
svai tiium idik fifikus pust | si tu id decreveris post
eisuk . | .......,

6 pun kahad avt num | cum incipiat aut ——,
neip putiiad punum kahad | nec possit, quandoque incipiat,
avt svai pid per- | aut si quid perficere
fa kum. | [incipiat] ..... nec]

7 putiiad nip hu[n]truis nip | possit; nec inferis nec
supruis aisusis putiians | superis sacrificiis possint, quid-
pidum putiians ufteis | quam optati possint (propinqui)
ud [Pakiui Kluvatiiui]| | [efficere Pacio Clovatio]

8 Valaimas puklui pun far | Valaemae filio; cum far
kahad nip putiiad edum | capiat nec possit edere
nip menvum limu | nec minuere famem
pi | [quoquam] ..... eorum]

9 pai humuns bivus karanter | quae homines vivi vescuntur.
suluh Pakis Kluvatiis | Omnino Pacius Clovatius
Valaims[2] puk turumiiad | Valaemae f. torqueatur.
| [Liberum] .... sit]

10 Vibiiai Akviiai svai puh | Vibiae Aquiae sive
aflakus Pakim Kluvatiium | detuleris Pacium Clovatium
Valaimas puklui[3] supr | Valaemae filium supra
| ..........

11 inim tuvai leginei [inim] | et tuae cohorti et
sakrim svai puh aflakus | hostiam, sive attuleris

---

[2] Read Valaimas.    [3] Read puklum.

huntrus teras huntrus     *infra* terra*m* infra . . .

a [Pakim Kluvatiium]|     [(*Devoveo*) *Pacium Clovatium*]

12 Valaimais[2] puklu[3] avt Keri     Valaemae filium aut Cereri

Aret[ikai] avt ulas     Ultrici aut illius

leginei *nuhturnaŝrutas*     cohorti . . .    ——

tus̀ *funk pakis klufalus val.um is. piuta*

Cf. Bücheler, Rh. M. 33, 1 ff. ; Bugge, Altitalische Studien (Christiania, 1878); Pascal, La tavola osca di esecrazione (Naples, 1894). On the curse-inscriptions in general cf. the convenient summary of contents by Battle, Proceed. Amer. Phil. Assoc. 26, LIV, and especially Wünsch, Defixionum tabellae Atticae (with additions in Rh. M. 55).

This inscription, as well as the following and also no. 40, belongs to a class of magical curses of which there are numerous examples among Greek and Latin inscriptions. Most of them, including the three Oscan, are written on thin lead plates, which were rolled up and placed in graves, in the belief that they gained access thus to the infernal deities invoked. They are written carelessly and often with intentional obscurity. Sometimes the natural order of words is changed, or a meaningless jumble of letters inserted. The curse is sometimes against an unknown person who has committed a wrong, but oftener one or more individuals are expressly named. Sometimes the cause of the curse is given, e.g. theft, cheating, assault, infidelity, a lawsuit, etc. The curse may be conditional, "if so-and-so does not (e.g. return a stolen object), may he . . .". The introduction in Latin inscriptions is usually "mando", "commendo","devoveo", "dedico", or a like word, followed by "diis inferis", "manibus inferis", or the name of some particular infernal deity. The punishments suggested are various, sometimes merely incapacity to eat, talk, or accomplish anything, but generally death with all sorts of tortures.

The person uttering the curse often takes the precaution to add a clause which shall avert from himself or herself any possible evil incidental to the curse. So frequently, in Greek inscriptions, ἐμοὶ δὲ ὅσια or ἐμοὶ δὲ καθαρόν.

Owing to the fragmentary character of our inscription, no complete interpretation of it is possible, but the general trend is clear. The author of the curse is Vibia, and its object Pacius Clovatius, and incidentally his relatives, who are also her enemies (l. 2 ; for usurs inim malaks another interpretation worthy of consideration is 'mulieres et liberos', connecting usurs with L. *uxor* and malaks with L. *mollis*). The appeal is to Ceres Ultrix and her cohort of spirits (cf. ἀνιεροῖ . . . Δάματρι, Κούρᾳ, Πλούτωνι, θεοῖς τοῖς παρὰ Δάματρι ἅπασι καὶ πάσαις, Collitz, 3536). In l. 1 pai probably introduces a relative clause of purpose, 'in order that she may direct her force and her cohort upon . . .'(?). The addition of the masculine pui is to be compared with Latin *si deus si dea*.

---

[2] Read Valaimas.      [3] Read puklum.

The cause of the curse is probably a theft, the object stolen being perhaps a slave (l. 3). If the object is not returned (l. 4) Vibia wishes Pacius Clovatius to be scourged (for **lamatir** see p. 238) and tortured (precise meaning of **kaispatar** and **krustatar** uncertain ; for the forms see **238**, *c*). But if it is otherwise decreed, she will be satisfied if he is incapacitated. So ll. 6-9. "When he either undertakes to ——, may he be powerless, when he undertakes it, or if he wishes to accomplish anything, may he be unable to ; nor shall (his relatives ?) avail him at all by sacrifices to either the infernal deities or those of the upper regions. When he takes food, may he not be able to eat nor allay his hunger by anything which men eat. In every way may Pacius Clovatius be tortured." But no harm must come to Vibia, in whichever way the curse is effected (ll. 10 f.).

The entire left-hand margin of the plate is broken off, so that the amount that is missing from the end of each line can only be inferred from restorations. But Pascal's restoration of **Pakim Kluvatiium** after **Ar[entikai** in l. 3 is well-nigh certain. For wherever the text is complete **Valaimas puklum** (or its variant) is preceded by this name (so in ll. 2, 9, 10). Bücheler, who restored l. 3 differently, thought that not over ten or eleven letters were missing.

The inscription has no double consonants (note **Keri** = **Kerri**, no. 45), no **í**, and probably no **ú** (if it had **V̇**, the dot is no longer visible). This, together with the style of the letters, shows that it is to be ranked among the earlier inscriptions, though not so old as no. 21 (contrast **aisusis**, l. 7, with **luisarifs**, no. 21), and there is no good reason for not dating it well back in the third century B.C.

**20.** On a lead plate found in the same place as the preceding. Now in the Naples Museum. Conway no. 131, v. Pl. no. 129.

| | |
|---|---|
| 1 Steni Klum. Vírriis | Stenius Clum. Verrius |
| Tr. . apíu Vírriis | Tr. —— Verrius |
| Plasis Bivellis | Plarius Bivellius |
| Úppiis Helleviis | Oppius Helvius |
| 5 Lúvikis Úhtavis | Lucius Octavius |
| 6 Statiis Gaviis nep fatíum nep | Statius Gavius nec fari nec |
| deíkum pútíans. \| | dicere possint. |
| 7 Lúvkis Úhtavis Núvellum | Lucius Octavius Novellum |
| Velliam \| | Velliam *(reddat. Si non,)* |
| 8 nep deíkum nep fatíum pútíad \| | nec dicere nec fari possit, |
| 9 nep memnim nep úlam sífeí | nec monumentum nec ollam sibi |
| heriiad. | capiat. |

With the phrase **nep fatíum nep deíkum pútíans** compare *nec loqui nec sermonare possit* in a Latin curse (CIL. I 818). Since praenomina in -iis are entirely irregular (**174**), one is tempted to read ll. 3-6 in columns (as Conway does for ll. 3-4), that is, **Plasis Úppiis, Lúvikis Statiis**, etc. But against this is **Lúvkis**

Úhtavis in l. 7. In ll. 7–8 Núvellum Velliam is without much doubt a proper name, but it is impossible to understand the construction without assuming an omission.

## 21–34. The Iovilae-Dedications

Cf. especially Bücheler, Rh. M. 39, 315 f., 43, 128 ff., 557 ff., 44, 321 ff., 45, 161 ff.; Conway, Ital. Dial. 101 ff.

Of these inscriptions, some are cut in blocks or thick slabs of coarse tufa (see photograph at end of book), while others are stamped on terra-cotta tiles. Many of the tiles bear the same inscription on both sides (nos. 23, 24, 25), and one of the tufa blocks is also inscribed on both sides (no. 31); while many of the tufa blocks belong in pairs which stood side by side, with inscriptions referring to the same dedicators and differing only in some details (nos. 27–28, 29–30, 32–33). Most of the inscriptions contain the word diuvila-, iúvila-, as the name of the object dedicated. This seems to be connected with the stem of L. *Iuppiter*, *Iovis* (257, 5), and in one inscription (no. 25) the iovilae are dedicated to Jupiter Flagius; there is also mention of *Ioviae* or Jupiter festivals (no. 29). It was, then, in all probability the technical name for some well-known and established Jupiter offering, — of just what nature we cannot tell. From the expression 'this iovila', 'these iovilae', we might assume that the stone was either itself the iovila, or else a pedestal for the iovila, which in that case would perhaps be a small statue. But the terra-cotta tiles could not be pedestals, and moreover the inscriptions on some of them seem to point to the iovilae as objects near by (nos. 21, 26).

The iovilae were dedicated by individuals (nos. 22, 25, 26, 32–33), by members of the same family (nos. 27–28), or of the same gens (nos. 21, 29–30, 34). Many of the inscriptions are accompanied by various devices which are undoubtedly heraldic emblems or coats of arms. Often the festivals or periods at which the iovilae were dedicated are mentioned. The púmperias were probably festivals of certain societies or family groups (cf. U. pumperias XII, II b 2; originally groups of five), and of these some were called Fisian and others Martian (nos. 27–28), apparently from the divinity in whose honor they were held (for Fiisiais cf. U. *Fisio-* beside *Fiso* '*Fiso, deo Fidio'). So too there were Fisian Ides (no. 21) and Martian Ides (no. 29). Other festivals are the Ioviae (no. 29, also 24) and, probably, the Vesulliae (nos. 26, 34). Some festivals were celebrated with a banquet, others with a sacrifice (contrast kerssnais and sakriss, no. 29, and kerssnasias, no. 27, with sakrasias, no. 28).

Most of these inscriptions, if not all, belong to the third century B.C. The mention of a meddix precludes a later date than the capture of Capua by the Romans in 211 B.C. Nos. 21–24, which lack the i and ú, belong to the beginning of the third or perhaps the end of the fourth century. No. 21 with its Dat.-Abl. Pl. luisarifs is one of the very earliest Oscan inscriptions, barring coin-legends. The other numbers have the letters i and ú, but they are used with great carelessness, and, moreover, the reading is often uncertain.

**21.** Conway no. 101, v. Pl. no. 130.

Diuvilam Tirentium      \*Iovilam Terentiorum
Magiium sulum muinikam      Magiorum omnium communem
Fisiais eiduis luisarifs      Fisiis idibus *lusoriis*
sakrvist. Iiuk destrst.      sacrabit. Ea dextra est.

It is altogether probable that luisarifs is related to L. *lūdō, lūsus*, as if L. \**lūsāribus*, though this connection is rejected by Bücheler. To 'consecrate the iovila at the festival of the Fisian Ides, which is celebrated with games' is the same as to 'consecrate with games'. Cf. the consecration with sacrifices and with banquets in no. 29.

**22.** Conway no. 102, v. Pl. no. 139.

Ek. diuvil. | Upfaleis | Saidiieis |      Hanc \*iovilam Ofelli Saedii
sakruvit | pustrei.      sacrat in postera(consecratione?).

**23.** Conway no. 105, v. Pl. no. 141.

*a.* Pumperias pustm[as      \*Quincuriae postremae
Kluvatiium.      Clovatiorum.

*b.* Pumperias pustm[as      \*Quincuriae postremae
Kluvatiium.      Clovatiorum.

**24.** Conway no. 103, v. Pl. no. 147.

*a.* Kluva . . .      Clovatiorum
Diuvia . . .      Ioviae
damu . . .      ———

*b.* Kluv . . .      Clovatiorum
damuse . . .      ———
Diuvia . . .      Ioviae

**25.** Conway no. 108, v. Pl. no. 138.

*a.* Ekas iúvilas Iuveí      Hae \*iovilae Iovi
Flagiuí stahínt. |      Flagio stant.
Minnieís Kaísillieís      Minii Caesillii
Minateís ner.      Minati f. principis
*b.* Minieís Kaísillieís      Minii Caesillii
Minateís ner. |      Minati f. principis
ekas iuvilas Iuveí Flagiuí |      hae \*iovilae Iovi Flagio
stahint.      stant.

Flagiuí is probably related to L. *flagrō* and so to be compared with such epithets of Jupiter as *Fulgur*, *Fulgurator*, *Fulguralis*, *Fulmen*, *Fulminaris* (Carter, de deorum Romanorum cognominibus, p. 44). Whether ner. is an abbreviation of a cognomen such as *Nero*, or of a title (cf. **IIII ner** 'quattuorvir') is uncertain, but the latter is more probable.

**26.** Conway no. 109. v. Pl. no. 134 a.

| | |
|---|---|
| **Tr. Vírriieís Ken-** | Tr. Verrii Cen- |
| **ssurineís ekas** | sorini hae |
| **iúvilas trís eh-** | *iovilae tres |
| **peílatasset Ve-** | erectae sunt Ve- |
| 5 **sulliaís.    Fertalis** | sulliis.  *Fertales |
| **stafiatasset** | statutae sunt |
| **Mi. Blússií(eís) Mi. m. t.** | Mi. Blossii Mi. f. in *meddicia tutica. |
| **Nessimas staíet** | Proximae stant |
| **veruís lúvkeí.** | portae in luco. |

It is not entirely clear whether **fertalis** is used substantively of certain ceremonies celebrated with cakes, being then in the Nom. Pl. and subject of a new sentence, or as an adjective agreeing with **Vesulliaís**. The spelling -is, not -ís, would be more surprising in the latter case than in the former (see **178, 7**).

**27.** Conway no. 115, v. Pl. no. 131.

| | |
|---|---|
| *Ek*. iúhil. Sp. **Ka**\|*lú*vieis | Haec *iovila Sp. Calovii |
| iním \| fratrúm m*uí*\|nik. | et fratrum communis |
| 5 est Fiísíais \| púmperiais | est Fisiis *quincuriis |
| pra\|i Mamerttiaís \| | quae prae Martiis |
| pas set.    Kerss*u*\|asías | sunt.  *Cenariae |
| L. Pettie*í*\|s meddíkia*í* \| | L. Pettii in *meddicia |
| 10 fufens. | fuerunt. |

**28.** Conway no. 116, v. Pl. no. 132.

| | |
|---|---|
| [iúvi]l [ek. Sp.] \| Kalúvieís | [*iovila haec Sp.] Calovii |
| iní\|m fratr*ú*m \| m*uí*nik. | et fratrum communis |
| 5 est \| Fiísíais púm\|periais | est Fisiis *quincuriis |
| pas pr\|ai Mamerttia\|ís | quae prae Martiis |
| set.    Sakrasía\|s L. | sunt.  *Sacrariae L. |
| 10 Pettieís me\|ddíkkiai fuf\|ens. | Pettii in *meddicia fuerunt. |

**29.** Conway no. 113, v. Pl. no. 133.

| | |
|---|---|
| Úpil. Vi. Pak. | Opilli Vibii Pacii |
| Tantrnnaiúm | Tanterneiorum |
| iúvilas sakran- | *iovilae sacran- |
| nas eidúis *Ma-* | dae idibus Mar- |
| 5 merttiaís.   Pún | tiis.   Cum |
| meddís *kapv* ad- | meddix *Capuanus* ad- |
| fust, Iúviass me- | erit, Iovias *me-* |
| ssímass taíef | *dioximas* —— |
| fud sakriss sa- | —— hostiis sa- |
| 10 krafír, avt | crato, at |
| últiumam ker- | ultimam ce- |
| ssnaís. | nis. |

For the reading of ll. 6–9, cf. I.F. 12, 17 ff.   Nothing satisfactory can be made out of the word between messimass and sakriss.

**30.** Conway no. 114, v. Pl. no. 134.

| | |
|---|---|
| Úpíl. Vi. Pak. | Opilli Vibii Pacii |
| Tantrnnaiúm | Tanterneiorum |
| iúvil. sakrans. | *iovilae sacrandae |
| Púmperiaís | *quincuriis |
| 5 súll , . . . . | soll . . . . . |
| pún medd. pís | Cum meddix quis |
| —— verehias | —— *iuventutis* |
| fust, sakrid | erit, hostia |
| sakrafír. | sacrato. |

**31.** Conway no. 117, v. Pl. no. 135.

| | |
|---|---|
| *a.* . . . arí . . . | . . . . . . |
| kas[it damsen]n- | decet —— |
| ias pas físet | —— quae fiunt |
| pústreí iúkleí | in postera *consecratione* |
| 5 eehiianasúm, | emittendarum, |
| avt sakrím | at hostiam |
| fakiiad kasit | faciat decet |
| medikk. túvtik. | in *meddicia tutica |
| Kapv. adpúd | Capuana quoad |
| 10 fiiet. | fiunt. |

| | |
|---|---|
| b. . . idat . . . . vií | ———— ———— |
| pag. medikid | ———— *meddicio |
| túvtik. daŕv. | tutico ———— |
| sakraítir kasít | sacretur decet |
| 5 damsennias | ———— |
| pas fiiet pústr. | quae fiunt in postera |
| iúklei vehiian. | *consecratione* emittendarum ; |
| medik. minive. | *in *meddicio minore.* |
| kersnaŕias. | *cenariae. |

What kind of offerings or celebrations are meant by **damsennias** is not clear, though the word (with **damuse**, no. 24) is very likely connected with L. *damium*, name of a sacrifice to Bona Dea, who was called Damia and Damiatrix. **Minive** in b 8 is perhaps an abbreviated form (Loc. Sg. for *minivei ?) from a stem *miniuvú-, as if L. *minuo-, with **iv** for **iuv** (31, b). Was there a 'minor meddix' in contrast to the 'meddix tuticus' ? The second letter of **avt**, a 6, is **e** corrected to **v**. In **eehiianasúm**, a 5, beside **vehiian.**, b 7, the error is almost certainly in the second form, though some assume the opposite.

    **32.** Conway no. 106, v. Pl. no. 136.

| | |
|---|---|
| Sepis \| Helevi \| púmpe. \| | Seppius Helvius *quincuriis |
| . Faler. \| iúvil. de. \| | Falerniis *iovilam *dedit* |
| Virriieís medikia[i]. | Verrii in *meddicia. |

    **33.** Conway no. 107, v. Pl. no. 137.

| | |
|---|---|
| Sepieís Heleviieís súm. | Seppii Helvii sum. |

| | |
|---|---|
| Mi. Anni\|ieí(s) medik\|kiaí | Mi. Annii in *meddicia |
| túv. \| iúvilam \| prúfts \| | tutica *iovilam probaverunt |
| púmper a | *quincuriae |
| Falenia s. | Falerniae. |

    The same **s** serves for the final of the last two words.

    **34.** Conway no. 110, v. Pl. no. 142.

| | |
|---|---|
| Viriium \| Vesuliais \| deivinais. | Verriorum Vesulliis divinis. |

### Other Capuan Inscriptions

    **35.** Painted epitaph. Conway no. 134, v. Pl. no. 156.

| | |
|---|---|
| Upfals patir Miínieis. | Ofellus pater Minii f. |

    **36.** Painted epitaph. Conway no. 135, v. Pl. no. 157.

| | |
|---|---|
| Upfals Salaviis Minies. | Ofellus Salvius Minii f. |

**37.** Painted epitaph.  Conway no. 136, v. Pl. nos. 161–162.

*a.* **Vibi[s] Smintiis**                      Vibius Smintius
    **Vibis Smintiis *sum*.** |          Vibius Smintius sum.
*b.* **Vibis Smintiis.**                        Vibius Smintius.

**38.** Gold finger-ring.  Conway no. 133, v. Pl. no. 165.

**Vibis | Urufiis.**                            Vibius Orfius.

This was formerly read upside down as **Arafiis Vibis.**

**39.** Small terra-cotta object of uncertain character.  v. Pl. no. 164 a.

**perkium | púiieh súm**          ... cuius sum ?

See footnote, p. 145.

## INSCRIPTIONS FROM OTHER CAMPANIAN TOWNS

**40.** Cumae (?).  Several fragments of a lead plate in the possession of the Naples Museum and believed to have come from Cumae.  It is evidently of the same character as nos. 19–20 from Capua.  The portion of the text given here is made up of two of the larger fragments.  Conway no. 137 c, f, g, v. Pl. no. 119 V (where the fragments are united).

[Upis?] **Mut[ti]lli[s** ..              [*Oppius*] Mutilius ... ,
[Gnai]**vs Fuvfdis Ma** ..           Gnaeus Fufidius ... ,
**Dekis Buttis,**                        Decius Botṭius,
**Dekis Rahiis Maraheis niir,**        Decius Raius *Marae* f. princeps,
  **kulupu**                     *culpa (eius est),*
5 *Dkuva* **Rahiis Upfalleis,**        —— Raius Ofelli f.,
**Marahis Rahiis Papeis,**             *Marius* Raius Papi f.,
**Dekis Hereiis Dekkieis Saipinaz,**   Decius Herius Decii f. Saepinas
**Maras Rufriis, Maras Blaisiis**      Maras Rubrius, Maras Blaesius
  **Marah[ei]s,**               *Marae* f.,
**Dekkieis Rahiieis, Uppiieis**        Decii Raii, Oppii
  **Muttillieis,**              Mutilii,
10 **Dekkieis Heriieis akkatus inim**  Decii Herii advocati et
  **tratus**                    testes
**sullus inim eisunk uhftis**          omnes et eorum voluntates
**sullum [s]ullas.**                   omnium omnes,

The akkatus inim trstus, correctly explained by Skutsch (B.B. 23, 100) as 'advocati et testes', shows that the occasion of this imprecation was a lawsuit. Cf. "nec illi hanc litem vincere possint . . . . . . sic nec advocati eorom eo[s def]endere (non) possint," from a Latin curse (Rh. M. 55, 241 ff.).

41. Herculaneum. On a marble table intended for offerings. Now in the Naples Museum. Conway no. 87, v. Pl. no. 117.

*a*. Herentateís súm.    Veneris sum.

*b*. L. Slabiis L. Aukíl   L. Stlabius L. f. Aucilus
 meddíss túvtíks    meddix tuticus
 Herentateí Herukinaí  Veneri Erycinae
 prúffed. |       posuit.

42. Nola. On a block of stone said to have been found under the ruins of a temple. Now in the Naples Museum. Conway no. 93, v. Pl. no. 124.

Ni]um*s*is Heírennis Niumsieís  Numerius Herennius Numerii f.
Ka . . . | Perkens Gaaviis    Ca . . ., Percennus Gavius
Perkedne[ís . . .] | meddíss   Percenni f. . . . meddices
degetasiús arag*et*[ud . . .    *decentarii argento . . . .

43. Nola. On a block of stone, possibly an altar. Conway no. 94, v. Pl. no. 125.

Paakul Mulukiis Marai.   Paculus Mulcius Mar. f.
meddís | degetasis aragetud  meddix *decentarius argento
multas[íkud.      multaticio.

44. Suessula. Incised on the inside of a glazed plate. Conway no. 97, v. Pl. no. 175.

Minis Beriis Anei upsatuh  Minius Berius Anei operati
 sent Tiianei. |      sunt Teani.

The third letter in the second word is a peculiar character which is read by some as l. The third word seems to be an abbreviation for another name, making up the plural subject of upsatuh sent, used here with active meaning.

INSCRIPTIONS OF SAMNIUM AND THE FRENTANI

## 45. The Dedicatory Tablet of Agnone

A small bronze tablet (about 11 by 6¼ inches), inscribed on both sides.
Now in the British Museum. Conway no. 175, v. Pl. no. 200.

A

| | |
|---|---|
| Statís pús set húrtín | (Di) qui erecti sunt in luco |
| Kerríín : Vezkeí statíf | Cereali : Vetusci statua, |
| Evklúí statíf, Kerrí statíf | Euclo statua, Cereri statua, |
| Futreí Kerríaí statíf | Genetrici Cereali statua, |
| 5 Anterstataí statíf | Interstitae statua, |
| Ammaí Kerríaí statíf | Ammae Cereali statua, |
| Diumpaís Kerríiaís statíf | Lumpis Cerealibus statua, |
| Líganakdíkeí Entraí statíf | Leg . . dici Interae statua, |
| Anafríss Kerríúís statíf | *Imbribus* Cerealibus statua, |
| 10 Maatúís Kerríúís statíf | Matis Cerealibus statua, |
| Diúyeí Verehasiúí statíf | Iovi *Versori* statua, |
| Diúveí Regatureí statíf | Iovi Rectori statua, |
| Hereklúí Kerríiúí statíf | Herculi Cereali statua, |
| Patanaí Piístíaí statíf | Pandae Fidiae statua, |
| 15 Deívaí Genetaí statíf. | Divae Genitae statua. |
| Aasaí purasiaí | In ara igniaria |
| saahtúm tefúrúm alttreí | crematio sancta *in altero* |
| púptereípíd akeneí . | *quoque anno* |
| Ssakahíter. | sacrificetur. |
| 20 Fiuusasiaís az húrtúm | Floralibus ad lucum |
| sakarater. | sacratur. |
| Pernaí Kerríiaí statíf | Pernae Cereali statua, |
| Ammaí Kerríiaí statíf | Ammae Cereali statua, |
| Fluusaí Kerríiaí statíf | Florae Cereali statua, |
| 25 Evklúí Patereí statíf. | Euclo Patri statua. |

**B**

| | |
|---|---|
| Aasas ekask eestínt | Arae hae exstant |
| húrtúí : | luco : |
| Vezkeí | Vetusci, |
| Evklúí | Euclo, |
| 30 Fuutreí | Genetrici, |
| Anterstataí | Interstitae, |
| Kerrí | Cereri, |
| Ammaí | Ammae, |
| Diumpaís | Lumpis, |
| 35 Líganakdíkeí Entraí | Leg .. dici Interae |
| Kerríiaí | Cereali, |
| Anafríss | *Imbribus,* |
| Maatúís | Matis, |
| Diúveí Verehasiú | Iovi *Versori,* |
| 40 Diúveí Piíhiúí Regatureí | Iovi Pio Rectori, |
| Hereklúí Kerriiúí | Herculi Cereali, |
| Patanaí Piístíaí | Pandae Fidiae, |
| Deívaí Genetaí. | Divae Genitae. |
| Aasaí purasiaí | In ara igniaria |
| 45 saahtúm tefúrúm | crematio sancta |
| alttreí pútereípíd | *in altero quoque* |
| akeneí. | *anno.* |
| Húrz Dekmanniúís staít. | Lucus *Decumaniis stat. |

Cf. especially Mommsen, Unterit. Dial., 128 ff.

The inscription contains an inventory of the statues (A) and altars (B) in a sacred grove devoted to the worship of rural divinities. Kerríú-, which is used as an epithet of several of the divinities and of the grove itself, does not mean simply 'pertaining to Ceres', though it is translated 'Cerealis' for convenience. It must have a wider sense, 'pertaining to the powers of generation', such as were Ceres and Cerrus, and might also be translated (with Mommsen) 'Genialis', since *Genius* was originally, like *Cerrus*, a personification of the power of generation.

Corresponding to the Floralia mentioned in l. 20, we probably have in Dekmanniúís of l. 48 the name of a December festival, like the Roman Consualia or Saturnalia. The phrase alttreí pútereípíd akeneí, in case akeneí is 'year' (159, *a*), must mean 'in every other year' (see 200, 2, *a*). Otherwise it is

'at each of the two festivals', referring to the Floralia and the Decumania.   In
l. 1 statús pús set means '(the gods) who are set up, i.e. honored with statues'.
Cf. Hor. Odes 4, 1, 20.

This is the earliest carefully written inscription of any size in the fully
developed alphabet and, judging from the style of the letters, must be at least
a century earlier than the Cippus Abellanus.   We may take 250 B.C. as a con-
servative date.

**46**. Bovianum Vetus.   Conway no. 171, v. Pl. no. 189.

| | |
|---|---|
| Nv. Vesullia\|ís Tr. m. t. \| | Nv. Vesullieius Tr. f. meddix tuticus |
| ekík sakara\|klúm | hoc templum |
| Búva\|ianúd \| aíkdafed. | ad Bovianum *decrevit.* |

On the last line, see **61**, 3, and **264**, 3.

**47**. Bovianum Vetus.   On fragments of a cornice.   Conway no. 174, v. Pl.
no. 190.

| | |
|---|---|
| Gn. *Staíís* Mh. Tafidins | Cn. Staius Mh. f. Tafidinus |
| metd. t. dadíkatted. \| | meddix tuticus dedicavit. |

**48**. Bovianum Vetus.   Conway no. 170, v. Pl. no. 192.

| | |
|---|---|
| Sten . . . . . meddíss | Stenius . . . meddix |
| túv[tík]s *úpsannam* | tuticus faciendam |
| deded \| iním *prúfatted.* | dedit et probavit. |

**49**. Bovianum Vetus.   Conway no. 173, v. Pl. no. 193.

| | |
|---|---|
| . . d Staatiis L. Klar . . | . . . Statius L. f. Clar . . . |
| . . d pestlúm úpsann[úm] | . . . templum faciendum . . . |

**50**. Bovianum Vetus.   Conway no. 169, v. Pl. no. 188.

| | |
|---|---|
| . . . p?]*úrtam* líís . . . . | . . . *portam* . . . |
| . . . d Safinim sak . . . . | . . . Samnium sac . . |
| . . upam íak úín . . . . | . . . eam un . . |
| ín]ím keenzstur . . . . | et censor(es?) |
| 5 M]aííeís Maráíieís . . . . | Maii Mareii |
| p]aam essuf úmb*n* . . . . | quam ipse . . . |
| a]vt pústíris esidu . . . | at posterius idem . . |
| d]uunated fíís . . . . . | donavit fan . . |
| í]ním leígúss samí . . . | et ———  ——— |
| 10 l?]úfríkúnúss fíf . . . . . | *liberigenos* . . . |

So much is lost that no certain restoration can be made.

*(handwritten top margin:)* ⟨ Ιν, εν(ς) -proprio, non altro cho, per l'appunto" n.8 1-44 ⟨ εα- Kent. ⟨ ειυι ⟨ ειυ ⟨ εγο.

**51.** Molise. Conway no. 163, v. Pl. no. 185.

Bn. Betitis Bn.      Bn. Betitius Bn. f.
  meddíss prúffed.      meddix posuit.

**52.** Aesernia. On a gold ring.    Conway no. 167, v. Pl. no. 187.

Stenis Kalaviis      Stenius Calvius
Anagtiai Diíviiai      Angitiae Diae
dunum deded.      donum dedit.

*(handwritten right margin:)* kuru ⟨ Κόπα Kent ⟨ ur. c ara cert Slei Καρυον, ako karabus Ref

**53.** Near Agnone. About the neck of a round pedestal. Conway no. 176, v. Pl. no. 201.

Mz. Húrtiis Km.      Mz. Hortius Cm. f.
Her. dúnúm.      *Herculi* donum.

    Her. for Hereklúí or Herentatei ?

*(handwritten right margin:)* ⟨ corona .. pialka londa Ribezzo. 4

**54.** Macchia di Valfortore. Conway no. 162, v. Pl. 180.

sakara]klum Maatreís      templum Matris
. . . ras Futre[ís      . . . Genetricis

    Known only from a copy. The last word appears as **Futre.e.**

*(handwritten right margin:)* kuru Kent Κόπα Ribezzo. carina erúk cara pietra.

**55.** Saepinum. Conway no. 164, v. Pl. no. 182.

pis tiú      Quis tu?
íív kúru      —— *glans*
púiiu Baíteís      cuia? Baeti
Aadiieís Aíífineís.      Adii Aedini.

    This is on an oval stone and is possibly an inscribed missile like the Roman *glandes plumbeae.* We have then a question "Who art thou and whose missile?" and the answer "(I am the missile) of Baetus Adius." But **íív** is hopeless and **kúru** is without known connection.

*(handwritten:)* Ribezzo · Neapolis II, 108   Chi (sei) tu? Io (sono) una pietra da getto. Di chi? Di Baetus adius adiinus

**56.** Aufidena. Conway no. 177, v. Pl. no. 199.

Pk. De. Pk. súvad      Pc. Decius Pc. f. sua
eítiv. upsed.      pecunia fecit.

*(handwritten right margin:)* Fay Rhe. di Fil. 43, 6 + quis. tu? spom S. III (testis) nux Cuia? Baeti. adii aedini

**57.** Conway no. 181, v. Pl. no. 203.

Mitl. Me|tiis Mh. |      Mitulus Mettius Mh. f.
Fíml. ups.      Fimulus fecit.

*(handwritten right margin:)* J. Friedrich I F. 1, 141 Ego glans.

**58.** Near Histonium.  Conway no. 190, v. Pl. no. 204.

| | |
|---|---|
| Kaal. Húsidiis Gaav . . . | Cal. Hosidius Gavii f. |
| Vifbis Úhtavis Úf . . . | Vibius Octavius Of. f. |
| kenzsur pa*tt* . . . | censores *patraverunt*. |

**59.** Near Histonium.  On the bottom of a bronze head.  Conway no. 191, v. Pl. no. 206.

Iúveís | Lúvfreís.       Iovis Liberi.

**60.** Conway no. 194, v. Pl. no. 208.

Pakis Tintiriis.       Pacius Tintirius.

**61.** Anxanum ?  On a bronze tablet of peculiar shape.  Conway no. 193, v. Pl. no. 209.

| | |
|---|---|
| Vereias Lúvkanateís | Iuventutis Lucanatis |
| aapas kaías Palanúd. | —— —— Pallano. |

The evidence for a town called Pallanum and a district called Lucania in the territory of the Frentani is given by Mommsen, Unterit. Dial. p. 169, Conway p. 210.  The first two words of l. 2 are wholly obscure.

## INSCRIPTIONS OF LUCANIA, BRUTTIUM, AND MESSANA

**62.** Messana.  Conway no. 1, v. Pl. no. 1.

| | |
|---|---|
| Στενις Καλινις Σταττιηις | Stenius Calinius Statii f. |
| Μαρας Πομπτιες Νιυμσδιηις | Maras Pontius Numerii f. |
| μεδδειξ ουπσενς | meddices fecerunt |
| εινειμ τωϝτο Μαμερτινο | et civitas Mamertina. |
| Απτελλουνηι σακορο. | Apollini sacra (est). |

The text is made up from two fragments, and an early copy from which are supplied the letters at the beginning of the lines.  The Mamertines were of Campanian origin.  The last word is probably Nom. Sg. F. or Nom. Pl. N., 'is' or 'are' being understood.  But possibly it is Nom. Sg. F. agreeing with τωϝτο.

**63.** On bricks in the museum at Messana.  Conway no. 2, v. Pl. no. 2.

Μαμερτινουμ.       Mamertinorum.

**64.** Bronze plate found in Monteleone (Bruttium).  Conway no. 5, v. Pl. no. 4.

Διουϝει Ϝερσορει ταυρομ.       Iovi Versori taurum.

**65.** Bronze helmet of unknown provenance, now in the museum of Palermo. Conway no. 6, v. Pl. no. 19.

Τρεβις Σ. Σεστιες δεδετ.　　　Trebius S. f. *F*estius dedit.

**66.** Bronze helmet of unknown provenance, now at Vienna. Conway no. 7, v. Pl. no. 18.

Σπεδις Μαμερεκιες　　　Spedius Mamercius
Σαιπινς αναΣακετ.　　　Saepinus dedicavit.

For the value of the character S in these last two inscriptions, see **24**, *b*.

Ϟ Ι Ο Υ Ϟ ο ι.　　　*Flusoi*

### COINS

Of the numerous examples of coin-legends the following may serve as specimens.

| | | |
|---|---|---|
| **67.** Aquilonia(?). | Akudunniad. | |
| **68.** Atella. | Aderl. | |
| **69.** Ausculum. | *a*) αυτυσκλι., *b*) αυσκλιν.., *c*) αυσκλα. | |
| **70.** Capua. | **Kapv.** | |
| **71.** Compulteria. | *a*) **Kupelternum**, *b*) **Kupelternúm.** | |
| **72.** Fistelia. | *a*) **Fistelú**, *b*) **Fistluis**, *c*) φιστελια, reverse **Fistluis.** | |
| **73.** Frentrum. | **Frentreí.** | |
| **74.** Messana. | Μαμερτινουμ. | |
| **75.** Lucania. | Λουκανομ. | |
| **76.** Nuceria Alfaterna. | **Nuvkrinum Alafaternum.** | |
| **77.** Teanum Sidicinum. | **Tíanud Sidikinud.** | |
| **78.** Teate. | **Tiiatium.** | |

**79.** Italia (coins of the Social War).

*a*) G. **Paapii** G. **Mutíl**, reverse **Víteliú.**　　　G. Papius G. f. Mutilus — Italia.

*b*) G. **Paapi** G., reverse **Mutíl embratur.**　　　G. Papius G. f. — Mutilus imperator.

**80.** Samnium (coins of the Social War).

G. **Mutíl**, reverse **Safinim.**　　　G. Mutilus — Samnium.

## UMBRIAN INSCRIPTIONS

## THE IGUVINIAN TABLES[1]

Seven bronze tablets, varying from about 16 by 12 inches to 25 by 15 inches, found at Gubbio, the ancient Iguvium, in 1444. Tables I–IV and V a–V b 7 are in the native alphabet, V b 7–18 and VI, VII, in the Latin alphabet. See also 8, 9, and below, p. 309; for the bibliography, see pp. xiii–xvi.

### V A, B

A Esuk frater Atiieřiur | eitipes
  plenasier urnasier uhtretie |
3 T. T. Kastruçiie. Ařfertur pisi
4 pumpe | fust eikvasese Atiie-
5 řier, ere ri esune | kuraia, pre-
  habia piřẹ uraku ri esuna |
6 si herte, et pure esune
7 sis. Sakreu | perakneu
  upetu, revestu, puře teřte, |
8 eru emantur herte,
9 et pihaklu pune | tribřiçu fu-
10 iest, akrutu revestu | emantu
  herte. Ařfertur pisi pumpe |
11 fust, erek esunesku vepurus
12 felsva | ařputrati fratru Atiie-
13 řiu prehubia, | et nuřpener
  prever pusti kastruvuf. |
14   Frater Atiieřiur esu eitipes
15 plenasier | urnasier uhtretie
  K. T. Kluviier. Kumnah|kle

Ita fratres Atiedii decreverunt plenariis *urnariis *auctura T. Castrucii T. f. Flamen quicumque erit *collegis* Atiediis, is rem sacram curet, praebeat quidquid ad illam rem sacram sit oportet, et qui in sacrificiis sint (oportet). Hostias sollemnis deligito, revisito, cum datur, (aliquae) earum accipiantur oportetne, et cum piaculorum ternio fiet, ex agro revisito accipiantur oportetne. Flamen quicumque erit, is ad sacrificia *sine igne holera* arbitratu fratrum Atiediorum praebeat, et ——pondiis singulis in *capita*.

Fratres Atiedii ita decreverunt plenariis *urnariis *auctura C. Cluvii T. f. In conventu

---

[1] Table V is given first, as a convenient starting-point for the beginner; then VI, VII, and with these are given at the bottom of the page the parallel passages of I, which is an earlier and shorter version of the same material; then I in a continuous text, for the sake of greater convenience for reference; lastly II–IV. These last, especially III and IV, are so difficult that they might be omitted in a work of this kind, were it not for the convenience of having the complete texts for reference.

The translation is in the main that of Bücheler, but with not a few departures in the rendering of certain words.

16 Atiieřie ukre eikvasese Ati-
17 ieřier, | ape apelust, muneklu
18 habia numer | prever pusti
   kastruvuf, et ape purtitu |
19 fust, muneklu habia numer
20 tupler |_pusti kastruvu, et ape
21 subra spafu fust, | muneklu
   habia numer tripler pusti |
22 kastruvu. Et ape frater çers-
23 natur furent,[1] | ehvelklu feia
24 fratreks ute kvestur, | sve
   rehte kuratu si.  Sve mestru
25 karu | fratru Atiieřiu, pure ulu
26 benurent, | prusikurent rehte
27 kuratu eru, eřek | prufe si. Sve
   mestru karu fratru Atiieř|iu,
28 pure ulu benurent, prusiku-
29 rent | kuratu rehte neip eru,
B  enuk fratru ‖ ehvelklu feia
2  fratreks | ute kvestur, panta
3  muta | arřferture si. Panta
4  muta fratru | Atiieřiu mestru
5  karu, pure ulu | benurent, ar̃-
6  ferture eru pepurkur|ent he-
7  rifi, etantu mutu arřferture | si. |
8  *Clauerniur dirsas herti*
   *fratrus Atiersir posti*
9  *acnu | farer opeter p. IIII*
   *agre Tlatie Piquier Martier*
10 *et šesna | homonus duir,*
   *puri far eiscurent, ote a. VI.*
11 *Clauerni | dirsans herti*
   *frater[2] Atiersiur sehmenier*
12 *dequrier | pelmner sorser*

Atiedio in arce, *collegis* Atiediis, ubi impenderit, sportulam
habeat nummis singulis in
*capita*, et ubi porrectum
erit, sportulam habeat nummis
binis in *capita*, et ubi
superiectum erit, sportulam
habeat nummis trinis in
*capita.* Et ubi fratres cenati erunt, sententiam roget
magister aut quaestor, si
recte curatum sit. Si maior
pars fratrum Atiediorum, qui illuc
venerint, pronuntiaverint recte
curatum esse, id probe sit. Si
maior pars fratrum Atiediorum,
qui illuc venerint, pronuntiaverint curatum recte non esse,
tum fratrum sententiam roget
magister aut quaestor, quanta
multa flamini sit. Quantam
multam fratrum Atiediorum maior
pars, qui illuc venerint, flamini esse oportuerit poposcerint,
tanta multa flamini sit.

Clavernii dent oportet
fratribus Atiediis in singulos
*annos* farris lecti pondo IIII
agri Latii Piquii Martii,
et cenam hominibus duobus,
qui far arcessierint, aut asses VI.
Claverniis dent oportet
fratres Atiedii sementivis
decuriis pulpamenti suilli

---

[1] Aes furent̃.     [2] Aes *frateer* with first *e* erased.

*posti acnu uef X cabri-*
13 *ner uef V, pretra | toco*
*postra fahe, et šesna*
*ote a. VI. Casilos dirsa her-*
14 *ti fratrus | Atiersir posti*
*acnu farer opeter p. VI agre*
15 *Casiler Piquier | Martier et*
*šesna homonus duir, puri*
*far eiscurent, ote a. VI. |*
16 *Casilate dirsans herti frateer*
*Atiersiur sehmenier dequ-*
17 *rier | pelmner sorser posti*
*acnu uef XV cabriner uef*
18 *VII s., et | šesna   ote*
*a. VI.*

in singulos *annos* partes X, caprini partes V, priores *sale* (*conditas*), posteriores ——, et cenam
aut asses VI. Casilas det oportet
fratribus Atiediis in singulos
*annos* farris lecti pondo VI agri
Casili     Piquii     Martii,     et
cenam hominibus duobus, qui
far arcessierint, aut asses VI.
Casilati    dent    oportet    fratres
Atiedii        sementivis        decuriis
pulpamenti suilli in singulos
*annos* partes XV, caprini partes
VII semissem, et cenam aut
asses VI.

## VI A

1    †*Este persclo aueis aser-*
*iater enetu, parfa curnase*
*dersua, peiqu peica merstu.*
2 *Poei angla aseriato | eest,*
*eso tremnu serse arsfer-*
*ture ehueltu:* '*stiplo aser-*
*iaia parfa dersua, curnaco*
3 *dersua, | peico mersto, peica*
*mersta, mersta auuei, mersta*
*angla esona'. Arfertur eso*
4 *anstiplatu: | 'ef     aserio*
*parfa dersua, curnaco ders-*
*ua, peico mersto, peica mers-*
*ta, mersta aueif, merstaf |*

Istud sacrificium avibus observatis inito, parra cornice
prospera, pico pica iusto.
Qui oscines observatum ibit,
sic in tabernaculo sedens flaminem iubeto: 'stipulare ut obser-
vem parram prosperam, cornicem
prosperam, picum iustum, picam
iustam, iustos avis, iustas
oscines divinas'. Flamen sic
instipulator: 'tum ibi observa
parram prosperam, cornicem prosperam, picum iustum, picam iustam, iustas avis, iustas

## I A

1    †**Este persklum aves anzer-**
2 **iates enetu | pernaies pusnaes.**

Istud sacrificium avibus observatis inito anticis posticis.

5 *anglaf esona mehe, tote Īo-*
*ueine, esmei stahmei stah-*
*meitei'. Sersi pirsi sesust,*

6 *poi angla | aseriato est, erse*
*neip mugatu nep arsir ander-*
*sistu, nersa courtust porsi*

7 *angla anseriato | iust. Sue*
*muieto fust ote pisi arsir*
*andersesust,*[1] *disleralinsust. |*

8 *Uerfale pufe arsfertur*
*trebeit ocrer peihaner, erse*
*stahmito eso tuderato est:*

9 *angluto | hondomu, porsei*
*nesimei asa deueia est,*
*anglome somo, porsei*
*nesimei uapersus auiehcleir |*

10 *est, eine angluto somo*
*uapefe auiehclu todcome*
*tuder, angluto hondomu*
*asame deueia todcome |*

11 *tuder. Eine todceir*
*tuderus seipodruhpei se-*
*ritu. |*

12 *Tuderor totcor: uapersus-*
*to auieclir ebetrafe, ooser-*
*clome, presoliafe Nurpier,*

13 *uasirslome, | smursime, tet-*
*tome Miletinar, tertiame pra-*
*co pracatarum; uapersusto*

14 *auieclir carsome | Uestisier,*
*randeme Rufrer, tettome No-*
*niar, tettome Salier, carsome*
*Hoier, pertome Padellar. |*

15 *Hondra esto tudero porsei*

oscines divinas mihi, civitati Iguvinae, huic statui sta-
tuto'. In sede cum sederit
qui oscines observatum ibit, tum
nec muttito nec *alius* \*intersidito, donec revorterit qui
oscines observatum ierit. Si
muttitum erit aut quis *alius*
\*intersederit, inritum fecerit.

Templum ubi flamen
versatur arcis piandae, id
statutum sic finitum est:
ab angulo imo qui
proxume ab ara divina est,
usque ad angulum summum qui
proxume ab sellis auguralibus
est, deinde ab angulo summo
iuxta sellas auguralis usque ad
urbicum finem, ab angulo imo
iuxta aram divinam usque ad
urbicum finem. Tum in urbicis
finibus seorsum utroque servato.

Fines urbici: ab sellis
auguralibus ad exitus, ad \*observaculum, ad ———— Nurpii,
ad ——, ad ————, ad ————
Miletinae, ad tertiam *sae-*
*pium saeptarum;* ab sellis
auguralibus ad ———— Vesticii,
ad ——— Rubri, ad ——— No-
niae, ad ——— Salii, ad ———
Hoii, ad ———— Patellae.
Infra istos finis qui

---

[1] *Aes andersesusp.*

*subra screihtor sent, parfa dersua, curnaco dersua*

16 *seritu. Subra esto | tudero peico mersto, peica mersta seritu.*

*Sue anclar procanurent,*

17 *eso tremnu serse | combifiatu, arsferturo nomne carsitu: 'parfa dersua, curnaco dersua, peico mersto, peica*

18 *meersta, | mersta aueif, mersta ancla eesona tefe, tote Iiouine, esmei stahmei stahmitei". Esisco esoneir seueir |*

19 *popler anferener et ocrer pihaner perca arsmatia habitu. Uasor uerisco Treblanir*

20 *porsi ocrer | pehaner paca ostensendi, eo iso ostendu, pusi pir pureto cehefi dia. Surur uerisco Tęsonocir. |*

21 *Surur uerisco Uehieir. |*

22 †*Pre uereir Treblaneir Iuue Grabouei buf treif fetu. Eso naratu uesteis: 'teio sub-*

23 *ocau suboco | Dei Graboui, ocriper Fisiu, totaper Iiouina, erer nomneper, erar nomneper; fos sei,*

24 *pacer sei ocre Fisei, | tote Iiouine, erer nomne, erar nomne. Arsie, tio subocau*

supra scripti sunt, parram prosperam, cornicem prosperam servato. Supra istos finis picum iustum, picam iustam servato.

Si oscines cecinerint, sic in tabernaculo sedens nuntiato, flaminem nomine appellato: 'parram prosperam, cornicem prosperam, picum iustum, picam iustam, iustas avis, iustas oscines sacras tibi, civitati Iguvinae, huic statui statuto'. Ad haec sacra omnia populi lustrandi et arcis piandae virgam ritualem habeto. Vasa ad portam Trebulanam quae arcis piandae causa ostendentur, ea sic ostendito, ut ignis ab igne *accensus sit* faciat. Item ad portam Tesenacam. Item ad portam Veiam.

Ante portam Trebulanam Iovi Grabovio boves tris facito. Sic narrato libans: 'te invoco invocationes Iovem Grabovium pro arce Fisia, pro civitate Iguvina, pro arcis nomine, pro civitatis nomine; favens sis, propitius sis arci Fisiae, civitati Iguvinae, arcis nomini, civitatis nomini. Sancte, te invoco

---

3 †Preveres Treplanes | Iuve Krapuvi tre buf fetu.

Ante portam Trebulanam Iovi Grabovio tris boves facito.

*suboco    Dei    Graboue,*    invocationes Iovem Grabovium,
25 *arsier frite tio subocau |*    sancti    fiducia    te    invoco
*suboco    Dei    Graboue.*    invocationes Iovem Grabovium.
*Di Grabouie, tio esu bue*    Iuppiter Grabovi, te hoc bove
*peracrei pihaclu ocreper Fi-*    opimo piaculo pro arce Fi-
*siu, totaper Iouina, irer*    sia, pro civitate Iguvina, pro arcis
26 *nomneper, | erar nomneper.*    nomine, pro civitatis nomine.
*Dei    Grabouie,    orer*    Iuppiter Grabovi, *huius (piaculi)*
*ose, persei ocre Fisie pir orto*    *opere,* si in arce Fisia ignis ortus
*est, toteme Iouine arsmor*    est, in civitate Iguvina ritus
27 *dersecor | subator sent, pusei*    debiti omissi sunt, (facito) quasi
*neip heritu. Dei Crabouie,*    non consulto. Iuppiter Grabovi,
*persei tuer perscler uaseto*    si tui sacrificii (quid) vitiatum
*est, pesetom est, peretom est, |*    est, peccatum est, peritum est,
28 *frosetom est, daetom est,*    fraudatum est, delictum est,
*tuer perscler uirseto auirseto*    tui sacrificii visum invisum
*uas est, Di Grabouie, persei*    vitium est, Iuppiter Grabovi, si
29 *mersei, esu bue | peracrei*    ius sit, hoc bove opimo
*pihaclu pihafei. Di Gra-*    piaculo piatum sit. Iuppiter Gra-
*bouie, pihatu ocre Fisei,*    bovi, piato arcem Fisiam,
*pihatu tota Iouina. Di*    piato civitatem Iguvinam. Iup-
*Grabouie, pihatu ocrer |*    piter Grabovi, piato arcis
30 *Fisier, totar Iouinar nome,*    Fisiae, civitatis Iguvinae nomen,
*nerf, arsmo, ueiro, pequo*    principes, ritus, viros, pec*uum*
*castruo, fri pihatu; futu fos*    *capita,* fruges piato ; esto favens
*pacer pase tua ocre Fisi, |*    propitius pace tua arci Fisiae,
31 *tote Iiouine, erer*[1] *nomne,*    civitati Iguvinae, arcis nomini,
*erar nomne. Di Grabo-*    civitatis nomini. Iuppiter Gra-
*uie, saluo seritu ocre Fisi,*    bovi, salvam servato arcem Fisiam,
*salua seritu tota Iioui-*    salvam servato civitatem Iguvi-
32 *na. Di | Grabouie, saluo*    nam. Iuppiter Grabovi, salvum
*seritu ocrer Fisier, totar*    servato arcis Fisiae, civitatis
*Iiouinar nome, nerf, arsmo,*    Iguvinae nomen, principes, ritus,
*ueiro, pequo castruo, fri*    viros, pec*uum capita,* fruges

---

[1] Aes *erir.*

33 *salua | seritu; futu fos pacer*
*pase tua ocre Fisi, tote*
*Iouine, erer nomne, erar*
*nomne. Di Grabouie, tio*
34 *esu bue | peracri pihaclu*
*ocreper Fisiu, totaper*
*Iouina, erer nomneper,*
*erar nomneper, Di*
*Grabouie, tio subocau.' |*
35 *'Di Grabouie, tio esu bue*
*peracri pihaclu etru ocreper*
*Fisiu, totaper Iouina, erer*
*nomneper, erar nomneper.*
36 *Di | Grabouie, orer*
*ose, persei ocre Fisie pir orto*
*est, tote Iouine arsmor*
*dersecor subator sent, pusei*
37 *neip | hereitu. Di Crabouie,*
*persi tuer perscler uasetom*
*est, pesetom est, peretomest,*
*frosetomest, daetomest,*
38 *tuer | perscler uirseto aui-*
*rseto uas est, Di Grabouie,*
*persi mersi, esu bue peracri*
*pihaclu etru pihafi. Di*
39 *Grabouie, | pihatu ocre Fisi,*
*pihatu tota Iouina. Di*
*Grabouie, pihatu ocrer*
*Fisier, totar Iiouinar nome,*
40 *nerf, arsmo, ueiro, | pequo*
*castruo, fri pihatu; futu fos*
*pacer pase tua ocre Fisie,*
*tote Iiouine, erer nomne,*
41 *erar nomne. Di | Gra-*
*bouie, saluo seritu ocre*

salvas servato; esto favens propitius pace tua arci Fisiae, civitati
Iguvinae, arcis nomini, civitatis
nomini. Iuppiter Grabovi, te
hoc bove opimo piaculo
pro arce Fisia, pro civitate
Iguvina, pro arcis nomine,
pro civitatis nomine, Iuppiter
Grabovi, te invoco.'

'Iuppiter Grabovi, te hoc bove
opimo piaculo altero pro arce
Fisia, pro civitate Iguvina, pro
arcis nomine, pro civitatis nomine.
Iuppiter Grabovi, *huius (piaculi)*
*opere,* si in arce Fisia ignis ortus
est, in civitate Iguvina ritus
debiti omissi sunt, (facito) quasi
non consulto. Iuppiter Grabovi,
si tui sacrificii (quid) vitiatum
est, peccatum est, peritum est,
fraudatum est, delictum est,
tui sacrificii visum invisum
vitium est, Iuppiter Grabovi,
si ius sit, hoc bove opimo
piaculo altero piatum sit. Iuppiter Grabovi, piato arcem Fisiam,
piato civitatem Iguvinam. Iuppiter Grabovi, piato arcis
Fisiae, civitatis Iguvinae nomen,
principes, ritus, viros, pecu*um*
*capita,* fruges piato; esto favens
propitius pace tua arci Fisiae,
civitati Iguvinae, arcis nomini,
civitatis nomini. Iuppiter Grabovi, salvam servato arcem

*Fisim, salua seritu totam Iiouina. Di Grabouie, saluuom seritu ocrer Fisier, to-*
42 *tar | Iiouinar nome, nerf, arsmo, uiro, pequo castruo, frif saluua seritu; futu fons pacer pase tuua ocre Fisi,*
43 *tote | Iiouine, erer nomne, erar nomne. Di Grabouie, tiom essu bue peracri pihaclu etru ocriper Fissiu,*
44 *totaper Iouina, erer | nomneper, erar nomneper, Di Grabouie, tiom subocau.' |*
45 *'Di Grabouie, tiom esu bue peracri pihaclu tertiu ocriper Fisiu, totaper Iiouina, erer nomneper, erar nom-*
46 *neper. Di | Grabouie, orer ose, pirse ocrem Fisiem pir ortom est, toteme Iouinem arsmor dersecor subator sent, pusi neip |*
47 *heritu. Di Grabouie, perse tuer pescler uasetom est, pesetom est, peretom est, frosetom est, daetom est,*
48 *tuer | pescler uirseto auirseto uas est, Di Grabouie, pirsi mersi, esu bue peracri pihaclu tertiu pihafi. Di*
49 *Grabouie, | pihatu ocrem Fisim, pihatu totam Iiouinam. Di Grabouie, pihatu ocrer Fisier, totar*

Fisiam, salvam servato civitatem Iguvinam. Iuppiter Grabovi, salvum servato arcis Fisiae, civitatis Iguvinae nomen, principes, ritus, viros, pecu*um* *capita*, fruges salvas servato; esto favens propitius pace tua arci Fisiae, civitati Iguvinae, arcis nomini, civitatis nomini. Iuppiter Grabovi, te hoc bove opimo piaculo altero pro arce Fisia, pro civitate Iguvina, pro arcis nomine, pro civitatis nomine, Iuppiter Grabovi, te invoco.'

'Iuppiter Grabovi, te hoc bove opimo piaculo tertio pro arce Fisia, pro civitate Iguvina, pro arcis nomine, pro civitatis nomine. Iuppiter Grabovi, *huius* (*piaculi*) *opere*, si in arce Fisia ignis ortus est, in civitate Iguvina ritus debiti omissi sunt, (facito) quasi non consulto. Iuppiter Grabovi, si tui sacrificii (quid) vitiatum est, peccatum est, peritum est, fraudatum est, delictum est, tui sacrificii visum invisum vitium est, Iuppiter Grabovi, si ius sit, hoc bove opimo piaculo tertio piatum sit. Iuppiter Grabovi, piato arcem Fisiam, piato civitatem Iguvinam. Iuppiter Grabovi, piato arcis Fisiae, civitatis

Iiouinar nome, nerf, asmo, | Iguvinae nomen, principes, ritus,
50 uiro, pequo castruo, fri viros, pecu*um capita*, fruges
pihatu; futu fons pacer piato; esto favens propitius
pase tua ocre Fisi, tote pace tua arci Fisiae, civitati
Iiouine, erer nomne, erar Iguvinae, arcis nomini, civitatis
51 nomne. Di | Grabouie, sal- nomini. Iuppiter Grabovi, sal-
uo seritu ocrem Fisim, vam servato arcem Fisiam,
saluam seritu totam Iio- salvam servato civitatem Iguuinam. Di Grabouie, sal- vinam. Iuppiter Grabovi, sal-
uom seritu ocrer Fisier, | vum servato arcis Fisiae,
52 totar Iiouinar nome, nerf, civitatis Iguvinae nomen, prin-
arsmo, uiro, pequo castruo, cipes, ritus, viros, pecu*um capita*,
frif salua seritu; futu fons fruges salvas servato; esto favens
pacer pase tua ocre Fisi, | propitius pace tua arci Fisiae,
53 tote Iiouine, erer nomne, civitati Iguvinae, arcis nomini,
erar nomne. Di Gra- civitatis nomini. Iuppiter Grabouie, tiom esu bue peracri bovi, te hoc bove opimo
pihaclu tertiu ocriper Fisiu, piaculo tertio pro arce Fisia,
54 totaper | Iiouina, erer nom- pro civitate Iguvina, pro arcis
neper, erar nomneper. nomine, pro civitatis nomine.
Di Grabouie, tio comohota Iuppiter Grabovi, te commoto
tribrisine buo peracrio[1] pi- ternione boum opimorum pi-
55 haclo | ocriper Fisiu, totaper aculorum pro arce Fisia, pro civi-
Iiouina, erer nomneper, tate Iguvina, pro arcis nomine,
erar nomneper, Di pro civitatis nomine, Iuppiter
Grabouie, tiom subocau.' Grabovi, te invoco.'
56 †Tases persnimu | seuom. Tacitus precator totum.
Surur purdouitu, proseseto Item porricito, prosecta

---

4 †Arvia ustentu, | vatuva fe- Frumenta ostendito, *exta in*
rine feitu, heris vinu heri puni, | *ferculo* facito, vel vino vel posca,
5 ukriper Fisiu, tutaper Iku- pro arce Fisia, pro civitate Igu-
6 vina feitu. Sevum | kutef vina facito. Totum murmurans
pesnimu arepes arves. | precator adipibus frumentis.

---

[1] Aes peracnio.

*naratu, prosesetir mefa spe-*
*fa, ficla arsueitu, aruio*
57 *fetu. Este | esono heri*
*uinu heri poni fetu. Uatuo*
*ferine fetu. |*

58 †*Post uerir Treblanir*
*si gomia trif fetu Trebo*
*Iouie ocriper Fisiu, tota-*
*per Iiouina. Persae*
*fetu, aruio fetu, |*
59 *pone fetu, tases persnimu.*
*Surur naratu puse pre uerir*
*Treblanir. Prosesetir strusla,*
*ficla arsueitu. |*

narrato, prosectis libum *spar-*
*sum,* offam addito, frumenta
facito. Istud sacrificium vel
vino vel posca facito. *Exta*
*in ferculo* facito.

Post portam Trebulanam
sues gravidas tris facito Trebo
Iovio pro arce Fisia, pro civitate Iguvina. (Sacrificium) *humi*
*stratum* facito, frumenta facito,
posca facito, tacitus precator.
Item narrato ut ante portam
Trebulanam. Prosectis struem,
offam addito.

## VI B

1 ‡*Pre uerir Tesenocir buf*
*trif fetu Marte Grabouei*
*ocriper Fisiu, totaper Iioui-*
*na. Aruio fetu, uatuo ferine*
2 *fetu, poni | fetu, tases persni-*
*mu. Prosesetir farsio, ficla*

Ante portam Tesenacam boves
tris facito Marti Grabovio pro
arce Fisia, pro civitate Iguvina.
Frumenta facito, *exta in ferculo*
facito, posca facito, tacitus precator. Prosectis farrea, offam

7 †**Pusveres Treplanes tref**
8 **sif kumiaf feitu | Trebe Iuvie**
**ukriper Fisiu, tutaper Ikuvi-**
9 **na. | Supa sumtu, arvia usten-**
10 **tu, puni fetu, | kutef**
**pesnimu arepes** [1] **arves.** [1] |
11 ‡**Preveres Tesenakes tre**
12 **buf fetu, Marte Krapuvi | fetu**
**ukripe Fisiu, tutaper Ikuvina.**
13 **Arviu ustentu, | vatuva ferine**
**fetu, puni fetu, kutef**
**pesnimu arpes arves. |**

Post portam Trebulanam tris
sues gravidas facito Trebo Iovio
pro arce Fisia, pro civitate Iguvina. Suppa sumito, frumenta ostendito, posca facito, murmurans
precator adipibus frumentis.

Ante portam Tesenacam tris
boves facito, Marti Grabovio facito pro arce Fisia, pro civitate Iguvina. Frumenta ostendito, *exta in*
*ferculo* facito, posca facito, murmurans precator adipibus frumentis.

---

[1] Aes are*arv*es.

*arsueitu. Surur naratu puse pre uerir Treblanir.* |

3    †*Post uerir Tesenocir sif filiu trif fetu Fiso Sansie ocriper*[1] *Fisiu, totaper Iouina. Poni feitu, persae fetu, aruio fetu.* |

4 *Surur naratu pusi pre uerir Treblanir. Tases persnimu. Mandraclo difue destre habi-*

5 *tu. Prosesetir ficla,* | *struɧla arsueitu. Ape sopo postro pe-perscust,uestisia et mefa spefa scalsie conegos*[2] *fetu Fisoui*

6 *Sansi*|*ocriper Fisiu, totaper Iouina.Eso persnimu uestisia uestis:* '*tio subocau suboco Fisoui Sansi, ocriper Fisiu,* |

7 *totaper Iiouina, erer nom-neper, erar nomneper, fons sir, pacer sir ocre Fisi, tote Iiouine, erer*

8 *nomne,* | *erar nomne. Arsie, tiom subocau suboco Fisoui Sansi, asier frite tiom sub-ocau suboco Fisoui Sansi.*'

*addito.* Item narrato ut ante portam Trebulanam. .

Post portam Tesenacam sues lactentes tris facito Fiso Sancio pro arce Fisia, pro civitate Igu-vina. Posca facito, (sacrificium) *humi stratum* facito, frumenta fa-cito. Item narrato ut ante portam Trebulanam. Tacitus precator. Mantele bifidum in dextra habe-to. Prosectis offam, struem addito. Ubi suppa retro *po-suerit,* libamento et libo *sparso* patera genu nixus facito Fisovio Sancio pro arce Fisia, pro civitate Iguvina. Sic precator libamentum libans: 'te invoco invocationes Fisovium Sancium, pro arce Fi-sia, pro civitate Iguvina, pro ar-cis nomine, pro civitatis nomine, favens sis, propitius sis arci Fisiae, civitati Iguvinae, arcis nomini, civitatis nomini. Sancte, te invoco invocationes Fisovium Sancium, sancti fiducia te invoco invocationes Fisovium Sancium.'

---

14   †Pusveres Tesenakes tref
15 sif feliuf fetu | Fise Saçi ukriper Fisiu, tutaper Iku-
16 vina. | Puni fetu, supa sumtu,
17 arviu ustentu.   Mefa, | ves-tiça ustetu, Fisuvi[3] fetu, ukriper Fisiu fetu, |

Post portam Tesenacam tris sues lactentis facito Fisio Sancio pro arce Fisia, pro civitate Iguvi-na. Posca facito, suppa sumito, frumenta ostendito. Libum, liba-mentum ostendito, Fisovio facito, pro arce Fisia facito,

---

[1] Aes ocrifer.    [2] Aes confgos.    [3] Aes fiiuvi.

9 *Suront|poni pesnimu. Mefa spefa eso persnimu: 'Fisouie Sanśie, tiom esa mefa spefa Fisouina ocriper Fisiu, totaper Iiouina, |*

10 *erer nomneper, erar nomneper. Fisouie Sanśie, ditu ocre Fisi, tote Iouine, ocrer Fisie, totar*

11 *Iouinar dupursus | ·peturpursus fato fito, perne postne, sepse sarsite, uouse auie esone; futu fons, pacer pase tua ocre Fisi, tote*

12 *Iiouine, | erer nomne, erar nomne. Fisouie Sanśie, saluo seritu ocrem Fisi, totam Iouinam. Fisouie*

13 *Sanśie, saluo seritu | ocrer Fisier, totar Iouinar nome, nerf, arsmo, uiro, pequo castruo, frif salua seritu;*

14 *futu fons, pacer pase | tua ocre Fisi, tote Iiouine, erer nomne, erar nomne. Fisouie Sanśie, tiom esa mefa spefa Fisouina ocriper Fisiu, |*

15 *totaper Iiouina, erer nomneper, erar nomneper. Fisouie Sanśie, tiom subocau, Fisouie frite[1] tiom subocau.'*

16 *Pesclu| semu uesticatu, atripursatu. Ape eam purdinsust, proseseto erus*

Item posca precator. Libo sparso sic precator: 'Fisovi Sançi, te hoc libo sparso Fisovino pro arce Fisia, pro civitate Iguvina, pro arcis nomine, pro civitatis nomine. Fisovi Sanci, dato arci Fisiae, civitati Iguvinae, arcis Fisiae, civitatis Iguvinae bipedibus quadrupedibus *factum fitum*, ante post, sane sarte, *voto* augurio sacrificio; esto favens propitius pace tua arci Fisiae, civitati Iguvinae, arcis nomini, civitatis nomini. Fisovi Sanci, salvam servato arcem Fisiam, civitatem Iguvinam. Fisovi Sanci, salvum servato arcis Fisiae, civitatis Iguvinae nomen, principes, ritus, viros, pecu*um capita*, fruges salvas servatò; esto favens propitius pace tua arci Fisiae, civitati Iguvinae, arcis nomini, civitatis nomini. Fisovi Sanci, te hoc libo *sparso* Fisovino pro arce Fisia, pro civitate Iguvina, pro arcis nomine, pro civitatis nomine. Fisovi Sanci, te invoco, Fisovii fiducia te invoco.' In precatione media libato, tripodato. Ubi id (libum) porrexerit, prosectorum *magmentum*

---

[1] Aes erite.

*ditu. Eno scalseto uestisiar*
17 *erus    conegos  |  dirstu.*
*Eno mefa, uestisia sopa*
*purome efurfatu, subra spah-*
*mu.    Eno serse comoltu, co-*
18 *matir persnihimu.  | †Capif*
*purdita dupla aitu, sacra*
*dupla aitu. |*
19   ‡*Pre uerir Uehier buf*
*trif      calersu      fetu*
*Uofione Grabouie ocriper*
*Fisiu,    totaper    Iiouina.*
*Uatuo ferine fetu.   Herie*
20 *uinu | herie poni fetu, aruio*
*fetu, tases persnimu.   Pro-*
*seseter mefa spefa, ficla*
*arsueitu. Suront naratu pusi*
21 *pre uerir | Treblanir. |*
22   §*Post uerir Uehier habina*
*trif fetu Tefrei Ioui ocriper*

dato.   Tum ex patera libamenti
*magmentum* genu nixus dato.
Tum libum, libamentum sub
ignem *expurgato*, superiacito.
Tum sedens commolito, commolitis    precator.    Capides
porrectas  binas  agito,  sacras
binas agito.

Ante portam Veiam boves
tris frontem albam habentis facito
Voviono  Grabovio  pro  arce
Fisia, pro civitate Iguvina.
*Exta  in  ferculo* facito.   Vel
vino vel posca facito, frumenta
facito, tacitus precator.   Prosectis libum *sparsum*, offam
addito.    Item    narrato    ut
ante .portam Trebulanam.

Post  portam  Veiam  *agnas*
tris facito Tefro Iovio pro arce

---

18 †kapiř ˙purtitaf sakref, etraf
19 purtitaf,  etraf |  sakref, tu-
·   taper Ikuvina.    Kutef pes-
nimu ařepes arves. |
20    ‡Preveres Vehiies tref buf
kaleřuf      fetu      Vufiune |
21 Krapuvi      ukriper      Fisiu,
22 tutaper Ikuvina. | Vatuva ferine
fetu,  heri vinu heri puni, |
23 arviu      ustentu,      kutef
pesnimu ařepes arves. |
24    §Pusveres Vehiies tref hapi-
25 naf fetu Tefre Iuvie | ukriper

capides porrectas sacras, alteras
porrectas, alteras sacras, pro civitate Iguvina.   Murmurans precator adipibus frumentis.

Ante portam Veiam tris boves
frontem albam habentis facito Voviono Grabovio pro arce Fisia,
pro civitate Iguvina. *Exta in fer-*
*culo* facito, vel vino vel posca,
frumenta ostendito, murmurans
precator adipibus frumentis.

Post  portam  Veiam  tris  *ag-*
*nas* facito Tefro Iovio pro arce

*Fisiu, totaper Iiouina.*
*Serse fetu, pelsana fetu,*
23 *aruio feitu, poni | fetu,*
*tasis pesnimu. Prosesetir*
*strusla, ficla arueitu. Suront*
*naratu puse uerisco Tre-*
*blanir. Ape habina pur-*
24 *dinsus, | eront poi habina*
*purdinsust, destruco persi*
*uestisia et pesondro sorsom*
*fetu. Capirse perso osatu,*
25 *eam mani | nertru tenitu,*
*arnipo uestisia uesticos.*
*Capirso subotu, isec perstico*[1]
*erus ditu. Esoc persnimu*
26 *uestis:* '*Tiom | subocau sub-*
*oco Tefro Ioui, ocriper*
*Fisiu, totaper Iiouina,*
*erer nomneper, erar nom-*
*neper; fonsir pacer si*
27 *ocre Fisi, tote | Iouine, erer*
*nomne, erar nomne. Arsie,*
*tiom subocau suboco Tefro*

Fisia, pro civitate Iguvina.
Sedens facito, *sepeliendas* facito,
frumenta facito, posca facito,
tacitus precator.   Prosectis
struem, offam addito.   Item
narrato ut ad portam Tre-
bulanam.   Ubi *agnas* porrexerit, idem qui *agnas*
porrexerit, ad dextrum pedem
libamentum et *figmentum suillum*
facito.   Capidi fossam facito,
eam manu sinistra teneto,
donec libamentum libaverit.
Capidem deponito, item ad pedem
*magmentum* dato.   Sic precator
libans: 'Te invoco invocationes Tefrum Iovium, pro arce
Fisia, pro civitate Iguvina,
pro arcis nomine, pro civitatis
nomine; favens sis propitius sis
arci Fisiae, civitati Iguvinae, arcis
nomini, civitatis nomini. Sancte,
te invoco invocationes Tefrum

---

**Fisiu, tutaper Ikuvina.  Puste**
26 **asiane fetu, zeřef fetu, | pelsana**
**fetu,  arvia  ustentu,  puni**
27 **fetu,  taçez pesnim|u ařiper**
**arvis.  Api habina purtiius,**
28 **suřum pesuntru | fetu, esmik**
**vestiçam    preve    fiktu,**
29 **Tefri Iuvi fetu ukri|per Fisiu,**
**tutaper    Ikuvina,    testruku**
**peři kapiře peřum feit|u.**

Fisia, pro civitate Iguvina. *Post*
—facito, sedens facito, *sepeliendas*
facito, frumenta ostendito, posca
facito, tacitus precator adipibus
frumentis. Ubi *agnas* porrexeris,
*figmentum suillum* facito, ei
libamentum singillatim figito,
Tefro Iovio facito pro arce Fisia,
pro civitate Iguvina, ad dextrum
pedem capidi fossam facito.

---

[1] Probably *persico*.

*Ioui, arsier frite tiom subo-*
*cau suboco Tefro Ioui.*
28 *Tefre | Iouie, tiom esu sorsu*
*persontru Tefrali pihaclu*
*ocriper Fisiu, totaper*
*Iiouina,. erer nomneper,*
*erar nomneper. Tefre |*
29 *Iouie, orer ose perse*
*ocre Fisie pir orto est, tote*
*Iiouine arsmor dersecor sub-*
*ator sent, pusi neip heritu.*
30 *Tefre Iouie, | perse touer*
*pescler uasetomest,¹ pesetom-*
*est, peretomest, frosetom-*
*est, daetomest, touer pescler*
*uirseto auirseto uas est, |*
31 *Tefre Iouie, perse mers est,*
*esu sorsu persondru pihaclu*
*pihafi. Tefre Iouie, pihatu*
*ocre Fisi, tota Iiouina.*
32 *Tefre Iouie, pihatu | ocrer*
*Fisier, totar Iiouinar nome,*
*nerf, arsmo, uiro, pequo²*
*castruo, fri pihatu; futu*
*fons pacer pase tua ocre*
33 *Fisi, tote | Iiouine, erer*
*nomne, erar nomne. Tefre*
*Iouie, saluo seritu ocre Fisi,*
*totam Iiouinam. Tefre Iouie,*
*saluom seritu ocrer Fisier, |*
34 *totar Iouinar nome, nerf,*
*arsmo, uiro, pequo castruo,*
*fri salua seritu; futu fons*
*pacer pase tua ocre Fisi,*

Iovium, sancti fiducia te invoco
invocationes Tefrum Iovium.
Tefer Iovi, te hoc *suillo*
*figmento,* Tefrali piaculo,
pro arce Fisia, pro civitate
Iguvina, pro arcis nomine,
pro civitatis nomine. Tefer
Iovi, *huius (piaculi) opere* si in
arce Fisia ignis ortus est, in civitate Iguvina ritus debiti omissi
sunt, (facito) quasi non consulto. Tefer Iovi, si tui
sacrificii (quid) vitiatum est, peccatum est, peritum est, fraudatum
est, delictum est, tui sacrificii
visum invisum vitium est,
Tefer Iovi, si ius est,
hoc *suillo figmento* piaculo
piatum sit. Tefer Iovi, piato
arcem Fisiam, civitatem Iguvinam. Tefer Iovi, piato arcis
Fisiae, civitatis Iguvinae nomen,
principes, ritus, viros, pecu*um*
*capita,* fruges piato; esto
favens propitius pace tua arci
Fisiae, civitati Iguvinae, arcis
nomini, civitatis nomini. Tefer
Iovi, salvam servato arcem Fisiam,
civitatem Iguvinam. Tefer Iovi,
salvum servato arcis Fisiae,
civitatis Iguvinae nomen, principes, ritus, viros, pecu*um capita,*
fruges salvas servato; esto favens
propitius pace tua arci Fisiae,

---

¹ Aes *uasetomesf.*      ² Aes *pfquo.*

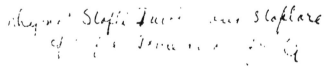

35 *tote Iiouine, erer | nomne,*
*erar nomne. Tefre Iiouie,*
*tiom esu sorsu persondru*
*Tefrali pihaclu ocriper*
*Fisiu, totaper Iiouina,*
36 *erer nomneper, erar | nom-*
*neper. Tefre Iouie, tiom*
*subocau.' Persclu sehemu*
*atropusatu.* |

37 †*Pesondro staflare ner-*
*truco persi fetu. Suront*
*capirse perso osatu, suror*
*persnimu puse sorsu. Ape*
38 *pesondro purdinsus, | pro-*
*seseto erus dirstu. Enom*
*uestisiar sorsalir destruco*
*persi persome erus dirs-*
*tu, pue sorso purdin-*
39 *sus. Enom | uestisiam*
*staflarem nertruco persi,*
*sururont erus dirstu. Enom*
*pesondro sorsalem persome,*
40 *pue persnis fust, ife | enden-*
*du, pelsatu. Enom pesondro*

civitati Iguvinae, arcis nomini,
civitatis nomini. Tefer Iovi,
te hoc *suillo* *figmento*
Tefrali piaculo pro arce
Fisia, pro civitate Iguvina,
pro• arcis nomine, pro civitatis
nomine. Tefer Iovi, te
invoco.' In precatione media
tripodato.

*Figmentum ovillum* ad sinistrum pedem facito. Item
capidi fossam facito, itidem
precator ut cum *suillo.* Ubi
*figmenta* porrexerit, prosectorum *magmentum* dato. Tum
libamenti *suilli* ad dextrum
pedem in fossam *magmentum* dato, ubi (*figmentum*) *suillum* porrexerit. Tum libamentum
*ovillum* ad sinistrum pedem,
itidem *magmentum* dato. Tum
*figmentum suillum* in fossam
ubi precatus erit ibi imponito, *sepelito.* Tum *figmentum*

---

30 †**Api eřek[1] purtiius, enuk**
**suřum pesuntrum feitu staf|lii[2]**
31 **uve, esmik[2] vestiça afiktu, ukri-**
32 **per Fisiu, tutaper Ikuvin|a[3] fei-**
**tu, nertruku peři kapiře peřum**
33 **feitu. Puni feitu. | Api su-**
**řuf purtiius,[4] enuk hapinaru**
34 **erus titu, zeřef | kumultu,**
**zeřef kumates[5] pesnimu.** |

Ubi id porrexeris, tunc
*figmentum* facito *ovillum,*
ei libamentum infigito, pro arce
Fisia, pro civitate Iguvina facito,
ad sinistrum pedem capidi fossam
facito. Posca facito. Ubi *fig-*
*menta* porrexeris, tum *agnarum*
*magmentum* dato, sedens commolito, sedens commolitis precator.

---

[1] Aes eřel.  [2] Aes stafli iuvesmik.  [3] Aes ikuvinp|a.  [4] Aes purtitius.  [5] Aes kumats.

*staflare persome, pue pesnis fus, ife endendu, pelsatu. Enom uaso porse pesondrisco*
41 *habus,* | *serse subra spahatu. Anderuomu sersitu, arnipo comatir pesnis fust. Serse pisher comoltu, serse comatir*
42 *persnimu.* | *Purdito fust.* |
43 † *Uocucom Iouiu, ponne oui furfant, uitlu toru trif fetu. Marte Horse fetu popluper totar Iiouinar, totaper Iiouina. Uatuo*
44 *ferine* | *fetu, poni fetu, aruio fetu, tases persnimu. Prosesetir fasio, ficla arsueitu. Suront naratu puse uerisco Treblanir.* |
45 ‡ *Uocucom Coredier uitlu toru trif fetu. Honde Serfi fetu popluper totar Iiouinar, totaper Iiouina.*[1]

ovillum in fossam, ubi precatus erit, ibi imponito, *sepelito*. Tum vasa quae ad *figmenta* habuerit, sedens superiacito. Inter —— sedeto, donicum commolitis precatus erit. Sedens quilibet commolito, sedens commolitis precator. Porrectum erit.

Ad aedem Ioviam, cum ovis *purgant*, vitulos tauros tris facito. Marti Hodio facito pro populo civitatis Iguvinae, pro civitate Iguvina. *Exta in ferculo* facito, posca facito, frumenta facito, tacitus precator. Prosectis farrea, offam addito. Item narrato ut ad portam Trebulanam.

Ad aedem Coredii vitulos tauros tris facito. Honto Cerrio facito pro populo civitatis Iguvinae, pro civitate Iguvina.

## I B

1 †Vukukum Iuviu, pune uvef
2 furfaθ, tref vitluf turuf | Marte Hurie fetu pupluper tutas Iiuvinas, tutaper Ikuvina. |
3 Vatuva ferine fetu, puni fetu, arvia ustentu, kutep
4 pesnimu | arepes arves.
    ‡Vukukum Kureties tref vitlup
5 turup Hunte Çe|fi feitu pupluper tutas Iiuvinas, tutaper

Ad aedem Ioviam, cum ovis purgant, tris vitulos tauros Marti Hodio facito pro populo civitatis Iguvinae, pro civitate Iguvina. *Exta in ferculo* facito, posca facito, frumenta ostendito, murmurans precator adipibus frumentis.

Ad aedem Coredii tris vitulos tauros Honto Cerrio facito pro populo civitatis Iguvinae, pro

---

[1] Aes *Iiouinar*.

*Uatuo*[1] *ferine fetu, aruio |*
46 *fetu, heri uinu heri poni*
*fetu, tases persnimu. Pro-*
*sesetir tesedi, ficla arsueitu.*[2]
*Suront naratu puse uerisco*
*Treblanir.*

47. †*Eno ocar | pihos fust.*
*Suepo esome esono ander-*
*uacose, uasetome fust;*
*auif aseriatu, uerofe Tre-*
*blano couertu, reste esono*
*feitu.* |

48 ‡*Pone poplo afero heries,*
*auif aseriato etu. Sururo*
*stiplatu pusi ocrer pihaner.*
*Sururont combifiatu. Erir-*
49 *ont tuderus auif | seritu.*
*Ape angla combifiansiust,*
*perca arsmatiam anouihimu.*

---

*Exta in ferculo* facito, frumenta
facito, vel vino vel posca
facito, tacitus precator. Prosectis ——, offam addito.
Item narrato ut ad portam
Trebulanam.

Tum    arx    piata    erit.
Sive horum sacrificiorum intervacatio *sit, in vitiatum erit;*
avis observato, ad portam Trebulanam revertito, instaurans sacrificium facito.

Cum populum lustrare volet,
avis observatum ito. Itidem
stipulator ut arcis piandae.
Itidem    nuntiato.    Isdem
finibus     avis     servato.
Ubi    oscines    nuntiaverit,
virgam    ritualem    induitor.

---

6 Iiuvina.    **Vatuva** | **ferine**
**fetu, arvia ustentu, tenzitim**
7 **arveitu, heris vinu heris** | **puni**
**feitu, kutef persnimu afri-**
**pes arvis.**

8 †**Inuk ukar pihaz fust.** | **Svepu**
**esumek esunu antervakaze,**
**vaçetumi se ;**[3] **avif azeriatu,** |
9 **verufe Treplanu kuvertu,**
**restef esunu feitu.** |    .

10 ‡**Pune puplum aferum heries,**
**avef anzeriatu**[4] **etu pernaia|f**
11 **pustnaiaf.    Pune kuvurtus,**

---

civitate Iguvina. *Exta in ferculo*
facito, frumenta ostendito, ——
addito, vel vino vel posca
facito, murmurans precator adipibus frumentis.

Tunc arx piata erit. Sive
horum sacrificiorum intervacatio
*sit, in vitiatum sit;* avis observato, ad portam Trebulanam revertito, instaurans sacrificium facito.

Cum populum lustrare voles,
avis observatum ito anticas
posticas.    Cum    reverteris,

---

[1] Aes *Uatue.*
[2] Aes *ficlmrsueitu.*
[3] Aes **vakazevaçetumiseavif.**
[4] Aes **anzvriatu.**

† *Cringatro hatu, destrame scapla anouihimu. Pir en-* 50 *dendu.* Pone | *esonome*[1] *Ferar,*[1] *pufe pir entelust, ere fertu poe perca arsmatiam habiest. Erihont aso destre onse fertu. Erucom* 51 *prinuatur dur* | *etuto, perca ponisiater habituto. Ennom stiplatu parfa desua seso, tote Iiouine. Sururont combifiatu uapefe auieclu. Neip* | 52 *amboltu, prepa desua combifiansi. Ape desua combifiansiust, uia auiecla esonome etuto com peracris sacris.* ‡ *Ape Acesoniame* | 53 *hebetafe benust, enom termnuco stahituto. Poi percam arsmatia habiest, eturstahmu. Eso eturstahmu: 'pisest* 54 *totar* | *Tarsinater, trifor*

Cinctum capito, in dextram scapulam induitor. Ignem imponito. Cum in sacrificium feratur, id in quo ignem imposuerit, is ferto qui virgam ritualem habebit. Idem arsum in dextro umero ferto. Cum eo legati duo eunto, virgas *calatoris* habento. Tum stipulator parram prosperam sibi, civitati Iguvinae. Itidem nuntiato ad sellas auguralis. Neve ambulato, priusquam prosperam nuntiaverit. Ubi prosperam nuntiaverit, via augurali in sacrificium eunto cum opimis hostiis. Ubi in Acedoniam ad exitus venerit, tum ad terminum stanto. Qui virgam ritualem habebit, exterminato. Sic exterminato: 'quisquis est civitatis Tadinatis, tribus

---

† **krenkatrum hatu. Enumek** | 12 **pir ahtimem ententu. Pune pir entelus ahtimem,** | 13 **enumek steplatu parfam** 14 **tesvam tefe, tute Ikuvine.** | **Vapefem avieklufe kumpifiatu. Vea** 15 **aviekla esunume etu.** | **Prinuvatu etutu, perkaf habetutu puniçate.** 16 ‡ **Pune menes** | **Akeřuniamem, enumek eturstamu tuta** 17 **Tařinate, trifu** | **Tařinate,**

cinctum capito. Tunc ignem ad caerimonium imponito. Cum ignem imposueris ad caerimonium, tunc stipulator parram prosperam tibi, civitati Iguvinae. Ad sellas auguralis nuntiato. Via augurali in sacrificium ito. Legati eunto, virgas habento *calatoris.* Cum venies in Acedoniam, tunc exterminato civitatem Tadinatem, tribum Tadinatem,

---

[1] Aes *esonomf ffrar.*

| | |
|---|---|
| *Tarsinater, Tuscer Naharcer* | Tadinatis,     Tusci     Narci |
| *Iabuscer nomner, eetu ehesu* | Iapudici nominis, ito ex hoc· |
| *poplu. Nosue ier ehe esu po-* | populo. Nisi *itum sit* ex hoc po- |
| 55 *plu,    sopir    habe* \| *esme*¹ | pulo, siquis *restat* in hoc |
| *pople,    portatu    ulo    pue* | populo, (eum) portato illuc quo |
| *mersest, fetu uru pirse mers* | ius est, facito illo quod ius |
| *est.' Trioper eheturstahamu.* | est.'     Ter     exterminato. |
| *Ifont termnuco com prinu-* | Ibidem ad terminum cum lega- |
| 56 *atir* \| *stahitu, eno deitu:* | tis     stato,     tum     dicito: |
| *'arsmahamo caterahamo Io-* | 'ordinamini *catervamini Igu- |
| *uinur'. Eno com prinuatir* | vini'.     Tum     cum     legatis |
| *peracris sacris ambretuto.·* | opimis     sacris     ambiunto. |
| 57 *Ape ambrefurent,* \| *termnome* | Ubi ambierint, ad terminum |
| *benurent,    termnuco    com* | venerint, apud terminum cum |
| *prinuatir eso persnimumo* | legatis     sic     precantor |
| *tasetur: 'Serfe Martie, Pre-* | taciti: 'Cerre Martie, Prae- |
| 58 *stota Serfia Serfer* \| *Martier,* | stita Cerria Cerri Martii, |
| *Tursa Serfia Serfer Martier,* | Torra Cerria Cerri Martii, |
| *totam Tarsinatem, trifo* | civitatem Tadinatem, tribum |
| *Tarsinatem, Tuscom Nahar-* | Tadinatem, Tuscum Narcum |
| 59 *com Iabuscom nome,* \| *totar* | Iapudicum    nomen,    civitatis |

| | |
|---|---|
| **Turskum, Naharkum numem,** | Tuscum,     Narcum     nomen, |
| 18 **Iapuzkum numem:** \| '**svepis** | Iapudicum nomen: 'siquis |
| **habe,    purtatulu    pue    mers** | *restat,* (eum) portato illuc quo ius |
| **est, feitu uru pere mers est'.** \| | est, facito illo quod ius est'. |
| 19 **Pune prinuvatus staheren term-** | Cum legati stabunt ad ter- |
| **nesku, enumek 'armamu**² \| | minos, tunc 'ordinamini |
| 20 **kateramu Ikuvinu'. Enumek** | *catervamini, Iguvini'. Tunc |
| **apretu tures et pure. Puni** | ambito tauris et igne. Cum |
| 21 **amprefu\|us,persnimu. Enumek** | ambieris, precator. Tunc |
| '**etatu Ikuvinus'. Triiuper am-** | 'itatote, Iguvini'. Ter am- |
| 22 **prehtu,** \| **triiuper pesnimu, triiu-** | bito, ter precator, ter |
| **per 'etatu Ikuvinus'. Enumek**\| | 'itatote,    Iguvini'.    Tunc |

¹ Aes *fsme.*        ² Aes **armanu.**

*Tarsinater, trifor Tarsinater,*
*Tuscer Naharcer Iabuscer*
*nomner nerf šihitu anšihi-*
60 *tu, iouie hostatu | anhos-*
*tatu tursitu tremitu, hondu*
*holtu, ninctu nepitu, sonitu*
*sauitu, preplotatu preui-*
61 *latu. | Serfe Martie, Pre-*
*stota Serfia Serfer Martier,*
*Tursa Serfia Serfer Martier,*
*fututo foner pacrer pase*
*uestra pople totar Iiouinar, |*
62 *tote Iiouine, ero nerus*
*sihitir anšihitir, iouies*
*hostatir anostatir, ero*
*nomne, erar nomne.' Ape*
63 *este dersicurent, eno | deitu*
*'etato Iiouinur', porse perca*
*arsmatia habiest. Ape este*
*dersicust, duti ambretuto*
64 *euront. Ape termnome | couor-*
*tuso, sururont pesnimumo.*
*Sururont deitu, etaians dei-*
*tu. Enom tertim ambretuto.*
*Ape termnome benuso, |*
65 *sururont pesnimumo, surur-*
*ont deitu etaias. †Eno pri-*
*nuatur šimo etuto erafont*
*uia, pora benuso. |*

Tadinatis, tribus Tadinatis,
Tusci Narci Iapudici
nominis principes cinctos incinc-
tos, iuvenes hastatos inhastatos
terreto tremefacito, *pessumdato*
*aboleto,* ninguito *inundato,* sonato
*sauciato, *praeplauditato *prae-*
vinculato. Cerre Martie, Praestita Cerria Cerri Martii,
Torra Cerria Cerri Martii,
estote faventes propitii pace
vestra populo civitatis Iguvinae,
civitati Iguvinae, eorum principibus cinctis incinctis, iuvenibus hastatis inhastatis, eorum
nomini, eius nomini.' Ubi
istud dixerint, tum dicito
'itatote Iguvini', qui virgam
ritualem habebit. Ubi istud
dixerit, iterum ambiunto
iidem. Ubi ad terminum rever-
sum erit, itidem precantor.
Itidem dicito, ut eant dicito. Tum tertium ambiunto.
Ubi ad terminum ventum erit,
itidem precantor, itidem
dicito ut eant. Tum le-
gati retro eunto eadem
via, qua ventum erit.

## VII A

1 *Sururont pesnimumo, su-*     Itidem precantor, itidem
*ruront deitu etaias. Eno*     dicito ut eant. Tum

23 †prinuvatus çimu etutu, erahunt    legati retro . eunto, eadem
**vea çimu etutu prinuvatus. |**    via retro eunto legati.

*prinuatur simo etuto erafont*
2 *uia, pora | benuso.*[1] |
3   †*Fondlire abrof trif fetu*
  *heriei rofu heriei peiu.*
  *Serfe*[2] *Martie feitu popluper*
  *totar Iiouinar, totaper |*
4 *Iiouina. Uatuo ferine feitu,*
  *poni fetu, aruio fetu,*
  *tases persnimu. Prosesetir*
  *mefa spefa, ficla arsueitu. |*
5 *Suront naratu puse uerisco*
  *Treblanir. Ape traha Saha-*
  *ta combifiansust, enom erus*
  *dirstu.* |
6   ‡*Rubine porca trif rofa ote*
  *peia fetu Prestote Serfie*
  *Serfer Martier popluper to-*
7 *tar Iiouinar, totaper | Iouina.*
  *Persaia fetu, poni fetu,*
  *aruio fetu. Suront naratu*
  *pusi pre uerir Treblanir.* ·

legati   retro   eunto   eadem
via, qua ventum erit.

In Fontulis apros tris facito
vel   rufos   vel   piceos.
Cerro Martio facito pro populo
civitatis Iguvinae, pro civitate
Iguvina. *Exta in ferculo* facito,
posca facito, frumenta facito,
tacitus   precator.   Prosectis
libum *sparsum*, offam addito.
Item   narrato   ut   ad   portam ·
Trebulanam.   Ubi   trans Sanctam nuntiaverit, tum *magmentum*
dato.

In Rubinia porcas tris rufas aut
piceas facito Praestitae Cerriae
Cerri Martii pro populo civitatis
Iguvinae, pro civitate Iguvina.
*Humi stratas* facito, posca facito,
arvia facito.   Item   narrato
ut ante portam Trebulanam.

---

24   †**Funtlere trif apruf rufru**
  **ute peiu feitu Çerfe Marti.** |
25 **Vatuvu ferine**[3] **fetu, arviu**
26 **ustentu, puni fetu,**[4] | **taçez**
  **pesnimu aŕepe arves.** |
27   ‡**Rupinie e tre purka rufra**
28 **ute peia fetu Prestate | Çer-**
  **fie Çerfe Marties.   Peŕaia fei-**
29 **tu, arviu ustentu, | kapi**
  **sakra aitu, vesklu vetu atru**
30 **alfu, puni fetu, | taçez pesnimu**
  **aŕeper arves.** |

In Fontulis tris apros rubros
aut piceos facito Cerro Martio.
*Exta in ferculo* facito, frumenta
ostendito, posca facito, tacitus
precator adipibus frumentis.

In Rubinia tris porcas rubras
aut piceas facito Praestitae Cerriae Cerri Martii. *Humi stratas* facito, frumenta ostendito, capides
sacras agito, vascula dividito atra
alba, posca facito, tacitus precator
adipibus frumentis.

---

[1] Repetition of last sentence of VI b to show connection of VII with VI.
[2] Aes *Serse*.          [3] Aes *ferime*.          [4] Aes *feiu*.

8 *Tases persnimu.* | *Prosesetir*
*struèla, ficla arsueitu. Ape*
*supo postro pepescus, enom*
*pesclu ruseme uesticatu*
9 *Prestote Serfie* | *Serfer Mar-*
*tier popluper totar Iouinar,*
*totaper Iouina. Enomuesclir*
*adrir ruseme eso persnihimu:*
10 *'Prestota* | *Serfia Serfer*
*Martier, tiom esir uesclir ad-*
*rir popluper totar Iiouinar,*
*totaper Iiouina, erer nom-*
11 *neper,* | *erar nomneper.*
*Prestota Serfia Serfer Mar-*
*tier, preuendu uia ecla atero*
*tote Tarsinate, trifo Tarsina-*
12 *te,* | *Tursce Naharce Iabusce*
*nomne, totar Tarsinater,*
*trifor Tarsinater, Tuscer*
*Naharcer Iabuscer nomner* |
13 *nerus sitir ansihitir, iouies*
*hostatir anostatir, ero nom-*
*ne. Prestota Serfia Serfer*
14 *Martier, futu fons | pacer pase*
*tua pople totar Iiouinar,*
*tote Iiouine, erom nomne,*
*erar nomne, erar nerus sihi-*
15 *tir ansihitir, iouies* | *hostatir*
*anostatir. Prestota Serfia*
*Serfer Martier, saluom seritu*
*poplom totar Iiouinar, salua*
16 *serituu* | *totam Iiouinam.*
*Prestota Serfia Serfer Mar-*
*tier, saluo seritu popler totar*
*Iiouinar, totar Iiouinar* |

Tacitus precator. Prosectis
struem, offam addito. Ubi
suppa retro *posuerit,* tum
precatione in ——— libato
Praestitae Cerriae Cerri Martii pro populo civitatis Iguvinae,
pro civitate Iguvina. Tum vasculis atris in —— sic precator:
'Praestita Cerria Cerri Martii, te his vasculis atris
pro populo civitatis Iguvinae,
pro civitate Iguvina, pro populi
nomine, pro civitatis nomine.
Praestita Cerria Cerri Martii,
advertito via omni malum
civitati Tadinati, tribui Tadinati, Tusco Narco Iapudico
nomini, civitatis Tadinatis,
tribus Tadinatis, Tusci
Narci Iapudici nominis
principibus cinctis incinctis, iuvenibus hastatis inhastatis, eorum
nomini. Praestita Cerria Cerri
Martii, esto favens propitia pace
tua populo civitatis Iguvinae,
civitati Iguvinae, eorum nomini,
eius nomini, eius principibus cinctis incinctis, iuvenibus hastatis
inhastatis. Praestita Cerria
Cerri Martii, salvum servato
populum civitatis Iguvinae, salvam servato civitatem Iguvinam.
Praestita Cerria Cerri Martii,
salvum servato populi civitatis
Iguvinae, civitatis Iguvinae

17 *nome,   nerf,  •arsmo,  uiro,*
   *pequo castruo, frif salua*
   *seritu; futu fons pacer pase*
   *tua pople totar Iiouinar,* |
18 *tote Iiouine, erer nomne,*
   *erar nomne.  Prestota Ser-*
   *fia Serfer Martier, tiom esir*
19 *uesclir adrer popluper* | *totar*
   *Iiouinar,   totaper  Iouina,*
   *erer nomneper, erar nomne-*
   *per.   Prestota Serfia Ser-*
20 *fer Martier, tiom* | *subocauu,*
   *Prestotar  Serfiar   Serfer*
   *Martier foner frite tiom sub-*
   *ocauu.'  Ennom persclu eso*
21 *deitu:* | *'Prestota Serfia Ser-*
   *fer Martier, tiom isir uesclir*
   *adrir, tiom plener popluper*
   *totar  Iiouinar,   totaper* |
22 *Iiouina,   erer   nomneper,*
   *erar nomneper.   Prestota*
   *Serfia*[1] *Serfer Martier, tiom*
23 *subocauu. Prestotar* | *Serfiar*
   *Serfer  Martier foner frite*
   *tiom subocauu. Enom uesti-*
   *catu, ahatripursatu.   Enom*
24 *ruseme* | *persclu uesticatu*
   *Prestote Serfie Serfer Marti-*
   *er popluper totar Iiouinar,*
   *totaper Iouina. Ennom ues-*
25 *clir* | *alfir persnimu, superne*
   *adro trahuorfi andendu, eso*
   *persnimu:* '*Prestota Serfia*
26 *Serfer Martier, tiom* | *esir*

nomen, principes, ritus, viros,
pecu*um capita*, fruges salvas
servato; esto favens propitia pace
tua populo civitatis Iguvinae,
civitati Iguvinae, populi nomini,
civitatis nomini.   Praestita Cerria   Cerri   Martii,   te   his
vasculis atris pro populo civitatis
Iguvinae, pro civitate Iguvina,
pro populi nomine, pro civitatis
nomine.  Praestita Cerria Cerri    Martii,    te    invoco,
Praestitae   Cerriae   Cerri
Martii faventis fiducia te invoco.'   Tum  precatione  sic
dicito:  'Praestita Cerria Cerri
Martii,    te    his    vasculis
atris,  te  plenis  pro  populo
civitatis Iguvinae, pro civitate
Iguvina,  pro  populi  nomine,
pro civitatis nomine.  Praestita
Cerria   Cerri   Martii,   te
invoco.   Praestitae   Cerriae
Cerri Martii faventis fiducia
te   invoco.    Tum    libato,   tripodato.     Tum
in ———— precatione libato
Praestitae Cerriae Cerri Martii
pro populo civitatis Iguvinae,
pro civitate Iguvina.  Tum vasculis  albis  precator,  super
atra transverse imponito, sic
precator:   'Praestita  Cerria
Cerri   Martii,   te   his

---

[1] Aes *Serfiar.*

*uesclir alfir popluper totar*
*Ïiouinar, totaper Ïiouina,*
*erer nomneper, erar nomne-*
27 *per. Prestota| Šerfia Šerfer*
 *Martier, ahauendu uia ecla*
 *atero pople totar Ïiouinar,*
 *tote Ïiouine, popler totar*
28 *Iouinar, | totar Ïiouinar*
 *nerus šihitir anšihitir, io-*
 *uies hostatir anhostatir, ero*
 *nomne, erar nomne. Prestota*
29 *Šerfia | Šerfer Martier, sal-*
 *uom seritu poplo totar Ïio-*
 *uinar, salua seritu totam*
 *Ïiouinam. Prestota Šerfia*
30 *Šerfer|Martier, saluom seritu*
 *popler totar Ïiouinar, totar*
 *Ïiouinar nome, nerf, arsmo,*
 *uiro, pequo castruo, frif |*
31 *salua seritu, futu fons pacer*
 *pase tua pople totar Ïio-*
 *uinar, tote Ïiouine, erer*
 *nomne, erar nomne. Pre-*
32 *stota | Šerfia Šerfer Martier,*
 *tiom ešir uesclir alfer poplu-*
 *per totar Ïiouinar, totaper*
 *Ïiouina, erer nomneper, erar |*
33 *nomneper. Prestota Šerfia*
 *Šerfer Martier, tiom subocauu,*
 *Prestotar Šerfiar Šerfer Mar-*
34 *tier foner frite tiom|subocauu.*
 *Ennom persclu eso persni-*
 *mu: 'Prestota Šerfia Šerfer*
 *Martier, tiom išir uesclir al-*
35 *fer, tiom plener | popluper to-*

vasculis albis pro populo civitatis
Iguvinae, pro civitate Iguvina,
pro populi nomine, pro civitatis
nomine. Praestita Cerria Cerri
Martii, avertito via omni
malum populo civitatis Iguvinae,
civitati Iguvinae, populi civitatis Iguvinae, civitatis Iguvinae
principibus cinctis. incinctis, iuvenibus hastatis inhastatis, eorum
nomini, eius nomini. Praestita
Cerria Cerri Martii, salvum
servato populum civitatis Iguvinae, salvam servato civitatem
Iguvinam. Praestita Cerria
Cerri Martii, salvum servato
populi civitatis Iguvinae, civitatis
Iguvinae nomen, principes, ritus,
viros, pecuum *capita*, fruges
salvas servato, esto favens propitia pace tua populo civitatis Iguvinae, civitati Iguvinae, populi
nomini, civitatis nomini. Praestita Cerria Cerri Martii,
te his vasculis albis pro populo civitatis Iguvinae, pro civitate
Iguvina, pro populi nomine, pro
civitatis nomine. Praestita Cerria
Cerri Martii, te invoco,
Praestitae Cerriae Cerri Martii faventis fiducia te invoco.'
Tum precatione sic preca-
tor : 'Praestita Cerria Cerri
Martii, te his vasculis albis,
te plenis pro populo civitatis

tar Iiouinar, totaper Iiouina,
erer nomneper, erar nomneper.  *Prestota Serfia Serfer*
36 *Martier,tiom | subocauu,Pre-*
*stotar Serfiar Serfer Martier*
*foner frite tiom subocauu'.*
*Enom uesticatu,ahatripursa-*
37 tu. | *Uestisa et mefa spefa*
*scalsie .conegos fetu Fisoui*
*Sansii      popluper      totar*
*Iiouinar, totaper Iiouina.*
38 *Suront | naratu puse post ue-*
*rir Tesonocir.  Uestisiar*
*erus ditu.  Enno uestisia*
*mefa spefa sopam purome*
39 *efurfatu, | subra spahamu,*
*traf Sahatam etu. Ape traha*
*Sahata couortus, ennom co-*
*moltu, comatir persnihimu.*
40 *Capif | sacra aitu. |*
41     † *Trahaf Sahate uitla trif*
*feetu Turse Serfie Serfer*
*Martier popluper totar Iio-*
*uinar,      totaper      Iiouina.*
42 *Persaea fetu, poni | fetu,*
*aruio fetu, tases persnimu.*
*Prosesetir strusla, ficlam*
*arsueitu. Suront naratu pu-*
*se uerisco Treblaneir. Ape |*

Iguvinae, pro civitate Iguvina,
pro populi nomine, pro civitatis
nomine.   Praestita Cerria Cerri
Martii,    te    invoco,    Praestitae   Cerriae   Cerri   Martii
faventis  fiducia  te  invoco'.
Tum      libato,      tripodato.
Libamentum et libum *sparsum*
in patera genu nixus facito Fisovio Sancio pro populo civitatis
Iguvinae, pro civitate Iguvina.
Item   narrato   ut   post   portam   Tesenacam.      Libamenti
*magmentum* dato. Tum libamentum,  libum  *sparsum*  sub  ignem   *expurgato*,   superiacito,
trans Sanctam ito.   Ubi trans
Sanctam  reverterit,  tum  commolito,   commolitis   precator.
Capides sacras agito.

Trans Sanctam vitulas tris
facito Torrae Cerriae Cerri
Martii pro populo civitatis Iguvinae,   pro   civitate   Iguvina.
*Humi stratas* facito, posca facito,
frumenta facito, tacitus precator.
Prosectis      struem,      offam
addito.   Item    narrato    ut
ad  portam  Trebulanam.   Ubi

---

31     † Tra Sate tref vitlaf feitu
Tuse Çerfie Çerfe Marties. |
32 Peřaia    feitu,    arviu    us-
tetu,  puni  fetu,  taçez  pes-
33 nimu | ařeper arves.  Pune

Trans Sanctam tris vitulas facito Torrae Cerriae Cerri Martii.
*Humi stratas* facito, frumenta ostendito, posca facito, tacitus precator adipibus frumentis.   Cum

43 †*purdinśiust, carsitu, pufe*
*abrons facurent, puse erus*
*dersa. Ape erus dirsust, pos-*
*tro combifiatu Rubiname,*
44 *erus | dersa. Enem traha*
*Sahatam combifiatu, erus*
*dersa. Enem Rubiname pos-*
*tro couertu, comoltu, comatir*
45 *persnimu et | capif sacra aitu.*
*Enom traha Sahatam couer-*
*tu, comoltu, comatir persnihi-*
*mu. Enom purditom fust.* |
46 *Postertio pane poplo*
*andirsafust, porse perca ars-*
*matia habiest et prinuatur*
*dur tefruto Tursar eso tasetur* |
47 *persnihimumo:* '*Tursa Iouia,*
*totam Tarsinatem, trifo Ta-*
*rsinatem, Tuscom Naharcom*
48 *Iapusco nome, totar | Tarsi-*
*nater, trifor Tarsinater,*
*Tuscer Naharcer Iapuscer*
*nomner nerf sihitu ansihitu,*

porrexerit, vocato, quo loco
apros fecerint, ut *magmentum*
det. Ubi *magmentum* dederit,
retro nuntiato in Rubiniam,
ut *magmentum* det. Tum trans
Sanctam nuntiato, *magmentum*
det. Tum in Rubiniam retro
revertito, commolito, commolitis
precator et capides sacras agito.
Tum trans Sanctam revertito,
commolito, commolitis precator.
Tum porrectum erit.

Postquam tertium populum
lustraverit, qui virgam ritualem habebit et legati
duo ex rogo Torrae sic taciti
precantor: 'Torra Iovia,
civitatem Tadinatem, tribum Tadinatem, Tuscum Narcum
Iapudicum nomen, civitatis Tadinatis, tribus Tadinatis,
Tusci Narci Iapudici
nominis principes cinctos incinc-

---

†*purtinçus, kaŕetu, pufe apruf* |
34 *fakurent, puze erus teŕa. Ape*
35 *erus teŕust, pustru | kupifia-*
*tu Rupiname, erus teŕa.*
*Ene tra Sahta kupifiaia,* |
36 *erus teŕa. Enu Rupiname*
37 *pustru kuvertu, antakre | ku-*
*mate pesnimu. Enu kapi*
*sakra aitu, vesklu vetu.* |
38 *Enu Satame kuvertu, anta-*
*kre kumate pesnimu. Enu*
39 *esunu | purtitu fust.* |

porrexeris, vocato, ubi apros
fecerint, ut *magmentum* det. Ubi
*magmentum* dederit, retro nuntiato in Rubiniam, *magmentum* det.
Tum trans Sanctam nunties,
magmentum det. Tum in Rubiniam retro revertito, integris commolitis precator. Tum capides
sacras agito, vascula dividito.
Tum in Sanctam revertito, integris commolitis precator. Tum
sacrificium porrectum erit.

*iouie hostatu anostatu* |
49 *tursitu tremitu, hondu holtu, ninctu nepitu, sunitu sauitu, preplohotatu preuislatu. Tursa Iouia, futu*
50 *fons* | *pacer pase tua pople totar Iouinar, tote Iouine, erar nerus sihitir ansihitir, iouies hostatir an-*
51 *hostatir, erom* | *nomne, erar nomne.' Este trioper deitu.*
†*Enom iuenga peracrio tursituto, porse perca arsmatia*
52 *habiest et* | *prinuatur. Hondra furo sehemeniar hatuto totar pisi heriest. Pafe trif promom haburent, eaf*
53 *Acersoniem* | *fetu Turse Iouie popluper totar Iiouinar, totaper Iouina. Suront naratu puse uerisco Treblanir.*
54 *Aruio fetu,* | *persaea fetu, strusla, ficla prosesetir arsueitu, tases persnimu, poni fetu.*|

tos, iuvenes hastatos inhastatos terreto tremefacito, *pessumdato aboleto,* ninguito *inundato,* sonato *sauciato,* \*praeplauditato \*praevinculato. Torra Iovia, esto favens propitia pace tua populo civitatis Iguvinae, civitati Iguvinae, eius principibus cinctis incinctis, iuvenibus hastatis inhastatis, eorum nomini, eius nomini.' Istud ter dicito. Tum iuvencas ex opimis fuganto, qui virgam ritualem habebit et ' legati. Infra forum seminarium capiunto civitatis quisquis volet. Quas tris primum ceperint, eas in Acedonia facito Torrae Ioviae pro populo civitatis Iguvinae, pro civitate Iguvina. Item narrato ut ad portam Trebulanam. Frumenta facito, *humi stratas* facito, struem, offam prosectis addito, tacitus precator, posca facito.

---

40 †**Pustertiu pane puplu aterafust, iveka perakre tusetu**[1]|
41 **super kumne arfertur, prinuva-**
42 **tu tuf tusetutu,** | **hutra furu sehmeniar hatutu. Eaf iveka**|
43 **tre Akerunie fetu Tuse**
44 **Iuvie. Arviu ustetu,** | **puni fetu, peraia fetu, taçez pesnimu arepe arves.** |
45 **Kvestretie usaie svesu Vuvçis Titis Teteies.**

Postquam tertium populum lustraverit, iuvencam opimam fugato super comitio flamen, legati duas fuganto, infra forum seminarium capiunto. Eas iuvencas tris Acedoniae facito Torrae Ioviae. Frumenta ostendito, posca facito, *humi stratas* facito, tacitus precator adipibus frumentis.
Quaestura —— sua *Lucius Tetteius Titi f.*

---

[1] Aes tuseiu.

## VII B

1   *Pisi panupei fratrex fra-*
*trus Atiersier fust, erec sueso*
*fratrecate portaia seuacne*
2 *fratrom | Atiersio desenduf,*
*pifi reper fratreca parsest*
*erom ehiato, ponne iuengar*
3 *-tursiandu hertei, | appei ar-*
*fertur Atiersir poplom an-*
*dersafust. Sue neip portust*
*issoc pusei subra screhto est, |*
4 *fratreci motar sins a. CCC.*

Quisquis quandoque magister fratribus Atiediis erit, is suo magisterio portet hostias fratrum Atiedium duodecim, quas pro re collegii par est esse emissas, cum iuvencae fugentur oportet, ubi flamen Atiediis populum lustrave- rit. Si non portaverit ita, uti supra scriptum est, magistro multae sint asses CCC.

## I A

1   Este persklum aves anzer-
2 iates enetu | pernaies pusnaes.
3   Preveres Treplanes | Iuve Krapuvi tre buf fetu.
4   Arvia ustentu, | vatuva fe- rinefeitu, heris vinu heri puni, |
5 ukriper Fisiu, tutaper Iku-
6 vina feitu. Sevum | kutef pesnimu arepes arves. |
7   Pusveres Treplanes tref
8 sif kumiaf feitu | Trebe Iuvie ukriper Fisiu, tutaper Ikuvi-
9 na. | Supa sumtu, arvia usten-
10 tu,   puni   fetu,  |   kutef pesnimu arepes [1] arves.[1] |
11   Preveres Tesenakes tre
12 buf fetu, Marte Krapuvi | fetu ukripe Fisiu, tutaper Ikuvina.
13 Arviu ustentu, | vatuva ferine

Istud sacrificium avibus obser- vatis inito anticis posticis.
Ante portam Trebulanam Iovi Grabovio tris boves facito.
Frumenta ostendito, *exta in ferculo* facito, vel vino vel posca, pro arce Fisia, pro civitate Igu- vina facito. Totum murmurans precator adipibus frumentis.
Post portam Trebulanam tris sues gravidas facito Trebo Iovio pro arce Fisia, pro civitate Iguvi- na. Suppa sumito, frumenta os- tendito, posca facito, murmurans precator adipibus frumentis.
Ante portam Tesenacam tris boves facito, Marti Grabovio faci- to pro arce Fisia, pro civitate Igu- vina. Frumenta ostendito, *exta in*

[1] Aes are•arv•es.

fetu, puni fetu, kutef pesnimu ařpes arves. |

14 Pusveres Tesenakes tref
15 sif feliuf fetu | Fise Saçi ukriper Fisiu, tutaper Iku-
16 vina. | Puni fetu, supa sumtu,
17 arviu ustentu. Mefa, | vestiça ustetu, Fisuvi [1] fetu,
18 ukriper Fisiu fetu, | kapiř purtitaf sakref, etraf pur-
19 titaf, etraf | sakref, tutaper Ikuvina. Kutef pesnimu ařepes arves. |

20 Preveres Vehiies tref buf kaleřuf fetu Vufiune |
21 Krapuvi ukriper Fisiu,
22 tutaper Ikuvina. | Vatuva ferine fetu, heri vinu heri puni, |
23 arviu ustentu, kutef pesnimu ařepes arves. |

24 Pusveres Vehiíes tref hapi-
25 naf fetu Tefre Iuvie | ukriper Fisiu, tutaper Ikuvina. Puste
26 asiane fetu, zeřef fetu, | pelsana fetu, arvia ustentu, puni
27 fetu, taçez pesnim|u ařiper arvis. Api habina purtiius,
28 surum pesuntru | fetu, esmik vestiçam preve fiktu,
29 Tefri Iuvi fetu ukri|per Fisiu, tutaper Ikuvina, testruku peři kapiře peřum feit|u.

30 Api eřek [2] purtiius, enuk surum pesuntrum feitu staf|lii

*ferculo* facito, posca facito, murmurans precator adipibus frumentis.

Post portam Tesenacam tris sues lactentis facito Fisio Sancio pro arce Fisia, pro civitate Iguvina. Posca facito, suppa sumito, frumenta ostendito. Libum, libamentum ostendito, Fisovio facito, pro arce Fisia facito, capides porrectas sacras, alteras porrectas, alteras sacras, pro civitate Iguvina. Murmurans precator adipibus frumentis.

Ante portam Veiam tris boves frontem albam habentis facito Voviono Grabovio pro arce Fisia, pro civitate Iguvina. *Exta in ferculo* facito, vel vino vel posca, frumenta ostendito, murmurans precator adipibus frumentis.

Post portam Veiam tris *agnas* facito Tefro Iovio pro arce Fisia, pro civitate Iguvina. *Post* —facito, sedens facito, *sepeliendas* facito, frumenta ostendito, posca facito, tacitus precator adipibus frumentis. Ubi *agnas* porrexeris, *figmentum suillum* facito, ei libamentum singillatim figito, Tefro Iovio facito pro arce Fisia, pro civitate Iguvina, ad dextrum pedem capidi fossam facito.

Ubi id porrexeris, tunc *figmentum* facito *ovillum,*

---

[1] Acs fiuvi.    [2] Aes efel.

31 uve, esmik[1] vestiça afiktu, ukri-
32 per Fisiu, tutaper Ikuvin|a[2] fei-
tu, nertruku peři kapiře peřum
33 feitu. Puni feitu. | Api su-
řuf purtiius,[3] enuk hapinaru
34 erus titu, zeřef | kumultu,
zeřef kumates[4] pesnimu. |

ei libamentum infigito, pro arce
Fisia, pro civitate Iguvina facito,
ad sinistrum pedem capidi fossam
facito. Posca facito. Ubi *figmenta* porrexeris, tum *agnarum
magmentum* dato, sedens commolito, sedens commolitis precator.

## I B

1 Vukukum Iuviu, pune uvef
2 furfaθ, tref vitluf turuf ⌊Marte
Huřie fetu pupluper tutas
Iiuvinas, tutaper Ikuvina. |
3 Vatuva ferine fetu, puni
fetu, arvia ustentu, kutep
4 pesnimu | ařepes arves.

Vukukum Kureties tref vitlup
5 turup Hunte Çe|fi feitu pu-
pluper tutas Iiuvinas, tutaper
6 Iiuvina. Vatuva | ferine
fetu, arvia ustentu, tenzitim
7 arveitu, heris vinu heris | puni
feitu, kutef persnimu aří-
pes arvis.
8 Inuk ukar pihaz fust. | Svepu
esumek esunu antervakaze,
vaçetumi se ;[5] avif azeriatu, |
9 verufe Treplanu kuvertu,
restef esunu feitu. |
10 ˙ Pune puplum aferum heries,
avef anzeriatu[6] etu pernaia|f
11 pustnaiaf. Pune kuvurtus,
krenkatrum hatu. Enumek |

Ad *aedem* Ioviam, cum ovis
purgant, tris vitulos tauros Marti
Hodio facito pro populo civitatis
Iguvinae, pro civitate Iguvina.
*Exta in ferculo* facitò, posca
facito, frumenta ostendito, murmurans precator adipibus frumentis.

Ad *aedem* Coredii tris vitulos
tauros Honto Cerrio facito pro
populo civitatis Iguvinae, pro
civitate Iguvina. *Exta in ferculo*
facito, frumenta ostendito, ——
addito, vel vino vel posca
facito, murmurans precator adipibus frumentis.

Tunc arx piata erit. Sive
*horum* sacrifici*orum* intervacatio
*sit, in vitiatum sit ;* avis observato, ad portam Trebulanam revertito, instaurans sacrificium facito.

Cum populum lustrare voles,
avis observatum ito anticas
posticas. Cum reverteris,
cinctum capito. Tunc

---

[1] Aes stafli iuvesmik.
[2] Aes ikuvinp|a.
[3] Aes purtitius.
[4] Aes kumats.
[5] Aes vakazevaçetumiseavif.
[6] Aes anzvriatu.

12 pir        ahtimem        ententu.
Pune pir entelus ahtimem, |
13 enumek        steplatu        parfam
14 tesvam tefe, tute Ikuvine. | Va-
pefem avieklufe kumpifiatu. Vea
15 aviekla esunume etu. | Prinuvatu
etutu, perkaf habetutu puniçate.
16 Pune menes | Akeřuniamem,
enumek        eturstamu        tuta
17 Tařinate,        trifu | Tařinate,
Turskum, Naharkum numem,
18 Iapuzkum numem : | 'svepis
habe, purtatulu pue mers
est, feitu uru pere mers est'. |
19 Pune prinuvatus staheren term-
nesku, enumek 'armamu [1] |
20 kateramu Ikuvinu'. Enumek
apretu tures et pure. Puni
21 amprefu|us, persnimu. Enumek
' etatu Ikuvinus'. Triiuper am-
22 prehtu, | triiuper pesnimu, triiu-
per 'etatu Ikuvinus'. Enumek|
28 prinuvatus çimu etutu, erahunt
vea çimu etutu prinuvatus. |
24        Funtlere trif apruf rufru
ute peiu feitu Çerfe Marti. |
25 Vatuvu ferine [2] fetu, arviu
26 ustentu, puni fetu, [3] | taçez
pesnimu arepe arves. |
27        Rupinie e tre purka rufra
28 ute peia fetu Prestate | Çer-
fie Çerfe Marties. Peřaia fei-
29 tu, arviu ustentu, | kapi
sakra aitu, vesklu vetu atru

ignem ad caerimonium imponito.
Cum ignem imposueris ad caerimonium, tunc stipulator parram
prosperam tibi, civitati Iguvinae.
Ad sellas auguralis nuntiato. Via
augurali in sacrificium ito. Legati eunto, virgas habento *calatoris.*
Cum venies in Acedoniam,
tunc exterminato civitatem
Tadinatem, tribum Tadinatem,
Tuscum, Narcum nomen,
Iapudicum nomen : 'siquis
*restat,* (eum) portato illuc quo ius
est, facito illo quod ius est'.
Cum legati stabunt ad ter-
minos, tunc 'ordinamini
*catervamini, Iguvini'. Tunc
ambito tauris et igne. Cum
ambieris, precator. Tunc
'itatote, Iguvini'. Ter ambito, ter precator, ter
'itatote, Iguvini'. Tunc
legati retro eunto, eadem
via retro eunto legati.

In Fontulis tris apros rubros
aut piceos facito Cerro Martio.
*Exta in ferculo* facito, frumenta
ostendito, posca facito, tacitus
precator adipibus frumentis.

In Rubinia tris porcas rubras
aut piceas facito Praestitae Cerriae Cerri Martii. *Humi stratas* facito, frumenta ostendito, capides
sacras agito, vascula dividito atra

---

[1] Aes armanu.        [2] Aes ferime.        [3] Aes feiu.

30 alfu, puni fetu, | taçez pesnimu ařeper arves. |

31     Tra Sate tref vitlaf feitu Tuse Çerfie Çerfe Marties. |

32 Peřaia feitu, arviu us-tetu, puni fetu, taçez pes-

33 nimu | ařeper arves. Pune purtinçus, kařetu, pufe apruf |

34 fakurent, puze erus teřa. Ape

35 erus teřust, pustru | kupifia-tu Rupiname, erus teřa. Ene tra Sahta kupifiaia, |

36 erus teřa. Enu Rupiname

37 pustru kuvertu, antakre | ku-mate pesnimu. Enu kapi sakra aitu, veaklu vetu. |

38 Enu Satame kuvertu, anta-kre kumate pesnimu. Enu

39 esunu | purtitu fust. |

40 Pustertiu pane puplu ateřafust, iveka perakre tusetu[1] |

41 super kumne ařfertur, prinuva-

42 tu tuf tusetutu, | hutra furu-sehmeniar hatutu. Eaf iveka |

43 tre Akeřunie fetu Tuse

44 Iuvie. Arviu ustetu, | puni fetu, peřaia fetu, taçez pesnimu ařepe arves. |

45 Kvestretie usaie svesu Vuvçis Titis Teteies.

alba, posca facito, tacitus precator adipibus frumentis.

Trans Sanctam tris vitulas faci-to Torrae Cerriae Cerri Martii. *Humi stratas* facito, frumenta os-tendito, posca facito, tacitus pre-cator adipibus frumentis. Cum porrexeris, vocato, ubi apros fecerint, ut *magmentum* det. Ubi *magmentum* dederit, retro nuntia-to in Rubiniam, *magmentum* det. Tum trans Sanctam nunties, magmentum det. Tum in Rubi-niam retro revertito, integris com-molitis precator. Tum capides sacras agito, vascula dividito. Tum in Sanctam revertito, inte-gris commolitis precator. Tum sacrificium porrectum erit.

Postquam tertium populum lustraverit, iuvencam opimam fu-gato super comitio flamen, lega-ti duas fuganto, infra forum seminarium capiunto. Eas iuven-cas tris Acedoniae facito Torrae Ioviae. Frumenta ostendito, pos-ca facito, *humi stratas* facito, taci-tus precator adipibus frumentis. Quaestura —— sua *Lucius Tetteius Titi f.*

---

[1] Aes tuseiu.

## II A

1 Pune karne speturie Atiieřie
2 aviekate naraklum | vurtus,
estu esunu fetu fratrusper
3 Atiieřie. Eu esunu | esu
naratu: 'peře karne spetu-
4 rie Atiieřie aviekate | aiu
urtu fefure, fetu puze neip
5 eretu'. Vestiçe Saçe | sa-
kre, Iuvepatre bum perakne,
Speture perakne restatu. |
6 Iuvie unu erietu sakre
pelsanu fetu. Arviu usten-
7 tu, | puni fetu, taçez pes-
nimu ařepe arves. Pune
8 purtiius, | unu suřu pesu-
tru fetu tikamne Iuvie,
9 kapiře | peřu preve fetu.
Ape purtiius suřu,[1] erus
10 tetu. Enu kuma|ltu, ku-
mate pesnimu. Ahtu Iuvip.
11 uve peraknem | peřaem
fetu, arviu ustentu, puni
fetu. Ahtu Marti abrunu |
12 perakne fetu, arviu uste-
tu, fasiu pruseçete ařveitu, |
13 peřae fetu, puni
fetu, trà ekvine fetu. |
14 Açetus perakne fetu. |
15 Huntia katle tiçel stakaz
16 est sume ustite | anter-
menzaru çersiaru. Heriiei
17 façiu ařfertur, avis | anzeriates
menzne kurçlasiu façia tiçit.

Cum carni *spectoriae Atiediae auspicatae nuntiatio mutaverit, ista sacrificia facito pro fratribus Atiediis. Ea sacrificia sic nuntiato: 'si carni *spectoriae Atiediae auspicatae *agitationes* ortae *fuerint*, facito quasi non consulto'. Vesticio Sancio hostiam, Iovi patri bovem sollemnem, Spectori hostiam instaurato. Iovio unum arietem sacrificum *sepeliendum* facito. Frumenta ostendito, posca facito, tacitus precator adipibus frumentis. Cum porrexeris, unum *suillum figmentum* facito dedicatione Iovio, capidi fossam singillatim facito. Ubi porrexeris *suillum*, *magmentum* dato. Tum commolito, commolitis precator. Actui Iovi patri ovem sollemnem *humi stratum* facito, frumenta ostendito, posca facito. Actui Marti aprum sollemnem facito, frumenta ostendito, farrea prosectis addito, (sacrificium) *humi stratum* facito, posca facito, trans *equinum* facito. *Ancitibus* hostiam facito.

Hontia catuli dedicatio statuta est summa *tempestate* intermenstruarum *cenariarum. Voluerit facere flamen, avibus observatis mense *ultimo* faciat decet.

---

[1] Aes purtiiusuřu.

18　Huntia fertu | katlu, ar-
　　via, struhçla, fikla, pune,
19　vinu, salu[1] maletu, | mantrah-
　　klu, veskla snata asnata,
20　umen fertu. Pir ase | an-
　　tentu. Esunu puni feitu.
　　　Hunte Iuvie ampentu ka-
21　tlu, | sakre sevakne, Petrunia-
　　per natine fratru Atiieřiu.
22　Esunu　|　peřae　futu.
　　Katles supa hahtu, sufafiaf
23　supaf hahtu. | Berus aplenies
　　pruseçia　kartu,　krematra
24　aplenia sutent|u. Peřu seri-
　　tu.[1] Arvia puni purtuvitu vesti-
25　katu ahtrepuřa|tu, pustin ançif
　　vinu. Nuvis ahtrepuřatu, 'tiu
26　puni tiu vinu' | teitu, berva
　　frehtef fertu. Puře nuvime
27　ferest, krematruf | sumel fertu.
　　Vestiçia peřume persnihmu.
28　Katles　tuva　tefra, | terti
　　erus　prusekatu.　Isunt
　　krematru prusektu. Struhçla |
29　fikla ařveitu. Katlu purtuvitu,
　　ampeřia persnihmu, aseçeta |
30　karne persnihmu, venpersun-
　　tra[2] persnihmu. Supa spantea |
31　pertentu. Veskles vufetes
　　persnihmu vestikatu ahtrepu-
32　řatu | ařpeltu statitatu. Supa
　　pustra perstu. Iepru erus
　　mani kuveitu. |

Hontia ferto catulum, frumenta, struem, offam, poscam,
vinum, salem molitum, mantele, vascula umecta non umecta,
unguen ferto. Ignem arae imponito. Sacrificium posca facito.

Honto Iovio impendito catulum, hostiam sollemnem, pro Petronia natione fratrum Atiedium.
Sacrificium *humi stratum* esto.
Catuli suppa capito, *partis exsertas* suppas capito. Veribus imple-
tis prosicias distribuito, *cremata
impleta supponito. *Pedem* servato. Frumenta posca porricito, libato,　tripodato,　in　vices
vino. Noviens tripodato, 'te
posca te vino' dicito, verua,
*fricta* ferto. Cum　nonum
feret, *cremata simul ferto.
Libamento in fossam precator.
Catuli duo carnes cremandas, tertium *magmentum* prosecato. Item
*cremata prosecato. Struem,
offam addito. Catulum porricito,
——— precator, non secta
carne precator, (carne) *ficticia* precator. Suppa lateralia
protendito. Vasculis votis
precator,　libato,　tripodato, admoveto, statuito. Suppa
retro *ponito.* ——— *magmentum* manu congerito.

---

[1] s expressed by the san (25, a).
[2] Aes eenpersuntra.

33 Spinamař etu. Tuvere
kapiřus pune fertu. Berva,
34 klavlaf a|anfehtaf, vesklu ena-
tu asnatu, umen fertu.
35 Kapiře Hunte | Iuvie vesti-
katu Petruniaper[1] natine fratru
36 Atiieřiu. Berus | sevaknis
persnihmu pert spinia. Isunt
37 klavles persnihmu. | Veskles
snate asnates sevaknis
spiniama persnihmu vestikatu |
38 ahtrepuřatu. Spina umtu,
umne sevakni persnihmu.
39 Manf easa | vutu.
Asama kuvertu. Asaku
vinu sevakni taçez persnihmu. |
40 Esuf pusme herter, erus
kuveitu teřtu. Vinu, pune
41 teřtu. | Struhçlas, fiklas, sufa-
fias kumaltu. Kapiře punes
42 vepuratu. | Antakres kuma-
tes persnihmu.[2] Amparihmu,
statita subahtu. Esunu |
43 purtitu futu. Katel asaku
pelsans futu. |
44 Kvestretie usaçe svesu Vuvçis Ti Teteies.

Ad *columnam* ito. Duabus in
capidibus poscam ferto. Verua,
clunis non coctas, vascula umecta non umecta, unguen ferto.
Capide Honto Iovio libato
pro Petronia natione fratrum
Atiedium. Veribus sollemnibus
precator trans *columnam*. Item
clunibus precator. Vasculis
umectis non umectis sollemnibus ad *columnam* precator, libato,
tripodato. *Columnam* unguito,
unguine sollemni precator.
Manus ex ara lavito.
Ad aram revertito. Apud aram
vino sollemni tacitus precator.
Ipse quem oportet, *magmentum*
congerito, dato. Vinum, poscam
dato. Struis, offae, *partis exser-*
*tae* commolito. Capide poscae
(*ignem*) *restinguito*. Integris commolitis precator. Surgito,
statuta deponito. Sacrificium
porrectum esto. Catulus apud
aram *sepeliendus* esto.
Quaestura —— sua *Lucius*
*Tetteius Ti. f.*

## II B

1 Semenies tekuries sim ka-
2 prum upetu. Tekvias | fameři-
as pumpeřias XII. 'Atiiеřiate,
3 etre Atiieřiate, | Klaverniie,
etre Klaverniie, Kureiate, etre

Sementivis decuriis suem, caprum deligito. Decuriales familiae *quincuriae XII. 'Atiediati,
alteri Atiediati, Claverniis,
alteris Claverniis, Curiati, alteri

---

[1] Aes petruniapert.       [2] Aes peramhniu.

4 Kureiate, | Satanes, etre Satane,    Curiati, Satanis, alteris Satanis,
Peieřiate, etre Peieřiate, Tale-    Peiediati, alteri Peiediati, Tale-
5 nate, | etre Talenate, Museiate,    nati, alteri Talenati, Musiati,
6 etre Museiate, Iuieskane, | etre    alteri Musiati, Iuiescanis, alteris
Iuieskanes, Kaselate, etre Kase-    Iuiescanis, Casilati, alteri Casi-
7 late, tertie Kaselate, | Peraz-    lati, tertiae Casilati, Peras-
nanie' teitu.    naniis' dicito.

Ařmune Iuve patre fetu.    Admoni Iovi patri facito.
8 Si pera|kne, sevakne upetu    Suem sollemnem, hostiam deli-
eveietu. Sevakne naratu.    gito, voveto. Hostiam nuntiato.
9 Arviu | ustetu, eu naratu    Frumenta ostendito, ea nuntiato
puze façefele[1] sevakne. Heri    quasi *sacrificabilem hostiam. Vel
10 puni | heri vinu fetu. Va-    posca vel vino facito. *Ture* (su-
putu Saçi ampetu. Ķapru    em) Sancio impendito. Caprum
11 perakne, seva|kne upetu, eve-    sollemnem, hostiam deligito, vo-
ietu, naratu. Çive ampetu,    veto, nuntiato. Citra impendito,
12 fesnere purtu|etu. Ife fertu,    in fano porricito. Eo ferto,
tafle e pir fertu, kapres pru-    in tabula ignem ferto, capri pro-
13 seçetu | ife ařveitu. Persutru    secta eo addito. *Figmentum*
vaputis, mefa, vistiça feta    *turibus*, libo, libamento facto
14 fertu. | Sviseve fertu pune,    ferto. In sino ferto poscam,
etre sviseve vinu fertu, tertie |    in altero sino vinum ferto, in ter-
15 sviseve utur fertu. Pistu    tio sino aquam ferto. Pistum
niru fertu, vepesutra fertu, |    — ferto, (carnem) *ficticiam* ferto,
16 mantraklu fertu, pune fertu.    mantele ferto, poscam ferto.
17 Pune fesnafe benus, | kabru    Cum in fanum veneris, caprum
purtuvetu. Vaputu Saçi Iuve-    porricito. *Ture* Sancio Iovi
18 patre prepesnimu. | Vepesu-    patri praefator. (Carne) *ficticia*
tra pesnimu, veskles pesnimu,    precator, vasculis precator,
19 atrepuřatu, | ařpeltu, statitatu.    tripodato, admoveto, statuito.
Vesklu pustru pestu, ranu |    Vascula retro *ponito*, ———
20 pesnimu, puni pesnimu, vinu    precator, posca precator, vino
21 pesnimu, une pesni|mu. Enu    precator, aqua precator. Tum
erus tetu.    *magmentum* dato.

---

[1] Aes façefete.

Vitlu vufru pune heries |
22 façu, eruhu tiçlu sestu
23 Iuvepatre. Pune seste, | urfeta
manuve habetu. Estu iuku
24 habetu : | 'Iupater Saçe, tefe
estu vitlu vufru sestu'. |
25 Purtifele triiuper teitu, triiu-
26 per vufru naratu, | fetu[1] Iu-
vepatre Vuçiiaper natine fratru
27 Atiieřiu. | Pune anpenes, kri-
katru testre e uze habetu.
28 Ape apel|us, mefe atentu.
Ape purtuvies, testre e uze
29 habetu | krikatru. Arviu us-
tetu, puni fetu.

Vitulum votivum cum voles
facere, eadem dedicatione sistito
Iovi patri. Cum sistis, orbitam
in manu habeto. Istas preces
habeto: 'Iuppiter Sanci, tibi
istum vitulum votivum sisto'.
*Porricibilem ter dicito, ter
votivum nuntiato, facito Iovi
patri pro *Lucia* natione fratrum
Atiedium. Cum impendes, cinctum in dextro umero habeto.
Ubi impenderis, libo imponito.
Ubi porricies, in dextro umero
habeto cinctum. Frumenta ostendito, posca facito.

## III, IV

III Esunu fuia herter sume |
2 ustite sestentasiaru | urna-
siaru. Huntak vuke prumu
4 pehatu. | Inuk uhturu urtes
5 puntis | frater ustentu-
6 ta, puře | fratru mersus
7 fust | kumnakle. Inuk
8 uhtur vapeře | kumnakle sistu.
9 Sakre, uvem uhtur | teitu,
puntes terkantur. Inumek
10 sakre, | uvem urtas puntes
11 fratrum upetuta. | Inumek
via mersuva arvamen etuta. |
12 Erak pir persklu uřetu.
13 Sakre, uvem | kletra fertuta
aituta. Arven kletram |
14 amparitu. Eruk esunu futu.

Sacrificium fiat oportet summa
*tempestate* sextantariarum *urna-
riarum. *Puteum in aede* primum
piato. Tum auctorem, surgentibus quinionibus, fratres ostend-
dunto, quomodo fratrum ex
moribus erit in conventu. Tum
auctor in sella in conventu con-
sidito. Hostiam, ovem auctor dicito, quiniones *suffragentur.* Tunc
hostiam, ovem surgentes quiniones fratrum deligunto. Tunc
via solita in arvum eunto.
Ea ignem cum precatione adoleto. Hostiam, ovem lectica fe-
runto, agunto. In arvo lecticam
conlocato. Illic sacrificium esto.

---

[1] Aes feiu.

15 Kletre tuplak | prumum an-
tentu, inuk çihçeřa ententu, |
16 inuk kazi ferime antentu. Isunt
17 feřehtru | antentu, isunt sufe-
18 řaklu antentu. Seples | ahesnes
tris kazi astintu, feřehtru
19 etres tris | ahesnes astintu,
20 suferaklu tuves ahesnes | an-
stintu. Inenek vukumen esu-
21 numen etu. Ap | vuku kukehes,
iepi persklumař kařitu. Vuke
22 pir | ase antentu. Sakre
sevakne upetu. Iuvepatre |
23 prumu ampentu testru sese
24 asa fratrusper | Atiieřies,
ahtisper eikvasatis, tutape
25 Iiuvina, | trefiper Iiuvina.
Tiçlu sevakni teitu. |
26 Inumek uvem sevakni upetu.
27 Puemune | Pupřike apentu.
Tiçlu sevakni naratu. |
28 Iuka mersuva uvikum habetu
29 fratruspe | Atiieřie, ahtisper
30 eikvasatis, tutaper | Iiu-
vina, trefiper Iiuvina. Sakre |
31 vatra ferine feitu, eruku
32 aruvia feitu. Uvem | pe-
řaem pelsanu feitu. Ererek
33 tuva tefra | spantimař
prusekatu, eřek peřume purtu-
34 vitu, | struçla ařveitu. Inumek
etrama . spanti tuva tefra |
35 prusekatu, eřek ereçluma
IV Puemune Pupřike ‖ purtuvitu,
erarunt struhçlas eskamitu

Lecticae *furcam* primum imponito, tum *cancellos* imponito,
tum —— —— imponito. Item
—— imponito, item ——
imponito. Simpulis ahenis
tribus —— distinguito, ——
alteris tribus ahenis distinguito,
—— duobus ahenis distin-
guito. Tum in *aedem* in sacrificium ito. Ubi *aedem incendet,
ibi* ad precationem vocato. In
*aede* ignem arae imponito. Hostiam sollemnem deligito. Iovi patri primum impendito dextrorsus
ab ara pro fratribus Atiediis, pro
*caerimoniis collegialibus*, pro civitate Iguvina, pro tribu Iguvina.
Dedicationem sollemnem dicito.
Tunc ovem sollemnem deligito.
Pomono Publico impendito. Dedicationem sollemnem narrato.
Preces solitas apud ovem habeto
pro fratribus Atiediis, pro *caerimoniis collegialibus*, pro civitate
Iguvina, pro tribu Iguvina. Hostiam *in extari ferculo* facito, cum
ea frumenta facito. Ovem *humi
stratum sepeliendum* facito. Eius
duo carnes cremandas ad latus
prosecato, tum in fossam porricito, struem addito. Tunc
alterum ad latus duo carnes
cremandas prosecato, tum ad
sacrarium Pomono Publico porricito, eiusdem struis ——

2 aveitu.  |  Inumek tertiama
spanti triia tefra prusekatu,  |
3 erek  supru  sese  erecluma
4 Vesune Puemunes  |  Pupŗiçes
purtuvitu, struhçla petenata
5 isek  |  aŗveitu.  Ererunt [1] ka-
6 piŗus Puemune,  |  Vesune pur-
tuvitu.  Asamaŗ erecŗlumaŗ [2]  |
7 aseçetes karnus,  iseçeles  et
8 vempesuntres, | supes sanes per-
9 tentu, persnimu, aŗpeltu,  | sta-
titatu.  Veskles snates asnates
10 sevakne  |  erecŗluma  persnimu
Puemune  Pupŗike,  Vesune  |
11 Puemunes Pupŗikes.  Klavles
12 persnihmu | Puemune Pupŗike [3]
13 et Vesune Puemunes  |  Pupŗikes
pustin  erecŗlu.  Inuk  ere-
14 çlu  umtu,  |  putrespe  erus.
Inuk     vestiçia,     mefa
15 Purtupite  |  skalçeta  kunikaz
16 apehtre esuf testru sese | asa
asama    purtuvitu,    sevakne
17 sukatu.  |  Inumek  vesteça, [4]
persuntru supu erecŗle Hule |
18 sevakne    skalçeta    kunikaz
19 purtuviθu.  Inumek [5] |  vestiçia
persuntru Turse super erecŗle
20 sevakne  |  skalçeta  kunikaz
pŗurtuvitu.  Inumek tehteŗim  |
21 etu veltu, eŗek persuntre an-
22 tentu. Inumek | arçlataf vasus
ufestne sevaknef purtuvitu.  |

addito.  Tunc   tertium   ad
latus tris carnes cremandas prosecato, tum sursus ad sacrarium
Vesonae    Pomoni    Publici
porricito,  struem  pectinatam
item addito.  Isdem capidibus
Pomono,  Vesonae  porricito.
Ad    aram    ad    sacrarium
non sectis carnibus, insectis et
*ficticiis*, suppis sanis protendito,
supplicato, admoveto, statuito.
Vasculis umectis non umectis sollemnibus ad sacrarium precator Pomono Publico, Vesonae
Pomoni ˙ Publici.    Clunibus
precator Pomono Publico et
Vesonae Pomoni Publici in singulis sacrariis.  Tunc sacrarium
unguito, utriusque *magmentum*
(dato).  Tunc libamentum, libum
*Porricienti* ex patera genu nixus
extrinsecus ipse dextrorsus ab
ara ad aram porricito, sollemne
declarato.   Tunc  libamentum,
*figmentum* sub sacrario Hulae
sollemne ex patera genu nixus
porricito.   Tunc  libamentum,
*figmentum* Torrae super sacrario
sollemne ex patera genu nixus
porricito.    Tunc   *tegumentum*
ito deligito, tum *figmentum* imponito.  Tunc arculatas vasis
*operculatis* sollemnis porricito.

---

[1] Aes erererunt.   [2] Aes erecŗlamaŗ.   [3] Aes pupŗikes.   [4] Aes vesveça.   [5] Aes inuntek.

23 Inumk pruzuře kebu sevakne
24 persnihmu | Puemune Pupřiçe.
25 Inumek kletra, veskles | vufetes
26 sevaknis, persnihmu[1] | Vesune
　　Puemunes Pupřçes.　Inumek
27 svepis heri, | ezariaf antentu.
28 Inumek erus taçez | tertu.
　　Inumek kumaltu, ařkani |
29 kanetu, kumates persnihmu.
30 Esuku | esunu uřetu, tapis-
31 tenu habetu, pune | frehtu
　　habetu.　Ap itek fakust,
32 purtitu | futu.　Huntak piři
33 prupehast, eřek | ures punes
　　neiřhabas.

Tunc *praestante* cibo sollemni
precator　Pomono　Publico.
Tunc　lectica,　vasculis　votis
sollemnibus,　precator　Vesonae Pomoni　Publici.　Tunc
siquis　vult,　*escas*　imponito.
Tunc *magmentum* tacitus dato.
Tunc　commolito,　cantum
canito, commolitis　precator.
Cum hoc sacrificium adoleto, *cal-*
*dariolam* habeto, poscam *calidam*
habeto.　Ubi　ita　fecerit,
porrectum esto.　*Puteum* cum
ante piabit, tum illis poscis
ne adhibeant.

---

[1] Aes persihmu.

BRIEF COMMENTARY[1] ON THE IGUVINIAN TABLES

## V

V a 1–13. First Decree. The flamen is to provide whatever is essential for the ceremony, and select the victims.

V a 2. **urnasier.** Probably 'Festival of the Urns'. The **plenasier urnasier** are distinguished from the **sestentasiaru urnasiaru** (III 2). But it is not certain whether the adjectives refer to the capacity of the vessels used, or to the time of year at which the festivals were held. In the latter case **plenasier** would refer to those occurring at the end of the year, and **sestentasiaru** to those occurring at the end of one sixth of the year, that is two months from the beginning.

V a 2–3. **uhtretie** etc. The **uhtur**, as appears from III 4–8, was not a regular official like the **kvestur** or **fratreks**, but one selected for a special occasion, perhaps a sort of chairman.

V a 4. **eikvasese**, perhaps related to L. *aequus* (**29**, *a*), but of obscure suffix-formation, probably means 'members of the brotherhood', equivalent to **fratrus**, or else, taken as Gen. Sg., denotes the brotherhood itself. In the Acta Arvalium we find both *magister fratrum Arvalium* and *magister conlegi fratrum Arvalium*. Cf. also **eikvasatis** III 24, 29.

V a 7 ff. "Let him select the sacrificial victims, and when they are given over let him inspect them to see if (see **316**) they (lit. any of them; see **366**) are to be accepted, and in case of a triple offering let him inspect them in the country to see if they are to be accepted." **puře teřte** is best taken as an impersonal construction, **puře** being the conjunction 'quod, cum' (**202**, 1).

V a 11. **felsva**, if connected with L. *holus* (**149**, *b*), might denote the 'garlands', or, more probably, the vegetables used in the case of 'fireless offerings' (**263**, 2), that is those which were not burnt-offerings.

V a 13. See **263**, 1, **299**, 7, footnote p. 236.

V a 14–b 7. Second Decree. Statement of the fees for the performance of certain rites (cf. CIL. VI 820). When the banquet of the brotherhood takes place (cf. the banquets of the Arval Brothers), the magister (**fratreks**) or quaestor (cf. *magister collegi* and *quaestores collegi*, CIL. III, p. 925) is to take a vote as to whether the banquet has been properly arranged, and, in case the majority of those present. declare that it has not been properly arranged, a further vote must be taken to determine the penalty for the flamen.

---

[1] Hardly more than a summary of contents. For most points the student must rely on the translation and the glossary, with the references there given.

V a 15-16.  **kumnahkle** and **ukre** may be Loc. Sg., or Dat. Sg. with the following verbs; **eikvasese** is Dat. Pl. with the following verbs, or Gen. Sg. (see note to l. 4) with **ukre**.

V a 17.  **apelust.**  This verb, as is clear from the succession of events here and in II b 27, is used of the initial ceremony in the sacrifice, preceding the laying of the victim upon the altar (**purtitu** l. 18).  But it is not clear precisely what the ceremony referred to is, whether the formal devotion of the victim to the god, or its preparation, or even the actual slaughter (cf. *inter caesa et porrecta*, Cic. Att. 5, 18, 1), though this last gets no support from the use of L. *impendō*.  The object expressed or understood is always an animal.[1]

V a 20.  **subra spafu**, see **308**, *b*.

V a 23 ff.  See **313, 316** ; on **prufe** si l. 27, see **307** ; on **pepurkurent herifi** b 5, 6, see **315**.

V b 8-18.  Statement of contributions to be made regularly by certain *gentes* to the Atiedian brothers, and of portions of flesh to be awarded them by the brothers on the occasion of the decurial festivals.  The two gentes mentioned here are among the ten (making up the decuria) enumerated in II b, and this passage is doubtless only the conclusion of a decree fixing the contributions and allotments of flesh for all ten, the main part being on one of the lost tables.

### VI, VII a, and I

#### *Purification of the Sacred Mount*

VI a 1—VI b 47 = I a 1—I b 9

VI a 1-21 (I a 1-2).  Introductory Auspices.  The sacrifice is to be preceded by the taking of auspices (so in I and VI).  Further details (only in VI): the formulae passed between the augur and flamen ; warning against interruption ; boundaries of the 'templum' ; formula of announcement of the auspices ; some general prescriptions applicable to all the following sacrifices.

VI a 6-7.  It is quite possible that **arsir** is not 'alius', but Dat.-Abl. Pl. of *arsie* 'sancte', meaning 'ceremonies'.  In this case the subject of *mugatu* as well as of *andersistu* is indefinite, and the use of *pisi* in l. 7 and not in l. 6 is due to the change from the passive impersonal construction.  The meaning would

---

[1] In II b 10 **vaputu** is commonly regarded as the object of **ampetu**, but it is better to understand **si** 'suem' and take **vaputu** as Abl. Sg. used like **vaputis** II b 13 (**293**).

then be " One shall not make a noise or interrupt the ceremonies until the augur returns. If there is a noise or any one interrupts the ceremonies, it will make the sacrifice void".

VI a 8–11. In spite of the most exhaustive discussion and comparison of passages in Latin authors bearing on the same subject, as Livy 1, 18, 6–9, there is the widest divergence of opinion as to the relations of the points mentioned. It seems clear however that l. 10 means not 'from the uppermost corner to the augural seats (and further) to the city limits', but 'from the uppermost corner at the augural seats to the city limits'. For l. 11, see **288**.

VI a 12–14. The words designate buildings and localities in the city and, naturally, are for the most part obscure.

VI a 20. See **315**.

VI a 22–57 (I a 2–6). First Sacrifice. Sacrifice of three oxen to Jupiter Grabovius in front of the Trebulan gate. A sort of preamble or opening prayer is followed by three long prayers in identical words for each of the three offerings, and these again by a brief general prayer in conclusion. All these prayers are given only in VI. Then come prescriptions for various rites connected with the sacrifice (also in I). For the phraseology of the prayers compare those given by Cato, De Agric. 132, 134, 139, 141; e.g. *Iuppiter, te hoc ferto ommovendo bonas preces precor, uti sies volens propitius mihi, domo, liberisque meis, familiaeque meae mactus hoc ferto.*

VI a 22. *sobocau suboco.* The interpretation 'invoco invocationes' (**279**) is, in spite of the unusual order, far more probable than 'invocavi invoco', which involves various grammatical difficulties.

VI a 26. *orer ose.* The interpretation is very doubtful. It has been taken as 'his (donis) macte', going with the preceding, as 'illius anni' going with the following, and as 'cuiuspiam opere' 'by any one's work'. This last suggestion gives the easiest solution for *ose* (cf. *osatu* 'operator') and suits well the context (if, by any one's doings, through any one's fault, etc.). But one hesitates to separate *orer* from the pronominal forms *uru, ures,* etc., for which the meaning 'any' cannot be maintained. The translation given in the text adopts the comparison of *ose* with *opere*, but retains for *orer* the meaning 'illius' or in this case better 'huius'. This could only refer to the piaculum, and the phrase would be an anticipation of what is given at the close of the sentence, *esu bue* etc. But no great confidence in this view is entertained.

*pir orto est.* The Arval Brothers institute a piaculum if the trees of the sacred grove are struck by lightning.

VI a 27. *pusei neip heritu.* See **294, a.**

VI a 30. For *castruo* the usual translation 'fundos' is in this passage ·more attractive than 'capita', but see footnote, p. 236 f.

VI a 32. See **322**.

VI a 54. See **17**, 17.

VI a 56. The *mefa spefa* (see **110**, 3 with *a*), for which **mefa** alone is used in the older tables, may mean simply 'libation cake,' but more probably 'cake besprinkled (with salt?)'. Cf. L. *mola salsa*.

VI a 57. The meaning of the frequently recurring *uatuo ferine fetu* is very uncertain, the translation given representing only one of several possibilities (for *ferine* see **178**, 6, note). Where the phrase is used, the victims are oxen, bull-calves, or boars.

### VI a 58–59 (I a 7–10). Second Sacrifice. Sacrifice of three pregnant sows to Trebus Iovius behind the Trebulan gate. The prayers used in the first sacrifice are to be repeated.

The sacrifice is to be made *persae*, a word which probably means 'stretched on the ground' (cf. *persom* 'solum, fossam'), referring to the manner in which the victims were slain. It is used of sows, sucking pigs, heifers, and heifer-calves, also of a sheep, a boar, and a dog. An accompanying operation in such cases was the removal of the *sopo* 'under parts' (Grk. ὕπτια), the mention of which is nearly always preceded by the statement that the sacrifice is to be *persae* (pefae etc.). Cf. especially II a 22–32. But one act implies the other, and VI a 58–59 has only *persae fetu*, while the parallel I a 7–10 has only **supa sumtu**.

### VI b 1–2 (I a 11–13). Third Sacrifice. Sacrifice of three oxen to Mars Grabovius in front of the Tesenacan gate. The prayers used in the first sacrifice are to be repeated.

### VI b 3–18 (I a 14–19). Fourth Sacrifice. Sacrifice of three sucking pigs to Fisus Sancius behind the Tesenacan gate. Prayers of the first sacrifice to be repeated. Then comes an offering of cakes etc. to Fisovius Sancius, accompanied by a prayer differing in some phrases from those used before. This is followed by some further special ceremonies.

VI b 4. *mandraclo* etc. At Rome the flamen sacrificed to Fides with the right hand wrapped in white cloth (Livy 1, 21, 4; Serv. ad Aen. 1, 292). Some Umbrian coins of Tuder bear the device of a right hand wrapped with a band about the wrist and base of fingers, crossing on the back (see Lepsius, Insc. Umbricae et Oscae, table **xxix**). The *difue* doubtless refers to the manner of binding.

VI b 5. For *sopo*, see above, on VI a 58; for the use of *postro*, see **306**.

VI b 11. See **325**.

VI b 16. *erus.* This denotes a supplementary offering by which the ceremony was completed. Sometimes it is used alone, sometimes with a Genitive designating the kind of offering to which it forms the complement, as here. Cf. especially VI b 38 ff. and VII a 43 ff. with notes. The word is probably from \*aisus, related to O. aisusis 'sacrificiis', U. esono-, etc. See **112**, *a*. The lack of rhotacism in the final may be attributed to the dissimilating influence of the preceding *r*.

VI b 17. *uestisia sopa purome*. See **306**. The meaning of *efurfatu* (and *furfant* VI b 43) is uncertain, but some such sense as 'purify' or 'consecrate' is probable. There is no plausible etymology.

VI b 19–21 (I a 20–23). Fifth Sacrifice. Sacrifice of three oxen with white foreheads to Vovionus Grabovius in front of the Veian gate. Prayers of the first sacrifice to be repeated.

VI b 22–42 (I a 24–34). Sixth Sacrifice. Sacrifice of three lambs (?) to Tefer Iovius behind the Veian gate. Prayers of the first sacrifice to be repeated. Then follow supplementary offerings, consisting probably of cakes made in the form of animals, with the usual prayers and various accompanying rites with the cups, the trench, etc.

VI b 22. *pelsana*. The most probable explanation is that this word refers to the burial of the remains of the victims. It is used also of a ram (II a 6), a dog (II a 43), and a sheep (III 32). And in VI b 40 the offerings called *pesondro* are to be put in the trench and buried. For the form see **262**, 1, *a*.

VI b 24 ff. *pesondro sorsom*. The first word, the etymology of which is wholly obscure, is most plausibly explained as referring to a symbolic offering, a sort of 'animal cracker' offered as a substitute for the animal itself. Cf. '*Et sciendum, in sacris simulata pro veris accipi. Unde cum de animalibus, quae difficile inveniuntur, est sacrificandum, de pane vel cera fiunt et pro veris accipiuntur*, Serv. ad Aen. 2, 116 ; *Tauri verbenaeque in commentario sacrorum significat ficta farinacea*, Festus ed. Thewrewk, p. 548.

*sorsom* (suŕum) is probably the same word as *sorser* 'suilli', V b 12, 17, while the contrasting *staflare* (VI b 37) refers to some animal kept in a stall, probably a sheep (cf. staflii uve I a 30 [1]). But the 'gingerbread pig' was the favorite form of the symbolic offering, so much so that in I a 30 suŕum pesuntrum is used as a generic term equivalent to the simple *pesondro* of VI b 40, the kind of animal to be represented, in this case not a pig, being shown by the following adjectives. Similarly Acc. Pl. suŕuf I a 33 is used substantively, equivalent to *pesondro* VI b 37, of the two kinds of cakes which had been mentioned, only one of which was in the form of a pig. The term *sorsom* is also found in its specific sense, as in VI b 37, 38; but in VI b 38, 39, we find also the extended form *sorsalir*, *sorsalem*, contrasted with *staflarem*.

---

[1] Aes stafli iuvesmik. To correct this to staflare esmik is entirely unnecessary, for staflii can be Acc. Sg. of a stem \*staßiio-, like *tertim*, terti, from \*tertio- (**91**, 1, **172**).

The order of events in this, the most complicated series of ceremonies, is as follows.

Sacrifice of the lambs with the usual prayers.

Offering of the *pesondro sorsom* at the right foot, with accompanying libation.

Making trench for the cup.

Offering of the libation and the *erus*.

Prayer to Tefer Iovius.

Offering of the *pesondro staflare* at the left foot.

Making trench for the cup.

Prayer repeated.

Offering of the *erus* of the *prosecta* (of the lambs).

Offering of the *erus* of the libation accompanying the *pesondro sorso*, in the trench at the right foot, where the *pesondro sorso* was offered.

Offering of the libation accompanying the *pesondro staflare* at the left foot, and offering of its *erus*.

Placing the *pesondro sorsalem* in the trench.

Placing the *pesondro staflare* in the trench.

Throwing on the vessels used in connection with the *pesondro*.

Breaking of cakes with prayers.

**VI b 43-44 `(I b 1-4). Seventh Sacrifice.** Sacrifice of three bull-calves to Mars Hodius at the Jovian temple (?). Prayers of the first sacrifice repeated.

**VI b 45-46 (I b 4-7). Eighth Sacrifice.** Sacrifice of three bull-calves to Hontus Cerrius at the temple (?) of Coredius. Prayers of the first sacrifice repeated.

**VI b 47 (I b 7-9). Conclusion.** Then shall the Mount be purified. In case of any omission the ceremony is vitiated and one must return to the Trebulan gate and begin anew.

The sentence *suepo esome* etc. is perfectly clear in its general meaning, but the exact construction is difficult. The most natural translation would be 'If this ceremony through any omission is vitiated, take auspices, etc.', taking *anderuacose* as a compound in the ablative. But there is no reasonable explanation of *uacose* as an ablative. This is rather to be taken (with Brugmann, Ber. sächs. Gesells. 1890, 217 ff.) as *uacos-se* 'vacatio sit', *uacos* being Nom. Sg. from *ụakāti-s*. *uasetom-e* will then be an adverbial phrase 'in vitiatum', like L. *incassum*. The corresponding phrase in I b *vaçetumise* is probably to be separated *vaçetum-i se*, the only difference being that the Present Subjunctive instead of the Future Indicative is used. But some take *ise* as a form of the verb 'to go'. *esome esono* (esumek esunu) is probably Gen. Pl., *ander* going with *uacos*, making a compound 'intervacatio'. But it has also been taken as Acc. Sg. governed by the following *ander*.

## Lustration of the People

### VI b 48—VII a 54 = I b 10-45

Compare the description of the Roman Lustration, Dionys. Hal. Antiq. Rom. 4, 22, which we quote here from the Latin translation of the Didot edition as follows : *Tunc igitur Tullius, censu perfecto, postquam iussit omnes cives cum armis adesse in campo, eorum qui sunt ante urbem maximo, et equites in turmas scripsit et pedites in acie collocavit, et milites levis armaturae in suis quosque centuriis, lustrationem instituit tauro, ariete, et hirco. Has hostias postquam ter circa exercitum circumagi iussit Marti, cui campus is sacer est, immolavit.*

VI b 48 — VII a 2 (I b 10-23). Introductory Ceremonies. Expulsion of the Aliens. Circuit of the People. The auspices are taken in the same way. as for the Purification of the Sacred Mount. After assuming the proper paraphernalia, the flamen and two assistants march with the victims by the Augural Way to the suburb Acedonia. Proclamation is made expelling the aliens. The Iguvinians are ordered to form in companies. The flamen and assistants march about them three times with the victims (bulls) and the fire. At the end of each circuit a prayer is made invoking misfortune upon the aliens and blessings upon the Iguvinians.

VI b 49-50. "One shall put on the fire. When it is carried to the ceremony, the one with the official staff shall carry the receptacle for the fire. He shall carry it lighted on his right shoulder." As stated in I b 20 the fire is carried about the people.

VI b 54-55 (I b 18). *nosue ier*, etc. There are widely different interpretations of this passage. Some take *habe* as meaning 'has possessions' and assume a concession to the metics or resident foreigners, who are to remove to a certain place and perform separate ceremonies. But in I b the proclamation begins with *svepis habe*, and it is more natural to take this as a threat than as a concession. The translation given in the text seems best suited to the two versions.

VI b 56 (I b 19-20). *arsmahamo caterahamo.* Compare the disposition of the Roman people in the passage quoted above.

VI b 60. For the verbs, some of which are obscure, see the Glossary.

VII a 3-5 (I b 24-26). Sacrifice of three bulls to Cerrus Martius at Fontuli, accompanied by the prayers used at the Trebulan gate.

VII a 5. The *erus* is not to be added until announcement is made of the third sacrifice. Cf. l. 43.

VII a 6–40 (I b 27–30).   Sacrifice of three sows to Praestita Cerria at Rubinia, with the prayers used at the Trebulan gate.   Ceremonies with the black vessels and the white vessels. ·With the former the prayer is to bring misfortune to the aliens, with the latter to avert misfortune from the Iguvinians.   Offering to Fisovius Sancius accompanied by the prayer used behind the Tesenacan gate.

VII a 11, 27.   *atero* clearly means ruin, though of uncertain etymology. Perhaps from *\*ap-terom* (by 121), a 'rubbing away' (L. *terō*), and so 'destruction'.   Cf. L. *dēleō* 'rub off, destroy'.[1]

VII a 41–45 (I b 31–39).   Sacrifice of three calves to˙Torra Cerria across the Sacred Way, with˙ the prayers used at the Trebulan gate.   When this is completed the order is given to add the *erus* at the place where the boars were sacrificed, then at Rubinia, then across the Sacred Way.   Then they return to Rubinia and pray with the broken cakes, after which they come back to the Sacred Way and do the same.

VII a 46–51.   Prayer to Torra Iovia in the same words as that made at the end of each circuit.   To be repeated three times.

VII a 46.   *tefru-to.*  ' From (the place of) the burnt-offering', that is, the place where the sacrifice mentioned in l. 41 took place.

VII a 51–54 (I b 40–44).   Pursuit and sacrifice of the heifers.

In the older version three heifers are let loose, one by the flamen, two by the assistants, and then caught and sacrificed.  In VII more than three (apparently twelve; cf. VII b) are let loose and the first three caught are sacrificed.

## VII b

Provision that the magister shall provide the victims.

VII b 1–2.   *seuacne . . . desenduf . . . ehiato.*   The general word for victims is used in the masculine (cf. *ehiato*) in spite of the fact that the heifers (*iuengar*) are meant.  ' He shall furnish the twelve victims which are to be let out on the occasion of the pursuit of the heifers.'

---

[1] Cf. I.F. 11, 14.

## II

**II a 1–14.** Sacrifices to be made in case of unfavorable auspices.

II a 1–2.  **naraklum vurtus.**  Cf. *extorum mutatio*, Cic. de div. 2, 35.

II a 3 f.  Parallel with VI a 26 etc.  See **128, a.**

**II a 15–43.** Dog-sacrifice to Hontus Iovius. Hontus was doubtless a divinity of the lower world and the rite one of purification.

krematra, krematruf, II a 23, 26, probably denote some sort of vessels used in roasting the meat (cf. L. *cremō*). But in II a 28 **krematru** as object of **prusektu** must be used of the meat itself.

**II b.** Sacrifices at the decurial festivals of the federated families. Ten *gentes* are named, some subdivided, making twenty families.

II b 14–15.  **sviseve** evidently denotes some sort of vessel for holding liquids, so that connection with L. *sinum* is attractive. The latter might be from \**s(u)it-s-no-* (cf. also *situla*), and the first part of U. **sviseve** might be from \**suit-s-*, but the suffix is wholly obscure.

## III–IV

The more private annual ceremonies of the brotherhood, like the festival of Dea Dia among the Arval brothers. Owing to the great number of technical terms not occurring elsewhere, the meaning of a considerable portion of these tables is obscure.

### *Relative Chronology of the Tables*

The universally adopted numbering of the Tables is that of Lepsius, though opinions vary as to the correctness of this order for I–IV. The probability, however, is that these tables were actually inscribed in this order. For in the form of the letters III and IV occupy a position midway between I and II on the one side and V a–b 7 on the other. But, as some or all may be copies of older inscriptions, this does not necessarily mean the same order of composition. Judging by orthographical peculiarities there is some evidence that III and IV are copies of inscriptions earlier than I and II, and that II a 15–end (dog-sacrifice) is earlier in composition than II a 1-14. Within I and II various divisions are to be noted, corresponding to subject-matter, namely I a–b 9 (Purification of Sacred Mount), I b 9–end (Lustration of People), II a 1-14 (offering in case of bad omens), II a 15–end (dog-sacrifice), II b (ceremonies of the Decurial Festivals). The order of composition is possibly, though by no means certainly, III–IV, II a 15–end, I a, b, II a 1-14, II b, V a–b 7, V b 8–end, VI, VII.

## MINOR INSCRIPTIONS

**82.** Tuder. On a bronze statue of a warrior. Conway no. 352, v. Pl. no. 292.

**ahaltrutitis dunum dede.**      — *Tr. Titius V.f.* donum 'dedit.

For ꟼ = *d* not *ř*, see **27, 131,** *c.*

**83.** On a bronze tablet found at Fossato di Vico, near the ancient Helvillum. Conway no. 354, v. Pl. no. 295.

| | |
|---|---|
| *Cubrar Matrer bio eso;* | Bonae Matris *sacellum* hoc ; |
| *oseto cisterno n. C↓V* | facta cisterna n. CLVIIII |
| *su maronato    IIII* | sub \*maronatu |
| *U. L. Uarie T. C. Fulonie.* | V. Varii L. f., T. Fullonii C. f. |

**84.** On a limestone block found near Assisi. Conway no 355, v. Pl. no. 296.

| | |
|---|---|
| *Ager emps et* | Ager emptus et |
| *termnas oht* | terminatus auct. |
| *C. U. Uistinie Ner. T. Babr.* | C. Vestinii V. f., Ner. Babrii T. f. |
| *maronatei* | in \*maronatu |
| *Uois. Ner. Propartie* | Vols. Propertii Ner. f., |
| *T. U. Uoisiener.* | T. Volsieni V. f. |
| *Sacre stahu.* | Sacrum sto. |

Cf. CIL. XI 5390 *Post. Mimesius C. f., T. Mimesius Sert. f., Ner. Capidas C. f. Ruf., Ner. Babrius T. f., C. Capidas T. f. C. n., V. Volsienus T. f., marones murum ab fornice ad circum et fornicem cisternamq. d. s. s. faciundum coiravere.* Marōn- was an official title among the Umbrians and Etruscans.

# GLOSSARY AND INDEX [1]

## OSCAN [2]

aa- 'ab-'. 77, 2, 264, 1.

Aadiieís 'Adii', gen. sg., gent., no. 55. 174.

Aadirans '*Adiranus', gent., no. 4. 81.

Aadiriís, Aadíriis 'Atrius', gent., nos. 14, 15. 81, 174.

aamanaffed 'mandavit, (faciendum) locavit', nos. 5, 6, 8, 9, 11. Cf. manafum. 77, 2, 80, 2, 88, 3, 223, 264, 1, 2.

aapas, meaning uncertain, no. 61.

aasaí 'in ara', loc. sg., no. 45 16, 44; — nom. pl. aasas, no. 45 26. 33.

Abellanú- 'Abellanus', no. 1. Dat. sg. m. -núí, acc. sg. f. -nam, nom. pl. m. -nús, gen. pl. m. -núm, dat. pl. m. [-núís]. 91, 2, 103, 3, 157, 1, 255, 4.

akkatus 'advocati', nom. pl., no. 40. 89, 3, 102, 3, 139, 1.

akeneí 'in anno' (⚥), loc. sg., no. 45 18, 47; —gen. pl. acunum, no. 2 31;—abbr. akun., no. 13. 81, 159, a.

akrid 'acriter', no. 19 4. 99, 3, 190, 4.

actud 'agito', imperat., no. 2 15; 32, 1, 143; — infin. acum, no. 2 24; 159, a.

Akudunniad, name of a Samnite town, abl. sg., no. 67. 144, a (nn by 162, 1). For the question of the identification with Aquilonia or modern Lacedogna see Conway, I, p. 172.

acum, see actud.

acunum, akun., see akeneí.

Akviiai 'Aquiae', dat. sg., gent. f., no. 19 10. 258, 3.

ad- 'ad-'. 299, 1.

Aderl. 'Atella' or 'Atellanorum', no. 68. 91, 2, 103, 3, 157, 2.

adfust 'aderit', no. 29. 299, 1.

adpúd 'quoad', no. 31. 202, 9.

aeteis 'partis', gen. sg., no. 2 12, 18, etc.; — gen. pl. [a]íttíúm, no. 1 53; 162, 1. 16, 1, 62, 187, 1, a.

Afaries 'Afarius', gent. 174.

---

See word Buck [handwritten marginalia]

[1] The references with "no." refer to the numbers of the preceding collection. Where no number is given, the form is from some fragment not included in the collection. The references in black type are to the sections of the grammar. Where several inflectional forms are included under one heading, references for the particular forms, when given, are put after each, while the references to the word as a whole are put at the end of the article. But it is not intended, of course, to give references for each inflectional form, except in special cases. References inclosed in ( ) refer to the particular form immediately preceding. Under compounds are sometimes given references to sections in which only the simplex is mentioned. And occasionally elsewhere reference is made to a section in which the word itself is not mentioned, but where parallel examples are given.

Besides the abbreviations used elsewhere, note praen. = praenomen, and gent. = gentile.

[2] Alphabetical order as in Latin, but with k under c. ú is given under o; likewise u = ú, o, when forms with ú or o also occur, otherwise under u. v is given after u, but consonantal u is given with v, and au and av, ou and úv, are treated as identical.

311

Avdiis 'Audius', gent., no. 10, also
Aϝδειες; 174; — Ahvdiu, no. 13,
probably dat. sg. (-u for -ui; see
171, 3, a). 61, 2, a.

Αυϝυσκλι., Αυσκλιν 'Ausculinorum',
Αυσκλα. 'Ausculanorum', no. 69. 61,
2, a.

auti 'aut', no. 2 (passim). 68, 92,
202, 17.

avt 'at, autem', nos. 1 (passim), 29, 31
(corrected from aet), 50 (a]vt); —
aut 'at, autem', no. 2 20; — avt 'aut',
no. 19 (passim). 68, 92, 202, 17.

az 'ad', no. 45 20. 137, 2, 299, 1.

Baiteis 'Baeti', gen. sg., praen., no. 55.

*Bansae* 'Bantiae', loc. sg., no. 2 (passim). 100, 3, c.

*Bantins* 'Bantinus', no. 2 19. 47, 255, 5.

Beriis 'Berius', gent., no. 44.

Betitis 'Betitius', gent., no. 51. 259, 1.

Bivellis 'Bivellius', gent., no. 20.

bivus 'vivi', nom. pl., no. 19 9. 101, 151.

Blaisiis 'Blaesius', gent., no. 40.

Blússii(eís) 'Blossii', gen. sg., gent.,
no. 26.

Bn., abbr. praen., no. 51.

Búvaianúd 'ad Bovianum', no. 46.
61, 3 with a and ftn., 253, 1, 298.

*brateis* 'gratiae', gen. sg., no. 2 6.  See
p. 235 with ftn.

Buttis 'Bottius', gent., no. 40.

-c, -k. 201, 1.

Kaal., abbr. praen., no. 58.

*cadeis* 'inimicitiae', gen. sg., no. 2 6.
See p. 235 with ftn.

kahad 'capiat', no. 19 6, 8 (in l. 6 probably 'incipiat'). 99, 3, 149, 213, 1, a.

kaías, meaning uncertain, no. 61.

kaíla 'aedem, templum', acc. sg., no. 3.
L. caelum(?).

Kaísillieís 'Caesilii', gen. sg., gent.,
no. 25 a, b.

kaispatar 'caedatur, glebis tunda-
tur'(?), no. 19 5. 238, 2, c.

Kalaviis 'Calvius', gent., no. 52. 80, 1,
258, 3.

Kαλινις 'Calinius', gent., no. 62.

Kaluvis '*Calovius, Calvius', gent.
(fragment); — gen. sg. Kalúvieis, nos.
27–28. 258, 4.

Kamp[aniis] 'Campanius', gent., no. 6.

Kapv., abbr. for Kapv(ad) 'Capua',
abl., or Kapv(anúm) 'Capuanorum',
no. 70; for Kapv(anai) or (anei), loc.
sg., no. 31; for Kapv(ans) 'Capua-
nus', no. 29 (but reading not certain).

karanter 'vescuntur', no. 19 9. 97.

*caria* 'panis'. "Carensis, pistoribus a
caria quam Oscorum lingua panem
esse dicunt." Placidus ed. Deuer-
ling, p. 25. 97.

*carneis* 'partis', no. 2 3, 7. 17, 3, 181, c.

kasit 'decet', no. 31. 17, 1, 78, 3, 112,
204, 7, 212, 3.

*casnar* 'senex'. "Casnar senex Oscorum lingua." Festus ed. Thewrewk,
p. 33. "Item significat in Atellanis
aliquot Pappum senem quod Osci
casnar appellant." Varro L. L. 7,
29. 114.

Kastríkiieís 'Castricii', gen. sg., cogn.,
no. 17. 174, 256, 3.

*castrid* 'capite'(?), no. 2 8; 59; — gen.
sg. *castrous*, no. 2 13; 71. 17, 2,
32, 1, 138, 184, 248, 4, a, p. 236.

*cebnust* 'venerit', no. 2 20. 88, 3, 224,
264, 1.

*censaum* 'censere', infin., no. 2 20; —
fut. 3 pl. *censazet*, no. 2 19; 221; —
imperat. pass. *censamur*, no. 2 19;
237, 279. 210, 3.

Kenssurineís 'Censorini', gen. sg.,
cogn., no. 26. 21, 246, 1.

*censtom-en* 'in censum', no. 2 20. 244,
1, a.

Dekis 'Decius', praen., nos. 10, 40
(passim); — gen. sg. Dekkieis, no. 40
(passim). **162, 1, 174.**

Dekmanniúís '*Decumaniis', probably
name of a festival, no. 45 48. **88, 8,
162, 1, 191, 10, 255, 4, p. 255.**

deded, see *didest.*

degetas-, see deketasiúí.

*deicum* 'dicere', infin., no. 2 10, deíkum,
no. 20; — pres. subj. 3 pl. *deicans*,
no. 2 9; — fut. perf. 3 sg. *dicust*, no.
2 14; **45, 224. 64, 95.**

Deívaí 'Divae', dat. sg., no. 45 15, 43.
**64.**

*deiuatud* 'iurato', imperat., no. 2 5; —
pres. subj. 3 sg. *deiuaid*, no. 2 11;
**232;** — fut. 3 sg. *deiuast*, no. 2 3;
**221;** — perf. pass. partic. nom. pl.
*deiuatuns* 'iurati', no. 2 9; **244, 2, a,
308, a. 16, 4, 262, 1.**

deivinais 'divinis', dat. pl. f., no. 34.
**47, 64, 101, 255, 5.**

destrst 'dextra est', no. 21. **84, 89, 1,
145, 1, 188, 2.**

*dicust*, see *deicum.*

*didest* 'dabit', fut. 3 sg., no. 2 16; **45,
221, 213, 4;** — perf. 3 sg. deded,
nos. 4, 7, 48, 52, δεδετ, no. 65; **223.**

d]iíkúlús, see *zicolom.*

Diíviiai 'Diae', dat. sg., no. 52. **95,** a,
ftn. p. 52.

Diúveí, Διουϝει, see Iúveís.

Diuvia.., see Iúviass.

diuvilam, see iúvilam.

Diumpaís 'Lumpis'. **56.**

*dolom* 'dolum', acc. sg., no. 2 5, 14,
*dolum*, no. 2 21; — abl. sg. dolud, no.
2 11, 20.

dúnúm 'donum', acc. sg., no. 53,
dunum, no. 52. **53, 107, 1, 251,
2.**

dunte.., meaning uncertain, no. 19 4.

d]uunated 'donavit', no. 59. **53,
228.**

ekak 'hanc', nos. 3, 4, 7, abbr. ek., no.
22; **108,** 2, *a*; — acc. sg. n. ekík,
no. 46; **196,** *a*; — nom. pl. f. ekas,
nos. 25 a, b, 26, ekask, no. 45 26; —
acc. pl. f. ekass, no. 3; — abbr. εk
for nom. sg. f., no. 27. **196.**

ekkum 'item', no. 1 27, 41. **139, 1, a,**
**201, 5.**

ekss 'ita, sic', no. 1 10, ἐx, no. 27. **196,** b.

eksuk 'hoc', abl. sg. n., nos. 14–18; —
abl. sg. f. *exac*, no. 2 8, 23; — loc. sg.
n. *exeic*, no. 2 (passim); — dat. abl. pl.
f. *exaisc-en*, no. 2 25. **145, 3, 196.**

edum 'edere', no. 19 8. **36, 1.**

ee-, eh- 'e-'. **77, 1, 142, a, 300, 4.**

eehiianasúm 'emittendarum', no. 81 a,
vehiian., no. 31 b (⌐ by mistake
for Ⅎ). **77, 1, 149, 163.**

eestínt 'exstant', no. 45 26; — ee[stit
'exstat', no. 1 52. **41,** b, **77, 1, 89, 2,
215, 2.**

*egmo* 'res', nom. sg., no. 2 4; — gen. sg.
*egm[as]*, no. 2 5; — abl. sg. *egmad*, no.
2 10; — gen. pl. *egmazum*, no. 2 24;
**270. 16, 5, 251, 3.**

ehpeílatas 'erectae, set up', perf. pass.
partic. nom. pl., no. 26. **64, 142, a,
262, 1.**

ehpreívíd. **142,** *a.*

ehtrad 'extra', no. 1 31. **142, 188, 2,
190, 3, 299, 3.**

eh[trúís? 'exterioribus', no. 1 14.

eídúís 'idibus', name of a festival, no.
29, eiduis, no. 21. **171, 14, p. 247.**

ειρεμ, see ínim.

eiseis 'eius', no. 1 20, eiseis, no. 19 4,
*eizeis*, no. 2 22; — loc. sg. n. eiseí,
no. 1 46, e[iseí, no. 1 51, eseí, mistake
for eiseí, no. 1 49, *eizeic*, no. 2 7, 21; —
loc. sg. f. e]ísaí, no. 1 57; — abl. sg. n.
eísúd, no. 1 13, *eizuc*, no. 2 29, 30,
*eizuc-en*, no. 2 16; — abl. sg. f. eísak,
no. 4, *eizac*, no. 2 10; — gen. pl. m.
eisunk, no. 40; — gen. pl. f. *eizazunc*,

no. 2 24; — abl. pl. m. *eizois*, no.
2 23; — abl. pl. f. *eizasc*, mistake for
*eizaisc*, no. 2 9.  **195.**  See also
*izic*.

eítiuvam 'pecuniam', no. 4, *eituam*,
no. 2 19; — gen. sg. *eituas*, no. 2 (passim); — abl. sg. eítiuvad, nos. 4, 5,
eítiu[vad], no. 6, abbr. eítiv., no.
56 (31, *b*); — acc. pl. *eituas*, no. 2 9;
— abbr. *ei.* for nom. sg., no. 2 22.
**16, 6, 56.**

eítuns 'eunto'(?), nos. 14, 17, 18, eítu[ns,
no. 16, abbr. eít., no. 15.  **236, 2,**
p. 242.  ~~quaesto gerego medeliatim~~
*eizeis, eizeíc,* etc., see eíseís.

embratur 'imperator', no. 79 b.  **89, 2,
157, 1, 246, 1.**

*en* 'in', no. 2 9, postpos. *-en.*  **301, 2.**
Entraí '*Interae', dat. sg., no. 45 8, 35.
**188, 2, 301, 2.**

eseí, see eíseís.

esídum, see ísídum.

essuf 'ipse', no. 50, *esuf*, no. 2 19, 21.
**110, 5, 122, 2, 197, 5.**

est, estud, *estud*, see súm.

*etanto* 'tanta', nom. sg. f., no. 2 11, 26.
**201, 7.**

Evklúí, dat. sg., no. 45 3, 25, 29.  **21,
70.**

*ex, exac,* etc., see eks, eksuk.

*ezum*, see súm.

faamat 'habitat, tendit, holds command', nos. 14, 15, (16), 17.  **99, 2,
204, 7, p. 242.** ~~with same meaning~~
~~command. C P 17, 12~~
fakiiad 'faciat', no. 31 a; 44, *a*; — imperat. 3 sg. *factud*, no. 2 9; **143, 216;**
— perf. subj. 3 sg. *fefacid*, no. 2 10;
**223;** — fut. perf. 3 sg. *fefacust*, no.
2 11, 17; **223.**  **32, 1, 99, 1, 136,
214, 2, 219.**

*facus* 'factus', no. 2 30.  **91, 1, 258, 1.**
Faler. 'Falerniis', no. 32; — nom. pl.
Falenias, no. 33.  **103, 2, *a*.**

famel 'famulus'.  "Famuli origo ab
Oscis dependét, apud quos servus
famel nominabatur, unde et familia
vocata."  Festus ed. Thewrewk,
p. 62.  Cf. also Pael. *famel inim
loufir* 'famulus et liber'.  **36, 2, 91,
2, *a*, 119, 2.**

*famelo* 'familia', no 2 22.  **100, 3, *c*,
250, 2.**

far 'far', no. 19 8.  **117, 182.**

fatíum 'fari', infin., no. 20.  **38, 1,
99, 2, 212, 1, 262, 2.**

feíhúss 'muros', no. 1 31; — abl. pl.
feíhúís, no. 1 45.  **16, 7, 64, 95,
136, 149.**

fertalis, ceremonies celebrated with
sacrificial cakes (L. *fertum*), nom.
pl. or dat. pl. (?), no. 26.  **178, 7,
257, 4, p. 249.**

Σεστιεϛ 'Festius', no. 65.  Also taken
as 'Sestius'.  **24, *b*.**

fifíkus 'decreveris'(?), no. 19 5.  **223**
with *a.* ~~I F 82, 7~~ ~~Herbig not from~~
fiiet, fiíet 'fiunt', no. 31 a, b.  **215, 2.**
Fiísíaís '*Fisiis', adj., no. 28, Fiisiais,
no. 27, Fisiais, no. 21.  **137, 1, 252, 1.**
fiísnú 'fanum', nom. sg., no. 1 30; —
acc. sg. fiísnam, no. 1 32, físnam,
no. 1 45; — fií..., no 1 24, fiís...,
no. 50.  **41, 99, 1, 114, 136, 251, 2.**
Fíml. '*Fimulus', no. 57.  **91, 2, *a*.**
Físanis '*Fisanius', no. 16.
Fistelú '*Fistelia', no. 72 a; — Fistluis
'*Fistulis', no. 72 b, c (φυστελια, no.
72 c, Greek, not Oscan).
Fiuusasiaís 'Floralibus', name of a
festival, no. 45 20.  **105, 1, *a*, 254.**
Flagiuí '*Flagio', dat. sg., no. 25 a, b.
See note, p. 249.
Fluusaí 'Florae', dat. sg., no. 45 24.
**53, 105, 1.**
*fortis* 'potius', no. 2 12.  **91, 1, 146,
188, 1.**
fratrúm 'fratrum', nos. 27, 28.  **33, 124.**

Frentreí '*Frentri', loc. sg., no. 73.

fruktatiuf 'fructus', no. 1 21. **58, 68,** 3, **153, 247,** 1.

fufans, fufens, *fuid,* fusíd, *fust,* see súm.

Fuutreí 'Genetrici', dat. sg., no. 45 30, Futreí, no. 45 4 ; — gen. sg. Futre[ís], no. 54. **58, 180,** *a* with ftn.

Fuvfdis 'Fufidius', gent., no. 40.

Gaaviis 'Gavius', gent., no. 42, Gaviis, no. 20 ; — gen. sg. **Gaav . . . ,** praen., no. 58.

Genetaí 'Genitae', dat. sg., no. 45 15, 43. **36,** 3.

Gnaivs 'Gnaeus', praen. (on fragment belonging with no. 40), [Gnai]vs, no. 40 ; — abbr. **Gn.,** no. 47. **147,** 2.

*hafiest* 'habebit', no. 2 8 (probably for *hapiest*); **218,** note ; — perf. subj. 3 sg. *hipid,* no. 2 (passim); **41, 218, 225 ;** — fut. perf. 3 sg. *hipust,* no. 2 11 ; **225. 99,** 1, **218.**

Heírennis 'Herennius'(?), gent., no. 42 ; cf. praen. Heírens.

Helleviis 'Helvius', gent., no. 20, Helevi., no. 32 ; — gen. sg. Heleviieís, no. 33. **80,** 1, **162,** 3, **174, 258,** 3. Her., no. 53, abbr. for Hereklúí or Herentateí.

Herekleís 'Herculis', no. 1 (passim) ; — dat. sg. Hereklúí, no. 45 13, 41. **21, 78,** *a,* **80,** 1.

Hereiis 'Herius', gent., no. 40 ; — gen. sg. Heriieis, no. 40. **176,** 5.

Herentateís 'Veneris', no. 41 ; — dat. sg. Herentateí, no. 41. **15,** 1, **251,** 5.

*herest* 'volet', no. 2 (passim). **100,** 3, *c,* **221.**

heriam 'vim', no. 19 1. **15,** 1, **250,** 1.

heriiad 'capiat', no. 20 ; **44,** *a* ; — imperf. subj. 3 pl. h]erríns, no. 1 54 ; **115,** 2, **216, 233. 149, 214,** 2.

Heriieís, see Hereiis.

Herukinaí 'Erycinae', dat. sg., no. 41. Epithet of Herentateí. **21, 149,** *a.*

*hipid, hipust,* see *hafiest.*

Húrtiis 'Hortius', gent., no. 53.

húrz 'hortus, lucus', no. 45 48 ; — acc. sg. húrtúm, no. 45 20 ; — dat. sg. húrtúí, no. 45 27 ; — loc. sg. húrtín, no. 45 1 ; **41,** *a,* **82,** 1, **171,** 7. **49, 149.**

Húsidiis 'Hosidius', gent., no. 58. **260,** 2.

humuns 'homines', nom. pl., no. 19 9. **90,** 1, **149, 181.**

hu[n]truis 'inferis', no. 19 7. **15,** 5, **149, 188,** 2.

huntrus 'infra'(?), no. 19 11 ; **299,** 4, *a.*

íak, see *izic.*

-*ic,* -*ík,* enclitic. **201,** 2.

*idic,* ídík, see *izic.*

Ieíis. 176, 1, 3.

íív, no. 55. ? ?  𝖨 𝖥 38, 171 Sommer.

imad-en 'ab imo', no. 3. **47, 114,** *d,* **189,** 1.

íním 'et', no. 1 (passim), íní, nos. 3, 14–17, iním, nos. 27, 28, inim, nos. 19 (passim), 40, *inim,* no. 2 6, εινειμ, no. 62 **(44),** abbr. *in.,* no. 2 (passim). **16,** 8, **202,** 16.

*ioc,* íúk, see *izic.*

iúkleí 'the formula of consecration', 'consecration'(?), loc. sg., no. 31 a, b. **249,** 1.

Iúvkiíúí '*Iovicio', dat. sg., gent., no. 1 4. **174, 256,** 3.

Iúveís 'Iovis', nos. 3, 59 ; — dat. sg. Iuveí, no. 25 a, b, Diúveí, no. 45 (passim), Διουϝει, no. 64 **(24).** **101, 134, 183** with *a.*

Iúviass '*Iovias', acc. pl., name of a festival, no. 29 ; — here probably Diuvia.., no. 24 a, b.

Iúviia 'Ioviam', adj., no. 3. **252,** 1.

iúvilam '*iovilam', no. 33, iúvil, no. 32, older diuvilam, no. 21, diuvil., no. 22 ; — nom. sg. iuvilu (on two fragments not included), iúhil., no. 27 (h by mistake); — nom. pl. iúvilas, nos. 25 a, 26, iuvilas, no. 25 b, iuvilas, no. 29, iúvil., no. 30. **134, 257,** 5, p. 247.

íp 'ibi', no. 1 34. **195,** *f.* 𐌍𐌖𐌋𐌀𐌏 .

isídum 'idem', nom. sg. m., no. 4, ísidu, nos. 7, 8, εισειδομ (fragment), esídum (fragment), esidu[m], no. 50 ; **44,** *c*; — nom. pl. m. íussu, íusu, no. 3 ; **53,** *a*, **139,** 1, *a*. **44,** *c*, **50, 195, 201,** 5.

íst, see súm.

íussu, see isídum.

izic 'is', no. 2 (passim); — nom. sg. f. *ioc*, no. 2 4, íúk, no. 1 37, 42, iiuk, no. 21 ; **31,** *a* ; — nom. acc. sg. n. *idic*, no. 2 6, 9, 30, ídík, no. 1 17, 18, idik, no. 19 3, 5 ; — acc. sg. m. *ionc*, no. 2 12, 17, 26 ; **49** ; — acc. sg. f. íak, no. 50 ; **108,** 2, *a* ; — nom. pl. m. *iusc*, no. 2 20 ; — nom. acc. pl. n. *ioc*, no. 2 5. See also eíseís. **195.**

L., see Lúvkis.

lamatir 'caedatur'(?), no. 2 21, lamatir, no. 19 4. **228, 238,** 2, **239,** p. 238.

Λαπονις 'Lamponius'. **108,** 2, *a*.

leginum 'legionem, cohortem', no. 19 3, legin[um, no. 19 1 ; —dat. sg. leginei, no. 19 4, 11, 12. **181.**

leígúss, meaning uncertain, no. 50.

licitud 'liceto', no. 2 (passim), líkítud, no. 1 36. **41, 44, 104, 212,** 3.

Líganakdíkeí, name of a goddess, dat. sg., no. 45 8, 35. **80,** 2, **263,** 1.

lígatúís 'legatis', dat. pl., no. 1 6, 7 ; — nom. pl. lígat[ús], no. 1 9. .**41.**

ligud 'lege', abl. sg., no. 2 19, 21 ; — loc. pl. *ligis*, no. 2 25. **41, 104.**

liimítú[m] 'limitum', gen. pl., no. 1 29. **47.**

líís.., no. 50. ? ?

limu 'famem', no. 19 8. **21.**

l?]úfríkúnúss '*liberigenos'(?), no. 50. Formation and meaning uncertain.

Λουκανομ 'Lucanorum', no. 75. **24, 71.**

Lúvkanateís '*Lucanatis', no. 61. **71, 259,** 3.

lúvkeí 'in luco', loc. sg., no. 26. **71, 104.**

Lúvkis 'Lucius', praen., no. 20 (Lúvikis, l. 5, probably mistake); — gen. sg. Luvcies ; **64,** *b*; — abbr. L., nos. 17, 27–28, 41, 49. **71.**

loufir 'vel', no. 2 8. **16,** 9, **71, 96, 104, 124, 202,** 18, **238,** 2, **239.**

Lúvfreís 'Liberi', gen. sg., no. 59. **71, 104, 136.**

luisarifs 'lusoriis'(?), no. 21. **124, 136, 178,** 9, **257,** 4, p. 248.

M., abbr. praen. (Maís ?), no. 3.

m., see meddikkiai.

Ma., abbr. praen. (Maís ?), nos. 11, 17.

Maatúís '*Matis', dat. pl., no. 45 10, 38. Cf. L. *Mātūta*.

Maatreís 'Matris', no. 54. **33, 81.**

*Maesius* 'mensis Maius'. "Maesius lingua Osca mensis Maius." Festus ed. Thewrewk, p. 109. **147,** 3, *a*.

Magiium 'Magiorum', gent., no. 21. **174, 176,** 1.

Mahii[s 'Maius'. **176,** 1.

maimas 'maximae', gen. sg., no. 2 3, 7. **114,** *b*, **147,** 3, *a*, **189,** 3.

mais 'magis, plus', adv., no. 2 5, 15, 25. **91,** 1, **147,** 3, **186,** 1, **289.**

Maís, Maís 'Maius', praen. (fragments); — dat. sg. Maiiúí, no. 1 1, 3 ; — gen. sg. [M]aíieís ?, no. 50 ; — abbr. Maí., no. 1 1, 4, Mh., nos. 47, 57 ; **176,** 1. Here also perhaps M. and Ma. **61,** 3, **91,** 1, **147,** 3, **176,** 1, 3.

malaks 'malevolos'(?), no. 19 2.  **176, 10, 256,** 6.

*mallom* 'malum', acc. sg., no. 2 5, 15, 22 ; — abl. sg. *mallud,* no. 2 20, *malud,* no. 2 11.  **100,** 3, *c.*

Μαμερκιεs 'Mamercius', gent., no. 66. Cf. praen. *Mamercus* quoted under *Mamers.*  **80,** 1, **174.**

*Mamers* 'Mars'.  " Mamers Mamertis facit, id est lingua Osca Mars Martis, unde et Mamertini in Sicilia dicti, qui Messanae habitant. Mamercus praenomen est Oscum ab eo quod hi Martem Mamertem dicunt." Festus ed. Thewrewk, pp. 98, 99.

Μαμερτινο 'Mamertina', adj. nom. sg. f., no. 62 ; — Μαμερτινουμ 'Mamertinorum', no. 63 (24).  **47, 255,** 5.

Mamerttiais 'Martiis', adj., nos. 27–29. **162,** 1, **252,** 1, p. 247.

manafum 'mandavi', no. 19 3.  **204,** 5, **223, 264,** 2.

*manim* 'manum', acc. sg., no. 2 24. **185,** 3.

Marahis 'Marius'(?), praen., no. 40 ; — gen. sg. Marahieis (fragment), abbr. **Marai.,** no. 43 (implying a spelling **Maraiieís,** as **Mai.** for **Maiieís** ; cf. foll.).  **176,** 4.

*Maraies* 'Marius'(?), gent. (fragment) ; — gen. sg. Maraiieís, no. 50.  **61,** 3, 176, 4, **253,** 1.

Maras '*Maras', praen., no. 40, Μαραs, no. 62 ; — ? gen. sg. Maraheis, no. 40 (and fragments) ; — abbr. **Mr.,** nos. 4, 14, 15, 17.  **169,** 12, **176,** 4.

Markas.  **169,** 12.

meddikkiai '*in meddicia, in the meddixship', loc. sg., no. 28, meddíkiaí, no. 27, medikkiaí, no. 33, medikia[i], no. 32 ; συτ μεδικιαι (fragment), **302** ; abbr. medik*k.*, medik., no. 31, m., no. 26.  **15,** 6, **162,** 1.

meddíss 'meddix', nos. 41, 48, 51, meddís, nos. 29, 43, *meddis,* no. 2 (passim) ; **145,** 2 ; — gen. sg. medíkeís, no. 3 ; — dat. sg. medíkeí, no. 1 5 ; — nom. pl. meddíss, no. 42, μεδδειξ, no. 62 (24) ; 90, 1, **145,** 2 ; — abbr. medd., no. 30, metd., no. 47, med., nos. 7–9. **15,** 6, **44, 163, 263,** 1, p. 229.

*medicatinom* 'iudicationem', no. 2 16. **15,** 6, **163.**

*medicatud* 'iudicato', abl. sg., no. 2 24. **15,** 6, **163.**

*medicim* '*meddicium, magistracy', nom. acc. sg., no. 2 30–33 ; **172** ; — abl. sg. *meddixud,* no. 2 13, 21 ; 100, 3, *c* ; — abl. sg. *medikid,* no. 31 b ; 173, 5.  **15,** 6, **163, 250,** 2.

Meeílíkiieís ' Μειλιχίου', no. 3.  **21.**

mefi[ú] 'media', nom. sg. f., no. 1 30 ; — loc. sg. f. mefiaí, no. 1 57.  **36,** 1, **136.**

memnim 'monumentum', no. 20.  **172, 250.**

Mener. 'Minervio'(?), no. 18.  **21.**

menvum 'minuere', no. 19 8.  **44,** *c.*

messímass 'medioximas, midmost'(?), no. 29.  **86,** 1, **138,** *a,* **189,** 1 (with ftn.).

Metiis 'Mettius', gent., no. 57.

**Mh.,** see Mais.

Mi., abbr. praen. (cf. the two following), no. 26.

Minaz 'Minatus', praen. (fragment) ; — gen. sg. Minateís, no. 25.  **259,** 1.

Minis 'Minius', praen., no. 44 ; — gen. sg. Minnieís, Minieís, no. 25, Miíneís, no. 35, Minies, no. 86.

minive, no. 31 b.  See note, p. 251.

*min[s]* 'minus', adv., no. 2 10.  **90,** 1, **315.**

*minstreis* 'minoris', gen. sg. m., no. 2 12, 27, *mistreis,* no. 2 18 (**108,** 2, *a*). **89,** 1, **187,** 1, *a,* **188,** 3.

Mitl. 'Mitulus', praen., no. 57.  **91,** 2, *a.*

múiníkú 'communis', adj., nom. sg. f., no. 1 22, abbr. múinik., nos. 27–28; — acc. sg. f. muinikam, no. 21; — abl. sg. f. múiníkad, no. 1 50; — nom. sg. n. múiní[kúm], no. 1 18; — loc. sg. n. múiníkeí, no. 1 19. 66, 187, 1, 256, 2. .

múltasíkad 'multaticia', adj., abl. sg. f., no. 5; — abl. sg. n. multas[íkud], no. 43. 49, 254.

*moltaum* 'multare', no. 2 (passim). 210, 1, 262, 1.

*molto* 'multa', nom. sg., no. 2 11, 26; — gen. sg. *moltas*, no. 2 13, 27; 269; — acc. sg. *moltam*, no. 2 2. 49, 146.

Mr., see Maras.

Mulukiis 'Mulcius', gent., no. 43. 80, 1.

Mutíl 'Mutilus', cogn., nos. 79–80. 119, 2, 171, 1.

Mut[ti]lli[s] 'Mutilius', gent., no. 40; — gen. sg. Muttillieis, no. 40. 171, 1.

Mz. 'Mettus', abbr. praen., nos. 10, 53. Cf. gent. Metiis.

N., see Niumsis.

*n.* 'nummi', no. 2 12, 26.

*ne* 'ne, nisi', no. 2 14, 25. 202, 20.

*nei* 'non', no. 2 20, 28. 202, 20.

*neip* 'neque, neve', no. 2 15, neip, no. 19 4, 5, 6. 202, 20.

*nep* 'neque, neve', no. 2 10, 28, nep, nos. 1 46–47, 20. 92, 202, 20.

ner., *nerum*, see niir.

nessimas 'proximae', nom. pl. f., no. 26; — gen. pl. *nesimum*, no. 2 17, 31; — dat.-abl. pl. *nesimois*, no. 2 25. 15, 8, 86, 1, 138, a, 189, 1, ftn. p. 134.

*ni* 'ne', no. 2 (passim). 202, 20.

Ni., see Niumsis.

niir 'vir, princeps, procer,' title of rank, no. 40 (and fragments); — gen. pl. *nerum*, no. 2 29, 32; — abbr. ner. for ner(eís), gen. sg., no. 25. 15, 7, 97, 180, 2, c.

nip 'neque, neve', no. 19 7, 8. 202, 20.

nistrus 'propinquos', no. 19 2. 38, 4, 138, a, 188, 2.

Niumeriis 'Numerius', gent. 21.

Ni]umsis 'Numerius', praen., no. 42; — gen. sg. Niumsieís, no. 42, Νιυμσδιης, no. 62 (24, c); abbr. Ni., nos. 9, 13; abbr. N., no. 3. 21, 56.

Nuvkrinum 'Nucerinorum', no. 76.

Núvellum 'Novellum', praen., no. 20.

Núvlanú- 'Nolanus', no. 1. Acc. sg. f. -nam; — dat. sg. m. -[núí]; — nom. pl. m. -nús; — gen. pl. m. -núm; — dat.-abl. pl. -núís.

Úf..., see Upfals.

Úhtavis 'Octavius', gent., nos. 20, 58. 142, 191, 8.

úín..., no. 50. ?

úíttiuf 'usus', no. 1 40, 43. 53, 66, 162, 1.

úlam 'ollam', no. 20. Perhaps borrowed from rustic Latin, for we should expect O. av (cf. the earlier Latin *aul(l)a*), not ú.

últiumam 'ultimam', no. 29. 49, 56, 86, 1, 189, 1.

úmbn..., no. 50. ?

úp 'apud', no. 1 13, op, no. 2 14, 23. 17, 7, 49, 300, 5.

Upfals 'Ofellus', praen., nos. 35–36; — gen. sg. Upfalleis, no. 40, Upfaleis, no. 22; — abbr. Úpf., no. 10; — here perhaps Úf..., no. 58. 119, 2.

Upils 'Opilius' (fragment); — abbr. Úpíl. for Úpíl(leís), nos. 29, 30. 119, 2.

Úppiis 'Oppius', praen., no. 20; — gen. sg. Uppiieis, no. 40; — Οπιες, cogn.

úpsannam 'operandam, faciendam', nos. 4, 48; úpsan., no. 7, úpsann[úm], no. 49, [úps]annu, no. 6; 135, 245; — perf. pass. partic. nom. pl. upsatuh, no. 44; 113, c, 308; —

perf. indic. 3 sg. upsed, no. 56, ups.,
no. 57, 3 pl. uupsens, no. 3, upsens,
no. 10, ουπσενς, no. 62 (**24**); **225** with
*a.* 17, 4, **49**, **68**, 3, **99**, 8, **122**, 3,
**211**, **262**, 1, **308**.
osii[ns] 'adsint', no. 2 4. **122**, 2, **232**.

Paakul '*Paculus', praen., no. 43 ; —
gent. Pakulliis 'Paculius'. **119**, 2,
**171**, 1.
Paapii, Paapi 'Papius', gent., no. 79.
**113**, *c.*
Pakis 'Pacius', praen., nos. 19 9, 60 ;
**172** ; — dat. sg. Pakiu, no. 19 2 ;
**171**, 3, *a* ; — acc. sg. Pakim, no.
19 10 ; **172** ; — abbr. Pak. for Pak-
(ieís), nos. 29, 30 ; — abbr. Pk., no.
56. **174**.
Πακϝηις 'Paqui', gen. sg., praen. Cf.**24**.
pag., no. 31 b. ?,
paí, *pae*, etc., see under pui.
Palanúd 'Pallano', no. 61.
pan 'quam', conj., no. 2 6, also in *pruter pan.* **135**, **190**, 6, **202**, 4.
Papeis 'Papi', gen. sg., praen., no. 40.
Cf. gent. Paapii.
passtata 'porticum', no. 7. **21**, **162**, 2.
Patanaí 'Pandae', dat. sg., no. 45 14, 42.
**81**.
patensíns 'panderent, aperirent', no.
1 50, 51. **99**, 4, **213**, 2, **233**. IF 30,33 8
patir 'pater', no. 35 ; **78**, 2 ; — dat. sg.
Patereí 'Patri', no. 45 25 ; **81**. **32**,
1, **97**, **246**, 2.
patt..., no. 58, perhaps patt[rafens
'patraverunt'.
Pk., see Pakis.
? pedú 'pedes', acc. pl. n., no. 1 56.
See p. 230.
per-. **299**, 5.

Perkens '*Percennus', praen., no. 42 ;
— gen. sg. Perkedne[ís], no. 42.
**135**, *a.*
perkium, meaning uncertain, nom. sg.
n., no. 39.
perek., per., abbr. for perek(aís) 'perticis', no. 3. A measure of length,
probably of about five feet. Cf.
Umbrian *perca* 'staff, rod'. **139**, 1.
peremust 'perceperit', fut. perf., no.
2 15. **224**, **299**, 5.
perfa[kium ?] 'perficere', no. 19 6.
Pernaí '*Pernae, Prorsae', dat. sg., no.
45 22. **300**, 8, *a.*
? pernúm, no. 1 29. **304**, p. 230.
pert 'trans', no. 1 33. **15**, 9, **299**, 5.
pert-, **299**, 5.
-pert, **192**, 2, **299**, 5.[1]
pertumum 'perimere, prohibere', infin.,
no. 2 7 ; **86**, 2 ; — fut. 3 sg. *pertemest*, no. 2 7 ; — fut. perf. 3 sg. *pertemust*, no. 2 4 ; **224**. **299**, 5, p. 235.
perum 'sine', prep., no. 2 5, 14, 21. **201**,
5, **299**, 6.
pestlúm 'templum', acc. sg. n., no. 49,
peessl[úm] (fragment). **76**, 2, **114**,
**116**, 3, **139**, 2, **162**, 2.
petiropert, petirupert 'quater', no. 2 14,
15. **34**, **81**, **100**, 3, *c*, **150**, **192**, 2.[1]
petora 'quattuor'. "Petoritum et Gal-
licum vehiculum esse et nomen eius
dictum esse existimant a numero IIII
rotarum ; alii Osce, quod hi quoque
petora quattuor vocent, alii Graece,
sed αιολικῶς dictum." Festus ed.
Thewrewk, p. 250. **191**, 4.
Pettieís, Pettieis 'Pettii', gen. sg.,
gent., nos. 27–28.
píd, pídum, see pís, *písum.
-píd '-que', indefinite particle. **201**, 4.

---

[1] Mention should perhaps have been made of another view, which has been revived
several times in recent years, namely that *-pert* is not to be compared with L. *-per* in
*semper* etc., but with Skt. *-kṛt* in *sakṛt* 'once' etc. We still regard the comparison
within the Italic as more probable.

Píihiúí 'Pio', dat. sg., no. 45 40. **48,
83, a, 102,** 2.

Piístíaí 'Fidiae', dat. sg., no. 45 14, 42.
**21.**

pís, píd 'quis, quid'.  Interrogative,
nom. sg. m. pis, no. 55.  Indefinite, nom. sg. m. *pis*, no. 2 (passim),
*pís*, no. 30; — acc. sg. m. *pim (phim)*,
no. 2 25; — nom.-acc. sg. n. **píd,**
no. 1 41, .pid, no. 19 6.  Indefinite
Relative, nom. sg. m. *pis*, no. 2 8,
19; — dat. sg. m. *piei*, no. 2 7.  **199.**

píspis 'quisquis' (fragment); — *pitpit*
'quidquid'.  "Pitpit Osce quicquid."
Festus ed. Thewrewk, p. 263. **200,** 1.

*písum, pídum 'quisquam, quicquam'.
Acc. sg. n. pídum, no. 1 47, pidum,
no. 19 7; — gen. sg. m. *pieisum*, no.
2 6.  ·199, **200,** 1, **201,** 5.

*pl.* in *tr. pl.* 'tribunus plebis', no. 2 29.

Plasis 'Plarius', praen., no. 20.

púkkapíd 'quandoque', no. 1 52, *pocapit,* no. 2 8 (**127,** 1, *a*), [*p*]*ocapid*
(Avellino fragment). **139,** 1, **201,** 4,
**202,** 13. IF 34, 405 Brugmann

pod, conjunction, in *pod . . . mín[s]*
'quominus', no. 2 10; **315;** — *suae . . .
pod* 'sive', no. 2 23, svai puh 'sive',
no. 19 10, 11 (**133,** *a*).  **190,** 6, **202,** 1.

puí 'qui', nom. sg. m., no. 19 1; —
nom. sg. f. paí, no. 1 34, pai, no. 19 1,
*pae, paei,* no. 2 22; — nom.-acc. sg.
n. púd, no. 1 12, 13, 14, 49, *pod,* no.
2 10; — gen. sg. m. púiieh, no. 39;
**61, 3, 64,** *b,* **113,** *c,* **199,** *b*; — acc.
sg. f. paam, no. 4, p]aam, no. 50,
pam, no. 1 38; — abl. sg. f. *poizad,*
no. 2 19; **199,** *d*; — nom. pl. m.
pús, no. 1 8, 45; — nom. pl. f. pas,
nos. 27, 28, 31 a, b; — nom. pl. f.
paí, no. 1 15, pai, no. 19 9.  **199.**

púiiu 'cuia', nom. sg. f., no. 55.  **61, 3,**
**199,** *b*.  For púiieh see pui.

*poizad,* see pui.

Púmpaiians 'Pompeianus', no.  4; —
gen. sg. m. Púmpaiianeís, no. 3; —
dat. sg. f. Púmpaiianaí, no. 4; —
acc. sg. f. Púmpaiiana, no. 3.  **61, 3,**
**253,** 1.

*pompe 'quinque'.  ·37, 150 with *a*.

púmperiaís '*quincuriis', name of a
festival, loc. pl., no. 30, púmperiais,
nos. 27–28, abbr. púmpe., no. 32; —
nom. pl. (or gen. sg.?) pumperias,
no. 23 a, b; — nom. pl. púmper(i)as,
no. 33.  **37, 150, 191,.5, 251,** 4, p.
247.  **Cl. Ph. I. 329,** lund

Πομπτιες 'Quintius, Pontius',[1] gent.,
no. 62, Púntiis, no. 3.  **146, 153,**
**174, 191,** 5.

*pomtis* 'quinquiens', no. 2 15.  **37,**
**146, 153, 191,** 5, **192,** 2.

pún 'cum', conjunction, nos. 1 50, 29,
30, pun, no. 19 6, 8, *pon,* no. 2
(passim).  **92, 135, 190,** 5, **202,** 3.

*púnttram* 'pontem', no. 3.  **162,** 1.  KZ 47,

Púpidiís 'Popidius, Cocidius', nos. 7–8.
Cf. Pupdiis, fragment. **89,** 1, **260,** 2.

?[p]úrtam 'portam', no. 50.

*posmom,* see pustm[as].

púst 'post', no. 1 45, pust, no. 19 5,
*post,* no. 2 8, 23, 29.  **300,** 6.

pússtíst 'positum est'(?), no. 1 33. **84,** *a*,
**162,** 2.  Also taken as 'post (adv.) est'.

pústin 'according to', prep., no. 1 34.
**15,** 10, **299,** 7.

púst iris 'posterius', adv., no. 50.  **44,** *b*,
**81, 88,** 4, **91,** 1, **188,** 1, **190,** 6.

pustm[as] 'postremae', nom. pl. (or
gen. sg.?), no. 23 a, b; — adv. *posmom,* no. 2 16; **190,** 5.  **114, 139,** 2,
**189,** 1.

---

[1] *Quintius* is the genuine Latin form, while *Pontius* is the latinized Oscan
form found on inscriptions of Campania and Samnium.  Cf. **246,** 1, *a*.

pústrei 'in postero', loc. sg., no. 31 a,
pustrei, no. 22, abbr. pústr., no. 31 b.
**81, 88, 4, 188, 2.**

pútereípíd 'in utroque', loc. sg., no.
45 18, 46 ; — nom. pl. pútúrúspíd, no.
19 ; — gen. pl. pútúrú[mpíd], no. 1 22.
**81, 88, 4, 188, 2,** a, **200, 2.**

pútíad 'possit', no. 20, putiiad, no.
19 6, 7, 8 ; — pútíans 'possint', no. 20,
putiians, no. 19 7. **88, 1, 262, 2.**

*pous*, see **puz.**

*pr.*, abbr. 'praetor', no. 2 (passim); for
gen. sg., no. 2 21.

*prae-* 'prae-', **300, 7.**

*praefucus* 'praefectus', no. 2 23. **86, 5,
258, 1.**

*praesentid* 'praesente', abl. sg., no. 2 21.
**62, 178, 5,** a.

prai 'prae', nos. 27-28. **62, 300, 7.**

prebai, meaning uncertain, dat. sg.,
no. 19 3.

*preiuatud* 'reo', abl. sg., no. 2 15, 16.
**17, 10, 64.**

prúfatted 'probavit', nos. 4, 8, 48, prúfattd, no. 7 (e omitted for want of
space); — prúfattens 'probaverunt',
no. 3, abbr. prúfts., no. 33. **102, 2,
228, 262, 1.**

prúffed 'posuit', nos. 41 b, 51 ; **88, 3, 223 ;**
— prúftú 'posita', no. 1 16 ; **69, 2,
244, 1.** Ftn. p. 170.

*pru* 'pro', no. 2 13, 24. **58, 300, 8.**

*pru-*, **17, 8, 300, 8.**

*pruhipid* 'prohibuerit', perf. subj. 3 sg.,
no. 2 25 ; — fut. perf. 3 sg. *pruhipust*, no. 2 26.　Cf. *hipid, hipust.*
**218.**

prupukid 'ex antepacto, by previous
agreement', no. 1 2. **17, 8, 86, 5,
173, 5, 250, 2.**

*pruter pan (pam)* 'priusquam', no.
2 4, 16. **188, 2, 202, 4.**

Pukalatúí 'Puclato', dat. sg., cogn.,
no. 1 4. **81, 259, 1.**

puklum 'puerum, filium', acc. sg., no.
19 4 (and so to be read in ll. 10, 12,
for puklui, puklu) ; — (?)dat. sg.
puklui, no. 19 8 ; — abbr. puk., nom.
sg., no. 19 9. **16, 10, 81, 248, 3.**

puf 'ubi', nos. 14-17. **55, 92, 200, 3,
202, 5.**

puh, see *pod.*

punum 'quandoque', no. 19 6. **201, 5,
202, 3.**

purasiaí 'in igniaria', loc. sg. f., no.
45 16, 44.　·**15, 11, 55, 99, 6.**

puz 'ut', conj., no. 1 17, *pous*, no. 2 9.
**55** with ftn., **137, 2, 200, 3, 202, 6.**

*q.*, abbr., 'quaestor', no. 2 2, 28-29.
Cf. **kvaisstur.**

Rahiis 'Raius', gent., no. 40 ; — gen.
sg. Rahiieis, no. 40.　**176, 2.**

Regatureí 'Rectori', no. 45 12, 40. **53,
103, 1, 246, 1.**

r[íhtúd] 'recto', abl. sg., no. 1 16.

Rufriis 'Rubrius', gent., no. 40.

saahtúm 'sanctum', nom. sg. n., no.
45 17, 45.　**73, 142.**

sakahíter 'sanciatur, sacrificetur', no.
45 19.　**210, 3, 232.**

sakaraklúm 'sacellum, templum', nos.
1 11, 46 ; — gen. sg. sakarakleís, no.
1 20 ; — abl. sg. sakaraklúd, no. 1 13.
**81, 248, 3.**

sakarater 'sacratur', no. 45 21 ; — pres.
subj. 3 sg. sakraftir, no. 31 b ; **238,
2,** b ; — perf. subj. 3 sg. sakrafír,
nos. 29, 30 ; **227, 234,** note, **238, 2,
239 ;** — gerundive nom. pl. f. sakrannas, no. 29, abbr. sakrann., no. 30.
**81.**

σακορο 'sacra', nom. sg. f. (?), no. 62.
**81, 257,** p. 258.

sakrasias '*sacrariae', nom. pl. f., no.
28. **254.**

sg. *toutam*, no. 2 19 ; — abl. sg. *toutad*, no. 2 14, 21.   **15, 2, 71.**

*tr.*, abbr., 'tribunus', no. 2 30.

**Trebiis** 'Trebius', gent., no. 9.

Τρεβις 'Trebius', praen., no. 65, abbr. Tr., nos. 9, 26, 46.

**tríbarakkiuf** 'aedificium', nom. sg. f., no. 1 37, 42.  **15, 14, 53, 162, 1, 247, 1, 263, 1.**

**tríibarak[avúm]** 'aedificare', no. 1 28, **tríbarakavúm**, no. 1 36 ; **50, 83 ;** — perf. subj. 3 pl. **tríbarakattíns**, no. 1 48; **228, 234,** note; — fut. perf. 3 pl. **tríbarakattuset**, no. 1 39, 42. **15, 14, 32, 3, 80, 1, 263, 1.**

**tríibúm** 'domum', acc. sg. f., no. 4, **[tr]íibu**, no. 17; — abl. sg. **tríbud**, no. 18.  **15, 14, 94, 171, 14.**

**trís** 'tres', nom. pl., no. 26.  **41, *a*, 82, 1, 191, 3.**

**tríataamentud** 'testamento', abl. sg., no. 4.  **91, 2, 247, 3, 290.**

**trstus** 'testes', nom. pl., no. 40.  **91, 2.**

*trutum* 'quartum'(?), acc. sg., no. 2 15 ; — **trutas**, case uncertain, no. 19 12. **191, 4,** p. 237.

**turumiiad** 'torqueatur, suffer torture', no. 19 9.  **38, 1, 80, 1, 146, 212, 1, 262, 2.**

**tuvai** 'tuae', dat. sg., no. 19 11.  **194.**

**udf...**, no. 19 7.  Possibly for ud*f*[akium 'efficere', but very doubtful (prefix *ud-*, Skt. *ud-*, not otherwise known in Italic).

**ufteis** 'optati, voluntatis', gen. sg., no. 19 7; — nom. pl. **uhftis** 'voluntates, wishes', no. 40.  **121** with note, **247, 1, *a*.**

**ulas** 'illius', no. 19 4, 12.  **197, 3.**

*-um*, enclitic particle.  **50, 201, 5.**

*ungulus* 'anulus'.  "Ungulus Oscorum lingua anulus."  Festus ed. Thewrewk, p. 570.

**Upfals, Upils,** see under **ú.**

**upsed, uupsens,** etc., see **úpsannam.**

**Urufiis** 'Orfius', gent., no. 38.  **80, 1, 174.**

*urust* 'oraverit, egerit', fut. perf. 3 sg., no. 2 14, 16.   **17, 16, 21, 211, 224.**

**uruvú** 'curva, flexa'(?), nom. sg. f., no. 1 56.  **80,** 1, p. 230.

**usurs** 'osores'(?), acc. pl., no. 19 2. **117,** *a*, **138, 178, 10.**

*ualaemom* 'optimum', acc. sg. n., no. 2 10.  **97, 189, 2.**

**Valaimas** 'Valaemae', gen. sg., no. 19 4, 8, 10 (and so to be read in ll. 2, 9, 12, for **Valamais, Valaims, Valaimais**).

**vehiian.**, see **eehiianasúm.**

**Velliam** 'Velliam', gent., no. 20. **169, 12.**

**Verehasiúí** '*Versori'(?),  no. 45 11, **Verehasiú,**  no. 45 39  (171,  3, *a*).    Cf. Διουϝει Ϝερσορει, no. 64, and Grk. Zεὺs Tρoραîos.  **80, 1, 149.**

**vereiiaí** 'iuventuti'(?),  no.  4 ; — gen. sg. **vereias,** no. 61, **verehias**(?), no. 30. **61, 3, 253, 2,** p. 240.

Ϝερσορει '*Versori', no. 64.  With Διουϝει Ϝερσορει compare Grk. Zεὺs Tρoραîos. **101, 115, 3, 138.**

**veru** 'portam', acc. pl. n., no. 15, **ver.**, no. 14 ; dat. abl. pl. **veruís,** no. 26. **15, 15.**

**Vestirikiíúí** 'Vestricio', dat. sg., no. 1 1. **81, 174, 246, 1, *a*, 256, 4.**

**Vesulliaís** '*Vesulliis', probably the name of a festival, no. 26, **Vesuliais,** no. 34.  **107, 3,** p. 247.

**Vesulliaís** '*Vesullieius', gent., no. 46. **176, 3, 253, 1.**

**Vezkeí** 'Vetusci'(?), no. 45 2, 28.  **256, 8.**

**Vibiiai** 'Vibiae', dat. sg., praen. (?), no. 19 3, 10.

**Vibis** 'Vibius', praen., nos. 37–38, **Viibis**, no. 58 ; — abbr. **V.**, nos. 4, 7, 8, 12, 14, 15, 17 ; — gen. sg., abbr. **Vi.**, nos. 29, 30.  **174.**

**Viinikiis** 'Viniclus', gent., no. 4.  **21, 174, 256,** 4.

*uincter* 'convincitur', no. 2 21.  **44, 143, 213,** 3.

**víú** 'via', nom. sg., no. 1 56, **víu,** no. 3 ; — acc. sg. **víam,** nos. 1 33, 3, **vía,** no. 3 ; **109,** 2 ; — loc. sg. **víaí,** no. 1 57 ; — acc. pl. **víass,** no. 3. **31,** *a*, **101.**

**Vírriis, Vírríiis** 'Verrius', gent., no. 20 ; — gen. sg. **Vírriieís,** no. 26, **Vírriieís,** no. 32 ; — gen. pl. **Viríium,** no. 34.  **38,** 2, **174, 176,** 5.

**Víteliú** 'Italia', no. 79 a, **Vítelliú** also found.  **5, 39,** 6, **162,** 1, **250,** 2.

*zicolom* 'diem', no. 2 14, *zico.*, no. 2 15 ; — loc. sg. *zicel*[*ei*, no. 2 7 ; — abl. sg. *ziculud*, no. 2 16 ; — nom. or acc. pl. d]**iíkúlús** (fragment) ; — gen. pl. *zicolom*, no. 2 17 ; **268** ; — abl. pl. *zicolois*, no. 2 25.  **81, 88,** 4, **100,** 3, *c*, **134,** *a*, **249,** 2.

## UMBRIAN [1]

*a.*, abbr., 'asses', v b 10 etc., vii b 4.

**aanfehtaf** 'infectas, non coctas' (?), ii a 33.  **73,** *a*, **263,** 2.

*abrof* 'apros', vii a 3, **apruf,** i b 24, 33.  **157,** 1, **171,** 11, *a*.

**abrunu** 'aprum', ii a 11 ; — acc. pl. *abrons*, vii a 43.  **157,** 1, **181,** *b*.

*Acesoniam-e* 'in Acedoniam' (Aquiloniam ?), a district of Iguvium, vi b 52 (**131,** *b*), **Akeŕuniam-em,** i b 16 ; — loc. sg. *Acersoniem,* vii a 52 (**109,** 1), **Akeŕunie,** i b 43.  **54, 144,** *a*.  See under O. **Akudunniad.**

*acnu* 'annos' (?), acc. pl. n., v b 8 etc.  **159,** *a*, **299,** 7.

**akrutu,** see *ager.*

*adro* 'atra,' acc. pl. n., vii a 25, **atru,** i b 29 ; — dat.-abl. *adrir*, vii a 9 etc., *adrer*, vii a 18.  **157,** 2.

*afero*, **aferum,** see **anferener.**

**afiktu** 'infigito', i a 31.  See **an-** and **fiktu.**

*ager* 'ager', no. 84 ; **91,** 2, **117** ; — gen. sg. *agre*, v b 9, 14 ; — abl. sg. **akru-tu,** v a 9.  **32,** 1.

*aha-, ah-, a-* 'ab-'.  **77,** 2, **264,** 1.

*ahatripursatu* '*abstripodato,tripodato', vii a 23, 36, *atripursatu,* vi b 16, *atropusatu,* vi b 36 (**66,** 7), **ahtrepuŕatu,** ii a 24 etc., **atrepuŕatu,** ii b 18.  **51,** *a*, **264,** 1.

*ahauendu* 'avertito', vii a 27.  Cf. **16,** 21, **161, 264,** 1.

**ahesnes** 'ahenis', iii 18, 19.  **83, 114, 255,** 3.

**ahtim-em** 'ad caerimonium' (?), i b 12 ; — **ahtis-per** 'pro caerimoniis', iii 24, 29.  **247,** 1, *a*.

**Ahtu** '*Actui, deo Agonio', ii a 10, 11.  **184, 251,** 6.

*aitu* 'agito', imperat. sg., vi b 18, vii a 40, 45, **aitu,** i b 29, 37, pl. **aituta,** iii 13.  **143.**

**aiu** 'agitationes, disturbances'(?), ii a 4.  **147,** 3.

**alfu** 'alba', acc. pl. n., i b 29 ; — dat.-abl. pl. *alfir,* vii a 25, 26, *alfer,* vii a 32, 34.  **124.**

*am-*, **an-, a-,** *ambr-,* **ampr-, apr-** 'amb-'.  **89,** 1, **161** with *a*.

---

[1] Alphabetical order as in Latin, but with **k** under *c*; **ŕ,** *rs,* after *r* ; **ç,** *ś,* after *s*.  **U** for *o* is put under *o* when forms with *o* are also found, otherwise under *u*.

H. Jacobsohn. Zur Ubl. Verbalbuplex K.Z.40,112/. an = (amphi) am or andf,
cf. ona, uzl = in umero thru syncope.

328　　　　　*Glossary and Index — Umbrian*　　　　　[amboltu-

*amboltu* 'ambulato', vi b 52. **161, 213, 1,** *a.* Glotta XI 252

*ambrefurent, ambretuto,* see **amprehtu.**

**amparitu** 'conlocato, set up', imperat., iii 14; — imperat. pass. **amparihmu** 'surgito, raise oneself', ii a 42. **215, 1, 264, 1, 308,** *b.*

**ampentu** 'impendito' (see p. 302), imperat. sg., ii a 20, iii 23, **ampetu,** ii b 10, 11, **apentu** iii 27 (cf. **108, 1, 135**); — fut. 2 sg. **anpenes,** ii b 27 (*n* from *nd* by **135**); — fut. perf. 2 sg. **apelus,** ii b 27, 3 sg. **apelust,** v a 17. **107, 3, 135, 236, 264, 1.**

**amperia,** a portion of the victim, perhaps the 'part about the foot', abl. sg., ii a 29. **161,** *a.*

**amprehtu** 'ambito', imperat. sg., i b 21, **apretu,** i b 20 (cf.**108,**1),pl.*ambretuto,* vi b 56, 63, 64; — fut. perf. 2 sg. **amprefuus,** i b 20, 3 pl. *ambrefurent,* vi b 56; **227. 161, 217, 4.**

*an-, a-* 'in-', verbal prefix. **264, 1.**

*an-, a-* 'in-', negative prefix. **98, 263, 2.**

*andendu* 'intendito, imponito', vii a 25, **antentu,** ii a 20, iii 15 etc., iv 21, 27, **atentu,** ii b 28. **135, 156, 264, 1.**

*ander-,* **anter-** 'inter-'. **98,** *c,* **156, 301, 1.**

*andersistu* '*intersidito, intervenito', vi a 6; **114;** — fut. perf. 3 sg. *andersesust,* vi a 7. **222,** note.

*anderuacose* '*intervacatio, intermissio sit'(?), vi b 47, **antervakaze,** i b 8. **35, 247, 1,** *a,* p. 306.

*anderuomu* 'inter———', abl. sg., vi b 41. **298.**

*andirsafust*'circumtulerit, lustraverit', vii a 46, *andersafust,* vii b 3, **aterafust,** i b 40. **131, 161,** *a,* **164,** *a,* **210,** *b,* **217, 227.**

*anferener* 'circumferendi, lustrandi', vi a 19; **135;** — infin. *afero,* vi b 48,

**aferum,** i b 10; **108, 1. 161,** *a,* **164,** *a,* **217.**

*anglaf* 'oscines', acc. pl., vi a 5, *angla,* vi a 1 etc., *ancla,* vi a 18; — nom. pl *anclar,* vi a 16. **16, 12, 155, 264, 1.**

*anglom-e* 'ad angulum', vi a 9; — *anglu-to* 'ab angulo', vi a 8, 10. **155.**

*anhostatu* 'non hastatos', vi b 60, *anostatu,* vii a 48; — dat. pl. **anhostatir,** vii a 28, 50, *anostatir,* vi b 62, vii a 13, 15. **98, 99, 3, 149,** *a,* **263, 2.**

*anouihimu* 'induitor', vi b 49. **16, 18, 215, 1, 237, 264, 1.**

**anpenes,** see **ampentu.**

*anseriato* 'observatum', supine, vi a 6, *aseriato,* vi a 1, 6, **anzeriatu,** i b 10; **57, 242;** — pres. subj. 1 sg. *aseriaia,* vi a 2; — pres. imperat. sg. *aserio,* vi a 4; **235;** — fut. imperat. sg. *aseriatu,* vi b 47, **azeriatu,** i b 8; — perf. pass. partic. abl. pl. *aseriater,* vi a 1, **anzeriates,** i a 1, ii a 17. **102, 4, 108, 1, 110, 1, 210,** *b,* **264, 1.**

**anstintu** 'distinguito', iii 20, **astintu,** iii 18, 19. **146, 153, 264, 1.**

*anstiplàtu* 'stipulator', vi a 3. **264, 1.**

**ançif,** in **pustin ançif,** probably 'in vices, by turns', ii a 25. **144, 299, 7.**

*ansihitu* 'non cinctos', vi b 59, *ansihitu,* vii a 48; — dat. pl. *ansihitir,* vi b 62, vii a 13 etc. **73, 144, 263, 2.**

**antakres** 'integris', abl. pl., ii a 42, **antakre,** i b 36, 38. Always in the phrase **antakres kumates** 'with the whole and the broken (cakes?)'. **32, 3, 263, 2, 325.**

**antentu,** see *andendu.*

**anter,** see *ander.*

**antermenzaru** 'intermenstruarum', ii a 16. **110, 1.**

**aterafust,** see *andirsafust.*

**anzeria-,** see *anseriato.*

*ape* 'cum, ubi' (always temporal), vi b 5 etc. (17 times), **ape,** i b 34 etc.

(8 times), **api**, i a 27, 30, 33, **ap**, iii 20, iv 31, *appei*, vii b 3. **16, 14, 189, 1, 202,** 8.

**apehtre** 'ab extra, extrinsecus', adv., iv 15. **142, 188,** 2, **268,** 3, *a*, **264,** 1.

**apelust, apentu,** see **ampentu.**

**aplenia** 'impleta', acc. pl. n., ii a 23; — dat.-abl. pl. **aplenies,** ii a 23. **161,** *a.*

**apretu,** see **amprehtu.**

**apruf,** see *abrof.*

**ar-, ar-** '**ad-**', see under *ars-, ar-*.

*arnipo* 'donec, until', vi b 25, 41. **202, 10, 319.**

**arçlataf** 'arculatas, circular cakes', iv 22. Cf. "arculata dicebantur circuli qui ex farina in sacrificiis fiebant." Festus ed. Thewrewk, p. 12. **154, 249,** 1.

**arvam-en** 'in arvum', iii 11; — loc. sg. **arven,** iii 13.

**arvia** '\*arvia, frumenta, fruits of the field', acc. pl. n., i a 3 etc. (7 times), **arviu,** i a 12 etc. (12 times), **aruvia,** iii 31 (**31,** *b*), *aruio*, vi a 56 etc. (12 times); — abl. pl. **arves,** i a 6 etc. (11 times), **arvis,** i a 27, i b 7 (**173,** 5). **31,** *a,* **102,** 1.

*ars-, ar-* '**ad-**'. **182** with *a*, **299,** 1.

**-ar, -a** 'ad'. **133,** *b,* **299,** 1.

**arkani** 'cantum', iv 28. **32, 3, 250,** 1.

**arepes** 'adipibus, fatty portions', abl. pl., i a 6 etc., **aripes,** i b 7, **arpes,** i a 13 (**132**), **areper,** i b 30, 33, **ariper,** i a 27, **arepe,** i b 26, 44, ii a 7. An *o*- or *ā*-stem, not a consonant-stem as in Latin. Occurs always in a phrase with following **arves** (see **325**), hence sometimes with final r even in Old Umbrian (cf. treatment before enclitics, **113,** *a*).

*arafertur* '\*adfertor, flamen', vi a 8, *arfertur*, vi a 3, vii b 3, **affertur,** i b 41, ii a 16, v a 3, 10 ; — dat. sg. *araferture,* vi a 2, **arferture,** v b 3, 5, 6 ; — acc.

sg. *araferturo*, vi a 17. **182** with *a*, **246,** 1.

*arsie* 'sancte', voc. sg., vi a 24, vi b 8, 27 ; — gen. sg. *arsier*, vi a 24, vi b 27, *asier*, vi b 8. Probably from the same root as *arsmor* 'ritus'.

*arsir* 'alius'(?), vi a 6, 7. **106,** *a*, p. 302.

*arsmahamo* 'ordinamini', vi b 56, **armamu,** i b 19 (**132,** *a*). **16, 15, 237,** *a,* **251,** 3.

*arsmatiam* 'ritualem, official', vi b 49, 50, *arsmatia*, vi a 19 etc. **16, 15, 251,** 3.

*arsmor* 'ritus', nom. pl., vi a 26 etc. (4 times), 171, 13 ; — acc. pl. *arsmo*, vi a 30 etc. (10 times), *asmo*, vi a 49. **16, 15, 251,** 3.

**Armune** '\*Admono' or '\*Admoni', epithet of Jupiter, dat. sg., ii b 7. **247,** 2, *a.* Perhaps from the same root as *arsmor.*

**arpeltu** 'adpellito, admoveto', ii a 32, ii b 19, iv 8. **132.**

**arputrati** 'arbitratu', v a 12. **59, 251,** 6.

*arsueitu* 'advehito, addito', vi a 56 etc. (11 times), **arveitu,** ii a 12 etc. (5 times), *arueitu*, vi b 23, **arveitu,** i b 6 (**132,** *a*), *aveitu*, iv 1. **182** with *a*, **143, 160.**

*asa* 'ara', abl. sg., vi a 9, **asa,** iii 23, iv 16, **e-asa** 'ex ara', ii a 38, **asa-ku** 'apud aram', ii a 39, 43 ; — **asam-ar** 'ad aram', iv 6, **asam-a,** ii a 39, iv 16, *asam-e* 'ad aram', vi a 10 (cf. **301,** 2); — dat. sg. **ase,** ii a 19, iii 22. **33, 112,** *a.*

*aseria-*, see *anseriato.*

**aseçeta** 'non secta', abl. sg., ii a 29 ; — abl. pl. **aseçetes,** iv 7. **211, 263,** 2.

**asiane,** meaning uncertain, probably loc. sg., i a 25.

*asier, asmo*, see *ars-.*

**asnata** 'non umecta', acc. pl. n., ii a 19, **asnatu,** ii a 34 ; — abl. pl. **asnates,** ii a 37, iv 9. **114, 263,** 2, **325.**

*aso* 'arsum', perf. pass. partic., ṿi b 50. **242**, *a*, **244**, 1, *c*.

astintu, see anstintu.

Açetus 'dis Ancitibus', ii a 14.

atentu, see *andendu*.

*atero* 'malum, ruin', acc. sg. n., vii a 11, 27. p. 308.

ateřafust, see *andirsafust*.

*Atiersir* 'Atiedius', adj., vii b 3 ; — dat. sg. n. Atiieřie, v a 16, ii a 1, 3 ; — nom. pl. *Atiersiur*, v b 11, 16, Atiie-řiur, v a 1, 14 ; — gen. pl. *Atiersio*, vii b 2, Atiieřiu, ii a 21, v a 12, etc. ; — dat.-abl. pl. *Atiersier*, vii b 1, *Ati-ersir*, v b 8, 14, Atiieřies, iii 24, Atiie-řier, v a 4, 16 (or gen. sg.?), Atiieřie, ii a 2, iii 29. **172**, **260**, 2.

Atiieřate 'Atiedati', dat. sg., ii b 2. **259**, 3.

*atripursatu*, *atropusatu*, etc., see *aha-tripursatu*.

atru, see *adro*.

*auie* 'augurio', dat. sg., vi b 11. **186**, **248**, 3, *a*.

aviekate 'auspicatae', dat. sg., ii a 1, 3. **248**, 3, *a*.

*auiecla* 'augurali', abl. sg. f., vi b 52, aviekla, i b 14 ; — acc. pl. m. *auiehclu*, vi a 10, *auieclu*, vi b 51, aviekluf-e, i b 14 ; — abl. pl. *auiehcleir*, vi a 9, *auieclir*, vi a 12, 13. **248**, 3, *a*.

*auif* 'avis', acc. pl., vi b 47, 48, *aueif*, vi a 4, 18, *auuei*, vi a 3 (**24**, *a*), avif, i b 8, avef, i b 10 ; — abl. pl. *aueis*, vi a 1 (**29**), avis, ii a 16, aves, i a 1. **101**.

*auirseto* 'non visum', vi a 28 etc., vi b 30. **244**, 4, **263**, 2.

azeriatu, see *anseriato*.

benus 'veneris', fut. perf. 2 sg., ii b 16, 3 sg. *benust*, vi b 53, 3 pl. *benurent*, vi b 57, benurent, v a 25, 28, v b 5 ; **224** ; — fut. perf. pass. *benuso* 'ven-tum erit', vi b 64, 65, vii a 2 ; **238**, 2 ;

—fut. 2 sg. menes, i b 15 ; **125**, 2, *a*, **164**, *a*. **151**.

berva 'verua', ii a 26, 33 ; — abl. pl. berus, ii a 23, 35. **151**.

*bio* 'sacellum' (?), no. 83. Cf. Pael. *biam*. Etym. uncertain.

bum 'bovem', ii a 5 ; — abl. sg. *bue*, vi a 25 etc. ; — acc. pl. *buf*, vi a 22, vi b 1, 19, buf, i a 3, 11, 20 ; — gen. pl. *buo*, vi a 54. **54**, **151**, **183** with *b*.

-c, -k, pronom. enclitic, **201**, 1.

*cabriner* 'caprini', gen. sg., v b 12, 17. **157**, 1, **255**, 5.

kabru 'caprum', ii b 17, kaprum, ii b 1, kapru, ii b 10 ; — gen. sg. kapres, ii b 12. **157**, 1.

*calersu* 'cal(l)idos, with a white fore-head', vi b 19, kaleřuf, i a 20. **260**, 1.

kanetu 'canito', iv 29. **88**, 1, **141**.

*capirse* 'capidi', dat. sg., vi b 24, 37, kapiře, i a 29, 32, ii a 8 ; — acc. sg. *capirso*, vi b 25 ; — abl. sg. kapiře, ii a 34, 41 ; — acc. pl. *capif*, vi b 18, vii a 39, 45 (**139**, 1), kapi, i b 29, 37, kapiř, i a 18 ; **139**, 1, **178**, 10 ; — abl. pl. kapiřus, ii a 33, iv 5.

kartu 'distribuito', ii a 23. **17**, 3.

karu 'pars', v a 24, 27, v b 4 ; — dat. sg. karne 'carni', ii a 1, 3 ; — abl. sg. karue 'carne', ii a 30 ; — abl. pl. kar-nus 'carnibus', iv 7. **17**, 3, **97**, **161** with *c*.

*carsitu* 'calato, appellato', imperat., vi a 17, vii a 43, kařetu, i b 33, kařitu, iii 21. **106**, **212**, *b*.

*carsom-e*, name of some building or locality at Iguvium, vi a 13, 14. Etym. uncertain.

*Casiler* '*Casili', gen. sg., v b 14.

*Casilos* '*Casilas', nom. sg., v b 13 ; — dat. sg. *Casilate*, v b 16, Kaselate, ii b 8. **85**, **259**, 3.

**Kastruçiie** '*Castrucii', gen. sg., gent., v a 3. **174, 256,** 5.

_castruo_ 'capita'(?), acc. pl., vi a 30 etc. (11 times), **kastruvuf,** v a 13, 18, **kastruvu,** v a 20, 22. **17,** 2, **32,** 1, **138, 171,** 13, **248,** 4, _a,_ ftn. p. 236 f.

**katel** 'catulus', ii a 43; — gen. sg. **katles,** ii a 22, 27, **katle,** ii a 15; — acc. sg. **katlu,** ii a 18, 20, 29. **88,** 4.

_caterahamo_ '*catervamini', form in troops,' vi b 56, **kateramu,** i b 20. **102,** 4, **237,** _a._

**kazi,** iii 16, 18, meaning and etym. uncertain.

**kebu** 'cibo', iv 23. **123, 144,** _a._

_cehefi_ 'accensum sit'(?), perf. subj. pass. 3 sg., vi a 20. **144,** _a,_ **227, 238,** 2, **239.**

_cisterno_ 'cisterna', nom. sg., no. 83.

_Clauerniur_ '*Clavernii', nom. pl., v b 8; — dat. pl. _Clauerni,_ v b 10, **Klaverniie,** ii b 3. **173,** 3.

**klavlaf** 'clunis', acc. pl., ii a 33; — abl. pl. **klavles,** ii a 36, iv 11. From *klā- _yelā-_ (cf. L. _clāva, clāvola_), by **88,** 4.

**kletram** 'lecticam', iii 13; — abl. sg. **kletra,** iii 13, iv 24; — dat. sg. **kletre,** iii 14. **248,** 4.

**Kluviier** 'Cluvii', gen. sg., gent., v a 15. **174.**

_com,_ -_co_(m), -**ku**(m) 'cum', prepos. **293** with _a._

_com-, co-,_ ku- 'con-'. **300,** 2.

_combifiatu_ 'nuntiato, mandato', imperat. sg., vi a 17 etc. (5 times), **kumpifiatu,** i b 14, **kupifiatu,** i b 35 (**108,** 1); — pres. subj. 2 sg. **kupifiaia,** i b 35; — perf. subj. 3 sg. _combifianši,_ vi b 52; **229;** — fut. perf. 3 sg. _combifianšiust,_ vi b 49, _combifianšiust,_ vi b 52, _combifianšust,_ vii a 5; **229. 16,** 16, **86,** 7, **136,** 161.

_comohota_ 'commota, brought, offered', abl. sg., vi a 54. **17,** 17, **244,** 4, _a._

_comoltu_ 'commolito, break in pieces' (cakes), imperat., vi b 17, 41, vii a 39, 44, 45, **kumaltu,** ii a 9, 41, iv 28, **kumultu,** i a 34; — perf. pass. partic. abl. pl. _comatir_ 'commolitis', vi b 17, 41, vii a 39, 44, 45, **kumates,** i a 34, ii a 42, iv a 29, **kumate,** i b 37, 38, ii a 10. **97, 105,** 2.

_conegos_ 'genu nixus', vi b 5, 16, vii a 37, **kunikaz,** iv 15, 18, 20. **35, 146,** _b,_ **153,** _b._

_Coredier_ '*Coredii', gen. sg., name of a god, vi b 45, **Kureties,** i b 4. **131,** _a,_ **260,** 2.

_couertu_ 'revertito', imperat., vi b 47, vii a 44, 45, **kuvertu,** i b 9, 36, 38, ii a 39; — fut. perf. 2 sg. **kuvurtus,** i b 11, 3 sg. _couortus,_ vii a 39, _courtust,_ vi a 6 (**51**); **224;** — fut. perf. pass. _couortuso,_ vi b 64; **238,** 2. **17,** 13, **97, 101, 300,** 2.

_Crabouie,_ **Krapuvi,** see _Grabouio-._

**krematra** '*crematra', acc. pl. n., ii a 23, **krematru,** ii a 28, **krematruf,** ii a 26; **171,** 13. **248,** 4, p. 309.

_cringatro_ 'cinctum', a sort of band worn about the shoulder as a token of office, acc. sg., vi b 49; **krenkatrum,** i b 11, **krikatru,** ii b 27, 29. **39,** 3, **161.**

_Cubrar_ 'Bonae', gen. sg., name of a goddess, no. 83. Cf. "Ciprum sabine bonum", Varro L. L. 5, 159. From the root of L. _cupiō_ (_br_ from _pr_ by **157,** 1).

**kukehes** 'incendet, light up'(?), fut. 3 sg., iii 21. **144,** _a._

**ku**(m), see _com._

**kumaltu** etc., see _comoltu._

**kumiaf,** see _gomia._

**kumnakle** 'in conventu', loc. sg., iii 7, 8, **kumnahkle,** v a 15. (Some prefer the dat. in v a 15, iii 7, and the gen. in iii 8.) **15,** 4, **248,** 3.

**kumne** 'comitio', loc. sg., i b 41. **15, 4,** **107,** 2 with ftn., **251,** 2.

**kunikaz,** see *conegos.*

**kupifiatu** etc., see *combiflatu.*

**kuraia** 'curet', pres. subj., v a 5; — perf. pass. part. **kuratu,** v a 24, 26, 29. **67,** 1, **112, 210,** 1, **262,** 1.

**Kureiate** '*Curiati', dat. sg., ii b 3. Cf. **259,** 3.

**Kureties,** see *Coredier.*

*curnaco* 'cornicem', vi a 2 etc. ; — abl. sg. *curnase,* vi a 1; **144. 51, 256,** 6.

**kurçlasiu** '*circulario, ultimo' (i.e. 'that which completes the circle', and so 'last' ?), abl. sg., ii a 17. **97, 295.**

**kutef** 'murmurans, speaking low', i a 6 etc., **kutep,** i b 3 (**25,** *a*). **262,** 2, **306.**

**kuveitu** 'convehito, congerito', ii a 32, 40. **143, 160, 300,** 2.

**kuvurtus,** see *couertu.*

**kvestretie** 'quaestura', abl. sg., i b 45, ii a 44. **246,** 1, *a*, **251,** 1.

**kvestur** 'quaestor', v a 23, v b 2. **21, 63.**

*daetom* 'delictum', vi a 28 etc., vi b 30. **300,** 3.

*Dei,* see *Di.*

*deitu* 'dicito', vi b 56 etc., **teitu,** ii a 26 etc. ; **143** ;—fut. perf. 3 sg. *dersicust,* vi b 63, 3 pl. *dersicurent,* vi b 62. **45, 95, 223.**

*dequrier* 'decuriis', festival of the decuriae, v b 11, 16, **tekuries,** ii b 1. **26, 191,** 10, *a*, **251,** 4.

*dersa,* see *dirsa.*

*dersecor* 'debiti', vi a 26 etc., vi b 29; **171,** 13. Probably from **de-deco-** (L. *decet*).

*dersicust, dersicurent,* see *deitu.*

*dersua* 'prosperam', vi a 2 etc., *desua,* vi b 51, 52, **tesvam,** i b 13. **132,** *b*, **258,** 2.

*desenduf* 'duodecim', acc. pl., vii b 2. **144, 191,** 10, 12, **263,** 3.

*destram-e* 'in dextram', vi b 49 ; — loc. sg. m. *destre,* vi b 50, **testre e,** ii b 27, 28 ; — loc. sg. f. *destre,* vi b 4 ; — *destru-co* 'ad dextrum', vi b 24, 38, **testru-ku,** i a 29 ; — adv. **testru sese** 'dextrorsum', iii 23, iv 15 ; **190,** 2, **307. 36,** 1, **89,** 1, **145,** 1, **188,** 2.

*deueia* 'divinam', vi a 10 ; — abl. sg. *deueia,* vi a 9. **253,** 2.

*Di* 'Iuppiter', voc. sg., vi a 25 etc. (29 times), *Dei,* vi a 26, 27 ; — acc. sg. *Dei* 'Iovem', vi a 23, 24, 25. **183** with *a*.

*dia* 'det, faciat', vi a 20. **102,** 3.

*difue* 'bifidum', acc. sg. n., vi b 4. **102,** 3, **173,** 1, **191,** 2, *a*, **263,** 1. •

*dirsa* 'det', pres. subj. 3 sg., v b 13, *dersa,* vii a 43, 44, **teřa,** i b 34 etc., 3 pl. *dirsans,* v b 11, 16, *dirsas,* v b 8 ; **45, 131, 213,** 4 ;— imperat. *dirstu,* vi b 17, 38, 39, **teřtu,** ii a 40 (**132**), **tertu,** iv 28 (**132,** *a*), *ditu,* vi b 10, 16, 25, vii a 38, **titu,** i a 33, **tetu,** ii a 9, ii b 21 ; **132** with note ; — perf. 3 sg. **dede,** no. 82 ; **131,** *c*, **223** ; — fut. perf. 3 sg. *dirsust,* vii a 43, **teřust,** i b 34 ; **223** ; — pres. pass. 3 sg. **teřte,** v a 7 ; **132, 238,** 1.

*disleralinsust* 'inritum fecerit', fut. perf., vi a 7. **114, 229, 262,** 3, **264,** 1.

*ditu,* see *dirsa.*

*dunum* 'donum', no. 82, also **dunu.** **107,** 1, **131,** *c*, **251,** 2.

*dur* 'duo', nom. m., vi b 50, vii a 46 ; **54, 82,** 2 ; — acc. f. **tuf,** i b 41 ; — acc. n. **tuva,** ii a 27, iii 32, 34 ; — dat.- abl. *duir,* v b 10, 15, **tuves,** iii 19, **tuver-e,** ii a 33 ; **31,** *b*. **191,** 2.

*dupla* 'binas', acc. pl. f., vi b 18 ; — abl. pl. m. **tupler,** v a 19. **191,** 2, *a*, **192,** 1.

*dupursus* 'bipedibus', vi b 10.  **54, 94,**
191, 2, *a*, **263,** 1.
*duti* 'iterum', adv.,  vi b 63.  **190,** 5,
**191,** 2.

e 'ex', see *ehe.*
*-e* 'in', see *-en.*
*-e, -ei*, pronom. enclitic.  **201,** 3.
*eam, eaf*, see *erec.*
*ebetraf-e* 'in exitus', vi a 12, *hebetafe,*
vi b 53 (*r* probably omitted by mistake).  **149,** *a.*
*-ec, -ek*, pronom. enclitic.  **201,** 2.
*ecla* 'omni', abl. sg. f., vii a 11, 27.
Etym. uncertain.
*ekvine,* loc. sg., ii a 13.  **141,** *a.*
*eest, eetu,* see *etu.*
*ef* 'ibi, tum ibi', adv., vi a 4.  **195,** *f.*
*efurfatu* 'expurgato'(?), vi b 17, vii a 38.
p. 305.
*ehe* 'ex', vi b 54, **e-asa** 'ex ara', ii a 38.
**300,** 4.
*ehe-, e-* 'ex-'.  **77,** 1, **300,** 4.
*eheturstahamu* 'exterminato, expellito',
vi b 55, **eturstahmu,** vi b 53, **etuřstamu,** i b 16.  **16, 20, 77,** 1, **131,** *a,*
**237, 262,** 1.
*ehiato* 'emissos', vii b 2.  **149, 171,**
11, *a*, p. 308.
**ehvelklu** 'sententiam' (**ehvelklu feia**
'take a vote'), v a 23, v b 1.  **36,** 2,
**248,** 3.
*ehueltu* 'iubeto', vi a 2.  **15,** 1, **217.**
**eikvasatis** 'collegialibus'(?), iii 24, 29.
**29,** *a.*
**eikvasese** 'collegis'(?), dat. pl. (or gen.
sg. 'collegii'?) v a 4, 16.  **29,** *a*, p. 301.
*eine,* see *enem.*
**eiscurent** 'arcessierint', v b 10, 15.  **29,** *a,*
**213,** 5, **224.**
**eitipes** 'decreverunt',  v a 2, 14.  **64,**
149, *a*, **213, 264,** 2.
**emantur** 'accipiantur', v a 8, **emantu,**
v a 10 ; — **emps** 'emptus', no. 84.  17, 9.

*en-.*  **301,** 2.
*-en, -em, -e* 'in'.  **109,** 1, **301,** 2.
*endendu* 'intendito, imponito', vi b 40,
49, **ententu,** i b 12, iii 15 ;  **135, 156 ;**
— fut. perf. 2 sg. **entelus,** i b 12, 3 sg.
**entelust,** vi b 50 ;  **107,** 3, **135, 236.**
*enem* 'tum, deinde', vii a 44, **ene,** i b 35,
**eine,** vi a 10, 11.  **202,** 16.
*enetu* 'inito', vi a 1, **enetu,** i a 1.
*enom* 'tum', vi b 38 etc. (16 times), *eno,̣*
vi b 16 etc. (9 times), *ennom,* vi b 51
etc. (5 times), *enno,* vii a 38, **enu,** i b
36 etc. (6 times) ; — **enuk,** i a 30 etc.
(3 times), **inuk,** i b 7 etc. (7 times),
**inumk,** iv 23 ; — **enumek,** i b 11 etc.
(7 times), **inumek,** iii 9 etc. (13
times).  **190,** 5, **202,** 16.
*erec* 'is', nom. sg. m., vii b 1, **erek,** v a
11, *ere*, vi b 50, **ere,** v a 4 (**201,** 1) ;—
nom.-acc. sg. n. *erse* 'id' (**201,** 1),
vi a 8 (adv. 'tum', vi a 6), **eřek,** i a
30, v a 26 (adv. 'tum', iii 33, 35, iv 3,
21, 39) ; — gen. sg. m. *erer* 'eius', vi a
23 etc. (34 times), *irer,* vi a 25, **erer-ek,**
iii 32 ; — gen. sg. f. *erar,* vi a 23 etc,̣
(41 times) ; — acc. sg. f. *eam,* vi b 16,
24 ; — abl. sg. m. n. *eru-com,* vi b 50,
**eru-ku,** iii 31 (**eruk,** adv., 'illic', iii
14) ; — abl. sg. f. **erak,** iii 12 ; — gen.
pl. *erom,* vii a 14, 50, *ero,* vi b 62, vii a
13, 28, **eru,** v a 8 (**266**) ; — acc. pl. f.
*eaf,* vii a 52, **eaf,** i b 42 ; — acc. pl. n.
*eo,* vi a 20, **eu,** ii a 2, ii b 9.  See also
*er-ont.*  **195.**
**ereçlu** 'sacrarium', 'shrine' or 'altar',
acc. sg., iv 13, **ereçlum-a,** iii 35, iv 3,
10, **ereclum-ař,** iv 6 (aes **ereçlam-ař**) ;
— loc. sg. **ereçle,** iv 17, 19.  **112,** *a.*
**eretu,** see **heri.**
**erietu** 'arietem', ii a 6.  **99,** 4.
*erom, eru,* see *est.*
*er-ont* 'idem', nom. sg. m., vi b 24,
*eri-hont,* vi b 50 ; — gen. sg. f. *erarunt,* iv 1 ; — abl. sg. m. *eru-hu,* ii b

---

22; **128**, 2, *a*; — abl. sg. f. **era-hunt,**
i b 23, *era-font,* vi b 65 **(201,** 6); —
nom. pl. m. *eur-ont,* vi b 63; — abl.
pl. m. *erir-ont,* vi b 48; — abl. pl. f.
**erer-unt,** iv 5. **195, 201,** 6.

**eruk** 'illic', adv., iii 14. Abl. sg. of
*erec* (cf. **190,** 2).

*erus* 'magmentum'(?), acc. sg., vi b 16,
25, etc. (12 times), erus, i a 33, i b 34,
etc. (12 times). **112,** *a,* p. 304 f.

*erse* 'tum', adv., vi a 6, e°rek, iii 33, 35,
iv 3, 21, 32. See *erec.* **190,** 6, **195,** *e.*

**eskamitu,** iv 1, name given to some
part of the struicula, but meaning
unknown.

*esmei* 'huic', vi a 5, 18, **esmik** 'ei', i a 28,
31; — loc. sg. *esme* 'in hoc', vi b 55.
**114, 195,** *c,* **197,** 1.

*eso* 'hic', nom. sg. f., no. 83; — abl. sg.
m. n. *essu,* vi a 43, *esu,* vi a 25 etc.
(13 times), **esu-ku,** iv 29; — abl. sg.
f. *esa,* vi b 9, 14; — gen. pl. (?) **esumek,** i b 8, *esom-e,* vi b 47; — abl. pl. n.
*esir,* vii a 10 etc., *isir,* vii a 21, 34
**(39,** 4), *esis-co,* vi a 18. **145, 3, 196.**

*esoc* 'ita', adv., vi b 25, *eso,* vi a 2 etc.
(14 times), *iso,* vi a 20 **(39,** 4), *issoc,*
vii b 3 **(39,** 4), **esuk,** v a 1, esu, ii a 3,
v a 14. **54, 190,** 2, **196,** *c.*

*esono-* 'sacer,' adj., and neut. subst.
'sacrum, sacrificium.' See *sacri-.*

1) Adj. Dat. sg., f. **esune,** v a 4;
— abl. sg. f. **esuna,** v a 5; — acc.
pl. f. **eesona,** vi a 18, *esona,* vi a
3, 5.

2) Subst. Nom.-Acc. sg. *esono,* vi a
57, **esunu,** i b 9, 38, ii a 20, 21, 42, iii 1, 14,
iv 30, *esonom-e,* vi b 50, 52, **esunum-e,**
i b 14, **esunum-en,** iii 20; — dat. sg.
*esone,* vi b 11; — loc. sg. **esune,** v a 6;
— gen. pl. (?) *esono,* vi b 47, **esunu,**
i b 8; — acc. pl. **esunu,** ii a 2; — abl.
pl. *esoneir,* vi a 18, **esunes-ku,** v a 11.
**15, 3, 112,** *a,* **255,** 6.

*est* 'est', vi a 8 etc. (very frequent), est,
i b 18, ii a 15; — *sent* 'sunt', vi a 15
etc.; — pres. subj. 2 sg. *sir,* vi b 7, 26,
*si,* vi b 26, *sei,* vi a 23, 3 sg. *si,* vi a
38, 48, si, v a 6 etc., *sei,* vi a 28 (see
also *anderuacose*), 3 pl. *sins* 'sint',
vii b 4, **sis,** v a 6; **232**; — pres. infin.
*erom* 'esse', vii b 2, **eru,** v a 26, 29,
v b 5; — fut. 3 sg. *fust,* vi a 7 etc.,
**fust,** i b 7 etc., *fus,* vi b 40, 3 pl.
**furent,** v a 22; **221**; — fut. perf. 3 pl.
**fefure** 'fuerint', ii a 4; **128,** 2, *a,* **223**;
— imperat. sg. *futu,* vi a 30 etc., **futu,**
ii a 22 etc., pl. *fututo,* vi b 61. **209.**

*est* 'ibit', see *etu.*

**estu** 'istum', acc. sg. m., ii b 24; —
acc. sg. n. *este* 'istud', vi a 1 etc.,
**este,** i a 1; — acc. pl. n. *esto,* vi a 15,
**estu,** ii a 2, ii b 23. **197,** 4.

**esuf** 'ipse', ii a 40, iv 15. **110,** 5, **122,**
2, **197,** 5.

*et,* et 'et', v b 9, v a 6 etc. (very frequent). **92, 202,** 15.

*etaians* 'itent', pres. subj. 3 pl., vi b 64,
*etaias,* vi b 65, vii a 1; — imperat. pl.
*etato,* vi b 63, **etatu,** i b 21, 22; **236,**
2, *a.* **210,** 2, **262,** 1.

**etantu** 'tanta', nom. sg., v b 6. Prefix
*e-* as in L. *e-quidem.*

**etram-a** 'alteram', iii 34; — dat. sg. f.
**etre,** ii b 2 etc.; — abl. sg. n. *etru,*
vi a 35, 38, 43; — loc. sg. **etre,** ii b 14;
— acc. pl. f. **etraf,** i a 18; — dat. pl.
m. **etre,** ii b 3, 4, 6; — abl. pl. n.
**etres,** iii 18. **188,** 2, *a,* **191,** 2.

*etu* 'ito', imperat. sg., vi b 48, vii a 39,
**eetu,** vi b 54, **etu,** i b 10 etc. **(65),** pl.
*etuto* 'eunto', vi b 51, 52, 65, vii a 1,
**etutu,** i b 15, 23, **etuta,** iii 11; — fut.
3 sg. *eest,* vi a 2, *est,* vi a 6; **221**; —
fut. perf. 3 sg. *iust,* vi a 7; **234,** *b;*
— pass. perf. subj. *ier* 'itum sit',
vi b 54; **238, 2, 239, 320. 209.**

*eturstahmu,* see *ehetursthahmu.*

**eu**, see *erec.*
*euront*, see *eront.*
**eveietu** 'voveto', ii b 8, 11. **148**, **212**, *b*.
**ezariaf** 'escas'(?), iv 27. **112**, *a*.

*fahe*, probably adv., v b 13. Meaning and etym. wholly uncertain.
**fameřias** 'familiae', nom. pl., ii b 2. **106**.
*far* 'far', v b 10, 15; — gen. sg. *farer*, v b 9, 14. **115**, 1, *a*, **117**, **182**.
*farsio* 'farrea', acc. pl. n., vi b 2, *fasio*, vi b 44, **fasiu**, ii a 12. **39**, 1, **115**, 1, **252**, 2.
**façefele** '*sacrificabilem', ii b 9. **261**.
**façia** 'faciat', ii a 17; **144**; — **feia** 'faciat', v a 23, v b 1; **219**; — infin. **façiu**, ii a 16, **façu**, ii b 22; **100**, 3, *b*, **144** with *b*; — imperat. sg. *fetu* 'facito', vi a 22 etc. (52 times), **fetu**, i a 3 etc. (48 times), *feitu*, vi b 3 etc. (5 times), **feitu**, i a 4 etc. (20 times), *feetu*, vii a 41; **99**, 1, **143**, **219** with note; — fut. perf. 3 sg. **fakust**, iv 31, 3 pl. *facurent*, vii a 43, **fakurent**, i b 34; — pass. partic. abl. sg. **feta**, ii b 13. **32**, 1, **136**, **214**, 2, **219**.
*fato* 'factum'(?), vi b 11. **325**.
**fefure**, see under *est.*
**feia**, *feitu*, see under **façia**.
**feliuf** 'lactentis', acc. pl., i a 14, *filiu*, vi b 3. **42**.
**felsva** 'holera'(?), v a 11. **21**, **149**, *b*, **258**, 2.
**ferime**, see following.
*ferine* 'in feretro, ferculo'(?), vi a 57, vi b 1, 19, 43, 45, vii a 4, **ferine**, i a 4, 13, 22, i b 3, 6, 25 (aes **ferime**), iii 16 (aes **ferime**, here retained by some, as a different word), iii 31. **178**, 6.
*fertu* 'ferto', imperat. sg., vi b 50, **fertu**, ii a 17 etc., pl. **fertuta**, iii 13; — fut. 3 sg. **ferest**, ii a 26; **221**; — pass. pres. subj. *ferar*, vi b 50; **238**, 2, **239**. **36**, 1, **124**, **217**.
**feřehtru**, meaning uncertain, acc. sg., iii 16, 18.
**fesnaf-e** 'in fanum', acc. pl., ii b 16; — loc. pl. **fesner-e** 'in fano', ii b 11. **99**, 1, **114**, **136**, **251**, 2.
**feta**, *fetu*, see **façia**.
*ficlam* 'offam, pellet, a kind of cake', vii a 42, *ficla*, vi a 56 etc. (11 times), **fikla**, ii a 18, 29; — gen. sg. **fiklas**, ii a 41; **266**. **248**, 3.
**fiktu** 'figito', i a 28. **153**.
*filiu*, see **feliuf**.
**Fise** 'Fiso, deo Fidio', dat. sg., i a 15, *Fiso*, vi b 3. **137**, 1, **171**, 3, *a*.
*Fisio-*, adj., epithet of *ocri-*, 'the Fisian Mount'. Gen. sg. *Fisier*, vi a 30 etc., *Fisie*, vi b 10; — dat. sg. *Fisie*, vi a 40, *Fisi*, vi a 30 etc. (12 times), *Fisei*, vi a 23 (**173**, 2); — acc. sg. *Fisim*, vi a 41, 49, 51, *Fisi*, vi a 31 etc., *Fisei*, vi a 29 (**29**); — abl. sg. *Fisiu*, vi a 23 etc., *Fissiu*, vi a 43, **Fisiu**, i a 5 etc.; — loc. sg. *Fisiem*, vi a 46 (**169**, 7, *a*), *Fisie*, vi a 26, 36, vi b 29. **252**, 1.
*Fisouina* 'pertaining to Fisovius', adj., abl. sg. f., vi b 9, 14.
*Fisouio-* '*Fisovius', name of a god. Gen. sg. *Fisouie*, vi b 15; — dat. sg. *Fisoui*, vi b 5, vii a 37, **Fisuvi**, i a 17; — acc. sg. *Fisoui*, vi b 6, 8; — voc. sg. *Fisouie*, vi b 9 etc. **258**, 4.
*fito* 'fitum'(?), vi b 11. **325**.
*Fondlir-e* 'in *Fontulis, at the Springs', vii a 3, **Funtler-e**, i b 24. **249**, 1.
*fons* 'favens', vi a 42 etc. (13 times), *fos*, vi a 23 etc. (4 times); — gen. sg. *foner*, vii a 20 etc.; — nom. pl. *foner*, vi b 61. **90**, 1, **255**, 2.
*-font*, see *-hont.*
*frater* 'fratres', nom. pl., v b 11, *fra-teer*, v b 16, **frater**, iii 5 etc.; **76**, 3, **90**, 1, **117**; — gen. pl. *fratrom*, vii b 1, **fratrum**, iii 10, **fratru**, ii a 21 etc. (9 times); — dat. pl. *fratrus*, v b 8,

13, vii b 1 ; — abl. pl. **fratrus-per,**
ii a 2, iii 23, 28. **33, 124, 246,** 2.

*fratreca* ' *fratrica, pertaining to the
brotherhood', abl. sg., vii b 2.

*fratrecate* ' magisterio, in the office of
*fratricus', loc. sg., vii b 1.     **259,**
2.

*fratrexs* ' *fratricus, fratrum magister',
vii b 1, **fratreks,** v a 23, v b 1; **145,** 2 ;
— dat. sg. *fratreci,* vii b 4 ; **144,** *a.*
**45, 256,** 2.

**frehtef** '*fricta', ' roasted pieces '(?),
acc. pl., ii a 26.   Also taken as pres.
partic. nom. sg. ' frigidans'.

**frehtu** ' frictum '(?), iv 31.  **pune frehtu**
' poscam et frictum' or ' poscam calidam '(?).  Also taken as ' frigidum'.

*frif* ' fruges', acc. pl., vi a 42 etc. (5
times), *fri,* vi a 30 etc. (6 times).
**59, 147,** 4.

*frite* ' fretu, fiducia', vi a 24 etc. **178,** 5,
**294.**

*frosetom* ' fraudatum', vi a 28 etc. **69,**
**138, 211, 262,** 1.

**fuia** ' fiat', iii 1 ; — fut. **fuiest** ' fiet', v a
9.  **215,** 3.

*Fulonie* ' Fullonii', no. 83.

**Funtler-e,** see *Fondlir-e.*

*furfant* ' purgant'(?), vi b 43, **furfaθ,**
i b 1 (**25,** *a*).  **204,** 2, p. 305.

*furo* ' forum', acc. sg., vii a 52, **furu,**
i b 42.  **51, 136.**

*fust,* **furent,** *futu,* etc., see *est.*

*gomia* ' gravidas', vi a 58, **kumiaf,** i a 7.
**16, 17, 94.**

*Grabouio-* ' *Grabovius', epithet of
Mars, Jupiter, and Vovionus.  Dat.
sg. *Grabouie,* vi b 19, *Grabouei,* vi a
22, vi b 1, **Krapuvi,** i a 3, 11, 21 ; —
acc. sg. *Graboui,* vi a 23, *Graboue,*
vi a 24, 25 ; — voc. sg. *Grabouie,* vi a
25 etc. (29 times), *Crabouie,* vi a 27,
37.  Connection with L. *Grādīvus*

attractive, but no satisfactory explanation of U. *b* : L. *d.*  **258,** 4,
~~Fraestochs~~. *f. Bezzenberger* (1921) *81-16.*

*habe* ' habet, restat'(?), vi b 54, **habe,**
i b 18 ; — pres. subj. **habia,** v a 17,
19, 21 ; — fut. *habiest,* vi b 50 etc. (5
times) ; **218** ; — imperat. sg. *habitu,*
vi a 19, vi b 4, **habetu,** ii b 23 etc.
(7 times), pl. *habituto,* vi b 51, **habe-**
**tutu,** i b 15 ; — fut. perf. 2 sg. *habus,*
vi b 40, 3 pl. *haburent* ' ceperint',
vii a 52.  **212, 3, 218.**

*habina* ' agnas'(?), acc. pl., vi b 22, 23, 24,
**habina,** i a 27, **hapinaf,** i a 24 ; — gen.
pl. **hapinaru,** i a 33.  **30, 6, 149,** *a,*
**151.**

**hahtu** ' capito', imperat. sg., ii a 22,
**hatu,** i b 11, *hatu,* vi b 49, pl. **hatutu**
' capiunto', i b 42, *hatuto,* vii a 52.
**121, 216, 218.**

*hebetafe,* see *ebetrafe.*

**heri** ' vult', iv 26 ; — fut. 2 sg. **heries,** i b
10, ii b 21, 3 sg. *heriest,* vii a 52, *heries,*
vi b 48 (127, 3) ; **221** ; — perf. subj.
3 sg. *heriiei,* ii a 16 ; **29, 42, 224,** *b,*
**234,** note, **320** ; — pres. indic. pass.
3 sg. **herter** ' oportet', ii a 40, iii 1,
**herte,** v a 6, 8, 10, *herti,* v b 8, 11, 13, 16,
*hertei,* vii b 2 ; **29, 39, 2, 216, 238,**
2, *a* ; — perf. subj. pass. 3 sg. **herifi**
' oportuerit', v b 6 ; **227, 238, 2, 239** ;
— perf. pass. partic. abl. sg. *heritu*
' optato, consulto', vi a 27, 47, vi b 29,
*hereitu,* vi a 37, **eretu,** ii a 4 (149, *a*);
**190, 2, 307.**   **15, 1, 149, 214,** 2.

*heriei* ' vel', vii a 3, *herie,* vi b 19, 20.
**203,** 19.

**heris** ' vel', i a 4, i b 6, **heri,** i a 4, 22, ii b
9, 10, *heri,* vi a 57, vi b 46.   **15, 1,**
**202,** 19.

*Hoier* ' *Hoii', gen. sg., name of a god,
vi a 14.

*holtu* ' aboleto'(?), imperat., vi b 60, vii a
49.  **149,** *a.*

*homonus* 'hominibus', v b 10, 15. **54, 149, 181** with *b*.

*Honde* '*Honto, deo inferno', dat. sg., vi b 45, **Hunte**, i b 4, ii a 20, 34.

*hondomu* 'infimo', abl. sg., vi a 9, 10. **15, 5, 86, 1, 149, 156, 189**, 1.

*hondra* 'infra', prep., vi a 15, vii a 52, **hutra**, i b 42. **15, 5, 149, 156, 188, 2, 190, 3, 299, 4**.

*hondu* 'pessumdato'(?), imperat., vi b 60, vii a 49. **264, 2**.

*-hont* '-dem', pronom. enclitic. **149,** *a*, **201, 6**.

*Horse* '*Hodio', dat. sg., name of a god, vi b 43, **Huřie**, i b 2.

*hostatu* 'hastatos', vi b 59, vii a 48; — dat. pl. *hostatir*, vi b 62, vii a 13 etc. **99, 3, 138,** *a*, **259,** 1.

**Hule** '*Holae', dat. sg., name of a goddess, iv 17. **149,** *a*.

**huntak** 'puteum'(?), iii 3, iv 32. **256, 6**.

**Huntia**, name of the festival in honor of the god Hontus, abl. sg., ii a 15, 17. Probably ablative of time (**295**), 'at the Hontus festival'.

**hutra**, see *hondra*.

*-i, -e, -ei*, pronom. enclitic. **201, 3**.
*-i = -en*. **39, 5**.

*Iapusco* '*Iapudicum', adj., acc. sg., vii a 47, *Iabuscom*, vi b 58, **Iapuzkum**, i b 17; — gen. sg. *Iapuscer*, vii a 48, *Iabuscer*, vi b 54, 59, vii a 12; — dat. sg. *Iabusce*, vii a 12. **256,** 1.

**Ikuvins** 'Iguvinus', coin-legend; — voc. pl. **Ikuvinus**, i b 21, 22, **Ikuvinu**, i b 20, *Iiouinur*, vi b 63, *Iouinur*, vi b 56; — acc. sg. f. *Iiouinam*, vi a 49 etc., *Iouinam*, vi b 12, *Iiouina*, vi a 31 etc., *Iouina*, vi a 29, 39; — gen. sg. f. **Iiuvinas**, i b 2, 5; *Iiouinar*, vi a 32 etc., *Iouinar*, vi a 30 etc. ; — dat. sg. f. **Ikuvine**, i b 13, *Iioueine*, vi a 5, *Iiouine*, vi a 18 etc., *Iouine*, vi a 33

etc.; — loc. sg. f. *Iouinem*, vi a 46 (**169,** 7, *a*), *Iiouine*, vi b 29, *Iouine*, vi a 26, 36; — abl. sg. f. **Ikuvina**, i a 5 etc., **Iiuvina**, i b 5 etc., *Iiouina*, vi a 23 etc., *Iouina*, vi a 25 etc. **48, 148, 187, 255, 5, 258, 4**.

**iepi** 'ibi, then'(?), iii 21. The form is not satisfactorily explained. **39,** 1, **195,** *d*.

**iepru**, meaning uncertain, ii a 32. Sometimes explained as 'pro iis', but this is very doubtful. **39,** 1, **195,** *d*.

**ier**, see *etu*.

*ife* 'ibi, eo, there', vi b 39, 40, **ife**, ii b 12, 13 ; — *ifont* 'ibidem', vi b 55; **201,** 6. **195,** *f*.

**inenek** 'tum', iii 20. Probably a mistake for **inemek** (cf. **inumek**). **202,** 16.

**inuk, inumek**, etc., see *enom*.

*iouies* 'iuvenibus', dat. pl. vi b 62 etc.; — acc. pl. *iouie*, vi b 59, vii a 48. **96, 100,** 1, **186**.

*Iouio-* 'Iovius', epithet of Tefer, Trebus, Hontus, and Torra. Also used without any other name, i b 1 (adj.), ii a 6, 8 (subst.). Dat. sg. m. **Iuvie**, i a 24 etc., **Iuvi**, i a 28, *Iouie*, vi a 58, *Ioui*, vi b 22 (**Iuvie**, i a 8, *Iouie*, vi a 58, taken by some as f.) ; — dat. sg. f. **Iuvie**, i b 43, *Iouie*, vii a 53 ; — acc. sg. m. *Ioui*, vi b 26, 27 ; — abl. sg. m. **Iuviu**, i b 1; — voc. sg. m. *Iouie*, vi b 28 etc., *Iiouie*, vi b 35 (this spelling after *Iiouine* etc.); — voc. sg. f. *Iouia*, vii a 47, 49. **252,** 1 with *a*.

**irer**, see *erec*.

*isec* 'item', adv., vi b 25, **isek**, iv 4. **39,** 4, **196,** *c*.

**iseçeles** 'insectis', abl. pl., iv 7. Probably mistake for **iseçetes**. **39, 5**.

*isir, iso, issoc*, see *eso, esoc*.

**isunt** 'item', ii a 28, 36, iii 16, 17. **39, 4**.

**itek** 'ita', iv 31.  **195,** *f.*

*iuka* 'preces', acc. pl. n., iii 28, **iuku,** ii b 23.  **249, 1.**

*iuengar* 'iuvencae', nom. pl., vii b 2; — acc. pl. *iuenga*, vii a 51, *iveka*, i b 40, 42 (**108,** 1).  **81,** *b,* **156.**

**Iuieskanes** '*Iuiescanis', dat. pl., ii b 6, **Iuieskane,** ii b 5.

**Iupater** 'Iuppiter', voc. sg., ii b 24; — dat. sg. **Iuvepatre,** ii a 5 etc. (5 times), **Iuve patre,** ii b 7, **Iuvip.,** ii a 10, **Iuve,** i a 3, *Iuue,* vi a 22.  Cf. also *Di.*  **183** with *a.*

*iust,* see *etu.*

**maletu** 'molitum', ii a 18.  **97, 244,** 4.

*mandraclo* 'mantele', acc. sg., vi b 4, **mantrahklu,** ii a 19, **mantraklu,** ii b 16.  **97, 263,** 1, p. 304.

*mani* 'manu', abl. sg., vi b 24, **mani,** ii a 32 (**59**) ; — loc. sg. **manuv-e,** ii b 23 ; **185,** 2 ; — acc. **manf,** ii a 38.  **185** with 8.

*maronatei* '*maronatu, office of maro', loc. sg., no. 84 ; — abl. sg. *maronato* (**171,** 6, *a*), no. 83.  **247,** 2, **259,** 2, **302,** p. 310.

*Marte* 'Marti', dat. sg., vi b 1, 43, **Marte,** i a 11, i b 2, **Marti,** ii a 11 (or possibly 'Martio', to foll.).

*Martio-* 'Martius', adj., usually epithet of Cerrus.  Gen. sg. *Martier,* v b 9, 15, vi b 58 etc. (31 times), **Marties,** i b 28, 31 ; — dat. sg. *Martie,* vii a 3, **Marti,** i b 24 ; — voc. sg. *Martie,* vi b 57, 61.

*Matrer* 'Matris', no. 83.  **33.**

*mefa* 'mensam, libum', acc. sg., vi a 56, vi b 17, 20, vii a 4, 38, **mefa,** i a 16, iv 14; — abl. sg. *mefa,* vi b 5, 9, 14, vii a 37, **mefa,** ii b 13 ; — dat. sg. **mefe,** ii b 28.  **110,** 3 with *a,* p. 304.

*mehe* 'mihi', vi a 5.  **193** with *a.*

**menes,** see **benus.**

**menzne** 'mense', ii a 17.  **110, 1.**

*mers* 'ius', vi b 31, (*mersest*), vi b 55, (*mersi, mersei = mers-si* 'ius sit'), vi a 28, 38, 48, **mers,** i b 18 ; — abl. pl. **mersus** 'ex moribus', iii 6 ; **132,** *a,* **287.  15, 6, 94, 132, 182.**

*mersto* 'iustum, prosperum' ('right, proper', and so 'favorable', used of birds of omen), acc. sg. m., vi a 3, 4, 16, 17 ; — acc. sg. f. *mersta,* vi a 3, 4, 16, *meersta,* vi a 17 (**76,** 1) ; — abl. sg. m. *merstu,* vi a 1 ; — acc. pl. f. *merstaf,* vi a 4, *mersta,* vi a 3, 4, 18.  **15, 6, 88,** 3, **259,** 1.

*mersuva* 'iusta, solita', abl. sg. f., iii 11 ; — acc. pl. m. **mersuva,** iii 28.  **15, 6, 132,** *a,* **258,** 2.

*mestru* 'maior', nom. sg. f., v a 24, 27, v b 4.  **147,** 3, *a,* **188,** 3.

*Miletinar* '*Miletinae', gen. sg., vi a 13.

*motar* 'multae', gen. sg., vii b 4 (**269,** *a*) ; — nom. sg. **muta,** v b 2, **mutu,** v b 6 ; — acc. sg. **muta,** v b 3.  **49, 105,** 2, **146.**

*mugatu* 'mugito, muttito, make a noise', imperat., vi a 6 ; — perf. pass. part. *muieto,* vi a 7.  **58, 148, 210,** 3, **211.**

**muneklu** 'munus, sportulam', v a 17, 19, 21.  **67,** 1, **248,** 3.

**Museiate** '*Musiati', dat. sg., ii b 5.  Cf. **259,** 3.

**muta,** see *motar.*

**n.,** abbr., 'nummis', no. 83.

*Naharcom* '*Narcum', acc. sg. n., vi b 58, vii a 47, **Naharkum,** i b 17 ; — gen. sg. *Naharcer,* vi b 54, 59, vii a 12, 48 ; **144,** *a ;* — dat. sg. *Naharce,* vii a 12.  **256,** 1.

**naraklum** 'nuntiatio, announcement' (of the results of inspecting the entrails), ii a 1.  **147,** 2, **248,** 3.

*nuratu* 'narrato, speak, announce', imperat., vi a 22, 56, 59, etc. (14 times),

naratu, ii a 3, ii b 8 etc. (5 times).
147, 2.

natine 'natione, gente', ii a 21, 35, ii b
26. 147, 2, 181, 247, 1.

*neip* 'non', vi a 27, 36, 46, vi b 29, vii b 3,
neip, v a 29, ii a 4 ; — prohib. *neip*
'neve', vi b 51, *neip . . . nep* 'nec . . .
nec', vi a 6. 29, *b*, 92, 202, 20.

neiřhabas 'ne adhibeant', iv 33. 29,
84, 202, 20, 318.

*nep*, see *neip*.

*nepitu* 'inundato', imperat., vi b 60, vii a
49. 212, *b*, 310.

*Ner.*, abbr. praen. (*Nero* or *Nerius*),
no. 84.

*nerf* 'principes, optimates', title of
rank, acc. pl., vi a 30 etc. (13 times) ;
— dat. pl. *nerus*, vi b 62 etc. (5 times).
15, 7, 130, 2, *c*.

*nertru* 'sinistro', abl. sg., vi b 25, *nertru-co*, vi b 37, 39, nertru-ku, i a 32.
16, 18, 188, 2.

*nersa* 'donec', vi a 6. 202, 11.

*nesimei* 'proxime', adv., vi a 9. 15, 8,
29, 42, 138, *a*, 189, 1 (with ftn.),
190, 1, 307.

*ninctu* 'ninguito' (transit., 'snow upon'), vi b 60, vii a 49. 114, *a*, 146,
153, 161, 213, 3, 310.

niru, meaning uncertain, acc. sg., ii b
15. Probably some sort of herb.

*nome* 'nomen', vi a 30 etc. (13 times),
numem, i b 17 (109, 1) ; — gen. sg.
*nomner*, vi b 54 etc. (4 times) ; — dat.
sg. *nomne*, vi a 24 etc. (40 times) ; —
abl. sg. *nomne*, vi a 17, *nomne-per*,
vi a 23 etc. (40 times). 54, 181, 247,
3.

*Noniar* 'Noniae', gen. sg., vi a 14.

*nosue* 'nisi', vi b 54. 67, 1, 95, 202, 14,
20.

numem, see *nome*.

numer 'nummis', abl. pl., v a 17, 19, 21.

*Nurpier* '*Nurpli', gen. sg., vi a 12.

*nuřpener* '— -pondiis', designation of a
small coin, abl. pl., v a 13. 94,
263, 1.

nuvime 'nonum', adv., ii a 26. 86, 1,
190, 1, 191, 9.

nuvis 'noviens', adv., ii a 25. 192, 2.

*ocar* 'arx, mons', the Sacred Mount of
Iguvium, nom. sg., vi b 46, ukar, i b 7 ;
91, 2, *b* ; — gen. sg. *ocrer*, vi a 8 etc.
(14 times) ; — dat. sg. *ocre*, vi a 23 etc.
(14 times) ; — acc. sg. *ocrem*, vi a 49,
51, vi b 12, *ocre*, vi a 29 etc. (6 times) ;
— abl. sg. *ocri-per*, vi a 23 etc. (17
times), *ocre-per*, vi a 25, 34, 35, ukriper, i a 5 etc. (8 times), ukri-pe, i a
12 ; — loc. sg. *ocrem*, vi a 46, *ocre*, vi a
26, 36, vi b 29, ukre, v a 16 (usually
taken as dat.). Cf. "ocrem antiqui,
. . . , montem confragosum dicebant."
Festus ed. Thewrewk, p. 196. 99,
3, 257, 2.

*oht*, see uhtretie.

*onse* 'in umero', loc. sg., vi b 50, uze,
ii b 27, 28. 110, 1.

*ooserclom-e* 'ad *observaculum'(?), vi a
12. 77, 3.

*opeter* 'lecti, choice', perf. pass. partic.
gen. sg. n., v b 9, 14 ; — imperat. sg.
upetu 'optato, deligito', v a 7, ii b 1,
8, 11, iii 22, 26, pl. upetuta iii 10.
212, *b*. For the meaning, cf. the
early and poetical use of L. *optō* in
sense of 'choose'.

*orer* 'illius'(?), vi a 26, 36, 46, vi b 29 ; —
abl. sg. m. *uru*, vi b 55, uru, i b 18 ; —
abl. sg. f. ura-ku, v a 5 ; — abl. pl.
ures, iv 33. 197, 2.

*ortom* 'ortum', nom. sg. n., vi a 46,
*orto*, vi a 26, 36, vi b 29 ; — nom. pl. n.
urtu 'orta', ii a 4 ; — nom. pl. f. urtas
'ortae, surgentes, standing up', iii
10 ; — abl. pl. urtes 'surgentibus', iii
4. 17, 11.

*osatu* 'operator, facito, make', imperat., vi b 24, 37 ; — pass. partic. nom. sg. f. *oseto*, no. 83. 17, 4, **49, 88,** 3, **122,** 3, **211, 262,** 1.

*ose* 'opere'(?), abl. sg., vi a 26, 36, 46, vi b 29. **182,** p. 303.

*ostendu* 'ostendito, set out, furnish', imperat. sg., vi a 20, ustentu, i a 3 etc. (12 times), ustetu, i a 17 etc. (6 times) (**108,** 1), pl. ustentuta, iii 5 ; **135, 156** ; — fut. pass. *ostensendi*, vi a 20 ; **39,** 2, **137,** 2, **156, 221.** 17, 15, **49, 122,** 1.

*ote* 'aut', v b 10 etc. (6 times), ute, v a 23 etc. (4 times). **43, 69, 92, 202,** 17.

*oui* 'ovis', acc. pl., vi b 43, uvef, i b 1 ; — acc. sg. uvem, iii 8 etc. (5 times), uve, ii a 10, i a 31. **101.**

*p.*, abbr., 'pondo', v b 9, 14.

*paca* 'causa', prepos., vi a 20. **304.**

*pacer* 'propitius', nom. sg. m., vi a 23 etc. (13 times) ; **91,** 2 ; — nom. sg. f. *pacer*, vii a 14, 17, 31, 50 ; **187,** 2, *a* ; — nom. pl. *pacrer*, vi b 61. **187,** 2, **257,** 2.

*Padellar* 'Patellae', gen. sg., vi a 14. **91,** 2, *a*, 107, 3, **158.**

*pafe*, see *poi.*

*pane* 'quam', adv., vii a 46, pane, i b 40. **92, 190,** 6, **202,** 4.

*panta* 'quanta', nom. sg. f., v b 2 ; — acc. sg. f. panta, v b 3. **150.**

*panupei* 'quandoque', vii b 1. **54, 201,** 4, **202,** 12.

*parfa* 'parram', vi a 2 etc. (5 times), parfam, i b 13 ; — abl. sg. *parfa*, vi a 1. **115,** 2.

*pars-est* 'par est', vii b 2. **117,** *b*, **182.**

*pase* 'pace', vi a 30 etc. (15 times). **144.**

*-pater* 'pater' in Iupater, voc. sg., ii b 24 ; — dat. sg. in Iuve patre, ii b 7 etc. **32,** 1.

*-pe, -pei* '-que', pronom. enclitic. **201,** 4.

**pehatu,** see *pihatu.*

*peica* 'picam', acc. sg., vi a 3 etc. (4 times) ; — abl. sg. *peica*, vi a 1. **48.**

*peico* 'picum', acc. sg., vi a 3 etc. (4 times); — abl. sg. *peiqu*, vi a 1 (**26**). **48.**

**Peieŕiate** '*Peiediati', dat. sg., ii b 4. Cf. **259,** 3.

*peiu* 'piceos', acc. pl. m., vii a 3, peiu, i b 24 ; — acc. pl. f. *peia*, vii a 6, peia, i b 27. **144,** *b.*

*pelmner* 'pulmenti, pulpamenti, meat', gen. sg., v b 12, 17. **36,** 2, **125,** 1.

*pelsatu* 'sepelito'(?), vi b 40 ; — gerundive nom. sg. m. pelsans, ii a 43, acc. sg. m. pelsanu, ii a 6, iii 32, acc. pl. f. *pelsana*, vi b 22, pelsana, i a 26. **262,** 1, *a*, p. 305.

*peperscust*, see perstu.

**pepurkurent** 'poposcerint', fut. perf., v b 5. **97, 145,** 1, **223.**

*pequo* 'pecuum', gen. pl. (?), vi a 30 etc. (11 times). **26, 184,** p. 236 f.

*per-.* **299,** 5.

*-per* 'pro'. **91,** 2, **300,** 8.

*-per* with numerals. **127,** 3, **192,** 2, **299,** 5. See ftn. p. 321.

*peracni-* 'sollemnem, sacrificial', and subst. 'hostia'. Acc. sg. m. peraknem, ii a 10, perakne, ii a 5, 12, ii b 7, 10 ; — acc. sg. n. (subst.) perakne 'hostiam,' ii a 5, 14 ; — acc. pl. n. perakneu, v a 7. For *peracnio,* vi a 54, see under *peracri-*. The meaning is not essentially different from that of *seuacni-*. The two words occur together only in ii b 8, 11, and here possibly sevakne is used substantively. **159,** *a,* **187,** 2, **263,** 1, *a.*

*peracri-* 'opimus, in perfect condition'. Acc. sg. perakre, i b 40 ; — abl. sg. *peracri*, vi a 34 etc. (7 times), *peracrei*, vi a 25, 29 ; — gen. pl. *peracrio,* vii a 51, vi a 54 (in vi a 54, aes *perac-nio*, but cf. *bue peracri*, vi a 34, 45, 53); — abl. pl. *peracris*, vi b 52, 56. **187, 2, 299,** 5.

**Peraznanie** '*\*Perasnaniis*', dat. pl., ii b 7.

*percam* 'virgam', vi b 53, *perca*, vi a 19 etc. (6 times); — acc. pl. *perca*, vi b 51, **perkaf**, i b 15. **139,** 1.

*peretom* 'peritum', vi a 27, 37, 47, vi b 30.

**pernaiaf** 'anticas', acc. pl. f., i b 10 ; — abl. pl. f. **pernaies**, i a 2. **61, 3, 253,** 1, **300,** 8, *a*.

*perne* 'ante,' adv., vi b 11. **300,** 8, *a*.

*persaea* etc., *perse, persi, perso*, see under *rs* = *ř*.

*persclo* 'precationem, sacrificium', acc. sg., vi a 1, **persklum**, i a 1, **persklum-ař**, iii 21 ; — gen. sg. *persler*, vi a 27 etc. (4 times), *pescler*, vi a 47 etc. (4 times) ; — abl. sg. *persclu*, vi b 36 etc. (4 times), *pesclu*, vi b 15, vii a 8, **persklu**, iii 12. **97, 116, 1, 129, 2, 145,** 1.

*persnimu* 'precator,' imperat. sg. pass. (dep.), vi a 55 etc. (20 times), *pers-nihimu*, vi b 17 etc. (4 times), *pes-nimu*, vi b 9, 23, **persnimu**, i b 7, 21, **persnihmu**, ii a 27 etc. (15 times), **pes-nimu**, i a 6 etc. (23 times), pl. *persni-mumo*, vi b 57, *persnihimumo*, vii a 47, *pesnimumo*, vi b 64, 65, vii a 1 ; — perf. pass. partic. nom. sg. m. *persnis*, vi b 39, *pesnis*, vi b 40, 41. **97, 116, 2, 145, 1, 146, 214, 1, 237, 262, 3.**

*persontro-* 'figmentum'(?), subst. m. Acc. sg. *pesondro*, vi b 24, 37, 39, 40, **pesuntru**, i a 27, **pesuntrum**, i a 30, **pesutru**, ii a 8, **persutru**, ii b 13, **per-suntru**, iv 17, 19 ; — dat. sg. **persun-tre**, iv 21 ; — abl. sg. *persontru*, vi b 28, *persondru*, vi b 31, 35 ; — acc. pl. *pesondro*, vi b 37 (171, 11, *a*) ; — abl. pl. *pesondris-co*, vi b 40. p. 305.

*perstico*, see under *persi*, below.

**perstu** 'ponito'(?), imperat., ii a 32, **pestu**, ii b 19 ; — fut. perf. 3 sg. *pe-perscust*, vi b 5, *pepescus*, vii a 8. **116, 3, 146, 213,** 5.

**pert** 'trans', ii a 36. **15, 9, 299,** 5.

**pertentu** 'protendito,' ii a 31, iv 8. **299,** 5.

*pertom-e*, acc. sg., vi a 14, name of some building or locality at Iguvium.

*persaeo-* 'humi stratus, pronus'(?), adj. Acc. pl. f. *persaea*, vii a 41, 54, *pe-rsaia*, vii a 7, **peřaia**, i b 28, 32, 44 ; — acc. sg. m. **peřaem**, ii a 11, iii 32 (173, 1); — nom. acc. sg. n. ('sacri-fice' being expressed or understood) *persae*, vi a 58, vi b 3, **peřae**, ii a 13, 22 (173, 1). **61, 3, 253,** 1, p. 304.

*persi*, **peře**, see *pirse.*

*persi* 'pede', abl. sg., vi b 24 etc., **peři**, i a 29, 32 ; — *persi-co* or *persei-co* 'ad pedem', vi b 25 (aes *perstico*) ; — acc. sg. **peřu**, ii a 24 (or 'fossam'?). **131, 178,** 5, *a*.

*perso* 'solum, fossam, trench for the libations', vi b 24, 37, *persom-e*, vi b 38 etc., **peřum**, i a 29, 32, **peřum-e**, ii a 27, iii 33, **peřu**, ii a 9. Cf. Grk. πέδον.

*pesetom* 'peccatum', vi a 27, 37, 47, vi b 30. **144, 211.**

**pestu**, see **perstu**.

**petenata** 'pectinatam, comb-shaped', iv 4. **259,** 1.

**Petrunia-per** 'pro Petronia', ii a 21, 35.

*peturpursus* 'quadrupedibus', vi b 11. **54, 94, 131, 150, 191, 4, *a*, 263,** 1.

*pihaclu* 'piaculo', abl. sg., vi a 25 etc. (12 times) ; — gen. pl. *pihaclo*, vi a 54, **pihaklu**, v a 8. **248,** 3.

*pihatu* 'piato', imperat., vi a 29 etc. (15 times), **pehatu**, iii 3 ; — perf. subj. pass. 3 sg. *pihafi*, vi a 38, 48, vi b 31, *pihafei*, vi a 29 ; **227, 238, 2, 239** ; — gerundive gen. sg. *pihaner*, vi a 19,

*pehaner*, vi a 20, *peihaner*, vi a 8 ; —
perf. pass. partic. nom. sg. m. *pihos*,
vi b 47, **pihaz**, i b 7; **35. 48, 83,** *a,*
**102, 2, 262, 1.**

*Piquier* '\*Piquii', gen. sg., v b 9, 14.
**258, 3.**

*pir* 'ignis, incendium', nom. sg., vi a
26 etc. (5 times) ; — acc. sg. *pir*, vi b
49, 50, pir, i b 12 etc. (6 times), *purom-e*
'in ignem', vi b 17, vii a 38 (**180,** *d*) ;
— abl. sg. *pure-to*, vi a 20, pure, i b 20.
**15, 11, 55, 59, 99, 6, 180,** *d.*

*pirse,* pe**ř**e, etc. 'quod, si, cum', conjunction.  *pirse*, vi a 46, vi b 55(?), *pirsi*,
vi a 5, 48, *persi*, vi a 37, 38, *perse*, vi a
47, vi b 29, 30, 31, *persei*, vi a 26, 27, 28,
36, pi**ř**i, iv 32, pe**ř**e, i b 18(?), ii a 3.
**45, 190, 6, 202, 2.**

*pis-est* 'quisquis est', vi b 53.  **113,** *a,*
**199.**

*pisher* 'quilibet', vi b 41.  **15, 1, 90, 2,**
**127, 3, 200, 1, 216.**

*pisi* 'quis, quisquis'.  **113,** *a,* **199, 200,** 1.
Indef. *pisi*, vi a 7.
Indef. rel. *pisi*, vii a 52, vii b 1,
'quisquis' ; **pisipumpe** 'quicumque,'
v a 3, 10 ; pi**ř**e 'quidquid', v a 5 ; —
acc. pl. *piři*, vii b 2 (with definite
antecedent).

**pistu** 'pistum', ii b 15.

**plenasier** '\*plenariis', loc. pl., v a 2, 14.
**42, 112,** *a,* **254.**   See **urnasier**.

*plener* 'plenis', abl. pl., vii a 21, 34.
**42, 255, 1.**

*podruhpei* 'utroque', adv., vi a 11 (in
*seipodruhpei* 'seorsum utroque') ; —
gen. sg. **putrespe** 'utriusque', iv 14.
**54, 88, 4, 157, 2, 188, 2,** *a,* **190, 2,**
**200, 2, 201, 4.**

*poi* 'qui,' nom. sg. m., vi a 5, vi b 24,
53, *poe*, vi b 50, *poei*, vi a 1 ; — dat.
sg. m. **pusme**, ii a 40 ; **114, 197, 1** ; —
abl. sg. f. *pora*, vi b 65, vii a 1; **67, 1,**
**199,** *d* ; — nom. pl. m. *puri*, v b 10,

15, pure, v a 6, 25, 28, v b 4 ; — acc. pl.
f. *pafe*, vii a 52.  **199.**   See also *porse.*

\**pompe* 'quinque'.  **37, 150** with *a.*

*poni* 'posca' (mixed wine and vine-
gar ?), abl. sg., vi a 57 etc. (12 times),
*pone*, vi a 59, **puni**, i a 4 etc.  (22
times) ; — acc. sg. **pune**, ii a 18 etc.
(6 times) ; — gen. sg. **punes**, ii a 41 ;
— dat. pl. **punes**, iv 33.  **54, 251, 2,** *a.*

*ponisiater* 'calatoris'(?), gen. sg., vi b
51, **puniçate**, i b 15.  **259, 1.**

*ponne* 'cum', conj., vi b 43, vii b 2, *pone*,
vi b 48, 49, **pune**, i b 1 etc. (14 times),
**puni**, i b 20.  **92, 135, 190, 5, 202, 3.**

*poplom* 'populum', acc. sg., vii a 15,
vii b 3, *poplo*, vi b 48, vii a 29, 46, puplum, i b 10, puplu, i b 40 ; — gen. sg.
*popler*, vi a 19 etc. (4 times) ; — dat.
sg. *pople*, vi b 61 etc. (6 times) ; —
abl. sg. *poplu*, vi b 54, *poplu-per*, vi b
43 etc. (15 times), poplu-per, i b 2, 5 ;
— loc. sg. *pople*, vi b 55.   **49.**

*pora*, see *poi.*

*porca* 'porcas', acc. pl., vii a 6, **purka**,
i b 27.

*portatu* 'portato', imperat., vi b 55, pur-
tatu, i b 18 ; — pres. subj. 3 sg. *portaia*, vii b 1 ; **232** ; — fut. perf. 3 sg.
*portust*, vii b 3 ; **211, 224.**

*porse*, pu**ř**e, conj., used also for some
cases of rel. pronoun.  pu**ř**e 'quod,
cum, quomodo', conj., ii a 26, iii 5,
v a 7 ; — used for nom. sg. m., *porse*,
vi b 63, vii a 46, 51, *porsi*, vi a 6, *porsei*,
vi a 9 ; — for nom. pl., *porsi*, vi a 19,
*porsei*, vi a 15 ; — for acc. pl., *porse*,
vi b 40.   **49, 190, 6, 199,** *f,* **202, 1.**

*post* 'post,' prep., vi a 58 etc. (4 times),
**pus**, i a 7, 14, 24 (**139,** 2) ; **puste**, i a
25 (or loc. sg. of a noun \**posti-* ?).
**49, 300, 6.**

*posti* 'pro, in, according to' (distrib.),
v b 8, 12, 14, 17, **pustin**, ii a 25, iv 13,
**pusti**, v a 13, 18, 20, 21.  **15, 10, 299, 7.**

*post-pane*'postquam', conj., in *postertio pane*'postquam tertium', vii a 46,
**pustertiu pane**, i b 40. **202, 4, 300,
6,** *a.*

**pustnaiaf**'posticas', acc. pl. f., i b 11 ;
— abl. pl. f. **pusnaes**, i a 2. **61, 3,
139, 2, 253, 1.**

*postne*'post', adv., vi b 11. **300, 6,** *a.*

*postra*'posteras, posteriores' (*pretra
. . . postra* 'the former . . . the latter'), acc. pl. f., v b 13 ;—acc. pl. n.,
used predicatively in sense of 'retro'
(**306**), *postro*, vi b 5, vii a 8, **pustru**,
ii b 19, **pustra**, ii a 32. **88, 4, 188,
2.**

*postro* 'retro', adv., vii a 43, 44, **pustru**,
i b 34, 36. **190, 6,** *a.*

*pracatarum* 'saeptarum'(?), vi a 13.

*praco*, name of some locality at Iguvium, gen. pl. (or acc. sg.?), vi a 13.
Possibly related to Low Latin *par-
cus* (whence Eng. *park* etc.) and
from the same root as L. *com-pescō*.

*pre*'prae', vi a 22 etc. (8 times), **pre**, i a
2, 11, 20. **63, 300, 7.**

*pre-*'prae-', **300, 7.**

**prehabia** 'praebeat', v a 5, **prehubia**,
v a 12. **86, 4.**

*prepa*'priusquam', vi b 52. **202, 4.**

**prepesnimu** 'praefator', ii b 17. **300, 7.**
See *persnimu.*

*preplotatu* '*praeplauditato, strike
down'(?), imperat., vi b 60, *preplohotatu*, vii a 49. **262, 1.**

*presoliaf-e*, name of some building or
locality in Iguvium, vi a 12.

*Prestota* 'Praesitita', voc. sg., vi b 57
etc. (19 times) ; — gen. sg. *Prestotar*,
vii a 20, 22, 33, 36 ;—dat. sg. *Prestote*,
vii a 6, 8, 24, **Prestate**, i b 27. **35,** *a.*

*pretra* 'priores' (see *postra*), acc. pl. f.,
v b 12. **188, 2.**

**preve** 'singillatim', adv., i a 28, ii a 9.
**190, 1.**

**prever** 'singulis', abl. pl. m., v a 13, 18.
17, 10, 65, **192,** 1.

*preuendu* 'advertito', vii a 11. 16, 21,
161.

*preuislatu* 'praevinculato', imperat.,
vii a 49, *preuilatu*, vi b 60. **144,
248, 1.**

*prinuatur* 'legati, deputies, assistants',
nom. pl., vi b 50 etc. (5 times), **prinuvatus**, i b 19, 23, **prinuvatu**, i b 15, 41;
— abl. pl. *prinuatir*, vi b 55, 56, 57.
No satisfactory etymology.

*pro-* 'pro-'. **300, 8.**

*procanurent* '*procinuerint', fut. perf.,
vi a 16. **32, 3, 224.**

*promom* 'primum', adv., vii a 52, **prumum**, iii 15, **prumu**, iii 3, 23. **189, 1,**
*a*, 190, 5, **191, 1.**

*Propartie* 'Propertii', gen. sg., gent.,
no. 84.

**prufe** 'probe', adv., v a 27. **190, 1, 307.**

**prupehast** 'ante piabit', iv 32. 17, 8,
**300, 8.** See *pihatu.*

**prusekatu** 'prosecato', imperat., ii a 28,
iii 33, 35, iv 2, **prusektu**, ii a 28 (**211**);
— perf. pass. partic. acc. pl. n. *proseseto*, vi a 56, **pruseçetu**, ii b 12,
gen. pl. *proseseto*, vi b 16, 38, dat.
pl. *prosesetir*, vi b 44, 46, *prosesetir*,
vi a 56 etc. (9 times), *proseseter*, vi b
20, **pruseçete**, ii a 12. **210, 3, 211.**

**pruseçia** 'prosicias', acc. pl., ii a 23.

**prusikurent** 'pronuntiaverint', fut.
perf., v a 26, 28. **94, 154, 225.**

**pruzuře** 'praestante'(?), iv 23. **94,
137, 2.**

*pue* 'ubi, where', adv., vi b 38, 39, 40, 55,
**pue**, i b 18. **54, 202, 7.**

**Puemune** 'Pomono' or 'Pomoni', dat.
sg. iii 26 etc. (6 times) ; — gen. sg.
**Puemunes**, iv 3 etc. (4 times). **83,
247, 2,** *a.*

*pufe* 'ubi', vi a 8, vi b 50, vii a 43, **pufe**,
i b 33. **55, 92, 200, 3, 202, 5.**

**pumpe** '-cumque' in **pisi pumpe** 'quicumque', v a 3, 10. **201, 4, 202,** 3.

**pumpeřias** '*quincuriae, groups of five', nom. pl., ii b 2. **37, 150, 191, 5, 251,** 4.

**puni** 'posca', see *poni*.

**puni** 'cum', see *ponne*.

**puntes** 'quiniones, pentads', nom. pl., iii 9, 10; — abl. pl. **puntis**, iii 4. **146, 153, 191, 5, 247,** 1, *a.* K7.47,2 //

**Pupřike** 'Publico'(?), epithet of **Puemune,** dat. sg., iii 27, 35, iv 10, 12, **Pupřiçe,** iv 24; — gen. sg. **Pupřikes,** iv 11, 13, **Pupřiçes,** iv 4, **Pupřçes,** iv 26. **106,** *a.*

*pur-* 'por-'. **264,** 1.

**purka,** see *porca*.

*purdouitu* 'porricito', imperat., vi a 56, **purtuvitu,** ii a 24 etc. (10 times; in iv 20 with θ = t; see **25,** *a*), **purtuvetu,** ii b 17, **purtuetu,** ii b 11 (**31,** *b*); — fut. 2 sg. **purtuvies,** ii b 28; **221;** — fut. perf. 2 sg. **purtiius,** i a 27 etc. (5 times; aes once **purtitius**); **224,** *b*; — fut. perf. 2 sg. **purtinçus,** i b 33, 3 sg. *purdinšiust*, vii a 43, *purdinšus*, vi b 23, 37, 38, *purdinsust*, vi b 16, 24; **144, 229, 264,** 1; — perf. pass. partic. *purditom* 'porrectum', nom. sg. n., vii a 45, *purdito*, vi b 42, **purtitu,** i b 39, ii a 43, iv 31, v a 18; — acc. pl. f. *purdita*, vi b 18, **purtitaf,** i a 18. **16, 19, 51, 96, 102, 3, 215,** 1. I£ʒ9,2/6

**pure,** *pureto, purome,* see *pir.*

**purtifele** '*porricibilem', ii b 25. **261.**

**Purtupite** 'Porricienti'(?), iv 14. Probably mistake for **Purtuvite.**

**puře,** see *porse.*

**pus,** see *post.*

*puše* 'ut', vi a 59 etc. (11 times), *puši*, vi a 20 etc. (7 times), *pusei*, vi a 27 etc. (3 times), **puze,** i b 34 etc. (3 times). **55, 137, 2, 200, 3, 202,** 6.

**pusme,** see under *poi.*

**puste, pustin, pustnaiaf,** see under *post* etc.

*randem-e,* name of some building or locality in Iguvium, vi a 14.

**ranu,** meaning uncertain, probably name of some kind of liquid, abl. sg., ii b 19.

*re-per* 'pro re', abl. sg., vii b 2, ri, v a 5; — dat. sg. ri, v a 4. **186.**

**re-** 're-'. **264,** 1.

**rehte** 'recte', adv., v a 24, 26, 29. **42, 142, 190,** 1.

**restatu** 'instaurato, offer anew', imperat., ii a 5; — pres. part. nom. sg. m. **restef,** i b 9, *reste*, vi b 47; **110, 4. 213, 4,** *a*, **264,** 1.

**revestu** 'revisito, inspicito', v a 7, 9. **137, 1, 264,** 1.

**ri,** see *re-per.*

*rofu* 'rufos', acc. pl. m., vii a 3; — acc. pl. f. *rofa*, vii a 6. **72, 96.**

*Rufrer* 'Rubri', gen. sg., vi a 14. **55.**

**rufru** 'rubros,' acc. pl. m., i b 24; — acc. pl. f. **rufra,** i b 27. **55, 96, 136, 257,** 1.

*Rubinam-e* 'in *Rubiniam', vii a 43, 44, **Rupinam-e,** i b 35, 36; loc. sg. *Rubine*, vii a 6, **Rupinie,** i b 27. **100, 3,** *b.*

*rusem-e,* meaning uncertain, vii a 8, 9, 23.

*s.,* abbr., 'semissem', v b 17.

*sacri-* 'sacrificial', adj., and neut. subst. 'hostia'. **187, 2, 257,** 2.

1) Adj. Acc. pl. f. **sakref,** i a 18, 19; — nom.-acc. sg. n. **sakre,** ii a 6 (possibly subst.), *sacre*, no. 84.

2) Subst. Nom.-acc. sg. **sakre,** ii a 5, 21, iii 8, 9, etc.; — acc. pl. **sakreu,** v a 6; — abl. pl. *sacris*, vi b 52, 56.

*sacru-* 'sacrificial'. Acc. pl. f. **sakra,** i b 29, 37, *sacra*, vi b 18, vii a 40, 45. **257,** 1.

Note that *esono-* means 'sacred' or, as subst., 'sacred rite, sacrifice' (i.e. the ceremony), while *sacri-*, *sacro-*, means 'pertaining to the sacrifice' (sacrificial cups etc.) or, as subst., the 'sacrifice' (i.e. the object sacrificed).

*Sahatam* 'Sanctam', probably the 'Sacred Way', acc. sg., vii a 39, 44, 45, *Sahata*, vii a 5, 39, **Sahta**, i b 35, **Satam-e**, i b 38 ; — loc. sg. *Sahate*, vii a 41, **Sate**, i b 31. **73, 75, 142.**

*Salier* 'Salii', gen. sg., vi a 14.

**salu** 'salem', ii a 18.

*saluom* 'salvum', acc. sg. m. n., vi a 51 etc. (5 times), *saluuom*, vi a 41 (**31**, *b*), *saluo*, vi a 31 etc. (8 times) ; — acc. sg. f. *saluam*, vi a 51, *salua*, vi a 31 etc. (4 times) ; — acc. pl. f. (see **322**) *salua*, vi a 32 etc. (6 times), *saluua*, vi a 42 (**31**, *b*). **258,** 1.

**sanes** 'sanis', abl. pl., iv 8.

*Sanðio-* '\*Sancius', usually epithet of Fisovius, but also of Fisus, Jupiter, and Vesticius. Once (ii b 10) used alone. Voc. sg. *Sanðie*, vi b 9 etc. (6 times), **Saçe**, ii b 24 ; — acc. sg. *Sanði*, vi b 8, *Sansi*, vi b 6 ; — dat. sg. *Sansie*, vi b 3, *Sansii*, vii a 37 (**173**, 2), *Sansi*, vi b 5, **Saçi**, i a 15, ii b 10, 17, **Saçe**, ii a 4. **144, 252,** 1, *a*.

*sarsite* 'sarte, wholly', adv., vi b 11. **244, 3, 325.**

**Saçe, Saçi,** see *Sanðio-*.

**Satanes** 'Satanis', dat. pl., ii b 4, **Satane**, ii b 4.

**Sate,** see *Sahatam*.

*sauitu* 'sauciato'(?), imperat., vi b 60, vii a 49. **212,** *b*.

*scalse-to* 'ex patera', vi b 16, **skalçe-ta**, iv 15, 18, 20 ; — loc. sg. *scalsie* 'in patera', vi b 16, vii a 37 ; **178, 6. 144.**

*scapla* 'scapulam', vi b 49.

*screhto* 'scriptum', nom. sg. n., vii b 3 ; — nom. pl. n. *screihtor*, vi a 15; **171, 13. 48, 121.**

*sehemeniar* 'seminarium', adj., acc. sg. n., vii a 52, **sehmeniar**, i b 42. **257, 4.**

*sehmenier* 'sementivis', dat. pl., v b 11, 16, **semenies**, ii b 1. The *sehmenier dequrier* were the seed-time festivals of the decuriae. Cf. L. *fēriae sēmentīvae*.

*sei* 'seorsum', adv., vi a 11 (in *seipodruhpei* 'seorsum utroque'). **200, 2, 263,** 2.

*sei* 'sis, sit', see *est*.

*semu* 'medio', abl. sg., vi b 16, *sehemu*, vi b 36. **189, 1,** *a*, **305.**

*sent,* see *est*.

**seples** 'simpulis', abl. pl., iii 17.

*sepse* 'sane, completely'(?), adv., vi b 11. **244,** 1, *b*, **325.**

*seritu* 'servato,' 'observe' and 'preserve', imperat., vi a 11 etc. (29 times), *serituu*, vii a 15, **seritu**, ii a 24. **102, 4.**

*sersi* 'sede,' abl. sg., vi a 5. **298.**

*sersitu* 'sedeto', imperat., vi b 41 ; — pres. partic. nom. sg. m. *serse*, vi a 2 etc. (7 times), **zeřef**, i a 25, 33, 34 (**137**, 2, note); **110, 4. 131, 212,** 3.

**sese** 'versus', adv., in **testru sese** 'dextroversus', iii 23, iv 15, and **supru sese** 'sursus', iv 3. **307.**

*seso* 'sibi', vi b 51. **193** with *b*.

**sestentasiaru** 'sextantariarum, bimonthly'(?), iii 2. **145,** 1, **191,** 6, p. 301.

*sestu* 'sisto', pres. indic. 1 sg., ii b 24, 2 sg. **seste**, ii b 22 (**90,** 2) ; — imperat. sg. **sestu**, ii b 22. **45, 213, 4.**

*sesust,* see *sistu*.

*seuacni-* 'sollemnis, sacrificial', and subst. 'hostia'. In many passages it is uncertain whether the form is used as adj. or subst. **159,** *a*, **187,** 2, **263,** 1 with *a*. See also *peracni-*.

1) Adj. Acc. sg. **sevakne**, ii a 21, iii 22, iv 16, 18, 19, **sevakni**, iii 25, 26, 27 ; — abl. sg. **sevakni**, ii a 38, 39, **sevakne**, iv 23 ; — acc. pl. **sevaknef**, iv 22 ; — abl. pl. **sevaknis**, ii a 36, 37, iv 25, **sevakne**, iv 9 (**178**, 9).

2) Subst. m. Acc. sg. **sevakne**, ii b 8, 9, 10 (adj. possible in all these); — acc. pl. *seuacne*, vii b 1.

*seuom* 'totum', acc. sg. n. (probably *persclo* understood; cognate acc. after *persnimu*), vi a 56, **sevum**, i a 5; — abl. pl. n. *seueir* 'omnibus', vi a 18. **15, 12, 258**, 1.

*sihitu*, see *ŝihitu*.

**sim** 'suem', acc. sg., ii b 1, **si**, ii b 7; — acc. pl. **sif**, i a 7, 14, *sif*, vi b 3, *si*, vi a 58. **59, 183**.

*sir, si, sins* 'sis, sit, sint', see *est*.

**sistu** 'sidito', iii 8; **114**; — fut. perf. 3 sg. *sesust* 'sederit' (given here rather than with *sersitu* on account of *andersesust* beside *andersistu*), vi a 5. **138, 222**, note.

*smursim-e*, name of some building or locality in Iguvium, acc. sg., vi a 13.

**snata** 'umecta', acc. pl. n., ii a 19, **snatu**, ii a 34 ; — abl. pl. **snates**, iv 9, **snate**, ii a 37. **114, 325**.

*somo* 'summum,' acc. sg. m., vi a 9 ; — — abl. sg. m. *somo*, vi a 10 ; **171**, 6, *a* ; — loc. sg. **sume**, ii a 15, iii 1. **57, 125**, 1, **189**, 1.

*sonitu* 'sonato' (transit., 'fill with noise, confuse'), imperat., vi b 60, *sunitu*, vii a 49. **37**, *a*, **51**, *b*, **212**, *b*, **310**.

*sopir* 'siquis'(?), vi b 54. **199, 202**, 14, *a*.

*sopo-* 'suppus, supinus, the under', adj. ; neut. pl. used subst., 'the under parts' (Grk. ὕπτια). Acc. sg. f. *sopa*, vi b 17, *sopam*, vii a 38 ; — acc. sg. m. **supu**, iv 17 ; — acc. pl. f. **supaf**, ii a 22 ; — acc. pl. n. *sopo*, vi b 5, *supo*, vii a 8, **supa**, i a 9, 16, ii a 22, 30, 32.

**57, 306**, p. 304. The adjective, except in ii a 22, is used predicatively, in sense equivalent to an adverb or preposition 'under'. See **306**.

*sorsalem* 'suillam'(?), adj., acc. sg. f., vi b 39 ; — gen. sg. f. *sorsalir*, vi b 38. **57, 260**, 1, p. 305.

*sorser* 'suilli', gen. sg., v b 12, 17 ; — here also, probably, acc. sg. *sorsom*, vi b 24, *sorso*, vi b 38, **suřum**, i a 27, 30, **suřu**, ii a 8, 9 ; — abl. sg. *sorsu*, vi b 28, 31, 35, 37 ; — acc. pl. m. used subst., **suřuf**, i a 33. **57, 260**, 1, p. 305.

*spahatu* 'iacito', imperat., vi b 41 ; — imperat. pass. (dep.) *spahmu*, vi b 17, *spahamu*, vii a 39 ; — perf. pass. partic. nom. sg. n. **spafu**, v a 20. **110**, 3 with *a*, **308**, *b*.

**spanti** 'latus', acc. sg., iii 34, iv 2, **spantim-ař**, iii 33. **247**, 1, *a*.

**spantea** 'lateralia', acc. pl. n., ii a 30.

*spefa* '*spensam, sparsam', acc. sg. f., vi a 56 etc. (4 times); — abl. sg. *spefa*, vi b 5 etc. (5 times). **110**, 3, p. 304.

**Speture** '*Spectori', name of a god, dat. sg., ii a 5. **142**.

**speturie** '*spectoriae', adj., dat. sg. f., ii a 1, 3. **246**, 1, *a*.

**spinia** 'columnam, barrier'(?), acc. sg., ii a 36, **spina**, ii a 38 (**100**, 3, *b*), **spiniam-a**, ii a 37, **spinam-ař**, ii a 33. Denotes some object, near the altar, which played a part in the ritual observances.

**stakaz** 'statutus', ii a 15. **262**, 1.

*staflarem* '*stabularem, ovillam'(?), adj., acc. sg. f., vi b 39 ; — acc. sg. m. *staflare*, vi b 37, 40. **136, 248**, 2, p. 305.

**staflii** '*stabularem, ovillum'(?), adj., acc. sg. m., i a 30. Footnote, p. 305.

*stahmei* 'statui', dat. sg., vi a 5, 18. **262**, 3.

*stahmito* 'statutum', nom. sg. n., vi a 8;
— dat. sg. *stahmitei*, vi a 18, *stahmei-tei*, vi a 5. **262**, 3.

*stahu* 'sto', no. 84; — imperat. sg.
*stahitu*, vi b 56, pl. *stahituto*, vi b 53;
— fut. 3 pl. **staheren**, i b 19; **128**, 2,
*a*. **83, 204, 6, 210, *a*, 215, 1.**

statita 'statuta', acc. pl. n., ii a 42.
**262**, 3.

statitatu 'statuito', imperat., ii a 32,
ii b 19, iv 9. **262**, 1.

*stiplo* 'stipulare', pres. imperat., vi a 2;
**235**; — fut. imperat. sg. *stiplatu*
'stipulator', vi b 48, 51, **steplatu**, i b
13. **45**.

*struƌla* '*struiculam, struem', a sort of
cake, acc. sg., vi a 59 etc. (6 times),
**struhçla**, ii a 18, 28, iv 4, **struçla**, iii 34;
— gen. sg. **struhçlas**, ii a 41 (**266**),
iv 1. **58, 144, 249, 2.**

*su* 'sub', no. 83. **302**.

*sub-*, su- 'sub-'. **302**.

**subahtu** 'deponito, set down, lay aside',
imperat., ii a 42, *subotu*, vi b 25 (? see
**35**, *a*); — perf. pass. partic. *subator*
'omissi', vi a 27, 36, 46, vi b 29; **171**,
13. **121, 218, 302.**

*subocau* 'invoco', vi a 22 etc. (15 times),
*subocauu*, vii a 20 etc. (8 times, all
in vii). Also taken by many as
perf. 'invocavi'. **102, 2, 153, *b*,
204, 6**, p. 303.

*suboco* 'invocationes', acc. pl. n., vi a
22 etc. (9 times). Also taken by
many as pres. 1 sg. 'invoco'. **279**,
p. 303.

*subotu*, see **subahtu**.

*subra* 'supra', adv., vi a 15, vi b 17, etc.,
**subra**, v a 20; — *subra*, prep., vi a 15;
**299, 8. 55, 157, 1, 188, 2, 190, 3.**

**sukatu** 'declarato'(?), iv 16. **94, 154.**

**sufafiaf** 'partis exsertas (hostiae), the
projecting parts'(?), acc. pl., ii a 22;
— gen. sg. **sufafias**, ii a 41; **266. 302.**

**sufeřaklu**, meaning uncertain, acc. sg.,
iii 17, 19. **302**.

**sume**, see *somo*.

**sumel** 'simul', ii a 27. **36, 2, 86, 3.**

**sumtu** 'sumito', imperat., i a 9, 16.
**114**, *c*.

**sunitu**, see *sonitu*.

**supa**, see *sopo-*.

**super** 'super', prep., i b 41, iv 19. **55,
301, 3.**

**superne** 'super', prep., vii a 25. **55,
301, 3.**

**supru sese** '*supro-versus, sursus', adv.,
iv 3. **157, 1, 190, 2, 307.**

**supu**, see *sopo-*.

**surur** 'item', vi a 20 etc. (6 times), *suror*,
vi b 37; — *sururont*, vi b 39 etc. (9
times), *sururo*, vi b 48 (**128, 2, *a*);** —
*suront*, vi b 8 etc. (11 times). **197,
6, 201, 6.**

**suřum**, see *sorser*.

**sutentu** 'subtendito, supponito', ii a 23.
**302**.

*sue* 'si', conj., vi a 7, 16, vii b 3, **sve**,
v a 24, 27. **63, 202, 14.**

**svepis** 'siquis', i b 18, iv 26. **199, 202,
14, *a*.**

**suepo** 'sive', vi b 47, **svepu**, i b 8. **133,
202, 1.**

*sueso* 'suo', poss. pron., loc. sg., vii b
1, **svesu**, i b 45, ii a 44. **194** with *b*.

**sviseve** 'in sino', loc. sg., ii b 14, 15.
p. 309.

*Šerfer* 'Cerri, Genii', gen. sg., vi b 57
etc. (25 times), *Serfer*, vi b 61 etc. (4
times), **Çerfe**, i b 28, 31; — dat. sg.
*Šerfe*, vii a 3, **Çerfe**, i b 24; — voc.
sg. *Serfe*, vi b 57, 61. **115, 2.**

*Šerfio-* '*Cerrius,' epithet of Praestita,
Torra, and Hontus. Gen. sg. f. *Šer-fiar*, vii a 20 etc. (4 times); — dat. sg.
f. *Šerfie*, vii a 6 etc. (4 times), **Çerfie**,
i b 28, 31; — dat. sg. m. *Šerfi*, vi b 45,

Çefi, i b 4 ; — voc. sg. f. *Serfia*, vi b 57 etc. (19 times), *Serfia*, vi b 61, vii a 16. **252**, 1 with *a*.

çersiaru 'feriarum epularium' (?), gen. pl., ii a 16.

çersnatur 'cenati', nom. pl., v a 22. **116, 2, 144.**

*ẟesna* 'cenam', v b 9, 13, 15, 18. **116, 2, 144, 251, 2,** *a*.

*ẟihitu* 'cinctos', acc. pl., vi b 59, *sihitu*, vii a 48 ; — dat. pl. *ẟihitir*, vii a 14, 28, 50, *sihitir*, vi b 62, *ẟitir*, vii a 13. **73, 144.**

çihçeřa 'cancellos' (?), acc. pl., iii 15. Possibly from *kinkedā-* (cf. Grk. κιγ- κλίδεϛ, L. *cingō*), but very uncertain.

*ẟimo* 'retro', adv., vi b 65, vii a 1, çimu, i b 23. **54, 189, 1,** *a*, **190, 2.**

çive 'citra', adv., ii b 11. **189, 1,** *a*, **190, 1, 258,** 1. 'On this side' is in this passage 'outside', contrasted with fesnere 'within the temple' of the following clause.

T., see **Titis.**

-ta, see *-to*.

tafle 'in tabula', loc. sg., ii b 12.

Talenate '*Talenati*', dat. sg., ii b 4, 5. **259, 3.**

tapistenu 'caldariolam' (?), iv 30. **99,** 4.

*Tarsinatem* 'Tadinatem', vi b 58, vii a 47, Tařinate, i b 16, 17 ; — gen. sg. *Tarsinater*, vi b 54 etc. (8 times) ; — dat. sg. *Tarsinate*, vii a 11. **259, 3.**

*tases* 'tacitus', vi a 55 etc. (11 times), *tasis*, vi b 23, taçez, i a 26 etc. (8 times) ; — nom. pl. *tasetur*, vi b 57, vii a 46. **137, 2, 144, 306.**

tekuries, see *dequrier*.

tekvias 'decuriales', nom. pl. f., ii b 1. **31,** *a*, **191, 10,** *a*.

*tefe* 'tibi', vi a 18, tefe, i b 13, ii b 24. **124, 193** with *a*.

*Tefrali* '*Tefrali*, pertaining to Tefer', adj., abl. sg., vi b 28, 35.

*Tefre* '*Tefer*,' voc. sg., vi b 27 etc. (10 times), **171,** 5 ; — acc. sg. *Tefro*, vi b 26, 27 ; — dat. sg. *Tefrei*, vi b 22, Tefre, i a 24, Tefri, i a 28.

*tefru-to* 'ex rogo, from the (place of the) burnt-offering', abl. sg., vii a 46 ; — acc. pl. n. tefra 'carnes cremandas', ii a 27, iii 32, 34, iv 2. **15, 13, 118.**

tehteřim 'tegumentum' (?), iv 20.

*teio*, see *tiom*.

teitu, see *deitu*.

tenitu 'teneto', vi b 25. **212,** 3.

tenzitim, meaning uncertain, acc. sg., i b 6, *tesedi*, vi b 46. **131,** *a*.

terkantur 'suffragentur' (?), pres. subj., iii 9. **308.** Possibly related to Grk. δέρκομαι, etc., the meaning being 'point out (with approval)'. Cf. Goth. *ga-tarhjan* 'point out'.

termnas 'terminatus', no. 84.

termnom-e 'ad terminum', acc. sg., vi b 57, 63, 64 ; — abl. sg. *termnu-co*, vi b 53, 55, 57 ; — abl. pl. termnes-ku, i b 19. **103,** 1.

*tertim* 'tertium', adv., vi b 64. **190,** 5, **191,** 3.

*tertio-* 'tertius', adj. Acc. sg. n. terti, ii a 28 ; **172, 173,** 1 ; — acc. sg. f. tertiam-e, vi a 13, tertiam-a, iv 2 ; — dat. sg. f. tertie, ii b 6 ; — abl. sg. n. *tertiu*, vi a 45 ; — loc. sg. tertie, ii b 14. **191,** 3.

*tertio* 'tertium', adv., vii a 46, tertiu, i b 40. **190, 2, 300,** 6, *a*.

teřte, teřust, etc., see *dirsa*.

*tesedi*, see tenzitim.

*Tesenocir* '*Tesenacis*,' abl. pl., vi b 1, 3, *Tesonocir*, vi a 20, vii a 38, Tesenakes, i a 11, 14. **35,** *a*, **256, 7.**

testre etc., see *destram-e*.

tesvàm, see *dersua*.

**Teteies** 'Tetteius' (?), i b 45, ii a 44. **61, 3, 253, 2.** Cf. also **174**, end.

*tettom-e*, name of some building in Iguvium, vi a 13, 14.

tetu, see *dirsa*.

Ti., see **Titis**.

**tikamne** 'dedicatione', ii a 8. **45, 107, 2, *a*, 247, 3.**

*tiom* 'te', acc. sg., vi a 43 etc. (33 times), *tio*, vi a 24 etc. (8 times), *teio*, vi a 22, **tiu**, ii a 25. **193** with *c*.

**tiçel** 'dedicatio', ii a 15 ; — acc. sg. **tiçlu**, iii 25, 27 ; — abl. sg. **tiçlu**, ii b 22. **45, 88, 4, 95, 144, 248, 1.**

**tiçit** 'decet', ii a 17. **39, 5, 144, 212, 3.**

**Titis**, praen., gen. sg., 'Titi' (?), i b 45 ; — abbr. **Ti.**, ii a 44, **T.**, v a 3, 15, *T.*, no. 84.

titu, see *dirsa*.

*Tlatie* 'Latii', gen. sg., v b 9. **129, 1.**

*-to, -ta, -tu* 'ex, ab'. **285, 300, 9.**

*toco* 'sale (conditas)' (?), probably adv., v b 13. Cf. L. *tuccēta* (pl.) and *tucca* (Corpus Gloss. Lat. II, p. 202 ; also *tur(e) tuc(ca) vin(o)*, CIL. V 2072).

*todcom-e* 'ad urbicum', acc. sg., vi a 10 ; — nom. pl. *totcor*, vi a 12 ; **171, 13** ; — abl. pl. *todceir*, vi a 11 ; **144, *a*. 15, 2, 89, 1, 153, 187, 1, 256, 2.**

*toru* 'tauros', acc. pl., vi b 43, 45, **turuf**, i b 1, **turup**, i b 4 (**25,** *a*) ; — abl. pl. **tures**, i b 20. **69.**

*totar* 'civitatis, urbis', gen. sg., vi a 30 etc. (44 times), **tutas**, i b 2, 5 ; — dat. sg. *tote*, vi a 5 etc. (24 times), **tute**, i b 13 ; — acc. sg. *totam*, vi a 41 etc. (9 times), *tota*, vi a 29 etc. (4 times), **tuta**, i b 16 ; — abl. sg. *tota-per*, vi a 23 etc. (35 times), **tuta-per**, i a 5 etc. (12 times), **tuta-pe**, iii 24 ; — loc. sg. *tote*, vi a 36, vi b 29, *toteme*, vi a 26, 46 (**169, 7,** *a*). **15, 2, 72.**

*touer*, see *tuer*.

*traf* 'trans', prepos., vii a 39, *trahaf*, vii a 41, *traha*, vii a 5, 39, 44, 45, **tra**, i b 31, 35, ii a 13. **110, 4, 301, 4.**

*trahuorfi* 'transverse', adv., vii a 25. **115, 8, 138, 190, 1, 301, 4.**

**Trebe** '*Trebo', dat. sg., i a 8, *Trebo*, vi a 58. **171, 3,** *a*.

*trebeit* 'versatur', vi a 8. **15, 14, 94, 212,** *b*.

*Treblanir* 'Trebulanis', adj., abl. pl., vi a 19 etc. (12 times), *Treblaneir*, vi a 22, **Treplanes**, i a 2, 7 ; — acc. pl. *Treblano*, vi b 47, **Treplanu**, i b 9. **255, 4.**

*tremitu* 'tremefacito', imperat., vi b 60, vii a 49. **212,** *b*, **310.**

*tremnu* 'tabernaculo', abl. sg., vi a 2, 16. **15, 14, 94, 125, 1, 251, 2, 298.**

**tribřiçu** 'ternio', nom. sg., v a 9 ; **110, 5** ; — abl. sg. *tribrisine*, vi a 54 ; **132,** *a*. **106,** *a*, **144, 181.**

*trif* 'tris', acc. pl. m. f., vi a 58 etc. (11 times), *treif*, vi a 22 (**74**), **trif**, i b 24, **tref**, i a 7 etc. (7 times), **tre**, i a 3 etc. (4 times) ; acc. pl. n. **triia**, iv 2 ; — abl. pl. **tris**, iii 18. **191, 3.**

*trifo* 'tribum', acc. sg., vi b 58, vii a 47, **trifu**, i b 16 ; — gen. sg. *trifor*, vi b 54 etc. (4 times) ; — dat. sg. *trifo*, vii a 11 ; — abl. sg. **trefi-per**, iii 25, 30. **184, 185.**

*trioper* 'ter', adv., vi b 55, vii a 51, **tri-iuper**, i b 21 etc. (5 times). **192, 2,** p. 321, ftn.

**tripler** 'trinis', abl. pl., v a 21. **192, 1.**

*-tu*, see *-to*.

*tuder* 'finem', acc. sg., vi a 10, 11 ; — nom. pl. *tuderor*, vi a 12 ; **171, 13** ; — acc. pl. *tudero*, vi a 15, 16 ; — dat.-abl. pl. *tuderus*, vi a 11 (**288**), vi b 48. **16, 20, 131,** *a*, **182.**

*tuderato* 'finitum', perf. pass. part. nom. sg. n., vi a 8. **16, 20, 131,** *a*, **262, 1.**

*tuer* 'tui', poss. pron., gen. sg., vi a 27 etc. (5 times), *touer*, vi b 30 (2 times) ;

P. Linde Gl. 3 (1912) 170-171 stellt die Forschung urnasier c 'or[?]narius' auf, indem er auf die Häufigkeit des Synkope ins u ...wie a... die V... dass ö im u sehr oft besonde nach r + Kona, ...u erscheint. plenasier, urnasier=

—abl. sg. f. *tua*, vi a 38 etc. (13 times), *tuua*, vi a 42 (31, b). **194** with a.

tuf, tupler, see under *d-*.

tuplak 'furcam'(?), acc. sg. n., iii 14. **32, 3, 178, 11, 179, 191, 2, a, 192, 1, 263, 1.**

tures, see *toru*.

*Tursa* '*Torra', voc. sg., vi b 58, 61, vii a 47, 49; — gen. sg. *Tursar*, vii a 46; — dat. sg. *Turse*, vii a 41, 53, Turse, iv 19, Tuse, i b 31, 43. Related to L. *terreð*, not *torreð*. Cf. *tursitu*.

Turskum 'Tuscum', adj., acc. sg. n., i b 17, *Tuscom*, vi b 58, vii a 47; — gen. sg. n. *Tuscer*, vi b 54 etc. (4 times); — dat. sg. n. *Tursce*, vii a 12. **256, 1, 116, 1.**

*tursitu* 'terreto', imperat., vi b 60, vii a 49, tusetu 'fugato', i b 40, pl. *tursituto*, vii a 51, tusetutu, i b 41; — pres. subj. 3 pl. *tursiandu* 'fugentur', vii b 2; **39, 1, 51, 156. 17, 12, 51, 97, 115, 1, 212, 2.**

tuta, tutas, etc., see *totar*.

tuva, tuves, etc., see *dur*.

u = v, see under v.

ukar, ukri-per, see *ocar*.

ufestne 'operculatis'(?), iv 22. **138, a.**

uhtretie '*auctura', loc. sg.(?), v a 2, 15. **246, 1, a, 251, 1, p. 301.**

uhtur 'auctor', title of an official, nom. sg., iii 7, 8; — acc. sg. uhturu, iii 4. **69, 142, p. 301.**

*ulo* 'illuc', adv., vi b 55, ulu, i b 18, v a 25, 28, v b 4. **54, 190, 2, 197, 3.**

umen 'unguen', acc. sg., ii a 19, 34; — abl. sg. umne, ii a 38. **125, 2, 151, 181.**

umtu 'unguito', ii a 38, iv 13. **153, a.**

une, see *utur*.

unu 'unum', acc. sg. m., ii a 6, 8. **67, 1, 191, 1.**

upetu, see *opeter*.

urfeta 'orbitam', a wheel-shaped object held in the hand as a token, ii b 23.

urnasier '*urnariis', abl. pl., v a 2, 15; — gen. pl. urnasiaru, iii 3. **112, a, 146, 254, p. 301.**

urtas, see *ortom*.

*uru, uru, ures*, see *orer*.

uretu 'adoleto', imperat., iii 12, iv 30. **106, 212, 3.**

usaçe, ii a 44, usaie, i b 45. **144, b.** Probably adj., loc. sg., but meaning and etym. wholly uncertain. Possibly from *opsākio-, as if L. *operācius.

ustentu, see *ostendu*.

ustite 'tempestate'(?), loc. sg., ii a 15, iii 2. Etym. unknown.

ute, see *ote*.

utur 'aquam', acc. sg., ii b 15; — abl. sg. une, ii b 20. **131, a, 135, a, 160, 2, d.**

uvem, see *oui*.

uze, see *onse*.

*U.*, abbr. praen., 'Vibius', nos. 83, 84

vakaze, uacose, see *anderuacose*.

vapeře 'sella', abl. sg., iii 7; — acc. pl. *uapef-e*, vi a 10, vi b 51, vapef-em, i b 14; — abl. pl. *uapersus*, vi a 9, uapersus-to, vi a 12, 13. **104.** Gl. 9,

vaputu 'ture'(?), abl. sg., ii b 10, 17 (for ii b 10, see footnote, p. 302); — abl. pl. vaputis, ii b 13. Probably connected with L. *vapor*.

*Uarie* 'Varii', gent., gen. sg., no. 83.

*uas* 'vitium', vi a 28, 38, 48. **145, 2.**

uasirslom-e, name of some locality in Iguvium, vi a 12.

uasor 'vasa', nom. pl., vi a 19; **171, 13;** — acc. pl. uaso, vi b 40; — abl. pl. vasus, iv 22. **182.**

uasetom 'vitiatum', perf. pass. partic. nom. sg. n., vi a 37, uasetom, vi a 47, vi b 30, uaseto, vi a 27; — acc. sg. n.

Charpentier, J in glotta 9 (1918) 53 *vaped-to ai. *up-ad < *up-ed das es in ai. úpala- 'obere Presstein, mörserkeule' vorfindet

*uasetom-e*, vi b 47, **vaçetum-i**, i b 8 (p. 306). **211.**

**vatra** 'extari'(?), adj., abl. sg. f., iii 31.

*uatuo* 'exta'(?), acc. pl. n., vi a 57 etc. (6 times), **vatuva**, i a 4 etc. (5 times), **vatuvu**, i b 25. Etym. wholly uncertain. See p. 304.

*uef* 'partis', acc. pl., v b 12, 17. **136,** *a.*

*Uehier* 'Veiis', abl. pl., vi b 19, 22, *Uehieir*, vi a 21, **Vehiies**, i a 20, 24.

*ueiro*, see *uiro*.

**veltu** 'deligito', imperat., iv 21. **36, 2, 105, 2, 217.**

**venpersuntra** 'ficticia'(?), adj., abl. sg. f., ii a 30, **vepesutra**, ii b 18; — acc. sg. f. **vepesutra**, ii b 15; — abl. pl. f. **vempesuntres**, iv 7. **263, 2.**

In ii a 30 the word agrees with *karne* of the preceding clause, similarly in iv 7 with *karnus*. In the other two passages it is used substantively, the word for flesh being understood.

**vepuratu** 'restinguito'(?), imperat., ii a 41. **262, 1.**

**vepurus** 'non igneis, (sacrifices) without fire'(?), adj., abl. pl., v a 11. **263, 2.**

*uerfale* 'templum', place marked off for taking the auspices, vi a 8. **136.** Cf. 'In terris dictum templum locus augurii aut auspicii causa quibusdam conceptis verbis finitus', Varro L. L. 7, 8.

*uerir* 'porta', abl. pl., vi a 58 etc. (11 times), *uereir*, vi a 22, **ueris-co**, vi a 19 etc. (9 times), **veres**, i a 2 etc. (6 times); — acc. pl. **uerof-e**, vi b 47, **veruf-e**, i b 9 (171, 13). **15, 15.**

**veskla** 'vascula', acc. pl., ii a 19, **vesklu**, i b 29, 37, ii a 34, ii b 19; — abl. pl. *uesclir*, vii a 9 etc. (8 times), **veskles**, ii a 31, 37, etc. (5 times). **88, 4, 99, 7, 144, 249, 2.**

**uesticatu** 'libato', imperat., vi b 16, vii a 8 etc. (5 times), **vestikatu**, ii a 24 etc. (4 times); — *uesticos* 'libaverit', vi b 25; **230,** *a,* **308,** *a.* **308,** *c.*

*uestis* 'libans', vi b 6, 25, *uesteis*, vi a 22. **308,** *c.*

**vestiçia** 'libamentum', acc. sg., iv 14, 19, **vestiçam**, i a 28, **vestiça**, i a 17, 31, **vesteça**, iv 17, *uestisiam*, vi b 39, *uestisia*, vi b 6 etc. (5 times); — gen. sg. *uestisiar*, vi b 16, 38, vii a 38; — abl. sg. **vestiçia**, ii a 27, **vistiça**, ii b 13 (39, 5), *uestisia*, vi b 5, *uestisa*, vii a 37. Like L. *libamentum*, not wholly confined to liquid offerings. **308,** *c.*

*Uestisier* '\*Vesticii', gen. sg., name of a god (probably of libation, like L. *Libasius*), vi a 14; — dat. sg. **Vestiçe**, ii a 4. **308,** *c.*

*uestra* 'vestra', abl. sg. f., vi b 61. **194.**

**Vesune** '\*Vesonae', dat. sg., name of a goddess, iv 3, 6, etc. **247, 2,** *a.*

**vetu** 'dividito', i b 29, 37. **136,** *a.*

*uia* 'via', abl. sg., vi b 52 etc., **via**, iii 11, **vea**, i b 14, 23. **31,** *a,* **101.**

**vinu** 'vinum', acc. sg., ii a 18, 40, ii b 14; — abl. sg. **vinu**, i a 4 etc., *uinu*, vi a 57, vi b 19, 46. **21.**

*uiro* 'viros', vi a 42 etc. (8 times), *ueiro*, vi a 30, 32, 39. **99, 5, 171, 11,** *a.*

*uirseto* 'visum', vi a 28, 38, 48, vi b 30. **45, 244, 4.**

*Uistinie* 'Vestinii', gent., gen. sg., no. 84.

**vitlaf** 'vitulas', acc. pl., i b 31, *uitla*, vii a 41.

**vitlu** 'vitulum', acc. sg., ii b 21, 24; — acc. pl. **vitluf**, i b 1, **vitlup** (**25,** *a*), i b 4, *uitlu*, vi b 43, 45. **39, 6, 88, 4.**

*uocu-com* 'ad aedem'(?), abl. sg., vi b 43, 45, **vuku-kum**, i b 1, 4; — acc. sg. **vuku**, iii 21, **vukum-en**, iii 20; — loc. sg. **vuke**, iii 3, 21. **67, 1.** Connection with L. *lūcus* (by **104**) is also held by some.

*Uoflone* '*Voviono' or '*Vovioni', 'deo votorum', dat. sg., vi b 19, **Vufiune**, i a 20. **247**, 2, *a.*

*Uois.*, abbr. praen., 'Volsii'(?), no. 84. Cf. **105**, 3.

*Uoisiener* 'Volsieni', gen. sg., no. 84. **105**, 3.

*uomu*, see *anderuomu.*

*uouse* 'voto'(?), dat. sg., vi b 11. **152**, *a.*

**vuke, vuku**, see *uocu-com.*

**vufetes** 'votis, consecratis', abl. pl., ii a 31, iv 25. **152.**

**Vufiune**, see *Uofione.*

**vufru** 'votivum', acc. sg. m., ii b 21, 24, 25. **152, 257**, 1.

**vurtus** 'mutaverit', fut. perf., ii a 2. **17**, 14.

**Vuçiia-per** 'pro Lucia'(?), adj., abl. sg. f., ii b 26. **72**, *a.*

**vutu** 'lavato', imperat., ii a 39. **104, 213**, 1, *a.*

**Vuvçis** 'Lucius'(?), i b 45, ii a 44. **72**, *a*, **104.**

**zeref**, see *sersitu.*

---

18 a. Notizie degli scavi 1916, 156 ff
Rivista indo-greco-italico = 58 ff
Buch, C.P 17, 111 ff.
Della Corte, Riv. i-i-i. VI 168
Ribezzo, " " VI 169

Restoration of Ribezzo:
1. eksud amvi[anud eituns]
set puz haf[rar treb.t[v.
ini viu mef[an ini turr[ja
neírak vefru urublanu
5 puis sent eipai i ai nert[rak
veru urublatu ini impi
mefira faament
L. Pupid L. Mr. Paril Mr.

PLATE I.

INSCRIPTION PAINTED IN RED ON THE FRONT OF THE "HOUSE OF PANSA" AT POMPEII. OUR NO. 15.

ONE OF THE IOVILAE-DEDICATIONS, NOW IN THE NAPLES MUSEUM. OUR NO. 29

ALCOVE OF OSCAN INSCRIPTIONS IN THE NAPLES MUSEUM.

446 Rebezzo, F., La nuova 'defixio' osca di
Cuma, Neapolis 2 (1914) 2.73.809
Stenim. Kalaviium tri- Jahresb. 1920/
aginas. urinss. ielna
fakinss. paácum (parykum Diruss.
brass tiltam. iftium i-
inamúm. rilatium ( cikis. nu i. 1. 2. dol.)
amiricum. úy. . . .

= Stenium Kalavium Tri- ugant
(exc. verbis, finajuls), urant (ela. lotiuia. 1,
iinu faiiart praccim (oda fuccum) to i-
ilamy úiúzciu, iieii uu, calalú in,
iiniricuiy ( 1. dialt) lupi!

Titi (ifim) ot fpart vin Kalaund.)
iy ip ipiiss fla inss, iiiuss = 'lii intiinii
iui = 'iffiiiie mitdif. icalniist. Jamii
cuu = inariiu iiiint iiiiiii iiii,
iiiiii = iiilindis Kiiiiiliiiii odiiiin 'ipi
iiidiyuum

iiiuita iiita
iiidulis iit

PLATE II.

FACSIMILE OF OSCAN INSCRIPTION FROM POMPEII, OUR NO. 4 (ZVETAIEFF).

urines f. *urvere, urvar = menare in giro (speciant, lorquant). comparing Sila, = silva, malako = *malvacos, vulg lat *malvax, frg mauvais but cf Walde Etym. WB² 457)

biagines, urinse, fakinse. Maurer betrachtet sie als ä Konjunktive eine 2. aoristo; Ribezzo dagegen ist der Anschauung das i dieser Formen gehe auf i aus io zurück und ihre Basis sei ein Praesensstamm; er vergleicht die lat. präs Optativ-formen sim, velim, edim temperint (Plaut. Truc. 60) und verberit (Fest p. 209 Th) Die Endung -nso für 3 Pl. tritt einzig in dieser Inschrift auf und zeugt vielleicht für die Aussprache der Endung in jener verhaltnismässig späten Zeit (nach 89. v. Chr. oo, gegen Ende des Bürgerkrieges!)

[illegible] the father's name. the following forms are acc plural forms.

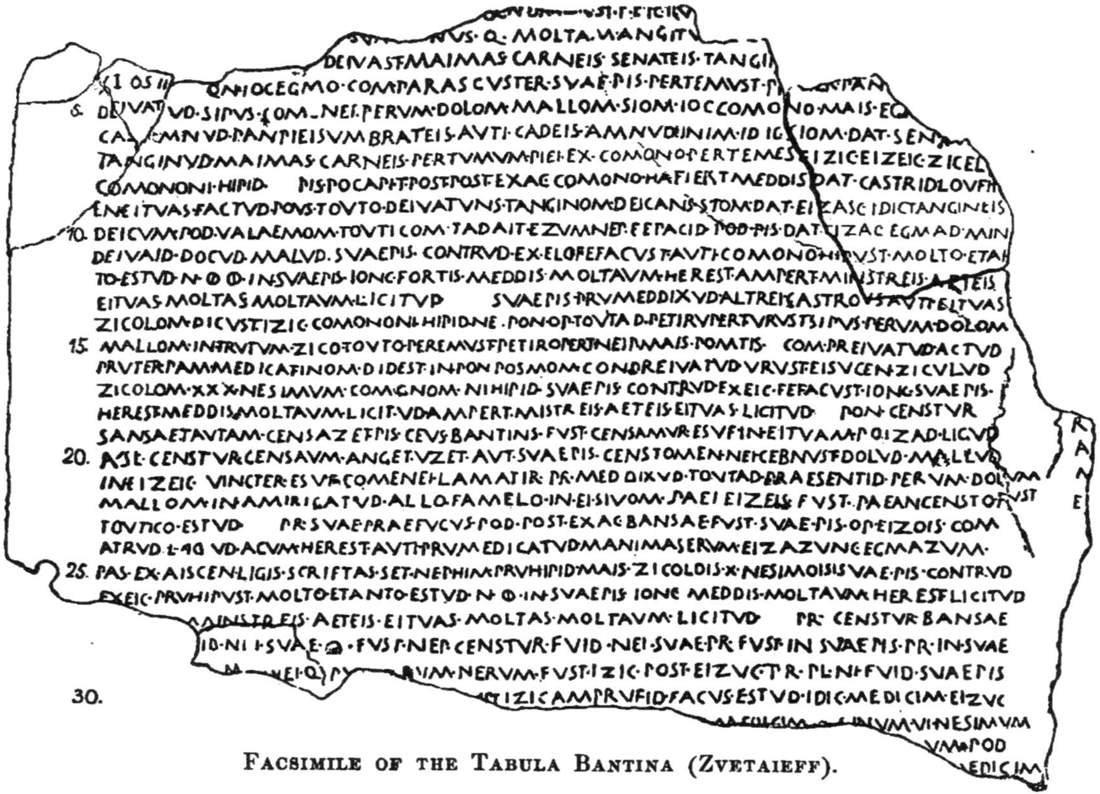

FACSIMILE OF THE TABULA BANTINA (ZVETAIEFF).

44a- Fritz Weege, Eine oskische Töpferfamilie
   in Bonner Jahrbücher 1909 p 275.

   vibiieisen : beruneis: anei : upsaluh : sent : tiianei :

d.l.  Im (officina)
   Ex (domo) Vibii   Berii   Anei (f) facti   sunt Teani.
   44 then would be.

   Minius Berius   Anei f.) facti  sunt Teani.

446. - Ibid.

   berumnen : anei : upsaluh : sent luanei.

d.h.  Beriorum ex (officina) Anei (filiorum) . Fachsunt Tea..

   For Vibius Virrius of 44a cf. Liv 23, 6; 26, 13
   descendant of above perhaps

Dasz unser Resultat, ein Brüderpaar Berius
Lato in Teano eine Vasenfabrik teth ..
richtig ist, hat auch mir bei meinem
letzten Besuch in Neapeles Museum
bestätigt. (44b = Inv. Nr. 130738)

PLATE IV.

CLAVERNIVR·DIR·SAS·HERTI·FRATRVS·ATIERSIR·POSTIACNV
FARER·OPETER·P·IIII·AGRE·TLATIE·PIQ·VIER·MARTIER·ET·SESNA
HOMONVS·DVIR·PVRI·FAR·EISCVRENT·OTE·A·VI·  CLAVERNI
DIR·SANS·HERTI·FRATRER·ATIER·SIVR·SEHMENIER·DEQVRIER
PELMNER·SOR·SER·POSTIACNV·VEF·X·CABRINER·VEF·V·PRETA
TO·CO·POSTRA·FAHE·ET·SESNA·OTE·A·VI·CASILOS·DIR·SA·HERTI·FRATRVS
ATIER·SIR·POSTIACNV·FARER·OPETER·P·VI·AGRE·CASILER·PIQ·VIER
MATIER·ET·SESNA·HOMONVS·DVIR·PVRI·FAR·EISCVRENT·OTE·A·VI
CASILATE·DIR·SANS·HERTI·FRATE·ER·ATIER·SIVR·SEHMENIER·DEQVRIER
PELMNER·SOR·SER·POSTIACNV·VEF·XV·CABRINER·VEF·VIIS·ET
SESNA·OTE·A·VI

PHOTOGRAPH OF Vb, IGUVINIAN TABLES (BREAL).

PLATE V.

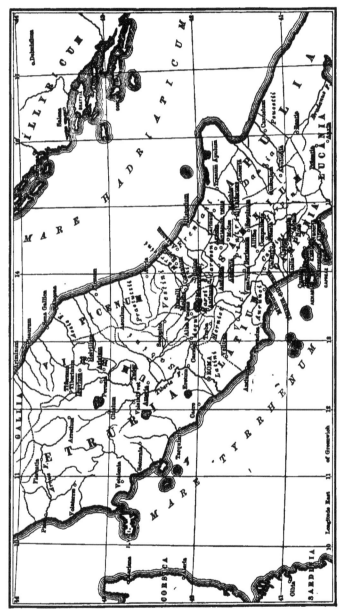

MAP OF CENTRAL ITALY

Showing places from which come inscriptions or coins in Oscan, Umbrian, or any of the minor Oscan-Umbrian dialects. The names of towns from which we have inscriptions are underscored, while the names of towns from which we have coins are marked with a line above. A few Oscan inscriptions come from places further south than the map shows, namely Tegeanum in southern Lucania, Vibo Valentia in Bruttium, and Messana in Sicily.

Lightning Source UK Ltd.
Milton Keynes UK
UKHW020628200721
387437UK00002B/174

9 780341 820932